The Language of Machines

An Introduction to Computability and Formal Languages

The Language of Machines

An Introduction to Computability and Formal Languages

Robert W Floyd
Stanford University

Richard Beigel
Yale University

Computer Science Press
An imprint of W. H. Freeman and Company
New York

Library of Congress Cataloging-in-Publication Data

Floyd, Robert W
The language of machines : an introduction to computability and formal languages / Robert W Floyd, Richard Beigel.
p. cm.
Includes index.
ISBN 0-7167-8266-9
1. Formal languages. 2. Machine theory. 3. Computable functions. I. Beigel, Richard. II. Title.
QA267.e.F56 1993
511'.3–dc20 93-3910
CIP

Printed in the United States of America

Computer Science Press

An imprint of W. H. Freeman and Company
The book publishing arm of *Scientific American*
41 Madison Avenue, New York, NY 10010
20 Beaumont Street, Oxford OX1 2NQ, England

1 2 3 4 5 6 7 8 9 0 RRD 9 9 8 7 6 5 4

CONTENTS

Preface xi

Acknowledgments xv

About the Authors xvii

0 **Mathematical Preliminaries** 1
0.1 Quantifiers and Two-Player Games 2
Exercises 5
0.2 Sets, Tuples, Sequences, Bags, Relations, and Functions 5
0.2.1 Sets 6
0.2.2 Set Extensions and Closures 9
0.2.3 Tuples 13
0.2.4 Sequences 15
0.2.5 Bags 16
0.2.6 Relations 18
0.2.7 Functions 24
0.3 Strings 29
0.3.1 Regular Operations 31
0.3.2 Miscellaneous String Operations and Relations 32
0.3.3 b-ary and b-adic Number Representations 33
0.4 Graphs 36
0.5 Big-O Notation 38
0.6 Induction 39
0.6.1 Strong Induction 51
0.6.2 Pigeonhole Principle 55
0.6.3 Recursive Definitions 60

1 **Introduction to Machines** 67

1.1 Programs . . . 68
1.2 Controls . . . 80
1.3 Unsigned Counters . . . 82
1.4 Signed Counters . . . 86
1.5 Stacks . . . 87
1.6 Two-Counter Machines . . . 89
1.7 Turing Machines . . . 91
1.8 Random Access Machines . . . 96
1.9 Determinism and Nondeterminism . . . 99
1.10 Chapter Summary . . . 107

2 **Devices, Machines, and Programs** 111

2.1 Representing Problems . . . 112
2.2 Devices . . . 115
2.3 Machines . . . 117
2.4 Instructions . . . 118
2.5 Initializers and Terminators . . . 120
2.6 Programs . . . 126
2.7 Running a Program . . . 132
2.7.1 Computations, Traces, and Histories . . . 133
2.7.2 Infinite Computations, Traces, and Histories . . . 136
2.8 Determinism and Blocking . . . 139
2.9 Three Important Kinds of Programs . . . 142
2.9.1 Acceptors . . . 142
2.9.2 Recognizers . . . 144
2.9.3 Transducers . . . 146
2.10 Chapter Summary . . . 151

3 **Simulation** 153

3.1 Simulation of Programs . . . 155
3.2 Lockstep Simulation . . . 156
3.2.1 One Control Simulates Two Controls (Pairing Construction) . . . 166
3.3 Simulation via Subprograms . . . 174
3.3.1 Eliminating the NONZERO Test from an Unsigned Counter . . . 180
3.3.2 An Unsigned Counter Simulates a Signed Counter . . . 184
3.3.3 Eliminating the EMPTY Test from a Stack . . . 190
3.4 Standardization . . . 194
3.4.1 Factoring Programs . . . 195
3.4.2 Eliminating the New Operations and Redundant Tests . . . 200

3.4.3 Eliminating Dead States and Unreachable States 204
3.4.4 Eliminating Null Instructions 208
3.4.5 Cleaning Up and Eliminating Blocking 212
3.5 Chapter Summary 214

4 **Finite Machines and Regular Languages** **217**
4.1 Standardizing Finite Machine Programs 219
4.2 Regular Expressions and Languages 220
*4.3 Regular Expressions in the Real World: egrep 225
4.4 Kleene's Theorem 229
4.4.1 Algorithms for Computing Regular Sets of Paths 232
4.4.2 NFA Languages Are Regular Languages 238
4.4.3 Pencil-and-Paper Algorithm 240
4.5 NFA Languages Are the Same as Regular Languages 247
4.6 Equivalence of NFAs and DFAs 250
4.7 Minimizing DFRs 258
4.7.1 Determining Equivalent States 267
4.8 Closure Properties 279
4.8.1 Closure under Finite Transductions 281
4.8.2 Composition Theorem 284
4.9 Pumping Theorems for Regular Languages 293
4.9.1 Al and Izzy Pump Strings 299
4.10 Chapter Summary 306

5 **Context-Free Languages** **313**
5.1 Defining Languages as Solutions to Equations 314
*5.2 Existence of Unique Minimal Solutions 322
5.3 CFGs and Their Standardizations 329
*5.4 Parse Trees 339
5.5 Derivations 342
5.6 CFLs Are the Same as NSA Languages 347
*5.7 The Chomsky Hierarchy 354
5.8 Pumping Theorems for CFLs 356
5.9 Ambiguity 369
*5.10 Greibach Normal Form 375
5.11 CYK Parsing Algorithm 389
*5.12 Earley's Parsing Algorithm 391
5.13 Chapter Summary 400

6 **Stack and Counter Machines** **401**
6.1 Closure Properties 402
6.2 DSA Languages Are DSR Languages 407
6.2.1 Eliminating PUSH–POP Pairs from DSAs 407

6.2.2 Making DSAs Halt 410
*6.3 Unambiguous Programs 414
*6.4 On-line Recognition 418
6.5 Two Counters Simulate a Stack 427
6.6 Two Counters Simulate Any Number of Counters 435
*6.7 Counter Languages and Prefix Equivalence 437
6.8 Chapter Summary 441

7 Computability **443**
7.1 Tapes and Turing Machines 445
7.1.1 One Tape Simulates k Tapes 447
7.1.2 Two Stacks Simulate a Tape 451
7.2 Putting the Argument on a Tape, Stack, or Counter 454
7.3 Random Access Memory 456
7.4 Universal Turing Machine Program 458
*7.5 Herbrand–Gödel Computability 461
7.6 Recursive and Recursively Enumerable Sets 467
7.7 The Halting Problem 478
7.8 Diagonalization 481
*7.8.1 The Real Numbers Are Uncountable 482
7.8.2 Recursively Inseparable Sets 486
*7.8.3 The Total Recursive Functions Cannot Be Enumerated Exactly 489
7.9 Many-One Reductions 490
*7.10 Rewriting Systems and Word Problems 498
*7.11 The Post Correspondence Problem 508
7.12 Undecidability of First-Order Logic 520
7.13 Valid and Invalid Computations 527
*7.14 Diophantine and Exponential Diophantine Equations 537
7.14.1 Some Diophantine and Exponential Diophantine Relations 541
7.14.2 Arithmetization of 3-Counter Machine Programs 546
7.15 Chapter Summary 553

8 Recursion Theory **557**
8.1 Rice's Theorem 558
8.2 The Recursion Theorem and the Fixed-Point Theorem 563
8.3 Gödel's Incompleteness Theorem 569
8.4 Oracles and Turing Reductions 574
8.4.1 Representational Issues 577
8.4.2 Relativization 578
8.4.3 Jumps 580
8.5 The Arithmetical Hierarchy 582

8.6 Chapter Summary 598

9 Feasible and Infeasible Problems **601**
9.1 Time-Bounded Computation: P and NP 602
9.2 NP-Completeness 611
9.3 Search and Optimization vs. Decision 616
9.4 Canonical NP-Complete Problems 621
9.5 Symbol Systems 624
9.6 Boolean Formula Satisfiability 631
9.7 NP-Complete Graph Problems 639
9.8 NP-Complete Problems Involving Sets, Vectors, and Numbers 653
*9.9 An NP-Complete Problem about DFRs 664
*9.10 Complexity of Some Problems Involving Regular Languages 670
9.11 Chapter Summary 679

10 Appendix **681**
10.1 Greek Symbols 681
10.2 Glossary 684
10.3 Common Acronyms 687
10.4 Program and Grammar Equivalences 690
10.5 Hierarchy of Partial Functions 692
10.6 Hierarchy of Relations 694
10.7 Closure Properties for Language Classes 695
10.8 Decision Problems for Language Classes 696

Index 697

PREFACE

The elementary theory of computability and of languages defined by formal grammars is a mature subject that has changed little since the mid-1960s. This theory underlies modern recursive function and complexity theory, as well as modern methods in the design of compilers for computer programming languages. Students of computer science, many of whom have little experience in the deductive algebraic side of mathematics, often find the subject difficult to follow and harder to apply. In response, we have reexamined the foundations of computability theory, asking ourselves how Turing, Gödel, Herbrand, Post, Kleene, and the other founders would have defined computability had they foreseen its entire development, along with the development of the corresponding arts and technologies of digital computer usage.

Our purpose is to make the subject easier for students and professionals in computer science and therefore more useful. Toward this end, we relate many of the paradigms of computability to concepts that are familiar to the average programmer. As much as possible we present definitions, proofs, and constructions informally first and formally second. The core of the text is written with third-year computer science undergraduates in mind. A substantial amount of optional material will appeal to more advanced students.

The Language of Machines is our proposal for the redefinition of computability and formal language theory. These are the major innovations we propose:

- A single definition encompasses all the familiar types of machine—finite automaton, Turing machine, counter, stack, and random-access machine—whether used as recognizer, acceptor, or transducer.
- We present nondeterminism and non-halting computations early, and in a natural, nontraumatic way.
- A mechanism is provided to combine machines, analogous to the way programs are combined through "pipes" by modern operating systems such as Unix on real computers.
- The capabilities of a machine type are separated from the details of

the specific algorithms. A machine type is a collection of "devices" capable of executing an infinite variety of programs. Because it is easier to design programs than to design hardware, the practical world replaced special-purpose computers by the general-purpose kind forty years ago; the theoretical world should follow.

- In practical programming as well as computability theory, it is important to be able to establish that one program simulates another. We define simulation in a way that captures the key intuitions and permits modularized proofs. The correct simulation of each part of a program is validated separately by verifying a mechanically generated condition. The same logical framework that supports showing that a two-counter machine simulates a Turing machine could, in principle, be used in showing that a microcode simulates the design specifications of a real computer.

  In a rigorous approach to automata theory, every simulation requires its own ad hoc induction. Our approach distills the ad hoc inductions into a single induction and confines the details to a single chapter so that subsequently the student may concentrate on the underlying ideas. We have supplemented the inductive proof with commutative diagrams that should appeal to all students regardless of mathematical background.

- Many proofs are facilitated by showing that programs for a machine can be standardized, i.e., put into a very restricted form. Proofs by standardization are more accessible than some of the classical proofs, because they appeal to programming insights. Such proofs can be validated by applying the formal definition of simulation.

In addition to these innovations in definitional framework, we have looked hard at the logical structure of traditional proofs. For example, by choosing the right induction hypothesis, the proof of Ogden's generalization of the classic pumping theorem becomes simpler than the classic proof of the special case. By expressing the halting problem for two-counter machines in first-order logic, we find an extremely simple proof that the set of theorems in first-order logic is undecidable. By expressing the set of computations of a two-stack machine as the intersection of two CFLs, we simplify the classic undecidability proofs for CFL properties. By introducing symbol systems, we are able to separate the key ideas of the Cook–Levin reduction from the technical encoding details.

In *The Language of Machines*, we assume that the reader is familiar with sets, functions, and relations, with the use of universal and existential quantifiers, with proof by induction, and with arithmetic congruences. Chapter 0 contains a quick review of this material. The most direct preparation would be a one-term course in discrete mathematics. In turn, we introduce the reader to some mathematical results of value outside computability, such as the Tarski–Knaster fixed-point theorem (important, for example, in denotational semantics). We believe that this book will properly prepare the student for subsequent courses in complexity theory and recursive function theory. This book is also valuable preparation for the study of modern programming languages, compilers, and interpreters.

We have made several judgment calls in defining the perimeter of our subject. We have ruled the theory of primitive recursive functions out as a historical dead end. We have returned to the original Herbrand–Gödel equational definition of the recursive functions, dropping the use of the μ-operator and the operation of primitive recursion as defined by Kleene. We make extensive use of finite transductions; however, homomorphisms, Moore machines, and Mealy machines per se are not needed and not mentioned. We present the core theory of NP-completeness but mostly resist the temptation to explore complexity theory.

We have tried to appeal to the reader's experience and intuition as much as possible without sacrificing mathematical rigor. Programs for all kinds of automata (not just finite automata) are presented informally as directed graphs labeled with actions to be performed so that they can be followed visually, although formally they are sets of tuples of partial functions. Our definitions are chosen to make algorithm design for automata seem as much like computer programming as possible. We have incorporated numerous concrete examples, some of practical value. Where possible, exercises explore historical variants of the theory.

The theory of computation uses a number of algorithms, e.g., to minimize a finite automaton or to put a context-free grammar into a normal form. We have made an effort to provide algorithms that are intelligible, feasible for execution by hand, and efficient on a real computer. Where these goals conflict, we emphasize the first two, citing the literature for the third.

We have taught this subject for many years and at several universities. Between the two of us, we have class-tested this formulation of the subject in nine classes. We are pleased by the level of student satisfaction. In an era of watered-down courses, we hope to revive the careful use of deductive methods in theory of computability.

Finally, we realize that we are asking teachers to overhaul their conceptual framework, but we think their effort will be amply repaid. Our unified approach to automata and languages will clarify the subject for teachers as well as students.

Notes: Exercises marked with an asterisk (*) are more challenging than others. Exercises marked with two asterisks (**) are much more challenging than others. Exercises marked with a dagger (†) are unsolved problems, to the best of our knowledge. Exercises marked with a plus (+) are used later.

Sections marked with an asterisk (*) contain material that we consider optional, although not necessarily more difficult than other material. As much as possible we have tried to make sections self-contained so that difficult material can be skipped with minimum consequences.

Robert W Floyd

Richard Beigel

November 1993

ACKNOWLEDGMENTS

We are grateful to a large number of colleagues, students, and friends for their assistance and support while we were preparing this textbook.

Students whose suggestions improved our early drafts include at Yale: Kostas Vassilakis, Tuija Kaisla, Jim Cowie, Nick Reingold, and Rebecca Wright; at Stanford: Brian Hagenbuch, Pat Lincoln, and Jim Hwang; at Johns Hopkins: Ashutosh Roy and others.

Some of the ideas for a unified approach to the theory of automata first appeared in a paper by Jonathan Goldstine. His advice as a reviewer has been exceptionally thorough and valuable.

We have had numerous helpful discussions with Rao Kosaraju and Mike Fischer. Bill Gasarch gave priceless, comprehensive advice on the manuscript and suggested numerous exercises. Terry Winograd provided some excellent general advice on the exposition. Udi Manber gave valuable advice on the presentation of mathematical induction. Ron Sigal, Nick Reingold, and Zohar Manna gave valuable advice on mathematical logic. We had helpful discussions with Sheila Greibach and Derick Wood on Greibach-normal-form grammars and other helpful discussions with Dana Angluin, Steven Rudich, Lance Fortnow, David Harel, Rod Downey, Steve Mahaney, Victor Miller, Sam Buss, Martin Davis, Greg Johnson, Neil Immerman, Ian Parberry, Gil Neiger, Christos Papadimitriou, Russell Impagliazzo, Ken Regan, Don Colton, Arny Rosenberg, Louxin Zhang, and Arthur Keller. Erann Gat helped us pick the colors for the stack of cafeteria trays.

We are grateful to John Rickard for the clever proof of Corollary 5.28. We are grateful to several researchers for showing us recent results that would not otherwise have made it into this manuscript: Exercise 2.9-7 is from a manuscript by Ken Regan; Exercise 4.7-15 is from a paper by Hing Leung; Exercise 5.8-1 is from a manuscript by Don Colton; Exercise 7.10-5(b) is from a paper by Louxin Zhang; Exercise 9.7-6(e) is from papers by Sam Buss and by Christos Papadimitriou and Mihalis Yannakakis.

The Internet provided valuable links between the two authors and to other educators. We are grateful to the National Science Foundation and agencies in other countries that support the Internet.

Bicoastal authorship required several extended visits to the east and west coasts, facilitated by Mike Fischer, Nick Reingold, Martin Schultz, Allen Cohn, Anna Karlin, Jeff Westbrook, Jeri and Ross Kirk, and Jane Reece, who also advised us on the publication process. The second author is also very grateful to his friends Clyde and Cathy Kruskal for their hospitality during the final preparation of the manuscript.

The manuscript was prepared using GNU Emacs and LaTeX. The diagrams were prepared by artists at Publication Services, based on roughs prepared using xfig, LaTeX, and Emacs. We are grateful to Richard Stallman for his assistance with Emacs. We are also grateful to Mike Fischer, Nick Reingold, and Donald Arseneau for their assistance with TeX and LaTeX. In addition to our home institutions, the University of California at San Diego and the University of Maryland at College Park provided computer time and other support. The National Science Foundation provided partial support for the second author's efforts through a Presidential Young Investigator award, number CCR-8958528.

RWF

RB

ABOUT THE AUTHORS

Robert Floyd studied the liberal arts, mathematics, and physics at the University of Chicago, earning a BA and a BS degree. He spent ten years as computer operator, programmer, and analyst, during which he developed widely used methods for translating programming languages. He has been a teacher and researcher in computer science since 1965, first at Carnegie–Mellon University and now at Stanford University. He was also the first Grace Murray Hopper Professor at the U.S. Naval Postgraduate School. His inventions include algorithms for finding shortest paths in a network, for parsing programming languages, for calculating quantiles, for printing shades of gray on a dot printer, and for selection of random permutations and combinations. He invented nondeterministic programming and systematic methods of program verification. He was given the Alan M. Turing Award of the Association for Computing Machinery in 1978 and the IEEE Computer Pioneer award in 1992. He is a fellow of the American Academy of Arts and Sciences, the ACM, and the American Association for the Advancement of Science. Nevertheless, he remains a simple unspoiled country boy.

Richard Beigel studied mathematics and computer science at Stanford University, where he received his BS, MS, and PhD. He has been a teacher and researcher in computer science since 1986, first at the Johns Hopkins University and now at Yale University. His research interests include complexity theory, circuits, algorithm design, and the mathematical theory of computation. In 1989 he received a Presidential Young Investigator Award from the National Science Foundation to further his research and teaching.

0

Mathematical Preliminaries

THIS CHAPTER PRESENTS the mathematical definitions, conventions, and foundations necessary for understanding this book. For a reader with experience in discrete mathematics, much of this material may be a review; however, this chapter will at least be worth skimming, especially Section 0.2.6 on relations.

0.1 QUANTIFIERS AND TWO-PLAYER GAMES

A *predicate* $p(u)$ is a statement about u that is either true or false for each u. For example, $p(u)$ could be the statement "$2 < u$ and $u < 17$."

We can precede a predicate $p(u)$ by the quantifier $(\forall u)$ (which we read as "for all u" or, informally, "for every u"), meaning that whatever value is chosen for u, $p(u)$ is true. (In this and the next few examples, u is an integer.)

EXAMPLE 0.1

- Let $p(u)$ be the predicate $u^2 - 1 = (u+1)(u-1)$. The predicate $(\forall u)p(u)$ is $(\forall u)[u^2 - 1 = (u+1)(u-1)]$, which is true.
- Let $q(u)$ be the predicate $u^2 > u$. The predicate $(\forall u)q(u)$ is $(\forall u)[u^2 > u]$, which is false because $q(1)$ is false, i.e., 1^2 is not greater than 1. ■■■

We may also precede $p(u)$ by the symbol $(\exists u)$ (which we read as "there exists u" or, informally, "for some u") to mean that a value of u can be chosen such that $p(u)$ is true.

EXAMPLE 0.2. Let $p(u)$ be the predicate $u^2 = 9$. The predicate $(\exists u)p(u)$ is $(\exists u)[u^2 = 9]$, which is true, because $p(3)$ is true, i.e., $3^2 = 9$. ■■■

The symbols $(\exists u)$ and $(\forall u)$ are called quantifiers. When a predicate has two arguments, quantifiers may be applied to both arguments.

EXAMPLE 0.3. The following predicates are true:

- $(\forall u)(\forall v)[u^2 - v^2 = (u+v)(u-v)]$.
- $(\exists u)(\exists v)[(u-1)^2 + (v-3)^2 = 0]$. ■■■

Life gets more exciting when we mix the two kinds of quantifiers. If we say $(\forall u)(\exists v)p(u,v)$, we are saying "for every u there exists a v such that $p(u,v)$ is true," i.e., "for every value given to u, a value depending on u can be given to v to make $p(u,v)$ true."

EXAMPLE 0.4. Let $p(u, v)$ be the predicate $|u - v| = 1$.

- Consider the predicate $(\forall u)(\exists v)p(u, v)$, which is

$$(\forall u)(\exists v)[|u - v| = 1].$$

  It says that for every u there is a number v, depending on u, that differs from u by exactly 1. That predicate is true because however u is chosen, we can choose v to be $u + 1$, so that $|u - v| = 1$.

- The predicate $(\exists v)(\forall u)p(u, v)$, which uses the same quantifiers in the reverse order, is a different matter entirely. It says there is a single value v (independent of u) that differs from every number u by exactly 1. That predicate is false. ■ ■ ■

We can illustrate the preceding example's distinction in terms of a game, with two players named Izzy ("there is") Existential and Al ("for all") Universal.

Al tries to make predicates false by choosing values for the arguments that have a $(\forall)$ quantifier. If $(\forall u)p(u)$ is true, Al can't win. If $(\forall u)p(u)$ is false, there is at least one value of u that makes $p(u)$ false, and Al can win by picking that value for u.

Izzy tries to make predicates true by choosing values for the arguments that have an $(\exists)$ quantifier. If $(\exists u)p(u)$ is true, Izzy can win by picking a value of u that makes $p(u)$ true. If $(\exists u)p(u)$ is false, Izzy can't find a value of u for which $p(u)$ is true, so Izzy loses.

If Al and Izzy play against each other, using a mixture of quantifiers, they take the quantifiers in left-to-right order.

EXAMPLE 0.5

- Consider the predicate

$$(\forall u)(\exists v)[u < v].$$

  Al goes first and tries to make the predicate false. However, he cannot win. Suppose Al picks some particular value for u. Now Izzy plays in turn and tries to pick v to make $u < v$. He picks

$v = u + 1$, making $u < v$, and wins. (For example, if Al picks $u = 17$, then Izzy picks $v = 18$.) The predicate is true, and if Izzy plays well, he can always win, no matter how clever Al is.

- Consider the predicate

$$(\exists v)(\forall u)[u < v].$$

Now the game is different, because Izzy has to go first. He must make his choice without knowing Al's. Suppose that Izzy picks some value for v. Now Al plays in turn. He picks $u = v$, so u is not less than v, and wins. (For example, if Izzy picks $v = 18$, then Al picks $u = 18$.) Al's winning strategy shows that the predicate is false. ■■■

In a truth table for $p(u, v)$, the entry in row u and column v is the value of $p(u, v)$. (See Figure 0.1 for an example.)

$(\forall u)(\forall v)p(u, v)$ means that Al chooses both u and v, but cannot find a "false" in the table; every entry is true. The same happens with $(\forall v)(\forall u)p(u, v)$. Al makes his choices in the opposite order, and they still do not make $p(u, v)$ false.

v

	F	F	F	T	T	F
	F	F	T	T	F	T
u	T	T	F	T	F	F
	F	F	F	T	F	F

FIGURE 0.1: A truth table where u takes on 4 possible values and v takes on 6 possible values. The entry in row u, column v denotes $p(u, v)$. T abbreviates "true," and F abbreviates "false." In this example the predicates $(\exists u)(\exists v)p(u, v)$, $(\forall u)(\exists v)p(u, v)$, $(\exists v)(\forall u)p(u, v)$, and $(\forall v)(\exists u)p(u, v)$ are true. The predicates $(\forall u)(\forall v)p(u, v)$ and $(\exists u)(\forall v)p(u, v)$ are false.

$(\exists u)(\exists v)p(u,v)$ means that Izzy can find a "true" in the table. So does $(\exists v)(\exists u)p(u,v)$. Some entry is true.

$(\exists u)(\forall v)p(u,v)$ means that Izzy can pick a row where Al cannot find a "false," i.e., some (at least one) row consists entirely of "true." Similarly, $(\exists v)(\forall u)p(u,v)$ means that some column consists entirely of "true."

$(\forall u)(\exists v)p(u,v)$ means that however Al picks a column, Izzy can find a "true" in it; there is at least one "true" in every column. Similarly, $(\forall v)(\exists u)p(u,v)$ means that there is at least one "true" in every row.

As a shorthand, we write $(\exists u \leq n)p(u)$ to denote $(\exists u)[u \leq n \text{ and } p(u)]$. We use similar shorthands with $<$, $\geq$, and $>$. For example, the predicate $(\exists u > 4)[u^2 = 25]$ is true, but the predicate $(\exists u > 5)[u^2 = 25]$ is false.

Exercises

0.1-1 Refer to the predicate $p(u,v)$ in Figure 0.1. Which of the following predicates are true?

(a) $(\exists v)(\exists u)p(u,v)$
(b) $(\forall v)(\forall u)p(u,v)$
(c) $(\forall u)(\exists v)p(v,u)$
(d) $(\exists v)(\forall u)p(v,u)$
(e) $(\forall v)(\exists u)p(v,u)$
(f) $(\exists u)(\forall v)p(v,u)$

Solution:

(a) true
(b) false
(c) true
(d) false
(e) true
(f) true

0.2 SETS, BAGS, RELATIONS, FUNCTIONS, AND SEQUENCES

In this section we review the mathematical notions of sets, bags, relations, functions, and sequences. Although this material will be familiar to most readers, it is important to at least skim the section on relations. Numerous examples are designed to familiarize the reader with postfix notation and certain operations on relations that facilitate studying the theory of languages and computation.

0.2.1 Sets

We assume that the reader is already familiar with sets.

EXAMPLE 0.6

- $\{\text{red}, \text{green}, \text{blue}\}$, the set of primary colors of light
- $\{\text{chocolate}, \text{vanilla}, \text{strawberry}\}$, the set of primary flavors of ice cream
- Z, the set of integers
- $\mathsf{Z}^+ = \{i \in \mathsf{Z} : i > 0\}$, the set of positive integers
- $\mathsf{Z}^- = \{i \in \mathsf{Z} : i < 0\}$, the set of negative integers
- $\mathsf{N} = \{i \in \mathsf{Z} : i \geq 0\}$, the set of natural numbers
- R, the set of real numbers ■ ■ ■

We review some basic notation:

- $x \in A$ means that x is an *element* of the set A.
- χ_A denotes the *characteristic function* of the set A.

  $\chi_A(x) = 1$ if $x \in A$, 0 if $x \notin A$.
- $\emptyset$ denotes the *empty set*.

  $(\forall x)[x \notin \emptyset]$.
- $A \cup B$ denotes the *union* of the sets A and B.

  $A \cup B = \{x : x \in A \text{ or } x \in B\}$.
- $A \cap B$ denotes the *intersection* of the sets A and B.

  $A \cap B = \{x : x \in A \text{ and } x \in B\}$.

- A and B are *disjoint* if $A \cap B = \emptyset$.
- $A \uplus B$ denotes the *union* of the sets A and B and also asserts that A and B are disjoint.

  $A \uplus B = A \cup B$ if A and B are disjoint, but is undefined otherwise.
- Nonempty sets $A_1, \ldots, A_k$ are said to *partition* a set A if we have $A = A_1 \uplus \cdots \uplus A_k$.
- $A - B$ denotes the *difference* of the sets A and B.

  $A - B = \{x : x \in A \text{ and } x \notin B\}$.
- $\overline{A}$ denotes the *complement* of the set A.

  $\overline{A} = U - A$, where U is a universal set containing all x of interest (the choice of the universal set will usually be clear from context).
- $A \subseteq B$ means that the set A is a *subset* of the set B.

  $A \subseteq B$ iff $(\forall x)[x \in A \Rightarrow x \in B]$.
- $A \subset B$ means that the set A is a *proper subset* of the set B.

  $A \subset B$ iff $A \subseteq B$ and $B \nsubseteq A$.
- $A = B$ means that the sets A and B contain the same elements.

  $A = B$ iff $A \subseteq B$ and $B \subseteq A$.
- $(x_1, \ldots, x_k)$ denotes the ordered k-tuple whose ith element is x_i, for $i = 1, \ldots, k$.
- In particular, (x, y) denotes the ordered pair whose first element is x and second element is y.
- $A \times B$ denotes the *Cartesian product* of the sets A and B.

  $A \times B = \{(x, y) : x \in A \text{ and } y \in B\}$.
- $|A|$ denotes the *cardinality* of the set A.

$|A|$ is the number of elements in A if A is finite, undefined otherwise.[1]

- 2^A denotes the *power set* of the set A, i.e., the set of all subsets of A.

  $2^A = \{B : B \subseteq A\}$.

One cannot hope to prove anything without knowing the definitions. When you run into an obstacle it often helps if you go back to the definitions to see what you have to prove. An example illustrates the steps involved in proving that two sets are equal.

EXAMPLE 0.7. Let $A = \{x \in \mathrm{R} : \sqrt{x} = x - 2\}$, and let $B = \{4\}$. Suppose that we want to prove that $A = B$. Then we have to prove two inclusions: $A \subseteq B$ and $B \subseteq A$.

To show that $A \subseteq B$, we show that $x \in A \Rightarrow x \in B$. Suppose that $x \in A$. Then $\sqrt{x} = x - 2$, so $x = x^2 - 4x + 4$, $x^2 - 5x + 4 = 0$, $(x-4)(x-1) = 0$. Therefore $x = 4$ or $x = 1$. But $\sqrt{1} \neq 1 - 2$, so $x = 4$. Therefore $x \in B$. Thus we have shown that $A \subseteq B$.

To show that $B \subseteq A$, we show that $x \in B \Rightarrow x \in A$. Suppose that $x \in B$. Then $x = 4$, so $\sqrt{x} = 2 = x - 2$. Therefore $x \in A$. Thus we have shown that $B \subseteq A$.

Having shown that $A \subseteq B$ and $B \subseteq A$, we conclude that $A = B$. ■■■

For reasonable predicates p, we can talk about the set of all x for which $p(x)$ is true, which is denoted $\{x : p(x)\}$ (Exercise 7.8-11 exhibits an unreasonable predicate). Several variants on this notation may be used when convenient. We may write $\{x \in A : p(x)\}$ to denote $\{x : x \in A \text{ and } p(x)\}$, and we may write $\{x \leq m : p(x)\}$ to denote $\{x : x \leq m \text{ and } p(x)\}$. As examples, we have $\{x \in \mathrm{Z} : x^2 < 7\} = \{-2, -1, 0, 1, 2\}$ and $\{x < 17 : x \text{ is prime}\} = \{2, 3, 5, 7, 11, 13\}$. (A positive integer n is *composite* if n is divisible by a positive integer other than n or 1. A positive integer n is *prime* if $n \neq 1$ and n is not composite.) Similarly, we write $(\exists x \in A)p(x)$ to denote $(\exists x)[x \in A \text{ and } p(x)]$.

---

[1] For the set theorist, $|A|$ is always defined, even for infinite sets. This need not concern us.

We will often consider the union or intersection of many sets, instead of just two as described earlier. Suppose that A_i is a set for each i, and suppose that $P(i)$ is a predicate. Then

$$\bigcup_{P(i)} A_i = \{x : (\exists i)[P(i) \text{ and } x \in A_i]\}.$$

EXAMPLE 0.8

- $\displaystyle\bigcup_{1 \le i \le 10} A_i = \bigcup_{i=1}^{10} A_i = A_1 \cup \cdots \cup A_{10}$.
- Let $A_i = \{x : (\exists y > 1)[x = iy]\}$, i.e., A_i contains all multiples of i greater than i. Then $\bigcup_{i \ge 2} A_i$ is the set of all composite numbers. ■ ■ ■

0.2.2 Set Extensions and Closures

If we have a binary operation $\oplus$ on elements, then we may *extend* that operation to apply to sets in the following general way:

$$A \oplus' B = \{a \oplus b : a \in A \text{ and } b \in B\}.$$

When no confusion can arise we abbreviate $\oplus'$ as $\oplus$, although these are technically different operations. In later sections we will present very important examples of set extensions. For now, let us consider some frivolous examples that will have no subsequent use.

EXAMPLE 0.9. We extend integer addition to sets of integers by defining

$$A + B = \{a + b : a \in A \text{ and } b \in B\}.$$

Then, for example

- $\{1, 2, 3\} + \{1, 2, 3\} = \{2, 3, 4, 5, 6\}$,
- $\{1\} + \{0, 2, 4, 6\} = \{1, 3, 5, 7\}$,
- $\{0, 1\} + \{0, 2, 4, 6\} = \{0, 1, 2, 3, 4, 5, 6, 7\}$,

- $\mathsf{Z}^+ + \mathsf{Z} = \mathsf{Z}$,
- $\mathsf{Z}^+ + \mathsf{Z}^- = \mathsf{Z}$, and
- $\emptyset + \{1, 2, 3\} = \emptyset$. ∎∎∎

If $\oplus$ is a unary operation, we extend it similarly:

$$\oplus' A = \{\oplus a : a \in A\}.$$

EXAMPLE 0.10. Let us extend the square root operation to sets of nonnegative reals:

$$\sqrt{A} = \{\sqrt{a} : a \in A\}.$$

Then, for example,

- If $A = \{0, 1, 4\}$ then $\sqrt{A} = \{0, 1, 2\}$.
- If $A = \{x \in \mathsf{R} : 4 < x \leq 25\}$ then $\sqrt{A} = \{x \in \mathsf{R} : 2 < x \leq 5\}$. ∎∎∎

A set A is *closed* under a binary operation $\oplus$ if for every pair of elements x and y (not necessarily distinct) of A, we have $x \oplus y \in A$, i.e., if $A \oplus A \subseteq A$. A set A is *closed* under a unary operation $\oplus$ if for every element x of A, we have $\oplus x \in A$, i.e., if $\oplus A \subseteq A$.

EXAMPLE 0.11

- The sets $\{0\}$, N, and Z^+ are closed under addition, but the set $\{0, 1\}$ is not.
- The sets $\{0, 1\}$, $\{x \in \mathsf{R} : 0 < x < 1\}$, and $\{x \in \mathsf{R} : x \geq 1\}$ are closed under square root, but the set $\{0, 1, 2\}$ is not. ∎∎∎

We may order sets by containment. That is, if $A \subseteq B$ then we think of A as being smaller than B or equal to it.[2] Let P be any property of sets,

[2] Technically, this is a partial order because there are sets like $\{0, 1\}$ and $\{1, 2, 3\}$, neither of which is a subset of the other.

e.g., finiteness, infiniteness, or closure under $\oplus$. We say that A is the *least* set with property P if

- A has property P, and
- if A' has property P, then $A \subseteq A'$.

EXAMPLE 0.12

- If $P(A)$ is the property $A \subseteq \mathsf{N}$, then the least set with property P is $\emptyset$.
- If $P(A)$ is the property "$|A|$ is even," then the least set with property P is also $\emptyset$.
- If $P(A)$ is the property $\{3, 6, 7\} \subseteq A$, then the least set with property P is $\{3, 6, 7\}$.
- If $P(A)$ is the property "$\{3, 6, 7\} \subseteq A$ and A is closed under negation," then the least set with property P is $\{3, 6, 7, -3, -6, -7\}$.
- If $P(A)$ is the property "$\{3, 6, 7\} \subseteq A$ and A is closed under addition," then the least set with property P is $\{3, 6, 7, 9, 10\} \cup \{x : x \geq 12\}$. ■■■

EXAMPLE 0.13. Sometimes, there is no least set with property P.

- If $P(A)$ is the property "$|A|$ is odd," then there is no least set with property P.
- If $P(A)$ is the property "A is infinite," then there is no least set with property P. ■■■

THEOREM 0.14. *If the least set with property P exists, then it is given by the following formula:*

$$\bigcap_{A \text{ has property } P} A.$$

Proof: Let L be the least set with property P. Let

$$B = \bigcap_{A \text{ has property } P} A.$$

Since L has property P, L is one of the terms in the intersection, so $B \subseteq L$. Since L is the *least* set with property P, L is contained in each term of the intersection, so $L \subseteq B$. Therefore $L = B$. ∎

EXAMPLE 0.15

- The intersection of all sets A with an even number of elements is $\emptyset$, which is also the least set A with an even number of elements.
- The intersection of all infinite sets is also $\emptyset$, which is not infinite, so there is no least infinite set. ∎∎∎

DEFINITION 0.16 (Closure). The *closure* of a set A under an operation $\oplus$ is the least set that contains A and is closed under $\oplus$, i.e., a set B satisfying

- $A \subseteq B$,
- B is closed under $\oplus$, and
- if $A \subseteq B'$ and B' is closed under $\oplus$, then $B \subseteq B'$.

EXAMPLE 0.17

- The closure of $\{1\}$ under addition is Z^+.
- The closure of $\{0, 2\}$ under addition is the set of nonnegative even integers.
- The closure of $\{x : 2 \leq x < 4\}$ under square root is the set $\{x : 1 < x < 4\}$. ∎∎∎

A binary operation $\oplus$ is called *associative* if, for every x, y, and z,

$$(x \oplus y) \oplus z = x \oplus (y \oplus z).$$

THEOREM 0.18. *The closure of A under $\oplus$ is given by formula (i) below. If $\oplus$ is a unary operation or an associative operation, then the closure of A under $\oplus$ is also given by formula (ii) below.*

(i) $$\bigcap_{\substack{A \subseteq B \text{ and} \\ B \text{ is closed under } \oplus}} B$$

(ii) $\bigcup_{i \geq 1} A^i$, *where A^k is the result of applying $\oplus$ to A k times, i.e., $A^1 = A$ and A^{k+1} is equal to $A \oplus A^k$ if $\oplus$ is a binary operation, $\oplus A^k$ if $\oplus$ is a unary operation.*

Proof: We present the proof assuming that $\oplus$ is an associative binary operator. The cases when $\oplus$ is unary or nonassociative are left as exercises. Let

$$A_1 = \bigcap_{\substack{A \subseteq B \text{ and} \\ B \text{ is closed under } \oplus}} B.$$

Let $A_2 = \bigcup_{i \geq 1} A^i$.

If $A \subseteq B$ and B is closed under $\oplus$, then $A^i \subseteq B$ for every i, so each term of A_2 is contained in each term of A_1. Therefore $A_2 \subseteq A_1$.

Suppose that x and y belong to A_2. Then $x \in A^i$ and $y \in A^j$ for some i and j. Therefore (by associativity) $x \oplus y \in A^{i+j}$, so $x \oplus y \in A_2$. Thus A_2 is closed under $\oplus$.

If B is closed under $\oplus$ then $A_1 \subseteq B$, because B is one of the terms of A_1. Therefore $A_2 \subseteq A_1 \subseteq B$, so A_2 is the least set that is closed under $\oplus$.

Since A_1 is contained in every set that is closed under $\oplus$, A_1 is contained in the closure of A under $\oplus$. We have already shown that A_1 contains the closure of A under $\oplus$ (because that is A_2). Therefore, A_1 is equal to the closure of A under $\oplus$. ■

0.2.3 Tuples

The differences and similarities between sets and tuples are worth noting.

First, order is completely unimportant in a set, e.g., the set $\{1, 2, 3\}$ is equal to the set $\{2, 1, 3\}$. In contrast, order matters somewhat in a tuple: the 3-tuple $(1, 2, 3)$ is not equal to the 3-tuple $(2, 1, 3)$.

Second, a set may not contain the same element twice, e.g., $\{1, 1, 2\}$ is equal to $\{1, 2\}$ (as a notational convention, we would always write the latter). In contrast, a tuple may contain two identical components; e.g., $(1, 1, 2)$ is a 3-tuple whereas $(1, 2)$ is a 2-tuple.

Third, many interesting general operations are defined on sets, e.g., membership, union, intersection, and complementation. In contrast, the only general operation defined on tuples is to select a particular component. When tuples contain specific kinds of data, then interesting functions may be defined on them in an ad hoc fashion. For example, the distance function is defined on 3-tuples that represent points in 3-dimensional space:

$$\text{dist}((x, y, z), (x', y', z')) = \sqrt{(x - x')^2 + (y - y')^2 + (z - z')^2}\,.$$

However, the distance function is not defined for general 3-tuples, because it would not make sense if the components of the 3-tuples were primary colors or flavors of ice cream, for example.

Next we describe a similarity between tuples and sets, which may be a bit surprising. Although we said that order matters somewhat in a tuple, it matters very little, as long as one is consistent about it. For example, there is no intrinsic reason that x-coordinates precede y-coordinates and y-coordinates precede z-coordinates in the 3-tuples that represent points in 3-dimensional space. Geometry works just as well if points are represented as (y-coordinate, x-coordinate, z-coordinate), provided that one is consistent about the representation. Similarly, in your personal phone directory you might store 3-tuples, each consisting of a name, home phone number, and work phone number. It does not matter whether the home phone number always comes second or always comes third; as long as you are consistent about the order, you will know what the 3-tuple means. In this sense, tuples are analogous to the "record" data structure in high-level programming languages. Order in a record is arbitrary, but it is important to be consistent about the order when storing the record in computer memory.

The phone directory example highlights one more distinction between sets and records. Elements of a set are all of the same type, whereas components of a tuple may have different types, like a name and a phone number.

0.2.4 Sequences

A *sequence* is an ordered list, which may contain repetitions. Examples are the sequence consisting of the decimal digits in increasing order $\langle\langle 0, 1, 2, 3, 4, 5, 6, 7, 8, 9\rangle\rangle$ and the sequence consisting of the first six Fibonacci numbers $\langle\langle 1, 1, 2, 3, 5, 8\rangle\rangle$. As with sets, the elements of a sequence are all of the same type. An important sequence is the *empty sequence*, which contains no elements and is denoted Λ. Sequences may be finite or infinite, but finite sequences are the most important for the study of computation.

There are two main differences between sequences and sets: sequences are ordered and may contain duplicates, whereas sets are unordered and may not contain duplicates.

The differences between sequences and tuples are more subtle: First, order matters a lot in sequences, e.g., $\langle\langle \texttt{p}, \texttt{a}, \texttt{l}, \texttt{e}\rangle\rangle$ and $\langle\langle \texttt{l}, \texttt{e}, \texttt{a}, \texttt{p}\rangle\rangle$, whereas order is merely a bookkeeping consideration in tuples. Second, lots of interesting general operations will be defined on sequences, e.g., concatenation, reversal, and shuffle, whereas most operations on tuples are ad hoc.

Usually we number the elements of a finite sequence s and write $s = \langle\langle x_1, \ldots, x_n\rangle\rangle$.[3] The number n is called the length of s, denoted $|s|$. There are two important operations on nonempty finite sequences: $\text{first}(s)$ is x_1, the first element of s; $\text{rest}(s)$ is the sequence $\langle\langle x_2, \ldots, x_n\rangle\rangle$. Two finite sequences $\langle\langle x_1, \ldots, x_m\rangle\rangle$ and $\langle\langle y_1, \ldots, y_n\rangle\rangle$ are equal if $m = n$ and $x_i = y_i$ for $i = 1, \ldots, m$.

It is possible to *concatenate* two finite sequences to obtain a longer sequence. If $s = \langle\langle s_1, \ldots, s_m\rangle\rangle$ and $t = \langle\langle t_1, \ldots, t_n\rangle\rangle$, then the concatenation of s and t (denoted $s \otimes t$) is the sequence $\langle\langle s_1, \ldots, s_m, t_1, \ldots, t_n\rangle\rangle$. When there is no possibility of confusion, we will identify a single element x with the sequence $\langle\langle x\rangle\rangle$. Under this convention, we have $s = \text{first}(s) \otimes \text{rest}(s)$. We note that concatenation is associative, i.e., $(s \otimes t) \otimes u$ is always equal to $s \otimes (t \otimes u)$. Therefore we may drop the parentheses and write $s \otimes t \otimes u$ for the concatenation of three sequences.

The operations $\text{first}()$, $\text{rest}()$, and $\otimes$ are also defined on infinite sequences. This will be useful when we discuss programs that do not terminate. Let $t = \langle\langle t_1, t_2, \ldots\rangle\rangle$. Then $\text{first}(t) = t_1$ and $\text{rest}(t) = \langle\langle t_2, t_3, \ldots\rangle\rangle$.

---

[3] Notes on the use of three-dots notation: When $n = 1$, $\langle\langle x_1, \ldots, x_n\rangle\rangle$ denotes $\langle\langle x_1\rangle\rangle$; when $n = 0$, $\langle\langle x_1, \ldots, x_n\rangle\rangle$ denotes Λ. More generally, when $i = j$, $\langle\langle x_i, \ldots, x_j\rangle\rangle$ denotes $\langle\langle x_i\rangle\rangle$; when $i = j + 1$, $\langle\langle x_i, \ldots, x_j\rangle\rangle$ denotes Λ.

If $s = \langle\langle s_1, \ldots, s_n \rangle\rangle$, then $s \otimes t = \langle\langle s_1, \ldots, s_n, t_1, t_2, \ldots \rangle\rangle$. In this book, we will not need to concatenate a sequence on the right of an infinite sequence, so we do not define $t \otimes u$ when t is an infinite sequence.

0.2.5 Bags

A *bag* is an unordered list. Like a sequence, a bag may contain duplicate elements. Like a sequence and a set, the elements of a bag are all of the same type. Historically, bags have been called multisets, because they are like sets that can contain multiple copies of the same element. An example is the bag that contains i copies of the number i for $0 \leq i \leq 4$: $\{1, 2, 2, 3, 3, 3, 4, 4, 4, 4\}$. This bag is equal to $\{1, 2, 3, 4, 2, 3, 4, 3, 4, 4\}$ because order is unimportant in bags.

The operations on bags are similar to the operations on sets, and we use set-theoretic notation to denote them:

- χ_A denotes the *characteristic function* of the bag A.

  $\chi_A(x)$ is the number of copies of x in bag A.

  For example, if $A = \{1, 2, 2, 3, 3, 3, 4, 4, 4, 4\}$, then $\chi_A(3) = 3$ and $\chi_A(5) = 0$.

- $x \in A$ means that x is an *element* of the bag A.

  $x \in A$ iff $\chi_A(x) \geq 1$.

  For example, if $A = \{1, 2, 2, 3, 3, 3, 4, 4, 4, 4\}$, then $3 \in A$ and $5 \notin A$.

- $A \subseteq B$ means that the bag A is a *sub-bag* of the bag B.

  $A \subseteq B$ iff B contains at least as many copies of each element as A contains, i.e., $(\forall x)[\chi_A(x) \leq \chi_B(x)]$.

  For example, $\{3, 3\} \subseteq \{1, 2, 2, 3, 3, 3, 4, 4, 4, 4\}$.

- $A = B$ means that the bags A and B contain the same number of copies of each element.

  $A = B$ iff $A \subseteq B$ and $B \subseteq A$.

  For example, $\{1, 2, 2, 3, 3, 3, 4, 4, 4, 4\} = \{4, 4, 4, 4, 3, 3, 3, 2, 2, 1\}$.

- $A \uplus B$ denotes the *disjoint union* of the bags A and B.

  $A \uplus B$ contains everything that is in A plus everything that is in B, i.e., $(\forall x)[\chi_{A \uplus B}(x) = \chi_A(x) + \chi_B(x)]$. Observe that this definition is meaningful for bags that have elements in common.

  For example, $\{1, 2, 2, 3, 3, 3\} \uplus \{1, 1, 3, 3, 5, 5\} = \{1, 1, 1, 2, 2, 3, 3, 3, 3, 3, 5, 5\}$.

- Nonempty bags $A_1, \ldots, A_k$ *partition* the bag A if A is the disjoint union of $A_1, \ldots, A_k$, i.e., if $A = A_1 \uplus \cdots \uplus A_k$.

  For example, the bags $\{1, 1, 1\}$, $\{1, 6\}$, and $\{3, 4, 5\}$ partition the bag $\{1, 1, 1, 1, 3, 4, 5, 6\}$.

- $\sum_{x \in A} f(x)$ denotes the sum, over all elements x in the bag A, counting multiplicities, of the function $f(x)$.

  $\sum_{x \in A} f(x) = \sum_x f(x)\chi_A(x)$, where the sum is over all distinct x.

  For example, if $A = \{1, 2, 2, 3, 3, 3, 4, 4, 4, 4\}$ then $\sum_{x \in A} x = 30$.

- $|A|$ denotes the *cardinality* of the bag A.

  $|A|$ is the number of elements of A, counting multiplicities, i.e., $|A| = \sum_x \chi_A(x)$, where the sum is over all distinct x.

  For example, if $A = \{1, 2, 2, 3, 3, 3, 4, 4, 4, 4\}$ then $|A| = 10$.

- $A \cup B$ denotes the *union* of the bags A and B.

  $\chi_{A \cup B}(x) = \max(\chi_A(x), \chi_B(x))$.

  For example, $\{1, 2, 2, 3, 3, 3\} \cup \{1, 1, 3, 3, 5, 5\} = \{1, 1, 2, 2, 3, 3, 3, 5, 5\}$.

- $A \cap B$ denotes the *intersection* of the bags A and B.

  $\chi_{A \cap B}(x) = \min(\chi_A(x), \chi_B(x))$.

  For example, $\{1, 2, 2, 3, 3, 3\} \cap \{1, 1, 3, 3, 5, 5\} = \{1, 3, 3\}$.

Exercises

0.2-1 Let $A = \{1, 2, 2, 3, 3, 3, 4, 4, 4, 4\}$. Find bags B and C such that B and C partition A, $\sum_{x \in B} x = \sum_{x \in C} x$, and $|B| = |C|$.

0.2-2 Let $A = \{1, 2, 2, 3, 3, 3, 4, 4, 4, 4, 5, 5, 5, 5, 5\}$. Prove that there do not exist bags B and C such that B and C partition A and $\sum_{x \in B} x = \sum_{x \in C} x$.

0.2.6 Relations

Formally,[4] a *relation* is a set of ordered pairs. For example, the less-than relation is $\{(x, y) : x < y\}$. Usually a relation ρ is understood to be a subset of $X \times Y$ for some sets X and Y. The set X is called the *source* of the relation, and the set Y is called the *target* of the relation. We say that ρ is a relation *from* X *to* Y; if $X = Y$, we say that ρ is a relation *on* X.

For example, the integer-part relation is

$$\{(x, y) : x \text{ is real, } y \text{ is an integer, and } y \leq x < y + 1\}.$$

Its source is R, its target Z. Another relation with source R and target Z is the round-off relation, $\{(x, y) : x \text{ is real, } y \text{ is an integer, and } |x - y| \leq \frac{1}{2}\}$. Usually the sets X and Y are understood from context, and they are not mentioned explicitly. But sometimes the sets X and Y truly matter. For example, there are really several different less-than relations: the less-than relation on integers is $\{(x, y) : x \text{ and } y \text{ are integers and } x < y\}$, and the less-than relation on real numbers is $\{(x, y) : x \text{ and } y \text{ are real numbers and } x < y\}$.

If the ordered pair (x, y) belongs to the relation ρ, we say that ρ *relates* x to y. In symbols, we can denote that in any of five ways:

(i) $(x, y) \in \rho$.

(ii) $x \ \rho \ y$.

---

[4] In many cases, we have a good intuitive notion of what something means, but it is still important to have a precise definition using mathematical formulas. Such a definition is called "formal." Both formal and informal definitions are valuable. Informal definitions can help us develop our intuition; formal definitions are needed so that we can verify our intuition via a mathematical proof.

(iii) $x \overset{\rho}{\mapsto} y$.

(iv) $y \in \rho(x)$.

(v) $y \in x\rho$.

The first notation reflects the formal definition of ρ as a set of ordered pairs. The second notation is probably the most familiar, because that is how we denote relations like equality ($x = y$) and less than ($x < y$); it would be confusing to write $(x, y) \in =$ or $(x, y) \in <$. The third notation suggests that the value x goes to the value y via ρ; it is used extensively in describing a program's effect on data. The fourth notation is similar to conventional notation for functions; we think of ρ as a multiple-valued function, i.e., a function that produces a set of values. The fifth notation is similar to postfix notation for functions, which we will discuss in Section 0.2.7.

Let us present some examples of relations on the set of all humans who have ever lived.

$$
\begin{aligned}
I &= \{(x, x) : x \text{ is a human}\}, \\
\text{is-parent} &= \{(x, y) : x \text{ is a parent of } y\}, \\
\text{is-grandfather} &= \{(x, y) : x \text{ is a grandfather of } y\}, \\
\text{is-grandmother} &= \{(x, y) : x \text{ is a grandmother of } y\}, \\
\text{is-grandparent} &= \{(x, y) : x \text{ is a grandparent of } y\}, \\
\text{is-greatgrandparent} &= \{(x, y) : x \text{ is a greatgrandparent of } y\}, \\
\text{is-father} &= \{(x, y) : x \text{ is the father of } y\}, \\
\text{is-mother} &= \{(x, y) : x \text{ is the mother of } y\}, \\
\text{is-child} &= \{(x, y) : x \text{ is a child of } y\}, \\
\text{is-son} &= \{(x, y) : x \text{ is a son of } y\}, \\
\text{is-daughter} &= \{(x, y) : x \text{ is a daughter of } y\}, \\
\text{is-sibling} &= \{(x, y) : x \text{ is a brother or sister of } y\}, \\
\text{is-brother} &= \{(x, y) : x \text{ is a brother of } y\}, \\
\text{is-sister} &= \{(x, y) : x \text{ is a sister of } y\}, \\
\text{is-ancestor} &= \{(x, y) : x \text{ is an ancestor of } y\}, \\
\text{is-descendant} &= \{(x, y) : x \text{ is a descendant of } y\}, \\
\text{is-relative} &= \{(x, y) : x \text{ is a blood relative of } y\}.
\end{aligned}
$$

The relation I is the identity relation on humans in this example. In general we write I_X to denote the identity relation on the set X; we write simply I if the set X is clear from context.

The *domain* of a relation ρ (denoted $\mathrm{Dom}(\rho)$) is $\{x : (\exists y)[x\ \rho\ y]\}$, and the *range* of ρ (denoted $\mathrm{Range}(\rho)$) is $\{y : (\exists x)[x\ \rho\ y]\}$. For example, the domain of is-daughter is the set of all human females ever born, and the range of is-mother is the set of all humans ever born.

The union of two relations is already defined, because relations are sets. For example, we have

$$\begin{aligned} \text{is-parent} &= \text{is-mother} \cup \text{is-father}, \\ \text{is-child} &= \text{is-son} \cup \text{is-daughter}. \end{aligned}$$

That is, x is a parent of y if and only if x is the mother of y or x is the father of y, and similarly for children. The notation $\subseteq$ and $\subset$ carry over from sets, and we have

$$\begin{aligned} \text{is-father} &\subset \text{is-parent}, \\ \text{is-daughter} &\subset \text{is-child}. \end{aligned}$$

The composition of two relations ρ and σ (denoted $\rho \circ \sigma$ or $\rho\sigma$) is defined as follows:

$$\rho \circ \sigma = \{(x, y) : (\exists t)[(x, t) \in \rho \text{ and } (t, y) \in \sigma]\}.$$

For example, we have

$$\begin{aligned} \text{is-grandmother} &= \text{is-mother} \circ \text{is-parent}, \\ \text{is-brother} &= (\text{is-son} \circ \text{is-mother}) \cap (\text{is-son} \circ \text{is-father}) - I. \end{aligned}$$

That is, x is a grandmother of y iff x is the mother of someone who is a parent of y. In the second line, x is a brother of y iff x is a son of the mother of y and x is a son of the father of y, but x is not the same person as y.

If A is any set then we define

$$A\rho = A \circ \rho = \{y : (\exists x \in A)[x\ \rho\ y]\}.$$

For example, if $A = \{1.0, 1.4, 1.9, 2.2\}$ and ρ is the round-off relation from reals to integers, then $A\rho = \{1, 2\}$. If $A = \{1, 3\}$ and ρ is the less-than relation on integers, then $A\rho = \{2, 3, 4, \ldots\}$. By convention, if A is a singleton set, then we may also write $x\rho$ to denote $\{x\}\rho$, which is equal to $\{y : x \; \rho \; y\}$.

We obtain the *converse* of a relation ρ (denoted ρ^{-1}) by reversing each of its elements. That is

$$\rho^{-1} = \{(x, y) : (y, x) \in \rho\}.$$

For example,

$$\begin{aligned} \text{is-mother}^{-1} &= \{(x, y) : y \text{ is the mother of } x\}, \\ \text{is-parent}^{-1} &= \text{is-child}, \\ \text{is-ancestor}^{-1} &= \text{is-descendant}. \end{aligned}$$

Note that is-ancestor $\circ$ is-ancestor$^{-1} \neq I$.

Transitive Closure A relation ρ is *transitive* if ρ is closed under $\circ$, i.e., $\rho \circ \rho \subseteq \rho$. Thus, for example, is-ancestor is transitive because your ancestor's ancestor is also your ancestor. I is transitive but is-parent is not.

The *transitive closure* of a relation ρ (denoted ρ^+) is the closure of ρ under $\circ$; i.e., it is the least relation that contains ρ and is also transitive. For example, the transitive closure of is-parent is is-ancestor. By Theorem 0.18 the transitive closure of ρ is equal to $\rho \cup \rho \circ \rho \cup \rho \circ \rho \circ \rho \cup \cdots$; e.g., is-ancestor $=$ is-parent $\cup$ is-grandparent $\cup$ is-greatgrandparent $\cup \cdots$.

A relation ρ is reflexive if $I \subseteq \rho$, i.e., if $x \; \rho \; x$ for all x. For example, the relations $=$ and $\leq$ are reflexive; on the other hand, the relations $<$ and is-son are not reflexive.

The *reflexive transitive closure* of ρ (denoted ρ^*) is the least relation that contains ρ and is reflexive and transitive. For example, the reflexive transitive closure of is-sibling is $I \cup$ is-sibling. In contrast, the transitive closure of is-sibling is $(I \cup \text{is-sibling}) - \{(x, x) : x \text{ is an only child}\}$.

THEOREM 0.19. *The reflexive transitive closure of ρ is equal to both of the following:*

- *the union of I and the transitive closure of ρ*
- *the transitive closure of $\rho \cup I$*

The proof of this theorem is left to the reader. ■

For example, the reflexive transitive closure of is-parent is $I \cup$ is-parent $\cup$ is-grandparent $\cup$ is-greatgrandparent $\cup \cdots$, which is equal to $I \cup$ is-ancestor.

When we have $x_1\ \rho_1\ x_2$ and $x_2\ \rho_2\ x_3$, we can write $x_1\ \rho_1\ x_2\ \rho_2\ x_3$. (For example, we can write $1 < 2 < 3$ or $2^9 < 2^{10} = 1024$.) If we know that $x_1\ \rho\ x_2\ \rho\ \cdots\ \rho\ x_n$, we can conclude that $x_1\ \rho^*\ x_i$ for $1 \leq i \leq n$. (For example, if x is-parent y is-parent z, then x is-ancestor z.) If ρ is reflexive and transitive, i.e., $\rho = \rho^*$, we can conclude further that $x_1\ \rho\ x_i$ for $1 \leq i \leq n$.

Equivalence Relations A relation ρ is *symmetric* if $\rho = \rho^{-1}$, i.e., if $x\ \rho\ y \Rightarrow y\ \rho\ x$. For example, is-sibling is symmetric. A relation ρ is an *equivalence relation* if ρ is reflexive, symmetric, and transitive.

EXAMPLE 0.20. The following are equivalence relations:

- I
- $\{(x, y)$: the numbers x and y have the same number of digits when written in base $10\}$
- $\{(x, y)$: the people x and y live on the same street$\}$

The following are not equivalence relations:

- is-sister, because it is not symmetric, reflexive, or transitive
- the relations is-sibling and is-relative, because they are not reflexive or transitive
- is-sister $\cup\ I$, because it is not symmetric

However, is-sibling $\cup\ I$ is an equivalence relation. ■ ■ ■

An important equivalence relation is congruence modulo m, explained below.

Arithmetic Congruence When we divide an integer n by a nonzero integer m, we obtain integers q and r such that $n = qm + r$ and $0 \leq r < m$. The number q is called the *quotient*, and r is called the *remainder*. The binary operation mod calculates this remainder, that is, $n \bmod m = r$, where r is the remainder upon dividing n by m. For example, we have $7 \bmod 5 = 2$, $7 \bmod 2 = 1$, and $14 \bmod 7 = 0$.

If $a \bmod m = b \bmod m$, then we say that a is *congruent* to b *modulo* m, which is denoted $a \equiv b \pmod{m}$. For example $7 \equiv 2 \pmod{5}$, n is odd iff $n \equiv 1 \pmod{2}$, and n is divisible by m iff $n \equiv 0 \bmod m$.

The relation *congruence modulo m* is $\{(x, y) : x \equiv y \pmod{m}\}$. The reader may verify that congruence modulo m is an equivalence relation.

Equivalence Classes Let ρ be an equivalence relation on a set A. We define the *equivalence class of a* (denoted $[a]$) to be $\{x \in A : x\ \rho\ a\}$.

EXAMPLE 0.21. If ρ is the congruence-modulo-5 relation, then ρ has 5 distinct equivalence classes. They are $[0] = \{x : x \equiv 0 \pmod{5}\}$, $[1] = \{x : x \equiv 1 \pmod{5}\}$, $[2] = \{x : x \equiv 2 \pmod{5}\}$, $[3] = \{x : x \equiv 3 \pmod{5}\}$, and $[4] = \{x : x \equiv 4 \pmod{5}\}$. Notice that in this example distinct equivalence classes have no elements in common. ■■■

In general, if $A = \bigcup_i B_i$ where every set B_i is nonempty and every pair B_i and B_j are disjoint if $i \neq j$, then we say that the sets B_i *partition* A. (This is slightly more general than our previous definition because we allow infinitely many B_i's.) Note that the equivalence classes of the congruence-modulo-5 relation partition the integers. This is a general phenomenon, as we now show:

THEOREM 0.22. *If ρ is an equivalence relation on A, then the distinct equivalence classes of ρ partition A.*

Proof: First we must show that $A = \bigcup_{a \in A} [a]$. Suppose that $x \in A$. Since ρ is reflexive, we have $x \in [x]$; therefore $x \in \bigcup_{a \in A} [a]$. Thus $A \subseteq \bigcup_{a \in A} [a]$. Conversely, $[a] \subseteq A$ for every a, so $\bigcup_{a \in A} [a] \subseteq A$.

Now we must show that $[a]$ and $[b]$ are either disjoint or equal. Suppose that $[a]$ and $[b]$ are not disjoint, i.e., that $[a] \cap [b] \neq \emptyset$. Then there exists

$x \in [a] \cap [b]$, i.e., $x \; \rho \; a$ and $x \; \rho \; b$. Suppose that $y \in [a]$. Then $y \; \rho \; a$. But then we have $y \; \rho \; a \; \rho \; x \; \rho \; b$, since ρ is symmetric. Since ρ is transitive, we have $y \; \rho \; b$, so $y \in [b]$. Thus $[a] \subseteq [b]$. Similarly, we have $[b] \subseteq [a]$, so $[a] = [b]$. ■

Partial Orders A relation ρ is *antisymmetric* if

$$a \; \rho \; b \text{ and } b \; \rho \; a \Rightarrow a = b.$$

A relation ρ is a *partial order* if ρ is transitive and antisymmetric.

EXAMPLE 0.23

- The relations $<$, $\leq$, $>$, $\geq$, $\subset$, $\subseteq$, and $=$ are partial orders. (Note that a partial order may or may not be reflexive.)
- Congruence modulo 5 is not a partial order, because it is not antisymmetric.
- The relation is-mother is not a partial order, because it is not transitive. ■ ■ ■

0.2.7 Functions

A relation ρ is a *function* if for every x in ρ's source there is a unique y in ρ's target such that $x \; \rho \; y$, i.e., if

$$(\forall x)\Big[|\{y : x \; \rho \; y\}| = 1\Big].$$

A relation ρ is a *partial function* if for every x in ρ's source there is at most one y in ρ's target such that $x \; \rho \; y$, i.e., if

$$(\forall x)\Big[|\{y : x \; \rho \; y\}| \leq 1\Big].$$

If a relation ρ is not a partial function, ρ is called *multiple-valued.*

Observe that, by the definitions above, every function is a partial function. If the relation ρ is a partial function but not a function, ρ is called a *strictly partial function*. Sometimes we call a function a *total function* to emphasize that it is not strictly partial.

EXAMPLE 0.24. The relation I is a function, called the identity function, and integer part is a function, but round-off is not even a partial function because round-off(x) has two values whenever x is an integer plus $\frac{1}{2}$. The relation is-mother^{-1} is a strictly partial function, because the first human had no human mother (whatever the origin of the human species may be). ■ ■ ■

In addition to the terminology and notation that apply to a relation ρ, we have special terminology and notation that apply only to functions. If ρ is a partial function such that $x\ \rho\ y$, then we say that ρ *maps* x to y, and we can denote that in two ways:

- $\rho(x) = y$,
- $x\rho = y$.

The former is the *prefix notation* for partial functions; the latter is the *postfix notation* for partial functions. We will typically use postfix notation with functions that denote some action. For example, suppose that, for all integers x, $x\rho = x + 1$ and $x\sigma = x * 2$. Then $x\rho\sigma$ is the result of adding 1 to x and then multiplying by 2. Observe that the function symbols are written in the same order as the actions are performed.

When composing functions, we write the function symbols in the same order as when we apply them. Thus $x\rho\sigma$, $x(\rho \circ \sigma)$, $\sigma(\rho(x))$, and $(\sigma \circ \rho)(x)$ all denote the same value, namely $2x + 2$. The first two expressions are in postfix notation, and the last two are in prefix notation.

We say that a partial function ρ is *one-to-one* (abbreviated *one-one*) if for every y there is at most one x such that $x\ \rho\ y$, i.e., if

$$(\forall y)\Big[|\{x : x\ \rho\ y\}| \leq 1\Big].$$

Equivalently, ρ is one-one iff ρ^{-1} is a partial function. This definition applies to all relations as well, although one-one functions are the most interesting.

For example, consider the function that maps an integer x to the real number that is "equal" to x:

$$\text{float} = \big\{(x, y) : x \in \mathsf{Z}, y \in \mathsf{R}, \text{and } x = y\big\}.$$

The function float is one-one. The function $x\rho = x^2$ from Z to Z is not one-one because $-2\ \rho\ 4$ and also $2\ \rho\ 4$. However the function $x\rho = x + 1$ from Z to Z is one-one.

We say that ρ is *onto* if for every y there is at least one x such that $x\ \rho\ y$, i.e., if

$$(\forall y)(\exists x)[x\ \rho\ y].$$

An equivalent definition is that ρ is onto if and only if its range is equal to its target.

The source and target sets are important in determining whether a function is one-one and whether it is onto.

EXAMPLE 0.25

- If we define a function ρ from Z to Z by $\rho(x) = x + 1$, then ρ is one-one and onto.
- But if we define ρ from N to N by the same formula, $\rho(x) = x + 1$, then ρ is one-one and not onto.
- If we define ρ from Z to Z by $\rho(x) = x^2$, then ρ is neither one-one nor onto.
- But if we define ρ from N to N by the same formula, $\rho(x) = x^2$, then ρ is one-one and not onto.
- The integer-part function from R to Z is onto, but not one-one. ■ ■ ■

A function that is both one-one and onto is called a *one-one* correspondence from its source to its target.

EXAMPLE 0.26

- If we define ρ by $\rho(\text{stop}) = \text{red}$, $\rho(\text{go}) = \text{green}$, and $\rho(\text{slow}) = \text{yellow}$, then ρ is a one-one correspondence from $\{\text{stop}, \text{go}, \text{slow}\}$ to $\{\text{red}, \text{green}, \text{yellow}\}$.
- If we define ρ by $\rho(x) = x + 1$, then ρ is a one-one correspondence from Z to Z.

- If we define ρ by

$$\rho(x) = \begin{cases} 2x & \text{if } x \geq 0, \\ -2x - 1 & \text{otherwise,} \end{cases}$$

then ρ is a one-one correspondence from Z to N. ∎∎∎

Suggestion: Many of the exercises in this book call for proofs. When a proof is more than one or two lines long, it is a good idea to begin your writeup with a one-paragraph summary of how your proof will proceed. This saves your grader lots of time when your proof differs from the one he or she had in mind. What's more, if your proof is incorrect in one or two inessential details, but the grader does not understand your approach, you might not get partial credit. You cannot expect any partial credit if your approach to the problem is hopeless or if your writeup is completely incomprehensible, but a short summary paragraph makes it possible for the grader to allot partial credit for a workable nonstandard approach that may be wrong in one or two correctable details. If your summary is clear enough, the grader might even choose not to check the details.

Exercises

0.2-3 Prove that $A - B = A \cap \overline{B}$.

0.2-4 (a) What is $2^{\{4,5\}}$?
(b) Prove that $|2^A| = 2^{|A|}$.

0.2-5 Which of the following sets—Z, the set of even integers, the set of odd integers—are closed under addition?

0.2-6 Let $\oplus x = 2x$. What is the set extension of $\oplus$? What is the closure of $\{1\}$ under $\oplus$?

0.2-7 (a) What is wrong with the following outline for a proof of Theorem 0.18 for associative operations? *Let A_0 be the closure of A under $\oplus$. Let A_1 and A_2 be as already defined. We show that $A_0 \subseteq A_2$, $A_2 \subseteq A_1$, and $A_1 \subseteq A_0$. The cycle of containments implies that $A_0 = A_2 = A_1$.*

(b) What is the correct expression in Theorem 0.18(ii) when $\oplus$ is a nonassociative binary operator? Prove the theorem for nonassociative relations.

(c) What is the correct expression in Theorem 0.18(ii) when $\oplus$ is unary? Prove the theorem for unary operations.

0.2-8 What is the relation (is-son $\circ$ is-mother) $\cup$ (is-son $\circ$ is-father) $-$ (is-brother $\cup I$)?

0.2-9 What is the relation is-mother $\circ$ is-parent $\circ$ is-parent?

0.2-10 What is is-ancestor^{-1} $\circ$ is-ancestor? What is is-ancestor $\circ$ is-ancestor^{-1}?

0.2-11 What is the converse of is-sibling?

0.2-12 Define relations is-grandchild and is-cousin. Express those relations in terms of the relations defined in this section.

0.2-13 Which of the following relations are transitive: is-descendant, is-brother, is-sibling?

0.2-14 What is the transitive closure of is-child? the reflexive transitive closure of is-child?

0.2-15 Prove Theorem 0.19.

0.2-16 Define symmetric closure. Give an equivalent formulation.

0.2-17 Prove that congruence modulo m is an equivalence relation.

0.2-18 Prove that $\sim$ is an equivalence relation if defined in any of the ways below:

(a) $x \sim y$ iff $f(x) = f(y)$, where f is a total function.

(b) $x \sim y$ iff $(\forall z)[f(x,z) = f(y,z)]$, where f is a total function.

(c) $x \sim y$ iff $x \approx y$ and $x \cong y$, where $\approx$ and $\cong$ are equivalence relations.

(d) $x \sim y$ iff $(\exists a, b)[f^{(a)}(x) = f^{(b)}(y)]$, where f is a total function. $f^{(n)}$ denotes f composed with itself n times if $n > 0$, f^{-1} composed with itself $-n$ times if $n < 0$, and I if $n = 0$.

Apply part (d) to the function $f(x) = x+m$, and conclude something interesting.

0.2-19 What is wrong with the following "proof" that every symmetric, transitive relation is an equivalence relation? *Assume that ρ is symmetric and transitive. Let a be an arbitrary element in the domain of ρ. Choose b such that $a\ \rho\ b$. By symmetry, $b\ \rho\ a$. By transitivity, $a\ \rho\ a$. Since that statement is true for arbitrary a, the relation ρ is reflexive. Therefore ρ is an equivalence relation.*

0.2-20 Prove that ρ is a one-one correspondence if and only if ρ^{-1} is a one-one correspondence.

0.2-21 The *equivalence* closure of a relation is its reflexive, symmetric, transitive closure. Prove that the equivalence closure of ρ is $(\rho \cup \rho^{-1})^*$.

Solution: Let R be any relation that contains ρ and is reflexive, symmetric, and transitive. Since R contains ρ and is symmetric, R contains the symmetric closure of ρ, i.e., $\rho \cup \rho^{-1}$. Since R contains $\rho \cup \rho^{-1}$ and is reflexive and transitive, R contains the reflexive transitive closure of $\rho \cup \rho^{-1}$, i.e., $(\rho \cup \rho^{-1})^*$.
If we can show that $(\rho \cup \rho^{-1})^*$ contains ρ and is an equivalence relation, then it will be the least relation with those properties, completing the proof. Clearly $(\rho \cup \rho^{-1})^*$ contains ρ. Since it is a reflexive transitive closure, it is reflexive and transitive. Finally, suppose that $(a, b) \in (\rho \cup \rho^{-1})^*$. Then

$$(a, b) = (a, c_1) \circ (c_1, c_2) \circ \cdots \circ (c_k, b)$$

where each ordered pair on the right-hand-side belongs to $\rho \cup \rho^{-1}$. Because $\rho \cup \rho^{-1}$ is symmetric, it also contains the ordered pairs $(b, c_k), \ldots, (c_2, c_1), (c_1, a)$, so $(\rho \cup \rho^{-1})^*$ contains (b, a). Therefore $(\rho \cup \rho^{-1})^*$ is symmetric, completing the proof.

0.3 STRINGS

The geometer begins with points and lines. We begin with characters and alphabets.[5] Although we usually think of characters as the roman letters,

[5] Historically, characters have been called symbols.

digits, and punctuation that usually appear on a keyboard, characters can be anything we want. An alphabet is a nonempty finite set of characters, e.g., $\{0, 1\}$, $\{a, b\}$, $\{0, \ldots, 9\}$, $\{a, \ldots, z\}$, and $\{\#, \$\}$.

DEFINITION 0.27 (Alphabets and Characters). An *alphabet* is any finite set. Elements of an alphabet are called *characters*.

We usually use the capital Greek letter Σ to denote an alphabet. In later chapters, we will also use the capital Greek letters Γ and Δ.

A finite sequence of characters is called a *string*. When writing a string, we usually leave out the angle brackets and the commas that ordinarily separate elements of the finite sequence. For example, abc, aba, word, and string are strings over the alphabet $\{a, \ldots, z\}$.

DEFINITION 0.28. Let Σ be an alphabet. A *string over* Σ is a finite sequence of characters that belong to Σ.

There are two main differences between sequences and strings: First, the elements of a string are taken from a finite set, whereas the elements of a sequence may be taken from a finite or infinite set. Second, strings always have finite length, whereas sequences may be finite or infinite.

A particularly important string is the finite sequence that contains no characters at all. This string is called the *empty string*, which we denote by Λ. Strings may also be defined recursively:

DEFINITION 0.29. Let Σ be an alphabet. s is a *string over* Σ if

- s is equal to the empty string, Λ, or
- $s = ct$, where c is a character belonging to Σ and t is a string over Σ.

The recursive definition is equivalent to the definition of strings as finite sequences of characters. We will talk more about recursive definitions in Section 0.6.3.

A *language* is a set of strings.[6] For example, {this, is, a, language} is a language; recall that order in sets is unimportant, so the language above is equal to $\{a, is, language, this\}$. The set of all strings over $\{a, b\}$

---

6 Such languages are also called *formal* languages, because the form of the strings is important, rather than their meaning.

that contain exactly one a is an example of an infinite language. The set of all grammatically correct sentences in English is another infinite language.

Often we will work with sets of languages. By convention a set of sets is usually called a *class* of sets. Because languages are sets themselves, a set of languages is typically called a class of languages.[7] Examples include the class of finite languages, the class of infinite languages, the class of languages containing the string boola, and the class of Indo-European languages.

If C is a class of languages, then co-C is the class of languages whose complement belongs to C, i.e.,

$$\text{co-}C = \{L : \overline{L} \in C\} = \{\overline{L} : L \in C\}.$$

For example, if C is the class of finite languages, then co-C is the class of languages whose complement is finite. Such languages are called *co-finite*, which is not the same as "infinite." For example, the language consisting of all strings over $\{\mathtt{a}, \mathtt{b}\}$ that end with a is infinite, but not co-finite, because the set of all strings over $\{\mathtt{a}, \mathtt{b}\}$ that do not end with a is also infinite. Thus, in this example, co-$C \neq \overline{C}$. The set of all strings over $\{\mathtt{a}, \mathtt{b}\}$ whose length is greater than 5 is an example of a co-finite language.

0.3.1 Regular Operations

The *regular operations* on languages are union, concatenation, and Kleene-closure.[8] From Section 0.2.1, the reader is already familiar with the union of two sets; we proceed to define the other two operations.

If s and t are strings, the concatenation of s and t is the string $s \otimes t$ obtained by writing the string s immediately followed by the string t. That is, if $s = s_1 \cdots s_m$ and $t = t_1 \cdots t_n$ then $s \otimes t = s_1 \cdots s_m t_1 \cdots t_n$. We usually write st to denote $s \otimes t$. For example, if $s =$ bed and $t =$ knob, then $st =$ bedknob and $ts =$ knobbed. The empty string is the identity element for string concatenation, i.e., $s\Lambda = \Lambda s = s$ for all strings s.

The concatenation of two languages A and B is the set extension of the concatenation operation on strings, i.e.,

$$A \otimes B = \{s \otimes t : s \in A \text{ and } t \in B\}.$$

---

[7] Classes of languages have historically been called "families" of languages.

[8] Kleene's name is pronounced "cleany."

For example,

$$\{\texttt{a}, \texttt{ab}\} \otimes \{\texttt{ba}, \texttt{aa}\} = \{\texttt{aba}, \texttt{aaa}, \texttt{abba}, \texttt{abaa}\}.$$

We usually write AB to denote $A \otimes B$. Frequently we want to concatenate a language with itself. As a shorthand we write $A^2 = AA$. More generally, we define A^k to be the set of strings obtained by concatenating exactly k elements of A (allowing duplicates). Formally, we have the definition

- $A^0 = \{\Lambda\}$
- $A^{k+1} = A \otimes A^k \quad (= A^k \otimes A)$

The Kleene-closure of a language L (denoted by L^*) is the closure of $L \cup \{\Lambda\}$ under concatenation, i.e., the least language that contains the string Λ, contains the language L, and is closed under concatenation. By Theorem 0.18, we have a practical formula for this:

$$L^* = \bigcup_{k \geq 0} L^k.$$

EXAMPLE 0.30

- $\{\texttt{a}\}^* = \{\texttt{a}^n : n \geq 0\}$
- $\{\texttt{aaa}\}^* = \{\texttt{a}^n : n \text{ is divisible by } 3\}$
- $\{\texttt{aa}, \texttt{aaaa}\}^* = \{\texttt{a}^n : n \text{ is divisible by } 2\}$
- $\{\texttt{aa}, \texttt{aaa}\}^* = \{\texttt{a}^n : n = 0 \text{ or } n \geq 2\}$ (which is less obvious)
- $\{\texttt{a}, \texttt{b}\}^*$ is the set of all strings over the alphabet $\{\texttt{a}, \texttt{b}\}$
- $\emptyset^* = \emptyset^0 = \{\Lambda\}$ ■ ■ ■

We abbreviate $\{c\}^*$ as c^*.

0.3.2 Miscellaneous String Operations and Relations

We say that the string s is a substring of t if the characters of s appear as consecutive characters of t. Thus, for example, `plane` is a substring of `interplanetary`. If the substring s appears at the beginning of t, then we call s a *prefix* of t; if s appears at the end of t, then we call s a *suffix* of t. Thus `inter` is a prefix and `ary` is a suffix of `interplanetary`.

DEFINITION 0.31. Let s and t be strings.

- s is a *substring* of t if there exist strings u and v such that $t = usv$.
- s is a *prefix* of t if there exists a string u such that $t = su$.
- s is a *suffix* of t if there exists a string v such that $t = vs$.

Note that Λ is a prefix, a suffix, and a substring of every string. In addition, every string is a prefix, a suffix, and a substring of itself. Furthermore, is-a-substring-of, is-a-prefix-of, and is-a-suffix-of are partial orders.

If s is a string, then the reversal of s (denoted s^R) is the string obtained by reversing the order of the characters in s. For example, if $s =$ `abc` then $s^R =$ `cba`. In general if $s = a_1 \cdots a_n$, then $s^R = b_1 \cdots b_n$, where $b_i = a_{n-i+1}$.[9]

We extend the string reversal operation to languages:

$$A^R = \{s^R : s \in A\}.$$

A palindrome is a string that reads the same forward and backward, like `ada`, `deed`, `radar`, `redivider`, `madamimadam`, and `madeupexampleelpmaxepuedam`.

DEFINITION 0.32. s is a *palindrome* if $s = s^R$.

0.3.3 b-ary and b-adic Number Representations

When we write numbers in base b, the string $a_k a_{k-1} \cdots a_0$ denotes the number $\sum_{0 \le i \le k} a_i b^i$. (When $k = -1$ this sum is 0, so Λ denotes the number 0.) Numbers are commonly written in base 10, although base 8, base 16, and base 2 are very important in computer applications. In computer theory, base 2 and base 1 are the most important.

---

[9] Informally we can also write $s^R = a_n \cdots a_1$. In most contexts the meaning will be intuitively clear; however, in some contexts $a_2 \cdots a_1$ means Λ. See footnote 3. The reader should beware of this potential ambiguity.

We can evaluate the base-b number $a_k \cdots a_0$ from left to right with the following algorithm:

```
n := 0;
for i := k down to 0 do
      n := b * n + a_i;
print n
```

We can also evaluate it from right to left as follows:

```
n := 0;  power := 1;
for i := 0 to k do begin
      n := n + a_i * power;  power := b * power;
end;
print n
```

These algorithms can be modified to compute n modulo m without computing large intermediate results.

The two most important base-2 representations for numbers are the familiar *binary* notation and the *dyadic* notation. In binary notation, we use the alphabet $\{0, 1\}$; a natural number is represented as $a_k a_{k-1} \cdots a_0$, where each a_i is 0 or 1. The binary representation of a natural number is not unique because of leading 0s; e.g., 10001 and 010001 both represent the number $1 \cdot 16 + 0 \cdot 8 + 0 \cdot 4 + 0 \cdot 2 + 1 \cdot 1 = 17$.

In dyadic notation, we use the alphabet $\{1, 2\}$; a natural number is represented as $a_k a_{k-1} \cdots a_0$, where each a_i is 1 or 2. For example, Λ represents the number 0 and 1121 represents the number $1 \cdot 8 + 1 \cdot 4 + 2 \cdot 2 + 1 \cdot 1 = 17$. Dyadic notation is very convenient because the dyadic representation of a natural number is unique. We write dyadic(s) to denote the number whose dyadic representation is s, so for example dyadic(1121) $= 17$ and $\text{dyadic}^{-1}(17) = 1121$.

In base 1, we have only the monadic notation, where we use the alphabet $\{1\}$, i.e., the string 1^n represents the number n. Monadic notation has also been loosely called unary notation.

In general, b-ary notation is base-b notation using $\{0, \ldots, b-1\}$ as the alphabet; b-adic notation is base-b notation using $\{1, \ldots, b\}$ as the alphabet. The b-adic representation of each natural number is unique. We write b-adic(x) to denote the number whose b-adic representation is x. For example, 3-adic(123) $= 18$, and 5-adic(123) $= 38$.

Exercises

0.3-1 Which of the following are alphabets? $\emptyset$, $\{0\}$, $\{17, 19, 23\}$, $\{0, 1, \ldots\}$, $\{\texttt{e}, \texttt{f}, \texttt{g}, \texttt{h}\}$, $\{q_1, q_2, \ldots, q_k\}$, $\{1, \ldots, 100\}$, the set of all real numbers between 1 and 100

Solution: They are all alphabets except for $\emptyset$, $\{0, 1, \ldots\}$, and the set of all real numbers between 1 and 100. Although we have to be careful to include commas when we write strings over $\{1, \ldots, 100\}$, it is still an alphabet.

0.3-2 Which of the following are strings over $\{\texttt{a}, \texttt{b}\}$? Which are languages over $\{\texttt{a}, \texttt{b}\}$? Λ, a, b, abc, abab, $\{\texttt{aa}, \texttt{ab}, \texttt{ba}, \texttt{bb}\}$, $\{\texttt{this}, \texttt{is}, \texttt{a}, \texttt{language}\}$

0.3-3 Which of the following are palindromes? Λ, a, b, aa, aaa, aca, abc, abab, ababa

0.3-4 Prove that x is a palindrome iff there exists a string w such that $x = ww^R$ or there exist a string w and a character a such that $x = waw^R$.

0.3-5 Prove that $A^k \otimes A = A \otimes A^k$.

0.3-6 What is $\{\texttt{aaa}, \texttt{aaaaaa}\}^*$? What is $\{\texttt{aaa}, \texttt{aaaa}\}^*$?

0.3-7 Is there a string operation whose set extension is Kleene-closure?

0.3-8 Prove that if s is a prefix of t and t is a prefix of s then $s = t$. What if s is a prefix of t and s is a suffix of t?

0.3-9 Prove that is-a-prefix-of is a partial order.

0.3-10 What is the sum of the dyadic numbers 1212 and 2121? Give your answer as a dyadic number.

0.3-11 When adding two binary numbers in the standard way, you carry either 0 or 1 into the next position. Describe a similar algorithm for adding two dyadic numbers. What values might be carried?

0.3-12 When adding two decimal numbers in the standard way, you carry either 0 or 1 into the next position. Describe a similar algorithm for adding two 10-adic numbers. (Use A to represent 10 if you like.) What values might be carried?

0.3-13 Modify the algorithms from this section to determine the value of n modulo m when n is represented in base b. You should not compute n itself, because n may be too large to store practically.

0.3-14 Prove that every natural number has a unique dyadic representation.

0.4 GRAPHS

A *directed graph* consists of vertices and edges that connect pairs of vertices. We think of the vertices as points, and the edges as arrows that connect the points, as in Figure 0.2. As indicated by the arrows, each edge has a direction; i.e., it goes from one vertex, called its *origin*, to another vertex, called its *destination* (possibly the same one). A directed graph is often called a *digraph* for short. The singular of vertices is *vertex*. A vertex may also be called a *node*.

We typically write G to denote a directed graph, V to denote the set of vertices, and E to denote the set of edges. Typically an edge is represented by the ordered pair of vertices that it connects. For example, the edge from vertex 1 to vertex 2 is represented as $(1, 2)$ and the edge from vertex 4 to itself is represented as $(4, 4)$. (An edge that goes from a node back to itself is called a *self-loop*.) Represented in this way, the edge set E may be thought of as a relation on the vertex set V.

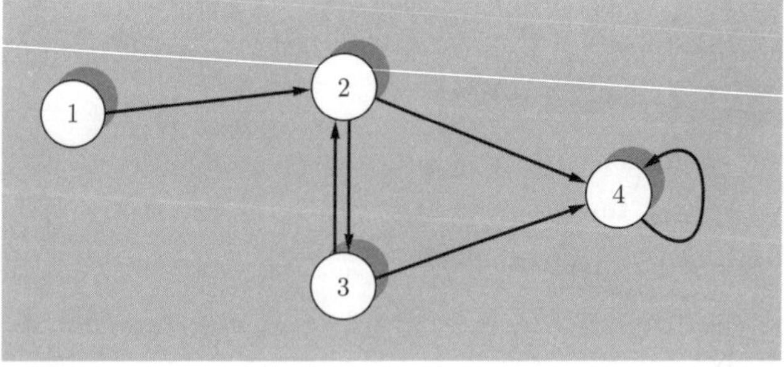

FIGURE 0.2: A directed graph. $V = \{1, 2, 3, 4\}$, $E = \{(1, 2), (2, 3), (2, 4), (3, 2), (3, 4), (4, 4)\}$.

A *path* in a digraph is a sequence of vertices each of which is connected to the next one by an edge. The *length* of a path is the number of edges. Like an edge, each path has an origin and a destination. The first element of a path is called its *origin*, and the last element is called its *destination*. A path is said to go from the origin to the destination. To be precise, a path is a sequence of vertices $\langle\langle v_0, \ldots, v_n \rangle\rangle$, with $n \geq 0$, such that the relation $v_i \; E \; v_{i+1}$ holds for each i. The length of that path is n.

In Figure 0.2, the sequence $\langle\langle 1, 2, 3, 2, 3, 4, 4 \rangle\rangle$ is a path; its source is 1, its destination is 4, and its length is 6. The sequence $\langle\langle 1, 2, 4, 3, 2 \rangle\rangle$ is not a path in that digraph, because there is no edge from 4 to 3.

We say that a vertex t is reachable from a vertex s if there is a path from s to t. For example, in Figure 0.2, vertex 4 is reachable from vertex 1, but vertex 1 is not reachable from vertex 4.

The distance from a vertex s in a digraph to a vertex t is the length of the shortest path from s to t or ∞ if there is no path from s to t. For example, in Figure 0.2, the distance from 1 to 4 is 2, the distance from 3 to 4 is 1, the distance from 2 to 2 is 0, and the distance from 4 to 1 is ∞.

We often write labels on the edges of a graph. Formally, a *labeled digraph* consists of a digraph and a mapping from the edge set E to the set of possible labels. Integral labels are often called weights; a digraph with weights on the edges is called a *weighted digraph*. The *cost* or *weighted length* of a path in a digraph is the sum of the weights on its edges. For example, a weighted digraph is shown in Figure 0.3; the cost of the path $\langle\langle 1, 2, 3, 2, 3, 4, 4 \rangle\rangle$ in that graph is $7 + 60 + 19 + 60 + 11 + 30 = 187$.

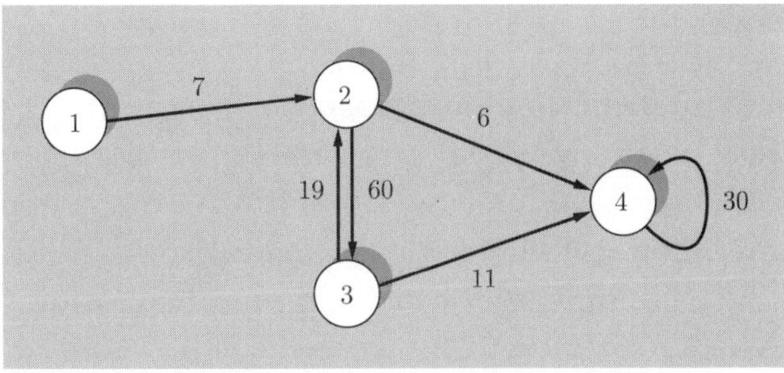

FIGURE 0.3: A weighted digraph.

0.5 BIG-O NOTATION

In this section we present a notation for describing numerical functions. This notation is very useful when discussing the running time of algorithms.

Let f and g be functions from $\mathbf{N}$ to $\mathbf{R}$. We use $O(\cdot)$ notation (pronounced "big oh") to indicate that, for large n, $f(n)$ is bounded by a constant times $g(n)$. More precisely,

$$f = O(g) \iff (\exists c)(\exists N)(\forall n \geq N)[f(n) \leq cg(n)].$$

We write $f \neq O(g)$ otherwise. Furthermore, although it may look like we are defining an object $O(g)$, we are not. The notation simply expresses a relationship between two functions f and g.

EXAMPLE 0.33. Let $f(n) = 2n$ and $g(n) = n^2$; for every $n \geq 0$, $f(n) = 2n \leq 2n^2 = 2g(n)$, so $f = O(g)$. However, for every c, if $n = \max(N, 2c + 1)$, then $g(n) = n^2 > 2cn = cf(c)$, so $g \neq O(f)$. ■■■

EXAMPLE 0.34. Let $f(n) = 3n^2 + 5n + 1$ and $g(n) = n^2$. Then, for all $n \geq 1, f(n) = 3n^2 + 5n + 1 \leq 9n^2 = 9g(n)$, so $f = O(g)$. Furthermore, for all $n \geq 0$, $g(n) = n^2 \leq f(n)$, so $g = O(f)$ as well. ■■■

Often one writes $f(n)$ to mean the function f rather than f's value at n. For this reason, it is conventional to write $f(n) = O(g(n))$ to mean that $f = O(g)$. For example, $3n^2 + 5n + 1 = O(n^2)$. In this example, the $O(\cdot)$ allowed us to simplify $3n^2 + 5n + 1$ by ignoring constants and low-order terms. That kind of simplification makes the notation useful.

See the exercises for some useful properties of $O(\cdot)$ notation.

Exercises

0.5-1 A *polynomial* is a function of the form

$$p(n) = a_k n^k + a_{k-1} n^{k-1} + \cdots + a_0$$

where k is a natural number and $a_0, \ldots, a_k$ are real numbers.

[+](a) Prove that if $p(n)$ is a polynomial, then $p(n) = O(n^k)$ for some natural number k.

Solution: If $p(n) = a_k n^k + a_{k-1} n^{k-1} + \cdots + a_0$, then let $a = |a_0| + \cdots + |a_k|$. Therefore, for $n \geq 1, p(n) \leq an^k$.

(b) If p is a polynomial, prove that $(\exists N)(\forall n \geq N)[p(n) \leq 2^n]$.

0.5-2 Prove the following:

(a) If $f(n) = O(g(n))$ and $g(n) = O(h(n))$, then $f(n) = O(h(n))$.

(b) If $f(n) = O(h(n))$ and $g(n) = O(h(n))$, then $f(n) + g(n) = O(h(n))$.

0.6 INDUCTION

Mathematical induction is an important technique for proving theorems. Suppose that $P(n)$ is some statement about the natural number n, and that we wish to prove the statement $(\forall n)P(n)$, i.e., that $P(n)$ is true for all n. The principle of induction says that it is sufficient to prove the following two statements:

Base case: $P(0)$ is true.

Inductive case: $(\forall n \geq 0)[P(n) \Rightarrow P(n+1)]$.

EXAMPLE 0.35. Suppose that we draw a finite collection of lines in the plane. These lines form the boundaries of regions in the plane, and we say that two regions are *contiguous* (adjacent) if they share two or more points, i.e., if they have a linear border in common. Examples are the checkerboard pattern of Figure 0.4 and the irregular pattern of Figure 0.5, where we have colored the regions black or white in such a way that contiguous regions have different colors. As our first example, we will prove that such a coloring is always possible.

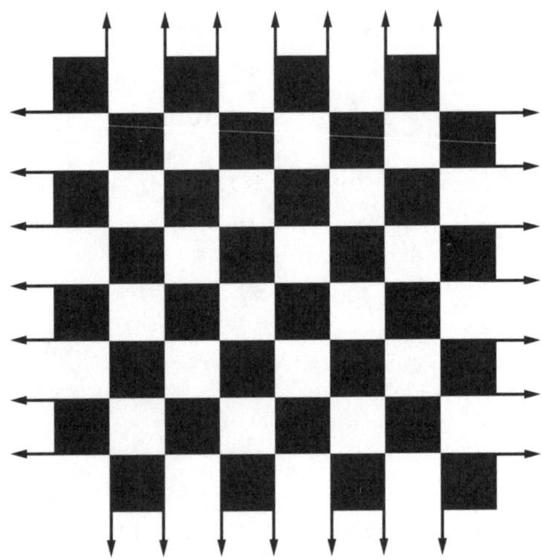

FIGURE 0.4: 2-coloring the regions of a checkerboard pattern.

FIGURE 0.5: 2-coloring the regions of an irregular pattern.

Our proof will be by induction on the number of lines drawn. Our assertion, for all n, is

If n lines are drawn in the plane, then it is possible to color regions black or white so that contiguous regions have different colors.

First we prove the assertion for $n = 0$, which is called the base case. If 0 lines are drawn in the plane, then there is only one region, namely the entire plane. For concreteness we may color it black. There are no contiguous regions, so the assertion is true for $n = 0$.

Second, we assume that the assertion is true for some particular $n \geq 0$, and we prove the assertion for $n+1$. Assume that when n lines are drawn in the plane, it is possible to color the regions black or white so that contiguous regions have different colors; this is called the inductive hypothesis.

Now suppose that $n + 1$ lines are drawn in the plane (Figure 0.6). Remove any one of those lines ℓ, so that only n lines remain. By the inductive hypothesis, it is possible to color the remaining regions black or white so that contiguous regions have different colors (Figure 0.7). Now put back the line ℓ that we removed, pick one side of ℓ, which we call the left side for concreteness, and reverse the colors on that side of ℓ, i.e., replace white with black and black with white everywhere on the left side of ℓ (Figure 0.8).

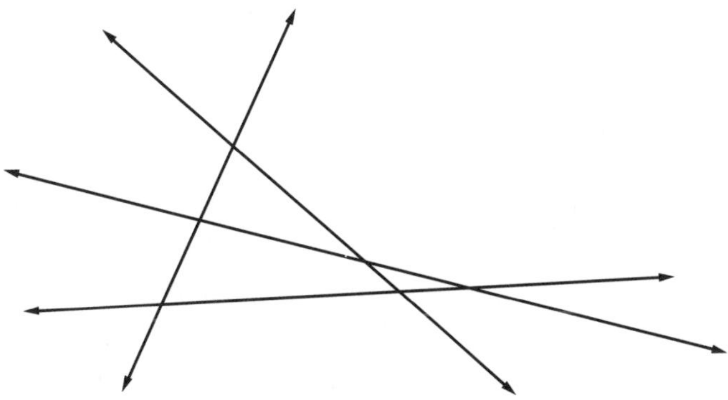

FIGURE 0.6: $n + 1$ lines in the plane.

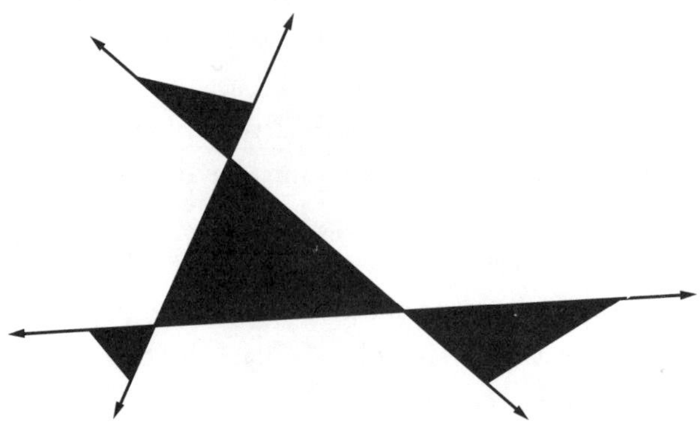

FIGURE 0.7: We remove one of the $n + 1$ lines and color the resulting figure.

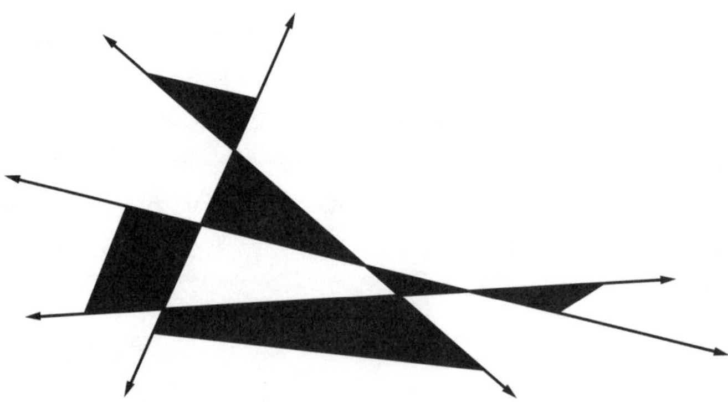

FIGURE 0.8: We replace the line and reverse the colors on one side of it.

Now all regions are colored black or white. We assert that contiguous regions are colored differently. Pick any two contiguous regions. If they are both on the right side of ℓ, then they were originally colored differently and their colors were not changed when we replaced ℓ, so they are still colored differently. If they are both on the left side of ℓ, then they were originally colored differently and their colors were reversed when we replaced ℓ, so they are still colored differently. The only remaining possibility is that the regions are on opposite sides of ℓ. Then their common border must be part of ℓ, so they were in the same region before ℓ was replaced. Therefore they had the same color before ℓ was replaced, but exactly one of them had its color reversed when ℓ was replaced, so now they have different colors. In every case, we have shown that two contiguous regions are colored differently.

Thus if $n + 1$ lines are drawn in the plane, it is possible to color the regions black or white so that contiguous regions are colored differently. This completes the inductive step of the proof. The assertion now follows for all n by the induction principle. ∎∎∎

EXAMPLE 0.36. Now let us consider an arithmetic identity. We wish to prove that $\sum_{0\le k\le n} k = \frac{1}{2}n(n+1)$. We could bolster our confidence in this statement by verifying it for small values of n.

$$
\begin{array}{lclclcl}
\sum_{0\le k\le 0} k &=& 0 &=& 0 &=& \frac{1}{2}0(0+1),\\
\sum_{0\le k\le 1} k &=& 0+1 &=& 1 &=& \frac{1}{2}1(1+1),\\
\sum_{0\le k\le 2} k &=& 0+1+2 &=& 3 &=& \frac{1}{2}2(2+1),\\
\sum_{0\le k\le 3} k &=& 0+1+2+3 &=& 6 &=& \frac{1}{2}3(3+1),\\
\sum_{0\le k\le 4} k &=& 0+1+2+3+4 &=& 10 &=& \frac{1}{2}4(4+1),\\
\sum_{0\le k\le 5} k &=& 0+1+2+3+4+5 &=& 15 &=& \frac{1}{2}5(5+1).
\end{array}
$$

Checking small values of n is a good way to weed out incorrect conjectures in practice, but it cannot prove the theorem, because infinitely many cases remain unverified. For a mathematical proof, we use the induction principle.

First we prove the base case, i.e., that $\sum_{0\le k\le 0} k = \frac{1}{2}0(0+1)$. Since the expressions on both sides of the equal sign evaluate to 0, the statement is true, so the base case is established.

Second, we prove the inductive case, i.e., if $\sum_{0\le k\le n} k = \frac{1}{2}n(n+1)$, then $\sum_{0\le k\le n+1} k = \frac{1}{2}(n+1)(n+1+1)$. In order to prove it, we assume that, for some fixed n, $\sum_{0\le k\le n} k = \frac{1}{2}n(n+1)$. (Note that it would be nonsensical to assume that the statement is true for all n, for that is exactly what we have set out to prove by induction.) Our assumption is called the *inductive hypothesis*. Identically,

$$\begin{aligned}
\sum_{0 \le k \le n+1} k &= (n+1) + \sum_{0 \le k \le n} k \\
&= (n+1) + \frac{1}{2}n(n+1) \qquad \text{by the inductive hypothesis} \\
&= (n+1)\left(1 + \frac{1}{2}n\right) \\
&= \frac{1}{2}(n+1)(n+2) \\
&= \frac{1}{2}(n+1)(n+1+1).
\end{aligned}$$

Thus the inductive case is established. That completes the proof by induction. ■■■

EXAMPLE 0.37. Next, let us consider the sum of the first n cubes. Notice that

$$\begin{aligned}
\textstyle\sum_{0 \le k \le 0} k^3 &= 0 &&= 0 &&= 0^2, \\
\textstyle\sum_{0 \le k \le 1} k^3 &= 0 + 1 &&= 1 &&= 1^2, \\
\textstyle\sum_{0 \le k \le 2} k^3 &= 0 + 1 + 8 &&= 9 &&= 3^2, \\
\textstyle\sum_{0 \le k \le 3} k^3 &= 0 + 1 + 8 + 27 &&= 36 &&= 6^2, \\
\textstyle\sum_{0 \le k \le 4} k^3 &= 0 + 1 + 8 + 27 + 64 &&= 100 &&= 10^2, \\
\textstyle\sum_{0 \le k \le 5} k^3 &= 0 + 1 + 8 + 27 + 64 + 125 &&= 225 &&= 15^2.
\end{aligned}$$

Thus we are led to conjecture that $\sum_{0 \le k \le n} k^3$ is always a square, i.e.,

$$(\forall n)(\exists m \in \mathsf{N})\left[\sum_{0 \le k \le n} k^3 = m^2\right].$$

Suppose that we tried to prove that statement directly by induction. For the inductive case, we would assume that $\sum_{0 \le k \le n} k^3 = m^2$ for some natural number m. Then we would reason that

$$\begin{aligned}\sum_{0\le k\le n+1} k^3 &= (n+1)^3 + \sum_{0\le k\le n} k^3 \\ &= (n+1)^3 + m^2 \qquad \text{by the inductive hypothesis.}\end{aligned}$$

Then we would be stuck, for it is not true for all n and m that $(n+1)^3+m^2$ is a square. What can we do? We need to know more about m in order to prove that $(n+1)^3+m^2$ is a square. Looking at the small cases again, we notice a pattern. In order to prove that $\sum_{0\le k\le n} k^3$ is a square, we prove something stronger, namely that

$$\sum_{0\le k\le n} k^3 = \left(\frac{1}{2}n(n+1)\right)^2.$$

First, the base case is easy, because both sides of the equal sign evaluate to 0.

Second, we assume that, for some fixed n, $\sum_{0\le k\le n} k^3 = \left(\frac{1}{2}n(n+1)\right)^2$. Identically,

$$\begin{aligned}\sum_{0\le k\le n+1} k^3 &= (n+1)^3 + \sum_{0\le k\le n} k^3 \\ &= (n+1)^3 + \left(\frac{1}{2}n(n+1)\right)^2 \qquad \text{by the inductive hypothesis} \\ &= (n+1)^2\left(n+1+\left(\frac{1}{2}n\right)^2\right) \\ &= (n+1)^2\left(\frac{1}{2}(n+2)\right)^2 \\ &= \left(\frac{1}{2}(n+1)(n+2)\right)^2.\end{aligned}$$

Thus, the inductive case is established. This completes the proof by induction that $\sum_{0\le k\le n} k^3 = \left(\frac{1}{2}n(n+1)\right)^2$ for all n. In particular, $\sum_{0\le k\le n} k^3$ is a square, as we originally set out to show.

This example demonstrates that when we use mathematical induction, it is sometimes easier to prove a stronger statement than a weaker statement. This is because, although the statement to be proved is stronger, the inductive hypothesis is stronger as well. ■ ■ ■

EXAMPLE 0.38. In this inductive proof, we will have the moral equivalent of two base cases. Let us prove that for all n, $2^n \geq 2n$. The proof is by induction on n. Observe that $2^0 = 1 > 0 = 2 \cdot 0$, so the base case is established. Our inductive hypothesis is that $2^n \geq 2n$ for some particular $n \geq 0$, and we wish to conclude that $2^{n+1} \geq 2(n+1)$. We have

$$2^{n+1} = 2 \cdot 2^n \geq 2 \cdot 2n = 4n = 2(n+1) + 2(n-1) \geq 2(n+1),$$

whenever $n \geq 1$. Thus we have proved that $2^n \geq 2n$ when $n = 0$, and we know that if it is true for $n = 1$ then it is true for $n = 2$, and then it is true for $n = 3$, and so on. However, we still have to prove it for $n = 1$. We do so as a special case: $2^1 = 2 = 2 \cdot 1$, so the case $n = 1$ is established. Therefore $2^n \geq 2n$ for all n.

Sometimes one must be careful when performing the inductive step for small values of n. In this example, we had a special case for $n = 1$. When some small values of n constitute special cases, we typically call them "base cases" and prove all of them first. ∎∎∎

EXAMPLE 0.39. In this inductive proof, we will have three base cases. Let us prove that for all n, $2^n \geq 3n - 2$. The base cases are $n = 0$, $n = 1$, and $n = 2$. Observe that $2^0 = 1 > -2 = 3 \cdot 0 - 2$, $2^1 = 2 > 1 = 3 \cdot 1 - 2$, and $2^2 = 4 = 3 \cdot 2 - 2$, establishing the base cases. The inductive hypothesis is that $2^n \geq 3n - 2$ for some particular $n \geq 2$. We have

$$2^{n+1} = 2 \cdot 2^n \geq 2 \cdot (3n-2) = 6n-4 = 3(n+1)-2+3n-5 > 3(n+1)-2,$$

because $n \geq 2$, establishing the inductive case. This completes the proof by induction. ∎∎∎

EXAMPLE 0.40. Sometimes we prove statements that are not true for small values of n, but only for sufficiently large n. Let us prove that for all $n \geq 4$, $2^n \geq 4n$. For the base case, we take the least value of n for which the statement is asserted, i.e., $n = 4$. We observe that $2^4 = 16 = 4 \cdot 4$, establishing the base case. The inductive hypothesis is that $2^n \geq 4n$ for some particular $n \geq 4$. We wish to prove that $2^{n+1} \geq 4(n+1)$. We have

$$2^{n+1} = 2 \cdot 2^n \geq 2 \cdot 4n = 8n = 4(n+1) + 4(n-1) \geq 4(n+1),$$

because $n \geq 4 \geq 1$. This completes the proof by induction. (Observe that in this example the inductive step worked fine for $n = 1, 2, 3$ as well, but the statement is not true for $n < 4$ for lack of a base case.) ■ ■ ■

Exercises

0.6-1 **Binomial Theorem.** Prove that $(x+1)^n = \sum_{0 \leq i \leq n} \binom{n}{i} x^i$, where $\binom{n}{i} = \frac{n(n-1)\cdots(n-i+1)}{i(i-1)\cdots 1}$. Hint: Use the fact that $\binom{n+1}{i+1} = \binom{n}{i+1} + \binom{n}{i}$ for all natural numbers n and i.

0.6-2 Prove that $\sum_{0 \leq k \leq n} \binom{k}{i} = \binom{n+1}{i+1}$. Hint: Use the fact that $\binom{n+1}{i+1} = \binom{n}{i+1} + \binom{n}{i}$ for all natural numbers n and i.

0.6-3 Prove that $\sum_{0 \leq k \leq n} k^2 = \frac{1}{24}(2n)(2n+1)(2n+2)$.

0.6-4 Prove that $\sum_{0 \leq k \leq n} k^4 = \frac{1}{30} n(n+1)(2n+1)(3n^2+3n-1)$.

0.6-5 Prove that $\sum_{0 \leq k \leq n} k^d \leq \frac{1}{d+1} n^{d+1} + n^d$, for $d \geq 1$.

Solution: The proof is by induction on n. When $n = 0$, the statement becomes $0 \leq 0$, so the base case is established. Assume for some particular n that $\sum_{0 \leq k \leq n} k^d \leq \frac{1}{d+1} n^{d+1} + n^d$. Identically,

$$
\begin{aligned}
\sum_{0 \leq k \leq n+1} k^d &= \sum_{0 \leq k \leq n} k^d + (n+1)^d \\
&\leq \frac{1}{d+1} n^{d+1} + n^d + (n+1)^d && \text{by the inductive hypothesis} \\
&\leq \frac{1}{d+1} (n+1)^{d+1} + (n+1)^d && \text{by the binomial theorem.}
\end{aligned}
$$

Thus the inductive case is established, which completes the proof.

0.6-6 (a) Let f be a function such that $f(0) = 1$ and $f(n+1) = 2f(n) + 1$ for all n. Prove that $f(n) = 2^{n+1} - 1$.

(b) **Towers of Hanoi.** You are given three pegs and n disks of different sizes. Initially the n disks are piled on one of the pegs, with the smallest on the top, then the second-smallest, ..., and the largest on the bottom. Your job is to move the n disks to one of the other two pegs. However, you are only allowed to move one disk at a time, and you cannot ever place a larger disk on top of a smaller disk. Let $H(n)$ denote the minimum number of moves in which your task can be accomplished. Prove that $H(n+1) \leq 2H(n)+1$.

*(c) Prove that $H(n+1) \geq 2H(n)+1$.

(d) Conclude that $2^{n+1}-1$ moves are necessary and sufficient in order to move all disks from one peg to another.

0.6-7 (a) Prove that for all n, $2^n \geq n^2 - 1$.
(b) Prove that for all $n \geq 4$, $2^n \geq n^2$.
(c) Prove that for all $n \geq 10$, $2^n \geq 100n$.

0.6-8 (a) Prove that $(\rho \cup \sigma)^* = \rho^*(\sigma\rho^*)^*$.
(b) Prove that $(\rho \cup \sigma)^* = \sigma^*(\rho\sigma^*)^*$.
$^+$(c) Prove that $(\rho \cup \sigma)^* = (\rho^*\sigma)^*\rho^*$.
(d) Prove that $(\rho \cup \sigma)^* = (\sigma^*\rho)^*\sigma^*$.

Solution

(a) First we show that $\rho^*(\sigma\rho^*)^* \subseteq (\rho \cup \sigma)^*$. Proof: Because $\rho \subseteq (\rho \cup \sigma)$ and $\sigma \subseteq (\rho \cup \sigma)^*$,

$$\begin{aligned} \rho^*(\sigma\rho^*)^* &\subseteq (\rho \cup \sigma)^*((\rho \cup \sigma)^*(\rho \cup \sigma)^*)^* \\ &\subseteq (\rho \cup \sigma)^* \end{aligned}$$

because $(\rho \cup \sigma)^*$ is reflexive and transitive.
Conversely, we show that $(\rho \cup \sigma)^* \subseteq \rho^*(\sigma\rho^*)^*$. For all k we assert that

$$(\rho \cup \sigma)^k \subseteq \rho^*(\sigma\rho^*)^*.$$

We prove the assertion by induction on k. The base case ($k = 0$) is established because

$$(\rho \cup \sigma)^0 = I \subseteq \rho^*(\sigma\rho^*)^*.$$

Assume that the assertion is true for k.

$(\rho \cup \sigma)^{k+1}$	$= (\rho \cup \sigma)(\rho \cup \sigma)^k$	
	$\subseteq (\rho \cup \sigma)\rho^*(\sigma\rho^*)^*$	by the inductive hypothesis
	$= \rho\rho^*(\sigma\rho^*)^* \cup \sigma\rho^*(\sigma\rho^*)^*$	by the distributive law for sets
	$\subseteq \rho^*(\sigma\rho^*)^* \cup (\sigma\rho^*)^*$	because $\tau\tau^* \subseteq \tau^*$ for all τ
	$= \rho^*(\sigma\rho^*)^*.$	

That completes the induction. Therefore,

$$
\begin{aligned}
(\rho \cup \sigma)^* &= \bigcup_{k \geq 0} (\rho \cup \sigma)^k \\
&\subseteq \bigcup_{k \geq 0} \rho^*(\sigma\rho^*)^* \\
&= \rho^*(\sigma\rho^*)^*.
\end{aligned}
$$

(b) $(\rho \cup \sigma)^* = (\sigma \cup \rho)^* = \sigma^*(\rho\sigma^*)^*$, by part (a).

(c) It is easily verified for all relations ρ and σ that $\rho^{-1}\sigma^{-1} = (\sigma\rho)^{-1}$, $\rho^{-1} \cup \sigma^{-1} = (\rho \cup \sigma)^{-1}$, and $(\rho^{-1})^* = (\rho^*)^{-1}$. By part (a),

$$(\rho^{-1} \cup \sigma^{-1})^* = (\rho^{-1})^*(\sigma^{-1}(\rho^{-1})^*)^*.$$

Taking the converse of both sides, we have

$$(\rho \cup \sigma)^* = ((\rho)^*\sigma)^*(\rho)^*.$$

(d) $(\rho \cup \sigma)^* = (\sigma \cup \rho)^* = ((\sigma)^*\rho)^*(\sigma)^*$, by part (c).

Alternatively, parts (b–d) may be proved analogously to part (a).

0.6-9 Suppose that n lines are drawn in the plane such that no two lines are parallel and no three lines go through the same point. These lines divide the plane into a number of regions r_n. Prove that $r_n = 1 + \frac{1}{2}n(n+1)$ for all n. Hint: Prove that $r_{n+1} = r_n + n + 1$.

0.6-10 Consider the following "proof" that all pigs are yellow. First, we buy a pig from a nearby farmer, and we paint it yellow. Next comes the hard part. We say that a set of pigs is *monochromatic* if all pigs in the set are the same color. We will prove that all finite sets of pigs are monochromatic. The proof is by induction on the size n of the set. The base case ($n = 0$) is trivial, because the empty set contains no pigs.

Inductive case: Assume that all sets consisting of n pigs are monochromatic for some particular n. We prove that all sets consisting of $n+1$ pigs are monochromatic. Let $\{\text{pig}_1, \ldots, \text{pig}_{n+1}\}$ be a set containing $n+1$ pigs. By the inductive hypothesis $\{\text{pig}_1, \ldots, \text{pig}_n\}$ is monochromatic. It remains to show that pig_{n+1} has the same color as pig_n, for then all $n+1$ pigs must have the same color. But $\{\text{pig}_2, \ldots, \text{pig}_{n+1}\}$ is a set consisting of n pigs, so by the inductive hypothesis it is monochromatic. Therefore pig_{n+1} has the same color as pig_n, so $\{\text{pig}_1, \ldots, \text{pig}_{n+1}\}$ is monochromatic, as desired. That completes the proof by induction.

Because all finite sets of pigs are monochromatic, in particular the set of all pigs is monochromatic. Because that set contains the pig we painted yellow, all pigs must be yellow.

Question: What is wrong with the proof given above?[10]

Solution: The inductive step is incorrect when $n = 1$, i.e., when we try to prove that every set consisting of two pigs is monochromatic. This is to be expected, because if every two pigs were the same color, then all pigs really would be the same color.

*0.6-11 An *undirected graph* is a digraph whose edge relation is symmetric; if (u, v) is an edge then u and v are called *neighbors*. A k-coloring of an undirected graph is a mapping from its vertex set to a set consisting of k colors such that neighbors are mapped to distinct colors. An undirected graph is *planar* if it can be drawn in the plane

[10] The earliest version of this paradox seems to be due to George Pólya, *Induction and Analogy in Mathematics*.

in such a way that no edges cross. Prove that every planar graph has a 6-coloring. Hint: every planar graph contains a vertex that has at most 5 neighbors.

Solution: We prove this by induction on the number of vertices in the graph. Base case: If there are no vertices then the graph has a trivial 6-coloring. Inductive hypothesis: Every planar graph containing n vertices has a 6-coloring. Let G be a planar graph containing $n + 1$ vertices. Because G is planar it contains a vertex v with at most 5 neighbors. Obtain G' by deleting v and all edges going to or from it. By the inductive hypothesis, G' has a 6-coloring. Map v to a color that none of its neighbors is mapped to.

0.6.1 Strong Induction

There is another form of induction, which appears more powerful than ordinary mathematical induction. Ordinary induction lets us assume a statement is true for n when proving it for $n + 1$; equivalently, it lets us assume a statement is true for $n - 1$ when proving it for n. However, the principle of *strong induction* lets us assume the statement is true for $0, 1, \ldots, n - 1$ when proving it for n. (Strong induction is also known as *course-of-values induction* or *complete induction*.) To be precise, suppose that we are trying to prove $(\forall x)P(x)$. The strong induction principle says that it is sufficient to prove the following single statement:

Inductive case: $(\forall n \geq 0)\Big[\big((\forall k < n)P(k)\big) \Rightarrow P(n)\Big]$.

More compactly, the strong induction principle says that

$$(\forall n)\Big[\big((\forall k < n)P(k)\big) \Rightarrow P(n)\Big] \Rightarrow (\forall x)P(x).$$

This principle is in fact equivalent to ordinary induction, but it is often easier to apply. First, the base case is part of the inductive case, rather than being proved separately. Second, we may assume $P(0), \ldots, P(n-1)$ when trying to prove $P(n)$, whereas ordinary induction only lets us assume $P(n - 1)$. This makes intuitive sense, because if we are proving the statements $P(0)$, $P(1), \ldots$ in order, then we have $P(0)$ through $P(n-1)$ at our disposal when it is time to prove $P(n)$.

Later in this section, we present some examples using the strong induction principle. But first, let us show that the strong induction principle is a logical consequence of the ordinary induction principle.

Proof of the strong induction principle: Let us use ordinary induction to prove the principle of strong induction. Assume that, for all n,

$$((\forall k < n)P(k)) \Rightarrow P(n). \tag{0.1}$$

We wish to prove $(\forall x)P(x)$. In fact we will prove something seemingly stronger. Let $Q(x)$ be the statement $(\forall y < x)P(y)$. In particular $Q(x+1) \Rightarrow P(x)$. Therefore it suffices to demonstrate $(\forall x)[Q(x)]$, which we prove by induction. First, we establish the base case, with $x = 0$, which says $(\forall y < 0)P(y)$. This statement is true because there are no values of y less than 0. (In that kind of situation we say that the statement is *vacuously* true.) Thus the base case is established.

Second, we establish the inductive case. Assume that $(\forall y < x)P(y)$, for some particular x. By equation (0.1), $P(x)$ is true. Therefore the statement $P(x) \wedge (\forall y < x)P(y)$ is true, but that is equivalent to the statement $(\forall y < x + 1)P(y)$, establishing the inductive case.

That completes the proof by induction. ■

EXAMPLE 0.41. We will prove that the recursive program below computes the identity function. Of course, there are easier ways to compute the identity function; our purpose here is to demonstrate the use of strong induction. Let f be a function on the natural numbers satisfying

$$f(n) = \begin{cases} 0 & \text{if } n = 0, \\ 2f(n/2) & \text{if } n \text{ is even and } n > 0, \\ f(n-1) + 1 & \text{if } n \text{ is odd.} \end{cases}$$

We wish to prove that f is the identity function, i.e., that $(\forall n)[f(n) = n]$. The proof is by strong induction. Assume that $(\forall k < n)[f(k) = k]$ for some particular n. We will show that $f(n) = n$. If $n = 0$, then $f(n) = 0$, as desired. Henceforth we may assume that $n > 0$. If n is even then $f(n) = 2f(n/2)$. By the inductive hypothesis, $f(n/2) = n/2$, so $f(n) = 2(n/2) = n$. If n is odd, then $f(n) = f(n-1) + 1$. By the inductive hypothesis, $f(n-1) = n-1$, so $f(n) = n - 1 + 1 = n$. Thus, in all cases, we have shown $f(n) = n$. That completes the proof by strong induction. ■■■

EXAMPLE 0.42. For a less trivial application of strong induction, we prove that the recursive program in Figure 0.9 computes the greatest common divisor of two natural numbers. The *greatest common divisor* of a and b is the largest natural number d such that a and b are both divisible by d; it is denoted by $\gcd(a, b)$. By convention $\gcd(0, 0) = 0$. Let Euclid be the function computed in Figure 0.9.

We assert that for all $a, b \geq 0$, $\text{Euclid}(a, b) = \gcd(a, b)$. Observe that when the function Euclid calls itself recursively, it uses a smaller value for one of the parameters, although their order might be reversed. In any case, the sum of the parameters to the recursive call is smaller. This is just what we need for a proof by strong induction. We prove that $\text{Euclid}(a, b) = \gcd(a, b)$ by strong induction on $a + b$.

Inductive hypothesis: For all a', b' such that $a' + b' < a + b$, $\text{Euclid}(a', b') = \gcd(a', b')$. (We wish to conclude that $\text{Euclid}(a, b) = \gcd(a, b)$.)

If $b > a$, then the first line will swap a and b; without loss of generality we assume henceforth that $a \geq b$. There are only two cases.

```
function Euclid(a, b);
begin
    if b > a then swap a and b; (* Henceforth a ≥ b *)
    if b = 0 then return a (* gcd(a, 0) = a *)
    else return Euclid(a − b, b); (* gcd(a, b) = gcd(a − b, b) *)
end;
```

FIGURE 0.9: The Euclidean algorithm for computing greatest common divisors. a and b are any natural numbers.

Case 1: $b = 0$. Then $\text{Euclid}(a, b) = a$. Clearly a is the largest divisor of a. Since every number is a divisor of 0, a is the largest divisor of a and 0, so $\text{Euclid}(a, b) = a = \gcd(a, b)$, as desired.

Case 2: $b > 0$. Then $\text{Euclid}(a, b) = \text{Euclid}(a-b, b)$. Since $(a-b)+b < a + b$, the inductive hypothesis says that $\text{Euclid}(a - b, b) = \gcd(a - b, b)$. Furthermore, if d is a divisor of a and b, then d is a divisor of $a - b$ as well. Therefore every divisor of a and b is a divisor of $a - b$ and b. Conversely, if d is a divisor of $a - b$ and b, then d is a divisor of $(a - b) + b = a$ as well. Therefore every divisor of $a - b$ and b is a divisor of a and b. Consequently, $\gcd(a - b, b) = \gcd(a, b)$. Thus,

$$\text{Euclid}(a, b) = \text{Euclid}(a - b, b) = \gcd(a - b, b) = \gcd(a, b),$$

as desired.

In both cases, $\text{Euclid}(a, b) = \gcd(a, b)$, so the inductive step is established. This completes the proof by strong induction. ■ ■ ■

Exercises

0.6-12 Let f be a function on natural numbers satisfying

$$f(n) = \begin{cases} 0 & \text{if } n = 0, \\ 4f(n/2) & \text{if } n \text{ is even and } n > 0, \\ f(n-1) + 2n - 1 & \text{if } n \text{ is odd.} \end{cases}$$

Prove that $f(n) = n^2$ for all $n \geq 0$.

0.6-13 Suppose that f is a function on integers satisfying

$$f(n) = \begin{cases} 0 & \text{if } n = 0, \\ 2f(n/2) & \text{if } n \text{ is even and } n > 0, \\ f(n-2) + 2 & \text{if } n \text{ is odd.} \end{cases}$$

Can you prove that $f(n) = n$ for all $n \geq 0$?

Solution: No. If we tried to apply the inductive proof given in this section, it would fail for $n = 1$, because the inductive hypothesis says nothing about $f(-1)$. For a concrete counterexample, note that any positive integer can be written as $2^k m$, where m is odd, and we may define $f(2^k m) = 2^k(m+1)$.

0.6-14 Use the strong induction principle to prove the ordinary induction principle.

0.6-15 A natural number is prime if it has exactly two distinct divisors, i.e., itself and 1. (That is, p is prime iff $p \geq 2$ and p is divisible only by 1 and p.) A *prime factorization* of n is a sequence of prime numbers $\langle\langle p_1, \ldots, p_k\rangle\rangle$, not necessarily distinct, such that

$$n = p_1 \cdot \cdots \cdot p_k.$$

Prove that if $n > 1$ then n has a prime factorization. (You need not prove that the prime factorization is unique.)

Solution: The proof is by strong induction on n.

Case 1: n is prime. Then $\langle\langle n\rangle\rangle$ is a prime factorization of n.

Case 2: n is not prime. Then n is divisible by some natural number d such that $1 < d < n$. Because $1 < d < n$, the inductive hypothesis says that there is a prime factorization $\langle\langle p_1, \ldots, p_i\rangle\rangle$ of d. Because $1 < n/d < n$, the inductive hypothesis says that there is a prime factorization $\langle\langle p'_1, \ldots, p'_j\rangle\rangle$ of n/d. Then

$$n = p_1 \cdot \cdots \cdot p_i \cdot p'_1 \cdot \cdots \cdot p'_j,$$

so $\langle\langle p_1, \ldots, p_i, p'_1, \ldots, p'_j\rangle\rangle$ is a prime factorization of n.

0.6.2 Pigeonhole Principle

The pigeonhole principle is a convenient version of the induction principle, which was discovered by the mathematically inclined daughter of a pigeon farmer.[11] Pigeons roost in homes called "holes." This particular farmer

[11] This farmer is also reported to raise yellow pigs.

built 100 holes for his pigeons, but he owned 101 pigeons. Each evening he would count 101 pigeons returning home to roost, and he would ask himself, "How can 101 pigeons live in 100 holes?" Needless to say, he was perplexed and concerned about his pigeons' welfare. His question was answered one evening when his daughter returned home from the university and observed the phenomenon. "Clearly," she said, "two of the pigeons must be in the same hole."

In general, the pigeonhole principle says that if p pigeons occupy h holes, where $p > h$, then two of the pigeons must occupy the same hole. More formally let P and H be finite sets such that $|P| > |H|$, and let f be a function from P to H; the pigeonhole principle says that f must not be one-one, i.e.,

$$(\exists i \in P)(\exists j \in P)[i \neq j \text{ and } f(i) = f(j)].$$

THEOREM 0.43 (Pigeonhole Principle). *Let P and H be finite sets such that $|P| > |H|$. If f is a function from P to H, then f is not one-one.*

Although the pigeonhole principle may seem too obvious to require a proof, it is in fact equivalent to the principle of mathematical induction (Exercise 0.6-22). In this section, we present several applications of the pigeonhole principle.

EXAMPLE 0.44. Suppose that we are given three integers x_1, x_2, x_3. We assert that the average of two of these numbers must be an integer; i.e., there exist x_i, x_j among the given numbers such that $(x_i + x_j)/2$ is an integer. We prove the assertion by the pigeonhole principle.

Note that $(x_i + x_j)/2$ is an integer if and only if $x_i \equiv x_j \pmod 2$. Let $f(x) = x \bmod 2$, so f maps to a range of size 2. Since we are given three integers, f must map two of them to the same value; i.e., there are distinct i and j such that $f(x_i) = f(x_j)$. Then $x_i \equiv x_j \pmod 2$, so the average of x_i and x_j is an integer. This completes the proof. ■ ■ ■

EXAMPLE 0.45. For a slightly more complicated application along the same lines, let us say that a point (x, y) in the plane is a *lattice point* if x and y are both integers. Suppose that we are given 5 lattice points $(x_1, y_1), \ldots, (x_5, y_5)$ in the plane. Find the midpoint of each of the 10 pairs of points. We assert that one of these midpoints must be a lattice point. We prove our assertion by the pigeonhole principle.

The midpoint of (x_i, y_i) and (x_j, y_j) is $((x_i + x_j)/2, (y_i + y_j)/2)$, which is a lattice point if and only if $x_i \equiv x_j \pmod 2$ and $y_i \equiv y_j \pmod 2$.

Let $f((x, y)) = (x \bmod 2, y \bmod 2)$. Then f maps to a range of size 4. Since there are 5 points, two of them must be mapped to the same value, i.e., we have $f((x_i, y_i)) = f((x_j, y_j))$. Then $x_i \equiv x_j \pmod 2$ and $y_i \equiv y_j \pmod 2$, so $((x_i + x_j)/2, (y_i + y_j)/2)$ is a lattice point. That completes the proof. ■■■

EXAMPLE 0.46. Suppose that we are given a set $A = \{x_1, \ldots, x_{10}\}$ consisting of 10 numbers between 1 and 100. A surprising fact is that there exist two distinct, disjoint subsets B and C of A whose elements sum to the same number, i.e., $B \neq C$, $B \subseteq A$, $C \subseteq A$, $B \cap C = \emptyset$, and $\sum_{x \in B} x = \sum_{x \in C} x$. We will prove this mathematical curiosity using the pigeonhole principle.

Let $A_1, \ldots, A_{1024}$ be a list of all subsets of A. Let $f(i)$ denote the sum of the elements of A_i, i.e., $f(i) = \sum_{x \in A_i} x$. The function f maps numbers in the domain $\{1, \ldots, 1024\}$ to numbers in the range $\{10, \ldots, 1000\}$. Therefore, by the pigeonhole principle, f cannot be one-one. In other words, there exist two distinct subsets A_i, A_j of A such that $\sum_{x \in A_i} x = \sum_{x \in A_j} x$. To obtain disjoint sets, we remove from A_i and A_j any elements they have in common. That is, let $B = A_i - (A_i \cap A_j)$ and $C = A_j - (A_i \cap A_j)$. Then $B \neq C$, $B \subseteq A$, $C \subseteq A$, $B \cap C = \emptyset$, and

$$\sum_{x \in B} x = \sum_{x \in A_i} x - \sum_{x \in A_i \cap A_j} x = \sum_{x \in A_j} x - \sum_{x \in A_i \cap A_j} x = \sum_{x \in C} x.$$

That completes the proof. ■■■

Exercises

0.6-16 The pigeon farmer's daughter has taken a summer job as a parking lot attendant. How would the pigeonhole principle be useful to her in this job?

0.6-17 (a) Let us say that a point (x, y, z) in Euclidean 3-space is a lattice point if all of its coordinates are integers. Suppose that we are given 9 lattice points. Construct the midpoints of all 36 pairs of points. Prove that at least one of these points is a lattice point.[12]

(b) Provide an example of 9 lattice points such that 35 of the midpoints are not lattice points.

0.6-18 Suppose that we are given a set $A = \{x_1, \ldots, x_{20}\}$ consisting of 20 numbers between 1 and 50,000. Prove that there exist two distinct, disjoint subsets B and C of A whose elements sum to the same number, i.e., $B \neq A$, $B \subseteq A$, $C \subseteq A$, $B \cap C = \emptyset$, and $\sum_{x \in B} x = \sum_{x \in C} x$.

0.6-19 Suppose that we are given 100 numbers $x_1, \ldots, x_{100}$ between 1 and $100,000,000,000$. Prove that for two of those numbers x_i and x_j, the sum of the base-10 digits of x_i is equal to the sum of the base-10 digits of x_j.

0.6-20 Suppose that we are given a set X containing n positive integers. Prove that there is a nonempty subset of X whose elements add up to a multiple of n.

0.6-21 The Fibonacci numbers are defined as follows:

$$f_n = \begin{cases} 1 & \text{if } n = 1, \\ 1 & \text{if } n = 2, \\ f_{n-1} + f_{n-2} & \text{if } n \geq 3. \end{cases}$$

We say that an infinite sequence $\langle\langle x_1, x_2, \ldots \rangle\rangle$ is *periodic* if there exists a number p called the *period* and a number ℓ called the *latency* such that $(\forall n \geq \ell)[x_n = x_{p+n}]$. Fix a positive integer m, and let $g_n = f_n \bmod m$.

(a) Prove that the sequence $\langle\langle g_1, g_2, \ldots \rangle\rangle$ is periodic. Hint: The period is less than or equal to m^2.

(b) Prove that the latency is 0. Hint: The recurrence can be run backwards, i.e., $f_n = f_{n+2} - f_{n+1}$.

(c) Prove that there is a Fibonacci number f_n, with $n \geq 1$, that is divisible by m. Hint: Define f_0.

---

[12] This problem originally appeared on the William Lowell Putnam mathematical competition.

0.6-22 (a) Use induction to prove the pigeonhole principle.

Solution: The proof is by induction on $|P|$. If $|P| = 0$, then it is impossible for $|P| > |H|$, so the base case is vacuously true. Assume that the pigeonhole principle is true whenever $|P| = n$, for some $n \geq 0$.

Now assume that $|P| = n + 1$. Because P is nonempty, there exists some element p in P. If there exists $q \in P$ such that $q \neq p$ and $f(p) = f(q)$, then f is not one-one, as we wished to prove. Otherwise, we may assume that for all $q \in P - \{p\}$, $f(p) \neq f(q)$. Let $P' = P - \{p\}$, $H' = H - \{f(p)\}$, and f' be the restriction of f to the domain P', i.e., $f'(x) = f(x)$ for all x in P' and f' is defined only on the points in P'. Since $f(q) \neq f(p)$ for all $q \in P'$, f' is a function from P' to H'. Because $|P'| = |P| - 1$ and $|H'| = |H| - 1$, $|P'| > |H'|$. By the inductive hypothesis, f' is not one-one, so there exist q and r in P' such that $q \neq r$ and $f'(q) = f'(r)$. But then q and r belong to P as well, and $f(q) = f'(q) = f'(r) = f(r)$, so f is not one-one. This establishes the inductive case, completing the proof by induction.

(b) Using the pigeonhole principle, prove the principle of mathematical induction; i.e., assume that for no finite sets P and H such that $|P| > |H|$ is there a one-one function from P to H, and prove for every predicate P

$$\Big(Q(0) \wedge (\forall n)[Q(n) \Rightarrow Q(n+1)]\Big) \Rightarrow (\forall n)Q(n).$$

Solution: Assume $Q(0) \wedge (\forall n)[Q(n) \Rightarrow Q(n+1)]$. Assume, for the sake of contradiction, that $Q(m)$ is false for some particular m. Define a function f from $\{0, \ldots, m\}$ to $\{0, \ldots, m-1\}$ as follows

$$f(x) = \begin{cases} x & \text{if } Q(x) \text{ is true and } 0 \leq x \leq m, \\ x - 1 & \text{if } Q(x) \text{ is false and } 0 \leq x \leq m. \end{cases}$$

Note that for all x, $f(x) \in \{x - 1, x\}$. We assert that f is one-one. Suppose that $i \neq j$. We wish to show that $f(i) \neq f(j)$.

Without loss of generality we can assume that $i \le j-1$. If $i \le j-2$ or $Q(i)$ is false, then $f(i) \le j-2 < f(j)$, so $f(i) \ne f(j)$. The only remaining possibility is that $i = j-1$ and $Q(i)$ is true. But $Q(i) \Rightarrow Q(i+1)$, by assumption. Therefore $Q(j)$ is true, so $f(j) = j$. Thus $f(i) = i = j-1 < j = f(j)$, so $f(i) \ne f(j)$. Thus f is one-one, as asserted.
But that contradicts the pigeonhole principle. Therefore, $Q(m)$ must in fact be true. Since our proof applies to every m, we have shown $(\forall n)Q(n)$.

0.6-23 We present yet a fourth principle that is equivalent to mathematical induction. The *least-element principle* says that every nonempty set of natural numbers has a least element, i.e., if $\emptyset \subset A \subseteq \mathsf{N}$ then $(\exists \ell)[\ell \in A \wedge (\forall x)[x \in A \Rightarrow \ell \le x]]$.

(a) Using mathematical induction, prove the least-element principle.

(b) Using the least-element principle, prove the induction principle.

0.6.3 Recursive Definitions

Often it is convenient to define concepts recursively.

EXAMPLE 0.47. Let us fix an alphabet Σ and define strings by the following two rules:

Rule 1: Λ is a string.

Rule 2: If s is a string and $c \in \Sigma$, then cs is a string.

An object is a string if and only if it can be proved to be a string by using rule 1 and rule 2 some number of times. For example, let us take $\Sigma = \{\mathsf{a}, \mathsf{b}\}$; then abab can be shown to be a string by applying rule 1 once and then applying rule 2 four times.

A third rule is implicit in the definition of strings given above: Nothing is a string unless it can be proved to be a string by rules 1 and 2. For this reason, the set of all strings is the least set of objects that satisfies rules 1 and 2. *This kind of rule is implicit in all recursive definitions and is rarely stated explicitly.* ■ ■ ■

EXAMPLE 0.48. Here is another recursive definition:

Rule 1: Λ is a pal.

Rule 2: If $c \in \Sigma$, then c is a pal.

Rule 3: If x is a pal and $c \in \Sigma$, then cxc is a pal.

For example, abba is shown to be a pal by applying rule 1 and then applying rule 3 twice; abbba is shown to be a pal by applying rule 2 and then applying rule 3 twice. ■■■

Theorems about recursively defined objects can often be proved by an induction that mimics the recursive definition.

EXAMPLE 0.49. Let us prove that if x is a pal then $x = x^R$. The proof is by induction on the number of times a rule is applied in order to show that x is a pal. (We call this kind of induction *structural*.)

Inductive hypothesis: If x can be shown to be a pal by k applications of rules 1–3, then $x = x^R$.

Base case: $k = 0$. No string x can be shown to be a pal without applying a rule at least once, so the base case is vacuously true.

Inductive case: $k \geq 1$. Rule 1, 2, or 3 is the last one applied in showing that x is a pal. If rule 1 or 2 is the last one applied, then $x = \Lambda$ or x is a single character, so $x = x^R$ as desired. Otherwise rule 3 is the last rule applied. So $x = cyc$ where y is shown to be a pal by $k - 1$ applications of the rules. By the inductive hypothesis $y = y^R$. Therefore $x^R = (cyc)^R = cy^Rc = cyc = x$, completing the inductive case. ■■■

Trees are structures with numerous uses in computer science. *Trees* have the following properties: Every tree contains a finite set of *nodes*, which are abstract objects that we will not define, like points or vertices. Exactly one node of the tree is called its *root*. Every node in the tree has a sequence of 0 or more *children*, which are nodes in the tree. Every node other than the root has a unique *parent*, which is a node in the tree. Children and parents satisfy the following relationship: c is a child of p iff p is the parent of c. In addition, if we connect each child to its parent by an edge, then there is a unique path from each node to the root. You can think of a tree as the family

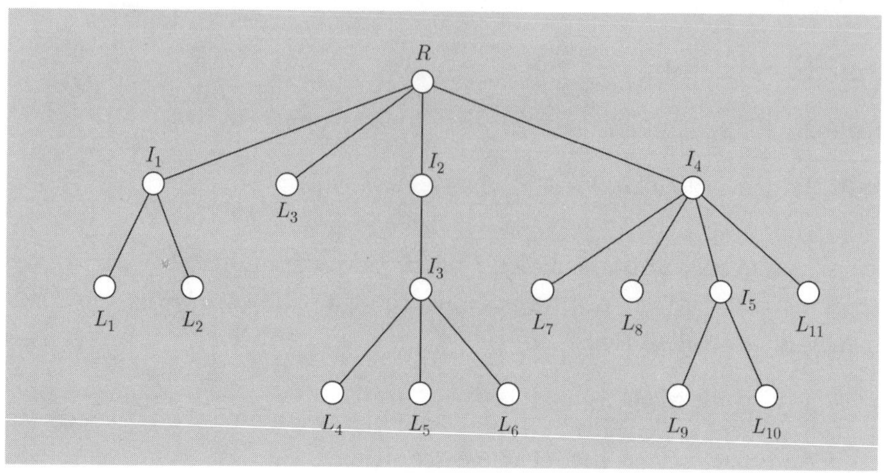

FIGURE 0.10: A tree. The root is R. The leaves are $L_1, \ldots, L_{11}$. The internal nodes are $R, I_1, \ldots, I_5$.

tree of an organism that reproduces asexually, such as the amoeba. You can think of the unique path from a node to the root as the node's lineage.

Trees are usually depicted as in Figure 0.10. Nodes are drawn as points. The topmost node in the diagram is the root of the tree.[13] Parents are connected to their children by edges, with the parent at the top of the edge and the child at the bottom. The children are ordered left to right. Some nodes have no children; they are called *leaves*. The tree in Figure 0.10 contains 17 nodes. R is the root. R's children are I_1, L_3, I_2, and I_4, in that order. I_1's children are L_1 and L_2, in that order. The parent of I_3 is I_2. The nodes labeled $L_1, \ldots, L_{11}$ are leaves. The non-leaves are called *internal* nodes; in this example, the internal nodes are labeled $R, I_1, \ldots, I_5$.

EXAMPLE 0.50. We can also define trees recursively. This recursive definition will provide a useful structure for inductive proofs.

Rule 1: If N is a node, then there is a tree whose only node is N. N is the tree's root. N has no parent and no children.

[13] Beware: Mathematicians draw their trees upside-down.

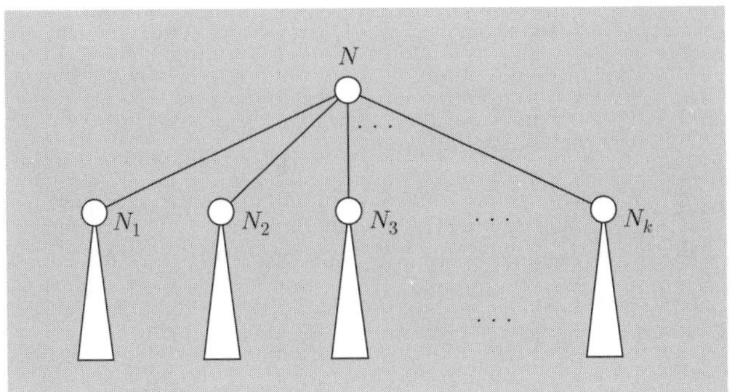

FIGURE 0.11: A recursively defined tree. The root is N. The subtrees' roots are $N_1, \ldots, N_k$.

Rule 2: Let N be a node. Let $T_1, \ldots, T_k$ be trees containing disjoint sets of nodes. Let $N_1, \ldots, N_k$ be the roots of $T_1, \ldots, T_k$, respectively. Then there is a tree whose nodes are N and all the nodes of $T_1, \ldots, T_k$. We call this tree T. T's root is N. N has no parent, and the children of N are $N_1, \ldots, N_k$, in that order. The parent of N_i is N for $i = 1, \ldots, k$. Other than that, the parents and children of nodes in T are the same as in $T_1, \ldots, T_k$, which are called the *subtrees* of T.

Rule 2 is illustrated in Figure 0.11. ■■■

Two nodes in a tree are called *adjacent* if either one is the parent of the other. In Figure 0.11, N is adjacent to N_1, but N_1 is not adjacent to N_2.

EXAMPLE 0.51. Let us prove by structural induction that every tree can be colored with two colors so that adjacent nodes are colored differently. In fact, we will prove something slightly stronger.

Inductive hypothesis: Let T be a tree produced by applying rules 1 and 2 at most k times. Then T can be colored with two colors so that the root has any desired color and adjacent nodes are colored differently.

Base case: $k = 0$. The base case is vacuous, as in Example 0.49.

Inductive case: $k \geq 1$. If rule 1 is the last rule applied in producing T, then T is a single node, which can be colored any desired color.

Otherwise, rule 2 is the last rule applied. Let N denote the root of T, and let $T_1, \ldots, T_k$ be the subtrees of the root. Color N the desired color, say "white" for concreteness. Call the other color "black" for concreteness. By the inductive hypothesis each of T's subtrees may be colored with two colors so that the root is colored "black" and adjacent nodes have different colors. This yields a coloring of T with two colors so that the root is colored the desired color and adjacent nodes have different colors. This completes the proof by structural induction.

Note: Since the base case ($k = 0$) is always vacuous in a structural induction, it is quite common to take $k = 1$ for the base case. ■ ■ ■

Exercises

0.6-23 Fix an alphabet Σ and let x be a string over Σ. Prove that if $x = x^R$ then x is a pal. Hint: Prove it by induction on the length of x. Conclude that the set of all pals is equal to the set of all palindromes.

0.6-24 For the purposes of this exercise, a tree is called *prolific* if every internal node has at least two children.

(a) Give a recursive definition of prolific trees.

(b) Prove that the number of leaves in a prolific tree is greater than the number of internal nodes.

0.6-25 A tree is called a *binary* tree if every internal node has exactly two children.

(a) Give a recursive definition of binary trees.

(b) Prove that the number of leaves in a binary tree is exactly one greater than the number of internal nodes.

(c) Prove that every binary tree contains an odd number of nodes.

(d) Prove that the number of leaves in a binary tree is equal to $(n + 1)/2$, where n is the number of nodes.

0.6-26 The *depth* of a node in a tree is its distance from the root, i.e., the number of edges on the unique path from the node to the root. A binary tree (see Exercise 0.6-25) is called *full* if every leaf has the same depth. Let T be a full binary tree in which each leaf has depth d.

(a) Prove that the number of leaves in T is 2^d.

(b) Prove that the number of nodes in T is $2^{d+1} - 1$.

0.6-27 Descendants are defined recursively. A node m is a *descendant* of a node n if $m = n$ or m is a descendant of a child of n. The *height* of a node n in a tree is the distance from n to its deepest descendant. The *height* of a tree is the height of its root.

(a) Restate the recursive definition of descendants using two rules (see the recursive definitions of strings, pals, and trees for examples).

(b) Suppose that the nodes of a binary tree are colored red, yellow, blue, orange, green, and violet. Let n be a node such that there are 33 leaves that are descendants of n. Prove that there are two nodes a and b such that a is a descendant of b, b is a descendant of n, and a and b have the same color. Hint: Use the pigeonhole principle.

Solution: Let T be the subtree whose root is n. If the height of T were 5 or less, then T would contain 32 leaves or fewer, by Exercise 0.6-26. Therefore the height of T is at least 6. Let c be the deepest descendant of n, so the path from n to c contains at least 6 edges. Then the path from n to c contains at least 7 nodes. But there are only 6 colors. By the pigeonhole principle, two of the nodes on this path have the same color. Let a be the deeper one, and let b be the other. Then a is a descendant of b; a and b are descendants of n.

0.6-28 Show how to restate any proof by structural induction on trees as a proof by strong induction on

(a) the number of nodes in a tree.

(b) the height of a tree.

*0.6-29 **Infinite trees.** An *infinite tree* consists of an infinite set of nodes, a root node R, and a partial function $p(\cdot)$ on the set of nodes such that $p(R)$ is undefined and for every node $N \neq R$ there exists i such that $p^i(N) = R$. That is, $p(\cdot)$ is the parent function, the root has no parent, and every node has a unique lineage from the root. A tree is *finite-branching* if each node has finitely many children, i.e., p is finite-to-one. An *infinite branch* in a tree T is a sequence $\langle\langle v_1, v_2, \ldots \rangle\rangle$ such that $v_1 = R$ and, for all i, v_i belongs to T and v_i is the parent of v_{i+1}, i.e., $v_i = p(v_{i+1})$.

The following result is called *König's tree lemma* or *König's compactness lemma*: Let T be a finite-branching, infinite tree. Prove that T contains an infinite branch. Hint: Construct the infinite branch iteratively.

Solution: If v is a node in T, let $T(v)$ denote the subtree rooted at v. We define an infinite branch in T as follows:

```
i := 1;
v_1 := the root of T;
while true do begin
    (* assertion: T(v_i) is infinite *)
    let v_{i+1} be a child of v_i such that T(v_{i+1}) is infinite;
    i := i + 1;
end;
```

We prove by induction on i that (1) v_i is well-defined and (2) the assertion is true for i. Base case: v_1 is well-defined and $T(v_1) = T$, which is infinite. Assume the two statements are true for i. The choice of v_{i+1} is possible, because if every child of v_i were the root of a finite tree, then v_i itself would be the root of a finite tree, contradicting the assertion for i. Because v_{i+1} is chosen so that $T(v_{i+1})$ is infinite, the assertion is true for $i + 1$. This completes the inductive proof. By construction $\langle\langle v_1, v_2, \ldots \rangle\rangle$ is an infinite branch in T.

1

Introduction to Machines

THE MOST FUNDAMENTAL question in theoretical computer science concerns computability: What problems can computers solve? Once we have determined that a particular problem indeed can be solved on a computer, the next natural question concerns complexity: How efficiently can computers solve it?

Although there are many approaches to answering these two questions, much of our understanding of the capabilities of computers arises from reasoning about the capabilities of computers with limited storage devices, such as finite memories, counters, stacks, and certain kinds of tapes.

In this chapter, we will informally describe some of the most important storage devices and present examples of programs that run on machines using those devices. Precise mathematical definitions of "device," "program," and "machine" are, however, postponed until Chapter 2.

1.1 PROGRAMS

We introduce programs by way of three examples.

EXAMPLE 1.1. Recall that a string x is a palindrome if x reads the same forwards as backwards, i.e., if $x = x^R$. Let us consider a special kind of palindrome, namely, strings of the form $w\#w^R$ where w is a string of a's and b's and # is a particular character. Such palindromes are called *palindromes with central marker*.

The following is an algorithm that recognizes palindromes with central marker:

Phase 1: Read characters of x and store them in the order read until a # is read, but don't store the #.

Phase 2: Read the remaining characters of x and compare them to the characters stored in Phase 1 in reverse order.

If a mismatch is detected or if a different number of characters are read than were stored in Phase 1, then indicate that x is not a palindrome with central marker. Otherwise, indicate that x is a palindrome with central marker.

The algorithm can be implemented as a program for a machine that has an input device and a last-in–first-out storage device, called a *stack*, which we describe by the following metaphor: In a certain cafeteria, trays are stored on a spring that is designed to make the topmost tray accessible, while keeping the others hidden. This cafeteria is rather upscale, and it uses trays of several different colors. The pattern of tray colors on the spring can encode useful information. We can add a tray of a particular color to the top of the pile or remove the tray from the top of the pile if it has the color we want. We can test visually whether the pile is empty. Such a pile of trays is informally called a stack.

Adding a tray of a particular color *c* to the stack is called "pushing" it and is denoted by PUSH*c*. Removing a tray of a particular color *c* from the stack is called "popping" it and is denoted by POP*c*. Suppose for concreteness that the trays are colored aqua, burgundy, and chartreuse. We could abbreviate aqua by a, burgundy by b, and chartreuse by c. If the stack has an aqua tray at the bottom, then two chartreuse trays, another aqua tray, and finally a burgundy tray at the top, we could represent the stack's contents by the string accab. If we apply the operation POPb to this string, we obtain the string acca. We could not, however, apply the operation POPa to the string accab because that would be like trying to remove an aqua tray when the top one is burgundy. If we apply the operation PUSHc to the string acca, we obtain the string accac.

The program that recognizes palindromes is presented graphically in Figure 1.1. The nodes labeled 1 and 2 correspond to phases 1 and 2, respectively, of the algorithm. Nodes 3 and 4, respectively, indicate that x is or is not a palindrome with central marker. Nodes are formally called *control states*; node 3 is called an *accepting control state*, and node 4 is called a *rejecting control state*. The set of all control states is called the *control set*. If the program stops in control state 3 we say that it *accepts* x, and if it stops in control state 4 we say that it *rejects* x. An edge indicates a transition from one phase to another, and the label on an edge indicates the operations performed on the input device and the stack simultaneously with the transition.[1] A slash (/) inside a label separates the input operation from the stack operation. When there is more than one label on a single edge, any one of them may specify the operations to be performed on the input device and the stack simultaneously with the transition (the program does not perform the operations specified by all the labels). Thus, an edge with several labels is a shorthand for several parallel edges, each with a single one of the labels.

The operation SCANa removes an a from the input; i.e., an edge labeled SCANa maps the input string ax to x, and the edge cannot be followed

[1] Our diagrams are not the same as conventional flowcharts. For example, we always label edges, rather than nodes, with operations.

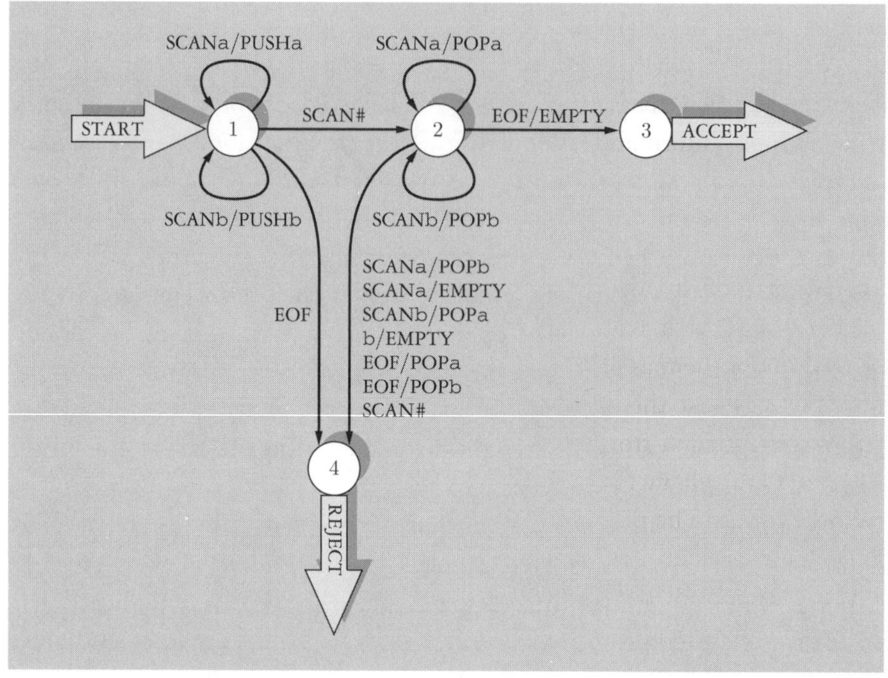

FIGURE 1.1: A program that recognizes palindromes with central marker.

except when the next input character is an a. Informally, SCANa can be expressed as

$$\mathtt{a}x \longrightarrow x,$$

where it is understood that the relation holds for all strings x over $\{\mathtt{a}, \mathtt{b}\}$. Analogously, the operation SCANb removes a b from the input; i.e., an edge labeled SCANb maps the input string bx to x, and the edge cannot be followed except when the next input character is a b. Informally, SCANb can be expressed as

$$\mathtt{b}x \longrightarrow x,$$

where it is understood that the relation holds for all strings x over $\{\mathtt{a}, \mathtt{b}\}$.

The operation EOF tests whether the input string has been scanned completely; i.e., an edge labeled EOF does not alter the input string, but it can be followed only when the input string has been exhausted. More precisely, the operation EOF maps the input string Λ to Λ and is undefined on other input strings. Informally, EOF can be expressed as

$$\Lambda \to \Lambda,$$

where it is understood that the relation holds for only this one pair.

Because SCAN`a`, SCAN`b`, and EOF are partial functions, it may be helpful to think of them as having preconditions and actions. The precondition for SCAN`a` is that the next input character be an `a`; the action of SCAN`a` is to remove that `a` from the input. The precondition for SCAN`b` is that the next input character be a `b`; the action of SCAN`b` is to remove that `b` from the input. The precondition for EOF is that the input be empty; EOF performs no action.

It is important to distinguish our SCANc and EOF operations from the input operations commonly encountered in real-world programming languages. For example, in Pascal `read(ch)` removes a character from the input and stores it in the variable parameter called `ch`. In contrast, our SCAN`a` removes the fixed character `a` from the input and does not store it anywhere. If the input does not start with an `a`, then an edge labeled SCAN`a` simply cannot be followed; the program has to follow a different edge or stop. For motivation, one may imagine that the first character of the input is always "visible" to the program; in that sense, the SCAN`a` operation is equivalent to

```
if the next input character is an a then it is OK to begin
      read forward to the next input character;
      follow this edge;
end else
      do not follow this edge;
```

Pascal's eof is a Boolean function that returns the value true iff the input has been exhausted. In contrast, our EOF operation does not return a Boolean value. An edge labeled EOF simply cannot be followed unless the input has been exhausted; if some input characters have not yet been scanned, the program must follow a different edge or stop. The effect of EOF can be viewed as

> if there is no next input character then it is OK to
> follow this edge
> else
> do not follow this edge

The operation PUSHa has no precondition; its action is to append an a to the string stored in the stack (the end appended to is conventionally called the *top* of the stack). Ordinarily, we append characters to the right end of a string, so the top of the stack is the right end of the string it holds. (We could just as well make the top of the stack the left end of the string it holds; this has no bearing on our convention of scanning the input string from left to right, which is firmly rooted in Western tradition.) Formally, the operation PUSHa maps the stack contents s to $s\mathtt{a}$. Informally, PUSHa can be expressed as

$$s \longrightarrow s\mathtt{a},$$

where it is understood that the relation holds for every string s over $\{\mathtt{a}, \mathtt{b}\}$.

The precondition for the operation POPa is that there be an a on the top of the stack (an edge labeled with POPa cannot be followed unless there is an a at the top of the stack); its action is to remove an a from the top of the stack. Formally, the operation POPa maps the stack contents $s\mathtt{a}$ to s. Informally, POPa can be expressed as

$$s\mathtt{a} \longrightarrow s,$$

where it is understood that the relation holds for every string s over $\{\mathtt{a}, \mathtt{b}\}$.

The precondition for the operation EMPTY is that the stack be empty; it performs no action. Informally, EMPTY tests whether the stack is empty; its practical effect is to prevent following an edge unless the stack is empty. Formally, the operation EMPTY maps the stack contents Λ to Λ. Informally, EMPTY can be expressed as

$$\Lambda \to \Lambda,$$

where it is understood that the relation holds for only this one pair.

Note that the labels on the edges enforce the following behaviors: In Phase 1 the same character that is read is pushed onto the stack. In Phase 2 the same character that is read is popped off of the stack. A transition from Phase 1 to Phase 2 is possible only when the character # is read. The accepting node is not reached unless the entire input has been read and the stack is empty.

Consider the behavior of this program on input `abb#bab`. During Phase 1, it will successively push the characters `a`, `b`, and `b` onto the top of the stack, so the stack holds the string `abb`. When the # is scanned, the program will enter Phase 2. Next, `b` is scanned and popped from the stack, leaving `ab` on the stack. When `a` is then scanned, a mismatch is detected and the program enters phase 4, rejecting `abb#bab`, which is not a palindrome.

The program in Figure 1.1 is called a *recognizer* for the language consisting of all palindromes with central marker, because it accepts all strings that are in the language and rejects all strings that are not in the language. In Figure 1.2 we present a simpler program with similar behavior: If the input x is a palindrome with central marker, then the program accepts x, but if x is not a palindrome with central marker, then the program at some time becomes unable to proceed and does not accept x. Such a program is called an *acceptor* for the set of palindromes with central marker.

Consider the behavior of the acceptor on input `abb#bab`. It behaves the same as the recognizer, until the second `a` is reached. Since it is not

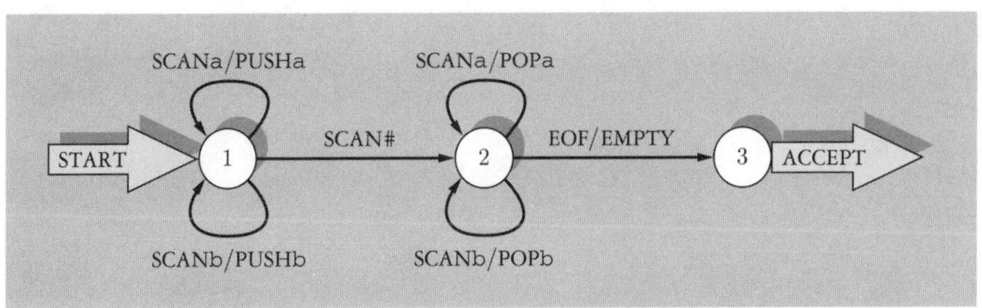

FIGURE 1.2: A program that accepts palindromes with central marker.

possible to scan a b or pop an a, neither edge can be followed, so the program cannot proceed. (When a program is in a nonfinal control state but is unable to proceed, we say that the program is *blocked*.) Thus the nonpalindrome abb#bab is not accepted. ■ ■ ■

EXAMPLE 1.2. Next we consider a simple kind of arithmetic calculation. The input is a sequence of monadic numbers separated by plus signs and minus signs, for example 111-11111+1111-111111. The output is a single signed monadic number representing the result of performing the indicated additions and subtractions. For the sample input above, the output is -1111.

An algorithm for performing this calculation is as follows: Set the variable **total** equal to the first number in the input. Each time a + is seen, add the next number to **total**. Each time a - is seen, subtract the next number from **total**. Finally, print out the value of **total**. This algorithm can be implemented as a program for a machine with an input device, an output device, and a signed counter, as shown in Figure 1.3. Slashes inside

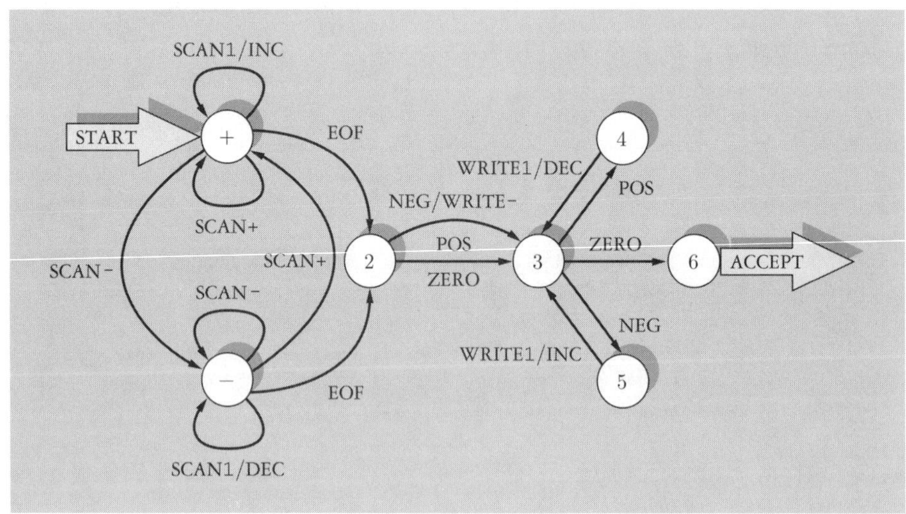

FIGURE 1.3: A program for monadic addition and subtraction.

labels separate operations on the different devices—in this case, the input, the output, and the counter.

A signed counter holds a single integer, which we call its state or its value. The operation INC (short for "increment") adds 1 to the state of the counter; the operation DEC (short for "decrement") subtracts 1. The operation ZERO maps the counter's state from 0 to 0; that is, it can be performed if the counter's state is zero. Similarly the operation POS can be performed if the counter's state is positive, and the operation NEG can be performed if it is negative.

We call operations like ZERO, POS, and NEG *tests* because they examine the counter's state but do not change it. Our usage of the word "test" is analogous to the usage in traditional programming languages, but not identical. In traditional usage, a test *selects* among two or more courses of action; in our usage, a test *permits* a single course of action, though there may be alternatives permitted by other tests.

The program adds by counting up by 1s; it subtracts by counting down by 1s. Addition is performed while in the control state labeled $+$, and subtraction is performed while in the control state labeled $-$. The counter's state, when the input is exhausted, is equal to the value to be written on the output device. If the counter's state is positive, we decrement and print 1 until the counter's state reaches zero. If the counter's state is negative we print a minus sign, and then we increment and print 1 until the counter's state reaches zero. If the counter's state is zero we print nothing. ■■■

EXAMPLE 1.3. A very practical problem is to determine where a pattern string p occurs as a substring of a text string x. For example, most text editors have some facility that permits searching for a word in a file. Recall that p is a substring of x if there exist (possibly empty) strings u and w such that $upw = x$.

For simplicity, we consider the related problem of determining, for a fixed pattern p, whether p is a substring of the input text x. We present an algorithm that solves this problem roughly as follows: We let y denote the prefix of the input that we have scanned so far. A *partial match* is a suffix of y that is also a prefix of p. We let q denote the longest partial match. It turns out that the only datum we need to keep track of is q, and that it is rather easy to update q when another input character is read.

p : ababb

q : abab

qa : ab<u>aba</u>

FIGURE 1.4: Determining the longest suffix of ababa that is a prefix of ababb.

For example, let p = ababb and let x = babababba. Suppose that we have read 5 characters of x so that y = babab. Then q = abab, the longest prefix of p that matches the characters most recently read.

Let us describe the algorithm more precisely: Initially q and y are both the empty string. At the start of the loop, if $q = p$ then we accept. Otherwise, if $y = x$ then we stop. Otherwise, we read the next character c from the input and set $y = yc$. The new value of q is the longest suffix of qc that is a prefix of p. Now we go back to the start of the loop. The proof of the algorithm's correctness is left as an exercise.

Continuing our example, suppose that we read the sixth character of x, which is a. Now qa = ababa, so aba is the longest prefix of p that is also a suffix of qa (Figure 1.4), and therefore q becomes aba. When we read the seventh and eighth characters of x, q takes successively the values abab and ababb; since the latter is equal to p, a complete match is detected.

Because p is fixed, this algorithm can be implemented as a program for a machine with only an input device and a finite number of control states. The program has one control state for each possible value of q, i.e., for each prefix of p, and a single accepting control state. One edge exits each of those control states for each character in the input alphabet; a single additional edge leads to the accepting control state. Since p has exactly $|p| + 1$ prefixes, the resulting program has $|p| + 2$ control states and $(|p| + 1)|\Sigma| + 1$ edges, where Σ is the input alphabet.

In Figure 1.5, we present a program that accepts exactly those strings containing the pattern p = ababb. Observe that the edges going from control state ababb ensure that the entire input string is scanned before

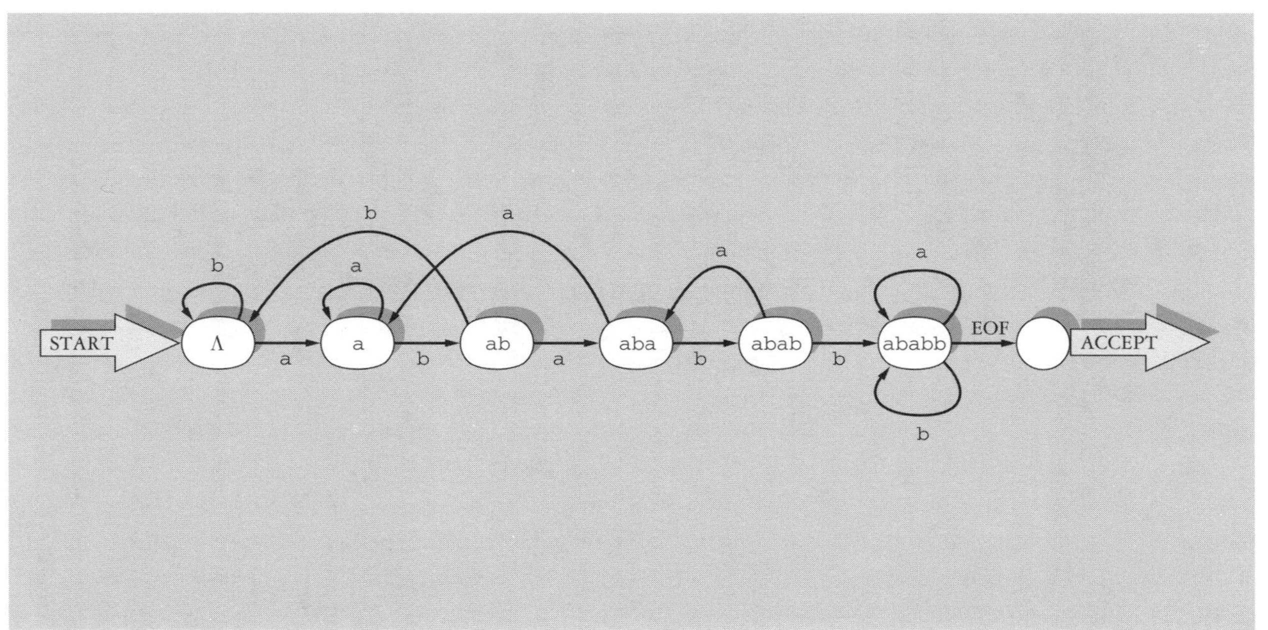

FIGURE 1.5: A pattern-matching program with p = `ababb`. Each control state corresponds to a partial match. After a complete match is found (state `ababb`), the remainder of the input is scanned and ignored. For brevity, we have written `a` for SCANa and `b` for SCANb; we have also omitted the state name from a node. These space-saving conventions may be used in diagrams when no confusion is possible.

the program accepts it. We will almost always require that programs scan the entire input before accepting. ■■■

Exercises

1.1-1 A *queue* (pronounced like the letter "q") is a storage device that can hold a string. Its operations are ENQUEUEc and DEQUEUEc, for each character c in some alphabet, and EMPTY. The operation ENQUEUEc appends a c to (the right end of) the queue's contents, mapping x to xc, and the operation DEQUEUEc removes a c from the left end of the queue's contents, mapping cx to x. The operation EMPTY tests whether the queue holds the empty string. Design a program, for a machine with an input device and a queue, that accepts exactly those strings of the form w#w for some string w over the alphabet $\{0, 1\}$.

1.1-2 Design a program for a machine with an input device, an output device, and a stack that performs the monadic addition and subtraction calculations described in this section.

1.1-3 Design a program for a machine with only an input device that accepts exactly those strings containing the substring `abbabbab`. Use only 10 control states.

1.1-4 Design a program for a machine with only an input device that accepts exactly those strings containing the substring `ababb` or `baaa`. Use only 10 control states.

Solution: The program is given in Figure 1.6.

1.1-5 In parts (c) and (d) "the algorithm" refers to the pattern-matching algorithm described in this section for pattern p.

(a) Prove that if p is a substring of x, then there exists y such that y is a prefix of x and p is a suffix of y.

(b) Suppose that q is the longest suffix of y that is a prefix of p. (1) Prove that p is a suffix of y iff $q = p$. (2) Prove that the longest suffix of qc that is a prefix of p is also the longest suffix of yc that is a prefix of p.

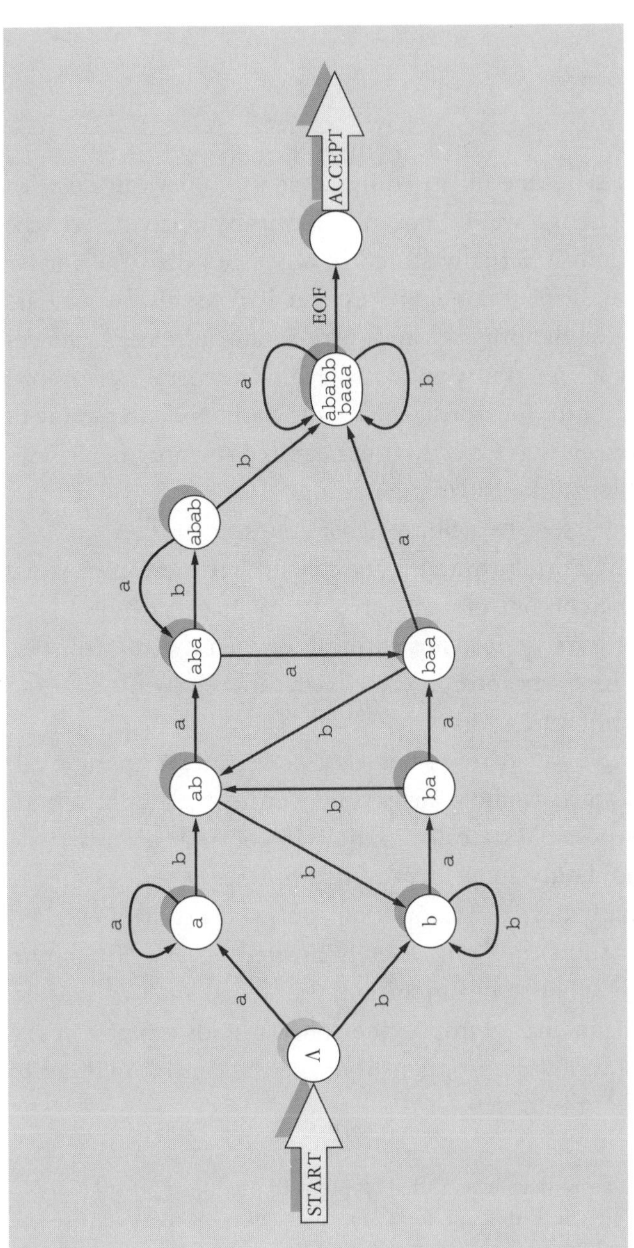

FIGURE 1.6: A program that accepts exactly those strings containing the substring ababb or baaa.

(c) Prove that if p is a substring of x, then the algorithm will accept input x.

(d) Prove that if p is not a substring of x, then the algorithm will not accept input x.

1.2 CONTROLS

In this section we will see some of the things that machines can do with very little memory. Although we did not mention it explicitly before, the control state of a program is actually stored in a device called the *control*. This control is the weakest of storage devices, but it is useful, because its value limits the action of the program to a very small number of choices at each step. Without it, programs would run out of control. A control can be thought of as a finite memory, which holds a bounded amount of information. We have seen that even this very limited memory device can be applied to real problems like pattern matching.

With a control, we associate a finite set of states $Q = \{q_1, \ldots, q_k\}$. When we represent a program as a digraph, the control states are represented by the nodes. For each pair of control states q_i, q_j there is an operation $q_i \to q_j$ that maps control state q_i to q_j; it is not applicable when the control state is different from q_i. The operations on the control are represented by the edges in the program digraph.

As storage devices go, a control is not very powerful. A counter can hold any integer, and a stack can hold any string over its stack alphabet; for both devices the set of possible states is infinite. In contrast, a control is a *finite* memory; it can hold only an element of its finite set Q.

A machine whose only devices are input, output, and a control is called a *finite machine* (FM, for short).[2] While severely limited in capability, finite machine programs can solve some important problems, such as pattern matching (Figure 1.5). In that example, the control holds a prefix of the pattern. In general, we can write programs that use the control in order to hold a bounded amount of information.

---

[2] Historically, finite machines have been called "finite state machines" (FSMs) or "finite automata" (FA). We think that the term "finite machine" is more concise and unpretentious.

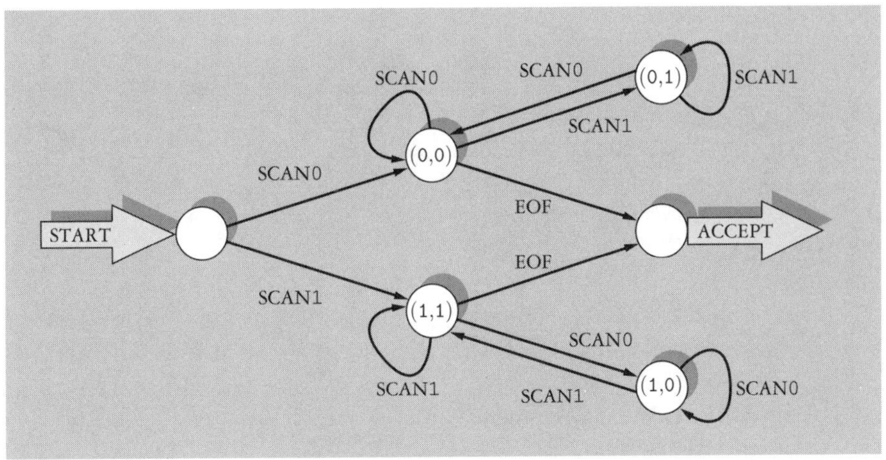

FIGURE 1.7: An FM program that accepts the language $\{awa : a \in \{0,1\},\ w \in \{0,1\}^*\} \cup \{0,1\}$.

EXAMPLE 1.4. A control can hold a pair of characters. Thus, by keeping track of the first character and the most recent character scanned, a finite machine program can test whether its input string begins and ends with the same character (Figure 1.7). ■ ■ ■

EXAMPLE 1.5. A control can also hold a single integer in the finite range $0, \ldots, m-1$. Because this makes it possible to count modulo m, a finite machine program can test whether the number of characters in its input is a multiple of m (Figure 1.8). ■ ■ ■

Exercises

1.2-1 Design an FM program that accepts exactly those strings over $\{0, 1\}^*$ containing an odd number of 1s.

1.2-2 Design an FM program that accepts exactly those strings over $\{0, 1\}^*$ containing a number of 1s that is congruent to 2 or 4 modulo 7.

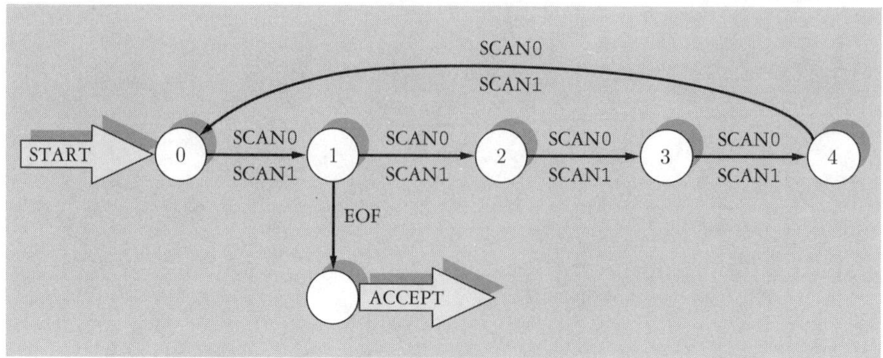

FIGURE 1.8: An FM program that accepts the language $\{w \in \{0,1\}^* : |w| \equiv 1 \pmod 5\}$.

1.3 UNSIGNED COUNTERS

In this section we will see some things that machines can do if we give them a little more memory. Except for the control, the weakest storage device we consider is the unsigned counter. We will see that a machine with a counter can solve real-world problems like checking whether parentheses balance properly.

An unsigned counter can hold any nonnegative integer. The operations on the unsigned counter are INC, DEC, ZERO, and NONZERO. The increment operation (INC) adds 1 to the counter's value. The decrement operation (DEC) subtracts 1; it is applicable only if the counter value is 1 or greater. The operation ZERO tests whether the counter value is 0; i.e., the operation does not affect the counter's value, and an edge labeled ZERO can only be followed when the counter holds the value 0. The operation NONZERO tests whether the counter value is different from 0 (i.e., whether the counter holds a positive integer); the operation does not affect the counter's value, and an edge labeled NONZERO can only be followed when the counter holds a value different from 0.

Notice that we allow very limited access to a counter's value. We can directly test only whether the value is 0 or not. For example, there is no operation that tests whether the counter holds the number 5 or whether the third bit from the left in its binary representation is a 0 (though we could write a program to determine the former—Exercise 1.3-9). A metaphor for this kind of counter exists in certain cafeterias that cannot afford multicolored trays. Identical trays are stored on a spring that is designed to make the topmost tray accessible while keeping any others hidden. Because the trays are identical, the only information stored in this way is the size of the pile. A tray may be added to the pile (INC) or removed from the pile if there are any left (DEC). One can visually determine whether there are any trays on the pile (NONZERO) or whether there are none (ZERO).

Remember that an edge can be followed only if all the operations labeling it can be performed. Thus an edge labeled DEC cannot be followed unless the counter holds a positive integer. If the counter holds 0, then the program must follow some other edge or stop.

A machine with a control and an unsigned counter is called an *unsigned counter machine* (UCM, for short). (Input and output (I/O) devices are storage devices because they hold strings, but the capabilities of a machine are usually dictated by its non-I/O devices. For that reason, we characterize a machine by its collection of non-I/O devices. For the remainder of this chapter, assume that all machines have input and output devices when necessary, though we may not say so explicitly.)

EXAMPLE 1.6. A program using a counter can determine whether the input is a string of a's followed by an equal number of b's (Figure 1.9). ■ ■ ■

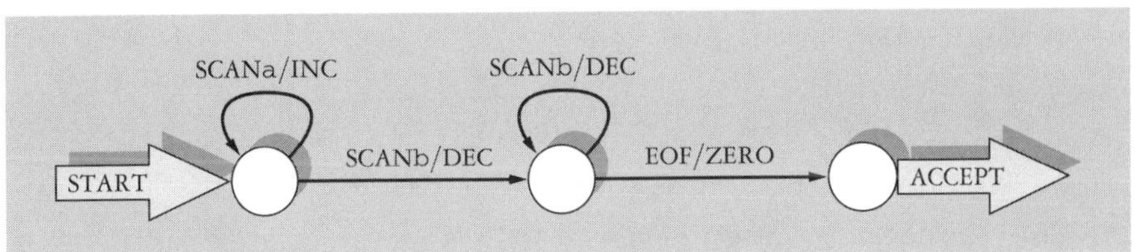

FIGURE 1.9: A UCM program that accepts $\{a^n b^n : n \geq 1\}$.

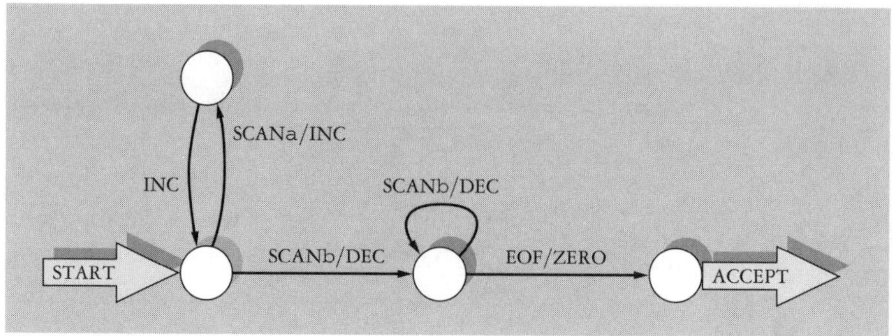

FIGURE 1.10: A UCM program that accepts $\{\mathtt{a}^n\mathtt{b}^{2n} : n \geq 1\}$.

EXAMPLE 1.7. To determine whether a string is of the form $\mathtt{a}^n\mathtt{b}^{2n}$, i.e., a string of a's followed by twice as many b's, we count each a twice and each b once, as shown in Figure 1.10. This program counts up twice as fast as it counts down. ■ ■ ■

When we write arithmetic expressions like $(7+2)(6+(3+1)(4+5))$, we use parentheses to force certain operations to be performed first. A sequence of parentheses that could be used in a well-formed arithmetic expression is called *balanced*. In the example above, the sequence of parentheses is ()(()()). By way of definition, we say that a string is balanced if it has one of the following three forms:

- Λ,
- (w), where w is balanced, or
- wx, where w and x are both nonempty and balanced.

The set consisting of all balanced strings of parentheses is called $L_{()}$. The following proposition is the key to designing a UCM program that tests whether its input belongs to $L_{()}$.

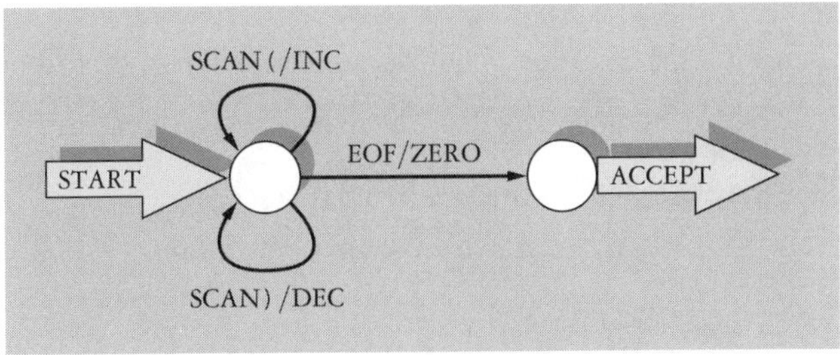

FIGURE 1.11: A UCM program that accepts $\{w : w \text{ is a balanced sequence of parentheses}\}$.

PROPOSITION 1.8. *w is a balanced string of parentheses if and only if*

- *w contains equal numbers of ('s and)'s, and*
- *every prefix of w contains at least as many ('s as)'s.*

The proof of this proposition is left as an exercise. ∎

EXAMPLE 1.9. By counting the number of ('s minus the number of)'s, a UCM can determine whether its input is a balanced string of parentheses (Figure 1.11). This program really exploits the fact that the counter value cannot become negative. Notice that if a prefix of the input contains more)'s than ('s, then the program becomes blocked, and so it does not accept. ∎ ∎ ∎

Exercises

1.3-1 For each unsigned counter operation, give its precondition and its action.

1.3-2 Design a UCM program that accepts $\{\mathtt{a}^n\mathtt{b}\mathtt{a}^n : n \geq 0\}$.

1.3-3 Design a UCM program that accepts $\{\mathtt{a}^n\mathtt{b}^n\mathtt{a}^m\mathtt{b}^m : m \geq 0 \text{ and } n \geq 0\}$.

1.3-4 Design a UCM program that accepts $\{\mathtt{a}^{2n}\mathtt{b}^{3n} : n \geq 0\}$.

1.3-5 Design a UCM program that *recognizes* $L_{()}$.

*+1.3-6 Design a UCM program that accepts the set of strings over $\{\mathtt{a}, \mathtt{b}\}$ that contain the same number of a's as b's.

1.3-7 Design another UCM program that accepts $\{\mathtt{a}^n\mathtt{b}^{2n} : n \geq 0\}$ by counting each a once and each pair of b's once.

*1.3-8 Prove Proposition 1.8.

1.3-9 In this exercise we will consider a UCM that starts with a number stored in its counter. Write a program that stops in an accepting control state if that number is 5, but never reaches an accepting control state if that number is different from 5.

1.4 SIGNED COUNTERS

Now let us see what we can do with a counter that can hold negative values, which we call a *signed counter*. Some problems are easier to solve using a signed counter, though we will see in Chapter 3 that any problem solvable with a signed counter can be solved with an unsigned counter via a slightly more complicated program.

A signed counter can hold any integer. Its operations are INC, DEC, ZERO, POS, and NEG. The operations INC and DEC, respectively, add and subtract 1 from the counter's value; the operations ZERO, POS, and NEG, respectively, test whether the counter's value is 0, positive, or negative. A machine with a control and a signed counter is called a *signed counter machine* (SCM, for short).

EXAMPLE 1.10. Since the counter is allowed to contain negative values, it is easy to design an SCM program that determines whether its input contains an equal number of a's and b's (Figure 1.12). ■■■

It is also possible to program a UCM to solve the problem in the preceding example (Exercise 1.3-6), though the solution is not as easy. In fact, in Chapter 3, we will see that a UCM can solve any problem that an SCM can solve, and vice versa.

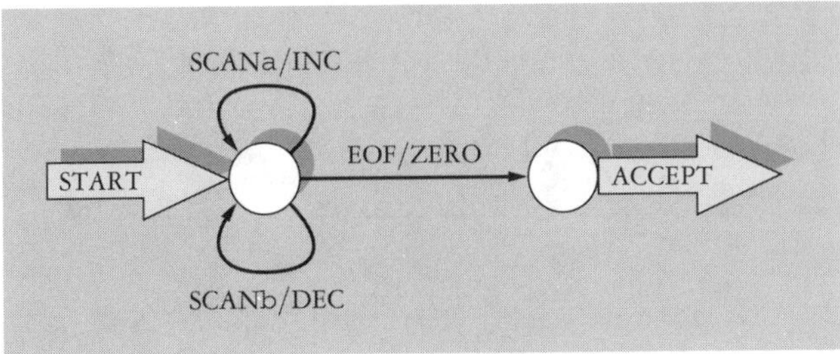

FIGURE 1.12: An SCM program that accepts $\{w : w \text{ contains an equal number of a's and b's}\}$.

Exercises

1.4-1 Suppose that the program of Figure 1.11 is run on an SCM. What language does the program accept then?

1.4-2 Design an SCM program that accepts exactly those strings containing more a's than b's.

1.4-3 Design an SCM program that accepts exactly those strings containing twice as many a's as b's.

1.4-4 Design an SCM program that accepts exactly those strings containing two-thirds as many a's as b's.

1.4-5 Design an SCM program that accepts $L_{()}$.

1.5 STACKS

In general, a *stack* uses a finite alphabet Γ. The stack can hold any string over Γ. For each character c belonging to Γ, the stack operation PUSHc pushes c onto the stack (maps x to xc), and the operation POPc pops c off the stack provided that the top character is in fact a c (maps xc to x). The stack operation EMPTY tests whether the stack holds the empty string (maps Λ

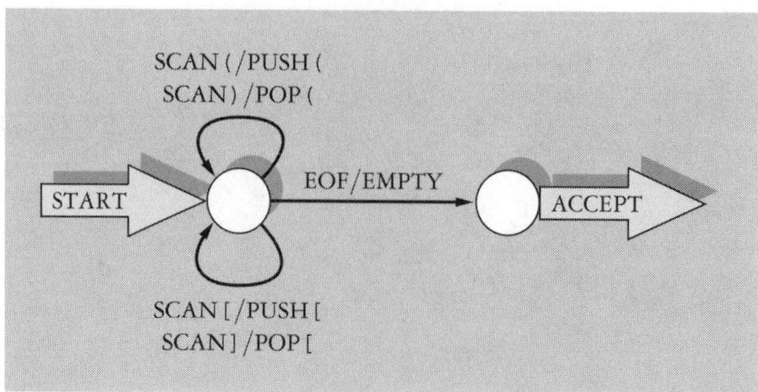

FIGURE 1.13: A stack machine program that accepts $\{w : w \text{ is a balanced sequence of parentheses and brackets}\}$.

to Λ). A machine with a control and a stack is called a *stack machine* (SM, for short).[3]

Remember that an edge can be followed only if all the operations labeling it can be performed. Thus an edge labeled POPc cannot be followed unless the top stack character is in fact a c. If the top of stack is some other character or if the stack is empty, then the program must follow some other edge or else stop.

A sequence of parentheses ( ) and brackets [ ] is *balanced* if it has one of the following forms:

- Λ,
- (w) or $[w]$ where w is balanced, or
- wx where w and x are both nonempty and balanced.

EXAMPLE 1.11. The set consisting of all balanced strings of parentheses and brackets is called $L_{()[]}$. In Figure 1.13 is a stack machine program that determines whether its input belongs to $L_{()[]}$. ■ ■ ■

---

[3] Other authors have defined stacks slightly differently, e.g., allowing several characters to be pushed at once. However, our stacks are computationally equivalent to theirs.

Exercises

1.5-1 Design a stack machine program that accepts $\{\texttt{a}^n\texttt{b}^m\texttt{a}^m\texttt{b}^n : m > 0 \text{ and } n \geq 0\}$.

1.6 TWO-COUNTER MACHINES

A 2-UCM (two-unsigned counter machine) has a control and two unsigned counters. It can use each of its counters independently in order to keep track of two numbers (Figure 1.14). The subscripts on the counter operations indicate which counter is affected.

Exercises

1.6-1 Construct a 2-UCM program that accepts

(a) $\{\texttt{a}^n\texttt{b}^n\texttt{c}^n : n \geq 1\}$

(b) $\{\texttt{a}^n\texttt{b}^n\texttt{c}^n\texttt{d}^n : n \geq 1\}$

**(c) $\{w\#w : w \in \{\texttt{a}, \texttt{b}\}^*\}$. Hint: If the input is $x\#y$, the first counter should hold $2^{\text{dyadic}(x)}3^{\text{dyadic}(y)}$.

1.6-2 A 2-stack machine has a control and two stacks. Construct a 2-stack machine program that

(a) recognizes $\{x\#x : x \in \{\texttt{a}, \texttt{b}\}^*\}$.

(b) takes as input $x\#y$ and outputs z where $\text{dyadic}(z^R) = \text{dyadic}(x) + \text{dyadic}(y)$.

*(c) takes as input $x\#y$ and outputs z where $\text{dyadic}(z) = \text{dyadic}(x) + \text{dyadic}(y)$.

Solution: Call the stacks S1 and S2. Because the control is a finite memory, it can hold two variables, each with a finite set of possible values. One variable, called "sum" holds 0, 1, or 2 depending on the result of adding a bit from x, a bit from y, and a carry bit. The other variable, called "done," holds either

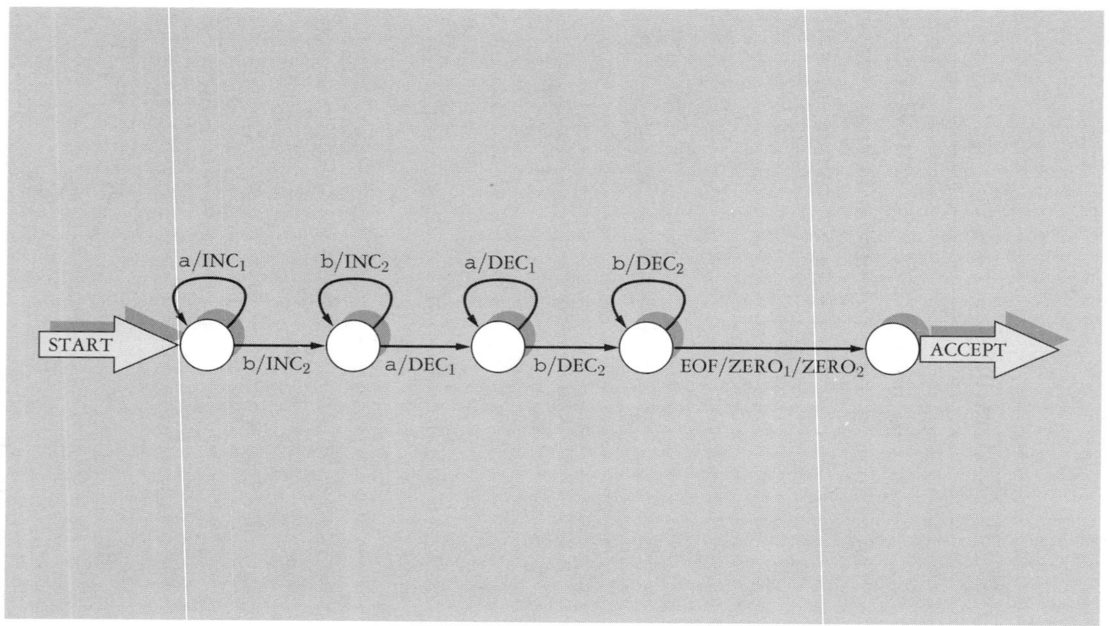

FIGURE 1.14: A 2-UCM program that accepts $\{a^n b^m a^n b^m : m > 0 \text{ and } n > 0\}$. The first counter counts the a's and the second counter counts the b's. The subscripts indicate which counter is being used.

"true" or "false." The control also keeps track of which step we are on in the following algorithm:

Step 1: Scan the input and push it onto S1, so S1 holds $x\#y$. Let sum = 0. Push a $ onto S2. Let done = true.

Step 2: If the top of the stack is #, then go to step 4, else let done = false.

Step 3: Pop the low-order digit of y and add it to sum. Pop the rest of y^R and push it onto S2.

Step 4: Pop the # and push it onto S2.

Step 5: If the stack is empty, then go to step 9, else let done = false.

Step 6: Pop the low-order digit of x and add it to sum.

Step 7: Pop everything above the $ from S2 and push it onto S1.

Step 8: Pop the $ from S2. Push sum mod 2 onto S2, and let sum = sum div 2. Push a $ onto S2.

Step 9: If done = false go to step 2.

Step 10: Pop the $ from S2. Pop the remaining characters from S2 and print them on the output.

1.7 TURING MACHINES

Alan Turing invented a machine that he intended to model human computation. His machine is now called a tape machine or a Turing machine. He observed that a person can keep only a limited amount of information in short-term memory but a virtually unlimited amount of information on pieces of paper.

Turing's machine uses a control and a new device called a *tape* or *Turing tape*. A tape is more powerful than any single device we have studied so far. Like a stack, a tape holds a finite string over a tape alphabet Γ (along with some additional information). Unlike a stack, access to the finite string is not restricted to the rightmost character. Access to the tape is governed by the read/write *head*, which indicates which character of the string is currently being operated on. This tape character is said to be *under* the tape head. An operation on a tape is any one of the following: examining the character under the tape head, overwriting the character under the head with a new character, moving the tape head one square to the right, moving the tape head one square to the left, or checking that the tape head is at the left end of the tape.

A machine with k tapes is called a k-tape *Turing machine.* A machine with one tape is commonly called a Turing machine, and a machine with an unspecified positive number of tapes is commonly called a multitape Turing machine. We usually write TM to abbreviate Turing machine.

(While stacks and counters are data structures in everyday use, tapes are not. One reason for this is that (limited versions of) stacks and counters are easier to design in hardware than tapes are. A second reason is that stacks and counters are less awkward to program with. Hence, one may wonder why tapes are mentioned at all in a course on computability. The answer is that, despite its awkwardness, one tape is computationally as powerful as any collection of known memory devices; we will prove so in Chapter 7. Thus, any problem that can be solved on any known computer can also be solved on a machine with a control and a single tape. Because Turing machines are very simple compared with computers in practical use, it is conceptually easier to prove impossibility results for Turing machines. These impossibility results apply as well to all known computers.)

We indicate the location of the tape head by drawing a box around the character that is under the tape head. For example, a tape string `abbabc` with the head on the fifth character is indicated by `abaa`$\boxed{\texttt{b}}$`c`. Let $\boxed{\Gamma}$ denote $\{\boxed{c} : c \in \Gamma\}$. Then the state of the tape is denoted by a string in $\Gamma^*\boxed{\Gamma}\Gamma^*$.

For each character c in the tape alphabet Γ, the tape operation PRINTc writes a c on the square under the tape head; i.e., it replaces the character previously under the head by a c. Thus if the tape state is $x\boxed{a}y$, then the operation PRINTc changes the tape state to $x\boxed{c}y$.

The operation SEEc tests that the character under the tape head is a c. Thus it maps the tape state $x\boxed{c}y$ to $x\boxed{c}y$. However, the operation SEEc cannot be performed if the character under the tape head is not a c, i.e., if the tape state is $x\boxed{a}y$ for some $a \neq c$.

Two additional operations move the tape head. The first is MOVEL, which moves the tape head one square to the left. If the tape state is $xa\boxed{b}y$, then the operation MOVEL produces the tape state $x\boxed{a}by$. The second is

MOVER, which moves the tape head one square to the right. If the tape state is $x\boxed{a}by$, then the operation MOVER produces the tape state $xa\boxed{b}y$.

Observant readers may wonder what happens if the tape head is moved right from the right end of the tape or left from the left end of the tape. We imagine that the tape extends infinitely far to the right, where previously unvisited squares hold blank characters (spaces). We denote the blank character by $\sqcup$. If the tape state is $x\boxed{a}$, then the operation MOVER produces the tape state $xa\boxed{\sqcup}$. In contrast, it is not possible to move left from the left end of the tape; i.e., if the tape state is $\boxed{b}y$, then the operation MOVEL cannot be performed. Because the tape extends infinitely only to the right, it is called "one-way" infinite.

The SEE, PRINT, and MOVE operations may, when convenient, be combined into a single operation, following the convention that seeing precedes printing and printing precedes moving. We use brackets [ ] to denote such a combination of tape operations; e.g., the operation [SEE a, PRINT b, MOVER] overwrites an a with a b and then moves right. It is also permissible to combine only two of the operations. For example, the operation [SEE a, MOVEL] moves left if the character under the tape head is an a. For consistency, brackets may enclose a single tape operation as well.

The operation ATHOME tests that the tape head is on the leftmost tape square, which we may think of as the home square on the tape. Thus ATHOME maps the tape state $\boxed{b}y$ to $\boxed{b}y$. However, the operation ATHOME cannot be performed if the tape head is not in the leftmost position, i.e., if the tape state is $x\boxed{c}y$ for some nonempty string x.

EXAMPLE 1.12. Let us see how a 1-tape Turing machine program can accept the set of all strings of the form $x\#y$ where $x = y$ (Figure 1.15). While in state 1, the program copies x from the input device to the tape. Then, while in state 2, the program moves the tape head back to the left end of the tape. While in state 3, the program compares x to y, one character at a time. ■ ■ ■

EXAMPLE 1.13. Let us use a 2-tape Turing machine to test whether a string is of the form ww (Figure 1.16). Using control states 1 and 2, the program copies the input string x onto tape 1, while at the same time writing $\frac{1}{2}|x|$ #'s on tape 2 (it becomes blocked if $|x|$ is not even). Using control states 3 and 4, it moves both tape heads to the home position. Using control state

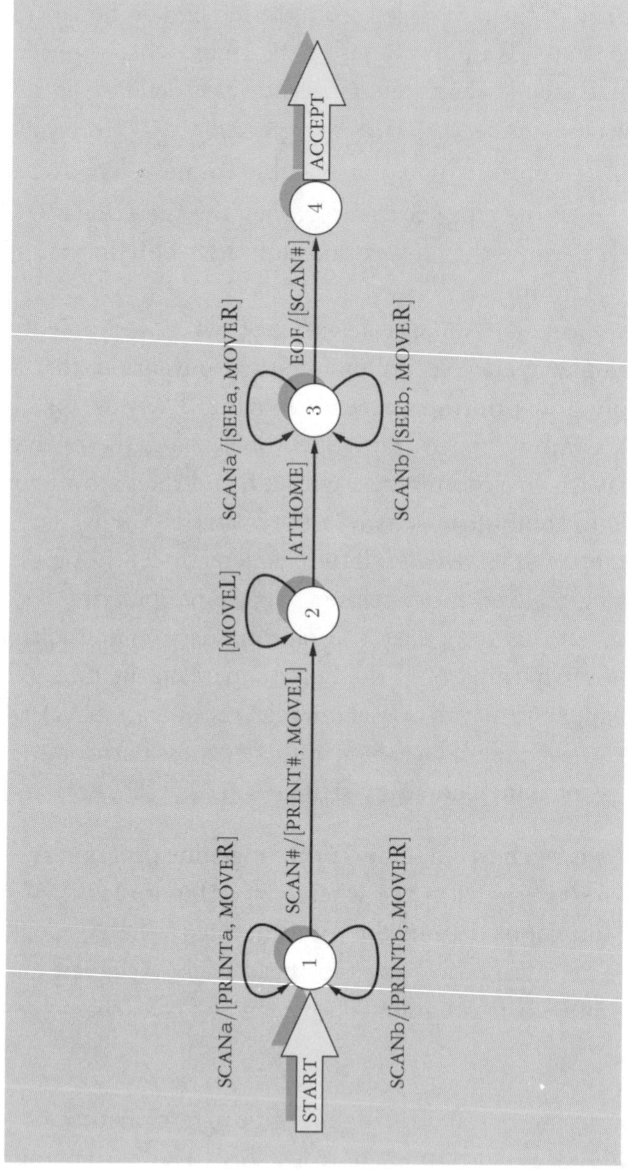

FIGURE 1.15: A 1-tape TM program that accepts $\{w\#w : w \in \{a,b\}^*\}$. This program copies the first part of the input onto the tape and then compares it to the second part of the input.

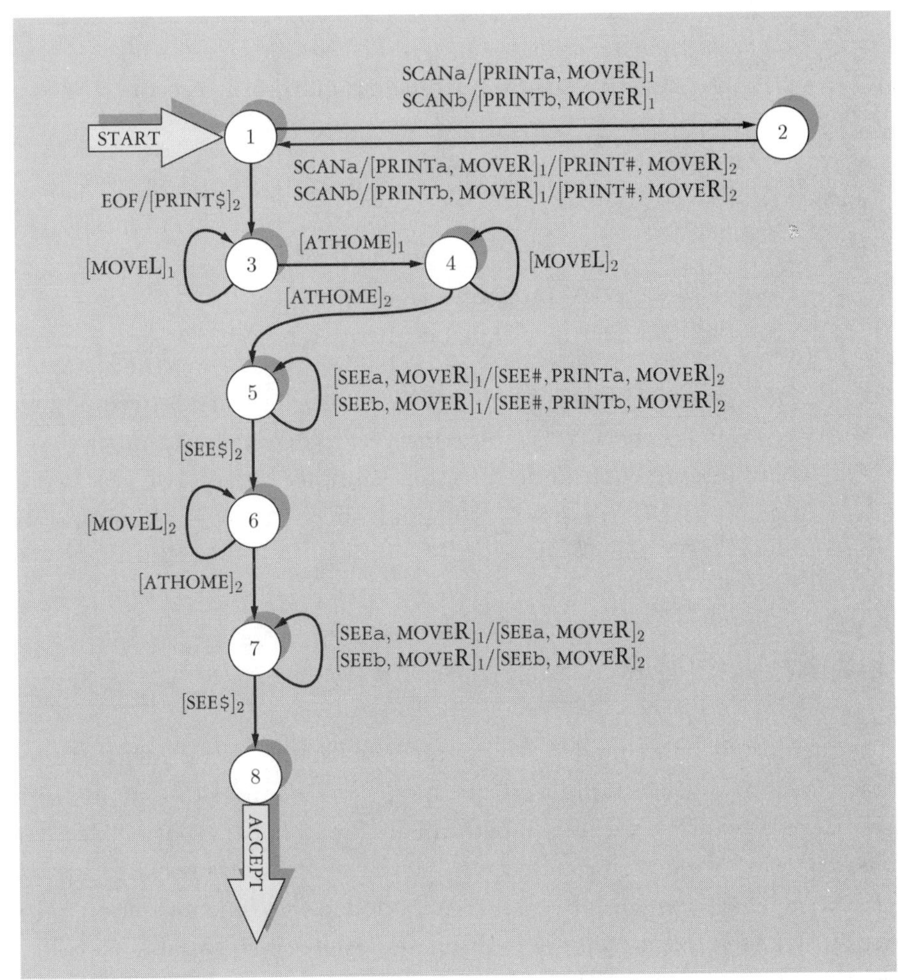

FIGURE 1.16: A 2-tape TM program that accepts $\{ww : w \in \{\mathtt{a},\mathtt{b}\}^*\}$.

5, it then copies the first half of x from tape 1 to tape 2, leaving the tape head in the middle of tape 1. Using control state 6, it moves the second tape's head to its home position. Finally, using control state 7, it compares the last half of x (on tape 1) to the first half of x (on tape 2). If the two halves are equal, the program accepts in control state 8. ■ ■ ■

Exercises

1.7-1 Design a 1-tape Turing machine program that accepts $\{x\#x^R : x \in \{\mathtt{a}, \mathtt{b}\}^*\}$.

1.7-2 Design a multitape Turing machine program that accepts $\{x \in \{\mathtt{a}, \mathtt{b}\}^* : x = x^R\}$.

1.7-3 Design a 1-tape TM program that accepts $\{x \in \{\mathtt{a}, \mathtt{b}\}^* : x = x^R\}$. Hint: Use a larger tape alphabet than $\{\mathtt{a}, \mathtt{b}\}$.

1.7-4 Design a multitape Turing machine program that adds two numbers given in binary. Let us write binary(s) to denote the number whose binary representation is s, so, for example, binary$(\mathtt{10011}) = 19$. On input $x\#y$ the program should output z, where binary$(z) =$ binary$(x) +$ binary(y).

1.8 RANDOM ACCESS MACHINES

The memory of most modern computers consists of several megabytes of static memory, where almost all of a program's data resides, along with several registers that are able to perform arithmetic operations on the data they contain. We describe an idealized device, called a *random access memory* (RAM, for short), which comprises an unbounded static memory and a finite set of registers. Each memory location and each register is able to hold a single natural number. A machine with a control and a random access memory is called a *random access machine* (also RAM, for short).

The operations consist of storing data from a register into memory and fetching data from memory into a register, along with several operations on numbers held in registers. These operations are addition, a restricted form of subtraction, division by 2 (with truncation), clearing a register to 0, setting a register to 1, testing whether a number is greater than another, testing whether two numbers are equal, testing whether a number is odd, and testing whether a number is even. While most practical computers also support negative numbers and multiplication, those can in fact be implemented efficiently using the RAM operations.

Let us consider a RAM with k registers. The numbers held in the registers are denoted $R_1, \ldots, R_k$. The ith location in the static memory is denoted MEM$[i]$, where i may be any natural number. We require that all memory locations initially hold the value 0. At any time only finitely many memory locations are nonzero, so a finite description is possible. If location n is the highest-numbered memory location that has been stored into, then the state of the RAM does not depend on any memory locations numbered higher than n. The state may thus be defined as a finite sequence: $\langle\langle R_1, \ldots, R_k, \text{MEM}[0], \ldots, \text{MEM}[n]\rangle\rangle$. The fetch and store operations are denoted

$$\begin{aligned} R_a &:= \text{MEM}[R_b], \\ \text{MEM}[R_a] &:= R_b, \end{aligned}$$

respectively. The fetch operation above is a total function, which maps $\langle\langle r_1, \ldots, r_a, \ldots, r_k, m_0, \ldots, m_n\rangle\rangle$ to $\langle\langle r_1, \ldots, m_{r_b}, \ldots, r_k, m_0, \ldots, m_n\rangle\rangle$.

The store operation is also a total function; if $r_a \leq n$, it maps $\langle\langle r_1, \ldots, r_k, m_0, \ldots, m_{r_a}, \ldots, m_n\rangle\rangle$ to $\langle\langle r_1, \ldots, r_k, m_0, \ldots, r_b, \ldots, m_n\rangle\rangle$. If $r_a > n$, it maps $\langle\langle r_1, \ldots, r_k, m_0, \ldots, m_n\rangle\rangle$ to $\langle\langle r_1, \ldots, r_k, m_0, \ldots, m_n, 0, \ldots, 0, r_b\rangle\rangle$.

The register operations are denoted

$$\begin{aligned} &R_a := R_b + R_c, \\ &R_a := R_b \dot{-} R_c, \\ &R_a := \lfloor R_b/2 \rfloor, \\ &R_a := 0, \\ &R_a := 1, \\ &R_a > R_b, \\ &R_a = R_b, \\ &R_a \text{ ODD}, \\ &R_a \text{ EVEN}. \end{aligned}$$

The addition operation maps $\langle\langle r_1, \ldots, r_a, \ldots, r_k, m_0, \ldots, m_n\rangle\rangle$ to $\langle\langle r_1, \ldots, r_b + r_c, \ldots, r_k, m_0, \ldots, m_n\rangle\rangle$. The monus operation (subtraction) maps $\langle\langle r_1, \ldots, r_a, \ldots, r_k, m_0, \ldots, m_n\rangle\rangle$ to $\langle\langle r_1, \ldots, r_b - r_c, \ldots, r_k,$

$m_0, \ldots, m_n\rangle\!\rangle$ if $r_b \geq r_c$, and to $\langle\!\langle r_1, \ldots, 0, \ldots, r_k, m_0, \ldots, m_n\rangle\!\rangle$ otherwise. The halving operation maps $\langle\!\langle r_1, \ldots, r_a, \ldots, r_k, m_0, \ldots, m_n\rangle\!\rangle$ to $\langle\!\langle r_1, \ldots, \lfloor r_b/2 \rfloor, \ldots, r_k, m_0, \ldots, m_n\rangle\!\rangle$. The greater-than operation maps $\langle\!\langle r_1, \ldots, r_k, m_0, \ldots, m_n\rangle\!\rangle$ to $\langle\!\langle r_1, \ldots, r_k, m_0, \ldots, m_n\rangle\!\rangle$ if $r_a > r_b$ and is undefined otherwise. The equality operation maps $\langle\!\langle r_1, \ldots, r_k, m_0, \ldots, m_n\rangle\!\rangle$ to $\langle\!\langle r_1, \ldots, r_k, m_0, \ldots, m_n\rangle\!\rangle$ if $r_a = r_b$ and is undefined otherwise. The oddness test maps $\langle\!\langle r_1, \ldots, r_k, m_0, \ldots, m_n\rangle\!\rangle$ to $\langle\!\langle r_1, \ldots, r_k, m_0, \ldots, m_n\rangle\!\rangle$ if r_a is odd and is undefined otherwise. The evenness test maps $\langle\!\langle r_1, \ldots, r_k, m_0, \ldots, m_n\rangle\!\rangle$ to $\langle\!\langle r_1, \ldots, r_k, m_0, \ldots, m_n\rangle\!\rangle$ if r_a is even and is undefined otherwise.

EXAMPLE 1.14. We present a RAM program that multiplies two natural numbers (Figure 1.17). This justifies our omission of multiplication from the repertory of a RAM. Our program implements the standard algorithm for binary multiplication. We assume that the numbers to be multiplied are initially in R_b and R_c. The product will be in R_a. The program uses

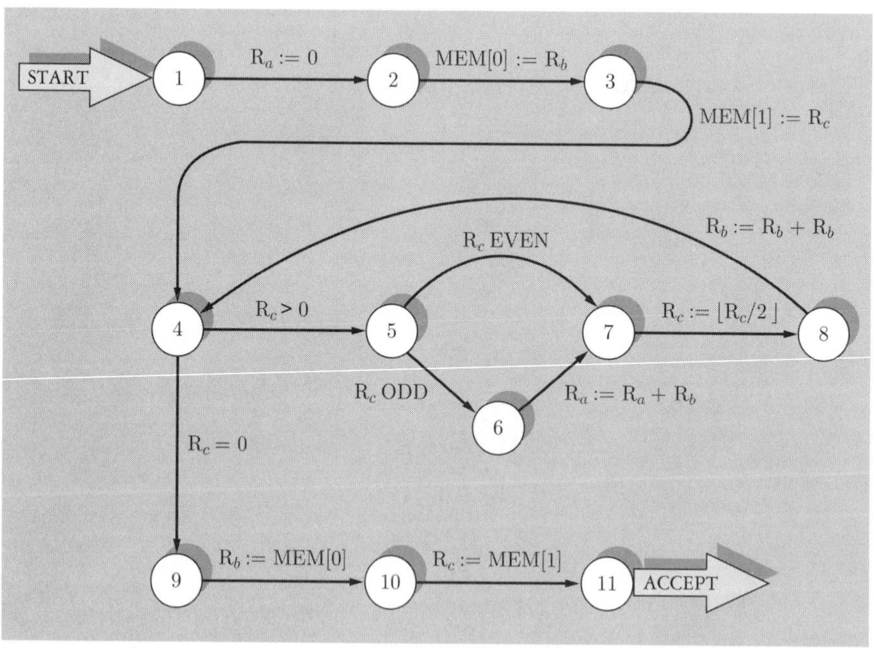

FIGURE 1.17: A RAM program that performs $R_a := R_b * R_c$.

MEM[0] and MEM[1] as temporary storage. In control states 1 through 3, the program clears R_a and saves the values of R_b and R_c in memory. In control states 4 through 8, the program performs the main loop of the multiplication. When R_c is 0, the multiplication is done; otherwise, the loop continues. If R_c is odd, then R_b is added to R_a. R_c is shifted right, R_b is shifted left, and then the loop is repeated. Once that loop is complete, the program restores the original values of R_b and R_c, in control states 9 through 11. ■ ■ ■

Exercises

1.8-1 Write a RAM program that computes x^n.

1.8-2 Write a RAM program that scans a number written in binary and stores the result in R_1.

1.8-3 Write a program that puts the value 17 into register 1.

1.9 DETERMINISM AND NONDETERMINISM

When a machine runs a program, we have come to expect the machine's behavior to be uniquely determined at each step by the contents of its storage devices. Programs having that property are called *deterministic*.[4] While we are most comfortable with programs whose behavior is uniquely determined and hence predictable, nondeterministic programs, which allow their machines a choice of actions in some configurations, are of fundamental importance in the study of computer science. Informally, we think of a nondeterministic program as being able to guess the correct way to proceed whenever it is faced with a choice.

[4] This name comes from the philosophy of determinism, which asserts that the entire universe's behavior at any time is uniquely determined by the universe's state at that time. In this light, nondeterministic programs may be thought of as having free will; however, it may be more illuminating to think of nondeterministic programs as prescient.

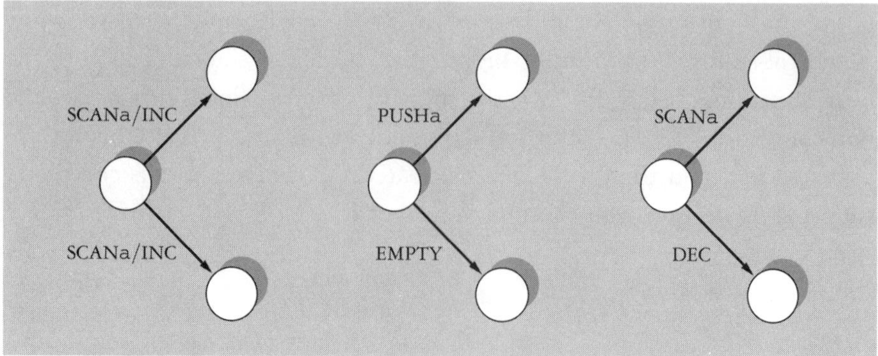

FIGURE 1.18: Three program fragments that are not deterministic.

EXAMPLE 1.15. It is easy enough to design a program that is not deterministic (Figure 1.18)—for example, we could draw two distinct edges out of control state 1 and label them identically. A program may also fail to be deterministic in subtler ways, e.g., by having two edges, one labeled "EMPTY" and the other labeled "PUSHa," emanate from a single control state (when the stack is empty, both operations are applicable). In some cases, a program may fail to be deterministic when edges leaving a single control state operate exclusively on different devices. ■■■

Nondeterminism is a mathematical construct that helps us to understand some important problems. We will see in Chapters 5 and 6 that nondeterministic programs for stack machines can be implemented efficiently on real computers. Nondeterministic programming is also the basis for declarative programming languages like Prolog. Lest the reader think that nondeterministic programs are always of practical use, however, we point out that no one has discovered a way to implement nondeterministic programs for general purpose machines efficiently on existing computers.

If we run a nondeterministic program several times on the same input x, then the program might very well give different results each time it is run. If every possible run results in x being accepted, then it is clear that we should say that the program accepts x, and similarly if every run results in x being rejected. In the case that some runs result in acceptance and others

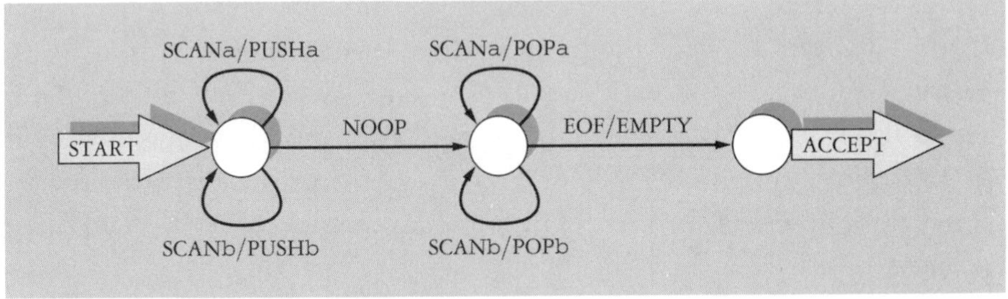

FIGURE 1.19: A nondeterministic SM program that accepts the language $\{ww^R : w \in \{\texttt{a,b}\}^*\}$.

do not, we have not yet defined whether the program accepts x. In order to make our theory turn out nicely, we make the following definition:

> *A nondeterministic program accepts a string x if at least one of its runs on input x results in acceptance.*

Thus a program is said to accept if *at least one* sequence of legal transitions leads to acceptance.[5] Informally, we may think of a nondeterministic program as having foreknowledge: When confronted with a choice of possible edges to follow, it will always make the "right choice" in the sense that it leads to acceptance if possible. Alternatively, we may think of the nondeterministic program as "guessing" the way to proceed. If its guesses lead to acceptance, then we say that it guessed correctly.

EXAMPLE 1.16. Recall that a stack machine program can test whether its input is of the form $w\#w^R$ by pushing each character that it scans until a # is encountered, then popping each character that it scans (Figure 1.2). The # indicates when to go from Phase 1 (pushing) to Phase 2 (popping). A nondeterministic stack machine program can test whether its input is an even-length palindrome, i.e., has the form ww^R, by using a similar technique (Figure 1.19). Since there is no marker to indicate when the middle of the

---

[5] There is a dual notion: programs that accept if *every* sequence of legal transitions leads to acceptance. A third possibility is to assign probabilities to transitions and thereby define the probability that a string is accepted. Although these modes of acceptance are of interest in the theory of computability, we do not address them in this book.

string has been reached, the program uses an edge nondeterministically to move from Phase 1 to Phase 2, "guessing" when the middle of the string has been reached. Although the program may have many ways to guess incorrectly, it needs only one way to guess correctly in order for the input to be accepted, by our definition of acceptance for nondeterministic programs. ■■■

EXAMPLE 1.17. Nondeterminism can help us to simplify FM programs by reducing the number of control states needed. The program in Figure 1.20 accepts any input string that has a 1 four characters from the end by nondeterministically guessing when it has read all but the last four characters. Note that the program must verify that it has guessed correctly, for otherwise it would accept all strings containing a 1 anywhere. To verify its guess, the program makes sure that there are at least four characters remaining in the input by scanning the next four characters (if there are fewer than four, then the program becomes blocked), and then it makes sure there is not a fifth character remaining by testing for EOF before accepting. As an exercise, the reader may consider the number of control states required by a deterministic FM program that accepts the same language (Exercise 1.9-3). ■■■

EXAMPLE 1.18. In Section 1.3 we saw that a deterministic UCM program can test whether its input consists of a string of a's followed by an equal number of b's. We also saw that a deterministic UCM program can test whether its input consists of a string of a's followed by twice as many b's. In Figure 1.21, we see how a nondeterministic UCM (NUCM) program can test whether its input satisfies at least one of those conditions. The nondeterministic program succeeds where no deterministic UCM program can by nondeterministically guessing whether to count up by ones or by twos. ■■■

EXAMPLE 1.19. We have seen how nondeterminism allows a program to test for the disjunction (OR) of two conditions. In this example we will convert the negation of a conjunction (AND) into a disjunction. The idea is that $\overline{L_1 \cap L_2} = \overline{L}_1 \cup \overline{L}_2$; if $\overline{L}_1$ and $\overline{L}_2$ are accepted nondeterministically, then so is $\overline{L}_1 \cup \overline{L}_2$. Consider the language $L = \{\mathsf{a}^i\mathsf{b}^j\mathsf{c}^k : \neg(i = j = k)\}$. By

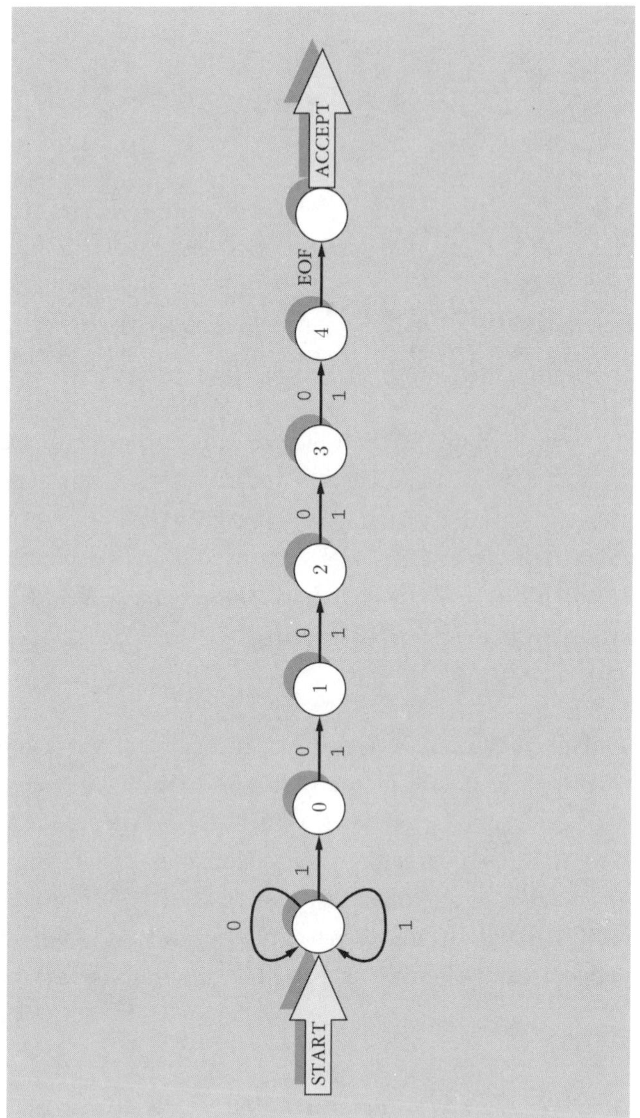

FIGURE 1.20: A 7-state nondeterministic FM program that accepts $\Sigma^*1\Sigma^4$, where $\Sigma = \{0, 1\}$.

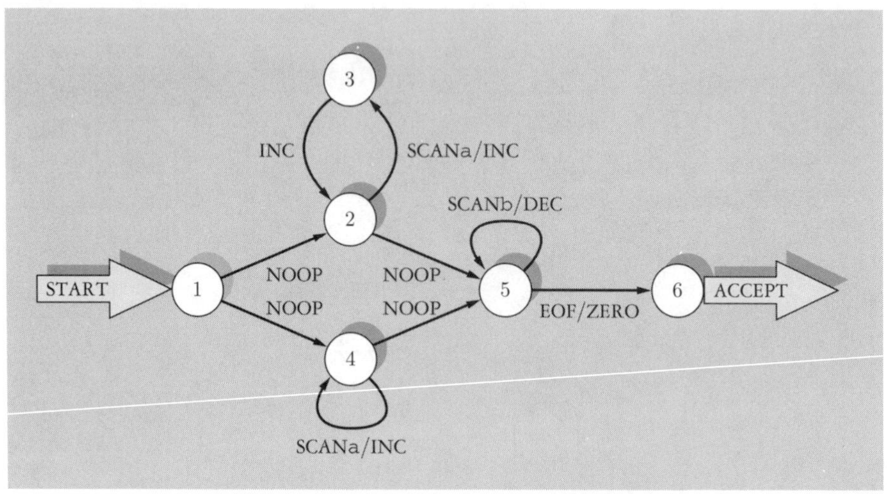

FIGURE 1.21: A nondeterministic UCM program that accepts the language $\{a^m b^n : n = m \text{ or } n = 2m\}$.

De Morgan's laws, $L = \{a^i b^j c^k : i \neq j \text{ or } i \neq k\}$. Now we can nondeterministically check each disjunct separately (Figure 1.22). ■■■

EXAMPLE 1.20. Finally, we use nondeterminism in order to test a large disjunction, i.e., to determine if one of many possibilities has occurred. We say that two strings x and y *agree* at position i if the ith character of x is equal to the ith character of y. Consider the language $L = \{x\#y : \text{the strings } x \text{ and } y \text{ agree in at least one position}\}$. We use nondeterminism in an NUCM program in order to guess a position in which x and y agree; if we guess correctly then we accept. The program is shown in Figure 1.23. ■■■

Determinism is a special case of nondeterminism. By historical accident, "nondeterministic" does not mean "not deterministic"; it means "not necessarily deterministic." For this reason, deterministic programs are a special case of nondeterministic programs in which there is at most one possible action in each configuration. Therefore, if a problem can be

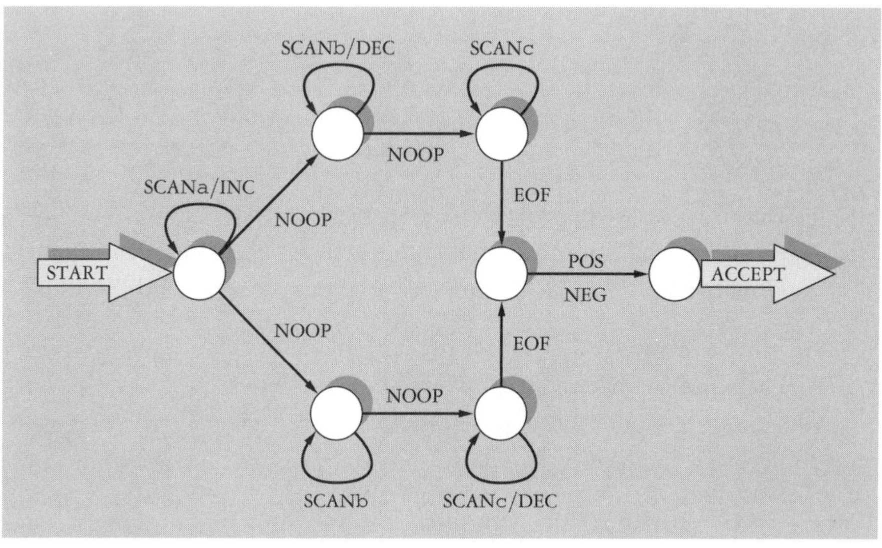

FIGURE 1.22: An NSCM program that accepts $\{\mathtt{a}^i\mathtt{b}^j\mathtt{c}^k : \neg(i = j = k)\}$.

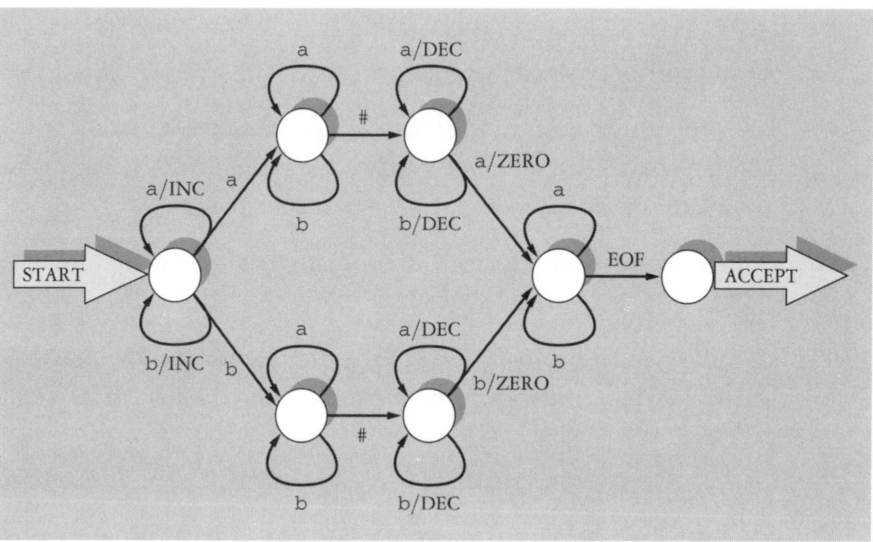

FIGURE 1.23: An NUCM program that accepts $\{x\#y : x \text{ and } y \text{ agree in at least one position}\}$.

solved by a deterministic program, then it can automatically be solved by a nondeterministic program.

Exercises

1.9-1 Recall that a string x is a palindrome iff $x = x^R$. Design a nondeterministic SM program that accepts the set of palindromes over the alphabet $\{0, 1, 2, 3\}$. (Don't forget about strings of odd length.)

1.9-2 Same as Exercise 1.9-1, but use a 2-character stack alphabet. Hint: Each number between 0 and 3 can be represented by a two-bit binary sequence, e.g., 2 is represented by 10. Use the control to convert between the binary representation and the base-4 representation.

1.9-3 (a) Construct a deterministic FM program that accepts $\Sigma^* 1 \Sigma^4$ where $\Sigma = \{0, 1\}$. Try to use as few control states as possible.

*(b) Prove that the number of control states you used in part (a) is as small as possible.

1.9-4 Design a nondeterministic SCM program that accepts the language $\{w : \#_a(w) = 2\#_b(w) \text{ or } 2\#_a(w) = \#_b(w)\}$, where $\#_c(x)$ denotes the number of c's in the string x.

1.9-5 The program of Figure 1.21 can make nondeterministic choices when in control state 2 or 4. Modify the program so that it makes a nondeterministic choice only when in control state 1.

1.9-6 Design a nondeterministic UCM program that accepts the language $\{a^m b^n : m \leq n \leq 2m\}$.

1.9-7 Design a nondeterministic SCM program that accepts the language $\{wx \in \{0, 1\}^* : |w| = |x| \text{ and } w \neq x\}$. Hint: Guess where w and x differ.

Solution: If w and x differ, then they differ somewhere, so $w \in \Sigma^i a \Sigma^j$ and $x \in \Sigma^i b \Sigma^j$ for some i and j, where $a \neq b$. Thus $wx \in \Sigma^i a \Sigma^k b \Sigma^j$ where $k = j + i$. Nondeterministically guess when the first i characters have been read and when the next k characters have been read. Use the counter to make sure that $k = j + i$.

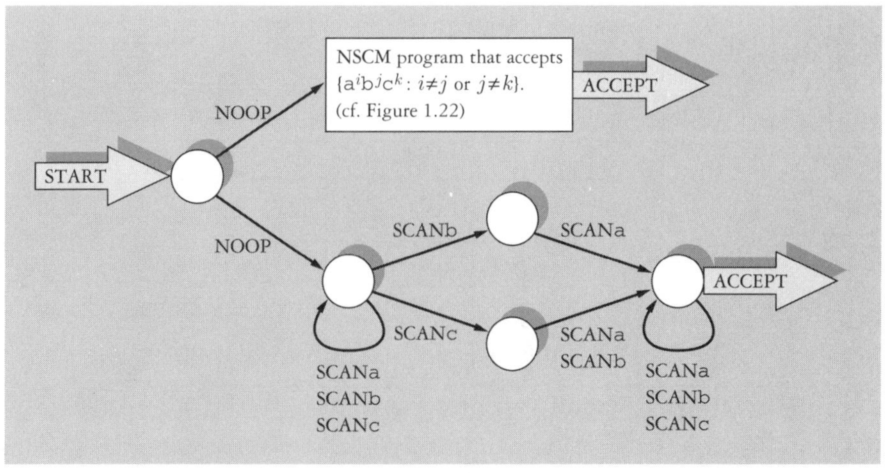

FIGURE 1.24: An NSCM program that accepts the complement of the language $\{\mathtt{a}^n\mathtt{b}^n\mathtt{c}^n : n \geq 0\}$.

1.9-8 Design a nondeterministic SCM program that accepts the set of all strings over the alphabet $\{\mathtt{a}, \mathtt{b}, \mathtt{c}\}$ that are not of the form $\mathtt{a}^n\mathtt{b}^n\mathtt{c}^n$. Suggestion: Handle strings like `cba` separately, using nondeterminism.

Solution: The program is given in Figure 1.24.

1.9-9 Speculate.

(a) How might one define the notion of a nondeterministic program computing a relation?

(b) How might one define the notion of a nondeterministic program computing a partial function?

1.10 CHAPTER SUMMARY

In this chapter, we introduced the most important storage devices—controls, inputs, outputs, stacks, counters, tapes, and RAMs—and we described how to write programs for machines equipped with these devices. We also introduced the notions of determinism and nondeterminism. Table 1.1 summarizes the operations on all of our important devices except the RAM.

Device	*Operations*				
Control	$q \longrightarrow r$				
Input	SCANc $cx \longrightarrow x$	EOF $\Lambda \longrightarrow \Lambda$			
Output	WRITEc $x \longrightarrow xc$				
Unsigned counter	INC $n \longrightarrow n+1$	DEC $n+1 \longrightarrow n$	ZERO $0 \longrightarrow 0$	NONZERO $n+1 \longrightarrow n+1$	
Signed counter	INC $z \longrightarrow z+1$	DEC $z \longrightarrow z-1$	ZERO $0 \longrightarrow 0$	POS $n+1 \longrightarrow n+1$	NEG $-n-1 \longrightarrow -n-1$
Stack	PUSHc $x \longrightarrow xc$	POPc $xc \longrightarrow x$	EMPTY $\Lambda \longrightarrow \Lambda$		
Tape	ATHOME $\boxed{a}x \longrightarrow \boxed{a}x$	SEEc $x\boxed{c}y \longrightarrow x\boxed{c}y$	PRINTc $x\boxed{a}y \longrightarrow x\boxed{c}y$	MOVEL $xa\boxed{b}y \longrightarrow x\boxed{a}by$	MOVER $x\boxed{a}by \longrightarrow xa\boxed{b}y$ $x\boxed{a} \longrightarrow xa\boxed{\sqcup}$

TABLE 1.1: Names and informal descriptions of control, input, output, counter, stack, and tape operations. Here, q and r mean arbitrary control states, x and y mean arbitrary strings over the device's alphabet, n means an arbitrary natural number, z means an arbitrary integer, and a, b, and c mean arbitrary characters in the device's alphabet.

Exercises

1.10-1 Let $\#_c(x)$ denote the number of c's in the string x. Design finite machine programs that accept the following languages:

(a) the set of all strings over $\{\mathtt{a}, \mathtt{b}\}$ that contain an odd number of a's

(b) the set of all strings over $\{\mathtt{a}, \mathtt{b}\}$ such that $\#_{\mathtt{a}}(x) \equiv 0 \pmod{5}$

(c) the set of all strings over $\{\mathtt{a}, \mathtt{b}\}$ such that $\#_{\mathtt{a}}(x) \equiv 0 \pmod{3}$ and $\#_{\mathtt{b}}(x) \equiv 1 \pmod{4}$

(d) the set of all strings over $\{\mathtt{a}, \mathtt{b}\}$ such that $\#_{\mathtt{a}}(x) \equiv 1 \pmod{6}$ or $\#_{\mathtt{b}}(x) \equiv 3 \pmod{7}$

1.10-2 Design UCM programs that accept the following languages:

(a) $\{\mathtt{a}^{pn}\mathtt{b}^{qn} : n \geq 0\}$, where p and q are fixed natural numbers

*(b) $\{w \in \{\mathtt{a}, \mathtt{b}\}^* : \#_{\mathtt{a}}(w) \neq \#_{\mathtt{b}}(w)\}$

1.10-3 Design SCM programs that accept the following languages:

(a) $\{w \in \{\mathtt{a,b,c}\}^* : 3\#_{\mathtt{a}}(w) = 4\#_{\mathtt{b}}(w)\}$

(b) $\{w \in \{\mathtt{a,b,c}\}^* : \#_{\mathtt{a}}(w) = 2.5\#_{\mathtt{b}}(w)\}$

1.10-4 Design a nondeterministic 1-tape TM program that accepts the language $\{ww : w \in \{\mathtt{a}, \mathtt{b}\}^*\}$.

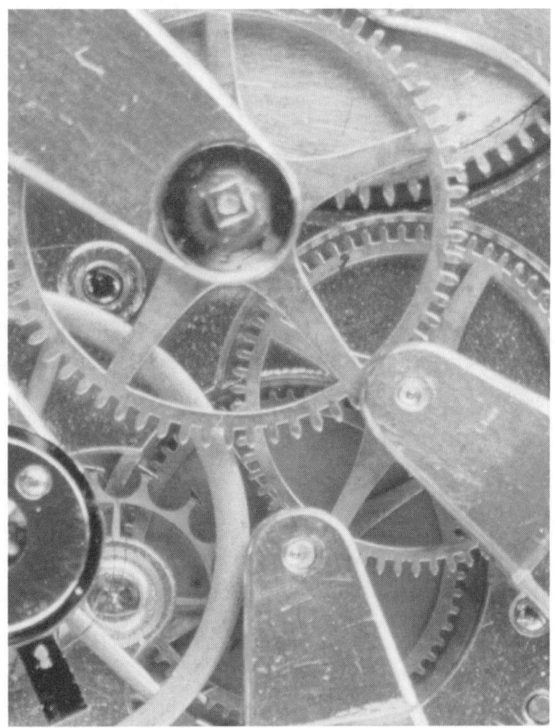

2 *Devices, Machines, and Programs*

IN THE PRECEDING chapter, we informally introduced machines, programs, and the most important memory devices. Many fundamental models of computation fall out of this framework. In this chapter, we will formalize our models of devices, machines, and programs. This treatment lays the foundation for the rest of the book, where we will prove important properties of languages and the machines that recognize them.

2.1 REPRESENTING PROBLEMS

Computer scientists consider a variety of problems, including many whose answers are yes or no: Is a string x a palindrome? Is a number n prime? Is a sequence of strings $\langle\langle x_1, \ldots, x_n\rangle\rangle$ sorted alphabetically in increasing order? Problems having a yes/no answer are called *decision problems*. Because there is exactly one correct answer and exactly one incorrect answer, this kind of problem is modeled as the membership problem for the set consisting of all the yes instances.

Some other problems call for a more substantial, but unique, answer, such as finding the longest prefix of x that is palindromic, finding the smallest prime factor of n, and sorting the sequence of strings $\langle\langle x_1, \ldots, x_n\rangle\rangle$ alphabetically in increasing order. Because the answer is unique, this kind of problem is usually modeled as the function that maps each instance to its unique answer.

A third kind of problem may have several correct answers or none. Examples include finding any palindromic substring of x having maximum length, finding any prime factor of x, and sorting the sequence of strings $\langle\langle x_1, \ldots, x_n\rangle\rangle$ into increasing order by length. Because the answer is not unique, this kind of problem is modeled as a relation.

Formally, a problem is a relation from a set of *instances* to a set of *answers*. Some examples follow:

Problem name: primality

Instance: a natural number n

Answer: yes if n has exactly two distinct positive divisors, no otherwise

The set of instances is N. The set of answers is $\{\text{yes}, \text{no}\}$.

Problem name: least prime factor

Instance: a natural number n

Answer: the least prime factor of n if $n \neq 1$, 1 otherwise

The set of instances is N. The set of answers is N.

Problem name: any prime factor

Instance: a natural number n

Answer: any prime factor of n if $n \neq 1$, otherwise 1

The set of instances is N. The set of answers is N.

Observe that problem instances may be of many types, such as strings, numbers, or sequences, but input devices hold only strings. In order to pass a nonstring argument to a program, we represent the argument as a string. In order to obtain a nonstring result from a program, we represent the result as a string. For example, a natural number can be represented in decimal, binary, dyadic, or monadic notation, to name a few. An ordered pair of strings over $\{\mathtt{a}, \mathtt{b}\}$ can be represented as a string over $\{\mathtt{a}, \mathtt{b}, \mathtt{(}, \mathtt{)}, \mathtt{,}\}$; e.g., $(\mathtt{baa}, \mathtt{baaaa})$ is represented as `(baa,baaaa)`. A sequence of strings over $\{\mathtt{a}, \mathtt{b}\}$ can be represented as a string over $\{\mathtt{a}, \mathtt{b}, \mathtt{<}, \mathtt{>}, \mathtt{,}\}$; e.g., $\langle\langle \mathtt{a}, \mathtt{baba}, \mathtt{baa} \rangle\rangle$ is represented as `<<a,baba,baa>>`. In fact, virtually anything you can write down can be represented as a string.

There are two popular ways to represent a set S of natural numbers. The first representation is the sequence of elements in S; we would represent $\{2, 3, 5, 7\}$ as $\langle\langle 2, 3, 5, 7 \rangle\rangle$. Sequences and numbers can be represented as above. The second representation, called the *bit-vector* representation, works for subsets of $\{1, \ldots, n\}$; we represent a set S by a string of 0's and 1's with a 1 in position i if and only if $i \in S$. If we take $n = 8$, we would represent $\{2, 3, 5, 7\}$ as 01101010.

There are three popular ways to represent graphs. Consider a graph with vertex set V and edge set E. Without loss of generality the vertex set V may be treated as a set of positive integers $\{1, \ldots, |V|\}$, so it need not be represented explicitly as long as the number $|V|$ is represented somehow. The edge set E may be represented in one of the following ways, which we illustrate for the graph in Figure 0.2:

edge list the sequence of edges in the set E, e.g., $\langle\langle (1, 2), (2, 3), (2, 4), (3, 2), (3, 4), (4, 4) \rangle\rangle$.

adjacency lists for each vertex v, the sequence of vertices adjacent to V, e.g., $\langle\langle \langle\langle 2 \rangle\rangle, \langle\langle 3, 4 \rangle\rangle, \langle\langle 2, 4 \rangle\rangle, \langle\langle 4 \rangle\rangle \rangle\rangle$.

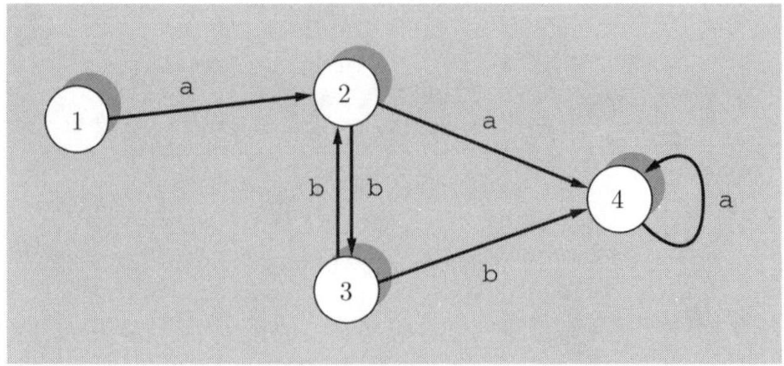

FIGURE 2.1: A labeled digraph.

adjacency matrix for each vertex v, the bit-vector representation of the set of vertices adjacent to V, e.g., $\langle\langle 0100, 0011, 0101, 0001 \rangle\rangle$

Sequences, ordered pairs, and numbers may be represented as above. If the edge-list representation is used, it is also necessary to represent $|V|$ explicitly; however this number is implicit in the other representations.

If the edges in a graph have labels, then we include the label along with the edge in the representation. For example, the graph in Figure 2.1 would be represented as

edge list $\langle\langle((1,2),\mathtt{a}),((2,3),\mathtt{b}),((2,4),\mathtt{a}),((3,2),\mathtt{b}),((3,4),\mathtt{b}), ((4,4),\mathtt{a})\rangle\rangle$.

adjacency lists $\langle\langle\langle\langle(2,\mathtt{a})\rangle\rangle,\langle\langle(3,\mathtt{b}),(4,\mathtt{a})\rangle\rangle,\langle\langle(2,\mathtt{b}),(4,\mathtt{b})\rangle\rangle,\langle\langle(4,\mathtt{a})\rangle\rangle\rangle\rangle$.

adjacency matrix $\langle\langle 0\mathtt{a}00, 00\mathtt{ba}, 0\mathtt{b}0\mathtt{b}, 000\mathtt{a}\rangle\rangle$.

Typically, numbers will be represented in b-adic or b-ary notation for some base b. Binary and dyadic notation are often the easiest to program with because they use only two distinct digits. However, some other base like 5, 8, or 10 can be used if it is appropriate to the problem at hand. Representing a number n in monadic notation is sometimes convenient, but the representation can be very long: n characters versus $\lfloor \log_b((b-1)n+1) \rfloor$ characters in b-adic notation or $\lfloor \log_b n + 1 \rfloor$ characters in b-ary notation with $b \geq 2$. In general, b-adic has a slight advantage over b-ary notation because each number has a unique b-adic representation; i.e., there are no leading zeroes.

A rational number r can be represented over $\{1, 2, /\}$ as the string n/d where n is the dyadic representation of r's numerator and d is the dyadic representation of r's denominator in lowest terms.

Exercises

2.1-1 Let $b \geq 2$.

(a) Prove that the number of characters in the b-ary representation of n is

$$\begin{cases} \lfloor \log_b n + 1 \rfloor & \text{if } n > 0, \\ 1 & \text{if } n = 0. \end{cases}$$

(b) Prove that the number of characters in the b-adic representation of n is $\lfloor \log_b ((b-1)n + 1) \rfloor$.

2.2 DEVICES

We run programs on machines, which consist of devices. We will define machines in Section 2.3 and programs in Section 2.4. First, it is necessary to define the building blocks of machines: devices.

Recall from the informal treatment in Chapter 1 that storage devices (henceforth "devices") can hold, test, and modify data. The value held by a device is called the device's *state*. The *realm* of a device is the set of values that the device can hold, i.e., the set consisting of all of the device's states. For example, the realm of an unsigned counter is N, and the realm of a signed counter is Z. A control is really a finite memory, so the realm of a control is some finite set, called the *control set* and conventionally denoted Q. The realm of an input device is Σ^* for some alphabet Σ, which we call the *input alphabet*. The realm of an output device is Δ^* for some alphabet Δ, which we call the *output alphabet*.

An *operation* is a partial function on the realm of a device. For example, SCANa is the partial function that maps strings of the form ax to x; it is undefined on strings that are not of the form ax. (It is important to read Sections 0.2.6 and 0.2.7 before continuing.)

One kind of operation is a test. A *test* is a partial identity function; i.e., a particular test is applicable only when the device's state belongs to a particular set, and it does not alter the device's state. For example, EOF, EMPTY, ZERO, POS, and NEG are tests (EOF $=$ EMPTY $= I_{\{\Lambda\}}$, ZERO $= I_{\{0\}}$, POS $= I_{\mathsf{Z}^+}$, and NEG $= I_{\mathsf{Z}^-}$).

The reader will notice that our notion of a test is different from a Boolean-valued function. Like any operation, a test is a partial function on a device's realm. For example, the test POS does not return a truth value—it returns a number, the same number it is applied to. An edge labeled with POS may be followed if the counter holds a positive integer, but the edge must not be followed otherwise.

The NOOP operation on a device leaves that device's value unchanged; i.e., NOOP denotes the identity function on a device's realm.

The *repertory* of a device is a set of operations on the device's realm. For example, the repertory of an unsigned counter is {INC, DEC, ZERO, NONZERO}, and the repertory of a signed counter is {INC, DEC, ZERO, POS, NEG}.

A *device* consists of a realm and a repertory of operations on the realm. For example, a stack with alphabet {a, b} consists of the realm $\{\mathtt{a}, \mathtt{b}\}^*$ and the repertory {POPa, POPb, PUSHa, PUSHb, EMPTY}. An input device with alphabet {a, b} consists of the realm $\{\mathtt{a}, \mathtt{b}\}^*$ and the repertory {SCANa, SCANb, EOF}.

Table 2.1 on page 123 shows the realm and repertory of most common devices other than the tape and the RAM. A formal treatment of tapes is postponed until Chapter 7.

Exercises

2.2-1 Consider a control with states q_1 and q_2. What is its realm? Its repertory?

2.2-2 A queue (pronounced like the letter "q") holds a string. The operations on a queue are

ENQUEUEc: Insert a c at the right end of the queue.

DEQUEUEc: Delete a c from the left end of the queue.

EMPTY: Test whether the queue is empty.

Fix a queue alphabet Γ.

(a) Define the realm of a queue formally.

(b) Express the queue operations informally using the $\rightarrow$ notation.

(c) Define the queue operations formally as relations.

2.2-3 A deque (pronounced "dek") is a double-ended queue that holds a string. The operations on a deque are

LEFT-INSERTc: Insert a c at the left end of the deque.

RIGHT-INSERTc: Insert a c at the right end of the deque.

LEFT-DELETEc: Delete a c from the left end of the deque.

RIGHT-DELETEc: Delete a c from the right end of the deque.

EMPTY: Test whether the deque is empty.

Fix a deque alphabet Γ.

(a) Define the realm of a deque formally.

(b) Express the deque operations informally using the $\rightarrow$ notation.

(c) Define the deque operations formally.

2.3 MACHINES

A *machine* M is an ordered tuple of devices $(d_1, \ldots, d_k)$. Because machines are a very important kind of tuple, we write "machine $[d_1, \ldots, d_k]$" to distinguish them from other kinds of tuples. For example, a machine [control, input, stack] is a stack machine with input but no output; a machine [control, input, output] is a finite machine with input and output; and a machine [control, output, counter, counter] is a 2-counter machine with output but no input. Since most interesting machines have a control, by convention the control is usually a machine's first device. The input and output devices, if present, are usually the machine's next two devices. Machines without input are sometimes called *inattentive*.

Two machines belong to the same *machine type* if, except for input and output, they have the same kinds and number of devices, although possibly in a different order. Machines of the simplest type are called *finite machines*. A finite machine can be a machine [control], a machine [control, input], a machine [control, output], or a machine [control, input, output]—or one of those machines with the devices in a different order. Another type of machine is the *stack machine*, which can be a machine [control, stack], a machine [control, input, stack], a machine [control, output, stack], or a machine [control, input, output, stack]—or one of those machines with the devices in a different order. An unsigned counter machine contains a control, an unsigned counter, and optional input and output devices. A signed counter machine contains a control, a signed counter, and optional input and output devices. A counter machine is either an unsigned counter machine or a signed counter machine. A 2-counter machine contains a control, two counters, and optional input and output devices.

A configuration of one of our machines carries information analogous to a core dump from a real-world machine. That is, a configuration of a machine is the aggregate of all information stored by the machine's devices. Whereas a core dump from a real machine consists of the values of all variables, a configuration of one of our machines M consists of the state of each of M's devices. Formally, a *configuration* is a k-tuple of states $(s_1, \ldots, s_k)$; it specifies that the state of device d_i is s_i for $i = 1, \ldots, k$.

EXAMPLE 2.1. Let M be a machine [control, input, stack] where the control set is $\{1, 2, 3, 4\}$, the input alphabet is $\{\mathtt{a}, \mathtt{b}, \#\}$, and the stack alphabet is $\{\mathtt{a}, \mathtt{b}\}$. Then $(2, \mathtt{abaa}, \mathtt{bbaa})$ is one configuration of M; the reader may verify that the program of Figure 1.1 enters this configuration on input `bbaaa#aabaa`. ■■■

2.4 INSTRUCTIONS

We can combine operations on individual devices to form an instruction, which operates on all of a machine's devices. A collection of instructions, together with mechanisms for the initialization of devices and the designation of results, forms a program. We define instructions formally in this section; we will define initializers, terminators, and programs formally in the next two sections.

An *instruction* for a machine M designates an operation for each device of M. Typically we apply an instruction to a configuration in order to obtain the next configuration of M. Formally, an instruction is a k-tuple $(f_1, \ldots, f_k)$ of operations, where each f_i is either NOOP or an operation belonging to the repertory of d_i. We identify instructions with partial functions on the set of M's configurations. That is, the instruction $(f_1, \ldots, f_k)$ maps the configuration $(s_1, \ldots, s_k)$ to the configuration $(s_1 f_1, \ldots, s_k f_k)$. We will explain how this definition causes devices to interact after an example.

EXAMPLE 2.2. Let us continue Example 2.1. Because M is a machine [control, input, stack], $(2 \rightarrow 4, \text{SCAN}\mathtt{a}, \text{POP}\mathtt{b})$ is an instruction for M. We call this instruction π. (π is the Greek letter for "p." We use it to denote an instruction, because instructions are the building blocks of programs.) We present π pictorially in Figure 2.2. The instruction π maps the configuration $(2, \mathtt{aaba}, \mathtt{aabb})$ to $(4, \mathtt{aba}, \mathtt{aab})$, i.e.,

$$(2, \mathtt{aaba}, \mathtt{aabb})\,\pi = (4, \mathtt{aba}, \mathtt{aab}).$$

■ ■ ■

It is possible that an instruction specifies an operation that cannot be performed on a device given the device's current state. For example, consider the configuration $(4, \mathtt{aba}, \mathtt{aab})$ and the instruction π as above. State 4 is not in the domain of the control operation $2 \rightarrow 4$, i.e., $4(2 \rightarrow 4)$ is undefined, and we say that $(4, \mathtt{aba}, \mathtt{aab})\pi$ is undefined simply because the

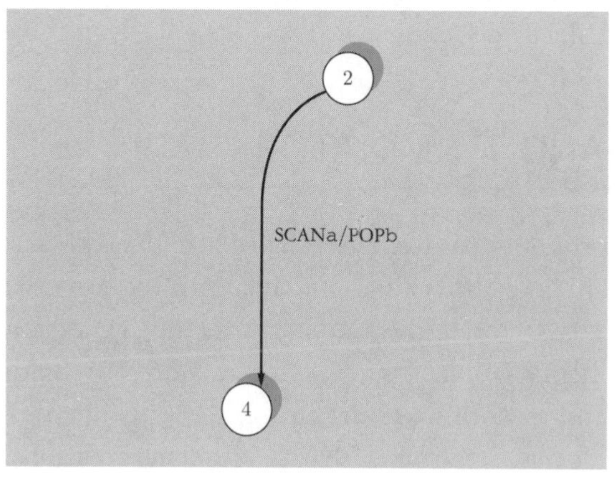

FIGURE 2.2: The instruction $(2 \rightarrow 4, \text{SCAN}\mathtt{a}, \text{POP}\mathtt{b})$. This edge was seen previously in Figure 1.1.

first component is undefined. The control prevents π from acting on the input and the stack because π cannot act on the control.

In general, $(s_1, \ldots, s_k)(f_1, \ldots, f_k)$ is undefined if $s_i f_i$ is undefined for some i. In this situation we say that the instruction $(f_1, \ldots, f_k)$ is *inapplicable* to the configuration $(s_1, \ldots, s_k)$.

EXAMPLE 2.3. Consider a machine [control, input], the configuration $(q_1, \texttt{abb})$, and the instruction $(q_1 \rightarrow q_2, \text{SCAN}\texttt{b})$; since $\texttt{abb}\,\text{SCAN}\texttt{b}$ is undefined, the instruction is inapplicable to the configuration. ■■■

We think of the configuration C as going by the instruction π to the new configuration C'. To capture this idea, we adopt the notation $C \overset{\pi}{\mapsto} C'$, which is equivalent to $C\ \pi\ C'$.

By convention, we do not allow an instruction to use the operation NOOP on the control. This makes it possible to depict each instruction as a single labeled edge. The reader may verify that this does not impose a significant limitation on programs (Exercise 2.4-2).

Exercises

2.4-1 What is the difference between the operation $4 \rightarrow 4$ and the operation NOOP on a control?

2.4-2 Suppose we allow the repertory of a control to include all partial functions from Q to Q. Show how to transform a program using this expanded repertory into a program that uses only the standard control operations like $q_i \rightarrow q_j$.

2.5 INITIALIZERS AND TERMINATORS

It is usually desirable for a program to initialize each of a machine's devices to some reasonable value before doing anything else. For example, we usually want a stack or output device to start empty (its state being Λ), a counter to start at zero (its state being 0), an input device to start out holding the program's argument, and a control to start in some specified state. In general, an *initializer* of a device determines that device's start state based on the argument; formally, the initializer maps an argument to a state of the device. Similarly, the *terminator* of a device relates the device's state to a result. A state s of a device d is called an *initial state* if s is in the range of d's initializer, and a *final state* if s is in the domain of d's terminator. A program can produce a result when all devices are in final states, but not otherwise.

Usually, controls start in their specified initial state and finish in one of their specified final states, input devices start holding the argument (or some reasonable encoding of the argument if the argument is not a string) and finish empty, and output devices start empty and finish holding the result (or some reasonable encoding of the result if the result is not a string). Unless explicitly stated otherwise, stacks start and finish empty, and counters start and finish at 0. Tapes start blank with the head at the left end and finish in arbitrary states. RAMs start with 0 in all registers and memory locations, and they finish in arbitrary states.

The initializer of a device maps each argument to a starting state of the device. The typical initializer of a control is $X \times \{q_{\text{start}}\}$, which maps each argument to the initial control state, q_{start}. The typical initializer of an input device is I_{Σ^*}, which maps each argument to itself. The typical initializer of an output device or a stack is $X \times \{\Lambda\}$, which maps each argument to the empty string. The typical initializer of a counter is $X \times \{0\}$, which maps each argument to 0.

The terminator of a device relates each final state of the device to a result. The typical terminator of a control is $Q_{\text{final}} \times Y$, which relates each final state to every possible result. The typical terminator of an input device is $\{\Lambda\} \times Y$, which relates the empty string to every possible result. The typical terminator of an output device is I_{Δ^*}, which maps each output string to itself. The typical terminators of a stack are $\{\Lambda\} \times Y$, which relates Λ to every possible result, and $\Gamma^* \times Y$, which relates each stack string to every possible result. The typical terminators of an unsigned counter are $\{0\} \times Y$, which relates 0 to every possible result, and $\mathsf{N} \times Y$, which relates each counter state to every possible result. The typical terminators of a signed counter are $\{0\} \times Y$, which relates 0 to every possible result, and $\mathsf{Z} \times Y$, which relates each counter state to every possible result.

Initializers and terminators are not meant to increase the computing ability of machines. They should only give machines a way to receive their arguments and communicate results. For example, an initializer that puts the control in state 1 if the argument is a palindrome but in state 2 if the input is not a palindrome would be unreasonable, because such an initializer is performing computation for the machine. In order to prevent this, we require that the initial state of each device either be the argument or else a fixed state that is independent of the argument. For example, if the argument is a number, then a counter could be initialized to hold it (although this would be unusual). Observe that the usual initializers put the argument into the input device and start all other devices in a fixed state independent of the argument.

If the set X of possible arguments is different from the device's realm, then the device may be initialized to hold a reasonable representation of the argument. For example, if the argument is a number, then an input device could be initialized to hold its dyadic or decimal representation. While there is no precise theory of what constitutes a reasonable representation, it should be computationally easy to convert from one reasonable representation to another. For example, representing a positive number n as $\text{dyadic}^{-1}(n)$ is generally considered reasonable, but representing n as $\text{dyadic}^{-1}(n)$#1 if n is prime but as $\text{dyadic}^{-1}(n)$#2 if n is not prime would be considered unreasonable in most contexts. Section 2.1 describes some representations that are generally considered reasonable.

A terminator that accepts if the input device holds a palindrome but rejects if the input device holds a nonpalindrome would be unreasonable, because it also performs computation for the machine. Similarly, a terminator that accepts if the counter holds a prime number but rejects if the counter holds a composite number would also be unreasonable. In order to prevent this, we put the following limitation on terminators: it must be possible, using a device's tests, to test whether the device is in a final state and to determine which result it gives. For input devices the test is EOF; for stacks the test is EMPTY; for counters the test is ZERO; for output devices, tapes, and RAMs the test is NOOP. For controls, it is necessary to use all the tests $q \to q$ for which q is a final state. The result may be either a fixed value, such as ACCEPT or REJECT, or else a reasonable representation of the device's state.

The usual initializers and terminators for common devices, except tapes and RAMs, are listed in Table 2.1. All programs will employ usual initializers and terminators unless explicitly stated otherwise.

Device	*Realm*	*Repertory*	*Usual Initializer*	*Usual Terminator*
Control with states $q_1, \ldots, q_n$	$Q = \{q_1, \ldots, q_n\}$	$\{q_i \rightarrow q_j : 1 \leq i, j \leq n\}$ (same as $Q \times Q$)	$X \times \{q_{\text{start}}\}$	$Q_{\text{accept}} \times Y$ (for an acceptor or transducer) or $Q_{\text{accept}} \times \text{ACCEPT}$ $\cup\, Q_{\text{reject}} \times \text{REJECT}$ (for a recognizer)
Input with alphabet Σ	Σ^*	$\{\text{SCAN}c : c \in \Sigma\} \cup \{\text{EOF}\}$	I_X	$\{\Lambda\} \times Y$
Output with alphabet Δ	Δ^*	$\{\text{WRITE}c : c \in \Delta\}$	$X \times \{\Lambda\}$	I_Y
Stack with alphabet Γ	Γ^*	$\{\text{PUSH}c : c \in \Gamma\} \cup \{\text{POP}c : c \in \Gamma\}$ $\cup \{\text{EMPTY}\}$	$X \times \{\Lambda\}$	$\{\Lambda\} \times Y$ or $\Gamma^* \times Y$
Unsigned Counter	N	$\{\text{INC}, \text{DEC}, \text{ZERO}, \text{NONZERO}\}$	$X \times \{0\}$	$\{0\} \times Y$ or $\mathsf{N} \times Y$
Signed Counter	Z	$\{\text{INC}, \text{DEC}, \text{ZERO}, \text{POS}, \text{NEG}\}$	$X \times \{0\}$	$\{0\} \times Y$ or $\mathsf{Z} \times Y$

TABLE 2.1: Realm, repertory, usual initializer, and usual terminator for common devices. X denotes the set of possible arguments, Y the set of possible results. For controls, q_{start} denotes an element of Q, Q_{accept} a subset of Q, and Q_{reject} a subset of Q that is disjoint from Q_{accept}.

An *initializer* for a machine is a one-one function that determines the machine's initial configuration. An initializer for M consists of an initializer for each of M's devices $d_1, \ldots, d_k$, which we denote $\alpha = (\alpha_1, \ldots, \alpha_k)$, where each α_i is an initializer for d_i. Typically x denotes the argument to the program. Then we have $x\alpha = (x\alpha_1, \ldots, x\alpha_k)$. ($\alpha$ is the first letter of the Greek alphabet; hence our choice of α to denote an initializer.)

When no confusion is possible, we may write α_d to denote the initializer of device d without referring to a particular numbering of devices. For example, α_{control}, α_{input}, α_{output}, α_{counter}, and α_{stack} denote the initializers of a control, input, output, counter, and stack, respectively. If, however, a machine has two counters, α_{counter} would be ambiguous notation; in this situation we can give the counters names like $K1$ and $K2$ and refer to their initializers as α_{K1} and α_{K2}. If the initializer α maps an argument x to a configuration C_0 of M, we call C_0 an *initial configuration*. We write $x \ \alpha \ C_0$ or, more descriptively, $x \overset{\alpha}{\mapsto} C_0$.

Equally important is a *terminator* for a machine, a partial function that we use to determine whether a program accepts and to extract the result of running it. A terminator for M consists of a terminator for each of M's devices. The machine's terminator maps the machine's configuration to a particular result if and only if each device's terminator relates that device's state to the same result. In particular, a result is not produced unless all devices are in a final state.

To be precise, let M's terminator $\omega = (\omega_1, \ldots, \omega_k)$, where each ω_i is a terminator for d_i, let $C = (s_1, \ldots, s_k)$ where each s_i is a state of d_i, and define the relation ω as follows:

$$C \ \omega \ y \iff s_1 \ \omega_1 \ y \text{ and } s_2 \ \omega_2 \ y \text{ and } \ldots \text{ and } s_k \ \omega_k \ y.$$

(ω is the last letter of the Greek alphabet; hence our choice of ω to denote a terminator.)

Although the individual ω_i's are relations, ω is required to be a partial function. This is typically accomplished by having one or more of the ω_i's be a partial function. If the terminator for a particular device is a partial function, then we say informally that that device determines the result. For example, if the program uses the output device to produce a result string, then the output device determines the result, and the output device's terminator is the identity function on Δ^*. For another example, in a DFR the result is determined by the control, and the control's terminator is the partial function that maps all accepting control states to ACCEPT and maps all rejecting control states to REJECT.

As with α, we may write ω_d to denote the terminator of device d without referring to a particular numbering of devices, provided that no confusion is possible. If the terminator ω maps the configuration C to some result y, i.e., if C is in the domain of ω, we call C a *final configuration*. We may also write $C \overset{\omega}{\mapsto} y$.

EXAMPLE 2.4. Let M be a machine [control, input, output, counter], and let the control set be $q_0, \ldots, q_k$. We define a typical initializer and terminator. The initial control state is q_0, and the final control state is q_k. The initial input state is x, the argument, and the final input state is Λ. The initial output state is Λ, and the final output state is y, the result. The initial and final counter states are both 0.

The devices' initializers are functions defined as follows:

- $x\alpha_{\text{control}} = q_0$,
- $x\alpha_{\text{input}} = x$,
- $x\alpha_{\text{output}} = \Lambda$,
- $x\alpha_{counter} = 0$.

M's initializer is the one-one function α defined by

$$x\alpha = (q_0, x, \Lambda, 0).$$

We can also denote this relation by $x \overset{\alpha}{\mapsto} (q_0, x, \Lambda, 0)$.

The devices' terminators are relations defined as follows:

- $q_k \; \omega_{\text{control}} \; y$, for all y,
- $\Lambda \; \omega_{\text{input}} \; y$, for all y,
- $y \; \omega_{\text{output}} \; y$, for all y,
- $0 \; \omega_{\text{counter}} \; y$, for all y.

M's terminator is the partial function ω defined by

$$(q_k, \Lambda, y, 0)\,\omega = y, \quad \text{for all } y.$$

(It is implicit in this definition that $(q, x, y, n)\,\omega$ is undefined for all other values.) We can also denote the relation above by $(q_k, \Lambda, y, 0) \overset{\omega}{\mapsto} y$.

Observe that in this example, ω is indeed a partial function, as required. In contrast, ω_{counter} merely forces the counter to be 0 in every final configuration but has no other effect on the program's result; since ω_{counter} relates 0 to every possible result, it is multiple-valued. So are ω_{control} and ω_{input}. Only ω_{output} is a partial function. ■ ■ ■

2.6 PROGRAMS

A *program* P for machine M consists of an initializer α, a terminator ω, and a finite set $\mathcal{I}$ of instructions for M.

EXAMPLE 2.5. Let M be a machine [control, input, stack] with control set $\{1, 2\}$, input alphabet $\{\mathtt{a}, \mathtt{b}, \#\}$, and stack alphabet $\{\mathtt{a}, \mathtt{b}\}$. Define α and ω by $x\alpha = (1, x, \Lambda)$ and $(2, \Lambda, \Lambda)\,\omega = \text{ACCEPT}$. We can specify a program P for M, consisting of initializer α, terminator ω, and instruction set $\mathcal{I}$ given below:

$$\left\{\begin{array}{lllllll}(& 1 \to 1 & , & \text{SCAN}\mathtt{a} & , & \text{PUSH}\mathtt{a} &),\\ (& 1 \to 1 & , & \text{SCAN}\mathtt{b} & , & \text{PUSH}\mathtt{b} &),\\ (& 1 \to 2 & , & \text{SCAN}\# & , & \text{NOOP} &),\\ (& 2 \to 2 & , & \text{SCAN}\mathtt{a} & , & \text{POP}\mathtt{a} &),\\ (& 2 \to 2 & , & \text{SCAN}\mathtt{b} & , & \text{POP}\mathtt{b} &)\end{array}\right\}.$$

It is represented graphically in Figure 2.3. ■ ■ ■

EXAMPLE 2.6. Let us design a program for a machine [control, input, output, stack] that adds one to a number. The argument will be repre-

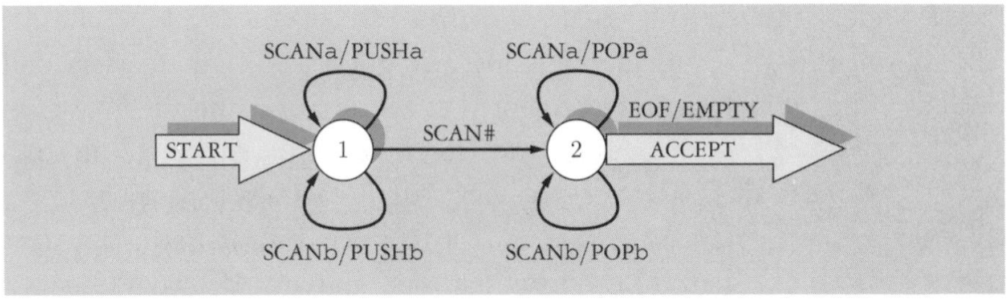

FIGURE 2.3: Another program that accepts palindromes with central marker.

sented as a binary numeral. However, the result will be represented as a binary numeral written in reverse. That is

$$\begin{aligned} \text{binary}(s)\ \alpha &= (q_{\text{start}}, s, \Lambda, \Lambda), \\ (q_{\text{accept}}, \Lambda, s, \Lambda)\ \omega &= \text{binary}(s^R), \end{aligned}$$

where q_{start} is the initial control state and q_{accept} is the final control state. The program is depicted in Figure 2.4. ∎∎∎

EXAMPLE 2.7. Let us consider another problem where the argument and result are not strings. We design a program to be used in a vending machine that sells three kinds of soda pop: cola, root beer, and grape.

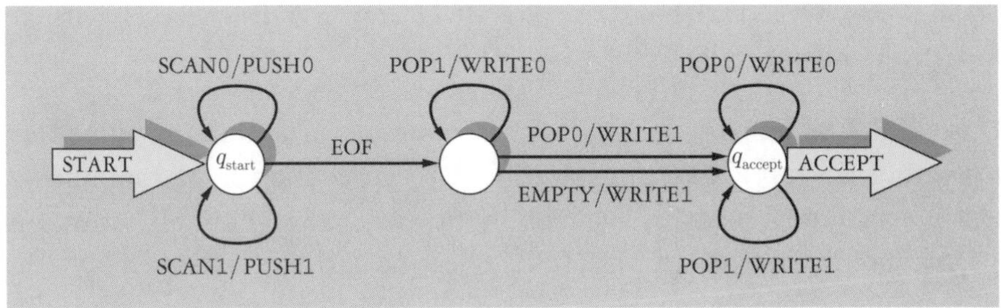

FIGURE 2.4: A program that reads n as a binary numeral and writes $n + 1$ as a binary numeral with the bits in reverse order.

The vending machine has a coin slot that takes nickels, dimes, and quarters, as well as three buttons that permit the user to choose a kind of soda. The argument to the program is a sequence of nickels, dimes, quarters, and button pushes, which can be represented as a string over the alphabet $\Sigma =$ {⑤, ⑩, ㉕, `c`, `r`, `g`}. Consider the function that maps a nickel to the character ⑤, a dime to the character ⑩, a quarter to the character ㉕, a push of the cola button to the character `c`, a push of the root beer button to the character `r`, and a push of the grape soda button to the character `g`. By extending that function to sequences, we obtain the initializer of the input device, α_{input}.

The result of the program is a sequence of sodas and change, which can be represented as a string over the same alphabet $\Delta =$ {⑤, ⑩, ㉕, `c`, `r`, `g`}. Consider the function that maps the character ⑤ to a nickel, the character ⑩ to a dime, the character ㉕ to a quarter, the character `c` to a can of cola, the character `r` to a can of root beer, and the character `g` to a can of grape soda. By extending that function to sequences, we obtain the terminator of the output device, ω_{output}.

The initializer and terminator for this program require specialized hardware, called a vending machine, which works properly only if restocked regularly. A finite machine program that sells 25-cent sodas is shown in Figure 2.5. ■ ■ ■

Thus far, we have defined devices, like controls, inputs, outputs, stacks, and counters. We have defined machines, which are composed of devices. We have defined instructions, which operate on machines. We have defined initializers, which provide, based on an argument, the initial values held by a machine's devices. We have defined terminators, which determine a result based on the final values held by the machine's devices. And we have defined programs, which consist of a set of instructions together with an initializer and a terminator.

EXAMPLE 2.8. Finally, let us design a program for a finite machine that recognizes the set of all strings over $\{\mathtt{a}, \mathtt{b}\}$ that contain an odd number of `a`'s. We will use a machine [control, input], where the input alphabet Σ is $\{\mathtt{a}, \mathtt{b}\}$ and the control set Q is $\{0, 1\}$. The initializer α is defined by

$$x \overset{\alpha}{\mapsto} (0, x).$$

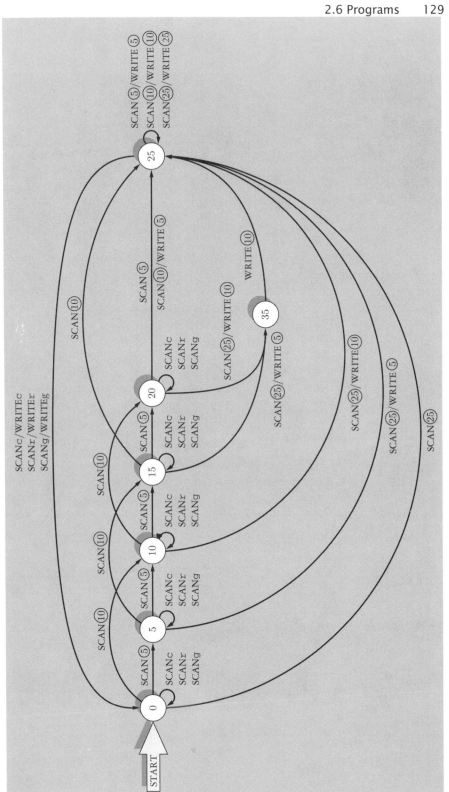

FIGURE 2.5: A finite machine program that operates a soda machine. All control states are accepting.

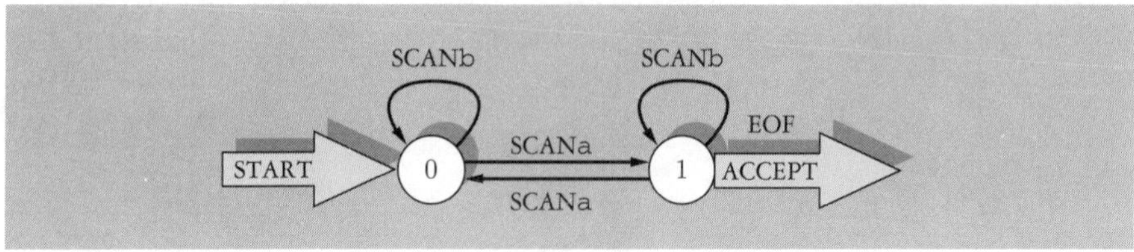

FIGURE 2.6: An FM program that accepts $\{x \in \{\mathtt{a,b}\}^* : \#_{\mathtt{a}}(x) \equiv 1 \pmod 2\}$.

The instruction set $\mathcal{I}$ is

$$\left\{\begin{array}{lcl} (\ 0 \to 1 & , & \mathrm{SCAN}\mathtt{a}\ ), \\ (\ 1 \to 0 & , & \mathrm{SCAN}\mathtt{a}\ ), \\ (\ 0 \to 0 & , & \mathrm{SCAN}\mathtt{b}\ ), \\ (\ 1 \to 1 & , & \mathrm{SCAN}\mathtt{b}\ ) \end{array}\right\}.$$

The terminator ω is defined by

$$(1, \Lambda) \overset{\omega}{\mapsto} \mathrm{ACCEPT}.$$

The program is depicted in Figure 2.6. ■ ■ ■

Exercises

2.6-1 What are the initializer and terminator of the program in Figure 1.19?

2.6-2 For each of the following types of arguments, choose an input alphabet and tell how you would initialize the input device:
(a) an integer
(b) an ordered pair of natural numbers

(c) a sequence of natural numbers

(d) a point in 3-dimensional space having integer coordinates

2.6-3 Consider the program represented in Figure 1.2.

(a) What are the machine's devices?

(b) What is the program's initializer?

(c) What is the program's instruction set?

(d) What is the program's terminator?

2.6-4 Repeat Exercise 2.6-3 for Figure 1.3.

2.6-5 Repeat Exercise 2.6-3 for Figure 1.12.

2.6-6 Repeat Exercise 2.6-3 for Figure 1.21.

2.6-7 Can a state be both an initial control state and a final control state? If so, give an example.

2.6-8 (a) Design a deterministic FM program that reads n as a dyadic numeral with the digits in reverse order and writes $n + 1$ as a dyadic numeral with the digits in reverse order.

(b) Design an NFM program that reads n as a dyadic numeral (with the digits in the normal order) and writes $n + 1$ as a dyadic numeral (with the digits in the normal order).

(c) Design a DSM program that reads n as a dyadic numeral (with the digits in the normal order) and writes $n + 1$ as a dyadic numeral with the digits in reverse order.

2.6-9 Repeat Exercise 2.6-8 for numbers written in 3-ary.

2.6-10 Repeat Exercise 2.6-8, but compute $n - 1$ instead of $n + 1$. The program should reject if $n = 0$.

2.6-11 Repeat Exercise 2.6-10 for numbers written in 3-ary.

2.6-12 Design an FM program to operate a vending machine that sells bubble gum for 15 cents and mints for 20 cents.

2.6-13 Design an FM program that takes a natural number as its argument and determines if the number is congruent to 0 modulo 5. Use the following input representation:

(a) monadic

(b) binary

(c) dyadic

(d) binary with the digits written in reverse order

(e) dyadic with the digits written in reverse order

(f) 5-ary

(g) 5-adic

(h) 5-ary with the digits written in reverse order

(i) 5-adic with the digits written in reverse order

(j) decimal

(k) 10-adic

(l) decimal with the digits written in reverse order

(m) 10-adic with the digits written in reverse order

2.7 RUNNING A PROGRAM

Informally, we *run* a program on argument x by determining the initial configuration and then repeatedly applying instructions to the current configuration in order to determine the next configuration. The general process is as follows:

Step 1: $C := x\alpha$ (we say that the initial configuration C is *entered*).

Step 2: If there is an instruction π such that $C\pi$ is defined and C is a final configuration, then go to step 3 or step 4, as you please. Otherwise, if there is an instruction π such that $C\pi$ is defined, then go to step 3. Otherwise, if C is a final configuration, then go to step 4. Otherwise, stop (no result is given if the program stops here; instead, we say that the program blocks).

Step 3: Choose any instruction π such that $C\pi$ is defined (we say that the instruction π is *executed*). $C := C\pi$ (we say that the configuration C is *entered*). Go to step 2.

Step 4: Stop and give the result $C\omega$ (we say that the program has run to completion).

The process of running a program may end at a final configuration, it may end at a nonfinal configuration (if no instruction is applicable), or it may go on forever. A result is only given if the program stops in a final configuration, i.e., runs to completion. If the program blocks or runs forever, then no result is given.

2.7.1 Computations, Traces, and Histories

Traces, computations, and histories summarize the entire behavior of a program, i.e., all instructions executed and all states of all devices while the program is run to completion. A trace of one of our programs, analogous to a debugging trace of a real-world program, consists of all the configurations entered while the program is run to completion. A computation consists of all the instructions executed while the program is run to completion. A history consists of a computation plus the corresponding trace, i.e., all configurations entered and instructions executed while the program is run to completion. Partial traces, partial computations, and partial histories summarize the behavior of a program up to a certain time, at which the program may still be running, may have run to completion, or may have blocked.

One can understand the behavior of individual programs without thinking about computations, traces, and histories as objects of study, but in later chapters we will find it useful to treat them as objects. They will provide powerful tools for understanding the capabilities of different types of machines.

Formally, a *partial history* of program P on argument x consists of x, α, and a finite sequence of configurations interleaved with the sequence of instructions that maps each configuration to the next, i.e., a finite sequence $\langle\langle x, \alpha, C_0, \pi_1, C_1, \pi_2, \ldots, \pi_n, C_n \rangle\rangle$, where $n \geq 0$, $C_0, \ldots, C_n$ are configurations, $\pi_1, \ldots, \pi_n$ are instructions belonging to P, $x \overset{\alpha}{\mapsto} C_0$, and $C_i \overset{\pi_{i+1}}{\mapsto} C_{i+1}$ for each i.

EXAMPLE 2.9. Recall the program P shown in Figure 2.3, which accepts palindromes with central marker. A partial history of the program P on argument a#a is:

$$\begin{array}{lll} \langle\!\langle\ \texttt{a\#a} & , & \alpha & , \\ (1, \texttt{a\#a}, \Lambda) & , & (1 \to 1, \text{SCAN}\texttt{a}, \text{PUSH}\texttt{a}) & , \\ (1, \texttt{\#a}, \texttt{a}) & , & (1 \to 2, \text{SCAN}\texttt{\#}, \text{NOOP}) & , \\ (2, \texttt{a}, \texttt{a}) & \rangle\!\rangle . \end{array}$$

■■■

A *history* (or *complete history*) of program P for argument x and result y consists of a partial history that ends in a final configuration, followed by ω and then the result y; i.e., a complete history is a finite sequence $\langle\!\langle x, \alpha, C_0, \pi_1, C_1, \pi_2, \ldots, \pi_n, C_n, \omega, y\rangle\!\rangle$, where $\langle\!\langle x, \alpha, C_0, \pi_1, C_1, \pi_2, \ldots, \pi_n, C_n\rangle\!\rangle$ is a partial history and $C_n \overset{\omega}{\mapsto} y$.

EXAMPLE 2.10. A history of the program P from the previous example on argument a#a is:

$$\begin{array}{lll} \langle\!\langle\ \texttt{a\#a} & , & \alpha & , \\ (1, \texttt{a\#a}, \Lambda) & , & (1 \to 1, \text{SCAN}\texttt{a}, \text{PUSH}\texttt{a}) & , \\ (1, \texttt{\#a}, \texttt{a}) & , & (1 \to 2, \text{SCAN}\texttt{\#}, \text{NOOP}) & , \\ (2, \texttt{a}, \texttt{a}) & , & (2 \to 2, \text{SCAN}\texttt{a}, \text{POP}\texttt{a}) & , \\ (2, \Lambda, \Lambda) & , & \omega & , \\ \text{ACCEPT} & \rangle\!\rangle . \end{array}$$

■■■

If a program has a complete history on argument x, then we say that the program *halts* on x. (The history must be complete; blocking does not imply halting.) If a history ends with ACCEPT, like the one above, we call the history *accepting*. If a program has an accepting history on argument x, then we say that the program *accepts* x.

Using histories, we can describe the acceptance mechanism for nondeterministic programs in terms of a simple game. The only player is Izzy. Let a nondeterministic program P and an argument x be given. Izzy tries to choose an accepting history of program P on input x. If Izzy succeeds, then the game is a win for Izzy. If it is possible for Izzy to win, then the nondeterministic program P accepts x. If it is not possible for Izzy to win, then P does not accept x.

We say that a configuration C is *blocked* in program P if C is neither in the domain of any instruction (it is impossible for the program to proceed) nor in the domain of ω (the program has not terminated). A partial history that ends in a blocked configuration obviously cannot be extended to any longer partial history or to a complete history. We will discuss blocking again in Section 2.8.

A computation is the sequence of instructions executed when a program is run. More precisely, if $\langle\langle x, \alpha, C_0, \pi_1, C_1, \pi_2, \ldots, \pi_n, C_n, \omega, y\rangle\rangle$ is a history of P, then the sequence of instructions $\langle\langle \pi_1, \ldots, \pi_n\rangle\rangle$ is called a *computation* of P for argument x and result y.

A trace of one of our programs is analogous to a debugging trace from a real-world program. That is, a trace is the sequence of configurations entered when the program is run. More precisely, if $\langle\langle x, \alpha, C_0, \pi_1, C_1, \pi_2, \ldots, \pi_n, C_n, \omega, y\rangle\rangle$ is a history of P, then the sequence of configurations $\langle\langle C_0, \ldots, C_n\rangle\rangle$ is called a *trace* of P for argument x and result y.

A computation or trace is called *accepting* if the associated history is. *Partial computations* and *partial traces* are similarly defined. A partial computation or partial trace is called *complete* if it is a computation or trace, respectively.

We can reach configuration C' from configuration C in one step of program P iff there exists some instruction $\pi \in \mathcal{I}$ such that $C \; \pi \; C'$. Equivalently, we can reach configuration C' from configuration C in one step of program P iff $C \; \Pi \; C'$ where $\Pi = \bigcup_{\pi \in \mathcal{I}} \pi$. We can reach configuration C' from C in exactly k steps iff $C \; \Pi^k \; C'$. We can reach C' from C (in a finite number of steps) iff $C \; \Pi^* \; C'$. Therefore, there is a computation of P on argument x with result y iff $x \; \alpha\Pi^*\omega \; y$.

If $C \; \Pi \; C'$, we say that C' is a *sequel* of C. The relation Π is called the *sequel relation* of P. The relation $\alpha \circ \Pi^* \circ \omega$, which relates arguments of P to results of P, is called the *transfer relation* of P and is denoted τ (the Greek letter for "t"):

$$\tau = \alpha \circ \Pi^* \circ \omega.$$

By convention, we write $C \overset{\Pi}{\mapsto} C'$, $C \overset{\Pi^k}{\mapsto} C'$, or $C \overset{\Pi^*}{\mapsto} C'$ to denote $C\ \Pi\ C'$, $C\ \Pi^k\ C'$, or $C\ \Pi^*\ C'$, respectively. We write $x \overset{\tau}{\mapsto} y$ to denote $x\ \tau\ y$. Thus in Example 2.10, we have a#a $\overset{\tau}{\mapsto}$ ACCEPT (and, in fact, $\tau = \{(x, \text{ACCEPT}) : x \text{ is a palindrome with central marker}\}$).

EXAMPLE 2.11. Consider the monadic calculation program in Figure 1.3. The unique history of that program on input 11-1+11 is given in Figure 2.7.

The transfer relation of the monadic calculation program is $\{(x, y) :$ x is a sequence of monadic numerals separated by plus and minus signs and y is the monadic numeral that results from performing the additions and subtractions$\}$. Observe that for every x there is at most one y such that $(x, y) \in \tau$; i.e., this program's transfer relation is a partial function. In fact, the transfer relation of a deterministic program is always a partial function. ■■■

Exercises

2.7-1 (a) What are the initializer, terminator, and instruction set of the program shown in Figure 1.10?

(b) What are that program's history, computation, and trace on input aabbbb?

2.7.2 Infinite Computations, Traces, and Histories

When a program is run, it may halt, block, or run forever. Running forever is formalized through the notion of infinite histories, computations, and traces. An infinite sequence $\langle\langle x, \alpha, C_0, \pi_1, C_1, \pi_2, C_2, \ldots\rangle\rangle$ is an *infinite history* if each prefix of the form $\langle\langle x, \alpha, C_0, \pi_1, C_1, \ldots, \pi_i, C_i\rangle\rangle$ is a partial history. Observe that an infinite history is not in fact a history. An infinite history of a program corresponds to the program's running forever without blocking or producing a result.

$$
\begin{array}{llll}
\langle\!\langle & \texttt{11-1+11} & , & \alpha \quad , \\
& (+, \texttt{11-1+11}, \Lambda, 0) & , & (+ \rightarrow +, \text{SCAN}\texttt{1}, \text{NOOP}, \text{INC}) \quad , \\
& (+, \texttt{1-1+11}, \Lambda, 1) & , & (+ \rightarrow +, \text{SCAN}\texttt{1}, \text{NOOP}, \text{INC}) \quad , \\
& (+, \texttt{-1+11}, \Lambda, 2) & , & (+ \rightarrow -, \text{SCAN}\texttt{-}, \text{NOOP}, \text{NOOP}) \quad , \\
& (-, \texttt{1+11}, \Lambda, 2) & , & (- \rightarrow -, \text{SCAN}\texttt{1}, \text{NOOP}, \text{DEC}) \quad , \\
& (-, \texttt{+11}, \Lambda, 1) & , & (- \rightarrow +, \text{SCAN}\texttt{+}, \text{NOOP}, \text{NOOP}) \quad , \\
& (+, \texttt{11}, \Lambda, 1) & , & (+ \rightarrow +, \text{SCAN}\texttt{1}, \text{NOOP}, \text{INC}) \quad , \\
& (+, \texttt{1}, \Lambda, 2) & , & (+ \rightarrow +, \text{SCAN}\texttt{1}, \text{NOOP}, \text{INC}) \quad , \\
& (+, \Lambda, \Lambda, 3) & , & (+ \rightarrow 2, \text{EOF}, \text{NOOP}, \text{NOOP}) \quad , \\
& (2, \Lambda, \Lambda, 3) & , & (2 \rightarrow 3, \text{NOOP}, \text{NOOP}, \text{POS}) \quad , \\
& (3, \Lambda, \Lambda, 3) & , & (3 \rightarrow 4, \text{NOOP}, \text{NOOP}, \text{POS}) \quad , \\
& (4, \Lambda, \Lambda, 3) & , & (4 \rightarrow 3, \text{NOOP}, \text{WRITE}\texttt{1}, \text{DEC}) \quad , \\
& (3, \Lambda, \texttt{1}, 2) & , & (3 \rightarrow 4, \text{NOOP}, \text{NOOP}, \text{POS}) \quad , \\
& (4, \Lambda, \texttt{1}, 2) & , & (4 \rightarrow 3, \text{NOOP}, \text{WRITE}\texttt{1}, \text{DEC}) \quad , \\
& (3, \Lambda, \texttt{11}, 1) & , & (3 \rightarrow 4, \text{NOOP}, \text{NOOP}, \text{POS}) \quad , \\
& (4, \Lambda, \texttt{11}, 1) & , & (4 \rightarrow 3, \text{NOOP}, \text{WRITE}\texttt{1}, \text{DEC}) \quad , \\
& (3, \Lambda, \texttt{111}, 0) & , & (3 \rightarrow 6, \text{NOOP}, \text{NOOP}, \text{ZERO}) \quad , \\
& (6, \Lambda, \texttt{111}, 0) & , & \omega \quad , \\
& \texttt{111} & \rangle\!\rangle . &
\end{array}
$$

FIGURE 2.7: The unique history of the program in Figure 1.3 on input `11-1+11`.

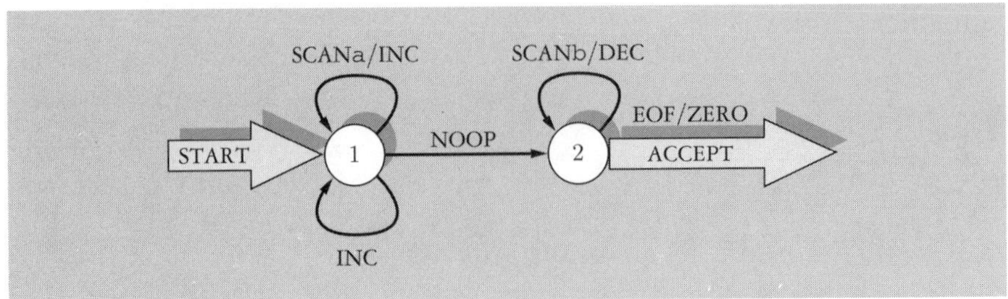

FIGURE 2.8: An NUCM program that accepts $\{\mathtt{a}^m\mathtt{b}^n : m \le n\}$.

For example, consider the NUCM program in Figure 2.8, which accepts the set of strings of the form $\mathtt{a}^m\mathtt{b}^n$ where $m \le n$. Its instruction set is

$$\left\{\begin{array}{lllllll} (& 1 \to 1 & , & \mathrm{SCAN}\mathtt{a} & , & \mathrm{INC} &), \\ (& 1 \to 1 & , & \mathrm{NOOP} & , & \mathrm{INC} &), \\ (& 1 \to 2 & , & \mathrm{NOOP} & , & \mathrm{NOOP} &), \\ (& 2 \to 2 & , & \mathrm{SCAN}\mathtt{b} & , & \mathrm{DEC} &) \end{array}\right\}.$$

This program can run forever, incrementing the counter without scanning anything. An infinite history on input ab is

$$\begin{array}{llll} \langle\!\langle & \mathtt{ab} & , \quad \alpha & , \\ & (1, \mathtt{ab}, 0) & , \quad (1 \to 1, \mathrm{NOOP}, \mathrm{INC}) & , \\ & (1, \mathtt{ab}, 1) & , \quad (1 \to 1, \mathrm{NOOP}, \mathrm{INC}) & , \\ & (1, \mathtt{ab}, 2) & , \quad (1 \to 1, \mathrm{NOOP}, \mathrm{INC}) & , \\ & & \vdots & \rangle\!\rangle. \end{array}$$

Infinite computations and infinite traces are defined analogously. An infinite sequence is an *infinite computation* if each of its prefixes is a partial computation. Equivalently, an infinite computation is the infinite sequence of instructions in some infinite history. An infinite sequence is an *infinite trace* if each of its prefixes is a partial trace. Equivalently, an infinite trace is the infinite sequence of configurations in some infinite history.

Exercises

2.7-1 What are the infinite computation and infinite trace that correspond to the infinite history presented in this section?

2.7-2 Present another infinite history of the program in Figure 2.8 on input ab. What are the corresponding infinite computation and infinite trace?

2.7-3 Design a deterministic UCM program that recognizes the language $\{\mathtt{a}^m\mathtt{b}^n : m \leq n\}$. Does your program have any infinite computations?

2.7-4 Present a deterministic program that has an infinite computation.

2.8 DETERMINISM AND BLOCKING

Recall from Section 1.9 that nondeterministic programs may perform one of several instructions at each step when they are run, but deterministic programs have at most one option at each step (zero options if the program is blocked). In this section, we formally describe the notions of determinism, nondeterminism, and blocking.

In a program, there may be more than one instruction applicable to a configuration, or an instruction may be applicable to a final configuration. Such a program could be faced with a choice of which instruction to perform next or whether to continue or halt. In such cases the program's behavior is not precisely determined. Such a situation may arise when two instructions $(\mu_1, \mu_2, \ldots, \mu_n)$ and $(\nu_1, \nu_2, \ldots, \nu_n)$ have overlapping domains, operation by operation, or when an instruction $(\mu_1, \mu_2, \ldots, \mu_n)$ and the terminator $(\omega_1, \omega_2, \ldots, \omega_n)$ have overlapping domains. When no such overlap occurs, a program is called *deterministic*. We say that determinism is a *syntactic* property because it does not depend on the behavior (semantics) of the program.

If a program is deterministic it has exactly one complete, blocked, or infinite computation on each input. In particular, it has at most one complete computation for each argument, so its transfer relation is a partial function (Exercise 2.8-2). The converse is not true; i.e., a program might not be deterministic, but still compute a partial function.

EXAMPLE 2.12. Consider the nondeterministic program in Figure 1.19 that accepts even-length palindromes. Its instructions are

$$\left\{\begin{array}{l}(\ 1 \to 1\ ,\ \mathrm{SCAN}\texttt{a}\ ,\ \mathrm{PUSH}\texttt{a}\ ),\\ (\ 1 \to 1\ ,\ \mathrm{SCAN}\texttt{b}\ ,\ \mathrm{PUSH}\texttt{b}\ ),\\ (\ 1 \to 2\ ,\ \mathrm{NOOP}\ ,\ \mathrm{NOOP}\ ),\\ (\ 2 \to 2\ ,\ \mathrm{SCAN}\texttt{a}\ ,\ \mathrm{POP}\texttt{a}\ ),\\ (\ 2 \to 2\ ,\ \mathrm{SCAN}\texttt{b}\ ,\ \mathrm{POP}\texttt{b}\ ),\\ (\ 2 \to 3\ ,\ \mathrm{EOF}\ ,\ \mathrm{EMPTY}\ )\end{array}\right\}.$$

Its terminator is $(2, \Lambda, \Lambda)\,\omega = \mathrm{ACCEPT}$. The program is not deterministic because the first and third instructions have overlapping domains; they are both applicable to configurations belonging to $\{1\} \times \texttt{a}\{\texttt{a}, \texttt{b}\}^* \times \{\texttt{a}, \texttt{b}\}^*$, i.e., in which the control state is 1, the next input character is a, and the stack contents can be anything. The second and third instructions also have overlapping domains. ■ ■ ■

EXAMPLE 2.13. Consider a program for a machine [control, input, stack, unsigned counter], whose instruction set is given below:

$$\left\{\begin{array}{l}(0 \to 1\ ,\ \mathrm{SCAN}\texttt{0}\ ,\ \mathrm{PUSH}\texttt{a}\ ,\ \mathrm{ZERO}),\\ (0 \to 1\ ,\ \mathrm{SCAN}\texttt{1}\ ,\ \mathrm{EMPTY}\ ,\ \mathrm{INC}\ ),\\ (1 \to 2\ ,\ \mathrm{NOOP}\ ,\ \mathrm{POP}\texttt{a}\ ,\ \mathrm{NOOP}),\\ (1 \to 3\ ,\ \mathrm{NOOP}\ ,\ \mathrm{NOOP}\ ,\ \mathrm{DEC}\ )\end{array}\right\}.$$

Its terminator is the everywhere-undefined partial function. See Figure 2.9.

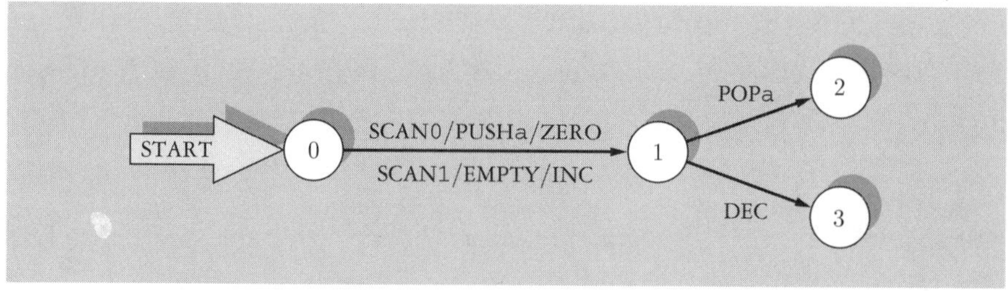

FIGURE 2.9: A program that is not deterministic but never has to choose.

This program is not deterministic because any configuration having the form $(1, x, s\mathtt{a}, n+1)$ is in the domain of both $(1 \rightarrow 2, \text{NOOP}, \text{POP}\mathtt{a}, \text{NOOP})$ and $(1 \rightarrow 3, \text{NOOP}, \text{NOOP}, \text{DEC})$; i.e., the program has the choice of popping an a or decrementing the counter.

Observe, however, that no configuration of the form $(1, x, s\mathtt{a}, n + 1)$ is actually reached during any partial computation that starts at control state 0, because the program can enter control state 1 only when the stack is empty or the counter is zero. Thus, when this program runs, it is never faced with a choice. However, it is not deterministic. By definition, determinism depends only on local properties of the instruction set and the terminator, rather than on the actual behavior of the program. This is important, because there is no general algorithm to determine which configurations of a program are actually entered, but we want to be able to decide easily whether a program is deterministic. ■■■

Recall from Section 1.9 that deterministic programs are a special case of nondeterministic programs. Nondeterministic means "not necessarily deterministic," as opposed to "not deterministic."

Blocking is another property that depends only on local properties of the instruction set and the terminator. Recall that a configuration C is *blocked* if C is not in the domain of any instruction or ω. A program is called *nonblocking* if no configuration is blocked. Like determinism, the nonblocking property does not depend on which configurations of the program are actually reachable.

Observe that the program in Example 2.12 is blocking because any configuration of the form $(2, \mathtt{a}x, \mathit{s}\mathtt{b})$ or $(2, \mathtt{b}x, \mathit{s}\mathtt{a})$ is not in the domain of any instruction or ω. In particular, $(2, \mathtt{a}, \mathtt{b})$ is a blocked configuration.

Exercises

2.8-1 For each nondeterministic program in Figures 1.19 through 1.23, tell which pairs of instructions have overlapping domains.

2.8-2 Prove that if a program is deterministic, then

(a) it has at most one computation on each argument.

(b) its transfer relation is a partial function.

The converses to (a) and (b) are not true. Give counterexamples.

2.9 THREE IMPORTANT KINDS OF PROGRAMS

Programs tend to fit into one of three paradigms: An acceptor is a nondeterministic program that takes a string as input and either accepts it or does not (it can fail to accept by blocking or running forever). A recognizer is a deterministic program that takes a string as input and either accepts it or rejects it. A transducer is a nondeterministic program in which each complete computation maps an input string to an output string.

Recognizers and acceptors are used for testing membership in a language. Transducers compute relations or partial functions on strings. Of course, all programs will be limited by the capabilities of the machines they run on.

2.9.1 Acceptors

A common application of programs is to test whether a string belongs to a language L. Informally, acceptors do so as follows: If the input x belongs to L, then the program has a complete computation on x with a result called ACCEPT (which can be thought of as "yes" or "true"); if x does not belong to L, then all computations of the program on x are blocked or infinite, producing no result. Acceptors can say yes, but they cannot say no. In symbols,

$$x \in L \iff x \overset{T}{\mapsto} \text{ACCEPT}.$$

Acceptors are nondeterministic. Therefore, for an input string in L, there may be more than one partial or complete computation. So long as there is at least one complete computation with result ACCEPT, the input string is *accepted*, even if other partial computations on that input are be blocked or infinite. In this convention, we say the program *accepts* the language L. We write $L(P)$ to denote the language accepted by program P.

Formally, an acceptor is a program that computes a partial function from Σ^* to $\{\text{ACCEPT}\}$ and obeys a certain input convention that we will specify. The program's argument is the initial state of the input device. Each non-input device is initialized to a particular initial state that is independent of the argument. That is, let M be a machine [control, input, $d_3, \ldots, d_k$] with input alphabet Σ. A program for M is an *acceptor* if its initializer satisfies the following conditions:

- The input's initial state is equal to the argument, i.e., $\alpha_{\text{input}} = I_{\Sigma^*}$.
- For $d \neq$ input, the initial state of d does not depend on the argument, i.e., $\alpha_d = \Sigma^* \times \{s_d\}$ for some state s_d in the realm of d.

The restrictions on α ensure that the program's only direct access to its argument is via the input device. If an acceptor P accepts a language L, then we call P an *acceptor for* L. For example, the programs presented in Figures 1.2, 1.5, 1.7, 1.8, 1.9, 1.10, 1.11, 1.12, 1.13, 1.14, 1.15, 1.16, 1.19, 1.20, 1.21, 1.22, and 1.23 are all acceptors.

An acceptor that runs on a finite machine is called a *nondeterministic finite acceptor* (NFA, for short). An acceptor that runs on a counter machine is called a *nondeterministic counter acceptor* (NCA, for short). An acceptor that runs on a stack machine is called a *nondeterministic stack acceptor* (NSA, for short). An acceptor that runs on a tape machine is called a *nondeterministic Turing acceptor* (NTA, for short). Deterministic acceptors running on those machines are called DFAs, DCAs, DSAs, and DTAs, respectively.

Exercises

2.9-1 Design deterministic acceptors that run on a machine [control, input] and accept the following languages:

(a) the set of numbers that are congruent to 1 modulo 5, written in monadic notation

(b) the set of numbers that are congruent to 1 modulo 5, written in dyadic notation

(c) the set of numbers that are congruent to 1 modulo 5, written in binary notation

(d) the set of numbers that are congruent to 1 modulo 2 and to 2 modulo 5, written in monadic notation

(e) the set of numbers that are congruent to 1 modulo 2 and to 2 modulo 5, written in dyadic notation

(f) the set of numbers that are congruent to 1 modulo 2 and to 2 modulo 5, written in binary notation

2.9.2 Recognizers

A second convention for programs that test membership in a language L requires that the program be nonblocking and deterministic and that it give a result for every input string. In particular, the program must have no infinite computations. Because the program is deterministic and gives a result for every string, its transfer relation is a function. The transfer function maps each string in the language L to a particular result, called ACCEPT (possibly synonymous with "yes" or "true"). The transfer function maps each string in $\overline{L}$, i.e., each string not in L, to a second particular result, called REJECT (possibly synonymous with "no" or "false"). In this convention, we say that the program *recognizes* L. In contrast with acceptors, recognizers can say yes or no. In symbols,

$$xT = \begin{cases} \text{ACCEPT} & \text{if } x \in L, \\ \text{REJECT} & \text{if } x \notin L. \end{cases}$$

We write $L(P)$ to denote the language recognized by program P.

A program that follows those conventions for recognizing a language and also obeys the same input convention as an acceptor is called a *recognizer*.

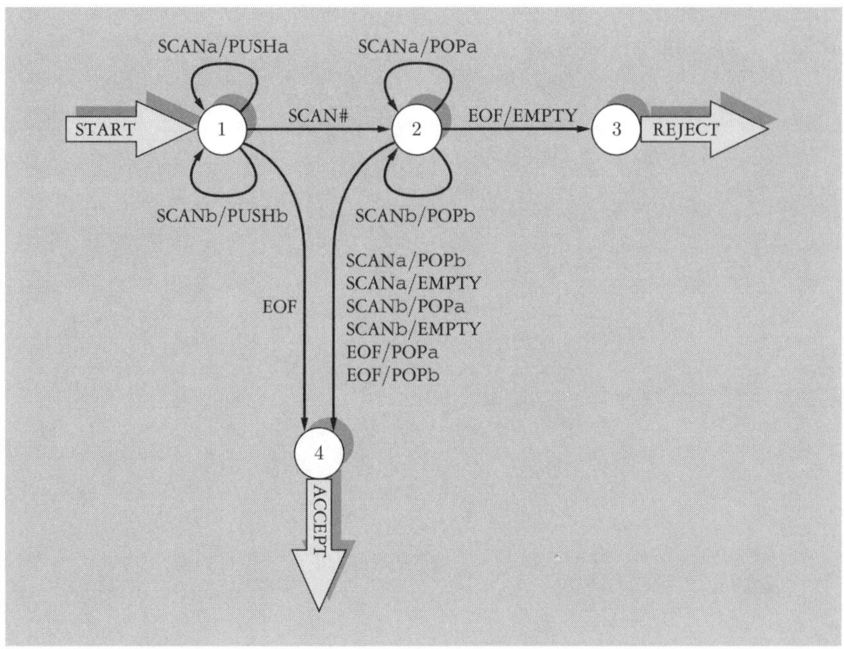

FIGURE 2.10: A recognizer for the set of strings that are not palindromes with central marker.

If a recognizer P recognizes a language L, then we call P a *recognizer for* L. For example, the program presented in Figure 1.1 is a recognizer for the set of palindromes with central marker.

Given a program that recognizes L, if we interchange ACCEPT and REJECT in the specification for the terminator ω, we obtain a program that recognizes $\overline{L}$. Therefore, a language is recognized by some program for a machine iff its complement is recognized by another (nearly identical) program for the same machine. In Figure 2.10, we apply this technique to convert the program in Figure 1.1 to a recognizer for the set of strings that are *not* palindromes with central marker.

Alternatively, if we delete from ω all ordered pairs whose second component is REJECT, we obtain a program that accepts L. Therefore, if a language is recognized by some program for a machine, then it is accepted by a nearly identical program for the same machine. (The converse need not

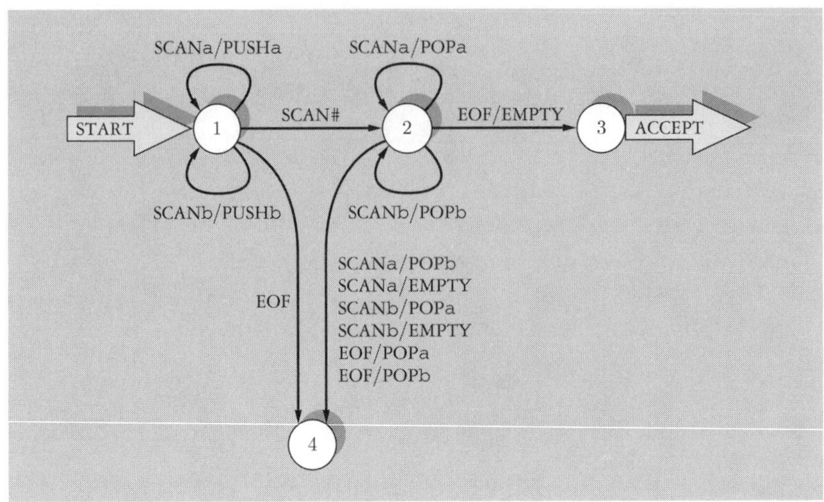

FIGURE 2.11: The result of converting the recognizer in Figure 1.1 to an acceptor.

be true, as we shall see in Chapters 6 and 7.) In Figure 2.11, we apply this technique to convert the program in Figure 1.1 to an acceptor for the set of palindromes with central marker. (We can also delete control state 4 and the edges leading to it, thereby obtaining a smaller program. See Figure 1.2.)

A recognizer that runs on a finite machine is called a *deterministic finite recognizer* (DFR, for short). A recognizer that runs on a counter machine is called a *deterministic counter recognizer* (DCR, for short). A recognizer that runs on a stack machine is called a *deterministic stack recognizer* (DSR, for short). A recognizer that runs on a tape machine is called a *deterministic Turing recognizer* (DTR, for short).

Exercises

2.9-2 Repeat Exercise 2.9-1 for recognizers.

2.9.3 Transducers

Another important application of programs is to compute a multiple-valued function, i.e., a relation. A transducer is a program that computes a relation from Σ^* to Δ^* and obeys certain input and output conventions that we will specify. The input device is initialized to hold the argument, and the output device holds the result. Each non-input device is initialized to a particular initial state that is independent of the input. Each non-output device has a particular set of final states, but the result does not depend on which final state any non-output device is in.

To be precise, let M be a machine [control, input, output, $d_4, \ldots, d_k$] with input alphabet Σ and output alphabet Δ. A program for M is a *transducer* if its initializer and terminator satisfy the following conditions:

- The input's initial state is equal to the argument, i.e., $\alpha_{\text{input}} = I_{\Sigma^*}$.
- For $d \neq$ input, the initial state of d does not depend on the argument, i.e., $\alpha_d = \Sigma^* \times \{s_d\}$ for some state s_d in the realm of d.
- The result is equal to the output's final state, i.e., $\omega_{\text{output}} = I_{\Delta^*}$.
- For $d \neq$ output, the result does not depend on the state that d ends up in, i.e., $\omega_d = S_d \times \Delta^*$ for some subset S_d of the realm of d.

The restrictions on α ensure that the program's only direct access to the input is via the input device. The restrictions on ω ensure that the result, if there is one, is not affected by any device but the output device. Note, however, that *the program produces no result unless it enters a final configuration, i.e, unless every device enters a final state.*

EXAMPLE 2.14. Consider the program for a machine [control, input, output, stack] in Figure 2.12. Its initializer is $x\alpha = (0, x, \Lambda, \Lambda)$, and its terminator is $(1, \Lambda, y, \Lambda)\,\omega = y$. The program is a transducer that maps strings of the form xx^R to x. The program does not accept any other inputs, so it does not produce any result when the input is not of the form xx^R. (In fact, any program with that initializer and terminator is a transducer.) ■ ■ ■

The program in Figure 1.3, which performs monadic addition and subtraction, is also a transducer.

FM transducers, also called *finite transducers*, transform strings while using a bounded amount of memory. The transfer relation of a (deterministic) finite transducer is called a (deterministic) *finite transduction*. Finite transductions will have many uses in subsequent chapters.

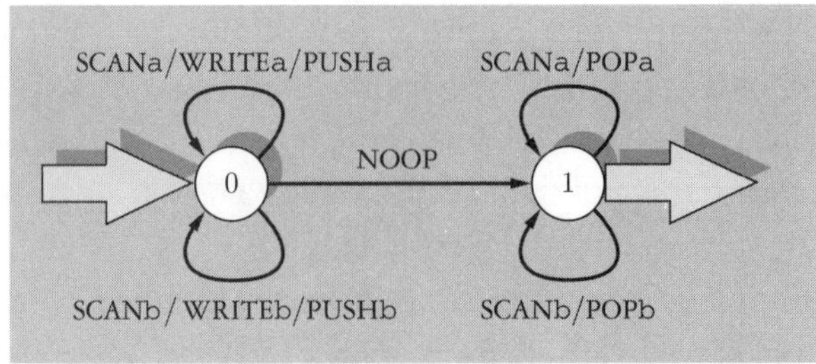

FIGURE 2.12: A program that maps strings of the form xx^R to x.

FIGURE 2.13: A deterministic finite transducer that maps x to $\mathtt{a}^{\#_\mathtt{a}(x)}$.

EXAMPLE 2.15. Let us design a deterministic finite transducer that maps each string x over $\{\mathtt{a}, \mathtt{b}\}$ to the string $\mathtt{a}^{\#_\mathtt{a}(x)}$ (recall that $\#_\mathtt{a}(x)$ is the number of a's in the string x). The transfer relation is $\{(x, y) \in \{\mathtt{a}, \mathtt{b}\}^* \times \mathtt{a}^*$: x and y contain equal numbers of a's$\}$ (a partial function). The program, shown in Figure 2.13, scans a's and copies them to the output device; it also scans b's but ignores them. ■ ■ ■

EXAMPLE 2.16. Let us design a nondeterministic finite transducer that relates each string x over $\{\mathtt{a}, \mathtt{b}\}$ to each string y over $\{\mathtt{a}, \mathtt{b}\}$ such that $\#_\mathtt{a}(x) = \#_\mathtt{a}(y)$, i.e., the output is any string that has the same number of a's as the input string. The transfer relation is $\{(x, y) \in \{\mathtt{a}, \mathtt{b}\}^* \times \{\mathtt{a}, \mathtt{b}\}^*$: x and y contain equal numbers of a's$\}$. The program, shown in Figure 2.14, scans a's and copies them to the output device, scans b's but ignores them, and also nondeterministically writes b's to the output device. ■ ■ ■

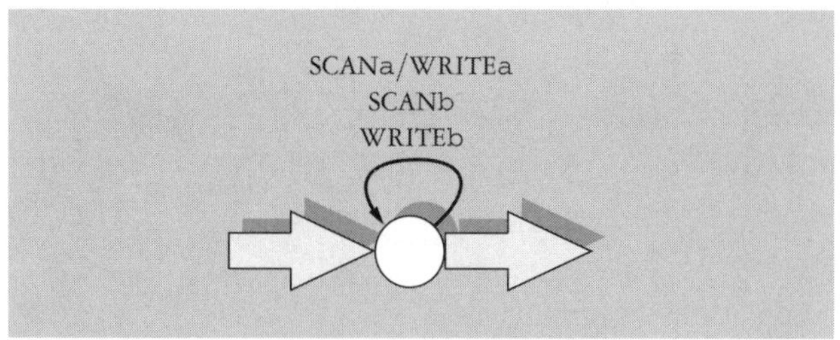

FIGURE 2.14: A nondeterministic finite transducer that relates x to any string with the same number of a's.

The behavior of acceptors, recognizers, and transducers is summarized in Figure 2.15.

Exercises

2.9-3 Design a stack transducer whose transfer relation is $\{(w, w^R): w \in \{\mathtt{a}, \mathtt{b}\}^*\}$.

2.9-4 Design a finite transducer that maps each string of the form $\mathtt{a}^i\#\mathtt{a}^j$ to $\mathtt{a}^i\mathtt{b}^j$.

2.9-5 Design a finite transducer that maps each string of the form $\mathtt{a}^i\mathtt{b}^j\mathtt{c}^k$ to $\mathtt{a}^j\mathtt{b}^k$.

2.9-6 **Filters**

(a) Let P be an acceptor for a language L. Show how to convert P into a transducer P', running on the same type of machine, whose transfer relation τ' is given by

$$x\tau' = \begin{cases} x & \text{if } x \in L, \\ \text{undefined} & \text{otherwise,} \end{cases}$$

i.e., $\tau' = I_L$. Such a program is called a *filter* for L, and we say that the program filters L.

$$\begin{array}{llllll}
\textit{Acceptor:} & x \in L & \Longleftrightarrow & x & \overset{\alpha}{\mapsto} & (q_{\text{start}}, x, \Lambda, \text{etc.}) \\
 & & & & \overset{\Pi^*}{\mapsto} & (q_{\text{accept}}, \Lambda, \Lambda, \text{etc.}) \\
 & & & & \overset{\omega}{\mapsto} & \text{ACCEPT.} \\
\textit{Recognizer:} & x \in L & \Longleftrightarrow & x & \overset{\alpha}{\mapsto} & (q_{\text{start}}, x, \Lambda, \text{etc.}) \\
 & & & & \overset{\Pi^*}{\mapsto} & (q_{\text{accept}}, \Lambda, \Lambda, \text{etc.}) \\
 & & & & \overset{\omega}{\mapsto} & \text{ACCEPT,} \\
 & x' \notin L & \Longleftrightarrow & x' & \overset{\alpha}{\mapsto} & (q_{\text{start}}, x', \Lambda, \text{etc.}) \\
 & & & & \overset{\Pi^*}{\mapsto} & (q_{\text{reject}}, \Lambda, \Lambda, \text{etc.}) \\
 & & & & \overset{\omega}{\mapsto} & \text{REJECT.} \\
\textit{Transducer:} & x \overset{\tau}{\mapsto} y & \Longleftrightarrow & x & \overset{\alpha}{\mapsto} & (q_{\text{start}}, x, \Lambda, \text{etc.}) \\
 & & & & \overset{\Pi^*}{\mapsto} & (q_{\text{final}}, \Lambda, y, \text{etc.}) \\
 & & & & \overset{\omega}{\mapsto} & y.
\end{array}$$

In short,

$$\begin{array}{llllll}
\textit{Acceptor:} & x \in L & \Longleftrightarrow & (q_{\text{start}}, x, \Lambda, \text{etc.}) & \overset{\Pi^*}{\mapsto} & (q_{\text{accept}}, \Lambda, \Lambda, \text{etc.}). \\
\textit{Recognizer:} & x \in L & \Longleftrightarrow & (q_{\text{start}}, x, \Lambda, \text{etc.}) & \overset{\Pi^*}{\mapsto} & (q_{\text{accept}}, \Lambda, \Lambda, \text{etc.}), \\
 & x' \notin L & \Longleftrightarrow & (q_{\text{start}}, x', \Lambda, \text{etc.}) & \overset{\Pi^*}{\mapsto} & (q_{\text{reject}}, \Lambda, \Lambda, \text{etc.}). \\
\textit{Transducer:} & x \overset{\tau}{\mapsto} y & \Longleftrightarrow & (q_{\text{start}}, x, \Lambda, \text{etc.}) & \overset{\Pi^*}{\mapsto} & (q_{\text{final}}, \Lambda, y, \text{etc.}).
\end{array}$$

FIGURE 2.15: The behavior of acceptors and recognizers for a language L and of transducers computing a relation τ. Assume that the programs run on a machine [control, input, output, $d_4, \ldots, d_k$] where $d_4, \ldots, d_k$ are devices other than input or output. We write "etc." as shorthand for the states of devices $d_4, \ldots, d_k$. q_{start} denotes the unique initial state; q_{accept}, q_{reject}, and q_{final} denote arbitrary accepting, rejecting, and final states, respectively. Recognizers must be deterministic. Note that the output device is not used by acceptors or recognizers, so it need not be present in their machines.

(b) Show how to convert a filter for L into an acceptor for L running on the same type of machine.

*2.9-7 Design a deterministic finite transducer with the following properties:

- If the input x is a balanced string of parentheses, then the program outputs a balanced string of parentheses having length $\frac{1}{2}|x|$ or less.
- If the input x is not a balanced string of parentheses, then the program either rejects or outputs an unbalanced string of parentheses having length $\frac{1}{2}|x|$ or less.

2.10 CHAPTER SUMMARY

In this chapter we showed how to represent problems, instances, and results. Then we formally defined many concepts that had already been presented informally in Chapter 1. It is important to remember that an operation is a partial function on the state of a device, a configuration captures all the state information needed to describe a machine at one moment, and an instruction is a partial function on the configuration of a machine.

Next we defined computations, histories, and traces, which record the behavior of a program. Finally, we defined three important kinds of programs: recognizers, acceptors, and transducers. Recognizers are always deterministic and test membership in languages. Acceptors are nondeterministic (although deterministic acceptors are an interesting special case) and also test membership in languages. Nondeterministic transducers compute relations, and deterministic transducers compute partial functions.

Throughout this book, it is important to remember that determinism is a special case of nondeterminism.

Exercises

2.10-1 Construct a DFR that scans a binary number x left to right and determines whether

(a) $x \equiv 0 \pmod 2$.

(b) $x \equiv 1 \pmod 3$.
(c) $x \equiv 5 \pmod 7$.

2.10-2 Repeat Exercise 2.10-1 for decimal numbers.

2.10-3 **Programs with nonstandard initializer**

(a) Construct a DUCM program that starts with a number x in the counter and determines whether $x \equiv 1 \pmod 3$.

(b) Construct a DSM program that starts with a string x on the stack and determines whether x contains the pattern `gram`. (Assume that the stack alphabet is $\{\mathtt{a}, \ldots, \mathtt{z}\}$, and use appropriate abbreviations when describing the program.)

(c) Construct a DSM program that starts with a string x on the stack and determines whether x contains the pattern `bbaba`. (Assume that the stack alphabet is $\{\mathtt{a}, \mathtt{b}\}$.)

In each part, be sure to define α.

2.10-4 **Generators**

(a) Let P be an acceptor for a language L. Assume that P does not use the EOF test. Show how to convert P into a program P', running on the same type of machine, that has no input but writes all strings belonging to L. To be precise, let the argument to P' be called START (since the argument is ignored, its name does not really matter). The transfer relation τ' of P' is given by

$$\text{START} \overset{\tau'}{\mapsto} x \iff x \in L.$$

Such a program is called a *generator* for L, and we say that the program *generates* L.

(b) Show how to convert a generator for L into an acceptor for L running on the same type of machine.

(c) Prove that if a program P generates an infinite language, then P has at least one infinite computation. Hint: Use König's tree lemma (Exercise 0.6-29).

3

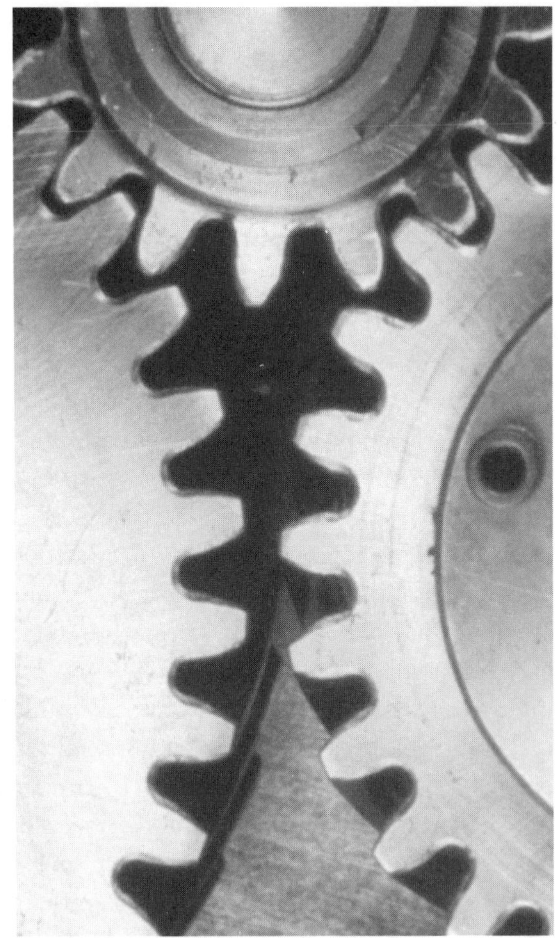

Simulation

SIMULATION IS A major topic in computer science, arising in hardware design, distributed systems, programming language semantics, and theory. In this chapter we will define what it means for one program to simulate another program. Although we do not present the most general notion of simulation, our simulation techniques suffice to prove many important theorems in computability theory. Furthermore, similar simulation techniques, beyond the scope of this book, are applicable to other areas of computer science. We begin by informally discussing some practical uses of simulation.

Suppose, for example, that your computer company wants to create a new Super Behemoth 2000 model of workstation to replace its popular Behemoth 1000 model. The design of a new real-world computer typically begins with the specification of an abstract machine that can hold certain kinds of information and perform instructions that affect that information. Next a network of wires and standard logic gates is designed (on paper) that behaves the same as the SB2000's specification. If correct, the design simulates the specification. Finally, the SB2000 is constructed from real hardware; if put together correctly, the SB2000 simulates the design and, by transitivity, simulates the specification. While the design and construction are going on, one may also write a program called a simulator that runs on the existing B1000 computer and simulates, instruction by instruction, programs for the SB2000. The simulator is likely to be slow, even compared to the B1000, because it may take several B1000 instructions to simulate one instruction of the SB2000, but the simulator makes it possible to write and debug software for the SB2000 even before it has been built.

Your company's SB2000 customers may depend on existing software written for the B1000. In order to keep them happy, it is useful to have a simulator that runs on the SB2000 and simulates B1000 programs. Because it may take several instructions of the SB2000 to simulate one instruction of the B1000, simulated programs will typically run slower than programs written expressly for the SB2000, but at least they will work.

Consumers who do much scientific computing will purchase chips that perform arithmetic on floating point numbers. However, most users will use floating point operations only occasionally; they do not mind if floating point is slow, and they do not want to pay extra for a special chip. For them it makes sense to provide subroutines that use the SB2000's instructions to perform floating point arithmetic. These subroutines simulate the operations performed by floating point chips.

In hardware design, one generally wants to prove that a design simulates its specification; in distributed systems, that a system simulates its specification; in programming language semantics, that a program meets its specification. Theory provides techniques to prove the correctness of simulations and hence that hardware, systems, and programs behave as desired.

3.1 SIMULATION OF PROGRAMS

A major topic of computability theory is comparing the relative computing power of different kinds of machines. For most of this book, we will measure the power of machines by which problems they can solve, regardless of how fast they can solve them; only in Chapter 9 will we make a formal study of running time.

We say that two programs P and P', possibly running on different machines, are *(computationally) equivalent* if P and P' have the same transfer relation; this is an equivalence relation on programs. We say that one machine M' is *at least as (computationally) powerful* as another machine M if every program P for machine M is equivalent to some program P' for machine M'; this is a partial order on machines.

We prove equivalence of programs so often that it is economical to find a standard proof framework into which we can plug the particulars of each proof. Usually we will prove the equivalence of programs P and P' by showing that their histories pass through some closely related configurations. Such similar behavior is called *simulation*. Proofs by simulation are desirable because the key ideas are computational rather than abstract.

If every program for a machine M can be simulated by a program for a machine M', then we say that the machine M is simulated by the machine M'. In particular, if a machine M' can simulate a machine M, then machine M' is at least as powerful as machine M.

In Section 3.2 we introduce a simple framework for proving simulation, called *lockstep simulation*, in which the behavior of P' corresponds to the behavior of P step for step. In Section 3.3, we describe a more general framework, using subprograms, in which P' may spend several steps simulating each step of P.

Simulation via subprograms will permit us to mechanize the details of almost every simulation we wish to verify in this book. That is not to say that simulations do not involve creativity. Some insight is usually needed in order to determine how the states of one machine's devices represent the states of another machine's devices. Given that insight, the details of the proof become routine.[1]

Typical simulation proofs can be explained informally. In later chapters they will be. The main purpose of this chapter is to develop formal tools so that you can take an informally explained simulation, describe it precisely, and formally prove its correctness. To understand Chapters 4 through 9, it suffices to have an informal understanding of simulation, especially the concrete examples that we will present in this chapter.

3.2 LOCKSTEP SIMULATION

In proving simulation we must first discover how the states of one machine's devices can effectively represent the states of another machine's devices, or, more succinctly, how the configuration of one machine can effectively represent the configuration of another machine. This is done on an ad hoc basis. After the correspondence between the configurations of the two machines is understood, we prove that the behavior of the programs preserves the correspondence. That part of the proof can often be performed in a purely mechanical way.

EXAMPLE 3.1. Let P be the program for a machine [control, input, unsigned counter] shown in Figure 3.1, which accepts $\{\mathtt{a}^n\mathtt{b}^n : n \geq 1\}$. Let P' be the DSA with a one-character stack alphabet, shown in Figure 3.2, which also accepts $\{\mathtt{a}^n\mathtt{b}^n : n \geq 1\}$. In fact, P' simulates P. The control state q in P is represented by the same state q in P'. The input state x in P is represented by the same state x in P'. The counter state i in P is represented by the stack state $\mathtt{1}^i$ in P'.

On argument x, the initial configuration of P is $(1, x, 0)$, which corresponds to the initial configuration $(1, x, \Lambda)$ in P'. The instruction $(1 \to 1, \text{SCAN}\,\mathtt{a}, \text{INC})$ in P maps the configuration $(1, \mathtt{a}x, i)$ to $(1, x, i+1)$; the instruction $(1 \to 1, \text{SCAN}\,\mathtt{a}, \text{PUSH}\,\mathtt{1})$ in P' maps the corresponding configuration $(1, \mathtt{a}x, \mathtt{1}^i)$ to $(1, x, \mathtt{1}^{i+1})$. The instruction $(1 \to 2, \text{SCAN}\,\mathtt{b}, \text{DEC})$ in P maps the configuration $(1, \mathtt{b}x, i+1)$ to $(2, x, i)$; the instruc-

[1] There is no general algorithm for obtaining proofs of equivalence, as we will prove in Chapter 7.

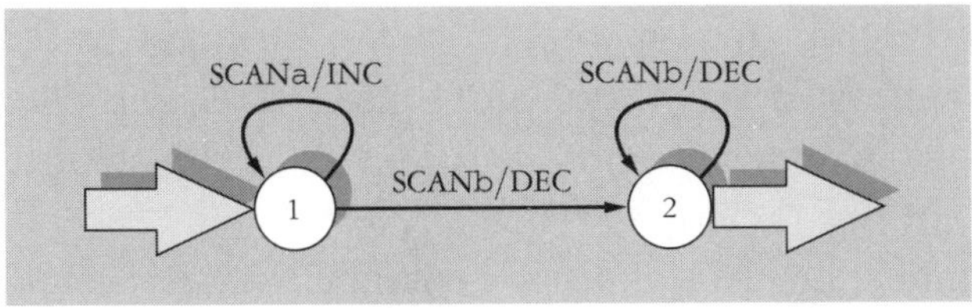

FIGURE 3.1: A DCA that accepts $\{\mathtt{a}^n\mathtt{b}^n : n \geq 1\}$.

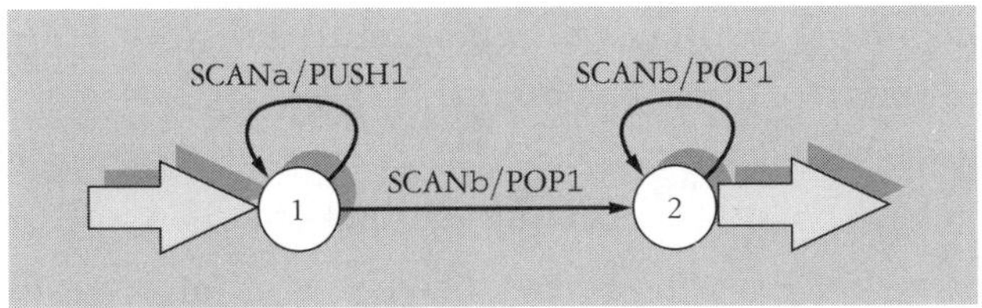

FIGURE 3.2: A DSA with a one-character stack alphabet that accepts $\{\mathtt{a}^n\mathtt{b}^n : n \geq 1\}$.

tion $(1 \to 2, \text{SCAN}\mathtt{b}, \text{POP}\mathtt{1})$ in P' maps the corresponding configuration $(1, \mathtt{b}x, \mathtt{1}^{i+1})$ to $(2, x, \mathtt{1}^i)$. The instruction $(2 \to 2, \text{SCAN}\mathtt{b}, \text{DEC})$ in P maps the configuration $(2, \mathtt{b}x, i + 1)$ to $(2, x, i)$; the instruction $(2 \to 2, \text{SCAN}\mathtt{b}, \text{POP}\mathtt{1})$ in P' maps the corresponding configuration $(2, \mathtt{b}x, \mathtt{1}^{i+1})$ to $(2, x, \mathtt{1}^i)$. The accepting configuration $(2, \Lambda, 0)$ in P corresponds to the accepting configuration $(2, \Lambda, \Lambda)$ in P'. ■■■

In this section we define a simple framework, called lockstep simulation, for proving simulation. Then we prove that lockstep simulation possesses the key feature of simulation: If one program simulates another in lockstep, then both programs have the same transfer relation. To prove lockstep simulation, it suffices to state how one program's configurations represent the other's and then to verify three equations involving this representation. The inductive part of the proof of program equivalence need be done only once and can be applied many times. Thus lockstep simulation eliminates the need for many tedious inductive proofs of program equivalence.

Let P be a program with initializer α, terminator ω, sequel relation Π, and transfer relation τ for a machine M whose control set is Q. Let P' be a program with initializer α', terminator ω', sequel relation Π', and transfer relation τ' for a machine M' whose control set is Q'. We want to prove that P' is equivalent to P, i.e., that $\tau' = \tau$.

In any simulation, we will define a relation ρ that relates configurations of M' to configurations of M. ρ is called the *relation of representation*. If C' is a configuration of M' and C is a configuration of M such that $C' \, \rho \, C$, we say that C' *represents* C. In the simplest kind of simulation, P' takes one step for each step of P, and the kth configuration of P' represents the kth configuration of P. We call this a *lockstep* simulation.

There are three conditions to establish in a lockstep simulation. First, we must show that the initial configuration of P' represents the initial configuration of P and no other configuration. That is, $x \overset{\alpha}{\mapsto} C_0$ if and only if $x \overset{\alpha'}{\mapsto} C_0'$ for some C_0' that represents C_0. Let us expand that formula:

$$x \, I \, x \overset{\alpha}{\longmapsto} C_0 \iff (\exists C_0')[x \overset{\alpha'}{\longmapsto} C_0' \, \rho \, C_0].$$

Stated in a diagram, this amounts to showing that the relations indicated by the dashed lines in Figure 3.3 are satisfied if and only if there exists C_0' such that the relations indicated by the dotted lines are satisfied. More compactly,

$$\alpha = \alpha' \circ \rho. \qquad (3.1)$$

We say that the diagram in Figure 3.3 *commutes* or is *commutative* because starting at the upper right hand corner one arrives at the same destination by following arrows down and then left as by following arrows left and then down.[2]

Second, we must show that a single instruction is simulated properly. That is, if C_i' represents C_i and C_{i+1} is a sequel of C_i, then there is a sequel C_{i+1}' of C_i' such that C_{i+1}' represents C_{i+1}; conversely, if C_{i+1}' is a sequel of

[2] Experienced travelers know that Manhattan streets form a commutative diagram, whereas Boston streets do not.

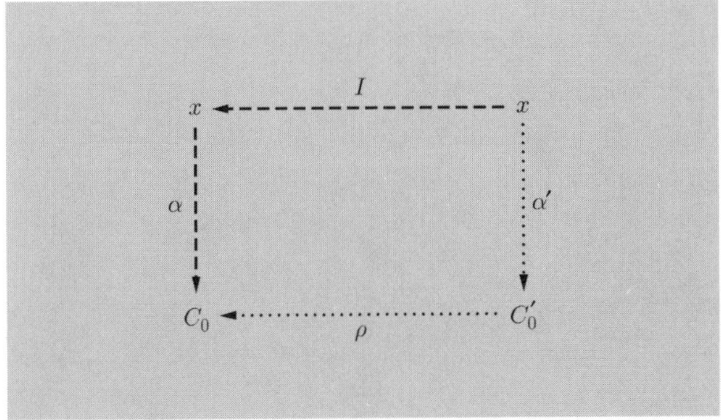

FIGURE 3.3: A commutative diagram demonstrating the simulation of α: $x \, I \, x \overset{\alpha}{\mapsto} C_0 \iff (\exists C_0')[x \overset{\alpha'}{\mapsto} C_0' \, \rho \, C_0]$.

C_i' and C_{i+1}' represents C_{i+1}, then there exists a configuration C_i such that C_i' represents C_i and C_{i+1} is a sequel of C_i. That is,

$$(\exists C_i)[C_i' \, \rho \, C_i \overset{\Pi}{\longmapsto} C_{i+1}] \iff (\exists C_{i+1}')[C_i' \overset{\Pi'}{\longmapsto} C_{i+1}' \, \rho \, C_{i+1}].$$

Stated in a diagram, this amounts to showing that there exists C_i satisfying the relations indicated by the dashed lines in Figure 3.4 if and only if there exists C_{i+1}' satisfying the relations indicated by the dotted lines. Much more compactly,

$$\rho \circ \Pi = \Pi' \circ \rho. \tag{3.2}$$

Third, we must show that every final configuration of P' represents a final configuration of P, and, conversely, every final configuration of P is represented by a final configuration of P'. That is, C_n' represents some configuration C_n such that $C_n \overset{\omega}{\mapsto} y$ if and only if $C_n' \overset{\omega'}{\mapsto} y$. Expanding that formula,

$$(\exists C_n)[C_n' \, \rho \, C_n \overset{\omega}{\longmapsto} y] \iff C_n' \overset{\omega'}{\longmapsto} y \, I \, y.$$

Diagrammatically, we show there exists C_n such that the relations indicated by the dashed lines in Figure 3.5 are satisfied if and only if the relations

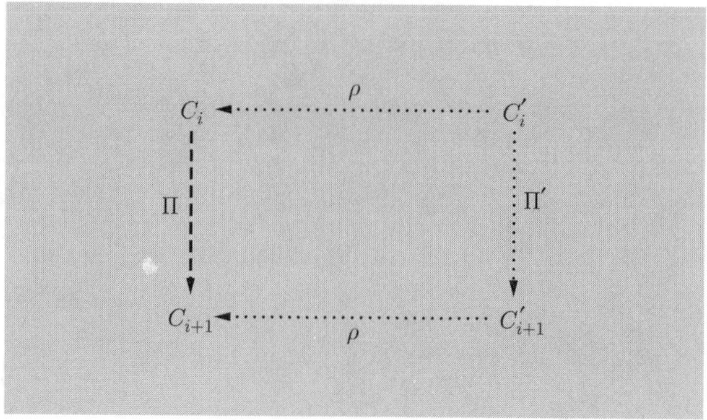

FIGURE 3.4: A commutative diagram demonstrating the simulation of Π: $(\exists C_i)[C_i' \,\rho\, C_i \overset{\Pi}{\mapsto} C_{i+1}] \iff (\exists C'_{i+1})[C_i' \overset{\Pi'}{\mapsto} C'_{i+1} \,\rho\, C_{i+1}]$.

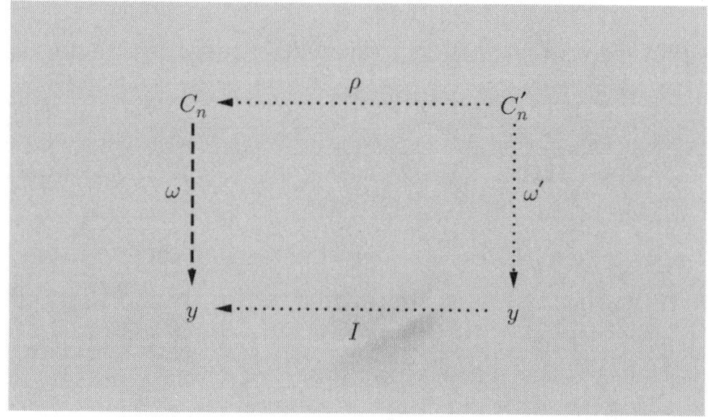

FIGURE 3.5: A commutative diagram demonstrating the simulation of ω: $(\exists C_n)[C_n' \,\rho\, C_n \overset{\omega}{\mapsto} y] \iff C_n' \overset{\omega'}{\mapsto} y \, I \, y$.

indicated by the dotted lines are satisfied. More compactly,

$$\rho \circ \omega = \omega'. \qquad (3.3)$$

Formally, we say that P' simulates P in lockstep if there is a relation ρ that satisfies equations (3.1–3.3). These three equations are summarized in Figure 3.6.

$$
\begin{aligned}
\alpha &= \alpha' \circ \rho, && (3.1)\\
\rho \circ \Pi &= \Pi' \circ \rho, && (3.2)\\
\rho \circ \omega &= \omega'. && (3.3)
\end{aligned}
$$

FIGURE 3.6: The three conditions of lockstep simulation.

Assume that equations (3.1–3.3) hold. First, we will prove by induction that $\rho \circ \Pi^k = (\Pi')^k \circ \rho$ for every $k \geq 0$. When $k = 0$, we have $\rho \circ \Pi^0 = \rho = (\Pi')^0 \circ \rho$, so the base case is established. Assume inductively that $\rho \circ \Pi^k = (\Pi')^k \circ \rho$ for some $k \geq 0$. Then, using (3.2),

$$\rho \circ \Pi^{k+1} = \rho \circ \Pi^k \circ \Pi = (\Pi')^k \circ \rho \circ \Pi = (\Pi')^k \circ \Pi' \circ \rho = (\Pi')^{k+1} \circ \rho,$$

completing the proof by induction. Then, for every k,

$$
\begin{aligned}
\alpha \circ \Pi^k \circ \omega &= \alpha' \circ \rho \circ \Pi^k \circ \omega && \text{by (3.1)}\\
&= \alpha' \circ (\Pi')^k \circ \rho \circ \omega\\
&= \alpha' \circ (\Pi')^k \circ \omega' && \text{by (3.3).}
\end{aligned}
$$

(This equality is depicted in Figure 3.7.) Therefore,

$$
\begin{aligned}
\tau &= \alpha \circ \Pi^* \circ \omega\\
&= \alpha \circ \left(\bigcup_{k\geq 0} \Pi^k \right) \circ \omega\\
&= \bigcup_{k\geq 0} \alpha \circ \Pi^k \circ \omega\\
&= \bigcup_{k\geq 0} \alpha' \circ (\Pi')^k \circ \omega'\\
&= \alpha' \circ \left(\bigcup_{k\geq 0} (\Pi')^k \right) \circ \omega'\\
&= \alpha' \circ (\Pi')^* \circ \omega'\\
&= \tau',
\end{aligned}
$$

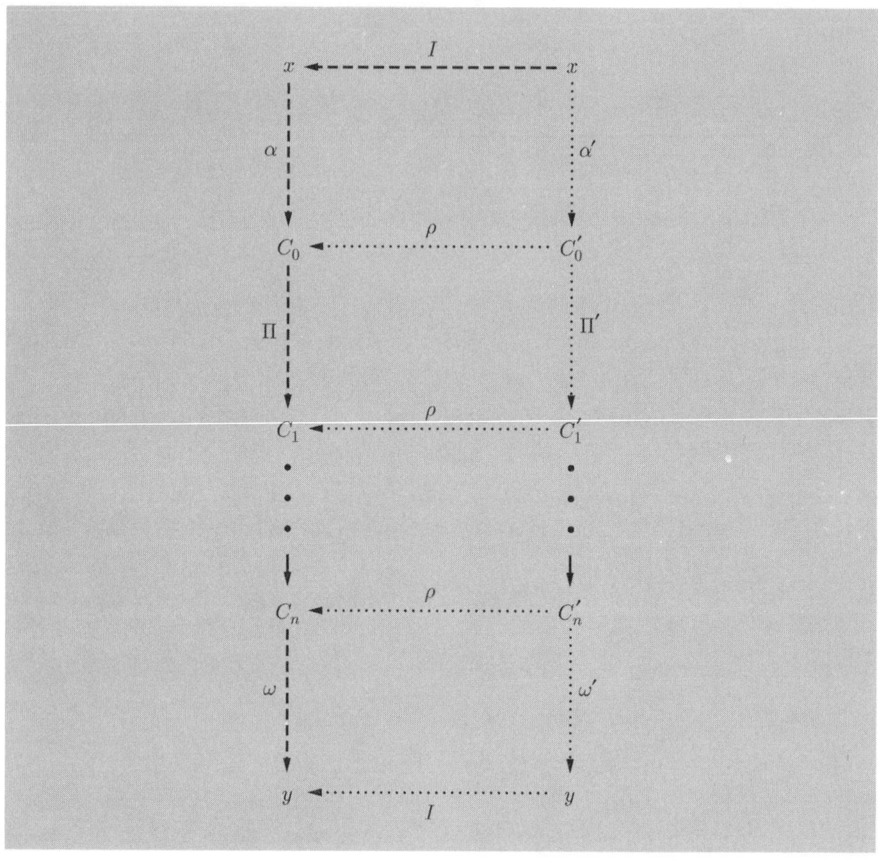

FIGURE 3.7: A commutative diagram demonstrating the simulation of an entire history: $(\exists C_0, \ldots, C_n)[x\ I\ x\ \alpha\ C_0\ \Pi\ C_1 \cdots C_n\ \omega\ y] \iff (\exists C_0', \ldots, C_n')[x\ \alpha'\ C_0'\ \Pi'\ C_1' \cdots C_n'\ \omega'\ y\ I\ y]$.

so P' and P have the same transfer relation. Thus equations (3.1–3.3) suffice to prove that P' is equivalent to P. We summarize this result:

THEOREM 3.2. *If P' simulates P in lockstep, then P and P' have the same transfer relation.*

Let us return to Example 3.1 and formally verify that it is a lockstep simulation. The relation of representation is given by

$$(q, x, 1^i)\ \rho\ (q, x, i).$$

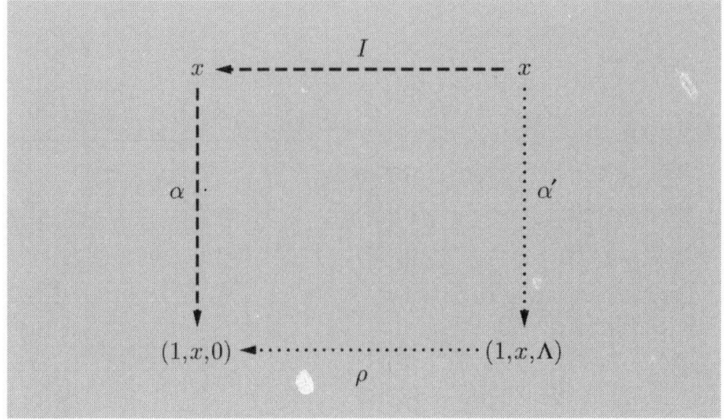

FIGURE 3.8: The simulation of α in Example 3.1.

Observe that ρ is a one-one, onto function; this will simplify the verification of equations (3.1–3.3).

Equation (3.1) requires that $\alpha = \alpha' \circ \rho$. For all x we have $x\alpha = (1, x, 0)$ and $x\alpha' = (1, x, \Lambda) = (1, x, 1^0)$. Therefore

$$x\alpha'\rho = (1, x, 1^0)\rho = (1, x, 0) = x\alpha.$$

Because that equality is true for every x, $\alpha'\rho = \alpha$, as required. This equality is diagrammed in Figure 3.8.

Equation (3.2) requires that $\rho \circ \Pi = \Pi' \circ \rho$. Let

$$\begin{aligned}
\pi_1 &= (1 \rightarrow 1, \text{SCAN}\,\texttt{a}, \text{INC}) \\
\pi_1' &= (1 \rightarrow 1, \text{SCAN}\,\texttt{a}, \text{PUSH}\,\texttt{1}) \\
\pi_2 &= (1 \rightarrow 2, \text{SCAN}\,\texttt{b}, \text{DEC}) \\
\pi_2' &= (1 \rightarrow 2, \text{SCAN}\,\texttt{b}, \text{POP}\,\texttt{1}) \\
\pi_3 &= (2 \rightarrow 2, \text{SCAN}\,\texttt{b}, \text{DEC}) \\
\pi_3' &= (2 \rightarrow 2, \text{SCAN}\,\texttt{b}, \text{POP}\,\texttt{1}),
\end{aligned}$$

so we have $\mathcal{I} = \{\pi_1, \pi_2, \pi_3\}$ and $\mathcal{I}' = \{\pi_1', \pi_2', \pi_3'\}$. We assert that $\rho\pi_1 = \pi_1'\rho$, $\rho\pi_2 = \pi_2'\rho$, and $\rho\pi_3 = \pi_3'\rho$. (We say that the instruction π_1'

simulates the instruction π_1, etc.) From this assertion it follows that

$$\begin{aligned} \rho\Pi &= \rho(\pi_1 \cup \pi_2 \cup \pi_3) &=& \rho\pi_1 \cup \rho\pi_2 \cup \rho\pi_3 \\ &= \pi_1'\rho \cup \pi_2'\rho \cup \pi_3'\rho &=& (\pi_1' \cup \pi_2' \cup \pi_3')\rho &=& \Pi'\rho, \end{aligned}$$

as desired. It remains to prove the assertion that $\rho\pi_i = \pi_i'\rho$ for $i = 1, 2, 3$. We prove it for π_1, but we leave π_2 and π_3 as exercises.

Consider any configuration $C' = (q, x, 1^i)$ of P'. Then $C'\rho = (q, x, i)$, so

$$C'\rho\pi_1 = \begin{cases} (1, y, i+1) & \text{if } q = 1 \text{ and } x \text{ has the form } ya, \\ \text{undefined} & \text{otherwise.} \end{cases}$$

On the other hand,

$$C'\pi_1' = \begin{cases} (1, y, 1^{i+1}) & \text{if } q = 1 \text{ and } x \text{ has the form } ya, \\ \text{undefined} & \text{otherwise,} \end{cases}$$

so

$$C'\pi_1'\rho = \begin{cases} (1, y, i+1) & \text{if } q = 1 \text{ and } x \text{ has the form } ya, \\ \text{undefined} & \text{otherwise.} \end{cases}$$

Therefore

$$C'\rho\pi_1 = C'\pi_1'\rho.$$

Because that equation is true for all configurations C', $\rho\pi_1 = \pi_1'\rho$, as required. This equality is diagrammed in Figure 3.9.

Equation (3.3) requires that $\rho \circ \omega = \omega'$. Let $C' = (q, x, 1^i)$ be any configuration of P'. Then $C'\rho = (q, x, i)$, so

$$C'\rho\omega = \begin{cases} \text{ACCEPT} & \text{if } q = 2,\ x = \Lambda, \text{ and } i = 0, \\ \text{undefined} & \text{otherwise.} \end{cases}$$

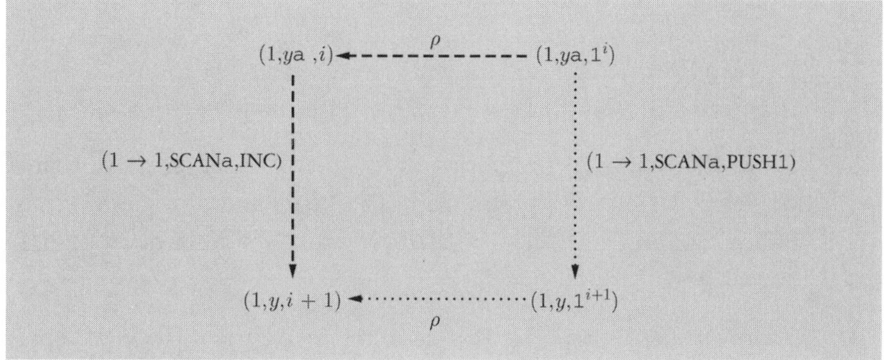

FIGURE 3.9: The simulation of π_1 in Example 3.1.

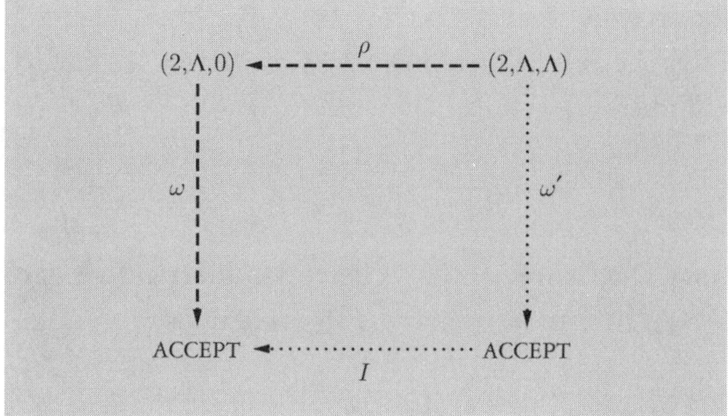

FIGURE 3.10: The simulation of ω in Example 3.1.

On the other hand,

$$C'\omega' = \begin{cases} \text{ACCEPT} & \text{if } q = 2, x = \Lambda, \text{and } i = 0, \\ \text{undefined} & \text{otherwise,} \end{cases}$$

so $C'\rho\omega = C'\omega'$. Because that equality is true for every configuration C', $\rho\omega = \omega'$, as required. This equality is diagrammed in Figure 3.10.

Exercises

3.2-1 Refer to Example 3.1 and its continuation after Theorem 3.2. Prove that $\rho\pi_2 = \pi'_2\rho$ and $\rho\pi_3 = \pi'_3\rho$.

3.2-2 Prove that lockstep simulation is transitive. That is, prove that if program A simulates program B in lockstep and program B simulates program C in lockstep, then program A simulates program C in lockstep.

Solution: Let A simulate B in lockstep using the relation of representation ρ_{AB}. Let B simulate C in lockstep using the relation of representation ρ_{BC}. Define $\rho_{AC} = \rho_{AB} \circ \rho_{BC}$. We will prove that A simulates C in lockstep using the relation of representation ρ_{AC}. Let α_P, Π_P, ω_P denote the initializer, sequel relation, and terminator of P, respectively.

(i) By the definition of lockstep simulation, we have $\alpha_A\rho_{AB} = \alpha_B$ and $\alpha_B\rho_{BC} = \alpha_C$. Therefore,

$$\alpha_A\rho_{AC} = \alpha_A\rho_{AB}\rho_{BC} = \alpha_B\rho_{BC} = \alpha_C.$$

(ii) By the definition of lockstep simulation, we have $\Pi_A\rho_{AB} = \rho_{AB}\Pi_B$ and $\Pi_B\rho_{BC} = \rho_{BC}\Pi_C$. Therefore,

$$\begin{aligned} \Pi_A\rho_{AC} &= \Pi_A\rho_{AB}\rho_{BC} \\ &= \rho_{AB}\Pi_B\rho_{BC} = \rho_{AB}\rho_{BC}\Pi_C = \rho_{AC}\Pi_C. \end{aligned}$$

(iii) By the definition of lockstep simulation, we have $\omega_A = \rho_{AB}\omega_B$ and $\omega_B = \rho_{BC}\omega_C$. Therefore,

$$\omega_A = \rho_{AB}\omega_B = \rho_{AB}\rho_{BC}\omega_C = \rho_{AC}\omega_C.$$

Thus we have proved the three conditions of lockstep simulation.

3.2.1 One Control Simulates Two Controls (Pairing Construction)

Let us present a simple example using the lockstep simulation framework developed in the preceding section. We show that one control can simulate two controls, in a sense that we will explain. For example, a machine [control, input] can simulate a machine [control, control, input].

We say that a collection of devices $d'_1, \ldots, d'_{k'}$ can *simulate* a collection of devices $d_1, \ldots, d_k$, if a machine $[d'_1, \ldots, d'_{k'}$, other] can simulate a machine $[d_1, \ldots, d_k$, other], for every choice of the device "other." A seemingly stronger but equivalent definition of device simulation allows a choice of more than one other device instead of just one (see Exercise 3.2-4).

Let M be a machine [Con1, Con2, other], where Con1 and Con2 are controls and "other" is any device. Given a program P for M, we want to write a program P' for a machine [control, other] that simulates P. Before writing a program, it is important to decide how the data are represented.[3] P' will hold in its control an ordered pair consisting of the state of Con1 and the state of Con2. The control set of P' will be the set of all such ordered pairs, i.e., the Cartesian product of the realms of Con1 and Con2. To be precise, assume that Q_1 is the realm of Con1 and Q_2 is the realm of Con2. Then we let the control set of P' be $Q_1 \times Q_2$. It should be clear how P' can hold the states of Con1 and Con2 in its single control and thus mimic the behavior of P.[4] In order to have a formal proof, it remains for us to write the program P' explicitly, state the relation of representation, and verify that equations (3.1–3.3) are satisfied.

Before writing the program P', we specify the relation of representation formally:

$$((a, b), s) \ \rho \ (a, b, s),$$

where a is any state of Con1, b is any state of Con2, and s is any state of the other device.

This relation of representation ρ is a one-one, onto function. Thus every configuration of M' corresponds to a unique configuration of M, and vice versa. This is not the only way to obtain lockstep simulations, but it is among the easiest. We proceed to write the program P' and prove that it simulates P.

---

[3] Would you want to buy software written by someone who disagrees with this principle?

[4] This kind of construction is called a pairing construction because the control states of the simulating machine are ordered pairs of control states of the simulated machines.

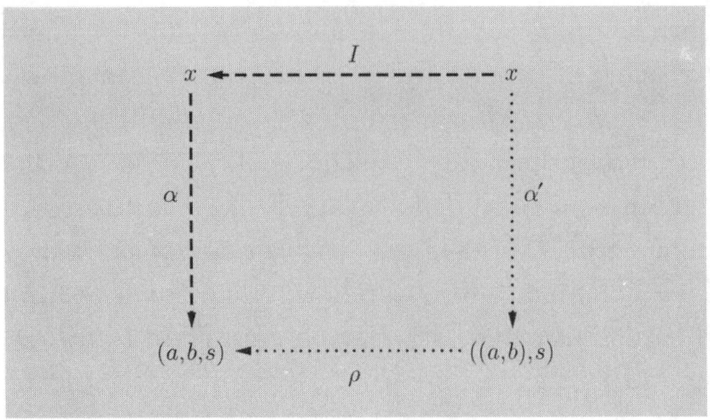

FIGURE 3.11: Simulating two controls with one (α).

First, if (a, b, s) is the initial configuration of P on argument x, we let $((a, b), s)$ be the initial configuration of P' on argument x. In the language of relations, this means $\alpha' = \alpha \circ \rho^{-1}$. Then $\alpha' \circ \rho = \alpha \circ \rho^{-1} \circ \rho$. Since ρ is a one-one, onto function, $\rho^{-1} \circ \rho = I$, so we have

$$\alpha = \alpha' \circ \rho,$$

i.e., condition (3.1) is satisfied (Figure 3.11).

Second, we convert an instruction of P that operates on two controls into an instruction of P' that operates in a corresponding way on the components of an ordered pair. For each instruction $\pi = (a_1 \rightarrow a_2,\ b_1 \rightarrow b_2,\ f)$ in P, where f is an operation on the other device, we let P' contain the instruction $\pi' = ((a_1, b_1) \rightarrow (a_2, b_2),\ f)$. Inspection of Figure 3.12 shows that

$$\rho \circ \pi = \pi' \circ \rho$$

for each instruction π in P. Therefore, $\rho \circ \Pi = \Pi' \circ \rho$, so (3.2) is satisfied.

Finally, for each final configuration (a, b, s) of P such that $(a, b, s)\ \omega\ y$ for some result y, we let $((a, b), s)$ be a final configuration of P' such that $((a, b), s)\ \omega'\ y$. In terms of relations, this means

$$\omega' = \rho \circ \omega,$$

so (3.3) is satisfied (Figure 3.13).

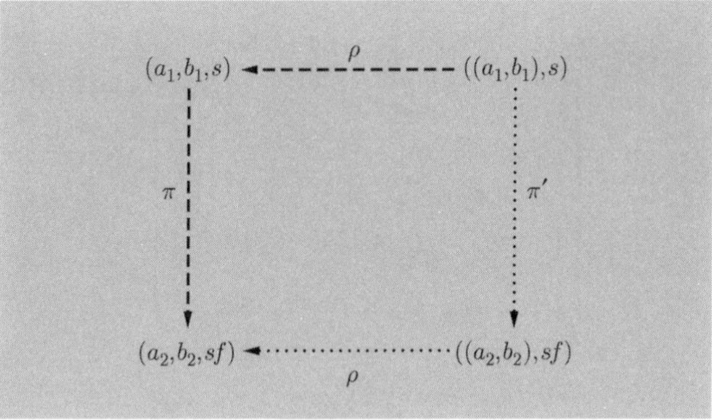

FIGURE 3.12: Simulating two controls with one (π).

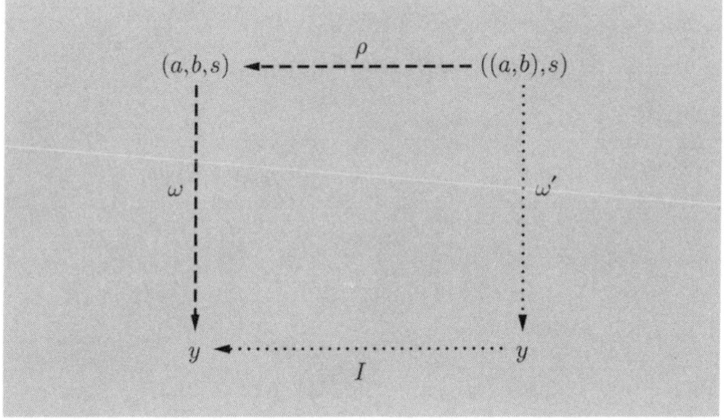

FIGURE 3.13: Simulating two controls with one (ω).

EXAMPLE 3.3. Let us design a DFA that accepts the set of strings over $\{\mathtt{a}, \mathtt{b}\}$ that contain an even number of a's and an odd number of b's. We begin by writing a program for a machine [control, control, input] that accepts that language. The first control will keep track of the number of a's mod 2, and the second control will keep track of the number of b's mod 2. Both controls are initialized to 0. The first control accepts in state 0, and the second control accepts in state 1. The instruction set is

$$\left\{\begin{array}{l}(0 \rightarrow 1\ ,\ \text{NOOP}\ ,\ \text{SCAN}\mathtt{a}),\\(1 \rightarrow 0\ ,\ \text{NOOP}\ ,\ \text{SCAN}\mathtt{a}),\\(\text{NOOP}\ ,\ 0 \rightarrow 1\ ,\ \text{SCAN}\mathtt{b}),\\(\text{NOOP}\ ,\ 1 \rightarrow 0\ ,\ \text{SCAN}\mathtt{b})\end{array}\right\}.$$

Before merging controls, we need to replace each NOOP by the pair of operations $0 \rightarrow 0$ and $1 \rightarrow 1$. The resulting program, called P, is shown in the left column of Table 3.1; an equivalent program, called P', for a machine [control, input] is shown in the right column. The DFA P' is diagrammed in Figure 3.14. ■■■

Instruction of P	*Instruction of P′*
$(0 \rightarrow 1\ ,\ 0 \rightarrow 0\ ,\ \text{SCAN}\mathtt{a})$	$((0,0) \rightarrow (1,0)\ ,\ \text{SCAN}\mathtt{a})$
$(0 \rightarrow 1\ ,\ 1 \rightarrow 1\ ,\ \text{SCAN}\mathtt{a})$	$((0,1) \rightarrow (1,1)\ ,\ \text{SCAN}\mathtt{a})$
$(1 \rightarrow 0\ ,\ 0 \rightarrow 0\ ,\ \text{SCAN}\mathtt{a})$	$((1,0) \rightarrow (0,0)\ ,\ \text{SCAN}\mathtt{a})$
$(1 \rightarrow 0\ ,\ 1 \rightarrow 1\ ,\ \text{SCAN}\mathtt{a})$	$((1,1) \rightarrow (0,1)\ ,\ \text{SCAN}\mathtt{a})$
$(0 \rightarrow 0\ ,\ 0 \rightarrow 1\ ,\ \text{SCAN}\mathtt{b})$	$((0,0) \rightarrow (0,1)\ ,\ \text{SCAN}\mathtt{b})$
$(1 \rightarrow 1\ ,\ 0 \rightarrow 1\ ,\ \text{SCAN}\mathtt{b})$	$((1,0) \rightarrow (1,1)\ ,\ \text{SCAN}\mathtt{b})$
$(0 \rightarrow 0\ ,\ 1 \rightarrow 0\ ,\ \text{SCAN}\mathtt{b})$	$((0,1) \rightarrow (0,0)\ ,\ \text{SCAN}\mathtt{b})$
$(1 \rightarrow 1\ ,\ 1 \rightarrow 0\ ,\ \text{SCAN}\mathtt{b})$	$((1,1) \rightarrow (1,0)\ ,\ \text{SCAN}\mathtt{b})$

TABLE 3.1: An example of merging two controls. The DFA P' simulates the program P. The initial control state of P' is $(0,0)$; the accepting control state of P' is $(0,1)$.

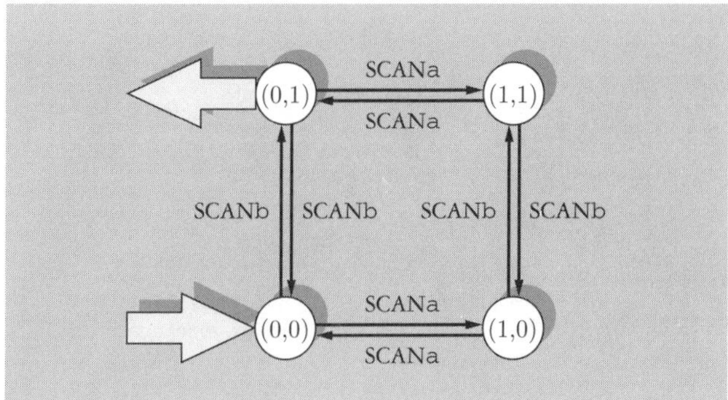

FIGURE 3.14: The result of merging two controls. P' is a DFA that accepts the set of all strings over {a,b} with an even number of a's and an odd number of b's.

By the same techniques, we can merge any number of controls.

EXAMPLE 3.4. Consider the program for a machine [control, control, control, input] shown in Figure 3.2.1, which accepts those strings over $\{a, b, c\}$ in which the first input character other than an a is equal to the last input character other than an a. The first control stores the program's location, the second control stores the first non-a in the input, and the third control stores the last non-a in the input. The second and third controls both have the realm $\{\Lambda, b, c\}$. They are both initialized to Λ. The first control accepts in state 3, the second and third controls accept in all states, and the input accepts when empty.

We can combine the three controls into a single control using the techniques developed in this section. We replace NOOP's on the second and third controls by three operations: $\Lambda \rightarrow \Lambda$, $b \rightarrow b$, and $c \rightarrow c$. Then we combine states of the three controls into ordered triples. The resulting program P' runs on a machine [control, input]. The program is given in Table 3.2. ∎∎∎

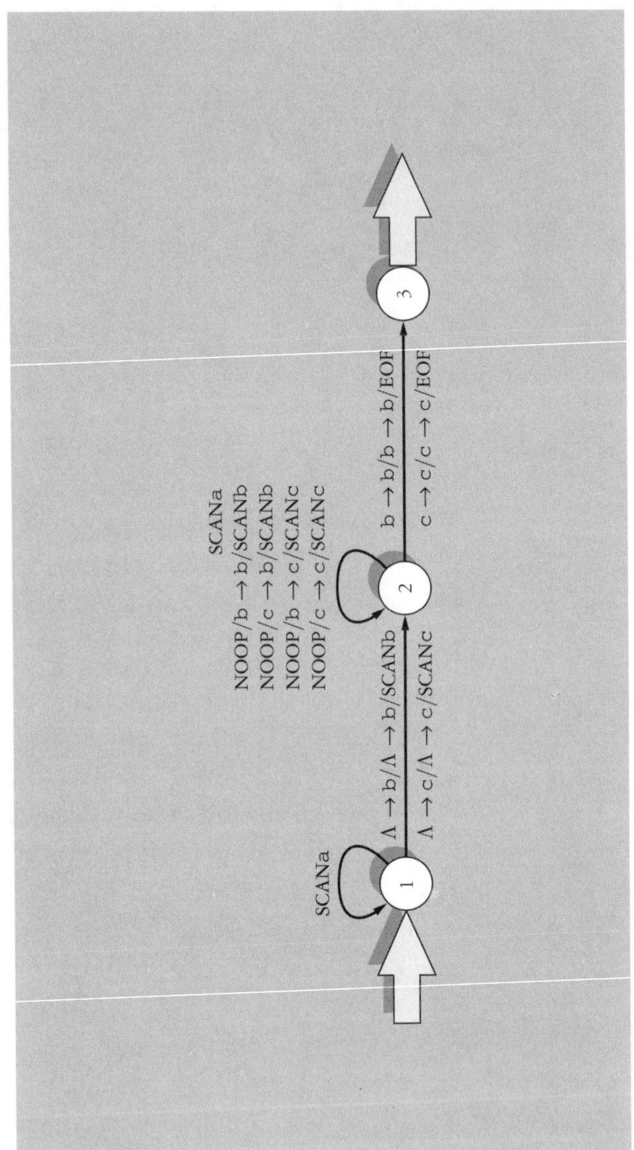

FIGURE 3.15: A program with three controls that accepts all strings over {a,b,c} in which the first non-a is equal to the last non-a.

Instruction of P	*Instruction of P′*
$(1 \to 1\ ,\ \Lambda \to \Lambda\ ,\ \Lambda \to \Lambda\ ,\ \text{SCAN}\,\mathtt{a})$	$((1,\Lambda,\Lambda) \to (1,\Lambda,\Lambda)\ ,\ \text{SCAN}\,\mathtt{a})$
$(1 \to 2\ ,\ \Lambda \to \mathtt{b}\ ,\ \Lambda \to \mathtt{b}\ ,\ \text{SCAN}\,\mathtt{b})$	$((1,\Lambda,\Lambda) \to (2,\mathtt{b},\mathtt{b})\ ,\ \text{SCAN}\,\mathtt{b})$
$(1 \to 2\ ,\ \Lambda \to \mathtt{c}\ ,\ \Lambda \to \mathtt{c}\ ,\ \text{SCAN}\,\mathtt{c})$	$((1,\Lambda,\Lambda) \to (2,\mathtt{c},\mathtt{c})\ ,\ \text{SCAN}\,\mathtt{c})$
$(2 \to 2\ ,\ \mathtt{b} \to \mathtt{b}\ ,\ \mathtt{b} \to \mathtt{b}\ ,\ \text{SCAN}\,\mathtt{a})$	$((2,\mathtt{b},\mathtt{b}) \to (2,\mathtt{b},\mathtt{b})\ ,\ \text{SCAN}\,\mathtt{a})$
$(2 \to 2\ ,\ \mathtt{b} \to \mathtt{b}\ ,\ \mathtt{c} \to \mathtt{c}\ ,\ \text{SCAN}\,\mathtt{a})$	$((2,\mathtt{b},\mathtt{c}) \to (2,\mathtt{b},\mathtt{c})\ ,\ \text{SCAN}\,\mathtt{a})$
$(2 \to 2\ ,\ \mathtt{c} \to \mathtt{c}\ ,\ \mathtt{b} \to \mathtt{b}\ ,\ \text{SCAN}\,\mathtt{a})$	$((2,\mathtt{c},\mathtt{b}) \to (2,\mathtt{c},\mathtt{b})\ ,\ \text{SCAN}\,\mathtt{a})$
$(2 \to 2\ ,\ \mathtt{c} \to \mathtt{c}\ ,\ \mathtt{c} \to \mathtt{c}\ ,\ \text{SCAN}\,\mathtt{a})$	$((2,\mathtt{c},\mathtt{c}) \to (2,\mathtt{c},\mathtt{c})\ ,\ \text{SCAN}\,\mathtt{a})$
$(2 \to 2\ ,\ \mathtt{b} \to \mathtt{b}\ ,\ \mathtt{b} \to \mathtt{b}\ ,\ \text{SCAN}\,\mathtt{b})$	$((2,\mathtt{b},\mathtt{b}) \to (2,\mathtt{b},\mathtt{b})\ ,\ \text{SCAN}\,\mathtt{b})$
$(2 \to 2\ ,\ \mathtt{b} \to \mathtt{b}\ ,\ \mathtt{c} \to \mathtt{b}\ ,\ \text{SCAN}\,\mathtt{b})$	$((2,\mathtt{b},\mathtt{c}) \to (2,\mathtt{b},\mathtt{b})\ ,\ \text{SCAN}\,\mathtt{b})$
$(2 \to 2\ ,\ \mathtt{c} \to \mathtt{c}\ ,\ \mathtt{b} \to \mathtt{b}\ ,\ \text{SCAN}\,\mathtt{b})$	$((2,\mathtt{c},\mathtt{b}) \to (2,\mathtt{c},\mathtt{b})\ ,\ \text{SCAN}\,\mathtt{b})$
$(2 \to 2\ ,\ \mathtt{c} \to \mathtt{c}\ ,\ \mathtt{c} \to \mathtt{b}\ ,\ \text{SCAN}\,\mathtt{b})$	$((2,\mathtt{c},\mathtt{c}) \to (2,\mathtt{c},\mathtt{b})\ ,\ \text{SCAN}\,\mathtt{b})$
$(2 \to 2\ ,\ \mathtt{b} \to \mathtt{b}\ ,\ \mathtt{b} \to \mathtt{c}\ ,\ \text{SCAN}\,\mathtt{c})$	$((2,\mathtt{b},\mathtt{b}) \to (2,\mathtt{b},\mathtt{c})\ ,\ \text{SCAN}\,\mathtt{c})$
$(2 \to 2\ ,\ \mathtt{b} \to \mathtt{b}\ ,\ \mathtt{c} \to \mathtt{c}\ ,\ \text{SCAN}\,\mathtt{c})$	$((2,\mathtt{b},\mathtt{c}) \to (2,\mathtt{b},\mathtt{c})\ ,\ \text{SCAN}\,\mathtt{c})$
$(2 \to 2\ ,\ \mathtt{c} \to \mathtt{c}\ ,\ \mathtt{b} \to \mathtt{c}\ ,\ \text{SCAN}\,\mathtt{c})$	$((2,\mathtt{c},\mathtt{b}) \to (2,\mathtt{c},\mathtt{c})\ ,\ \text{SCAN}\,\mathtt{c})$
$(2 \to 2\ ,\ \mathtt{c} \to \mathtt{c}\ ,\ \mathtt{c} \to \mathtt{c}\ ,\ \text{SCAN}\,\mathtt{c})$	$((2,\mathtt{c},\mathtt{c}) \to (2,\mathtt{c},\mathtt{c})\ ,\ \text{SCAN}\,\mathtt{c})$
$(2 \to 3\ ,\ \mathtt{b} \to \mathtt{b}\ ,\ \mathtt{b} \to \mathtt{b}\ ,\ \text{EOF})$	$((2,\mathtt{b},\mathtt{b}) \to (3,\mathtt{b},\mathtt{b})\ ,\ \text{EOF})$
$(2 \to 3\ ,\ \mathtt{c} \to \mathtt{c}\ ,\ \mathtt{c} \to \mathtt{c}\ ,\ \text{EOF})$	$((2,\mathtt{c},\mathtt{c}) \to (3,\mathtt{c},\mathtt{c})\ ,\ \text{EOF})$

TABLE 3.2: An example of merging three controls. The DFA P' simulates the program P. The initial control state of P' is $(1, \Lambda, \Lambda)$. We have omitted instructions that go from unreachable control states. The accepting control states of P' are (3,b,b), (3,b,c), (3,c,b), and (3,c,c). Note that only two of the accepting control states are reachable: (3,b,b) and (3,c,c).

Exercises

3.2-3 (a) Prove that a machine [control, input, stack] where the stack has a one-character alphabet can simulate a machine [control, input, unsigned counter].

(b) Prove that a machine [control, input, unsigned counter] can simulate a machine [control, input, stack] where the stack has a one-character alphabet.

3.2-4 In this exercise we consider extending the definition of simulating a collection of devices to allow a list of more than one "other" device. Say that one collection of devices $d'_1, \ldots, d'_{k'}$ *simulates a collection of devices* $d_1, \ldots, d_k$ if every machine $[d'_1, \ldots, d'_{k'}, e_1, \ldots, e_j]$ simulates a machine $[d_1, \ldots, d_k, e_1, \ldots, e_j]$. Although this definition may seem more restrictive than the one in the text, prove that they are in fact equivalent. Your proof should apply to any kind of simulation, not just lockstep.

3.3 SIMULATION VIA SUBPROGRAMS

In the previous examples, each step of program P was simulated by executing one step of program P'. Usually, however, some steps of P will be simulated by several steps of P'. To keep the proofs of simulation simple, we try to partition the program P' into subprograms where each step of P is simulated by executing a subprogram of P'.

EXAMPLE 3.5. In Figure 3.16, we present a DCA P that accepts the set of all nonempty strings over $\{\mathtt{a}, \mathtt{b}\}$ in which every nonempty prefix contains more a's than b's. In Figure 3.17, we present another DCA P' that accepts the same language. (Both counters are unsigned.) The configuration (q, x, n) in P is represented by the same configuration in P'. The instructions $(1 \rightarrow 2, \text{SCAN}\,\mathtt{a}, \text{INC})$, $(2 \rightarrow 2, \text{SCAN}\,\mathtt{a}, \text{INC})$, and $(2 \rightarrow 3, \text{SCAN}\,\mathtt{b}, \text{DEC})$ in P are simulated by the same instructions in P'. The instruction $(3 \rightarrow 2, \text{NOOP}, \text{NONZERO})$ is simulated by a *pair* of instructions—$(3 \rightarrow \nu, \text{NOOP}, \text{DEC})$ and $(\nu \rightarrow 3, \text{NOOP}, \text{INC})$—in P'. We call that pair of instructions a subprogram. Why does the simulation work?

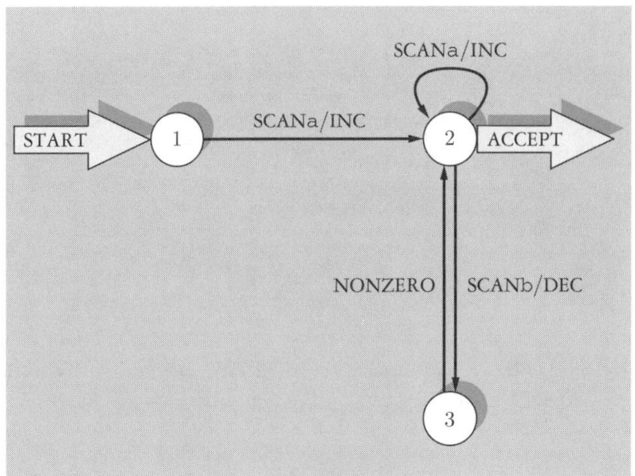

FIGURE 3.16: A DCA that accepts the set of all strings in $\{a,b\}^+$ such that every nonempty prefix contains more a's than b's.

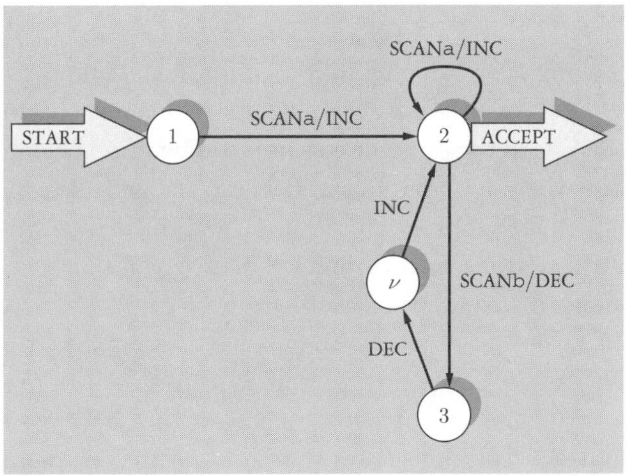

FIGURE 3.17: A DCA without the NONZERO test that accepts the set of all strings in $\{a,b\}^+$ such that every nonempty prefix contains more a's than b's.

The DEC operation can be performed exactly when the counter value is positive, and the subsequent INC restores the counter to its previous value. This simulation will be discussed in greater generality and formality in Section 3.3.1.

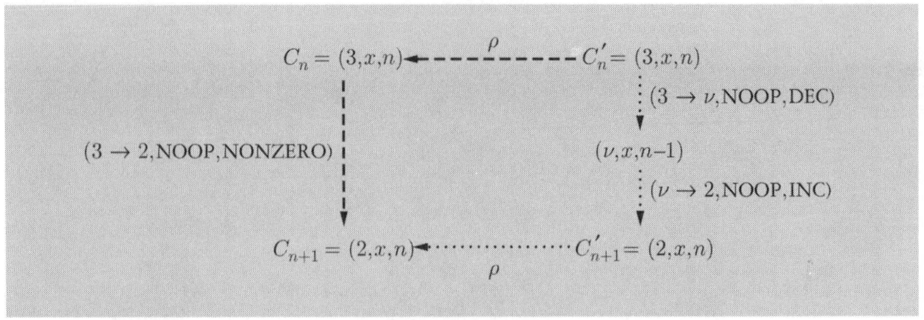

FIGURE 3.18: A commutative diagram for simulating the instruction $(3 \to 2, \text{NOOP}, \text{NONZERO})$ by a subprogram.

The simulation of the instruction $(3 \to 2, \text{NOOP}, \text{NONZERO})$ is shown in a commutative diagram in Figure 3.18. ■ ■ ■

When proving simulation by subprograms, it is useful to preserve in P' the control states Q of program P, while introducing a set N of new control states as needed, as in the preceding example. The states belonging to Q (Q states) indicate where subprograms in P' begin and end. Reaching a Q state marks the end of one subprogram execution and the beginning of the next. The sequence of Q states reached in a simulating computation is the same as in the simulated computation.

We identify the subprograms themselves as sets of instructions. We say that an instruction *uses* a control state if it goes to or from that control state. Two instructions *meet* at a control state if they both use that control state. If two instructions meet at a state ν in N, they belong to the same subprogram. (The Greek letter ν is pronounced "new.") The subprograms can be determined graphically by drawing the state digraph for P' and cutting it at the Q states. This cuts the digraph into three kinds of pieces: The piece that starts at the initial state of P' and ends at a Q state is called the *initial subprogram*; a piece that starts and ends at Q states is called an *ordinary subprogram*; a piece that starts at a Q state and ends at a final state of P' is called a *final subprogram*. If the initial state of P' is a Q state, then the initial subprogram contains no instructions and is called *trivial*. If a final state of P' is a Q state, then its final subprogram contains no instructions and is called *trivial*.

A *computation* of a subprogram is an executable sequence of instructions of that subprogram, beginning at an initial state of P' or a Q state and ending at a Q state or a final state of P'. The transfer relation σ'_S of a subprogram S is the relation between configurations at the beginning and end of such a computation. We write σ'_{init} to denote the transfer relation of the initial subprogram. The relation $\sigma' = \bigcup_{S \text{ is an ordinary subprogram}} \sigma'_S$ gives the effect of executing any single ordinary subprogram. The relation $\sigma'_{\text{final}} = \bigcup_{S \text{ is a final subprogram}} \sigma'_S$ gives the effect of executing any single final subprogram. A complete computation of P' can be cut into a sequence of subprogram computations, so informally we may treat subprograms as if they were single instructions.

The three conditions of lockstep simulation translate readily into the framework of simulation by subprograms. They become

$$\alpha = \alpha' \circ \sigma'_{\text{init}} \circ \rho \tag{3.1*}$$

$$\rho \circ \Pi = \sigma' \circ \rho \tag{3.2*}$$

$$\rho \circ \omega = \sigma'_{\text{final}} \circ \omega'. \tag{3.3*}$$

The first condition indicates that the initializer of P is simulated by the initializer of P' followed by its initial subprogram. The second condition indicates that each instruction of P is simulated by a single subprogram of P'. The third condition indicates that the terminator of P is simulated by a final subprogram of P' followed by its terminator.

By a simple induction, as in the preceding section, these three conditions imply that

$$\tau = \alpha \circ \Pi^* \circ \omega = \alpha' \circ \sigma'_{\text{init}} \circ (\sigma')^* \circ \sigma'_{\text{final}} \circ \omega'.$$

It remains only to show that

$$\alpha' \circ \sigma'_{\text{init}} \circ (\sigma')^* \circ \sigma'_{\text{final}} \circ \omega' = \tau'.$$

Clearly σ'_{init}, σ', and σ'_{final} are contained in $(\Pi')^*$, so $\sigma'_{\text{init}} \circ (\sigma')^* \circ \sigma'_{\text{final}} \subseteq (\Pi')^*$, and therefore

$$\alpha' \circ \sigma'_{\text{init}} \circ (\sigma')^* \circ \sigma'_{\text{final}} \circ \omega' \subseteq \alpha' \circ (\Pi')^* \circ \omega' = \tau'.$$

For the reverse containment, suppose that $(x, y) \in \alpha' \circ (\Pi')^* \circ \omega'$. Then there is a computation mapping x to y. That computation can be broken, at the Q states, into a computation of the initial subprogram, followed by some computations of the ordinary subprograms, and finally a computation of the final subprogram; therefore, $(x, y) \in \alpha' \circ \sigma'_{\text{init}} \circ (\sigma')^* \circ \sigma'_{\text{final}} \circ \omega'$. Therefore,

$$\alpha' \circ (\Pi')^* \circ \omega' \subseteq \alpha' \circ \sigma'_{\text{init}} \circ (\sigma')^* \circ \sigma'_{\text{final}} \circ \omega',$$

completing the proof that

$$\tau' = \alpha' \circ (\Pi')^* \circ \omega' = \alpha' \circ \sigma'_{\text{init}} \circ (\sigma')^* \circ \sigma'_{\text{final}} \circ \omega'.$$

We will define ρ so that every configuration of M is represented by a configuration of M'; i.e., ρ will be an onto function. Furthermore, every configuration of M' with a control state in Q will represent a unique configuration of M with the same control state.

When proving simulation by subprograms, the instructions on the right side of a single box in the commutative diagram are limited to a single subprogram. Figure 3.19 diagrams the simulation of the initializer α by α' and the initial subprogram. We must show that the rectangle in that figure can be traversed left and then down if and only if it can be traversed down

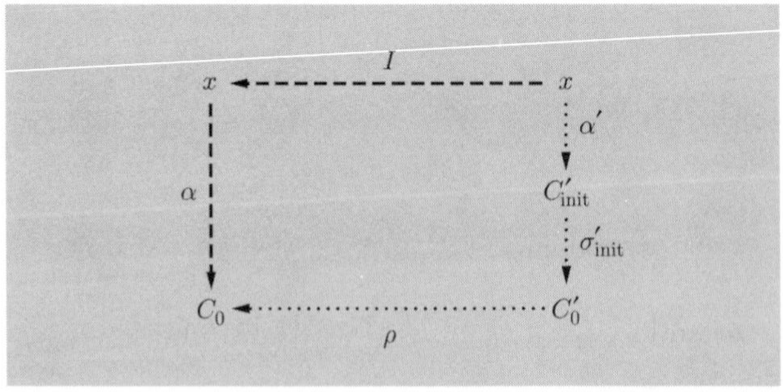

FIGURE 3.19: Showing that $\alpha = \alpha' \circ \sigma'_{\text{init}} \circ \rho$.

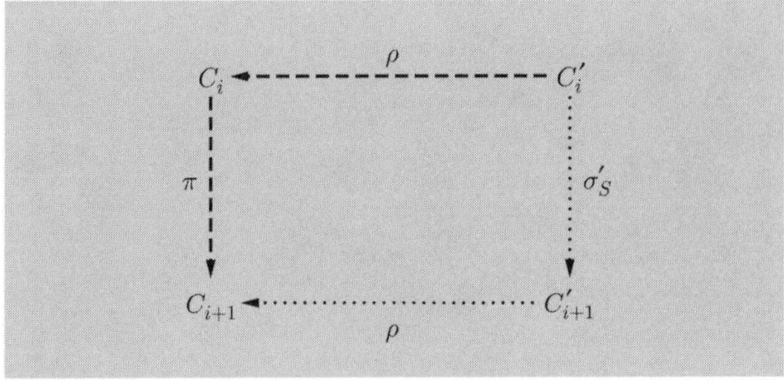

FIGURE 3.20: Showing that $\rho \circ \pi = \sigma'_S \circ \rho$.

and then left. That is, we show that $x \overset{\alpha}{\mapsto} C_0$ if and only if

$$x \overset{\alpha'}{\longmapsto} C'_{\text{init}} \overset{\sigma'_{\text{init}}}{\longmapsto} C'_0$$

and C'_0 represents C_0. In many simulations, e.g., Example 3.5, the initial state of P' will be a Q state and σ'_{init} will be a trivial subprogram; then $\sigma'_{\text{init}} = I_{\{C'_0\}}$, so the simulation of α is no different from lockstep simulation.

Figure 3.20 diagrams the simulation of an instruction π by an ordinary subprogram S. We must show that the rectangle in that figure can be traversed left and then down if and only if it can be traversed down and then left. That is, we show that if C'_i represents C_i and $C_i \overset{\pi}{\mapsto} C_{i+1}$, then there exists C'_{i+1} such that

$$C'_i \overset{\sigma'_S}{\longmapsto} C'_{i+1}$$

and C'_{i+1} represents C_{i+1}; conversely, if

$$C'_i \overset{\sigma'_S}{\longmapsto} C'_{i+1}$$

and C'_{i+1} represents C_{i+1} then there exists a configuration C_i such that C'_i represents C_i and

$$C_i \overset{\pi}{\mapsto} C_{i+1}.$$

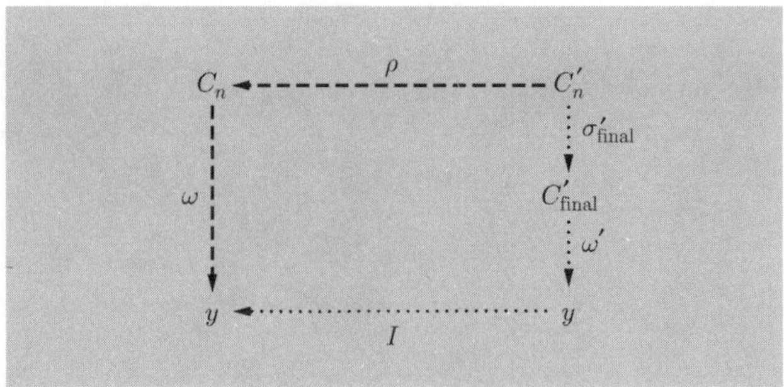

FIGURE 3.21: Showing that $\rho \circ \omega = \sigma'_{\text{final}} \circ \omega'$.

Figure 3.21 diagrams the simulation of the terminator ω by a final subprogram and ω'. We must show that the rectangle in that figure can be traversed left and then down if and only if it can be traversed down and then left. That is, we show that if C'_n represents a configuration C_n such that $C_n \overset{\omega}{\mapsto} y$, then there exists C'_{final} such that $C'_n \xmapsto{\sigma'_{\text{final}}} C'_{\text{final}} \overset{\omega'}{\mapsto} y$; conversely if $C'_n \xmapsto{\sigma'_{\text{final}}} C'_{\text{final}} \overset{\omega'}{\mapsto} y$, then there exists C_n such that C'_n represents C_n and $C_n \overset{\omega}{\mapsto} y$. (Although σ'_{final} is the union of several programs, exactly one of them corresponds to each final state of P.) In many simulations, e.g., Example 3.5, the final states of P' will be Q states and each final subprogram will be a trivial subprogram; then σ'_{final} is the identity function on final configurations, so the simulation of ω is no different from lockstep simulation.

Simulation via subprograms is a very useful technique: It will enable us to standardize programs in Section 3.4 and to classify machines according to their computing power in later chapters.

3.3.1 Eliminating the NONZERO Test from an Unsigned Counter

In this section we will show that an unsigned counter that does not use the NONZERO operation can simulate an unsigned counter that does use the NONZERO operation. This generalizes Example 3.5. In this simulation, as in many simulations via subprograms, each subprogram will simulate exactly one instruction, and each instruction will be simulated by exactly one subprogram; i.e., there will be a one-one correspondence between subprograms and instructions. For that reason, each subprogram will have exactly one initial control state and exactly one final control state, which correspond to the simulated instruction's origin and destination. (A contrast will be seen in Sections 3.4.1 and 6.5, where a single subprogram will simulate several instructions.) In addition, the initializer and terminator will be simulated by trivial subprograms.

Let M be a machine [control, unsigned counter, input] in which the counter's repertory is $\{\text{INC}, \text{DEC}, \text{ZERO}, \text{NONZERO}\}$. Let M' be a machine [control, unsigned counter, input] in which the counter's repertory is $\{\text{INC}, \text{DEC}, \text{ZERO}\}$; i.e., the counter in M' cannot perform the NONZERO test. Obviously M is at least as powerful as M', because every program for M' is also a program for M. We wish to show that M' is at least as powerful as M.

Let P be any program for M. We want to find a program P' for M' such that the transfer relations τ and τ' are the same. We can simulate the NONZERO operation by performing a DEC, which ensures that the counter value is positive, followed by an INC, which changes the counter value back to what it was before it was decremented. Another way to see this is because NONZERO $=$ DEC $\circ$ INC, i.e.,

$$n+1 \xmapsto{\text{NONZERO}} n+1 \iff n+1 \xmapsto{\text{DEC}} n \xmapsto{\text{INC}} n+1.$$

We will produce P' from P by replacing each instruction of P that uses the NONZERO operation by a pair of instructions in P'; the first of these instructions uses the DEC operation, and the second uses the INC operation.

Let $Q' = Q \uplus N$, where N is a set of new control states, let $\alpha' = \alpha$, and let $\omega' = \omega$. (Recall that $A \uplus B$ denotes the union of sets A and B that are guaranteed to be disjoint.) For each instruction π of P that does not use the NONZERO operation, let P' contain the same instruction π, so that π is simulated by the single-instruction subprogram $\{\pi\}$.

In addition, P may contain some instructions π of the form $(q_1 \to q_2, \text{NONZERO}, f)$, where f is an arbitrary input operation (Figure 3.22). In this case, let P' contain instead the pair of instructions $\pi'_1 = (q_1 \to \nu, \text{DEC}, f)$ and $\pi'_2 = (\nu \to q_2, \text{INC}, \text{NOOP})$, where $\nu \in N$ (as shown in Figure 3.23). The instruction π is simulated by the subprogram $\{\pi'_1, \pi'_2\}$. (Note that we need one new control state ν in P' for each occurrence of the NONZERO operation in P. We do not reuse the same state ν in

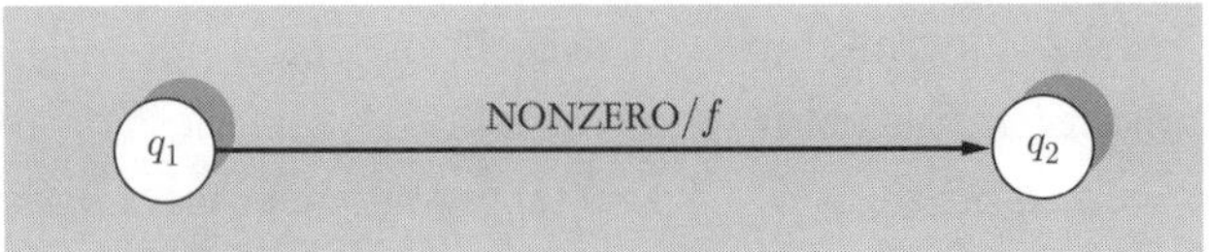

FIGURE 3.22: An instruction that uses the NONZERO operation.

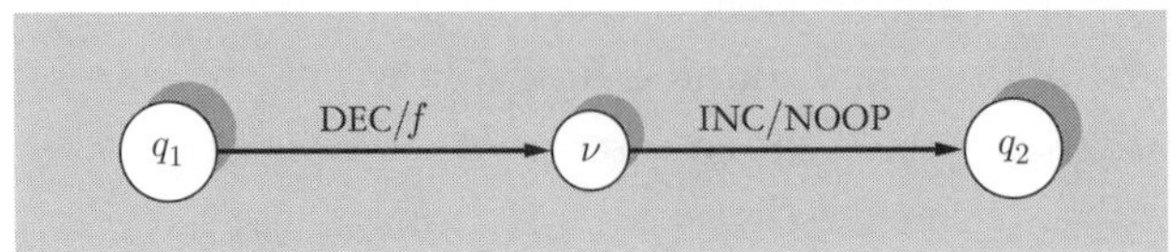

FIGURE 3.23: Simulating the NONZERO operation by a subprogram.

simulating each instruction that uses NONZERO. This is usually clear from context, but if there is a chance of confusion, the new state can be called ν_π to distinguish it from the new states used in simulating other instructions.)

If in a history of P we have $C_1 \overset{\pi}{\mapsto} C_2$, where π does not use the NONZERO operation, then in the corresponding history of P' we also have $C_1 \overset{\pi}{\mapsto} C_2$, because π is simulated by the single-instruction subprogram $\{\pi\}$. On the other hand, suppose that in a history of P we have $(q_1, n, x) \overset{\pi}{\mapsto} (q_2, n, xf)$, where π uses the NONZERO operation. Then $n \geq 1$. In the corresponding history of P' we have

$$(q_1, n, x) \overset{\pi_1'}{\longmapsto} (\nu, n-1, xf) \overset{\pi_2'}{\longmapsto} (q_2, n, xf).$$

Because state ν is used only in these two instructions and is not an initial or final state, the two instructions can only be used together, and their composition is $\pi_1' \circ \pi_2' = \pi$, so P' has no histories that do not correspond to histories of P.

In this example, the closely related configurations are those with control states in Q; the configurations are in fact identical. Configurations of P' with control states in N do not correspond to configurations of P. In this example, P and P' have the same initializer and terminator. In general, however, it is not necessary for corresponding configurations in a simulation to be identical, nor for the initializers and terminators to be the same.

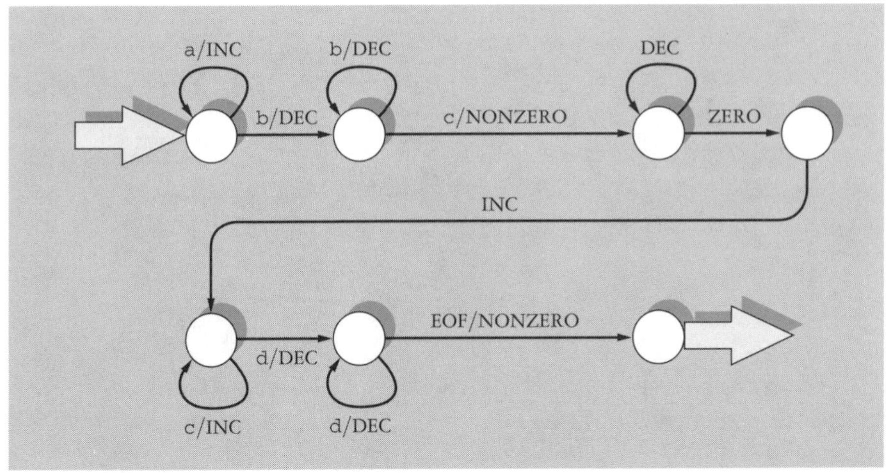

FIGURE 3.24: A UCA that accepts all strings of the form $\mathtt{a}^i\mathtt{b}^j\mathtt{c}^k\mathtt{d}^\ell$, where $i > j$ and $k > \ell$. All counter states are accepting.

Until we prove their equivalence, we will want to distinguish between signed and unsigned counters. In this section and Section 3.3.2 we will use the acronyms UCA and SCA to denote acceptors running on a machine [control, input, unsigned counter] and a machine [control, input, signed counter], respectively.

EXAMPLE 3.6. The UCA in Figure 3.24 accepts strings of the form $\mathtt{a}^i\mathtt{b}^j\mathtt{c}^k\mathtt{d}^\ell$, where $i > j$ and $k > \ell$. All states of the counter are accepting states. In Figure 3.25 we present an equivalent UCA that does not use the NONZERO operation. ■ ■ ■

Exercises

3.3-1 Define a relation on instructions as follows: π_1 *is related to* π_2 if π_1 and π_2 meet at a state belonging to N.

(a) Prove that "is related to" is symmetric.

(b) Let $\sim$ be the reflective, transitive closure of "is related to." Prove that $\sim$ is an equivalence relation.

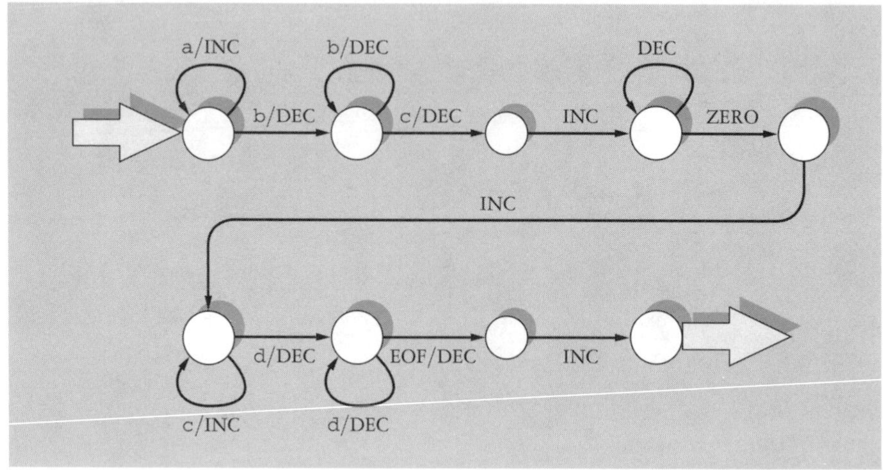

FIGURE 3.25: A UCA without the NONZERO test that accepts strings of the form $a^i b^j c^k d^\ell$, where $i > j$ and $k > \ell$.

(c) Prove that, in general, the subprograms of P' are exactly the equivalence classes of $\sim$.

(d) Prove that each state in N belongs to exactly one subprogram.

3.3-2 (a) Would it be correct to simulate the UCM instruction $(q_1 \rightarrow q_2, \text{NONZERO}, f)$ by the following subprogram?

$$\left\{\begin{matrix} (q_1 \rightarrow \nu\ , & \text{DEC}\ , & \text{NOOP}), \\ (\nu \rightarrow q_2\ , & \text{INC}\ , & f \qquad) \end{matrix}\right\}$$

(b) What disadvantage does this simulation have?

Solution: It does not preserve determinism.

3.3.2 An Unsigned Counter Simulates a Signed Counter

As another simple example, we show how any program for a machine with a signed counter can be simulated by a program for a machine with an unsigned counter and an extra control. (If desired, we can merge controls using the techniques of Section 3.2.1.) When the signed counter holds an integer n, the unsigned counter simulating it will hold $|n|$ and the extra control will hold the sign of n. When the sign is positive, we simulate INC by incrementing $|n|$ and we simulate DEC by decrementing $|n|$. However, when the sign is negative, we simulate INC by decrementing $|n|$ and we simulate DEC by incrementing $|n|$. As in Section 3.3.1, the initializer and terminator will be simulated by trivial subprograms.

Let M be a machine [control, signed counter, other], where the realm of M's control is Q. Let M' be a machine [control, sign, unsigned counter, other] where the control has realm $Q' = Q \uplus N$ for some set N of new states that we will specify shortly, and where the sign is a control device with two states denoted "+" and "−". By the preceding section's simulation, we may assume without loss of generality that the unsigned counter of M' is equipped with the operation NONZERO. We will use the sign to distinguish positive numbers from negative numbers. The initial and final control states of subprograms of P' will be the elements of Q, and the internal control states will be the elements of N. The representation relation ρ is given below for $n \geq 0$, $q \in Q$, and s any state of the "other" device:

$$\begin{aligned}(q, +, n, s) \quad &\rho \quad (q, n, s),\\ (q, -, n, s) \quad &\rho \quad (q, -n, s).\end{aligned}$$

Notice that ρ is a partial function from configurations of M' to configurations of M. ρ is not total because M' has more control states than M. ρ is onto, but ρ is not one-one because $(q, +, 0, s)$ and $(q, -, 0, s)$ both represent $(q, 0, s)$.

Each kind of instruction of P is listed in the left column of Table 3.3. The right column lists the instructions of the corresponding subprogram of P', where ν denotes a previously unused control state. (By convention we use different ν's to simulate different instructions unless otherwise specified. For example, the control state ν used for simulating the INC instruction below is meant to be distinct from the control state ν used for simulating the DEC instruction. If there are several INC instructions or several DEC instructions, they all use different new states.) The initial control state for each subprogram below is the origin of the instruction being simulated, and the final control state for each subprogram is the destination of the instruction being simulated.

Instruction of P	*Subprogram of P′*
$(q_1 \to q_2$, INC , $f)$	$(q_1 \to \nu$, NOOP , NOOP , f)
	$(\nu \to q_2$, $+ \to +$, INC , NOOP)
	$(\nu \to q_2$, $- \to -$, DEC , NOOP)
	$(\nu \to \nu$, $- \to +$, ZERO , NOOP)
$(q_1 \to q_2$, DEC , $f)$	$(q_1 \to \nu$, NOOP , NOOP , f)
	$(\nu \to q_2$, $+ \to +$, DEC , NOOP)
	$(\nu \to q_2$, $- \to -$, INC , NOOP)
	$(\nu \to \nu$, $+ \to -$, ZERO , NOOP)
$(q_1 \to q_2$, ZERO , $f)$	$(q_1 \to q_2$, NOOP , ZERO , f)
$(q_1 \to q_2$, POS , $f)$	$(q_1 \to q_2$, $+ \to +$, NONZERO , f)
$(q_1 \to q_2$, NEG , $f)$	$(q_1 \to q_2$, $- \to -$, NONZERO , f)

TABLE 3.3: An unsigned counter simulates a signed counter via subprograms. A generic instruction of the SCM is shown in the first column; a subprogram that simulates it is shown in the second column.

We present one of these subprograms in Figure 3.26; an INC instruction for the signed counter is shown on the left, and the subprogram that simulates it is shown on the right.

On the right side of a commutative diagram we will show a computation of a subprogram that corresponds to a single instruction π of P. The computation of the subprogram may depend on the configuration to which π is applied; we show commutative diagrams for each possible case. We

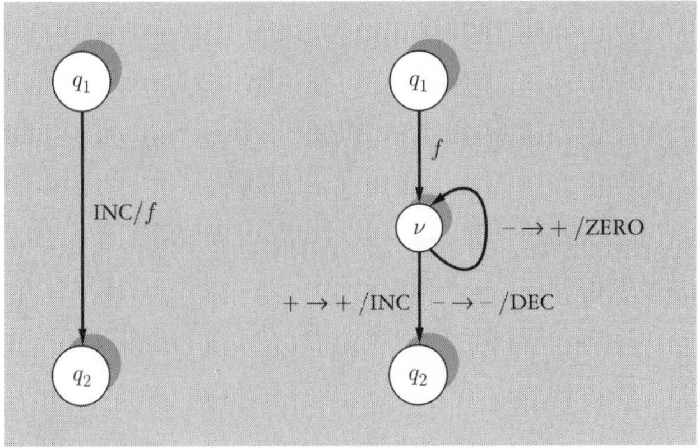

FIGURE 3.26: Simulating an INC instruction by a subprogram.

must also be sure to account for every computation of the subprogram, lest the subprogram do more than intended.

The computation that simulates the ZERO operation is only a single instruction in length, but there are two cases, depending on the value of sign, as shown in Figure 3.27. The computations of subprograms that simulate INC and DEC are two or three instructions long, depending on the values of sign and of the unsigned counter of M'. The three cases of simulating the INC operation, depending on whether the sign and counter of M' are $(+, n)$ where $n \geq 0$, $(-, n)$ where $n > 0$, or $(-, 0)$ are shown in Figure 3.28. It is necessary only to confirm that all the relations shown are satisfied and that there are no other computations of the subprograms.

Similar diagrams, which the reader may construct, apply to the other signed counter operations. We note that this simulation preserves determinism (Exercise 3.3-3).

EXAMPLE 3.7. Consider the SCA shown in Figure 1.12, which accepts those strings over $\{\mathtt{a}, \mathtt{b}\}$ that contain an equal number of a's and b's. By replacing each instruction in P with a UCM subprogram that simulates it, we construct an equivalent UCA (Figure 3.29). ■ ■ ■

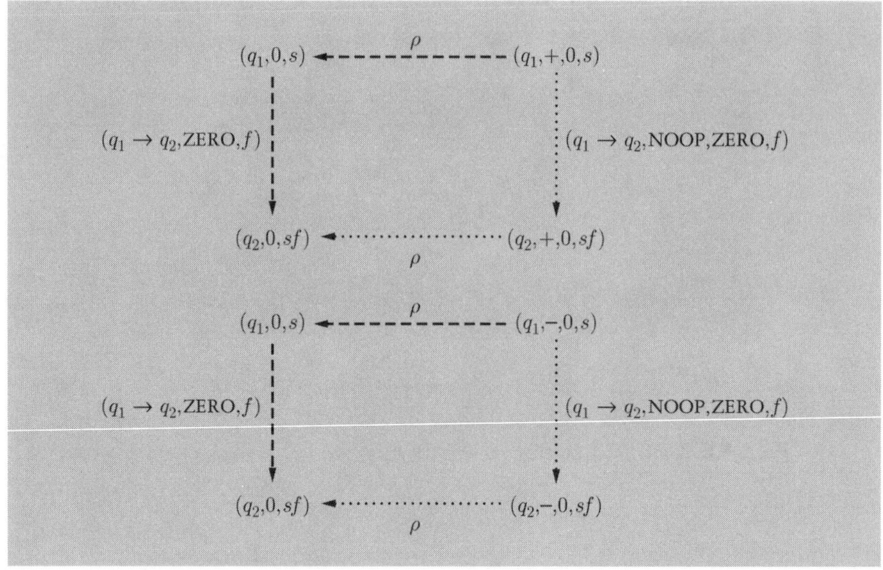

FIGURE 3.27: Simulating the ZERO test of a signed counter.

Exercises

3.3-3 Prove that this section's simulation of a signed counter via an unsigned counter preserves determinism.

3.3-4 Show informally how to simulate a signed counter via an unsigned counter and a control with realm $\{+, -\}$ as in this section but without augmenting Q with any new control states N. Does your simulation preserve determinism?

3.3-5 Show informally how to simulate a signed counter via an unsigned counter and a control with realm $\{+, -\}$ as in this section, using subprograms that take at most two steps to simulate an instruction of P. Your simulation should preserve determinism. In your construction, how many subprograms of P' simulate a single instruction of P?

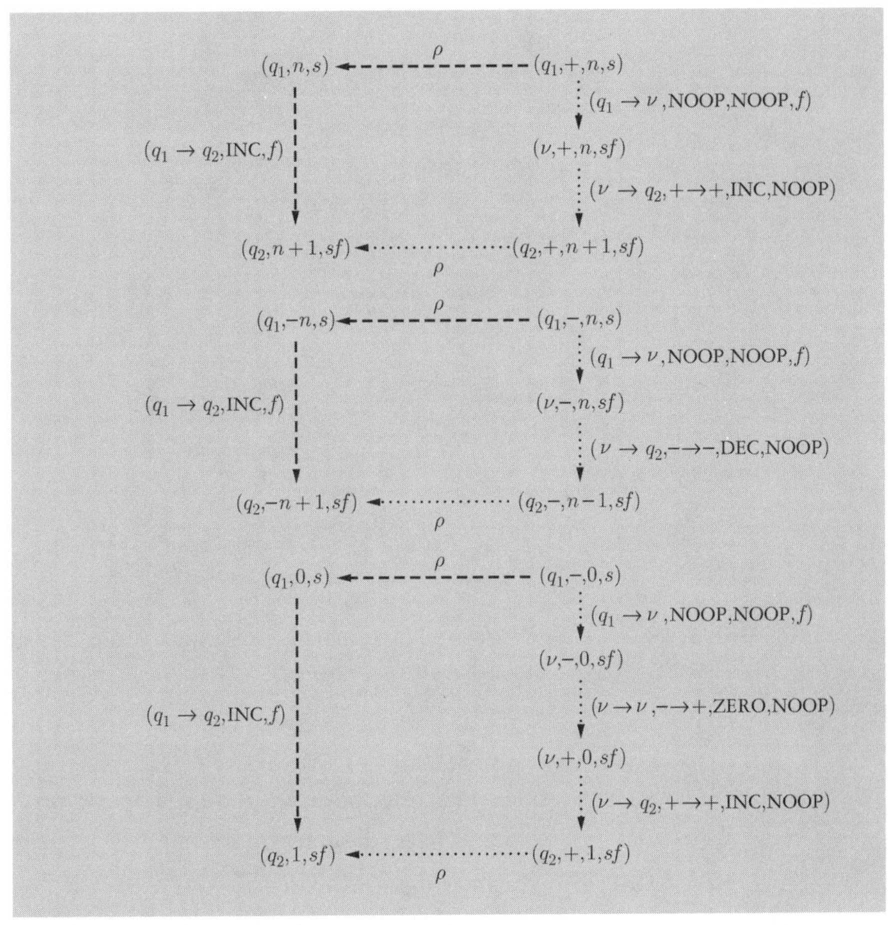

FIGURE 3.28: The three cases of simulating INC.

*3.3-6 Design a simulation of a signed counter by an unsigned counter using a relation of representation that is one-one.

3.3-7 Refer to the simulation of a signed counter by an unsigned counter and a control called "sign," as explained in this section.

(a) Define α' and ω' appropriately. What do we need to prove about those two partial functions? Prove it.

(b) Construct the commutative diagram corresponding to the NEG operation.

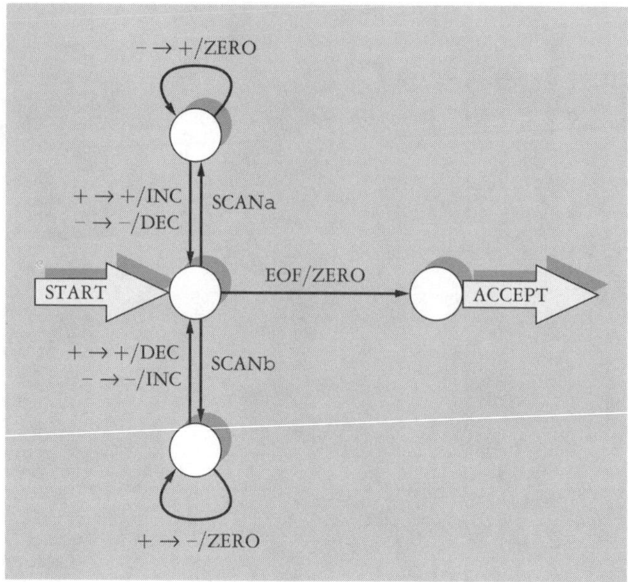

FIGURE 3.29: A UCA that accepts $\{w : w \text{ contains an equal number of a's and b's}\}$. The new states are depicted slightly smaller.

(c) Draw the subprogram corresponding to the DEC operation.

(d) Construct the commutative diagram corresponding to the DEC operation.

3.3-8 Prove that there is a UCA that does not use the NONZERO test which accepts $\{x : \#_a(x) \neq \#_b(x)\}$.

Solution: It is easy to construct an SCA that accepts that language. The SCA can be converted to an equivalent UCA, which can in turn be converted to a UCA that does not use the NONZERO test.

3.3-9 Show how to simulate an unsigned counter by a signed counter.

3.3.3 Eliminating the EMPTY Test from a Stack

In this section we show how any stack machine program can be simulated by a one that does not use the EMPTY test. The construction is simple. If

P is a stack machine program, the simulating program P' will use a new character Z to mark the bottom of the stack. P' will start by pushing a Z onto the stack, P' will simulate the EMPTY test by popping the Z and then pushing it back onto the stack, and P' will finish by popping the Z so that the stack ends up empty. Unlike the previous two sections, this simulation uses nontrivial subprograms to simulate the initializer and terminator.

Let M be a machine [control, stack, other] in which the stack alphabet is Γ and the stack has the usual initializer, terminator, and repertory. Let M' be a machine [control, stack, other] in which the stack alphabet is $\Gamma \cup \{\text{Z}\}$, where Z is a new character, and the stack has the usual initializer, terminator, and repertory except that it is unable to perform the EMPTY test. We wish to show that M' is at least as powerful as M.

The configuration (q, s, v) of P will be represented by the configuration $(q, \text{Z}s, v)$ of P', i.e.,

$$(q, \text{Z}s, v)\ \rho\ (q, s, v).$$

Let P be a program for M. If the initial configuration of P is $(q_{\text{start}}, \Lambda, v)$, let the initial configuration of P' be $(\nu_{\text{start}}, \Lambda, v)$. P's initializer is simulated by the subprogram consisting of the single instruction $(\nu_{\text{start}} \to q_{\text{start}}, \text{PUSHZ}, \text{NOOP})$, as shown below:

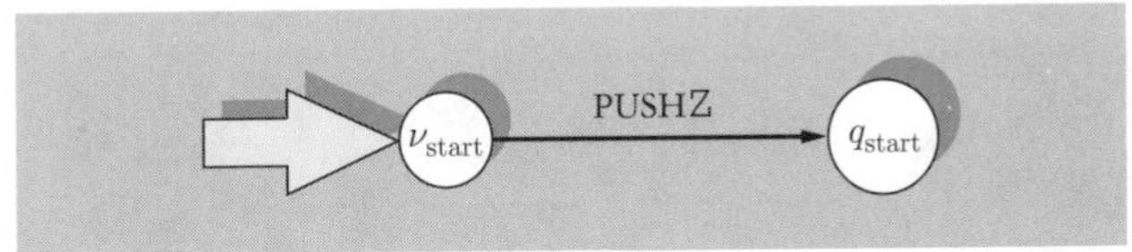

Each instruction of P that does not use the EMPTY test is simulated by the same instruction in P.

Because the character Z can appear only at the bottom of the stack, the instruction $(q \to r, \text{EMPTY}, f)$ in P can be simulated by the pair of instructions $(q \rightarrow \nu, \text{POP}Z, f)$ and $(\nu \rightarrow r, \text{PUSH}Z, \text{NOOP})$ in P', as shown below:

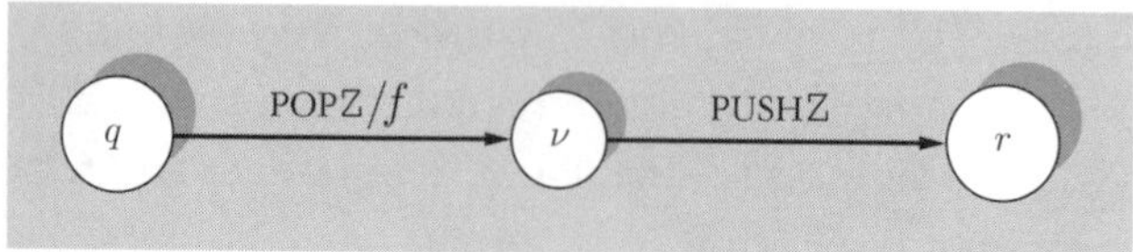

If q_{final} is an accepting (rejecting) state of P, let ν_{final} be a new accepting (rejecting) state in P'. For each such final state, let P' contain a subprogram that consists of the single instruction $(q_{\text{final}} \rightarrow \nu_{\text{final}}, \text{POP}Z, \text{NOOP})$, as shown below:

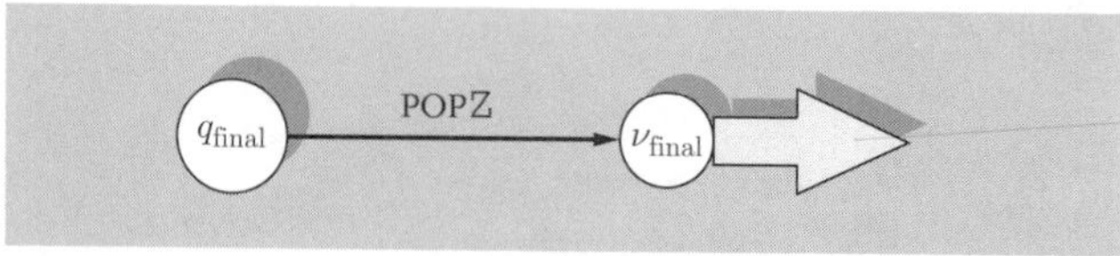

To prove the simulation's correctness we construct commutative diagrams for α, ω, and each kind of stack operation. These are presented in Figures 3.30 through 3.34. In Figure 3.33, we implicitly use the fact that Z can appear only at the bottom of the stack.

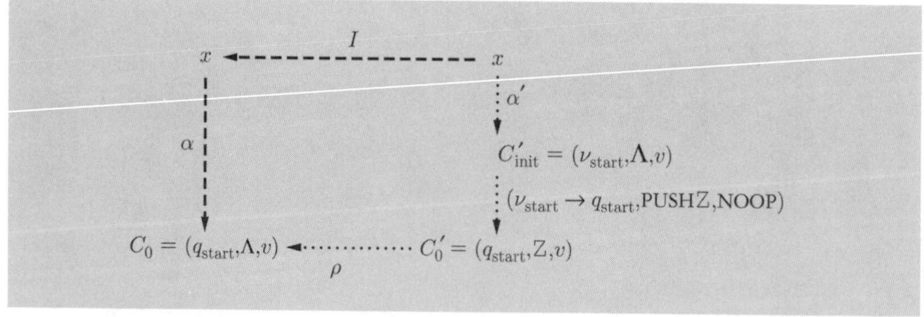

FIGURE 3.30: Eliminating the EMPTY operation from a stack: verifying the simulation of α.

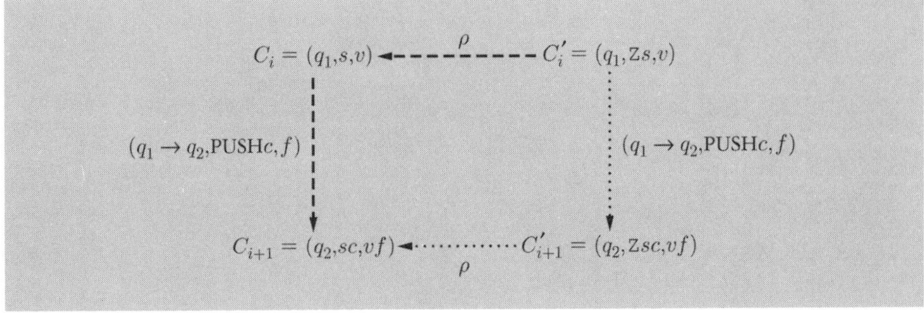

FIGURE 3.31: Eliminating the EMPTY operation from a stack: verifying the simulation of PUSHc.

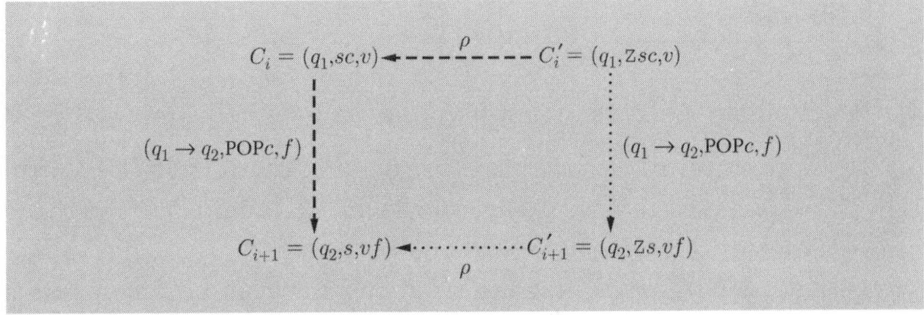

FIGURE 3.32: Eliminating the EMPTY operation from a stack: verifying the simulation of POPc.

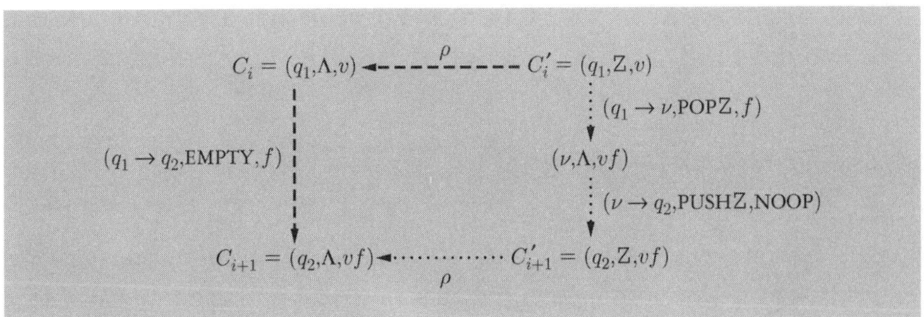

FIGURE 3.33: Eliminating the EMPTY operation from a stack: verifying the simulation of EMPTY.

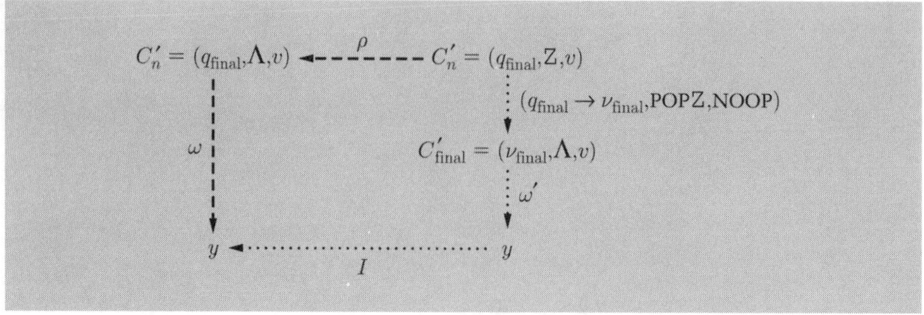

FIGURE 3.34: Eliminating the EMPTY operation from a stack: verifying the simulation of ω.

Exercises

3.3-9 Eliminate the EMPTY test from the program in Figure 1.1.

3.3-10 Since programs can have more than one final control state, Dr. Curtin has proposed that we change the definition of initializers so that a program can have more than one initial control state. Prove that a nondeterministic program for a machine [control, other] with a standard initializer can simulate a nondeterministic program for a machine [control, other] with Dr. Curtin's kind of initializer.

3.3-11 Often it is desirable to put a particular number in one of a RAM's registers. The operation of putting the number n into register a is denoted $R_a := n$. Given a and n, design a subprogram that simulates $R_a := n$ using only standard RAM operations.

3.4 STANDARDIZATION

In this section we present systematic sequences of transformations on programs that put them into increasingly restricted form. Each transformation changes a program into one that simulates it, so a sequence of transformations will yield an equivalent program, i.e., one with the same transfer relation. Usually the transformations preserve or introduce certain desirable properties, such as determinism, absence of blocking, and absence of infinite computations. Programs that have been transformed into a restricted form are said to be *standardized*.

Often we will want to prove that no program for a certain machine can perform a certain task, i.e., have a certain transfer relation. Since standardization preserves transfer relations, we will see that any task that can be performed by a program for a certain machine can, in fact, be performed by a standardized program for the same machine. Therefore, we need only show that no standardized program for the machine can perform the task. Thus, standardizations can illuminate the limitations of a machine type.

We have already seen some standardizations in this chapter. For example, in Section 3.3.1 we showed that every UCM program can be converted to an equivalent UCM program that does not use the NONZERO operation.

3.4.1 Factoring Programs

Proving things about programs is simpler if each instruction does only one thing at a time. It is easy to split each instruction into separate instructions, each of which operates on only one device other than the control. However, doing so in a naive fashion may destroy determinism. Consider the deterministic program fragments in Figure 3.35. If we always perform the input operations first, then the second fragment does not remain deterministic. If we always perform the stack operations first, then the first fragment does not remain deterministic.

In this section we will develop a way to split instructions without destroying determinism. We illustrate the key idea in terms of the input device. Instead of using the SCAN operation to access the next input character, we will store the next character in a look-ahead buffer. This buffer is implemented as an extra control. That way we can see what character is next without actually performing any input operations. Similar ideas apply to outputs, stacks, counters, tapes, and RAMs. We will spend the rest of this section and the next filling in the details of this standardization.

If an instruction operates only on the control and a device d other than the control, then we say that the instruction is *dedicated* to device d. An instruction with control operation $q_1 \rightarrow q_2$ is said to *go* (or be) *from* q_1 *to* q_2. If all instructions that go from control state q are dedicated to the same non-control device d, we say that the control state q is *dedicated* to d. The

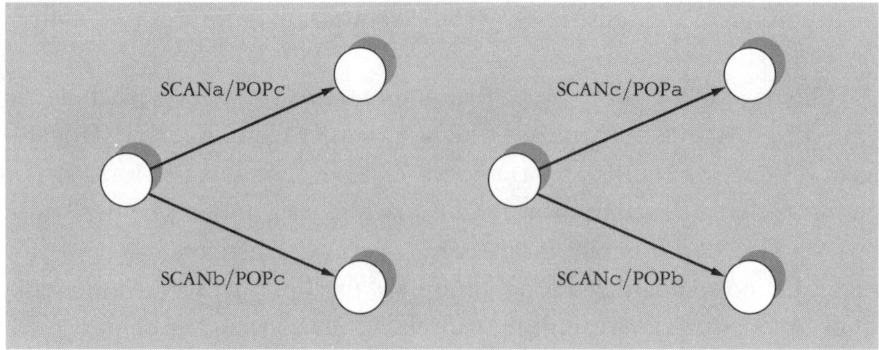

FIGURE 3.35: Two deterministic program fragments. We wish to split each instruction into separate instructions, each of which operates on only one device other than the control. However, if we always perform the input operations first, the second fragment does not remain deterministic. If we always perform the stack operations first, the first fragment does not remain deterministic.

first standardization we present ensures that each control state is dedicated to one device. Such a program is called *factored*.

For each non-control device we define a set of *partitioning tests* that determine which operations are applicable on that device. Some partitioning tests are operations that have already been presented. In addition, we define the tests NEXT$c = I_{c\Sigma *}$ on the input device and TOP$c = I_{\Gamma * c}$ on the stack. The operation NEXTc tests whether the next input character is a c without actually consuming it; the operation TOPc tests whether whether the top stack character is a c without actually popping it. As the name suggests, the partitioning tests on a device are exhaustive and mutually exclusive. The partitioning tests for an input device, a stack, a counter, and an output device are listed in Table 3.4. The partitioning tests for tapes and RAMs are left as Exercises 3.4-4 and 3.4-5.

To factor a program, replace the set of instructions from each control state with a subprogram that uses the partitioning tests to find an applicable instruction and then performs that instruction, one operation at a time. Determinism is preserved; i.e., a deterministic program, when factored, remains deterministic.

Device	*Partitioning Tests*	*Applicable Operations*
Input	NEXTa	NEXTa, SCANa
	NEXTb	NEXTb, SCANb
	EOF	EOF
Stack	TOPa	TOPa, POPa, PUSHa, PUSHb
	TOPb	TOPb, POPb, PUSHa, PUSHb
	EMPTY	EMPTY, PUSHa, PUSHb
Counter	ZERO	ZERO, INC
	NONZERO	DEC, INC
Output	NOOP	WRITEa, WRITEb

TABLE 3.4: Partitioning tests.

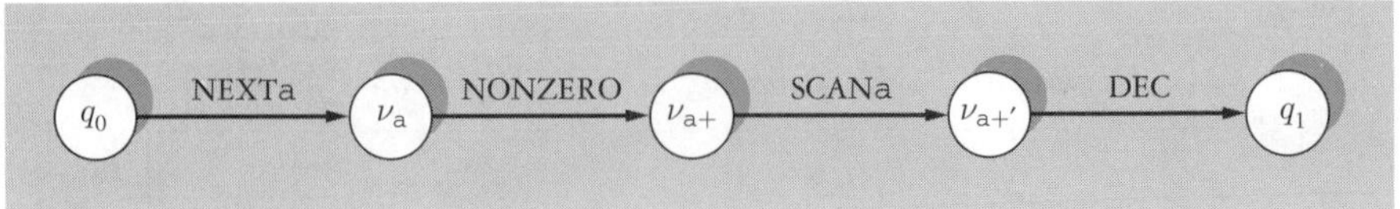

FIGURE 3.36: Factoring $(q_0 \rightarrow q_1, \text{SCAN}\mathtt{a}, \text{DEC})$.

EXAMPLE 3.8. Consider a machine [control, input, unsigned counter]. We factor the instruction $(q_0 \rightarrow q_1, \text{SCAN}\mathtt{a}, \text{DEC})$ into four instructions:

$$\begin{aligned}
&(q_0 \rightarrow \nu_a &&, \text{NEXT}\mathtt{a}, \text{NOOP} &&)\\
&(\nu_a \rightarrow \nu_{a+} &&, \text{NOOP} &&, \text{NONZERO})\\
&(\nu_{a+} \rightarrow \nu_{a+'} &&, \text{SCAN}\mathtt{a}, \text{NOOP} &&)\\
&(\nu_{a+'} \rightarrow q_1 &&, \text{NOOP} &&, \text{DEC} &&)
\end{aligned}$$

These instructions are shown in Figure 3.36. The first two instructions check that SCANa and DEC are both applicable. If so, the last two instructions perform those operations. ■ ■ ■

In general, there may be several instructions going from a single control state. We factor those instructions all together; i.e., the factored instructions share some new states.

EXAMPLE 3.9. Suppose that P contains five instructions that go from q_1, as shown in Figure 3.37. The transformed subprogram in P' is shown in Figure 3.38. Notice that P' is not deterministic, because a choice is possible from control state ν_{b0}. This choice was present in the original program.

Obviously the subprogram in Figure 3.38 can be simplified. The lower third could be simply

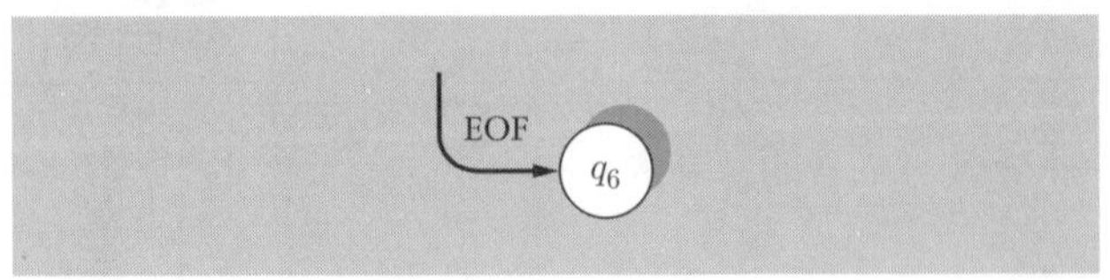

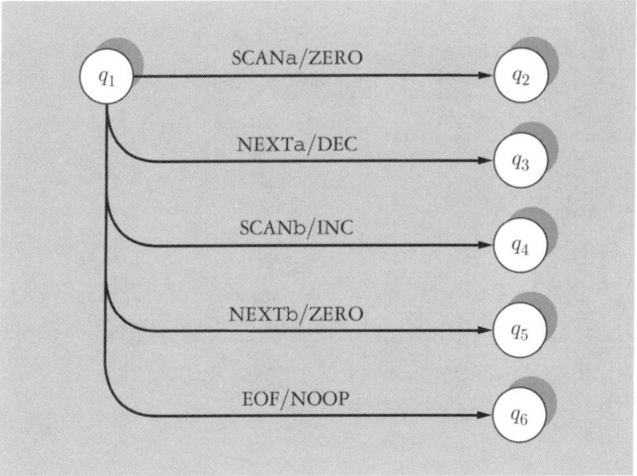

FIGURE 3.37: Before factoring.

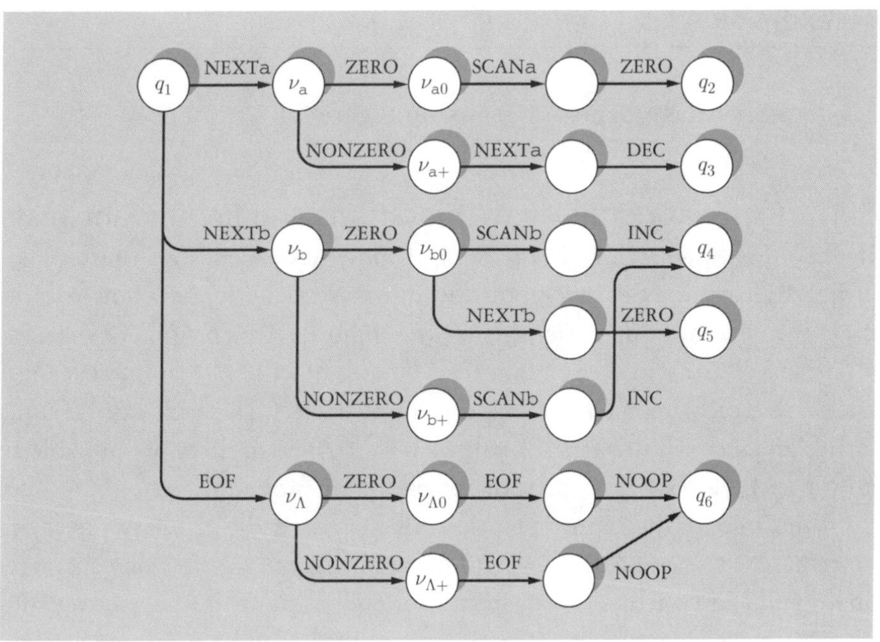

FIGURE 3.38: After factoring the instructions in Figure 3.37.

and the first line could be

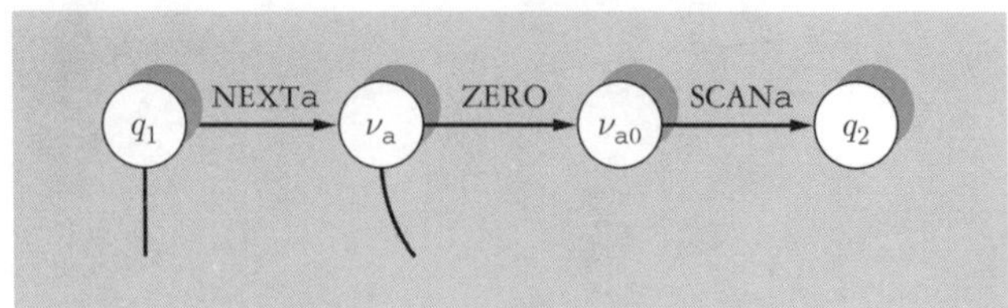

When actually transforming a program into standardized form, common sense indicates simplifying where possible. However, when proving that standardizing transformations are possible, we use the simplest transformation rules rather than trying to produce the simplest programs. ■ ■ ■

The transformation presented in this section—factoring a program—is an example of simulation by subprograms. Proving the simulation's correctness is routine and not interesting enough to include here.

Exercises

3.4-1 Factor the program presented in Figure 1.13.

3.4.2 Eliminating the New Operations and Redundant Tests

In the preceding section we introduced some new operations that are not ordinarily part of a device's repertory. In this section we show how to simulate the new input operations using the input device's original operations while also eliminating redundant tests (i.e., EOF will be performed at most once). We call this *standardizing* the input device. (A stack can be similarly standardized; this is left as an exercise.) As a corollary, we are able to eliminate EOF tests from any nondeterministic program.

We simulate the input operation NEXTc using the ordinary input operations: SCANc and EOF. The simulating program will stay one character ahead and keep track of this character (or end of input) in the control, so it always knows what the "next" input character is. To be precise, we introduce an additional control device, which we call the *buffer*, which can hold Λ, an element of the input alphabet Σ, or a special value z that does not

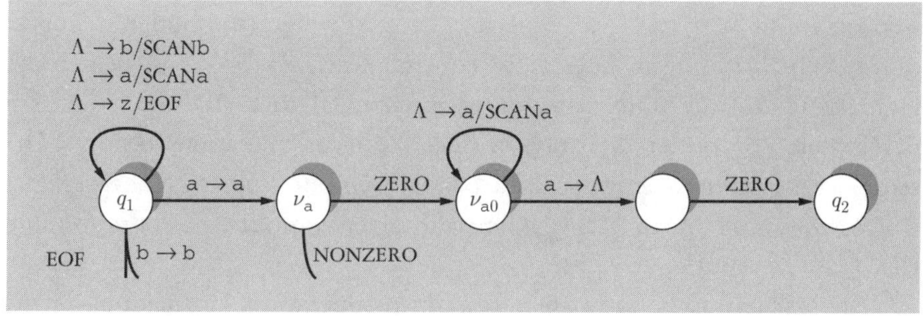

FIGURE 3.39: Standardizing the input in the top line of Figure 3.38.

belong to Σ. Let M be a machine [control, input, other] and let M' be a machine [control, buffer, input, other]. We transform program P (running on M) to P' (running on M'), where P' scans one character ahead of P, saving the look-ahead character in the buffer. If P' detects the end of input, it records that fact by storing $\mathtt{z}$ in the buffer.

The relation of representation ρ is the partial function given by

$$\begin{aligned} (q, c, x, s)\,\rho &= (q, cx, s) \qquad \text{where } c \in \Sigma \text{ or } c = \Lambda, \\ (q, \mathtt{z}, \Lambda, s)\,\rho &= (q, \Lambda, s) \end{aligned}$$

(and $C'\rho$ is undefined for all other configurations C').

The initial and final relations of P' will agree with those of P on the devices that they both have; i.e., $\alpha'_{\text{control}} = \alpha_{\text{control}}$, $\omega'_{\text{control}} = \omega_{\text{control}}$, $\alpha'_{\text{input}} = \alpha_{\text{input}}$, $\omega'_{\text{input}} = \omega_{\text{input}}$, $\alpha'_{\text{other}} = \alpha_{\text{other}}$, and $\omega'_{\text{other}} = \omega_{\text{other}}$. The buffer used by P' must start empty and finish holding the character $\mathtt{z}$ that denotes empty input. The instructions are simulated as in Table 3.5. (Note that the self-loops on Q states may belong to several subprograms.

If P is in factored form, then each instruction of P' will operate on a single device other than the control and the buffer. We can merge the buffer with the control of P', so that P' will also be in factored form. Standardizing the input device in this way also preserves determinism.

We apply this transformation to the top line of Figure 3.38; the result is shown in Figure 3.39.

In a factored program with standardized input, a complete computation on input $x = a_1 \cdots a_n$ consists of a part where the buffer is not z, during which the input operations consist of exactly $|x|$ scans; next there is an EOF, during which the buffer is changed to z; finally, there is a part where the buffer is always z and no input operations occur. The sequence of input operations in a partial computation is some prefix of $\langle\langle \text{SCAN}a_1, \ldots, \text{SCAN}a_n, \text{EOF} \rangle\rangle$. Thus no partial computation contains more than $|x| + 1$ input operations.

An instruction consisting of only a control operation, i.e., having NOOPs on all other devices, is called a *null instruction* (cf. Section 3.4.4). If we can bound the number of instructions dedicated to each device and also bound the number of null instructions, then we can bound the total number of

Instruction of P	*Instructions of P′*
$(q_i \to q_j$, SCANc, NOOP$)$	$(q_i \to q_i$, $\Lambda \to c$, SCANc, NOOP$)$
	$(q_i \to q_j$, $c \to \Lambda$, NOOP, NOOP$)$
$(q_i \to q_j$, NEXTc, NOOP$)$	$(q_i \to q_i$, $\Lambda \to c$, SCANc, NOOP$)$
	$(q_i \to q_j$, $c \to c$, NOOP, NOOP$)$
$(q_i \to q_j$, EOF, NOOP$)$	$(q_i \to q_i$, $\Lambda \to$ z, EOF, NOOP$)$
	$(q_i \to q_j$, z $\to$ z, NOOP, NOOP$)$
$(q_i \to q_j$, NOOP, $f)$	$(q_i \to q_j$, $c \to c$, NOOP, $f)$
	$(q_i \to q_j$, z $\to$ z, NOOP, $f)$
	$(q_i \to q_j$, $\Lambda \to \Lambda$, NOOP, $f)$

TABLE 3.5: Standardizing the input. Here q_i and q_j denote any control states, and c denotes any character in the input alphabet. In effect, each instruction is broken into two parts: One part fills the buffer if necessary, and the second part acts depending on the contents of the nonempty buffer.

instructions in any partial computation. In particular, we will eliminate infinite computations. Although this is not possible for every kind of machine, it is possible for some machines, and standardizing the input is the first step in this direction.

Now we can eliminate the EOF operation entirely from nondeterministic programs, relying instead on the input device's terminator to ensure that the input is exhausted. In a nondeterministic program with standardized input, we replace each occurrence of EOF by NOOP, effectively guessing when the input has been exhausted. Because the program will place a `z` in the buffer, no further scanning will occur, even if the guess is wrong. The input device's terminator will check that the guess is correct.

Eliminating EOF in this way does not preserve determinism; however, specialized techniques work for DFRs (Section 5.4.1), DCRs (Exercise 6.4-9), DSRs (Section 6.4), and DTRs (Exercise 7.2-4).

Exercises

3.4-2 In order to standardize a stack, we must eliminate the TOP operations and also ensure that any two occurrences of EMPTY in a partial computation are separated by at least one PUSH. Show how to perform this standardization. Be sure to preserve factored form.

3.4-3 In the program you produced for Exercise 3.4-1, standardize the input and the stack.

3.4-4 Define partitioning tests for a tape with alphabet {`a`, `b`}, and show how to simulate them using ordinary tape operations.

Solution: In order to know which tape operations are applicable, it is necessary to know the character under the tape head and also whether the head is on the leftmost square. There are four possibilities, which we test for with the following new operations: SEE`a`-ATHOME, SEE`a`-NOT-ATHOME, SEE`b`-ATHOME, and SEE`b`-NOT-ATHOME. SEE*c*-ATHOME is simulated by performing SEE*c* followed by ATHOME. SEE*c*-NOT-ATHOME is simulated by performing SEEc, followed by MOVEL, followed by MOVER.

3.4-5 Define partitioning tests for a RAM, and show how to simulate them using ordinary RAM operations.

3.4-6 Prove that factoring preserves determinism.

3.4-7 Prove that factoring does not introduce infinite computations.

3.4.3 Eliminating Dead States and Unreachable States

Eliminating dead states A control state q is a *live state* in program P if there is a directed path from q to a final control state in the graph of P (regardless of the labels on the edges); q is a *dead state* otherwise. More formally, q is a live state if there is a final control state f and sequence of instructions $\pi^1, \ldots, \pi^k$ in P such that $q\pi^1_{\text{control}} \cdots \pi^k_{\text{control}} = f$. Although there is no general way to determine whether there is a computation fragment that goes from q to a final state (Chapter 7), it is possible to determine whether q is live because liveness depends only on the control operations. We say that liveness is a *syntactic* property because it does not depend on the behavior (semantics) of the program.

If all of a program's control states are dead, then it has no computations; it is equivalent to a program with no instructions and a single dead control state. If a program has at least one live state, our next transformation eliminates all dead states and all instructions going to or from dead states. A valuable side effect is the elimination of some kinds of infinite computations (Section 6.2.2).

Let Q_{final} denote the set of final control states, and let κ be the relation that is the union of all control operations in the program. Thus $q_1\ \kappa\ q_2$ if and only if there is an edge from q_1 to q_2 in the graph of P, and $q_1\ \kappa^*\ q_2$ if and only if there is a directed path from q_1 to q_2 in the graph of P.

Then the set of live control states Q_{live} is $Q_{\text{final}}(\kappa^{-1})^*$. We call an instruction *live* if it goes to a live state, and we denote the set of live instructions $\mathcal{I}_{\text{live}}$. Note that every instruction that goes to a live state must go from a live state as well (Exercise 3.4-9).

Assume that P has at least one live state. We eliminate dead states from P by keeping only the live states and the live instructions, i.e., we let $\alpha' = \alpha$, $\omega' = \omega$, $Q' = Q_{\text{live}}$, and $\mathcal{I}' = \mathcal{I}_{\text{live}}$. Since all control states and

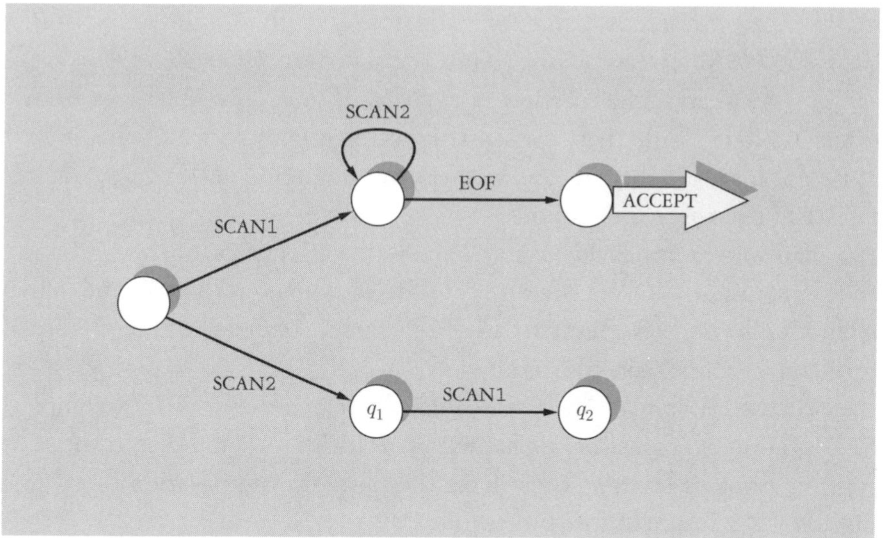

FIGURE 3.40: The control states labeled q_1 and q_2 are dead.

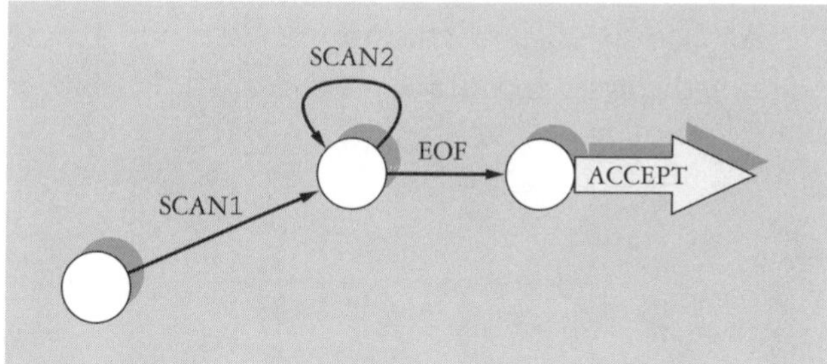

FIGURE 3.41: The dead states in Figure 3.40 have been removed.

instructions that appear in complete computations are live, P' has the same computations as P, so P' has the same transfer relation as P.

EXAMPLE 3.10. Consider the program shown in Figure 3.40, which accepts 12^*. It has two dead states, labeled q_1 and q_2, which we eliminate in Figure 3.41. ■ ■ ■

Eliminating unreachable states A control state q in a program P is a *reachable state* if there is a directed path from q_{start} to q in the graph of P; q is an *unreachable state* otherwise. Thus the set of reachable states is $q_{\text{start}}\kappa^*$.

We say that an instruction is *reachable* if and only if it goes from a reachable state. Note that every instruction that goes from a reachable state must go to a reachable state as well (Exercise 3.4-11). Let $\mathcal{I}_{\text{reachable}}$ denote the set of reachable instructions.

To eliminate unreachable states from P, we let $Q' = q_{\text{start}}\kappa^*$, $\alpha' = \alpha$, and $\mathcal{I}' = \mathcal{I}_{\text{reachable}}$. We obtain ω' by deleting from ω any element that references an unreachable state; i.e., if a control state is eliminated, then it is no longer a final control state.

Because all control states and instructions that appear in a complete computation of P must be reachable, the resulting program P' has the same computations as P, so P' must have the same transfer relation as P. (See Figures 3.44 and 3.45 for an example.)

Because the deletion of instructions cannot create new choices, this standardization preserves determinism.

Technically, we have omitted one important step in eliminating dead states and unreachable states: determining which states are live and which are reachable. An algorithm for determining dead and live states can be based on the graph-theoretic techniques of Section 4.4 (see Exercise 4.4-9).

Exercises

3.4-8 Eliminate dead states from the program depicted in Figure 3.42.

3.4-9 Prove that if π goes to a live state, then π goes from a live state.

3.4-10 Using lockstep simulation, obtain yet another correctness proof for the procedure to eliminate dead states. Hint: Define ρ to be the identity relation on configurations of P', i.e., $C \ \rho \ C'$ if and only if C' is a configuration of P' and $C = C'$. Prove that P simulates P', rather than the other way around.

3.4-11 Prove that if an instruction goes to an unreachable control state, then it goes from an unreachable control state.

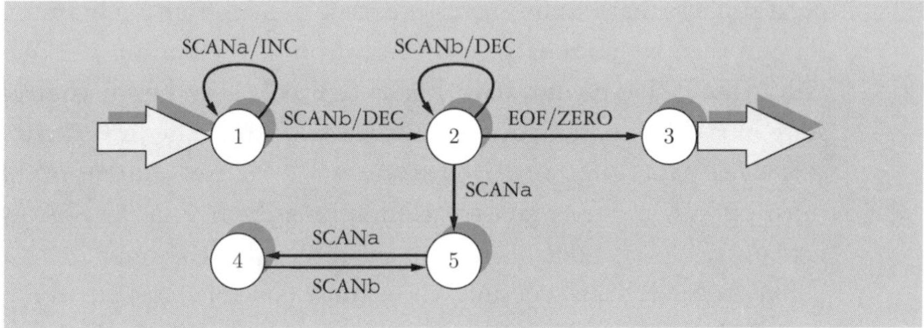

FIGURE 3.42: For use with Exercise 3.4-9.

3.4-12 Using lockstep simulation, obtain an alternate correctness proof for the procedure to eliminate unreachable states. Hint: Define ρ to be the identity relation on configurations of P'; i.e., $C' \ \rho \ C$ if and only if C' is a configuration of P' and $C' = C$.

3.4-13 If we want to eliminate dead states and eliminate unreachable states from P, does the order in which we perform this section's transformations matter?

Solution: No. The transformations may be applied in either order to obtain a program with no dead or unreachable states.

Suppose that we eliminate dead states from P, obtaining P', and then we eliminate unreachable states from P', obtaining P''. We assert that P'' has no dead states. Proof: Let q be any control state in P''. By construction, q must be a control state in P'; hence q is a live state in P'. Therefore there is an accepting state q_{accept} in P' that is reachable from q. Because q is a control state in P'', q must be reachable in P''; by construction, q is reachable in P'. Since q is reachable in P', every control state on the directed path from q to q_{accept} is reachable in P'. By construction, all of those control states are in P'', so q_{accept} is reachable from q in P'', so q is live in P''. Thus we have shown that if we eliminate dead states and then eliminate unreachable states, the resulting program has no dead states. Obviously it has no unreachable states.

Next suppose that we eliminate unreachable states from P, obtaining P', and then we eliminate dead states from P', obtaining P''. We assert that P'' has no unreachable states. Proof: Let q be any control state in P''. By construction, q must be a control state in P'; hence q is a reachable state in P'. Because q is a control state of P'', q must be live in P''; by construction, q must be live in P'. Since q is live in P', every control state on the directed path from q_{start} to q is live in P'. By construction, all of those control states are in P'', so q is reachable in P''. Thus we have shown that if we eliminate unreachable states and then eliminate dead states, the resulting program has no unreachable states. Obviously it has no dead states.

3.4-14 Construct a program in which every control state is reachable in the syntactic sense described in this section, but one of the control states is not entered in any partial computation.

3.4.4 Eliminating Null Instructions

An instruction consisting of only a control operation, i.e., having NOOPs on all devices other than the control, is called a *null instruction*. In this section, we show how to eliminate null instructions from any program.

Informally, we will look for paths in the program's digraph labeled "NOOP, ..., NOOP, π" where π is a non-null instruction. We replace every such path by a single edge labeled π. In addition, if a path labeled "NOOP, ..., NOOP" ends in a final control state, then we change the control state at the beginning of that path to a final control state.

Formally, let Π_Λ be the union of the null instructions in P, and let Π_+ be the union of the remaining (non-null) instructions. The transfer relation τ is $\alpha \circ \Pi^* \circ \omega = \alpha \circ (\Pi_\Lambda \cup \Pi_+)^* \circ \omega$. By Exercise 0.6-8(c), $(\rho_1 \cup \rho_2)^* = (\rho_1^* \rho_2)^* \rho_1^*$ for all relations ρ_1, ρ_2. Therefore $\tau = \alpha \circ (\Pi_\Lambda^* \Pi_+)^* \Pi_\Lambda^* \circ \omega$.

Let $\alpha' = \alpha$, so P' will have the same initial configuration as P. Let $\omega' = \Pi_\Lambda^* \circ \omega$. Since Π_Λ operates only on the control, this amounts to letting the final control states of P' consist of all control states from which a sequence of null instructions leads to a final control state of P.

For each non-null instruction π_+ in P, let P' contain all the instructions in $\Pi_\Lambda^* \circ \pi_+$, so that $\Pi' = \Pi_\Lambda^* \circ \Pi_+$. That is, the instruction $(q_j \to q_k, f)$ is simulated by the set of instructions of the form $(q_i \to q_k, f)$ such that q_j is reachable from q_i by a sequence of null instructions. Since each instruction in P' belongs to $\Pi_\Lambda^* \circ \Pi_+$, none of them is null.

By our construction,

$$\tau' = \alpha' \circ (\Pi')^* \circ \omega' = \alpha \circ (\Pi_\Lambda^* \Pi_+)^* \circ (\Pi_\Lambda^* \omega) = \alpha \circ (\Pi_\Lambda^* \Pi_+)^* \Pi_\Lambda^* \circ \omega = \tau,$$

so P' simulates P.

We are not quite done with our standardization, however, because our transformation may make some states unreachable. We remove the unreachable states as in Section 3.4.3. Since the elimination of unreachable states does not introduce any new instructions, there are still no null instructions.

EXAMPLE 3.11. Consider the program in Figure 3.43, which contains several null instructions. Eliminating the null instructions results in the program in Figure 3.44, which contains two unreachable states; eliminating those unreachable states results in the program in Figure 3.45. ■ ■ ■

The elimination of null instructions has a subtle effect on nondeterministic programs that are in factored form. Suppose that P is in factored form, and we construct P' by eliminating null instructions. Clearly, each instruction in P' operates on only one device other than the control. This arrangement is useful; however, control states may no longer be dedicated to a single device (Figure 3.46).

Fortunately, the elimination of null instructions from *deterministic* programs does preserve factored form. The elimination of null instructions also preserves determinism. Why? Let P be a deterministic program. If a null instruction goes from some control state, then no other instruction can go from that control state. Let q be any control state in P. If a non-null instruction is reachable from q then, by a simple induction, there is a unique sequence (possibly empty) of null instructions in P that starts at q and finishes at some control state r such that only non-null instructions go from r. Let P' be obtained by eliminating null instructions from P but not unreachable states. The set of instructions that go from q in P' is equal to the set of instructions that go from r in P, except for renaming the source. If r is dedicated to a single device in P, q is dedicated to a single device in P'; thus P' is factored if P is factored. Similarly, P' is deterministic because P is deterministic. Eliminating unreachable states from P' preserves factored form and determinism. Thus, we have shown that the elimination

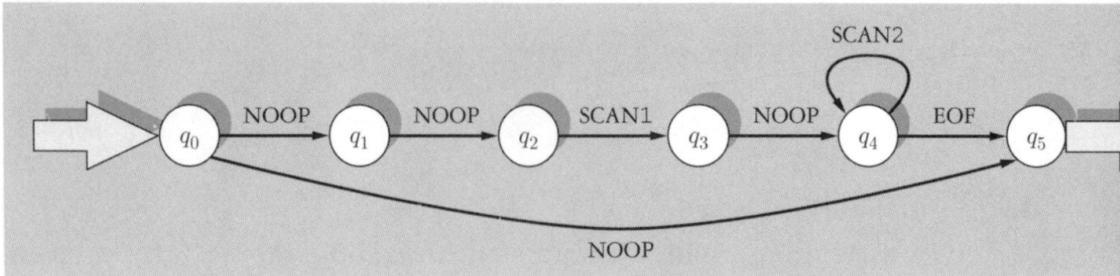

FIGURE 3.43: A program with some null instructions.

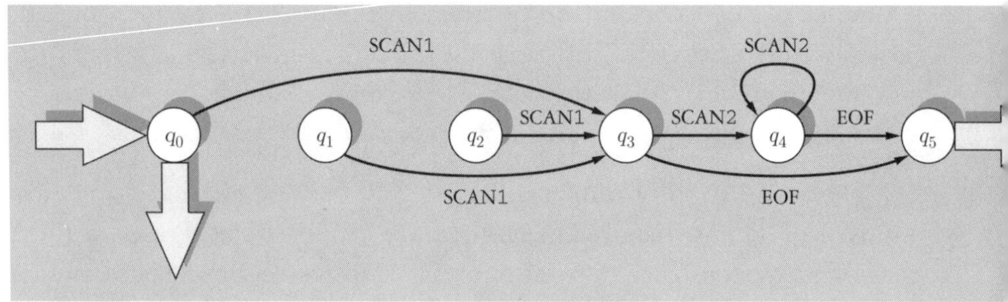

FIGURE 3.44: Null instructions are eliminated from the program in Figure 3.43. For example, the instruction $(q_0 \to q_3, \text{SCAN}1)$ was formed by combining the instructions $(q_0 \to q_1, \text{NOOP})$, $(q_1 \to q_2, \text{NOOP})$, and $(q_2 \to q_3, \text{SCAN}1)$. Observe that q_1 and q_2 are now unreachable.

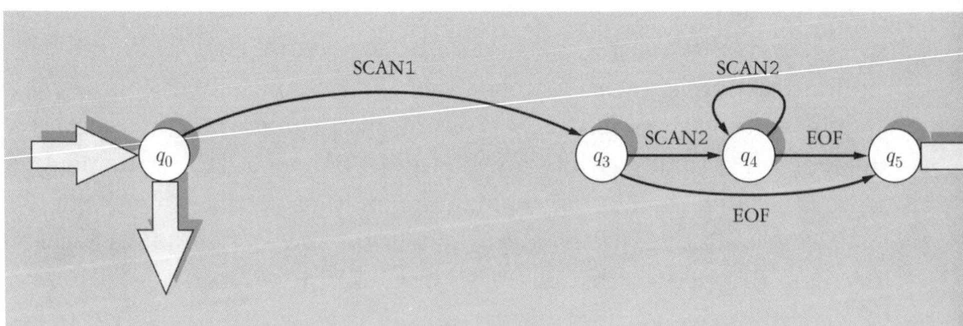

FIGURE 3.45: The unreachable states, q_1 and q_2, are removed from the program in Figure 3.44, along with all instructions going to or from those states.

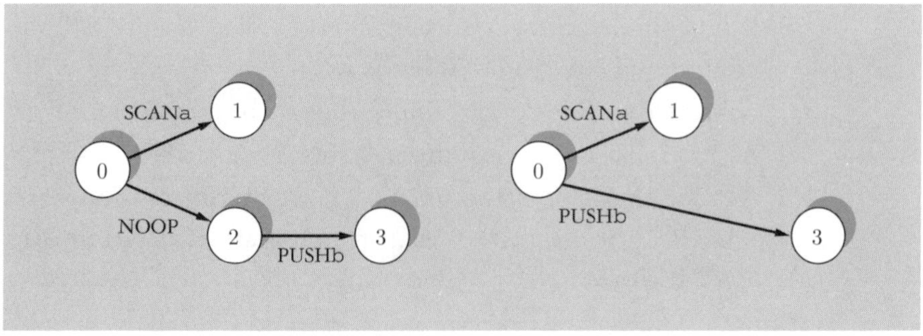

FIGURE 3.46: Eliminating null instructions from nondeterministic programs does not preserve factored form. On the left we have a fragment of a nondeterministic factored program that contains a null instruction. On the right we have eliminated the null instruction. Each instruction still operates on a single device, but the control state 0 is no longer dedicated to a single device.

of null instructions preserves determinism and that the elimination of null instructions from a deterministic program preserves factored form.

Exercises

3.4-15 Eliminate the null instructions from the programs in the following figures:

(a) Figure 1.19

(b) Figure 1.21

(c) Figure 1.22

3.4-16 Given a program P, we wish to construct a program P' such that $\alpha' = \alpha\Pi_\Lambda^*$, $\Pi' = \Pi_+\Pi_\Lambda^*$, and $\omega' = \omega$.

(a) Show how to construct P'.

(b) Prove that P' has the same transfer relation as P.

(c) Can P' contain dead states?

(d) Can P' contain unreachable states?

(e) If P is nondeterministic, then P' may violate a standard programming convention. What is it?

(f) Assume that P is nonblocking. Must P' be nonblocking?

(g) Assume that P is deterministic. Must P' be deterministic?

(h) Assume that P is deterministic. If we eliminate dead states from P', prove that the resulting program is deterministic. Does it violate the programming convention you noted in part (e)?

3.4.5 Cleaning Up and Eliminating Blocking

Cleaning Up Suppose that the terminator for a program does not depend on the contents of some particular devices; e.g., the program may terminate regardless of the input state, rather than requiring the input to be exhausted. We show how to convert such a program to one with the same transfer relation that leaves each device except the control and the output in some standard state, usually 0 or Λ. We illustrate the method for a machine with an input, a stack, and two unsigned counters. Similar ideas apply to machines with any number of inputs, stacks, signed counters, unsigned counters, tapes, and RAMs (Exercise 3.4-17). This standardization is called *cleaning up*.

For each final control state q, we construct a *cleanup subprogram* that first verifies that the program is in a final configuration and then proceeds to clear (empty) all devices except control and output. The final states of all devices except control and output are changed to 0 or Λ. The particular final state of the control is changed to q', and the control's terminator is changed accordingly. One such cleanup subprogram is shown in Figure 3.47 for a machine [control, input, stack, unsigned counter, unsigned counter] that accepts in state q_{accept} whenever the first counter is zero.

Eliminating Blocking We can also convert a program to one that accepts the same strings but never blocks (its former blocking computations will become rejecting computations). Nonblocking is a highly desirable property. Since transformed programs will reject rather than block, this standardization can change the transfer relation; for that reason it is not actually a simulation. It is, however, an important step in converting cer-

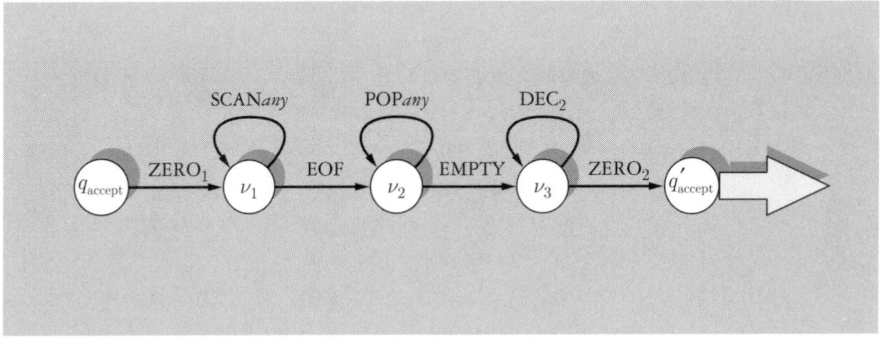

FIGURE 3.47: A cleanup subprogram that clears the input, the stack, and the second unsigned counter. The first counter is required to already hold 0 as a condition of acceptance. SCAN*any* is shorthand for SCANa, SCANb, etc.

tain kinds of deterministic acceptors, which may block on some inputs, into recognizers, which reject all inputs that are not accepted. If P is a deterministic acceptor with no infinite computations, then the elimination of blocking converts P to a recognizer for the same language.

We give the construction for an input device. Similar ideas work for stacks, unsigned counters, signed counters, tapes, and RAMs (Exercise 3.4-18).

To eliminate blocking, we introduce a single new rejecting state r. From any state where blocking can occur, as in Figure 3.48 for example, we introduce appropriate alternative instructions that verify that blocking would have occurred and go directly to the rejecting state r. Then blocking does not occur.

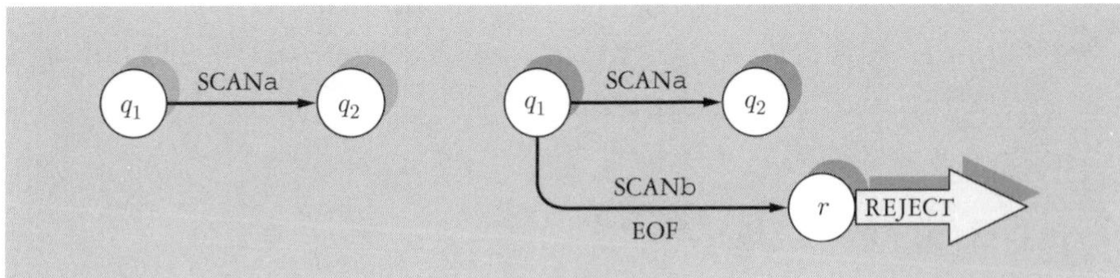

FIGURE 3.48: On the left side, blocking occurs if the remaining input does not start with a. On the right side, blocking has been eliminated.

Exercises

3.4-17 (a) A signed counter is clean if it holds 0. Show how to clean up a signed counter.
(b) A tape is clean if all squares are blank and the head is in the home position. Show how to clean up a tape.
(c) A RAM is clean if all registers and memory locations hold 0. Show how to clean up a RAM.

Hint: In all three parts, the program will need to remember some extra information that is needed only for cleaning up. What is it?

3.4-18 Show how to eliminate blocking from a program that uses a
(a) stack
(b) unsigned counter
(c) signed counter
(d) tape
(e) RAM

3.4-19 Eliminate blocking from your program for Exercise 3.4-9.

3.4-20 How many new control states do we introduce when we eliminate blocking from a program P that runs on a machine [control, input, stack], assuming that P might block in k different control states?

3.4-21 Show how to eliminate blocking from any program for a machine with arbitrary devices without affecting the transfer relation. Hint: The simulation may introduce undesirable properties, like null instructions and infinite computations.

3.4-22 Suppose that P is a deterministic program that does not block. Must P have a computation for every input?

Solution: No. P might have only infinite computations. For example, consider a program with initial control state 1 and only one instruction, $(1 \rightarrow 1, \text{NOOP}, \text{INC})$.

3.5 CHAPTER SUMMARY

In this chapter we described informally what it means for one program to simulate the behavior of another. Then we presented two specific kinds of simulation: lockstep simulation and simulation by subprograms. One machine or machine type simulates another if every program for the latter is simulated by a program for the former. Thus, simulation allows us to prove that one type of machine is at least as powerful as another. It also allows us to construct standard forms for programs, which will facilitate proofs. Although the mathematical details of simulation are not necessary to understand the rest of this book, an informal understanding of simulation will be very important.

Exercises

3.5-1 Chaos Computing is designing a new line of computers that have no control device. Because of your expertise in simulation, you have been hired to consult on the project. Assume that the control to be simulated has realm Q. Be careful not to use any controls in your simulation.

(a) Show how to simulate the control using a tape.

(b) Show how to simulate the control using two stacks.

(c) Show how to simulate the control using $|Q|$ unsigned counters. You may use the NONZERO instruction on the counters.

(d) Show how to simulate the control using unsigned counters without the NONZERO test.

(e) What effects do your simulations in parts (a–d) have on programs that are in factored form?

(f) Show how to simulate a machine [control, stack, stack] by a machine [stack, stack, stack].

3.5-2 Devices 'R Us® is marketing a new-and-improved counter. Their new device has all the ordinary operations and two additional operations: INC2, which adds 2 to the counter's state, and DEC2, which subtracts 2 from the counter's state. Their ads say that their new device will speed up counter machine programs by a factor of 2. Their competitors, the Itty Bitty Machine Corporation, have countered by providing a free control with every purchase of an ordinary counter. They have hired you—an independent researcher—to prove that an ordinary counter together with a control is just as good and just as fast as a new-and-improved counter.

Show how to simulate a new-and-improved counter, in lockstep, using an ordinary counter and a control.

4

Finite Machines and Regular Languages

IN THIS CHAPTER we examine finite machines, i.e., machines with no storage devices other than the control. Although computationally quite limited, finite machines are nonetheless useful. The control is a finite memory, so it can store a bounded amount of information, such as a number between 1 and 100, the last five input characters scanned, or a 16-bit binary sequence. Furthermore, the control can store a bounded number of different pieces of information as long as each is bounded in size.

Every real computer has a fixed, finite amount of memory, so finite machines can, in principle, simulate real computers. Thus, in principle, real computers are subject to the limitations of finite machines. However, in practice, finite machines are a useful model of computers with only small amounts of memory; RAMs, which have infinite memory, are a more useful model for real computers.

Finite machines are useful for pattern matching, as we saw in Example 1.3. They are also useful in the lexical analysis phase of parsing computer languages, when the input is separated into reserved words, identifiers, operators, and punctuation. Finite machines are used in the theory of distributed computing, where they model individual processes that have a small number of states. From a theoretical viewpoint, finite machines can also help us to understand more complicated machines. Finite machines are easy to build in hardware, easy to simulate on real computers, and also easy to analyze.

Let us recall some terminology from Chapter 2. If P is a nondeterministic acceptor running on a finite machine, then P is called an *NFA* (nondeterministic finite acceptor). If P is a recognizer running on a finite machine, then P is called a *DFR* (deterministic finite recognizer). If P is a deterministic acceptor running on a finite machine, then P is called a *DFA* (deterministic finite acceptor). If P is a nondeterministic transducer running on a finite machine, then P is called a *finite transducer*. If P is a deterministic transducer running on a finite machine, then P is called a *deterministic finite transducer*.

In this chapter we define the regular expressions, which generate languages called regular languages. We prove that the class of regular languages is equal to the class of languages accepted by NFAs. This is the first illustration of a major paradigm in the theory of computability: the correspondence between grammar-based and machine-based definitions of languages.

Then we prove that the class of languages accepted by NFAs is equal to the class of languages recognized by DFRs. (The analogous statement is false for machines with counters, stacks, or tapes.) Thus, regular languages can be represented by regular expressions, NFAs, or DFRs. None of these representations for regular languages is always better than another; each is useful for different applications.

Finally, we develop three tools for proving that certain languages are not regular: the Myhill–Nerode theorem, closure properties, and pumping theorems.

4.1 STANDARDIZING FINITE MACHINE PROGRAMS

In this section we present some standardizations for NFAs that we will use, as needed, in this chapter. Recall that in Chapter 3 we saw how to eliminate null instructions, dead control states, and unreachable control states from any program.

We saw how to eliminate the EOF test from acceptors in Section 3.4.2. It will also be useful to eliminate the EOF test from DFRs. To do so, we first eliminate null instructions and standardize the input as in Section 3.4.2. If such a standardized program contains the instruction $(q \to r, \text{EOF})$, then there are no instructions going from control state r. Because the program is deterministic, q is not a final state and there is at most one such r. Delete the instruction $(q \to r, \text{EOF})$. Make q an accepting state if r is accepting and a rejecting state if r is rejecting. The terminator will make sure that the input is exhausted before accepting or rejecting. This transformation will be useful in Section 4.7.

Thus we may assume that all instructions in an NFA or a DFR perform a SCAN operation on the input, i.e., that all instructions have the form $(q \to r, \text{SCAN}c)$. Similarly, we may assume that all instructions in a finite transducer perform a SCAN or a NOOP on the input device. Because dead states and unreachable states can be eliminated, we may further assume that every control state is on a path from the initial control state to a final control state.

A simple transformation ensures that no instructions go to the initial control state q_{start} of any program (Exercise 4.1-1). At the price of introducing null instructions and destroying determinism, we might also ensure that an acceptor has a unique accepting control state q_{accept} such that no instructions go from q_{accept} (Exercise 4.1-2). These transformations of NFAs will be useful in Sections 4.4 and 4.5.

Exercises

4.1-1 Show how to convert any program into an equivalent program in which the initial control state has no edge going to it. Your transformation should preserve determinism.

4.1-2 Show how to convert any program into an equivalent program with a unique accepting state that has no edge going from it. Your transformation may introduce null instructions.

4.1-3 Is it possible to eliminate the EOF test from deterministic finite transducers (while preserving determinism)?

Solution: No. Consider a deterministic finite transducer that maps each string x to x#. Assume that it does not use the EOF test. Because it maps Λ to #, it must write # before performing any input operations. Therefore all of its results begin with #, a contradiction.

4.2 REGULAR EXPRESSIONS AND LANGUAGES

In this section we define regular expressions and languages. Some important parts of programming languages, such as tokens, numbers, and identifiers, are regular languages. Regular expressions are important because they provide a succinct way to represent regular languages. In particular, they are useful in specifying programming languages and in pattern matching.

Recall that a set of strings is called a *language* and that the operations union ($\cup$), concatenation ($\otimes$), and Kleene-closure (*) on languages are called *regular operations*. We say that a language is *regular* if it can be obtained by applying a finite number of regular operations to the empty set and the sets containing just the empty string or a single character. We restate this definition formally below (this would be a good time to read Section 0.3.1 on regular operations and Section 0.6.3 on recursive definitions if you have not already done so):

DEFINITION 4.1 (Regular Languages). We define regular languages recursively:

(i) $\emptyset$ is a regular language.

(ii) $\{\Lambda\}$ is a regular language.

(iii) If c is a character (1-character string), then $\{c\}$ is a regular language.

(iv) If L_1 and L_2 are regular languages, then $L_1 \cup L_2$ is a regular language.

(v) If L_1 and L_2 are regular languages, then $L_1 \otimes L_2$ is a regular language.

(vi) If L_1 is a regular language, then L_1^* is a regular language.

For example,

$$\begin{aligned}\{\texttt{a}, \texttt{ab}\}^* &= (\{\texttt{a}\} \cup \{\texttt{ab}\})^* \\ &= (\{\texttt{a}\} \cup (\{\texttt{a}\} \otimes \{\texttt{b}\}))^*,\end{aligned}$$

so $\{\texttt{a}, \texttt{ab}\}^*$ is regular.

Regular expressions, defined next, are a shorthand way of describing regular languages.

DEFINITION 4.2 (Regular Expressions). We define regular expressions recursively:

(i) $\emptyset$ is a regular expression.

(ii) Λ is a regular expression.

(iii) If c is a character (1-character string), then c is a regular expression.

(iv) If r_1 and r_2 are regular expressions, then $(r_1) \cup (r_2)$ is a regular expression.

(v) If r_1 and r_2 are regular expressions, then $(r_1)(r_2)$ is a regular expression.

(vi) If r is a regular expression, then $(r)^*$ is a regular expression.

The language *generated* by a regular expression r (denoted $L(r)$) is defined recursively as follows:

(i) $L(\emptyset) = \emptyset$.

(ii) $L(\Lambda) = \{\Lambda\}$.

(iii) If c is a character, then $L(c) = \{c\}$.

(iv) $L((r_1) \cup (r_2)) = L(r_1) \cup L(r_2)$.

(v) $L((r_1)(r_2)) = L(r_1) \otimes L(r_2)$.

(vi) $L((r)^*) = (L(r))^*$.

For example, $((\mathtt{a}) \cup ((\mathtt{a})(\mathtt{b})))^*$ is a regular expression, and

$$L(((\mathtt{a}) \cup ((\mathtt{a})(\mathtt{b})))^*) = \{\mathtt{a}, \mathtt{ab}\}^*.$$

We adopt precedence rules in order to reduce the need for parentheses in regular expressions. Kleene-closure (*) has the highest priority, concatenation has the next highest priority, and union ($\cup$) has the lowest priority. Thus, for example,

$$((\mathtt{a}) \cup ((\mathtt{a})(\mathtt{b})))^* = (\mathtt{a} \cup \mathtt{ab})^*.$$

Because concatenation distributes over union in the same way that multiplication distributes over addition, we have the following rules for manipulating regular expressions:

- $L(r(s \cup t)) = L(rs \cup rt)$.
- $L((s \cup t)r) = L(sr \cup tr)$.

The justification for these rules and others is left as Exercise 4.2-1.

We often write S^+ to denote the set of strings obtained by concatenating a positive number of strings from S, i.e., $S^+ = SS^*$. If S is regular, then S^+ is regular, because S^+ is defined via Kleene-closure and concatenation. For example, $\mathtt{a}^+ = \{\mathtt{a}^i : i \geq 1\}$, which is a regular language.

Exercises

4.2-1 Let R, S, T be any sets of strings. Prove the following identities:
(a) **Distributive law.** $R(S \cup T) = RS \cup RT$
(b) **Distributive law.** $(S \cup T)R = SR \cup TR$

(c) $(S \cup T)^* = (S^* T^*)^*$
(d) $(S \cup T)^* = S^* \cup (S^* T S^*)^+$
(e) $(S \cup T)^* = S^* (T S^*)^*$
(f) $(S \cup T)^* = T^* (S T^*)^*$
(g) $(S \cup T)^* = (T^* S)^* T^*$
(h) $(S \cup T)^* = (S^* T)^* S^*$
(i) $(R \cup S)(T \cup V) = RT \cup RV \cup ST \cup SV$

4.2-2 Write regular expressions that generate the following languages:
(a) the set of all strings over $\{\mathtt{a}, \mathtt{b}\}$ that contain exactly two a's
(b) the set of all strings over $\{\mathtt{a}, \mathtt{b}\}$ that contain at least two a's
(c) the set of all strings over $\{\mathtt{a}, \mathtt{b}\}$ whose length is divisible by 3

4.2-3 Prove that the following definition of regular languages is equivalent to Definition 4.1.
A language is *regular* if it can be shown to be regular by a finite number of applications of the rules below:
(a) Every finite set is regular.
(b) $L_1 \cup L_2$ is regular if L_1 and L_2 are regular.
(c) $L_1 \otimes L_2$ is regular if L_1 and L_2 are regular.
(d) L_1^* is regular if L_1 is regular.

4.2-4 Recursively define a function f from regular expressions to natural numbers as follows:

$$\begin{aligned}
f(\mathtt{a}) &= 1 \\
f(\mathtt{b}) &= 1 \\
f(\Lambda) &= 0 \\
f((r_1) \cup (r_2)) &= \min(f(r_1), f(r_2)) \\
f((r_1)(r_2)) &= f(r_1) + f(r_2) \\
f((r)^*) &= 0.
\end{aligned}$$

Prove that $f(r)$ is equal to the length of the shortest string generated by r, i.e.,

$$f(r) = \min_{x \in L(r)} |x|.$$

4.2-5 Define a function f from regular expressions to natural numbers:

$$\begin{aligned} f(\mathtt{a}) &= 1 \\ f(\mathtt{b}) &= 0 \\ f(\Lambda) &= 0 \\ f((r_1) \cup (r_2)) &= \min(f(r_1), f(r_2)) \\ f((r_1)(r_2)) &= f(r_1) + f(r_2) \\ f((r)^*) &= 0. \end{aligned}$$

Prove that $f(r)$ is equal to the smallest number of a's in any string generated by r, i.e.,

$$f(r) = \min_{x \in L(r)} \#_{\mathtt{a}}(x).$$

4.2-6 Give a recursive algorithm to determine whether the language generated by a regular expression is empty, finite but nonempty, or infinite.

Solution: Knowing whether r_1 and r_2 are empty, finite, or infinite is enough to determine whether $r_1 r_2$ and $r_1 \cup r_2$ are empty, finite, or infinite. However, knowing whether r is empty, finite, or infinite is not enought to determine whether r^* is finite. Why? Because $\{\Lambda\}$ and $\{\mathtt{a}\}$ are finite languages, but $\{\Lambda\}^*$ is finite whereas $\{\mathtt{a}\}^*$ is infinite. Thus we will also need to determine whether $L(r) = \{\Lambda\}$.

Fix an alphabet Σ. Let

$$f(r) = \begin{cases} \emptyset & \text{if } L(r) = \emptyset, \\ \Lambda & \text{if } L(r) = \{\Lambda\}, \\ F & \text{if } L(r) \text{ is any other finite language,} \\ I & \text{if } L(r) \text{ is infinite.} \end{cases}$$

Then $L(r)$ is empty if $f(r) = \emptyset$, finite but nonempty if $f(r) = \Lambda$

or $f(r) = F$, infinite if $f(r) = I$. We compute $f(\cdot)$ by a recursive algorithm whose structure mimics the definition of $L(\cdot)$.

$$
\begin{aligned}
f(\emptyset) &= \emptyset, \\
f(\Lambda) &= \Lambda, \\
f(c) &= F && \text{for each } c \in \Sigma, \\
f((r_1) \cup (r_2)) &= \max\,(f(r_1), f(r_2)) && \text{using the order } \emptyset < \Lambda < F < I, \\
f((r_1)(r_2)) &= \max\,(f(r_1), f(r_2)) && \text{using the order } \Lambda < F < I < \emptyset, \\
f((r)^*) &= \begin{cases} \Lambda & \text{if } f(r) = \emptyset \text{ or } f(r) = \Lambda, \\ I & \text{if } f(r) = F \text{ or } f(r) = I. \end{cases}
\end{aligned}
$$

4.2-7 How would you represent a regular expression as a string?

Solution: Suppose that the regular expression's alphabet is Σ. When we write down the regular expression, we use the characters in Σ and the special characters $\emptyset$, Λ, $\cup$, *, (, and). That is, we represent the regular expression as a string over the alphabet Σ', where Σ' consists of the characters in Σ and the six special characters mentioned above.

*4.3 REGULAR EXPRESSIONS IN THE REAL WORLD: EGREP

(This section is optional; it is intended only for students with access to Unix®.) If you have used the Unix operating system, you may have used the program fgrep, grep, or egrep[1] in order to search for a string or a more complex pattern in a file. Regular expressions provide a convenient, compact way of expressing patterns. This section describes the use of egrep. (The internal workings of egrep are based on finite machines; although we will

[1] The name "egrep" is an acronym for "extended global regular expression print."

develop some of the relevant theory later in this chapter, the algorithmic details are beyond the scope of this book.)

We say that a string s *matches* a regular expression r if s belongs to the language generated by r, i.e., if $s \in L(r)$. Given a regular expression and a file name, egrep will print out every line (of the file) that contains a substring that matches the regular expression. The command format is

`grep '`*regexp*`'` *file*

where *file* is a file name and *regexp* is a regular expression whose format we will describe below. (The single quotes around the regular expression are not strictly necessary, but they prevent undesired preprocessing by the Unix command shell.)

EXAMPLE 4.3. The command

```
% grep 'depend' /usr/dict/words
```

searches the dictionary for all words containing `depend` as a substring. The result:

```
depend
dependent
independent
```

∎∎∎

Because of the limitations of standard keyboards, we must write regular expressions slightly differently when using egrep (Table 4.1). The Kleene-closure operator (*) is denoted by `*` (not a superscript), union ($\cup$) is denoted by a vertical bar (`|`), and concatenation is denoted by adjacency in the ordinary way. Parentheses have their usual meaning as grouping operators. The alphabet (Σ) is denoted by a period (`.`), i.e., `.` matches any character.

For example, the regular expression $(\mathtt{ab} \cup \mathtt{c})^*$ would be denoted `(ab|c)*`, and Σ^* would be denoted `.*`.

There is no way to express the empty string in egrep; e.g., `()` is not permitted. Instead, r? denotes zero or one occurrences of the regular expression r, so the empty string is not needed in practice.

Egrep understands other special characters, of which we will mention only two more. Imagine that a line starts with an invisible character, which we call *beginning-of-line*, and ends with an invisible character, which we call *end-of-line*. These are not standard characters, though they are loosely related to the carriage return/line feed pairs that separate lines of text in real files. In egrep, beginning-of-line is denoted by ^, and end-of-line is denoted by $. Thus ^*r*$ matches an entire line of text rather than a substring, though ^.**r*.*$ is equivalent to *r*.

EXAMPLE 4.4. To find words of two or more letters that begin and end with y, we could type

```
% egrep '^y.*y$' /usr/dict/words
yeasty
yeomanry
yesterday
```

In contrast, the command

```
% egrep 'y.*y' /usr/dict/words
```

Expression	*Egrep Notation*
r^*	*r**
r^+	*r*+
$r \cup \Lambda$	*r*?
$r \cup s$	*r*|*s*
rs	*rs*
(r)	(*r*)
Σ	.
c	*c*
d	*d*
beginning-of-line	^
end-of-line	$

TABLE 4.1: Egrep notation (*r* and *s* denote nonempty regular expressions; *c* denotes an ordinary character; *d* denotes a special character).

results in a list of 113 words, going all the way from `alleyway` to `yesteryear`. ∎∎∎

EXAMPLE 4.5. For help with spelling we might type

```
% egrep '^rec(ei|ie)ve$' /usr/dict/words
receive
```
∎∎∎

EXAMPLE 4.6. For help with a crossword puzzle

s			u		t			e

we might type

```
% egrep '^s..u.t..e$' /usr/dict/words
seductive
structure
```
∎∎∎

If one wants to specify the character `(` rather than use it as a grouping operator, one types `\(`. A character with a special meaning can be quoted by preceding it with `\`.

EXAMPLE 4.7. To search for all occurrences of the string `f(x)` in a file called ch4.tex, we could type

```
% egrep 'f\(x\)' ch4.tex
string \verb:f(x): in a file called ch4.tex, we could type
```
∎∎∎

EXAMPLE 4.8. Egrep is also useful in checking files for common grammatical errors. The following command looks for two consecutive occurrences of the word `the` separated by one or more spaces:

```
% egrep '(^| )the +the( |$)' myfile.txt
```
∎∎∎

This short section explains only a few of the capabilities of egrep. For additional information consult your Unix documentation or type the Unix command

```
% man egrep
```

Exercises

4.3-1 A common grammatical error is to write the word a followed by a word beginning with a vowel. Write a Unix command using egrep that checks myfile.txt for this error, assuming that the error occurs inside a single line.

Solution:

```
egrep '(^| )(a|A) +(a|e|i|o|u)' myfile.txt
```

4.3-2 Write a command using egrep that searches myfile.txt for all lines that contain the letter a and the letter b.

Solution:

```
egrep 'a.*b|b.*a' myfile.txt
```

4.3-3 Write a command using egrep that searches myfile.txt for all lines that contain at least two y's or at least two z's.

4.3-4 Write a command using egrep that searches myfile.txt for all lines that contain the string Bob and do not start with %. Hint: [^%] matches each character other than %.

4.4 KLEENE'S THEOREM

In our diagrams, we have represented programs as labeled digraphs. This metaphor for programs is very powerful. In this section, we present a fundamental theorem about directed graphs. Using the relationship between digraphs and programs, we then show that every NFA language is a regular language.

Recall that the first element of a path is called its origin, and the last element is called its destination. A path of length 0, such as $\langle\langle v \rangle\rangle$, will be identified with the vertex v. A path of length 1, such as $\langle\langle v_0, v_1 \rangle\rangle$, will be identified with the edge (v_0, v_1).

The *catenation* operation (denoted $\overrightarrow{\otimes}$) on paths is very similar to the *con*catenation operation on sequences. If one path's destination is another path's origin, then the catenation operation joins the two paths at that vertex; if one path ends at a different vertex from where the other path starts, then it is impossible to join the paths and their catenation is undefined. Formally, we have

$$\langle\langle u_1, \ldots, u_i \rangle\rangle \overrightarrow{\otimes} \langle\langle v_1, \ldots, v_j \rangle\rangle = \begin{cases} \langle\langle u_1, \ldots, u_i, v_2, \ldots, v_j \rangle\rangle & \text{if } u_i = v_1 \\ \text{undefined} & \text{otherwise.} \end{cases}$$

We extend the catenation operation to sets of paths in the standard way, so $S_1 \overrightarrow{\otimes} S_2 = \{s_1 \overrightarrow{\otimes} s_2 : s_1 \in S_1 \text{ and } s_2 \in S_2\}$. Henceforth we treat catenation as an operation on sets of paths. Catenation is easily seen to be associative, and the vertex set V (which is the same as the set of paths of length 0) is an identity element for catenation; i.e., for every set S of paths,

$$V \overrightarrow{\otimes} S = S \overrightarrow{\otimes} V = S.$$

We define successive powers of S inductively: $S^0 = V$ and $S^{i+1} = S^i \overrightarrow{\otimes} S$. (Observe that $S^1 = S$.) By Theorem 0.18, the closure of $V \cup S$ under catenation (denoted S^*) is given by

$$S^* = \bigcup_{i \geq 0} S^i.$$

S^* is sometimes called simply the *closure of* S.

Let G be a digraph with vertex set $V = \{1, \ldots, m\}$ and edge relation E. We show how to compute the set of paths with origin i and destination k. Let $P_{i,j,k}$ denote the set of paths with origin i and destination k that do not pass through any intermediate vertices greater than j, i.e., all paths $\langle\langle v_1, \ldots, v_n \rangle\rangle$ such that $v_1 = i, v_n = k$, and $v_a \leq j$ for $1 < a < n$. Note that even if i and k are greater than j, $P_{i,j,k}$ may contain many paths; for example, if $(i, k) \in E$, then $\langle\langle i, k \rangle\rangle \in P_{i,j,k}$ for all j. Similarly, $P_{i,j,i}$ always contains the path $\langle\langle i \rangle\rangle$ having length 0.

The sets $P_{i,j,k}$ can be computed for all i, j, k by recursion on j. Since G has no vertices numbered greater than m, the set of paths with origin i and destination k is exactly $P_{i,m,k}$. When $j = 0$, no paths may pass through any intermediate vertex, so the only possible paths are of length 0 or 1. That is, $P_{i,0,k}$ contains $\langle\langle i \rangle\rangle$ if $i = k$, it contains $\langle\langle i, k \rangle\rangle$ if $(i, k) \in E$, and it contains nothing else; in particular,

$$P_{i,0,k} \subseteq \{\langle\langle i \rangle\rangle, \langle\langle i, k \rangle\rangle\}. \tag{4.1}$$

Now assume that $j \geq 1$. Some paths in $P_{i,j,k}$ do not pass through j, while others pass through j one or more times. The former paths are exactly those belonging to $P_{i,j-1,k}$. Each of the latter kind consists of (1) a segment from i to the first occurrence of j on the path, then (2) a nonnegative number of segments, each going from one occurrence of j to the next, and finally (3) a segment going from the last occurrence of j to k. Since the vertex j appears only at the start or end of a segment (or both), the latter set of paths is exactly $P_{i,j-1,j} \overrightarrow{\otimes} (P_{j,j-1,j})^* \overrightarrow{\otimes} P_{j,j-1,k}$. Combining the two cases, we have

$$P_{i,j,k} = P_{i,j-1,k} \cup P_{i,j-1,j} \overrightarrow{\otimes} (P_{j,j-1,j})^* \overrightarrow{\otimes} P_{j,j-1,k}. \tag{4.2}$$

Before presenting an actual algorithm to compute the set of paths with origin i and destination k, we will prove an important theorem about digraphs that is due to Kleene.

If each edge in a digraph is labeled with a character from some alphabet, then each path is labeled with a string over that alphabet. We will extend our definition of regular operations to apply to paths in digraphs. Then we will prove a theorem about regular sets of paths and use it to draw conclusions about regular sets of strings.

In our definition of regular sets of paths, the edge set E will play the role of the alphabet Σ in our definition of regular sets of strings. Catenation will play the role of concatenation. V will play the role of Λ.

We call the operations union ($\cup$), catenation ($\overrightarrow{\otimes}$), and closure (*) on sets of paths *regular operations*. We say that a set P of paths on a vertex set V is *regular* if P can be obtained by applying a finite number of regular operations to the empty set and sets consisting of a single vertex or a single edge. (Recall that we identify a sequence of length 0 with a vertex and a sequence of length 1 with an edge.) Formally, we define a regular set of paths recursively:

(i) $\emptyset$ is a regular set of paths.

(ii) If v is a vertex, then $\{v\}$ is a regular set of paths.

(iii) If v_0 and v_1 are vertices, then $\{(v_0, v_1)\}$ is a regular set of paths.

(iv) If P_1 and P_2 are regular sets of paths, then $P_1 \cup P_2$ is a regular set of paths.

(v) If P_1 and P_2 are regular sets of paths, then $P_1 \vec{\otimes} P_2$ is a regular set of paths.

(vi) If P is a regular set of paths, then P^* is a regular set of paths.

We are now ready to state and prove Kleene's theorem for digraphs.

THEOREM 4.9 (Kleene's Theorem for Digraphs). *Let G be a digraph. The set of paths in G with origin i and destination k is a regular set of paths.*

Proof: Assume that G has m vertices. Define $P_{i,j,k}$ as above. Then the set of paths with origin i and destination k is equal to $P_{i,m,k}$. We prove by induction on j that $P_{i,j,k}$ is regular for every i and every k. The theorem follows by taking $j = m$. For the base case, assume that $j = 0$. Then $P_{i,0,k}$ is either $\emptyset$, $\{i\}$, $\{(i,k)\}$, or $\{i\} \cup \{(i,k)\}$ by equation (4.1), so $P_{i,0,k}$ is regular by rules (i–iv). For the inductive case, assume that $P_{i,j-1,k}$ is regular for every i and every k. In particular, $P_{i,j-1,k}$, $P_{i,j-1,j}$, $P_{j,j-1,j}$, and $P_{j,j-1,k}$ are regular for every i and every k. By equation (4.2),

$$P_{i,j,k} = P_{i,j-1,k} \cup P_{i,j-1,j} \vec{\otimes} (P_{j,j-1,j})^* \vec{\otimes} P_{j,j-1,k},$$

so $P_{i,j,k}$ is regular for every i and every k by rules (iv–vi). ∎

4.4.1 Algorithms for Computing Regular Sets of Paths

Kleene's theorem is of fundamental importance in understanding the class of languages accepted by NFAs. Before discussing this application, we present an algorithm for determining the set of paths in a digraph with origin i and destination k.

Equation (4.2) provides a simple recurrence for $P_{i,j,k}$. We solve this recurrence via the recursive algorithm of Figure 4.1, thus computing the set of paths with origin i and destination k. In the algorithm, the set of paths can be represented by a regular expression involving union, catenation, and closure.

The remainder of this section is devoted to finding more efficient algorithms than the recursive algorithm in Figure 4.1. The technique we will use is known as dynamic programming. Dynamic programming has many important applications; in particular, we will use it again in Section 5.11.

```
procedure P(i, j, k);
local S: set of paths;
      if j = 0 then begin
            S := ∅;
            if i = k then
                  S := S ∪ {i};
            if (i, k) ∈ E then
                  S := S ∪ {(i, k)};
            return S;
      end else
            return P(i, j − 1, k) ∪
                  P(i, j − 1, j) ⊗→ (P(j, j − 1, j))* ⊗→ P(j, j − 1, k);
end procedure P;

begin main
      return P(i, m, k);
end main
```

FIGURE 4.1: A recursive algorithm for the set of paths from i to k.

Observe that the recursive algorithm will wastefully evaluate $P_{i,0,k}$ a huge number of times, even though its value does not change. Therefore, it is economical to redesign the algorithm so that it does not recompute any values. The algorithm in Figure 4.2 stores the value of $P_{i,j,k}$ the first time it is computed in order to avoid recomputation.

Since the values of $P_{i,j,k}$ are computed in order of increasing j, we may replace our algorithm with a simple iterative algorithm, shown in Figure 4.3. Algorithms like this one, which fill in a table of values iteratively (instead of computing the single desired value recursively), are called *dynamic programming*.

Finally, we make a simple practical improvement to our iterative algorithm by considering only paths of length 1 or greater. Let $\hat{P}_{i,j,k}$ denote the set of paths of length 1 or greater from i to k that pass through no intermediate vertex numbered higher than j. Then $\hat{P}_{i,0,k} = \{(i,k)\}$ if $(i,k) \in E$,

```
global Parray[m, m, m]: set of paths;
global Known[m, m, m]: boolean;

procedure P(i, j, k);
local S: set of paths;
    if Known[i, j, k] then return Parray[i, j, k];
    if j = 0 then begin
        S := ∅;
        if i = k then
            S := S ∪ {i};
        if (i, k) ∈ E then
            S := S ∪ {(i, k)};
    end else
        S := P(i, j − 1, k) ∪
            P(i, j − 1, j) ⊗→ (P(j, j − 1, j))* ⊗→ P(j, j − 1, k);
    Known[i, j, k] := true;
    Parray[i, j, k] := S;
    return S;
end procedure P;

begin main
    for i := 1 to m do
        for j := 0 to m do
            for k := 1 to m do
                Known[i, j, k] := false;
    return P(i, m, k);
end main
```

FIGURE 4.2: Avoiding recomputation in the recursive algorithm of Figure 4.1 for the set of paths from i to k.

and $\hat{P}_{i,0,k} = \emptyset$ otherwise. As an exercise, the reader may verify that the recurrence of equation (4.2) applies as well to $\hat{P}_{i,j,k}$, i.e., that

$$\hat{P}_{i,j,k} = \hat{P}_{i,j-1,k} \cup \hat{P}_{i,j-1,j} \overset{\rightarrow}{\otimes} (\hat{P}_{j,j-1,j})^* \overset{\rightarrow}{\otimes} \hat{P}_{j,j-1,k}. \tag{4.3}$$

```
global Parray[m, m, m]: set of paths;

for i := 1 to m do
    for k := 1 to m do begin
        Parray[i, 0, k] := ∅;
        if i = k then
            Parray[i, 0, k] := Parray[i, 0, k] ∪ {i};
        if (i, k) ∈ E then
            Parray[i, 0, k] := Parray[i, 0, k] ∪ {(i, k)};
    end;

for j := 1 to m do
    for i := 1 to m do
        for k := 1 to m do
            Parray[i, j, k] := Parray[i, j − 1, k] ∪
               Parray[i, j − 1, j] ⊗→ (Parray[j, j − 1, j])*
                                   ⊗→ Parray[j, j − 1, k];

return Parray[i, m, k];
```

FIGURE 4.3: An iterative algorithm for the set of paths from i to k.

We solve this recurrence via the algorithm in Figure 4.4. If i is equal to k, then we include the length-0 path from i to k at the very end.

EXAMPLE 4.10. Let us consider the complete digraph on two vertices shown in Figure 4.5 (we say that a digraph is *complete* if it contains all possible edges on the vertex set). The edges are labeled a, b, c, and d; henceforth we will identify an edge with its label.

Abusing our standard notation, we identify a singleton set with the element it contains, so that we can write, for example, c to denote $\{c\}$. We also drop the symbol $\overrightarrow{\otimes}$, writing ST in place of $S \overrightarrow{\otimes} T$. Applying the algorithm of Figure 4.4, we obtain the formulas shown in Figure 4.6. ■ ■ ■

global Phat$[m, m, m]$: set of paths;

for $i := 1$ to m do
  for $k := 1$ to m do
    if $(i, k) \in E$ then Phat$[i, 0, k] := \{(i, k)\}$
    else Phat$[i, 0, k] := \emptyset$;

for $j := 1$ to m do
  for $i := 1$ to m do
    for $k := 1$ to m do
      Phat$[i, j, k] :=$ Phat$[i, j-1, k] \cup$
        Phat$[i, j-1, j] \overrightarrow{\otimes}$ (Phat$[j, j-1, j])^*$
          $\overrightarrow{\otimes}$ Phat$[j, j-1, k]$;

if $i = k$ then
  return Parray$[i, m, k] \cup \{i\}$
else
  return Parray$[i, m, k]$;

FIGURE 4.4: An improved iterative algorithm for the set of paths from i to k.

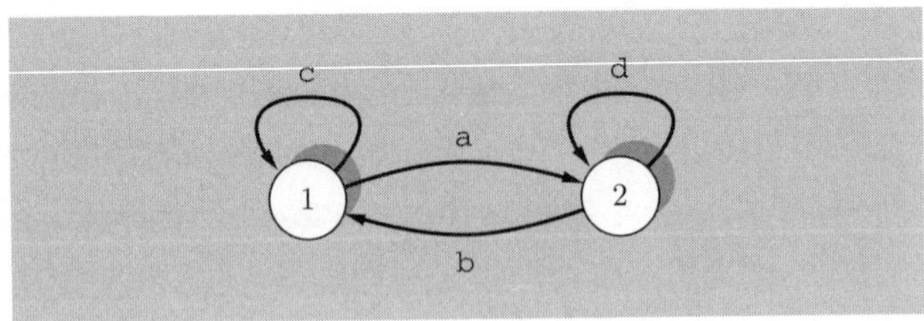

FIGURE 4.5: The complete digraph on two vertices.

$$
\begin{aligned}
\hat{P}_{1,0,1} &= c, \\
\hat{P}_{1,0,2} &= a, \\
\hat{P}_{2,0,1} &= b, \\
\hat{P}_{2,0,2} &= d, \\
\hat{P}_{1,1,1} &= c \cup cc^*c = c(c^0 \cup c^*c) = cc^*, \\
\hat{P}_{1,1,2} &= a \cup cc^*a = (c^0 \cup cc^*)a = c^*a, \\
\hat{P}_{2,1,1} &= b \cup bc^*c = b(c^0 \cup c^*c) = bc^*, \\
\hat{P}_{2,1,2} &= d \cup bc^*a, \\
\hat{P}_{1,2,1} &= cc^* \cup c^*a(d \cup bc^*a)^*bc^*, \\
\hat{P}_{1,2,2} &= c^*a \cup c^*a(d \cup bc^*a)^*(d \cup bc^*a) = c^*a(d \cup bc^*a)^*, \\
\hat{P}_{2,2,1} &= bc^* \cup (d \cup bc^*a)(d \cup bc^*a)^*bc^* = (d \cup bc^*a)^*bc^*, \\
\hat{P}_{2,2,2} &= d \cup bc^*a \cup (d \cup bc^*a)(d \cup bc^*a)^*(d \cup bc^*a) \\
&= (d \cup bc^*a)(d \cup bc^*a)^*, \\
P_{1,2,1} &= cc^* \cup c^*a(d \cup bc^*a)^*bc^* \cup 1, \\
P_{1,2,2} &= c^*a(d \cup bc^*a)^*, \\
P_{2,2,1} &= (d \cup bc^*a)^*bc^*, \\
P_{2,2,2} &= (d \cup bc^*a)(d \cup bc^*a)^* \cup 2.
\end{aligned}
$$

FIGURE 4.6: The results of applying the algorithm of Figure 4.4 to the complete digraph on two vertices shown in Figure 4.5. The first 12 formulas give the values in the array Phat. (We have simplified the formulas at each step in order to prevent them from becoming unmanageably long.) The last four formulas give the sets of paths from 1 to 1, from 1 to 2, from 2 to 1, and from 2 to 2, respectively.

EXAMPLE 4.11. To obtain formulas for sets of paths in other digraphs on the vertex set $\{1, 2\}$, we can simply replace the name of any omitted edge by $\emptyset$ in the preceding formulas. For example, in the digraph shown in Figure 4.7, the set of paths from 1 to 2 is given by

$$\emptyset^*a(d \cup b\emptyset^*a)^* = a(d \cup ba)^*.$$

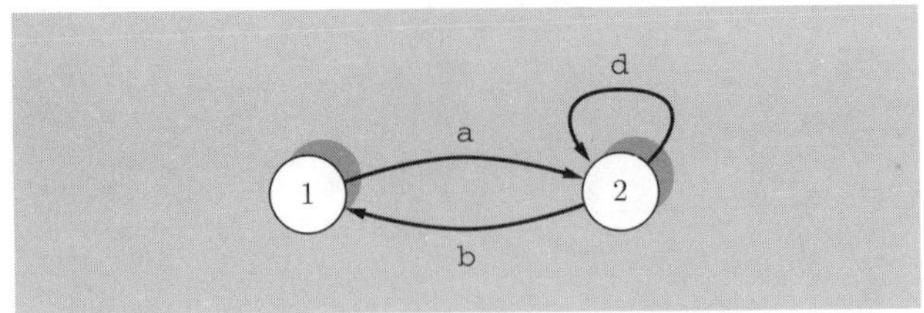

FIGURE 4.7: A proper subset of the complete digraph on two vertices.

That formula may also be obtained directly with somewhat less work by the techniques of Section 4.4.3. ■■■

4.4.2 NFA Languages Are Regular Languages

In this section we show that the set of computations of a standardized NFA is a regular language and that the set of strings accepted by any NFA is a regular language.

Recall that we represent programs as digraphs, where the labels on the edges indicate noncontrol operations. A computation corresponds to a path from an initial state to a final state in the program's digraph. The sequence of control operations performed is just the sequence of edges in the path. The sequence of noncontrol operations is just the sequence of labels on the edges.

EXAMPLE 4.12. In Figure 4.8, we show the digraph of a DFA. Consider the computation

$$\langle\!\langle \alpha, (1 \to 1, \text{SCAN}\mathtt{e}), (1 \to 2, \text{SCAN}\mathtt{f}), (2 \to 2, \text{SCAN}\mathtt{g}), \\ (2 \to 1, \text{SCAN}\mathtt{f}), (1 \to 2, \text{SCAN}\mathtt{f}), \omega \rangle\!\rangle.$$

The corresponding path is $\langle\!\langle 1, 1, 2, 2, 1, 2 \rangle\!\rangle$, which can be written as the catenation of five edges: $(1, 1)(1, 2)(2, 2)(2, 1)(1, 2)$. The sequence of noncontrol operations is the sequence of labels of these edges $\langle\!\langle \text{SCAN}\mathtt{e}, \text{SCAN}\mathtt{f}, \text{SCAN}\mathtt{g}, \text{SCAN}\mathtt{f}, \text{SCAN}\mathtt{f} \rangle\!\rangle$, and the string scanned is `efgff`. ■■■

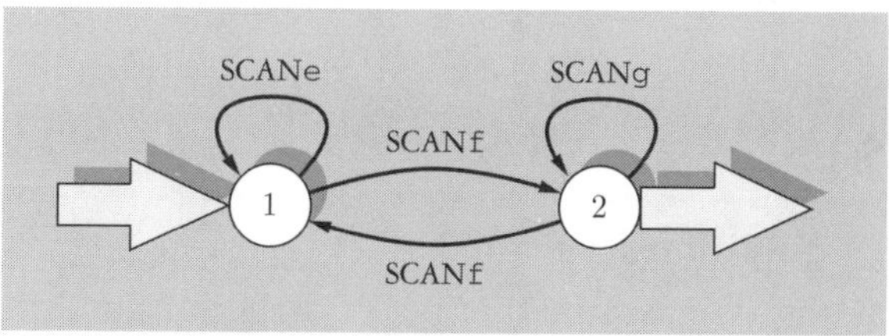

FIGURE 4.8: A DFA.

For every computation of any program P, there is a path in P's digraph from an initial state to an accepting state, which is labeled by the noncontrol operations performed during the computation. Conversely, assuming that P is an FM program, consider any path in P's digraph from an initial state to an accepting state. This path is labeled by a sequence of input operations. Provided that null instructions and EOF operations have been eliminated from P (cf. Sections 3.4.4 and 3.4.2), this sequence of operations must have the form $\langle\langle \text{SCAN}x_1, \ldots, \text{SCAN}x_n \rangle\rangle$. Thus, this path corresponds to an accepting computation on input $x_1 \cdots x_n$. Therefore, we can determine the set of accepting computations of a standardized finite machine program by forming its digraph, determining the set of all paths that go from the initial control state to an accepting control state, and replacing each edge in a path by the corresponding instruction. If we wish to determine the set of strings accepted by a standardized NFA, we can simply replace each edge in a path by the character scanned by the corresponding instruction.

EXAMPLE 4.13. The set of accepting computations of the program in Figure 4.8 is obtained by substituting the names of the instructions into Figure 4.6's formula for $P_{1,2,2}$, the set of paths with origin 1 and destination 2:

$$(1 \to 1, \text{SCAN}\texttt{e})^*(1 \to 2, \text{SCAN}\texttt{f})$$
$$\Big((2 \to 2, \text{SCAN}\texttt{g}) \cup (2 \to 1, \text{SCAN}\texttt{f})(1 \to 1, \text{SCAN}\texttt{e})^*(1 \to 2, \text{SCAN}\texttt{f})\Big)^*.$$

Therefore the set of strings accepted by that program is

$$\texttt{e}^*\texttt{f}(\texttt{g} \cup \texttt{fe}^*\texttt{f})^*.$$

■ ■ ■

Kleene's theorem for digraphs yields a nice corollary about NFA languages.

COROLLARY 4.14. *If P is an NFA, then P accepts a regular language.*

Proof: Let q_{start} be P's initial state, and let Q_{accept} be the set consisting of P's accepting states. We assume that null instructions and EOF operations have been eliminated from P. Let G be the digraph of P, and let paths(i, k) denote the set of paths whose origin is i and whose destination is k. The set of paths whose origin is an initial state and whose destination is a final state is given by

$$\bigcup_{k \in Q_{\text{accept}}} \text{paths}(q_{\text{start}}, k).$$

Because paths(i, k) is a regular set of paths for each i and each k by Theorem 4.9, so is the finite union above. In the expression for that regular set of paths, we replace each edge by the character scanned while traversing that edge, we replace each vertex by Λ, and we replace $\overrightarrow{\otimes}$ by $\otimes$. Thus we obtain the set of strings accepted by P. Since that set is constructed from $\emptyset$, Λ, and individual characters by a finite number of regular operations, it is a regular language. ∎

Exercises

4.4-1 Let P be any NFA. Prove that the set of computations of P is a regular language.

4.4-2 Let L be a language filtered or generated by a finite machine program (for definitions, see Exercises 2.9-6 and 2.10-4). Prove that L is a regular language.

4.4.3 Pencil-and-Paper Algorithm

In order to convert an NFA to an equivalent regular expression, we can use the algorithm in Figure 4.4. That algorithm is suitable for use on real computers, but it is not so easy to work by hand. In this section, we describe an algorithm that is suitable for pencil-and-paper calculation.

First, we standardize the NFA so that (1) no EOF operations are used, (2) the initial control state has no edges going to it (Exercise 4.1-1), and (3) there is a unique accepting control state with no edges going from it (Exercise 4.1-2). Assume that the control states of the standardized program are numbered 1 through m, where $m - 1$ is the initial control state and m is the unique accepting control state. Because there are no edges to $m - 1$ or from m, they cannot be intermediate vertices, so $\hat{P}_{m-1,m,m} = \hat{P}_{m-1,m-2,m}$.

Construct the digraph representation of program P, but instead of labeling edges SCANc or NOOP, label them c or Λ, respectively. Thus each edge is labeled by the string scanned when that edge is traversed.

Suppose that in the course of executing the algorithm of Figure 4.4 we have computed $\hat{P}_{i,j,k}$ for every i, k. Then clearly we need no longer store $\hat{P}_{i,j-1,k}$ for any i, k. In addition, since our goal is only to compute $\hat{P}_{m-1,m-2,m}$, we need not compute $\hat{P}_{i,j,k}$ if $i \leq j$ or $k \leq j$, because these values will not be needed in later computations. Thus, each pass through the outermost for-loop corresponds to eliminating vertex j and its incident edges, while maintaining for each $i, k > j$ that $\hat{P}_{i,j,k}$ is the set of paths from i to k whose intermediate vertices have already been eliminated. Finally, when all vertices but $m - 1$ and m have been removed, the digraph is reduced to a single edge from the start state to the accepting state, which is labeled by the set of paths from $m - 1$ to m.

Since the noninitial, nonfinal vertices can be numbered arbitrarily, we may in fact eliminate them in any order that pleases us. Because this algorithm repeatedly simplifies the digraph, it is particularly amenable to pencil-and-paper computation.

Step 1: Standardize the start and accepting state.

Step 2: For every pair of vertices r and t, if there is more than one edge from r to t, then combine them into a single edge, which is labeled with the union of the labels of the individual edges (Figure 4.9).

Step 3: After parallel edges have been merged, remove any vertex s except the initial vertex or the accepting vertex. For every pair of vertices r and t, see if $\langle\langle r, s, t\rangle\rangle$ is a path in the digraph. If so, there are four cases, depending on whether there is an edge from r to t and whether there is an edge from s to s. These cases are shown in Figure 4.10. When eliminating s from the old digraph, put the correspondingly labeled edge from r to t in the new digraph (replacing the old edge from r to t if it already exists).

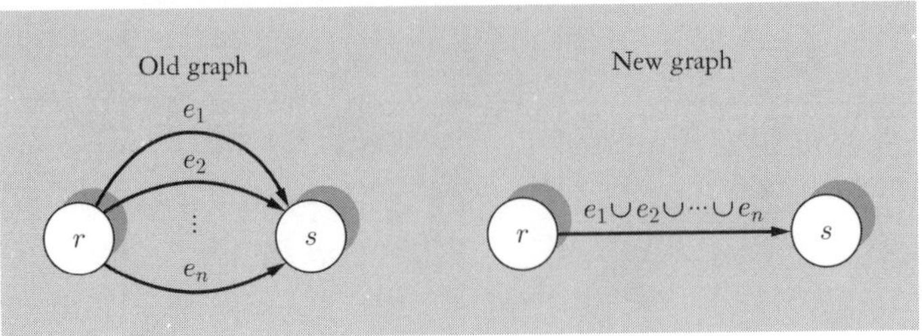

FIGURE 4.9: Merging parallel edges.

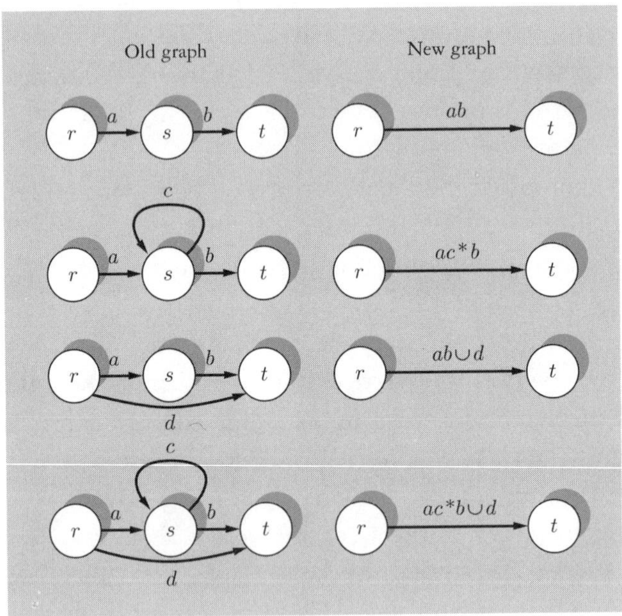

FIGURE 4.10: Four cases when eliminating vertex s.

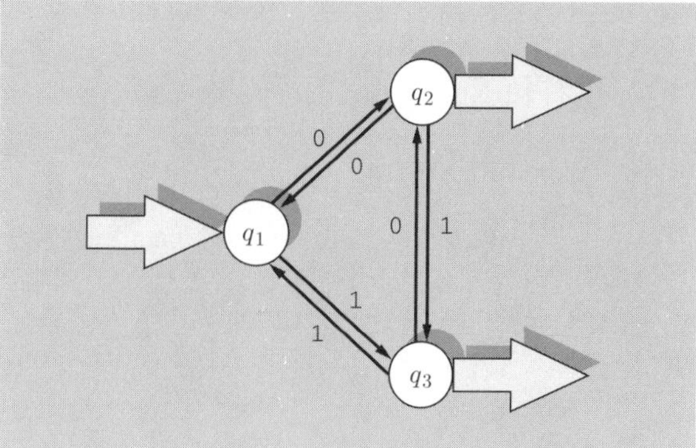

FIGURE 4.11: A finite acceptor.

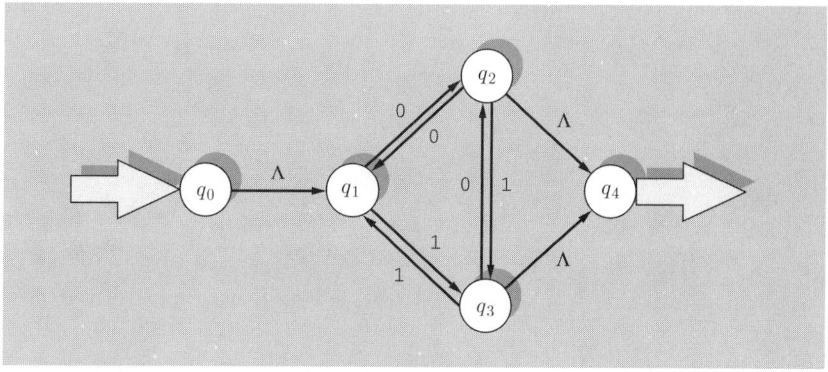

FIGURE 4.12: Standardizing the initial and final states.

Now repeat step 3 — removing a single vertex and the incident edges — until only the start and the final vertex remain. A single edge must join them and be labeled with the language accepted by the original program.

EXAMPLE 4.15. We apply this technique to the program in Figure 4.11. We introduce a new initial state with no edges going to it and a new unique final state with no edges going from it (Figure 4.12). Since there are no parallel edges, we go immediately to step 3, where we eliminate control state q_1 (Figure 4.13). Then we eliminate control state q_2 (Figure 4.14).

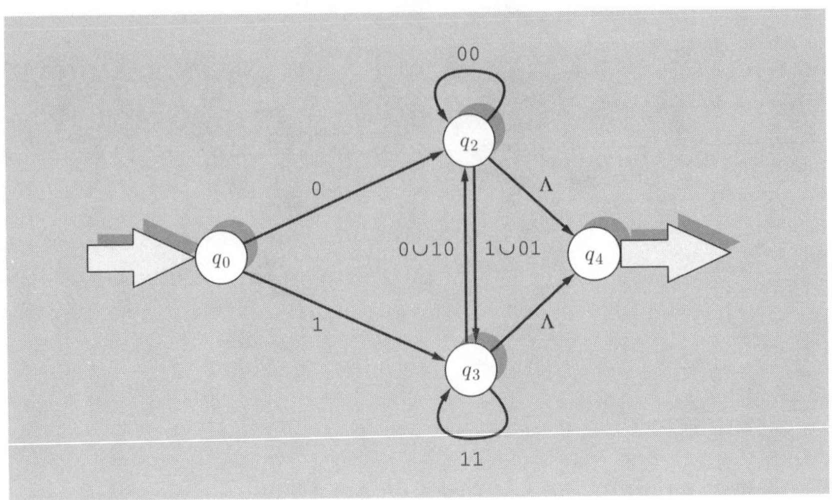

FIGURE 4.13: Eliminating q_1.

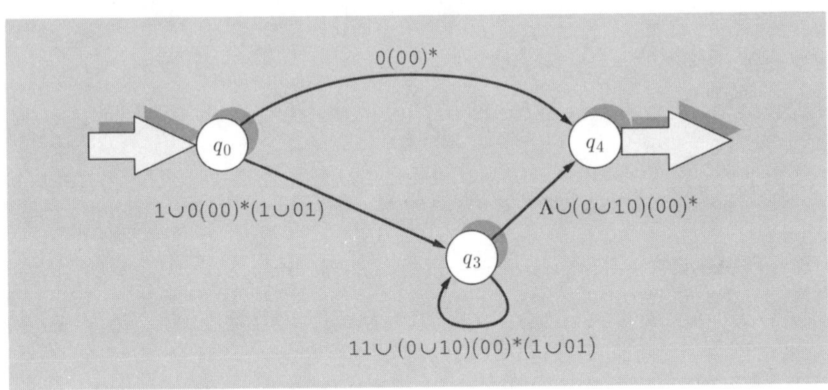

FIGURE 4.14: Eliminating q_2.

It is helpful to simplify the regular expressions (Figure 4.15) if one can see how to, although this is not strictly necessary and may not always be easy. Finally, we eliminate q_3 (Figure 4.16). ■ ■ ■

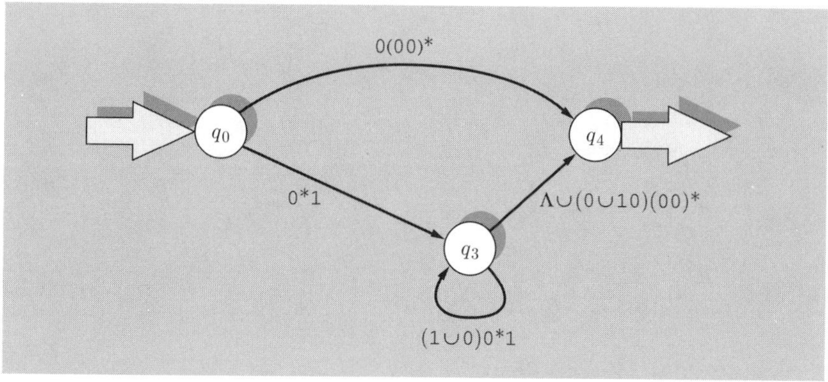

FIGURE 4.15: Simplifying the regular expressions.

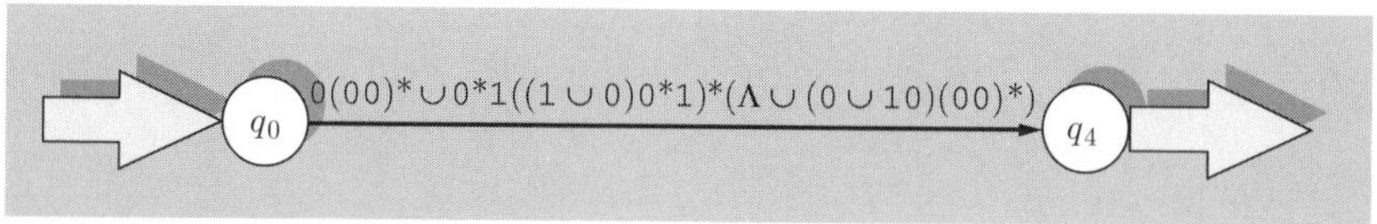

FIGURE 4.16: Eliminating q_3.

Exercises

4.4-3 Prove equation (4.3).

4.4-4 Let R and S each be any language. Prove that $R \cup RSS^* = RS^*$.

4.4-5 Use our pencil-and-paper algorithm to determine the regular language accepted by the NFA in Figure 1.5. Show your work.

4.4-6 Use our pencil-and-paper algorithm to determine the regular language accepted by the NFA in Figure 4.17. Show your work.

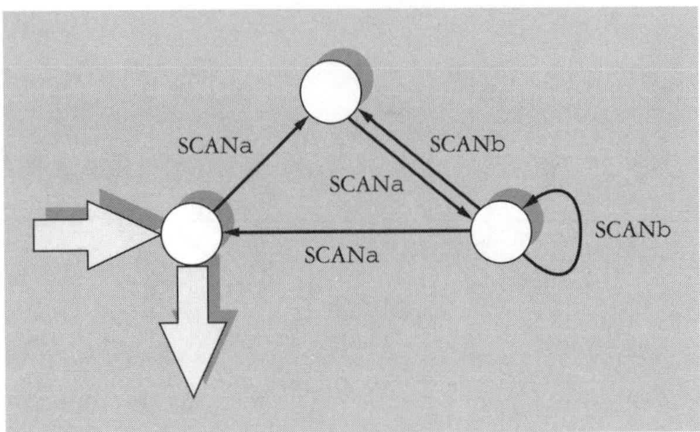

FIGURE 4.17: An NFA.

+4.4-7 If L is a nonempty language accepted by an NFA with N states, prove that L contains a string whose length is less than N.

4.4-8 Let $L \subseteq \mathsf{a}^*$ be accepted by a DFA with N states. Prove that there exist a natural number $M \leq N$ and sets $F, F' \subseteq \{0, \ldots, N-1\}$ such that

$$L = \{\mathsf{a}^i : i \in F \text{ or } (i \geq N \text{ and } (i \bmod M) \in F')\}.$$

4.4-9 **Reachability**

(a) Design an efficient algorithm that will determine for every pair of vertices s, t in a directed graph whether there is a path from s to t. Hint: One approach is to label the edges by Λ and apply Kleene's algorithm, although somewhat faster algorithms are possible.

(b) Design an algorithm to determine which of a program's states are live.

(c) Design an algorithm to determine which of a program's states are reachable.

4.4-10 **All-pairs shortest path.** Design an efficient algorithm that will determine for every pair of vertices s, t in a weighted digraph the minimum weighted length of a path from s to t. Hint: Replace $\otimes$ by *addition* and replace $\cup$ by *minimum* in Kleene's algorithm.

4.5 NFA LANGUAGES ARE THE SAME AS REGULAR LANGUAGES

In the preceding section, we proved that every NFA language is a regular language. We now prove the converse; hence we conclude that the class of NFA languages is exactly equal to the class of regular languages.

LEMMA 4.16. *Every regular language is an NFA language.*

Proof: If L is regular, then L is built from $\emptyset$, $\{\Lambda\}$, and sets containing a single character $\{c\}$ by applying the regular operations union ($\cup$), concatenation ($\otimes$), and Kleene-closure (*). We prove that L is an NFA language by induction on the number of applications of the regular operations used in building L.

Let L be a regular language. If L is $\emptyset$, $\{\Lambda\}$, or $\{c\}$, where c is any character, then clearly L is an NFA language (the desired NFA has one or two control states and is easily constructed). Otherwise, L is equal to $L_1 \cup L_2$, $L_1 \otimes L_2$, or L_1^* for some regular languages L_1 and L_2 that are built up using one fewer application of the regular operations. By the inductive hypothesis, L_1 and L_2 are NFA languages. By our standardizations (Exercise 4.1-2) we may assume that L_1 and L_2 are accepted by NFAs P_1 and P_2, respectively, with start states q_{1-} and q_{2-} and unique accepting control states q_{1+} and q_{2+}.

In each of three cases, we construct a program P with start state q_- and accepting state q_+. If $L = L_1 \cup L_2$, then we connect the start state of P by null instructions to the start states for P_1 and P_2; similarly, we connect the accepting states of P_1 and P_2 to the accepting state of P (Figure 4.18). If $L = L_1 \otimes L_2$, then we connect the start state of P to the start state of P_1, the accepting state of P_1 to the start state of P_2, and the accepting state of P_2 to the accepting state of P (Figure 4.5). If $L = L_1^*$, then we connect the start state of P to the start state of P_1, the accepting state of P_1 to the accepting state of P, and the accepting state of P_1 to the start state of P_1; we also connect the start state of P directly to the accepting state of P, in order to accept Λ (Figure 4.20). (A more compact construction for Kleene-closure is possible. See Exercise 4.5-2.)

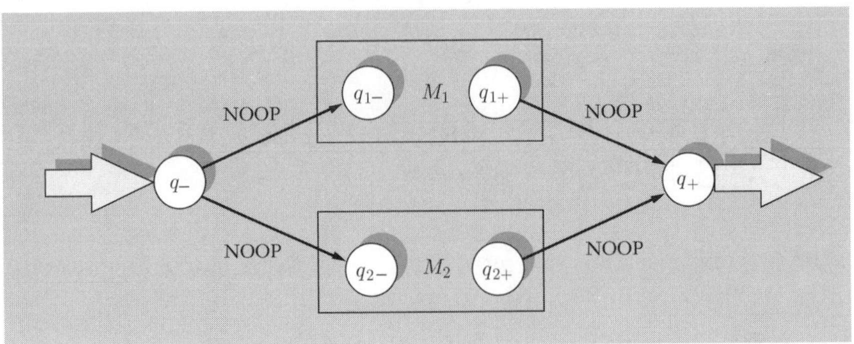

FIGURE 4.18: An NFA that accepts $L_1 \cup L_2$.

The NFA P so constructed accepts L; therefore L is an NFA language. ■

THEOREM 4.17 (Kleene). *L is a regular language if and only if L is an NFA language.*

Proof: By Corollary 4.14, if L is an NFA language, then L is a regular language. By Lemma 4.16, if L is a regular language, then L is an NFA language. ■

Exercises

4.5-1 Use Lemma 4.16 to construct NFAs that accept the following languages:

(a) $\Lambda \cup \mathtt{a}(\mathtt{a} \cup \mathtt{b})^*$

(b) $(\mathtt{ab}^*)^*$

(c) $(\mathtt{ab}^*)^* \cup (\mathtt{ba}^*)^*$

4.5-2 In Figure 4.20, we introduced four new edges in order to construct an NFA for L_1^* with start state q_- and accepting state q_+. Show how to do the construction with only three new edges, still ensuring

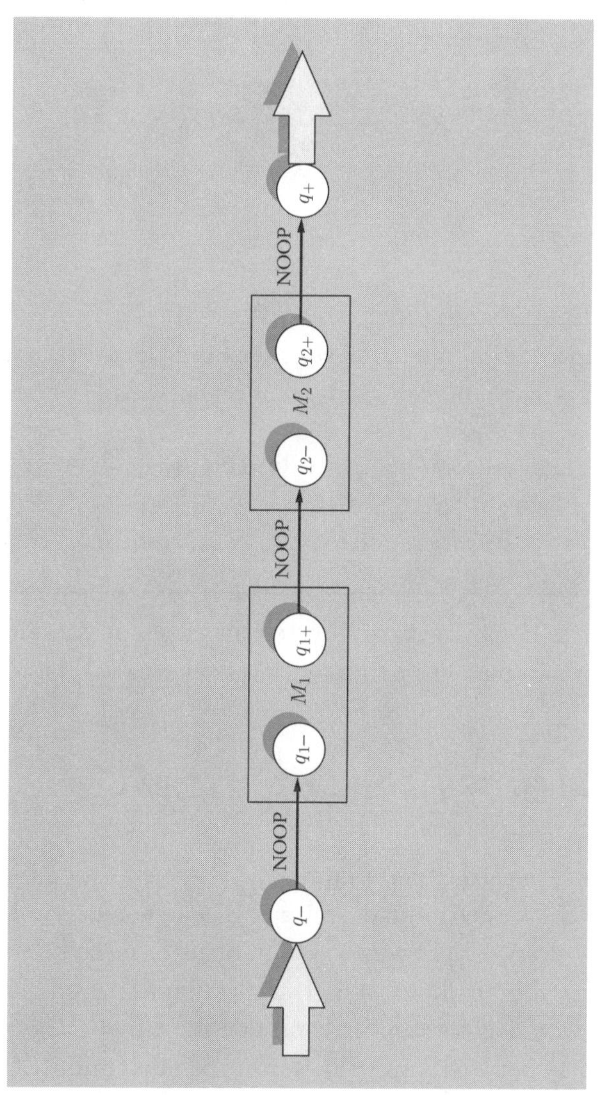

FIGURE 4.19: An NFA that accepts $L_1 \otimes L_2$.

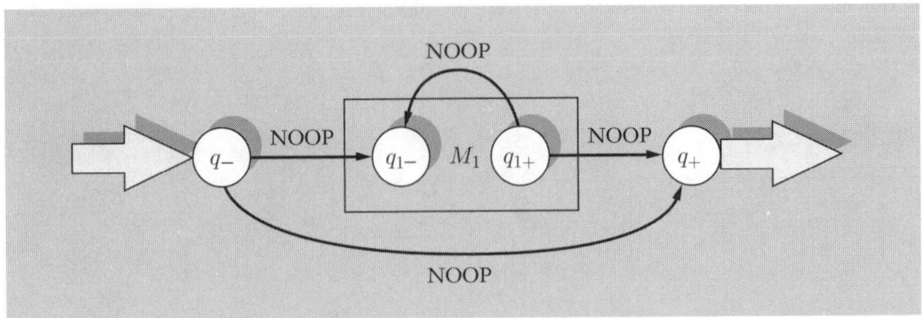

FIGURE 4.20: An NFA that accepts L_1^*.

that no instructions go to the start state or from the accepting state. If we drop that condition, show that one new edge suffices.

4.5-3 A program is called *planar* if its digraph can be drawn in the plane without having any edges cross.

(a) Prove that every regular language is accepted by a planar NFA.

*(b) Construct a regular language that is not accepted by any planar DFA. Hint: Every undirected planar graph contains a vertex with at most five neighbors (cf. Exercise 0.6-11).

4.6 EQUIVALENCE OF NFAs AND DFAs

A very important concern in computer science is the relation between the computing power of deterministic programs and nondeterministic programs. Because every deterministic program for a machine M is also a nondeterministic program for M, it is clear that nondeterministic programs are at least as powerful as deterministic programs. Although nondeterministic programs may be strictly more powerful than deterministic programs running on the same kind of machine, we will show in this section that this is not the case for finite acceptors. We will show that any NFA with n control states can be simulated by a DFA with 2^n control states. Although 2^n is much larger than n, it is still finite. (In some cases, the exponential blowup in control states is unavoidable.)

The ability of a DFA to simulate an NFA is very important because it gives us additional characterizations of the regular languages: They are exactly the set of DFA languages and, because DFAs and DFRs are equivalent, they are exactly the set of DFR languages. However, it is also worth noting that deterministic finite *transducers* cannot simulate all nondeterministic finite transducers (Exercise 4.6-2).

THEOREM 4.18. *L is a regular language if and only if L is a DFA language.*

Proof: By Theorem 4.17, the class of regular languages is equal to the class of NFA languages, so it suffices to prove the equivalence of NFAs and DFAs. Every DFA is also an NFA; therefore every DFA language is an NFA language. For the converse, let L be accepted by an NFA P with control set Q. We assume that all null instructions and EOF operations have been eliminated from P.

After P has scanned a string w, P can be in one of many different control states, because P is nondeterministic. We construct a corresponding deterministic program P' such that, after reading w, P' will be in a control state that represents the set of all possible control states that P could be in after reading w. In fact, we let Q' consist of all subsets of Q, so the control state of P' will *be* the set of all possible control states that P could be in after reading w.

We let $Q' = 2^Q$, where Q is the set of control states of P. Then Q' is finite. (Recall that 2^Q denotes the set of all subsets of Q, also known as the power set of Q. If Q is finite, then 2^Q is finite and in fact $|2^Q| = 2^{|Q|}$.)

Let t_c be the union of all the control operations that accompany SCANc in P. Then for every $S \subseteq Q$ and every character $c \in \Sigma$, let P' contain the instruction

$$(S \rightarrow St_c, \text{SCAN}c). \tag{4.4}$$

(St_c is the set of states of P that are reachable from an element of S via a single SCANc instruction. Since S and St_c are single states of P', (4.4) is a single instruction of P', not a set of instructions.)

Let q_{start} denote the initial state of P, and let Q_{accept} denote the set of accepting states of P. The initial state of P' is $\{q_{\text{start}}\}$. A control state S of

P' is accepting if and only if it contains an accepting state of P, i.e., if and only if $S \cap Q_{\text{accept}} \neq \emptyset$.

It is not hard to prove that P' simulates P in lockstep. The details are left as an exercise for the reader.

We prove that P' is deterministic. Suppose that $(S_1 \to S_1 t_c, \text{SCAN}c)$ and $(S_2 \to S_2 t_d, \text{SCAN}d)$ are two instructions of P' with overlapping domains. Then the control operations have overlapping domains, so $S_1 = S_2$; the input operations have overlapping domains, so $c = d$. Thus the two instructions are identical. Therefore P' is deterministic. ■

The construction in the preceding proof is known as the "subset construction" because Q' is the set of all subsets of Q.

EXAMPLE 4.19. Consider the NFA shown in Figure 4.21, which accepts those strings over $\{\mathtt{a}, \mathtt{b}\}$ that have an a two characters from the end. Its initial control state is 1, and its unique accepting control state is 4.

To construct an equivalent DFA P', we could just write the instructions $(S \to St_{\mathtt{a}}, \text{SCAN}\mathtt{a})$ and $(S \to St_{\mathtt{b}}, \text{SCAN}\mathtt{b})$ for every $S \subseteq Q$. However, in order to save some work we construct only the reachable states of P'. The initial state of P' is $\{1\}$. From $\{1\}$ we can go to $\{1\}t_{\mathtt{a}} = \{1, 2\}$ and $\{1\}t_{\mathtt{b}} = \{1\}$; hence we include the two instructions $(\{1\} \to \{1, 2\}, \text{SCAN}\mathtt{a})$ and $(\{1\} \to \{1\}, \text{SCAN}\mathtt{b})$ in P'. From $\{1, 2\}$ we can go to $\{1, 2\}t_{\mathtt{a}} = \{1, 2, 3\}$ and $\{1, 2\}t_{\mathtt{b}} = \{1, 3\}$; hence we include the two instructions $(\{1, 2\} \to \{1, 2, 3\}, \text{SCAN}\mathtt{a})$ and

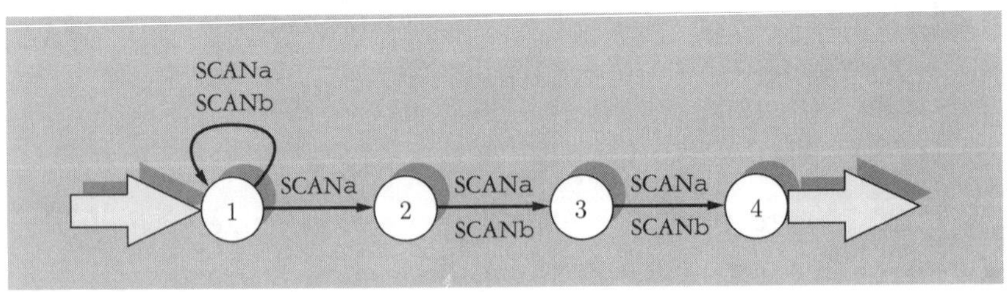

FIGURE 4.21: An NFA that accepts $\{\mathtt{a}, \mathtt{b}\}^*\mathtt{a}\{\mathtt{a}, \mathtt{b}\}^2$.

$(\{1,2\} \to \{1,3\}, \text{SCAN}\mathtt{b})$ in P'. Continuing this process, we obtain the entire instruction set of P':

$$\left\{\begin{array}{ll}
(\{1\} \to \{1,2\} & , \text{SCAN}\mathtt{a}), \\
(\{1\} \to \{1\} & , \text{SCAN}\mathtt{b}), \\
(\{1,2\} \to \{1,2,3\} & , \text{SCAN}\mathtt{a}), \\
(\{1,2\} \to \{1,3\} & , \text{SCAN}\mathtt{b}), \\
(\{1,2,3\} \to \{1,2,3,4\} & , \text{SCAN}\mathtt{a}), \\
(\{1,2,3\} \to \{1,3,4\} & , \text{SCAN}\mathtt{b}), \\
(\{1,3\} \to \{1,2,4\} & , \text{SCAN}\mathtt{a}), \\
(\{1,3\} \to \{1,4\} & , \text{SCAN}\mathtt{b}), \\
(\{1,2,3,4\} \to \{1,2,3,4\} & , \text{SCAN}\mathtt{a}), \\
(\{1,2,3,4\} \to \{1,3,4\} & , \text{SCAN}\mathtt{b}), \\
(\{1,3,4\} \to \{1,2,4\} & , \text{SCAN}\mathtt{a}), \\
(\{1,3,4\} \to \{1,4\} & , \text{SCAN}\mathtt{b}), \\
(\{1,2,4\} \to \{1,2,3\} & , \text{SCAN}\mathtt{a}), \\
(\{1,2,4\} \to \{1,3\} & , \text{SCAN}\mathtt{b}), \\
(\{1,4\} \to \{1,2\} & , \text{SCAN}\mathtt{a}), \\
(\{1,4\} \to \{1\} & , \text{SCAN}\mathtt{b})
\end{array}\right\}.$$

The accepting control states are $\{4\}$, $\{1,4\}$, $\{2,4\}$, $\{3,4\}$, $\{1,2,4\}$, $\{1,3,4\}$, $\{2,3,4\}$, and $\{1,2,3,4\}$. Note that only four of them are reachable. ■■■

COROLLARY 4.20. *L is a regular language if and only if L is a DFR language.*

Proof: By Theorem 4.18 it suffices to prove that L is a DFA language iff L is a DFR language. We can convert a DFR to a DFA for the same language by making rejecting states nonfinal. Conversely, given a DFA, we can eliminate blocking. Then we eliminate null instructions and EOF tests, so that each instruction scans a character; this rules out infinite computations, so the resulting program is a DFR. ■

The final step of converting an NFA to a DFR is actually simpler than the proof of Corollary 4.20 suggests. Theorem 4.18's construction actually produces a DFA that has no null instructions and does not use the EOF test, so it cannot have infinite computations. Furthermore, for every state S and every character c there is an instruction $(S \to St_c, \text{SCAN}c)$, so the DFA cannot block except when the input is exhausted. To eliminate blocking, it suffices to convert nonaccepting states to rejecting states, thus producing an equivalent DFR.

EXAMPLE 4.21. Figure 4.22 shows an NFA P and Figure 4.23 shows the equivalent DFR P' produced by this method. Some states of P', such as $\{1, 2\}$, are not shown because they are unreachable from the initial state $\{1\}$. ■ ■ ■

The DFR that we construct from a k-state NFA may have as many as 2^k states. For some languages, this exponential blowup is unavoidable, i.e., there are languages that are accepted by a k-state NFA but are not recognized by any $(2^k - 1)$-state DFR. This will be discussed further in Section 4.7 (Corollary 4.28 and Exercise 4.7-15).

Exercises

4.6-1 (a) Can every nondeterministic finite transducer be simulated by a deterministic transducer running on some type of machine? Hint: Deterministic transducers compute partial functions.

(b) Suppose that we replace the input device by an output device in this section's proof that an NFA without null instructions can be simulated by a DFA. Where does this introduce an error in the proof?

4.6-2 (a) Let τ be the partial function that maps xc to cx for every string $x \in \{\mathtt{a}, \mathtt{b}\}^*$ and every character $c \in \{\mathtt{a}, \mathtt{b}\}$. Prove that τ is a nondeterministic finite transduction.

*(b) Prove that τ is not a deterministic finite transduction.

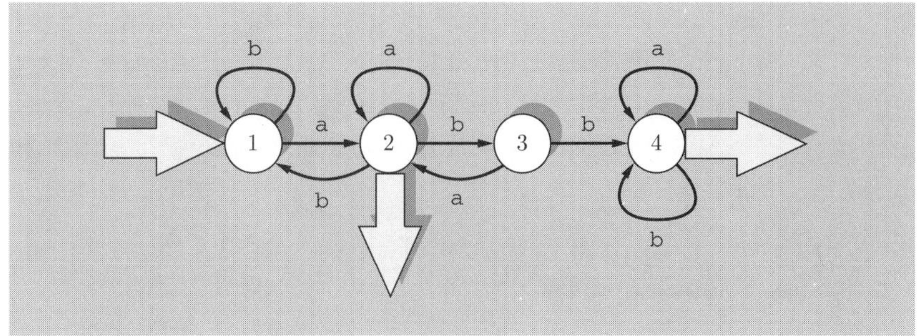

FIGURE 4.22: An NFA.

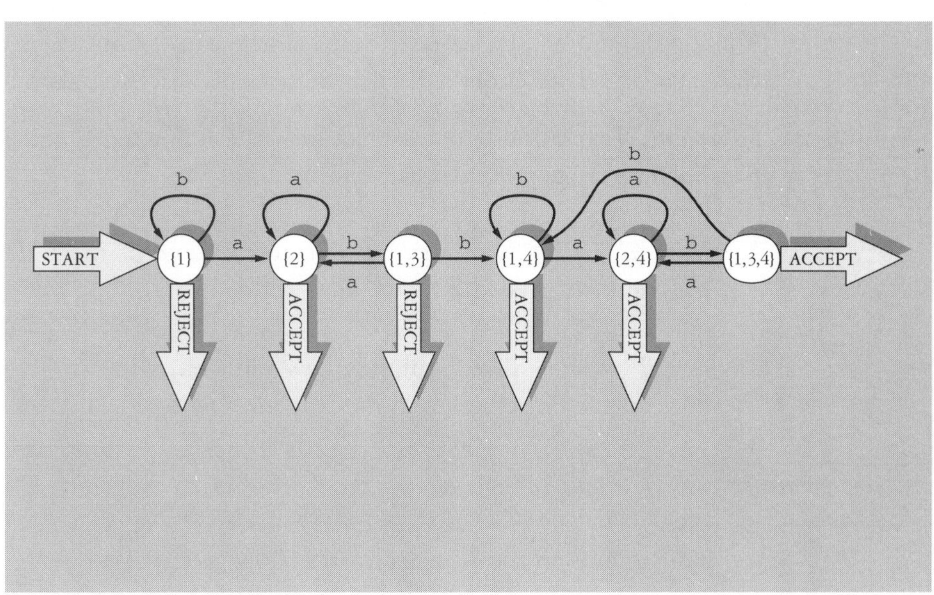

FIGURE 4.23: A DFR that accepts the same language.

*(c) Prove that $\mathcal{T}$ is not even computed by a deterministic program for a machine [control, input, output, stack]. Hint: Prove that the program must scan the entire input before writing anything. In addition, you may use the fact that $\{xcx : x \in \{\mathtt{a},\mathtt{b}\}^*$ and $c \in \{\mathtt{a},\mathtt{b}\}\}$ is not accepted by any NSA, although you will not be able to prove it until Chapter 5.

4.6-3 Prove the correctness of the simulation of an NFA by a DFA in the proof of Theorem 4.18.

4.6-4 Prove that the set of NFA languages is closed under complementation.

4.6-5 Use the techniques of this section to convert the NFAs you constructed in Exercise 4.5-1 to DFRs.

4.6-6 Design an efficient algorithm to solve the following problem:

Problem name: NFA acceptance
Instance: a string x and a k-state NFA P
Question: Does P accept x?

You should assume that $|x|$ is not much larger than k. Hint: Observe that only $|x|+1$ states of the DFR P' are actually reached on input x.

Solution: With suitable data structures, the following algorithm runs in time $O(|\mathcal{I}| \cdot |X|) = O(k^2|x|)$:

```
S := {q_start}; (* S holds the set of states P could be in *)
while not eof do begin
    read(c);
    T := ∅; (* T will hold the new value of S *)
    for each instruction in P of the form (q → q', SCANc) do
        if q ∈ S then T := T ∪ {q'};
    S := T;
end;
if S contains an accepting state of P then accept else reject;
```

*4.6-7 An *alternating finite machine program* (AFM program) has two kinds of states, existential (nondeterministic) and universal. Informally, an AFM program accepts when started in an existential state if at least one of its choices leads to acceptance; it accepts when started in a universal state if all of its choices lead to acceptance.

Formally, an AFM program is a directed graph where each edge is labeled SCANc for some character c and each node is labeled existential or universal. A subset of the nodes are accepting states. t_c is defined as in the proof of Theorem 4.18. An AFM program accepts a string x iff $A(q_0, x)$ is true, where q_0 is the start state and the predicate A is defined recursively as follows:

- $A(q, \Lambda)$ is true iff q is an accepting state.
- If q is an existential state, then

$$A(q, cx) = \bigvee_{q' \in qt_c} A(q', x).$$

- If q is a universal state, then

$$A(q, cx) = \bigwedge_{q' \in qt_c} A(q', x).$$

Prove that every AFM language is regular. Hint: Construct a DFR whose control set is the set of functions from Q to $\{\text{true}, \text{false}\}$.

4.6-8 (a) In this problem we define a notion of acceptance that is dual to nondeterministic acceptance. An $\forall$FA (pronounced "all-eff-ay") is like an NFA except that it accepts an input x iff all computations on input x are accepting and there are no infinite computations or blocked partial computations on input x. Show how to convert an $\forall$FA to an equivalent DFR.

(b) Lucy and Charlie are sitting at a table. On the table is a square tray with four glasses at the corners. Charlie's goal is to turn all the glasses either right-side up or upside down. However, Charlie is blindfolded and he is wearing mittens. He does not know the initial state of the glasses. If they are initially all turned the same way, then Charlie automatically wins. In his turn, Charlie may grab one or two glasses and turn them over; however, because of the blindfold and mittens he cannot see or feel whether the glasses he grabbed are right-side up or upside down. He can, however, choose whether to grab adjacent glasses or diagonally opposite glasses. If the glasses are all turned the same direction, Lucy announces that Charlie has won. Otherwise, Lucy may rotate the tray, just to make Charlie's goal harder.

Find the shortest sequence of actions by Charlie that is guaranteed to win the game, no matter how Lucy plays. Prove that your solution is correct and is the shortest possible.

4.7 MINIMIZING DFRs

Computer scientists put a lot of effort into finding optimal programs for tasks, where "optimal" means "using the minimum amount of some resource." Some important resources are time and memory, so we may look for real programs that run as fast as possible or use as little storage as possible. Although it is difficult or impossible to optimize programs for real-world computers, it is possible to optimize DFRs. This is useful in designing compilers and hardware.

Suppose that L is the language recognized by a DFR P. We say that the program P is *minimal* if no DFR for L has fewer control states than P. Given a DFR P, we will show how to find a minimal DFR for $L(P)$.

Step 1: Standardize. We eliminate null instructions and then EOF tests (Section 4.1), so that every instruction of the DFR performs a SCAN on the input device. Next we eliminate unreachable states as in Section 3.4.3. Call the resulting program P.

Recall that a recognizer may contain nonfinal control states. We assert that every control state in P is in fact final. Why? Let q be a control state in P. Then q is reachable via some path labeled SCAN$x_1, \ldots,$ SCANx_n. Let $x = x_1 \cdots x_n$. On input x, the program P must reach q and stop there, because every instruction scans a character. Because a recognizer must give a result for every input, the control state q must be either accepting or rejecting.

Step 2: Merge equivalent states. In this paragraph, we think of P's initial state as variable; only P's final states and instruction set are fixed. We say that two control states q_1 and q_2 are *equivalent* if for every string

x, P accepts x when started in state q_1 iff P accepts x when started in state q_2, i.e., iff P produces the same result whether it is started in state q_1 or q_2. If q_1 is reached in the middle of running P and q_2 is equivalent to q_1 then the computation could continue from q_2 without changing the result. Thus, if q_1 and q_2 are equivalent then they can both be replaced by a single state without changing the language accepted. Furthermore, we will prove that every program that accepts $L(P)$ has at least as many control states as P has inequivalent states. Thus, merging equivalent states into a single state produces the minimal program that is equivalent to P.

We give the details of how to merge equivalent states, and then we prove that the resulting program is in fact a DFR and is minimal. In the next section, we will give an algorithm for determining which states are equivalent.

How to merge equivalent states Let E denote the equivalence relation on states defined above, i.e., $q_1 \; E \; q_2$ if and only q_1 is equivalent to q_2.

We merge states as follows: Let $[q]$ denote the set of control states that are equivalent to q, i.e.,

$$[q] = \{q' : q' \; E \; q\}.$$

In the minimal program P', the single state $[q]$ will replace all the states that are equivalent to q in P; we let

$$Q' = \{[q] : q \in Q\}.$$

Instructions that use q in P will be converted to instructions that use $[q]$ in P'. To be precise, for each instruction $(q_1 \to q_2, \text{SCAN}c)$ in P, let P' contain the instruction $([q_1] \to [q_2], \text{SCAN}c)$. If q is the initial state of P, we make $[q]$ the initial state of P'. If q is an accepting state in P, we make $[q]$ an accepting state in P'. If q is a rejecting state in P, we make $[q]$ a rejecting state in P'. That completes the minimization algorithm. The reader may verify that P' simulates P in lockstep (Exercise 4.7-4).

Proving that P' is deterministic For each string $u \in \Sigma^*$, we define a partial function t_u from Q to Q. The partial function t_u maps each control state q to the control state that P would finish in if it were started in control state q with input u. (Because P is deterministic and has no null instructions,

t_u is a partial function. If P were nondeterministic or had null instructions, then we could say only that t_u would be a relation.) Observe that if P is in control state q' at some time in a computation and then the string v is scanned, P will be in the control state $q't_v$ immediately afterward. Therefore $qt_{uv} = qt_u t_v$.

If control states q_1 and q_2 are equivalent and u is any string then we assert that the control states $q_1 t_u$ and $q_2 t_u$ must also be equivalent. Why? Let x be any string. Because q_1 and q_2 are equivalent, P produces the same result on input ux whether started in state q_1 or state q_2. Therefore $q_1 t_{ux} = q_2 t_{ux}$, so

$$q_1 t_u t_x \;=\; q_1 t_{ux} \;=\; q_2 t_{ux} \;=\; q_2 t_u t_x.$$

Since this is true for every x, $q_1 t_u$ and $q_2 t_u$ are equivalent control states.

Now we show that P' is deterministic. For the sake of contradiction, assume that P' is not deterministic. Then P' contains two instructions of the form $([q_1] \to [q_2], \text{SCAN}c)$ and $([q_1] \to [q_3], \text{SCAN}c)$. We must show that $[q_2] = [q_3]$, so that these are really the same instruction. In order for these instructions to belong to P', the original program P must contain the instructions $(q_{10} \to q_{20}, \text{SCAN}c)$ and $(q_{11} \to q_{31}, \text{SCAN}c)$ where $q_{10}\ E\ q_1$, $q_{20}\ E\ q_2$, $q_{11}\ E\ q_1$, and $q_{31}\ E\ q_3$. Because E is an equivalence relation, $q_{10}\ E\ q_{11}$, so $q_{10}t_c\ E\ q_{11}t_c$. Therefore,

$$q_2\ E\ q_{20} \;=\; q_{10}t_c\ E\ q_{11}t_c \;=\; q_{31}\ E\ q_3.$$

Because $q_2\ E\ q_3$, $[q_2] = [q_3]$.

Proving that P′ is minimal Next we show that P' has the fewest states of any DFR that is equivalent to P.

DEFINITION 4.22 (Prefix Equivalence). Let L be a language. Two strings x_1 and x_2 are *prefix equivalent* with respect to L (denoted $x_1 \sim_L x_2$) if

$$(\forall u \in \Sigma^*)[x_1 u \in L \iff x_2 u \in L].$$

The reader may verify that $\sim_L$ is an equivalence relation. If strings $x_1, \ldots, x_k$ are all prefix inequivalent with respect to L, then, on an informal level, any DFR that recognizes L needs to be able to tell those strings apart, and it needs at least k control states in order to do so. This is made precise in the theorem and proof below.

THEOREM 4.23 (Myhill–Nerode Theorem). *The number of control states in any minimal DFR for a language L is equal to the number of equivalence classes of* $\sim_L$. *(Such a DFR exists if and only if the number of equivalence classes of* $\sim_L$ *is finite.)*

Proof: First, if P is any DFR that recognizes L, we show that P has at least as many control states as $\sim_L$ has equivalence classes. Let $x_1, \ldots, x_k$ be strings that belong to distinct equivalence classes of $\sim_L$. We show that $q_{\text{start}}t_{x_1}, \ldots, q_{\text{start}}t_{x_k}$ are distinct control states of P. The proof is by contradiction. Suppose that $q_{\text{start}}t_{x_i} = q_{\text{start}}t_{x_j}$ for distinct i and j. Then for every string u,

$$\begin{aligned} x_iu \in L \quad &\Longleftrightarrow \quad q_{\text{start}}t_{x_i}t_u\omega_{\text{control}} = \text{ACCEPT} \\ &\Longleftrightarrow \quad q_{\text{start}}t_{x_j}t_u\omega_{\text{control}} = \text{ACCEPT} \\ &\Longleftrightarrow \quad x_ju \in L. \end{aligned}$$

Therefore, $x_i \sim_L x_j$, which is a contradiction.

If $\sim_L$ has a finite number k of equivalence classes, we construct a DFR P that recognizes L and has exactly k control states. In its control, this program P keeps track of which equivalence class the input belongs to, as follows. For each string $x \in \Sigma^*$, let

$$[x] = \{x' : x' \sim_L x\}.$$

P's control set is $\{[x] : x \in \Sigma^*\}$, which has exactly k elements. State $[x]$ is accepting if $x \in L$, rejecting otherwise. P's instruction set consists of all instructions of the form

$$([x] \to [xc], \text{SCAN}c).$$

The reader may verify that the program is deterministic, and that after an input x is scanned the control state is in fact $[x]$ (Exercise 4.7-6). ∎

COROLLARY 4.24. *Let P be a DFR in which all control states are reachable, and let E be the equivalence relation on states defined in this section. Any DFR that is equivalent to P has at least as many control states as E has equivalence classes.*

Proof: Let the initial control state of P be q_{start}, and let the distinct equivalence classes of E be $[q_1], \ldots, [q_k]$. For each i choose u_i such that $q_{\text{start}} t_{u_i} = q_i$. (These strings must exist because each state q_i is reachable in P.) If $i \neq j$, then q_i and q_j are not equivalent, i.e., $q_i \not{E}\, q_j$, so there exists a string v such that $q_i t_v \omega_{\text{control}} \neq q_j t_v \omega_{\text{control}}$. But

$$\begin{aligned} u_i v \in L &\iff q_{\text{start}} t_{u_i} t_v \omega_{\text{control}} = \text{ACCEPT} \\ &\iff q_i t_v \omega_{\text{control}} = \text{ACCEPT} \\ &\iff q_j t_v \omega_{\text{control}} = \text{REJECT} \\ &\iff q_{\text{start}} t_{u_j} t_v \omega_{\text{control}} = \text{REJECT} \\ &\iff u_j v \notin L. \end{aligned}$$

so $u_i \not\sim_L u_j$. Since this holds for all i and j, we have shown that $u_1, \ldots, u_k$ belong to different equivalence classes of $\sim_L$. By the Myhill–Nerode theorem, any DFR that recognizes L must have at least k states. ■

Corollary 4.24 implies that the program P' constructed by our algorithm actually contains the minimum number of states possible for any DFR that is equivalent to P.

EXAMPLE 4.25. Let L be the set of strings over $\{\texttt{a}, \texttt{b}\}$ that contain at least one occurrence of `abbaba` or `bbaabb` as a substring. Using ideas from Figure 1.5, we have designed a DFR that recognizes L. The program is presented in Figure 4.25. We will use the Myhill–Nerode theorem to prove that this DFR is in fact minimal.

We say that a string u *distinguishes* two control states q_1 and q_2 in a DFR P if, on input u, P produces different results depending on whether it starts in control state q_1 or control state q_2. Such a string proves that q_1 and q_2 are inequivalent.

Let $p_i(x)$ denote the prefix of x having length i, and let $s_i(x)$ denote the suffix of x obtained by deleting $p_i(x)$ from the beginning. Note that all rejecting states have been labeled with the string $p_i(\texttt{abbaba})$ or $p_i(\texttt{bbaabb})$ for some $i \leq 5$. Let x be `abbaba` or `bbaabb`; then $p_i(x)$ is distinguished from each other state by the string $s_i(x)$. Because all states of this DFR are inequivalent, it has the minimum possible number of states. ■ ■ ■

The Myhill–Nerode theorem can be used to prove that certain languages are not regular.

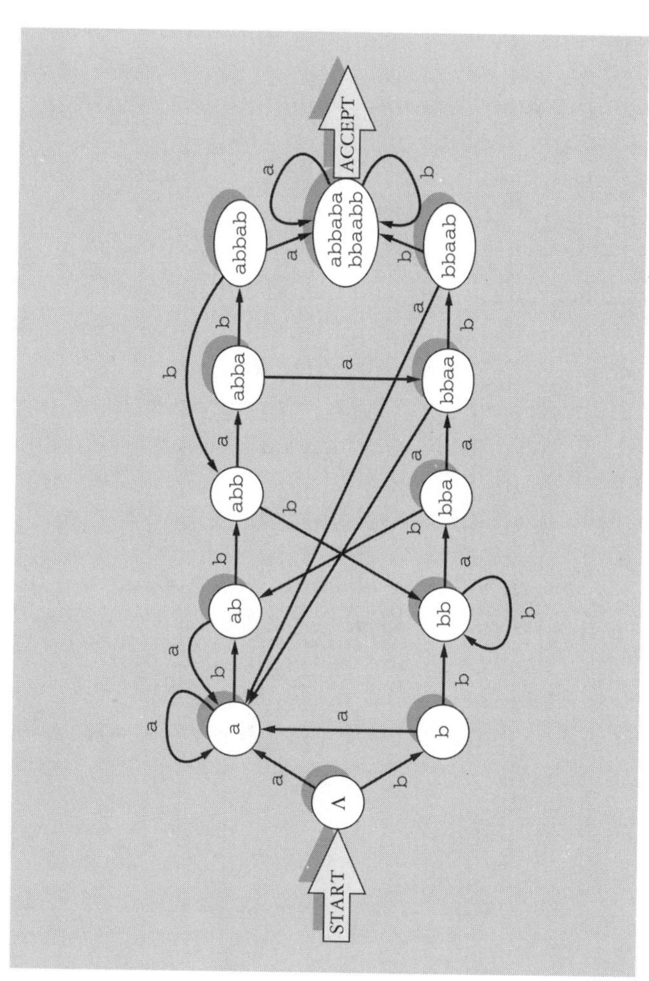

FIGURE 4.24: A program that recognizes $\{a, b\}^*(abbaba \cup bbaabb)\{a, b\}^*$. All states are rejecting unless marked accepting.

EXAMPLE 4.26. Let $L = \{a^n b^n : n \geq 0\}$. None of the strings $\Lambda, a, a^2, \ldots$ are equivalent under $\sim_L$, because $a^i b^i \in L$ but $a^j b^i \notin L$ for $i \neq j$. Therefore $\sim_L$ has infinitely many different equivalence classes, so L cannot be recognized by a DFR. Therefore L is not regular. ■■■

In Section 4.9, we will present another method for proving that certain languages are not regular.

EXAMPLE 4.27. We can also use the Myhill–Nerode theorem to obtain lower bounds on the size of DFRs for certain languages. For example, fix a positive integer n and let $L = \{a, b\}^* a \{a, b\}^{n-1}$. Let x and y be two distinct strings in $\{a, b\}^n$; then x and y differ in at least one character, say the ith. Therefore $xb^{i-1} \in L \iff yb^{i-1} \notin L$, because one of them has an a $n - 1$ characters from the end, and the other has a b $n - 1$ characters from the end. Therefore $\sim_L$ has at least 2^n distinct equivalence classes, so any DFR that recognizes L requires at least 2^n states.

In contrast, L is accepted by an NFA with only $n + 1$ control states. Thus we see that an exponential blowup may be necessary when simulating an NFA by a DFR. ■■■

COROLLARY 4.28. *For every $k \geq 1$ there is a language accepted by an NFA with k states but not recognized by any DFR with fewer than 2^{k-1} states.*

Proof: Let $n = k - 1$, and define L as in Example 4.27. L is accepted by an NFA with $n + 1 = k$ states (Exercise 4.7-12) but is not recognized by any DFR with fewer than $2^n = 2^{k-1}$ states. ■

Exercises

4.7-1 Repeat Example 4.25 for substrings abbaba and bbaaba.

4.7-2 Prove rigorously that $t_{uv} = t_u t_v$ for all strings u and v.

4.7-3 Prove that E is an equivalence relation.

4.7-4 Prove that the minimal equivalent DFR P' constructed by the techniques of this section recognizes the same language as P.

4.7-5 Prove that $\sim_L$ is an equivalence relation.

4.7-6 Let P be the k-state DFR constructed in the second half of the proof of Theorem 4.23.

(a) Prove that P is deterministic.

(b) Prove, by induction on $|x|$, that on input x the program P halts in state $[x]$.

4.7-7 Let L be recognized by a DFR P that has no null instructions, EOF tests, or unreachable states. Let q_{start} be the initial state of P.

(a) Prove that if $q_{\text{start}}t_x = q_{\text{start}}t_y$, then $x \sim_L y$.

(b) Give a counterexample to show that $x \sim_L y$ does not imply $q_{\text{start}}t_x = q_{\text{start}}t_y$.

(c) Define the *infix equivalence relation* for L (denoted $\approx_L$) by $x \approx_L y$ if and only if

$$(\forall u)(\forall v)[uxv \in L \iff uyv \in L].$$

Prove that if $t_x = t_y$ then $x \approx_L y$.

(d) Give a counterexample to show that $x \approx_L y$ does not imply $t_x = t_y$.

(e) Now assume that P is minimal. Prove that

$$q_{\text{start}}t_x = q_{\text{start}}t_y \iff x \sim_L y$$

and

$$t_x = t_y \iff x \approx_L y.$$

4.7-8 Refer to the definition of infix equivalence in Exercise 4.7-7(c).

(a) Prove that if $x_1 \sim_L x_2$ and $y_1 \approx_L y_2$ then $x_1y_1 \sim_L x_2y_2$.

(b) Prove that if $x_1 \approx_L x_2$ and $y_1 \approx_L y_2$ then $x_1y_1 \approx_L x_2y_2$.

(c) Prove that $y_1 \approx_L y_2$ if and only if

$$(\forall x_1, x_2)[x_1 \sim_L x_2 \Rightarrow x_1y_1 \sim_L x_2y_2].$$

4.7-9 Refer to the definition of infix equivalence in Exercise 4.7-7(c).

(a) Prove that $\approx_L$ is an equivalence relation.

(b) Prove that L is recognized by a DFR if and only if $\approx_L$ has finitely many equivalence classes.

4.7-10 Refer to the definition of infix equivalence in Exercise 4.7-7(c). Give an algorithm to determine whether $x \approx_L y$.

4.7-11 Use the Myhill–Nerode theorem to prove that the following languages are not regular:
(a) $\{\mathtt{a}^n\mathtt{b}\mathtt{a}^n : n \geq 0\}$
(b) $\{\mathtt{a}^{n^2} : n \geq 0\}$

4.7-12 Construct an NFA with $n+1$ states that accepts $\{\mathtt{a},\mathtt{b}\}^*\mathtt{a}\{\mathtt{a},\mathtt{b}\}^n$. Hint: See Figure 1.17.

4.7-13 Let L_n be the set of all strings $x_1\#x_2\#\cdots x_m\#\#x$ such that $x_1, x_2, \ldots, x_m$ and x are each n characters long and there exists i such that $x = x_i$.
(a) Prove that every DFR that recognizes L_n must have at least 2^{2^n} control states.
(b) Refer to Exercise 4.6-7 for the definition of AFM programs. Prove that L_n is accepted by an AFM program with $O(n)$ control states.

4.7-14 Let $L = \{x : \#_{\mathtt{a}}(x) \equiv 0 \pmod{k}\}$.
(a) Prove that L is recognized by a DFR with k control states but not by any DFR with fewer than k control states.
(b) Prove that L is not recognized by any NFA with fewer than k control states.

4.7-15 Prove that for every $k \geq 3$ there is a language accepted by an NFA with k states but not recognized by any DFR with fewer than 2^k states. Hint: Consider an NFA N with control set $\{0, \ldots, k-1\}$, initial state 0, accepting state 0, and the following instructions:

$$(i \to (i+1) \bmod k, \text{SCAN}\,\mathtt{a}) \quad \text{for } 0 \leq i \leq k-1$$

$$(i \to i, \text{SCAN}\,\mathtt{b}) \quad \text{for } 1 \leq i \leq k-1$$

$$(0 \to 0, \text{SCAN}\,\mathtt{a}).$$

(Such an NFA, with $k = 6$, is shown in Figure 4.25.) Construct an equivalent DFR D via the subset construction but without eliminating unreachable states. Then D's control set consists of all subsets

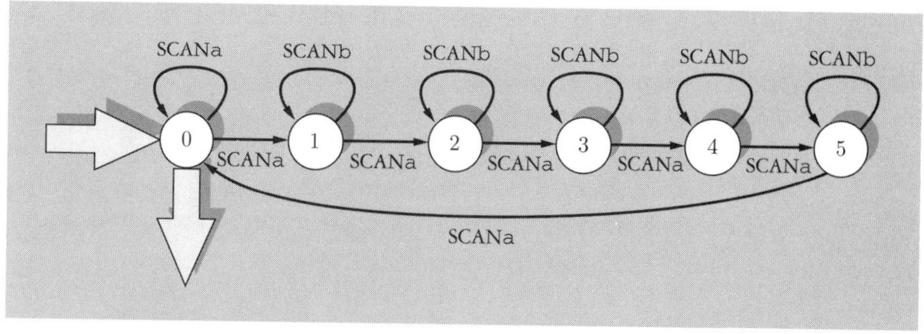

FIGURE 4.25: An NFA with 6 states that is not equivalent to any DFR with fewer than 64 states.

of N's control set. If S and S' are distinct control states of D prove that S and S' are not prefix equivalent. Prove that every subset of $\{0, \ldots, k-1\}$ is a reachable state in D. Therefore D is a minimal DFR, so every equivalent DFR requires at least 2^k states.

4.7-16 Let R and S be regular languages recognized by DFRs with r control states and s control states, respectively. By using the pairing construction, we can produce DFRs with rs control states that recognize the languages $R \cap S$ and $R \cup S$. Prove that these constructions are optimal, i.e., for every r and s, there exist regular languages R and S recognized by DFRs with r control states and s control states, respectively, such that

(a) every DFR that recognizes $R \cap S$ has at least rs control states.

(b) every DFR that recognizes $R \cup S$ has at least rs control states.

4.7-17 *(a) Re-do Exercise 4.7-16(a) for NFAs.

(b) Is Exercise 4.7-16(b) true for NFAs?

4.7.1 Determining Equivalent States

In this section, we give an algorithm for the difficult step in DFR minimization, namely, computing the equivalence classes of the relation E. We compute these equivalence classes by successive refinement, first considering inputs of length at most zero, then at most one, then at most two, and so on. That is, we define $q_1\ E_\ell\ q_2$ if for all strings x of length ℓ or less, P accepts x when started in state q_1 if and only if P accepts x when started in state q_2. It is easy to see that E_ℓ is an equivalence relation. In symbols, we have $q_1\ E_\ell\ q_2$ if and only if

$$(\forall u \in (\Sigma \cup \Lambda)^\ell)\big[q_1 t_u \omega_{\text{control}} = q_2 t_u \omega_{\text{control}}\big].$$

As we consider more inputs, we distinguish more states, so we obtain more but smaller equivalence classes. By definition,

$$E = \bigcap_{\ell \geq 0} E_\ell.$$

To compute E_0, note that if $|u| = 0$ then $u = \Lambda$, so $t_u = I$; thus

$$q_1\ E_0\ q_2 \iff q_1 \omega_{\text{control}} = q_2 \omega_{\text{control}},$$

i.e., $q_1\ E_0\ q_2$ iff control states q_1 and q_2 are both accepting or both rejecting.

Suppose that we have computed E_ℓ and wish to compute $E_{\ell+1}$. We have $q_1\ E_{\ell+1}\ q_2$ iff (1) $q_1\ E_\ell\ q_2$ and (2) for every string u of length $\ell + 1$, $q_1 t_u \omega_{\text{control}} = q_2 t_u \omega_{\text{control}}$. We rewrite condition (2) in symbols:

$$\begin{aligned}
&(\forall u \in \Sigma^{\ell+1})\big[q_1 t_u \omega_{\text{control}} = q_2 t_u \omega_{\text{control}}\big] \\
&\iff (\forall c \in \Sigma)(\forall v \in \Sigma^\ell)\big[q_1 t_{cv} \omega_{\text{control}} = q_2 t_{cv} \omega_{\text{control}}\big] \\
&\iff (\forall c \in \Sigma)(\forall v \in \Sigma^\ell)\big[q_1 t_c t_v \omega_{\text{control}} = q_2 t_c t_v \omega_{\text{control}}\big] \\
&\iff (\forall c \in \Sigma)\big[(q_1 t_c)\ E_\ell\ (q_2 t_c)\big].
\end{aligned}$$

Thus

$$q_1\ E_{\ell+1}\ q_2 \iff q_1\ E_\ell\ q_2 \text{ and } (\forall c \in \Sigma)\big[(q_1 t_c)\ E_\ell\ (q_2 t_c)\big].$$

Observe that $E \subseteq E_{\ell+1} \subseteq E_\ell$ for all ℓ. Since $E_{\ell+1}$ and E_ℓ are both equivalence relations, $E_{\ell+1}$ must have at least as many equivalence classes as E_ℓ. The relation E_0 has at least one equivalence class, and the relation E has at most $|Q|$ equivalence classes. Therefore, by the pigeonhole principle, there must exist $k \leq |Q| - 1$ such that E_{k+1} and E_k have the same number of equivalence classes. Then E_{k+1} and E_k are equal. Because E_{k+2} is computed from E_{k+1} in the same way that E_{k+1} is computed from E_k, it follows that

$E_{k+2} = E_{k+1} = E_k$. In fact, a simple induction (Exercise 4.7-21) shows that $E_\ell = E_k$ for every $\ell \geq k$. Since $E_k \subseteq E_\ell$ for every $\ell \leq k$, we have

$$E = \bigcap_{\ell \geq 0} E_\ell = E_k.$$

Thus we can compute E by computing E_ℓ for $\ell = 1, 2, \ldots,$ stopping as soon as we find k such that $E_k = E_{k+1}$.

EXAMPLE 4.29. Consider the DFR shown in Figure 4.26, which recognizes the set of all strings over $\{\mathtt{a}\}$ whose length is 1 or 5 modulo 8. The relation E_0 partitions the control set into two equivalence classes: $C_{00} = \{1, 5\}$, the set of accepting states, and $C_{01} = \{0, 2, 3, 4, 6, 7\}$, the set of rejecting states.

The equivalence classes of E_1 partition the equivalence classes of E_0. To determine how an equivalence class of E_0 is partitioned, we apply $t_{\mathtt{a}}$ to each of its elements and see if any of the resulting states belong to distinct

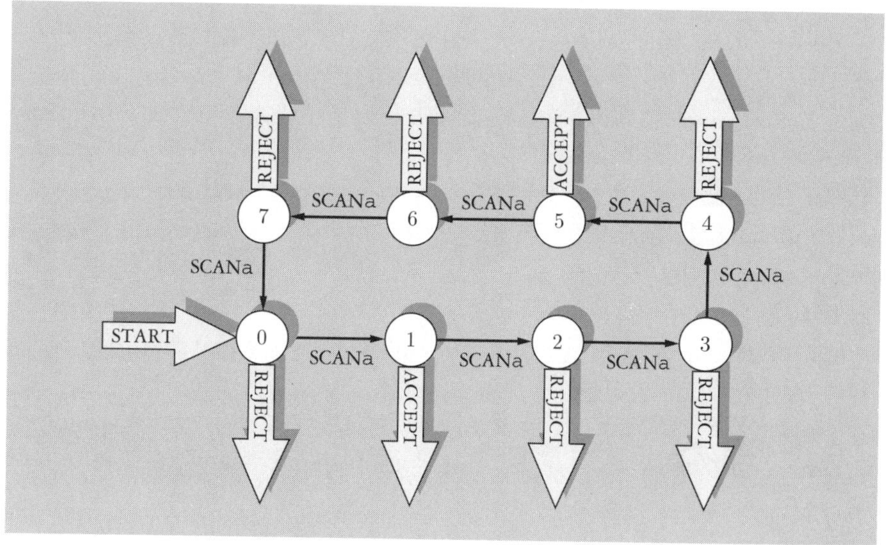

FIGURE 4.26: A DFR that recognizes the set of all strings over $\{\mathtt{a}\}$ whose length is 1 or 5 modulo 8. The control state records the length of the input modulo 8.

equivalence classes of E_0. In general, $it_{\mathrm{a}} = (i+1) \bmod 8$. Let us see how C_{00} is partitioned. We find $1t_{\mathrm{a}} = 2$ and $5t_{\mathrm{a}} = 6$; because 2 and 6 belong to the same equivalence class of E_0, this does not lead to any partitioning of C_{00}, so $C_{10} = C_{00} = \{1, 5\}$.

Now let us see how C_{01} is partitioned. We have $0t_{\mathrm{a}} = 1$, $2t_{\mathrm{a}} = 3$, $3t_{\mathrm{a}} = 4$, $4t_{\mathrm{a}} = 5$, $6t_{\mathrm{a}} = 7$, and $7t_{\mathrm{a}} = 0$; because 1 and 5 belong to a different equivalence class from 3, 4, 7, and 0, we have distinguished the states 0 and 4 from 2, 3, 6, and 7. Thus C_{01} is partitioned into $C_{11} = \{0, 4\}$ and $C_{12} = \{2, 3, 6, 7\}$.

By repeating this process, we determine the equivalence classes of E_2. Let us see how C_{10} is partitioned. We get $1t_{\mathrm{a}} = 2$ and $5t_{\mathrm{a}} = 6$; because 2 and 6 belong to the same equivalence class of E_1, this does not lead to any partitioning of C_{10}, so $C_{20} = C_{10} = \{1, 5\}$.

Now let us see how C_{11} is partitioned. We have $0t_{\mathrm{a}} = 1$ and $4t_{\mathrm{a}} = 5$; because 1 and 5 belong to the same equivalence class of E_1, this does not lead to any partitioning of C_{11}, so $C_{21} = C_{11} = \{0, 4\}$.

Next let us see how C_{12} is partitioned. We find $2t_{\mathrm{a}} = 3$, $3t_{\mathrm{a}} = 4$, $6t_{\mathrm{a}} = 7$, and $7t_{\mathrm{a}} = 0$; because 3 and 7 belong to a different equivalence class from 4 and 0, we have distinguished the states 2 and 6 from 3 and 7. Thus C_{12} is partitioned into $C_{22} = \{2, 6\}$ and $C_{23} = \{3, 7\}$.

By repeating this process, we determine the equivalence classes of E_3. Let us see how C_{20} is partitioned. We have $1t_{\mathrm{a}} = 2$ and $5t_{\mathrm{a}} = 6$; because 2 and 6 belong to the same equivalence class of E_2, this does not lead to any partitioning of C_{20}, so $C_{30} = C_{20} = \{1, 5\}$.

For C_{21}, we get $0t_{\mathrm{a}} = 1$ and $4t_{\mathrm{a}} = 5$; because 1 and 5 belong to the same equivalence class of E_2, this does not lead to any partitioning of C_{21}, so $C_{31} = C_{21} = \{0, 4\}$.

For C_{22}, we find $2t_{\mathrm{a}} = 3$ and $6t_{\mathrm{a}} = 7$; because 3 and 7 belong to the same equivalence class of E_2, this does not lead to any partitioning of C_{22}, so $C_{32} = \{3, 7\}$.

Finally, for C_{23} have $3t_{\mathrm{a}} = 4$ and $7t_{\mathrm{a}} = 0$; because 4 and 0 belong to the same equivalence class of E_2, this does not lead to any partitioning of C_{23}, so $C_{33} = C_{23} = \{3, 7\}$.

Because E_3 has the same equivalence classes as E_2, the relation E_3 must be equal to E_2; therefore $E_3 = E$ and no more partitioning is possible. The control states of the minimal DFR are $\{0, 4\}$, $\{1, 5\}$, $\{2, 6\}$, and $\{3, 7\}$, the

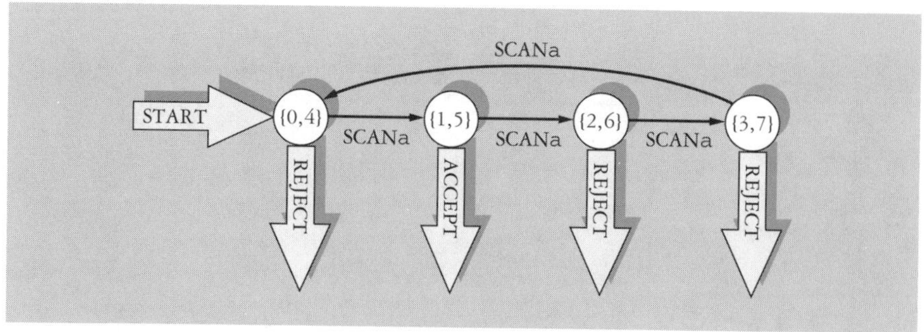

FIGURE 4.27: A minimal DFR that recognizes the set of all strings over $\{\mathtt{a}\}$ whose length is 1 or 5 modulo 8. The control state records the length of the input modulo 4.

four equivalence classes into which E partitions the original control set. The instruction $(0 \to 1, \text{SCAN}\mathtt{a})$ becomes $(\{0,4\} \to \{1,5\}, \text{SCAN}\mathtt{a})$ in the minimal program; $(1 \to 2, \text{SCAN}\mathtt{a})$ becomes $(\{1,5\} \to \{2,6\}, \text{SCAN}\mathtt{a})$; and so on. The minimal DFR is shown in Figure 4.27. ■■■

EXAMPLE 4.30. Consider the DFR shown in Figure 4.28, which recognizes the set of all strings over $\{\mathtt{a}, \mathtt{b}\}$ such that the number of $\mathtt{a}$'s is the same as the number of $\mathtt{b}$'s modulo 3.

The relation E_0 partitions the control set into two equivalence classes:

$$C_{00} = \{(0,0), (1,1), (2,2)\},$$

the set of accepting states, and

$$C_{01} = \{(0,1), (0,2), (1,0), (1,2), (2,0), (2,1)\},$$

the set of rejecting states.

The equivalence classes of E_1 partition the equivalence classes of E_0. To determine how an equivalence class of E_0 is partitioned, we apply $t_{\mathtt{a}}$ to each of its elements and see if any of the resulting states belong to distinct equivalence classes of E_0; then we do the same with $t_{\mathtt{b}}$. In general, $(i,j)t_{\mathtt{a}} = ((i+1) \bmod 3, j)$ and $(i,j)t_{\mathtt{b}} = (i, (j+1) \bmod 3)$. Let us see how C_{00}

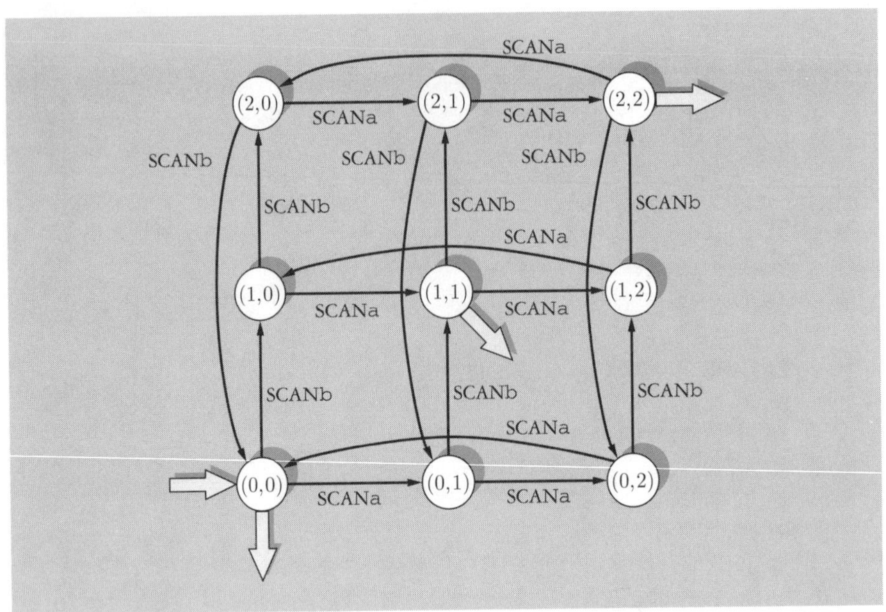

FIGURE 4.28: A DFR that recognizes the language $\{x \in \{\mathtt{a},\mathtt{b}\}^* : \#_{\mathtt{a}}(x) \equiv \#_{\mathtt{b}}(x) \pmod 3\}$. The control stores the number of a's and b's modulo 3 seen so far. The initial control state is $(0, 0)$. The accepting control states are $(0, 0)$, $(1, 1)$, and $(2, 2)$; the other six control states are rejecting.

is partitioned. We get $(0, 0)t_{\mathtt{a}} = (1, 0)$, $(1, 1)t_{\mathtt{a}} = (2, 1)$, and $(2, 2)t_{\mathtt{a}} = (0, 2)$; because $(1, 0)$, $(2, 1)$, and $(0, 2)$ belong to the same equivalence class of E_0, this does not lead to any partitioning of C_{00}. In addition, $(0, 0)t_{\mathtt{b}} = (0, 1)$, $(1, 1)t_{\mathtt{b}} = (1, 2)$, and $(2, 2)t_{\mathtt{b}} = (2, 0)$; because $(0, 1)$, $(1, 2)$, and $(2, 0)$ belong to the same equivalence class of E_0, this does not lead to any partitioning of C_{00} either, so $C_{10} = C_{00} = \{(0, 0), (1, 1), (2, 2)\}$.

Now let us see how C_{01} is partitioned. We find $(0, 1)t_{\mathtt{a}} = (1, 1)$, $(0, 2)t_{\mathtt{a}} = (1, 2)$, $(1, 0)t_{\mathtt{a}} = (2, 0)$, $(1, 2)t_{\mathtt{a}} = (2, 2)$, $(2, 0)t_{\mathtt{a}} = (0, 0)$, and $(2, 1)t_{\mathtt{a}} = (0, 1)$; because $(1, 1)$, $(2, 2)$, and $(0, 0)$ belong to a different equivalence class from $(1, 2)$, $(2, 0)$, and $(0, 1)$, we have distinguished the states $(0,1)$, $(1,2)$, and $(2,0)$ from the states $(0,2)$, $(1,0)$, and $(2,1)$. In addition, $(0,1)t_\mathtt{b} = (0,2)$, $(0,2)t_\mathtt{b} = (0,0)$, $(1,0)t_\mathtt{b} = (1,1)$, $(1,2)t_\mathtt{b} = (1,0)$, $(2,0)t_\mathtt{b} = (2,1)$, and $(2,1)t_\mathtt{b} = (2,2)$; because $(0,0)$, $(1,1)$, and $(2,2)$ belong to a different equivalence class from $(0,2)$, $(1,0)$, and $(2,1)$, we have distinguished the states $(0,2)$, $(1,0)$, and $(2,1)$ from $(0,1)$, $(1,2)$, and $(2,0)$. Coincidentally, we discovered exactly the same thing by examining $t_\mathtt{a}$. Thus C_{01} is partitioned into $C_{11} = \{(0,2),(1,0),(2,1)\}$ and $C_{12} = \{(0,1),(1,2),(2,0)\}$.

By repeating that process, we determine the equivalence classes of E_2. Let us see how C_{10} is partitioned. We find that $(0,0)t_\mathtt{a} = (1,0)$, $(1,1)t_\mathtt{a} = (2,1)$, and $(2,2)t_\mathtt{a} = (0,2)$; because $(1,0)$, $(2,1)$, and $(0,2)$ belong to the same equivalence class of E_1, this does not lead to any partitioning of C_{10}. In addition, $(0,0)t_\mathtt{b} = (0,1)$, $(1,1)t_\mathtt{b} = (1,2)$, and $(2,2)t_\mathtt{b} = (2,0)$; because $(0,1)$, $(1,2)$, and $(2,0)$ belong to the same equivalence class of E_1, this does not lead to any partitioning of C_{10} either, so $C_{20} = C_{10} = \{(0,0),(1,1),(2,2)\}$.

Now let us see how C_{11} is partitioned. We get $(0,2)t_\mathtt{a} = (1,2)$, $(1,0)t_\mathtt{a} = (2,0)$, and $(2,1)t_\mathtt{a} = (0,1)$; because $(1,2)$, $(2,0)$, and $(0,1)$ belong to the same equivalence class of E_1, this does not lead to any partitioning of C_{11}. In addition, $(0,2)t_\mathtt{b} = (0,0)$, $(1,0)t_\mathtt{b} = (1,1)$, and $(2,1)t_\mathtt{b} = (2,2)$; because $(0,0)$, $(1,1)$, and $(2,2)$ belong to the same equivalence class of E_1, this does not lead to any partitioning of C_{11}. Thus $C_{21} = C_{11} = \{(0,2),(1,0),(2,1)\}$.

Finally, let us see how C_{12} is partitioned. We have $(2,0)t_\mathtt{a} = (0,0)$, $(0,1)t_\mathtt{a} = (1,1)$, and $(1,2)t_\mathtt{a} = (2,2)$; because $(0,0)$, $(1,1)$, and $(2,2)$ belong to the same equivalence class of E_1, this does not lead to any partitioning of C_{12}. In addition, $(2,0)t_\mathtt{b} = (2,1)$, $(0,1)t_\mathtt{b} = (0,2)$, and $(1,2)t_\mathtt{b} = (1,0)$; because $(2,1)$, $(0,2)$, and $(1,0)$ belong to the same equivalence class of E_1, this does not lead to any partitioning of C_{12}. Thus $C_{22} = C_{12} = \{(2,0),(0,1),(1,2)\}$.

Because E_2 has the same equivalence classes as E_1, the relation E_2 must be equal to E_1; therefore $E_2 = E$ and no more partitioning is possible. Let $C_0 = \{(0,0),(1,1),(2,2)\}$, $C_1 = \{(0,2),(1,0),(2,1)\}$, and $C_2 = \{(2,0),(0,1),(1,2)\}$, the three equivalence classes into which E partitions the control set. The instruction $((0,0) \to (0,1), \text{SCAN}\,\mathtt{a})$ becomes $(C_0 \to C_2, \text{SCAN}\,\mathtt{a})$ in the minimal program; $((0,0) \to (1,0), \text{SCAN}\,\mathtt{b})$

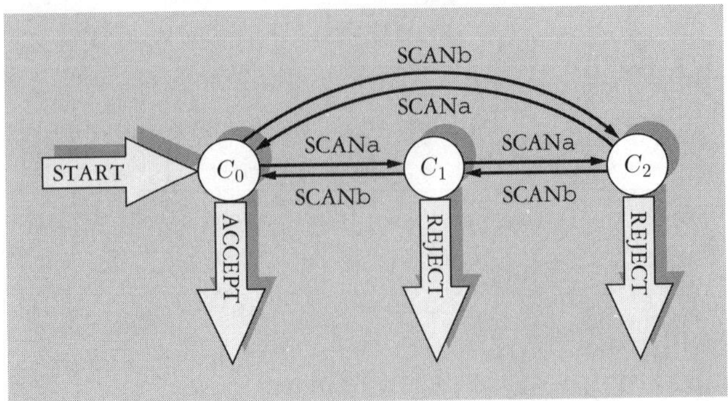

FIGURE 4.29: A minimal DFR that recognizes the set of all strings over {a,b} that contain equal numbers of a's and b's modulo 3. The control set records the number of a's minus the number of b's modulo 3.

becomes $(C_0 \to C_1, \text{SCAN}\mathtt{b})$; and so on. The minimal DFR is shown in Figure 4.29. ■ ■ ■

EXAMPLE 4.31. We minimize the DFR shown in Figure 4.30. By examining the terminator, we see that the equivalence classes of E_0 are $\{1, 3\}$ and $\{2, 4\}$. We find that $E_1 = E_0$, so $E = E_0$. The equivalence classes of E are therefore $\{1, 3\}$ and $\{2, 4\}$. The instruction $(1 \to 2, \text{SCAN}\mathtt{a})$ becomes $(\{1, 3\} \to \{2, 4\}, \text{SCAN}\mathtt{a})$ in the minimal program, the instruction $(2 \to 4, \text{SCAN}\mathtt{b})$ becomes $(\{2, 4\} \to \{2, 4\}, \text{SCAN}\mathtt{b})$, and so forth. The minimal DFR is shown in Figure 4.31. ■ ■ ■

The minimization algorithm is very handy. For example, we can use it in order to determine whether two DFRs P_1 and P_2 recognize the same language. Rename the control states of P_2 if necessary so that P_1 and P_2 have no control states in common. Eliminate null instructions and EOF tests from both programs. Combine P_1 and P_2 into a single program P with control states being all the control states of P_1 and P_2; the instructions are all the instructions of P_1 and P_2; the final states are all the final states of P_1 and P_2. Do not identify initial states or eliminate unreachable states. P is deterministic because P_1 and P_2 are deterministic and have no control states in common. Construct E for the combined program. P_1 and P_2 are

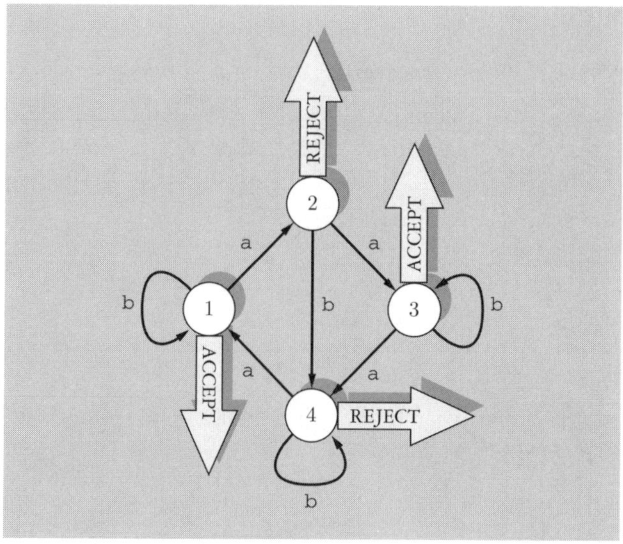

FIGURE 4.30: A DFR.

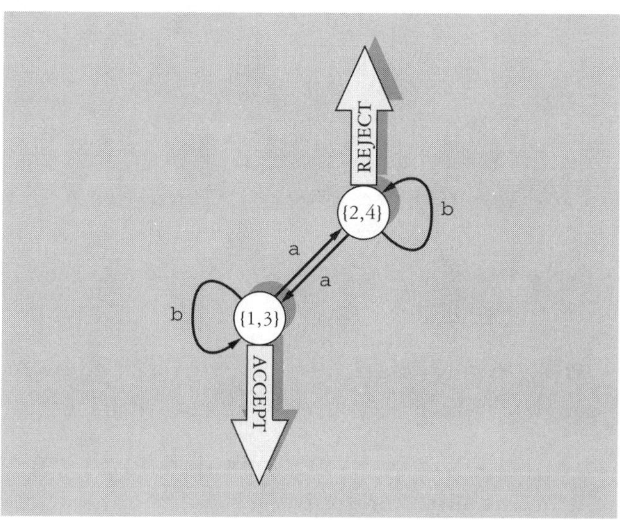

FIGURE 4.31: The minimal equivalent DFR.

equivalent if and only if their start states are equivalent under E. Thus we have the following corollary.

COROLLARY 4.32. *There is an algorithm to determine whether two DFRs are equivalent.* ■

For each DFR P, the minimal equivalent DFR is essentially unique (Exercise 4.7-24).

Exercises

4.7-18 Construct a minimal DFR equivalent to the following:
  (a) the DFR in Figure 4.32
  (b) the DFR in Figure 4.33
  (c) the DFR in Figure 4.7-18

4.7-19 Using this section's algorithm, minimize the DFR in Figure 3.45.

4.7-20 Minimize the DFRs that you produced in Exercise 4.6-5.

4.7-21 (a) Let n be a natural number, and let f be any function. Let g be a strictly decreasing function from sets to natural numbers, i.e.,

$$X \subset Y \Rightarrow g(X) > g(Y).$$

Let $S_0, S_1, \ldots$ be sets satisfying $S_{i+1} = f(S_i) \supseteq S_i$ and $1 \leq g(S_i) \leq n$ for all $i \geq 0$. Prove that $S_i = S_{n-1}$ for all $i \geq n-1$.

  (b) Prove that $E_\ell = E_k$ for every $\ell \geq k$ (see the algorithm for computing E).

4.7-22 Give an algorithm that determines whether two NFAs accept the same language. Your algorithm need not be efficient.

4.7-23 A *classifier* is like a recognizer except that there are more than two possible results. More precisely, each device starts in its usual initial state, the program is deterministic and gives a result for all inputs, and the result depends only on the final control state.

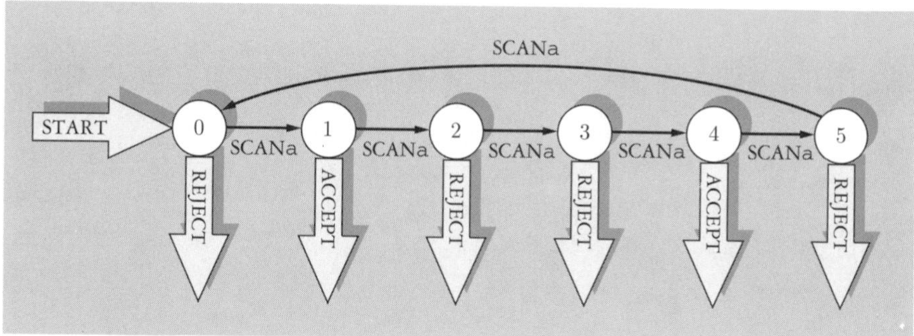

FIGURE 4.32: A DFR that recognizes the set of all strings over $\{\mathtt{a}\}$ whose length is 1 or 4 modulo 6. The control state records the length of the input modulo 6.

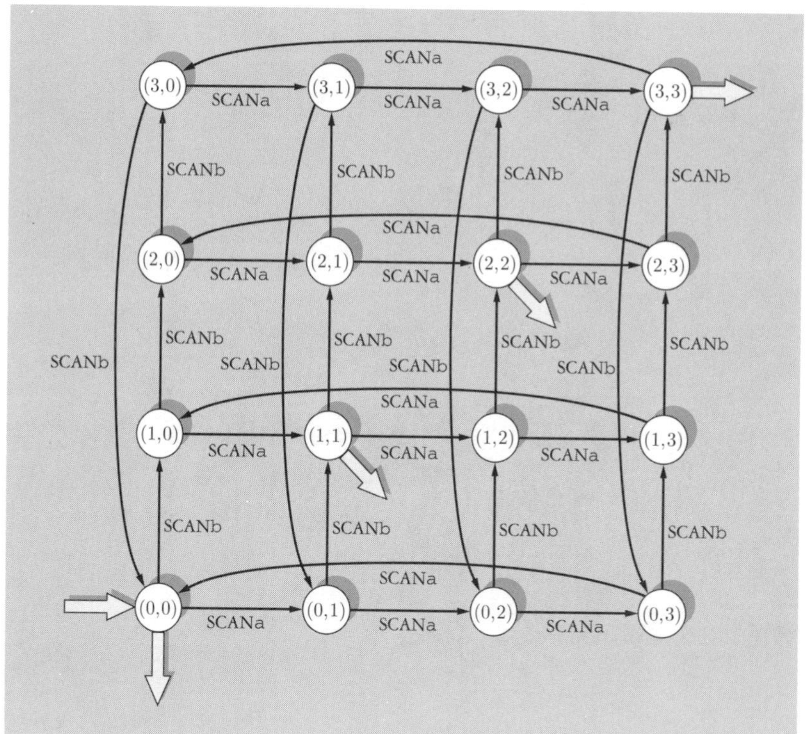

FIGURE 4.33: A DFR that recognizes the language $\{x \in \{\mathtt{a}, \mathtt{b}\}^* : \#_{\mathtt{a}}(x) \equiv \#_{\mathtt{b}}(x) \pmod 4\}$. The control stores the number of a's and b's modulo 4 seen so far. The initial control state is $(0, 0)$. The accepting control states are $(0, 0)$, $(1, 1)$, $(2, 2)$, and $(3, 3)$; the other 12 control states are rejecting.

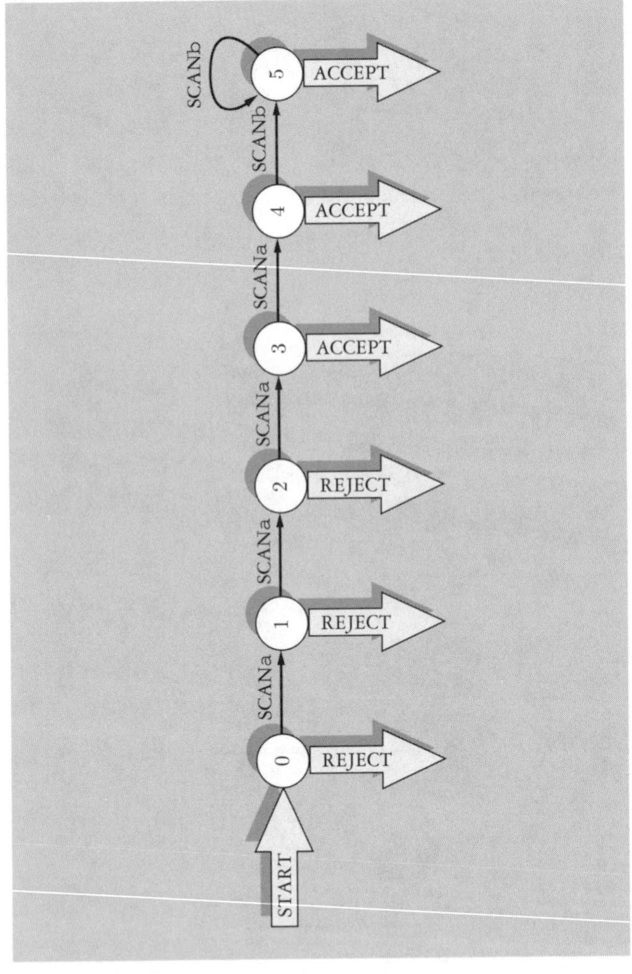

FIGURE 4.34: A DFR to be minimized.

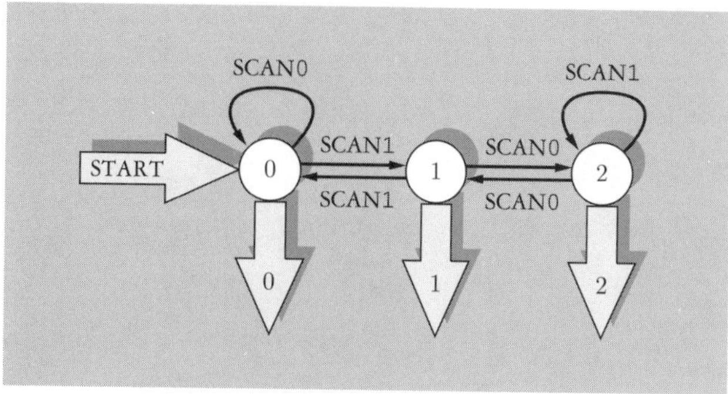

FIGURE 4.35: A program that computes x mod 3, where x is a binary numeral.

(a) Construct a classifier that determines the remainder modulo 3 of a nonnegative number written in binary.

Solution: The program is shown in Figure 4.35.

(b) Prove an analogue of the Myhill–Nerode theorem for classifiers.

(c) Show how to minimize a classifier.

4.7-24 (a) Let P_1 and P_2 be two minimal DFRs that do not use the EOF test and recognize the same language. Prove that P_1 and P_2 are identical except for the renaming of control states.

(b) Using part (a), present another algorithm that determines whether two DFRs recognize the same language.

4.8 CLOSURE PROPERTIES

In this section we prove that the class of regular languages is closed under several important operations: union, intersection, complementation, Kleene-closure, reversal, and quotient by arbitrary languages. Another very important property of regular languages is closure under finite transductions. Furthermore, the class of languages accepted by programs for machines with any fixed set of devices is closed under finite transductions;

this general property of machines will be useful when we study NSA languages in Section 6.1.

THEOREM 4.33. *The class of regular languages is closed under the following operations:*

- *Boolean operations (e.g., union, intersection, and complementation)*
- *concatenation*
- *Kleene-closure (*)*
- *reversal*

Proof: Closure under union, concatenation, and Kleene-closure follows directly from the definition of regular languages. Closure under complementation is implied because the regular languages are the DFR languages. Closure under the remaining Boolean operations follows from closure under union and complementation. Closure under reversal is obtained by reversing the edges in an NFA. ∎

We can use these closure properties to prove that certain languages are not regular.

EXAMPLE 4.34. Let L be the set of all strings over $\{\mathtt{a}, \mathtt{b}\}$ that have different numbers of a's and b's. Suppose that L is regular. Then $\overline{L}$ is regular. Now, $\overline{L}$ is the set of all strings with the same number of a's and b's. Then $L' = \overline{L} \cap \mathtt{a}^*\mathtt{b}^*$ is regular. But $L' = \{\mathtt{a}^n\mathtt{b}^n : n \geq 0\}$, which was proved not regular in Example 4.26. This contradiction implies that L is not regular. ∎∎∎

DEFINITION 4.35 (Quotient). If R and S are languages, the *quotient* of R by S (denoted R/S) is $\{x : (\exists y \in S)[xy \in R]\}$.

Intuitively, we have $x \in R/S$ if it is possible to extend x by a string in S to obtain a string in R or, equivalently, if x can be obtained by deleting a string in S from the end of a string in R. We prove that if R is regular and S is any language whatsoever, then R/S is regular.

THEOREM 4.36. *The class of regular languages is closed under quotient by arbitrary languages.*

Proof: Let R be a regular language, and let S be any language. Then there is a DFR P that recognizes R. The language R/S will be recognized by a DFR P' with the same initial control state and the same instruction set as P. Only the accepting states of P' will be different. We let q be an accepting control state in P' if and only if there exists $y \in S$ such that qt_y is an accepting control state of P. ■

Unlike the earlier proofs of closure properties, this proof is nonconstructive because we did not give an algorithm to determine whether there exists $y \in S$ such that qt_y is an accepting control state of P. In fact, no such algorithm is possible (there may not even be an algorithm to determine which strings belong to S). However, the proof can be made constructive if S is regular. See Corollary 4.41.

Exercises

4.8-1 Let R be a regular language over an alphabet Σ. Let

$$C = \{R/L : L \subseteq \Sigma^*\}.$$

Prove that C is a finite set of languages.

4.8.1 Closure under Finite Transductions

Recall that transducers running on finite machines are called *finite transducers* and their transfer relations are called *finite transductions*.[2] Finite transductions are very important in obtaining closure properties for general classes of languages. We will use them in this section to obtain closure properties for regular languages. We will also use them in Section 6.1 to obtain closure properties for NSA languages.

By interchanging SCAN and WRITE, we can convert a program that computes τ into a program that computes τ^{-1}.

[2] Historically finite transducers have been called "generalized sequential machines" (gsm's) and finite transductions have been called "gsm maps."

LEMMA 4.37. *If τ is a finite transduction, then τ^{-1} is a finite transduction; i.e., the class of finite transductions is closed under converse.*

Proof: Let P be a finite transducer with transfer relation τ. Eliminate the EOF instruction, as in Section 3.4.2. Replace each SCANc by a WRITEc and each WRITEc by a SCANc to obtain a finite transducer P' with transfer relation τ'. If P scans a string x and writes y, then P' writes x and scans y; thus $x \; \tau \; y$ if and only if $y \; \tau' \; x$. Therefore $\tau' = \tau^{-1}$, so τ^{-1} is a finite transduction. ■

The following theorem says that very general classes of languages defined in terms of machines are closed under finite transductions.

THEOREM 4.38

(i) Let C be the class of languages accepted by nondeterministic programs for a machine [control, input, $d_1, \ldots, d_k$]. *C is closed under finite transductions.*

(ii) Let D be the class of languages accepted by deterministic programs for a machine [control, input, $d_1, \ldots, d_k$]. *D is closed under the converses of deterministic finite transductions; i.e., if $L \in D$ and τ is a deterministic finite transduction, then $L\tau^{-1} \in D$.*

(iii) Let D be the class of languages recognized by deterministic programs for a machine [control, input, $d_1, \ldots, d_k$]. *D is closed under the converses of deterministic finite transductions; i.e., if $L \in D$ and τ is a deterministic finite transduction, then $L\tau^{-1} \in D$.*

The proof of Theorem 4.38 will be given in Section 4.8.2. For now, let us explore some interesting corollaries.

COROLLARY 4.39. *The class of regular languages is closed under finite transductions.*

Proof: The class of regular languages is equal to the class of languages accepted by nondeterministic programs for a machine [control, input]. Apply Theorem 4.38(i). ■

Suppose that R is a regular language. Then there is a DFA that accepts R. By replacing each SCANc operation in that DFA by SCANc/WRITEc, we construct a deterministic finite transducer whose transfer relation τ is given by

$$x\tau = \begin{cases} x & \text{if } x \in R, \\ \text{undefined} & \text{otherwise.} \end{cases}$$

(Such a program is called a *filter* for R (cf. Exercise 2.9-6), and we say that the program filters R.) For every language L, $L \cap R = L\tau$. If L is regular, this result must be regular by the preceding corollary. This yields another proof that the class of regular languages is closed under intersection. For yet a third proof, see Exercise 4.8-2.

COROLLARY 4.40

(*i*) *Let C be the class of languages accepted by nondeterministic programs for a machine* [control, input, $d_1, \ldots, d_k$]. *C is closed under intersection with regular languages.*

(*ii*) *Let D be the class of languages accepted by deterministic programs for a machine* [control, input, $d_1, \ldots, d_k$]. *D is closed under intersection with regular languages.*

(*iii*) *Let D be the class of languages recognized by deterministic programs for a machine* [control, input, $d_1, \ldots, d_k$]. *D is closed under intersection with regular languages.*

Proof: If R is a regular language, then R is filtered by a deterministic FM program, as described above. Let τ be that program's transfer relation. Apply Theorem 4.38. In parts (ii) and (iii), note that $\tau = \tau^{-1}$. ■

Similarly, if R is a regular language, then there is a finite transduction τ satisfying $L\tau = L/R$ for every L (Figure 4.36). This yields a constructive proof that the class of regular languages is closed under quotient by regular languages.

COROLLARY 4.41. *Let C be the class of languages accepted by programs for a machine* [control, input, $d_1, \ldots, d_k$]. *C is closed under quotient with regular languages. Furthermore, the proof is constructive.*

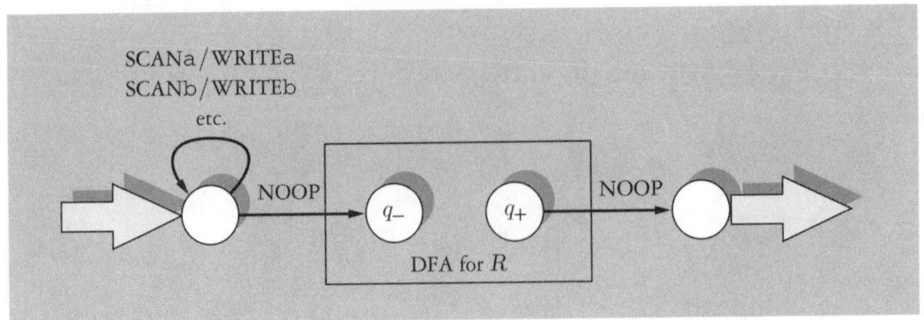

FIGURE 4.36: A finite transducer such that $L\tau = L/R$ for all L. This program copies a prefix of the input and then checks that the remainder is a string in R. q_- denotes the initial state of R's acceptor, and q_+ denotes its final state, which is assumed to be unique.

Proof: Let τ be the transfer relation of the program constructed as in Figure 4.36. Apply Theorem 4.38(i) to τ. ∎

Corollary 4.39 also allows us to prove that certain languages are not regular.

EXAMPLE 4.42. Let $L = \{(\mathtt{ab})^n\mathtt{c}^n : n \geq 0\}$. Assume that L is regular. It is easy to construct a finite transduction τ that maps $(\mathtt{ab})^i\mathtt{c}^j$ to $\mathtt{a}^i\mathtt{b}^j$ (Figure 4.37). Then $L\tau = \{\mathtt{a}^n\mathtt{b}^n : n \geq 0\}$, which must be regular. But by Example 4.26 that language is not regular. This contradiction implies that L must not be regular. ∎∎∎

EXAMPLE 4.43. Let L be the set of all strings over $\{\mathtt{a}, \mathtt{b}\}$ that contain more a's than b's. Assume that L is regular. Let L' be the set of all strings over $\{\mathtt{a}, \mathtt{b}\}$ that contain more b's than a's. It is easy to construct a finite transduction that replaces a with b and vice versa, so L' must be regular. Therefore $L \cup L'$ must be regular. But $L \cup L'$ is the set of all strings with unequal numbers of a's and b's, which is not regular by Example 4.34. This contradiction implies that L is not regular. ∎∎∎

4.8.2 Composition Theorem

In this section, we prove an important theorem about machines in general. Recall that the composition of two relations τ_1 and τ_2 (denoted $\tau_1 \circ \tau_2$) is

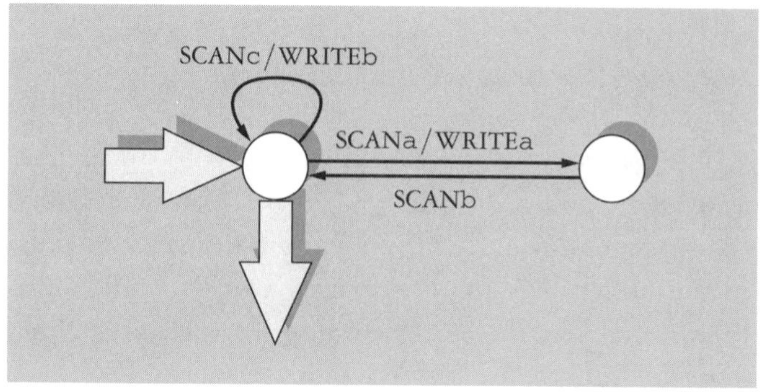

FIGURE 4.37: A finite transducer that takes strings of the form $(\texttt{ab} \cup \texttt{c})^*$ and replaces all occurrences of ab by a and all occurrences of c by b. In particular, it maps $(\texttt{ab})^i\texttt{c}^j$ to $\texttt{a}^i\texttt{b}^j$.

$\{(x, z) : (\exists y)[x\ \tau_1\ y \text{ and } y\ \tau_2\ z]\}$. It is often convenient to define relations as the composition of simpler relations. Therefore we investigate the difficulty of computing the composition of two relations compared to computing the individual relations.

Suppose that τ_1 is computed by a program P_1 for a machine M_1 and τ_2 is computed by a program P_2 for a machine M_2. By combining these programs and machines we create a program P that uses the devices of M_1 and M_2 and computes $\tau_1 \circ \tau_2$. This is especially useful when M_1 (or M_2) is a finite machine and M_2 (or M_1) contains a control, because the controls can be merged; then the program P can be run on a machine of the same type as M_2 (or M_1); no additional computing power is required.

In order to preserve determinism when composing programs, we will need to assume that their terminators are well-behaved. A terminator for a program is called *well-behaved* if it is possible, using operations for each device, to test whether that device is in an accepting, rejecting, or nonfinal state. This is possible for the usual devices, because we can test whether a stack or input device is empty, whether a counter holds 0, and whether a control holds a specific state; furthermore, all states of tapes and RAMs are accepting.

LEMMA 4.44. *Let τ_1 be the transfer relation of a program P_1 for a machine* [output, d_1] *and τ_2 be the transfer relation of a program P_2 for a* *machine* [input, d_2]. *Then* $\tau_1 \circ \tau_2$ *is the transfer relation of a program P for a machine* [control, d_1, d_2]. *Furthermore, if* P_1 *and* P_2 *are deterministic and the terminator of* P_1 *is well-behaved, then P is deterministic.*

Proof: We will use an extra control called the buffer to support communication between P_1 and P_2. When an instruction of P_1 would write a character on its output device, the corresponding instruction of P stores the character in the buffer. When an instruction of P_2 would scan a character from its input device, the corresponding instruction of P removes the character from the buffer.

In order to handle an EOF test of P_2 deterministically, we use the hypothesis that we can test whether d_1 is in a final state. Thus when P_1 would be in a final configuration, a corresponding instruction of P stores a z in the buffer, where z is a new character that does not belong to the output alphabet of P_1 or the input alphabet of P_2. Let accept$_1$ denote an operation that tests whether d_1 is in an accepting state. (For example, accept$_1$ is EMPTY if d_1 is a stack, EOF if d_1 is an input device, ZERO if d_1 is a counter, and NOOP if d_1 is a tape or a RAM. If d_1 is a control, accept$_1$ is shorthand for the collection of operations $\{(q, q) : q \text{ is a final control state}\}$.) We let P contain the instruction

$$(\Lambda \to \mathtt{z},\ \text{accept}_1,\ \text{NOOP}).$$

If we allow P to be nondeterministic, then we need make no assumption about the final states of d_1. Instead, we let P contain the instruction $(\Lambda \to \mathtt{z}, \text{NOOP}, \text{NOOP})$. In this case P guesses that P_1 has finished writing. If P guesses wrong, then P will block.

Table 4.2 shows generic instructions of P_1 or P_2 and the corresponding instruction of P. The initial and final states of P's buffer are Λ. The initial and final states of d_1 are the same as in P_1; the initial and final states of d_2 are the same as in P_2. ∎

The devices d_1 and d_2 in the preceding lemma can be replaced by collections of devices.

THEOREM 4.45 (Composition Theorem). *Let* τ_1 *be the transfer relation of a program* P_1 *for a machine* [output, $d_{11}, \ldots, d_{1j}$] *and* τ_2 *be the transfer relation of a*

Instruction of P_1	*Instruction of* P_2	*Instruction of* P
(NOOP , f_1)		($\Lambda \to \Lambda$, f_1 , NOOP)
(WRITEc , f_1)		($\Lambda \to c$, f_1 , NOOP)
	(NOOP , f_2)	($c \to c$, NOOP , f_2)
	(SCANc , f_2)	($c \to \Lambda$, NOOP , f_2)
	(EOF , f_2)	($\mathtt{z} \to \mathtt{z}$, NOOP , f_2)

TABLE 4.2: Composing two transductions. P's transfer relation τ is equal to $\tau_1 \circ \tau_2$. f_1 denotes an operation on d_1 and f_2 denotes an operation on d_2. c denotes any character in P_1's output alphabet (P_2's input alphabet). $\mathtt{z}$ is a special character placed in the buffer to indicate that P_1's computation is complete.

program P_2 for a machine $[\text{input}, d_{21}, \ldots, d_{2k}]$. *Then $\tau_1 \circ \tau_2$ is the transfer relation of a program P for a machine* $[\text{control}, d_{11}, \ldots, d_{1j}, d_{21}, \ldots, d_{2k}]$. *Furthermore, if P_1 and P_2 are deterministic and P_1's terminator is well-behaved, then P is deterministic.*

Proof: We combine the devices $d_{11}, \ldots, d_{1j}$ into a new device d_1. The realm of d_1 is the Cartesian product of the realms of $d_{11}, \ldots, d_{1j}$. The repertory of d_1 is formed by combining the operations of $d_{11}, \ldots, d_{1j}$ in the natural way. Define

$$(x_1, \ldots, x_j)\ (f_1, \ldots, f_j)\ (y_1, \ldots, y_j) \iff (x_1\ f_1\ y_1) \wedge \cdots \wedge (x_j\ f_j\ y_j).$$

Then the repertory of d_1 is the Cartesian product of the repertories of $d_{11}, \ldots, d_{1j}$. The terminators can be combined analogously and will remain well-behaved.

We combine the devices $d_{21}, \ldots, d_{2k}$ into a new device d_2 similarly. Clearly a machine $[\text{output}, d_{11}, \ldots, d_{1j}]$ is equivalent to a machine $[\text{output}, d_1]$, and a machine $[\text{input}, d_{21}, \ldots, d_{2k}]$ is equivalent to a machine $[\text{input}, d_2]$.

Therefore τ_1 is computed by a program for a machine $[\text{output}, d_1]$ and τ_2 is computed by a program for a machine $[\text{input}, d_2]$. By Lemma 4.44, $\tau_1 \circ \tau_2$ is computed by a program for a machine $[\text{control}, d_1, d_2]$, which is equivalent to a machine $[\text{control}, d_{11}, \ldots, d_{1j}, d_{21}, \ldots, d_{2k}]$. ■

When P_1 and P_2 are finite transducers we obtain a nice consequence.

COROLLARY 4.46. *The class of finite transductions is closed under composition, i.e., if τ_1 and τ_2 are finite transductions, then $\tau_1 \circ \tau_2$ is a finite transduction.*

Proof: Let τ_1 and τ_2 be programs for a machine [input, output, control]. Applying the composition theorem (4.45), we find that $\tau_1 \circ \tau_2$ is the transfer relation of a program for a machine [control, input, control, output, control]. The three controls can be merged into a single control, so $\tau_1 \circ \tau_2$ is the transfer relation of a program for a finite machine. ■

When only τ_2 is a finite transduction, we obtain a very important consequence, namely the proof of Theorem 4.38.

Proof of Theorem 4.38: First we prove that C is closed under the converses of finite transductions and that D is closed under the converses of deterministic finite transductions. Let τ be computed by a finite transducer T, which runs on a machine [control, input, output]; let L be accepted by program P for a machine $[\text{control}, \text{input}, d_1, \ldots, d_k]$.

Let τ_L be the transfer relation of the program that accepts L. By the composition theorem, $\tau \circ \tau_L$ is the transfer relation of a program for a machine $[\text{control}, \text{control}, \text{input}, d_1, \ldots, d_k]$. Now merge controls, so $\tau \circ \tau_L$ is the transfer relation of a program for a machine $[\text{control}, \text{input}, d_1, \ldots, d_k]$. Call that program P'. We assert that P' accepts $L\tau^{-1}$. Why? It suffices to show that the transfer relation of P' is $\{(x, \text{ACCEPT}) : x \in L\tau^{-1}\}$. The transfer relation of P' is

$$\begin{aligned} \tau \circ \tau_L &= \{(x, y) : x \; \tau \; y\} \circ \{(y, \text{ACCEPT}) : y \in L\} \\ &= \{(x, \text{ACCEPT}) : (\exists y)[x \; \tau \; y \text{ and } y \in L]\} \\ &= \{(x, \text{ACCEPT}) : x \in L\tau^{-1}\}. \end{aligned}$$

If T and P are deterministic, then P' is deterministic as well. This proves part (ii).

To prove part (i), observe that if $\mathcal{T}$ is a finite transduction, then $\mathcal{T}^{-1}$ is a finite transduction as well; $L\mathcal{T} = L(\mathcal{T}^{-1})^{-1}$, which we showed is accepted by a program for a machine [control, input, $d_1, \ldots, d_k$].

To prove part (iii), eliminate EOF and dead states from T so that it has no infinite computations (every state in an infinite loop must be dead because T is deterministic). Construct the deterministic program P' that accepts $L\mathcal{T}^{-1}$ as above; it has no infinite computations because T and P have none; by eliminating blocking, we convert P' to a recognizer for $L\mathcal{T}^{-1}$. ∎

An alternative proof of part (i) may be more intuitive: Let L be a language accepted by a program for a machine [control, input, $d_1, \ldots, d_k$]. By replacing each SCANc in that program by a WRITEc, we construct a nondeterministic program without input that writes all the strings belonging to L (one per computation). (We call such a program a *generator* for L, and we say that the program *generates* L.) Thus L is generated by a program for a machine [control, output, $d_1, \ldots, d_k$]; call that program's transfer relation $\mathcal{T}_L$. Let $\mathcal{T}$ be a finite transduction. Then $\mathcal{T}$ is the transfer relation for a machine [control, input, output]. By the composition theorem, there is a program for a machine [control, control, $d_1, \ldots, d_k$, control, output] whose transfer relation is $\mathcal{T}_L \circ \mathcal{T}$. That program generates $L\mathcal{T}$. By merging controls, we obtain a program for a machine [control, output, $d_1, \ldots, d_k$] that generates $L\mathcal{T}$. By replacing WRITEc operations with SCANc operations, we construct a program for a machine [control, input, $d_1, \ldots, d_k$] that accepts $L\mathcal{T}$.

Exercises

4.8-2 One can emulate the behavior of two FM programs by using two controls. These controls can be merged into one using the pairing construction described in Section 3.2.1. Use pairing constructions to prove the following theorems directly:

(a) The intersection of two DFR languages is a DFR language.
(b) The union of two DFR languages is a DFR language.
(c) The difference of two DFR languages is a DFR language.
(d) The symmetric difference of two DFR languages is a DFR language.

(e) The intersection of two NFA languages is an NFA language.

(f) The union of two NFA languages is an NFA language.

4.8-3 Let L_1 and L_2 be accepted by NFAs having k_1 and k_2 control states, respectively. How many control states might be required if we constructed an NFA for $L_1 \cap L_2$ as in the proof of Theorem 4.33? If we constructed it by composing a filter for L_1 with an acceptor for L_2? If we constructed it by composing a generator for L_1 with a filter for L_2? If we constructed it via the pairing construction of Section 3.2.1?

4.8-4 Prove directly from the definition that the class of regular languages is closed under reversal.

4.8-5 A derivative is like a quotient on the left. More precisely, if R and S are languages, the *derivative* of R by S is $\{x : (\exists y \in S)[yx \in R]\}$. We write $D_S(R)$ to denote the derivative of R by S.

(a) Prove that the class of regular languages is closed under derivative by arbitrary languages.

(b) Give a constructive proof that the class of regular languages is closed under derivative by regular languages.

(c) Let R be a regular language over an alphabet Σ. Let

$$C = \{D_L(R) : L \subseteq \Sigma^*\}.$$

Prove that C is a finite set of languages.

4.8-6 Use the Myhill–Nerode theorem to prove that the class of regular languages is closed under quotient by any language S.

4.8-7 Is the class of deterministic finite transductions closed under composition?

4.8-8 (a) Let R be a regular language. Construct a finite transduction τ such that $L\tau = LR$ for every language L.

(b) What is $L\tau^{-1}$? Give an alternative constructive proof that the class of regular languages is closed under quotient.

4.8-9 For strings x and y, define the *shuffle* of x and y (denoted $x \clubsuit y$) to be the set of all strings formed by interleaving the characters of x and y any number at a time. Formally,

$$x \clubsuit y = \{x_1 y_1 \cdots x_m y_m : x_1 \cdots x_m = x \text{ and } y_1 \cdots y_m = y\},$$

where $x_1, \ldots, x_m, y_1, \ldots, y_m$ denote strings of any length, including 0. We extend the shuffle operation to languages as follows:

$$L \clubsuit R = \bigcup_{x \in L,\, y \in R} x \clubsuit y.$$

If R is a regular language, construct a finite transduction τ such that $L\tau = L \clubsuit R$ for all languages L. Prove that the set of regular languages is closed under shuffle.

Solution: We construct a transducer that copies the input string to the output while nondeterministically shuffling it with a string in R. Let P be an NFA that accepts the regular language R. Standardize P so that it does not use the EOF test. At each step the transducer either (a) copies a character from its input to its output or else (b) simulates P for one step without scanning anything, writing a character that P might scan. To make the construction precise, replace each SCAN in P by WRITE (this takes care of (b)). For each control state q and each character c include the instruction $(q \to q, \text{SCAN}c, \text{WRITE}c)$ as well (this takes care of (a)).

4.8-10 For strings x and y of equal length, define the *perfect shuffle* of x and y (denoted $x \spadesuit y$) to be the string formed by interleaving the characters of x and y one at a time. Formally,

$$x \spadesuit y = x_1 y_1 \cdots x_m y_m$$

where $x_1 \cdots x_m = x$, $y_1 \cdots y_m = y$, and $x_1, \ldots, x_m, y_1, \ldots, y_m$ denote single characters. We extend the perfect shuffle operation to languages in the standard way:

$$L \spadesuit R = \{x \spadesuit y : x \in L, y \in R, \text{ and } |x| = |y|\}.$$

If R is a regular language, construct a finite transduction τ such that $L\tau = L \spadesuit R$ for all languages L. Prove that the set of regular languages is closed under perfect shuffle.

4.8-11 Let PREFIX(L) be the set of all prefixes of strings belonging to L. Prove that if L is regular then PREFIX(L) is regular. Your proof should be constructive.

4.8-12 Prove that the set of all strings over $\{\mathtt{a}, \mathtt{b}, \mathtt{c}\}$ with equal numbers of b's and c's is not regular.

4.8-13 A *permutation* of a set S is a one-one function from S to S. We define the PERM operation on strings and languages. If $x = x_1 \cdots x_n$ is a string of n characters, then $\text{PERM}(x) = \{x_{\sigma(1)} \cdots x_{\sigma(n)} : \sigma \text{ is a permutation of } \{1, \ldots, n\}\}$. That is, PERM($x$) is the set of all anagrams of the string x. If L is a language, then $\text{PERM}(L) = \bigcup_{x \in L} \text{PERM}(x)$. For example,

$$\text{PERM}(\{\mathtt{aba}, \mathtt{aa}\}) = \{\mathtt{aab}, \mathtt{aba}, \mathtt{baa}, \mathtt{aa}\}.$$

Is the class of regular languages closed under PERM?

4.8-14 Recall from Exercise 4.8-11 that if L is regular then PREFIX(L) is regular. Prove that if PREFIX(L) is regular then L is not necessarily regular.

4.8-15 Recall that when a transducer blocks or runs forever, the computation produces no result, although it may have performed some WRITE operations during its partial or infinite computation. This has been described quaintly as "reneging" on the characters already written. Let us define a *reneging* output device that has the ability to erase the entire string written so far and start writing again from scratch. Its operations are WRITEc for each $c \in \Delta$ and ERASE. The ERASE operation is defined for all strings y by

$$y\text{ERASE} = \Lambda.$$

(a) Prove that the reneging output device does not add any computational power to nondeterministic finite transducers. That is, prove that if τ is any transduction computed by a nondeterministic program for a machine [control, input, reneging output], then τ is computed by a nondeterministic program for a machine [control, input, output].

(b) Prove that the reneging output device does add computational power to deterministic finite transducers. That is, construct a transduction that can be computed by a deterministic program for a machine [control, input, reneging output] but not by any deterministic program for a machine [control, input, output].

(c) A transduction computed by a deterministic program for a machine [control, input, reneging output] is called a *Pratt transduction*. Let D be the class of languages accepted by deterministic programs for a machine [control, input, $d_1, \ldots, d_k$]. Prove that D is closed under the converses of Pratt transductions.

(d) Let D be the class of languages recognized by deterministic programs for a machine [control, input, $d_1, \ldots, d_k$]. Prove that D is closed under the converses of Pratt transductions.

†(e) Prove a new closure property using Pratt transductions.

4.9 PUMPING THEOREMS FOR REGULAR LANGUAGES

In Section 4.7, we showed how to use the Myhill–Nerode theorem in order to prove that certain languages are not regular. In this section we will develop handier tools for proving that certain languages are not regular.

THEOREM 4.47 (First Pumping Theorem for Regular Languages). *Let L be a regular language. There exists a natural number N (depending on L) such that if $z \in L$ and $|z| \geq N$, then there exist strings u, v, w satisfying the following conditions:*

- $z = uvw$
- $v \neq \Lambda$
- $|uv| \leq N$
- *for all* $i \geq 0$, $uv^iw \in L$

N is informally called a *pumping number* for L.

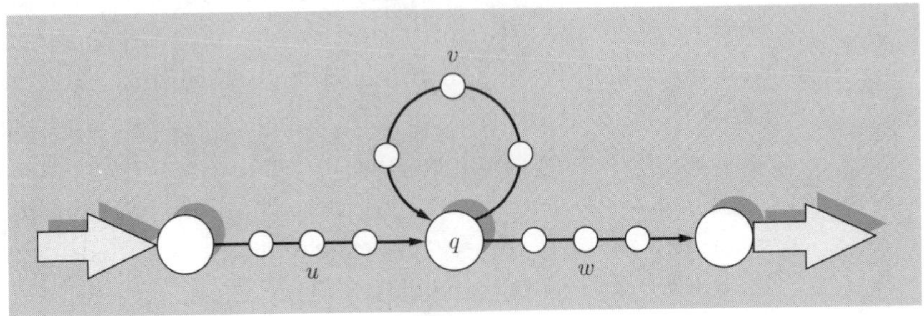

FIGURE 4.38: The control state q is repeated during the computation. u is the string scanned on the way from the initial control state to q. v is the string scanned on the way from q back to itself. w is the string scanned on the way from q to an accepting state.

Proof: Since L is regular, there is a DFA P that accepts L. Let N be the number of control states of P. Let the input string $z = z_1 \cdots z_\ell$, where each z_m is a character and $\ell \geq N$. Let $(q_m, z_{m+1} \cdots z_\ell)$ be the configuration of P immediately after $z_1 \cdots z_m$ has been scanned. By the pigeonhole principle two of the $N+1$ control states $q_0, \ldots, q_N$ must be equal. That is, $q_j = q_k = q$ for some j and k with $0 \leq j < k \leq N$. Let

$$\begin{aligned} u &= z_1 \cdots z_j, \\ v &= z_{j+1} \cdots z_k, \\ w &= z_{k+1} \cdots z_\ell. \end{aligned}$$

(This situation is depicted in Figure 4.38.) We assert that P accepts uv^iw for all $i \geq 0$. After scanning u, P is in control state q. Each time it scans a copy of v, it proceeds from control state q back to q. When it scans w, it proceeds from q to an accepting state. Thus $uv^iw \in L$. ∎

The proof of the first pumping theorem is illustrated with a concrete example in Figure 4.39.

A language is informally called *pumpable* if it satisfies the conclusions of the first pumping theorem, i.e., if it has a pumping number as defined in that theorem. The first pumping theorem says that every regular language is pumpable. Therefore, if we prove that a language is not pumpable, then we have a proof by contradiction that the language must not be regular.

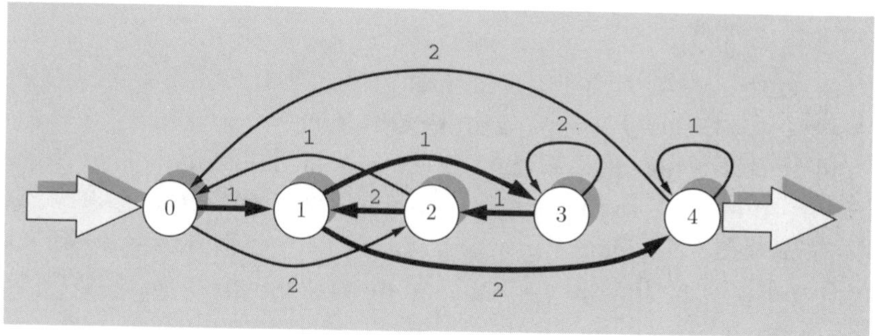

FIGURE 4.39: A concrete example of the loop guaranteed by the proof of the first pumping theorem. The DFA program accepts the language L consisting of all dyadic numerals whose value is congruent to 4 modulo 5. The number of control states, N, is 5. Consider the input string 11122, whose length is exactly N. The edges followed when that input string is scanned have been drawn thicker. Observe the loop going from state 1 to state 3 to state 2 and back to state 1. This loop can be repeated any nonnegative number of times to obtain an accepting trace on any input of the form $1(112)^i2$.

EXAMPLE 4.48. Suppose, for the sake of contradiction, that the following language is regular:

$$L = \{\mathtt{a}^i\mathtt{b}^i : i \geq 0\}.$$

Then L has a pumping number N as in the first pumping theorem. Let $z = \mathtt{a}^N\mathtt{b}^N$. Since $z \in L$ and $|z| \geq N$, we can obtain u, v, w satisfying the conclusions of Theorem 4.47: $z = uvw$, $v \neq \Lambda$, $|uv| \leq N$, and $uv^iw \in L$ for all $i \geq 0$. We do not get to pick u and v, but however they are picked, both u and v must be substrings of $\mathtt{a}^N$ because $|uv| \leq N$. That is, $u = \mathtt{a}^j$ for some $j \geq 0$ and $v = \mathtt{a}^k$ for some $k \geq 1$ (because $v \neq \Lambda$). Now $uv^0w = \mathtt{a}^{N-k}\mathtt{b}^N$, which has fewer a's than b's, so $uv^0w \notin L$. Taking $i = 0$, this contradicts the statement that $uv^iw \in L$ for all $i \geq 0$. Therefore L must not be a regular language. (When we take $i = 0$ in the pumping theorem, we say that we are "pumping (the string) down." We could also reach a contradiction by considering uv^2w, which has more a's than b's. When we take some $i > 1$, we say that we are "pumping up" $i - 1$ times. When we take $i = 1$, we are just being silly.)

■ ■ ■

Caveat: When using the first pumping theorem, we choose z and i. We do not choose u, v, w, or N.

EXAMPLE 4.49. Let L be the set of palindromes over $\{\mathtt{a}, \mathtt{b}\}$. Suppose, for the sake of contradiction, that L is a regular language. Then L has a pumping number N as in the first pumping theorem. Let $z = \mathtt{a}^N\mathtt{b}\mathtt{a}^N$ and apply Theorem 4.47. However u and v are picked, we have $u = \mathtt{a}^j$ for some $j \geq 0$ and $v = \mathtt{a}^k$ for some $k \geq 1$. Pumping down, $uv^0w = \mathtt{a}^{N-k}\mathtt{b}\mathtt{a}^N$, which is not a palindrome. This contradicts Theorem 4.47, so L must not be a regular language. ■■■

EXAMPLE 4.50. Let L be the set $\{ww : w \in \{\mathtt{a}, \mathtt{b}\}^*\}$. If L were regular, it would have a pumping number N as in the first pumping theorem. Let $z = \mathtt{a}^N\mathtt{b}\mathtt{a}^N\mathtt{b}$ and apply Theorem 4.47. However u and v are picked, we have $u = \mathtt{a}^j$ and $v = \mathtt{a}^k$ for some $k \geq 1$. Pumping down, $uv^0w = \mathtt{a}^{N-k}\mathtt{b}\mathtt{a}^N\mathtt{b}$, which is not in L. This contradicts Theorem 4.47, so L must not be a regular language. ■■■

Note that in applying Theorem 4.47 we pick the string z from L however we like, provided that $|z| \geq N$. If we chose $z = \mathtt{a}^{2N}$ in the preceding example, we would not obtain a contradiction because v could be $\mathtt{aa}$. Alternatively, if we chose $z = \mathtt{abab}$, we would not obtain a contradiction because $|z|$ could be less than N. We must choose z so that $z \in L$ and $|z| \geq N$, and then we must obtain a contradiction for all possible choices of u, v, and w satisfying $z = uvw$, $v \neq \Lambda$, and $|uv| \leq N$. *Note that we do not choose v; rather we must derive a contradiction for* all *legal choices of v.*

EXAMPLE 4.51. Let L be the set $\{\mathtt{a}^n : n \text{ is prime}\}$. If L were regular, it would have a pumping number N as in the first pumping theorem. Let $z = \mathtt{a}^p$ where p is any prime greater than or equal to N, and apply Theorem 4.47. However u, v, and w are picked, we have $v = \mathtt{a}^i$ where $i \geq 1$. Pumping up p times, $uv^{p+1}w = uvv^pw = uvwv^p = \mathtt{a}^p\mathtt{a}^{ip} = \mathtt{a}^{p(i+1)}$, which does not belong to L because $p(i+1)$ is not prime. This contradicts Theorem 4.47, so L must not be a regular language. ■■■

The reader may use the first pumping theorem to prove that the following languages are not regular (see Exercises 4.9-5 and 4.9-6):

- $\{\mathtt{a}^n : n \text{ is composite}\}$
- $\{w : w \text{ is the decimal representation of an integer squared}\}$
- $\{w : w \text{ is the decimal representation of a prime number}\}$
- $\{w : w \text{ contains more } \mathtt{a}\text{'s than } \mathtt{b}\text{'s}\}$

Closure properties can also be used in combination with pumping to prove nonregularity.

EXAMPLE 4.52. Let L consist of all strings of the form $\mathtt{a}^*\mathtt{b}^n\mathtt{c}^n \cup \mathtt{b}^*\mathtt{c}^*$ where $n \geq 0$, i.e.,

$$L = \{\mathtt{a}^i\mathtt{b}^j\mathtt{c}^k : j = k \text{ or } i = 0\}.$$

Although we will show that L is not regular, the first pumping theorem will not prove it directly, because every nonempty string in L is pumpable, as we now show. If z is a nonempty string in L, we can let $u = \Lambda$, $v =$ the first character of z, and $w =$ the rest of z. Then $uv^iw \in L$ for all $i \geq 0$. For example, if $z = \mathtt{ab}^{10}\mathtt{c}^{10}$, we take $u = \Lambda$, $v = \mathtt{a}$, and $w = \mathtt{b}^{10}\mathtt{c}^{10}$. Then $uv^iw = \mathtt{a}^i\mathtt{b}^{10}\mathtt{c}^{10} \in L$ for all $i \geq 0$.

We will prove a better pumping theorem later in this section, which will suffice to prove that L is not regular. But first let us use another technique, based on closure properties, which has widespread importance. We construct a finite transducer that accepts only strings of the form $\mathtt{a}w$, where $w \in \{\mathtt{b}, \mathtt{c}\}^*$, and maps them to w (Figure 4.40).

Let τ be the transfer relation of that finite transducer. Then

$$L\tau = \{\mathtt{b}^j\mathtt{c}^k : j = k\} = \{\mathtt{b}^n\mathtt{c}^n : n \geq 0\}.$$

A second finite transduction (Figure 4.41) maps $L\tau$ to $\{\mathtt{a}^n\mathtt{b}^n : n \geq 0\}$, which we proved nonregular earlier in this section. Recall that the class of regular languages is closed under finite transductions. If L were regular, then $\{\mathtt{a}^n\mathtt{b}^n : n \geq 0\}$ would be regular, contradicting Example 4.48. Therefore L is not regular.

■ ■ ■

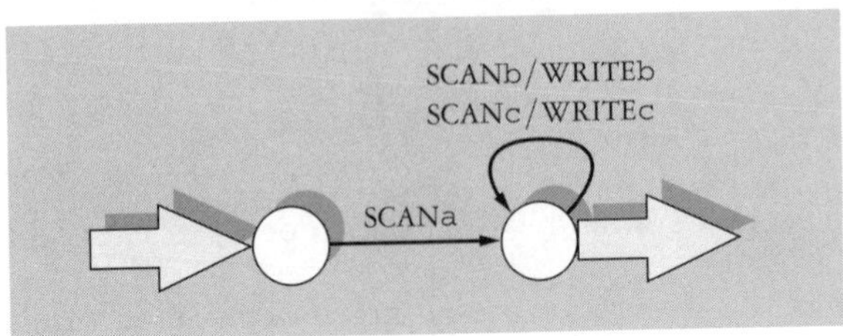

FIGURE 4.40: A finite transducer that maps aw to w if $w \in \{\mathtt{b},\mathtt{c}\}^*$.

FIGURE 4.41: A finite transducer that replaces b's with a's and replaces c's with b's.

The first pumping theorem says that we can pump near the beginning of a string belonging to a regular language. The second pumping theorem gives us more control over which part of the string gets pumped.

THEOREM 4.53 (Second Pumping Theorem for Regular Languages) *Let L be a regular language. There exists a natural number N (depending on L) such that if x_1, x_2, and x_3 are strings with $x_1x_2x_3 \in L$ and $|x_2| \geq N$, then there exist strings u, v, w satisfying the following conditions:*

- $x_2 = uvw$
- $v \neq \Lambda$
- $|uv| \leq N$
- *for all* $i \geq 0$, $x_1uv^iwx_3 \in L$

N is informally called a *pumping number* for L.

Proof: Since L is regular, there is a DFA P that accepts L. Let N be the number of control states of P. Let the input string be $x_1x_2x_3$, and let $x_2 = z_1 \cdots z_\ell$, where each z_m is a character and $\ell \geq N$. Let $(q_m, z_{m+1} \cdots z_\ell x_3)$ be the configuration of P immediately after $x_1 z_1 \cdots z_m$ has been scanned. By the pigeonhole principle two of the $N+1$ control states $q_0, \ldots, q_N$ must be equal. That is, $q_j = q_k = q$ for some j and k with $0 \leq j < k \leq N$. Let

$$\begin{aligned} u &= z_1 \cdots z_j, \\ v &= z_{j+1} \cdots z_k, \\ w &= z_{k+1} \cdots z_\ell. \end{aligned}$$

We assert that P accepts $x_1 uv^i wx_3$ for all $i \geq 0$. After scanning $x_1 u$, P is in control state q. Each time it scans a copy of v, it proceeds from control state q back to q. When it scans wx_3, it proceeds from q to an accepting state. Thus P accepts $x_1 uv^i wx_3$, so $x_1 uv^i wx_3 \in L$. ■

EXAMPLE 4.54. Let us apply this theorem to the language

$$L = \{\mathtt{a}^i \mathtt{b}^j \mathtt{c}^k : i = 0 \text{ or } j = k\}$$

to prove that L is not regular. Let N be a pumping number for L as in the second pumping theorem. Let $z = \mathtt{ab}^N\mathtt{c}^N$, $x_1 = \mathtt{a}$, $x_2 = \mathtt{b}^N$, and $x_3 = \mathtt{c}^N$. By the second pumping theorem, there exist u, v, w such that $x_2 = uvw$, $v \neq \Lambda$, and $\mathtt{a}uv^i w\mathtt{c}^N \in L$ for all $i \geq 0$. Then $v = \mathtt{b}^k$ for some $k \geq 1$. Pumping up once, $\mathtt{a}uv^2w\mathtt{c}^N = \mathtt{ab}^{N+k}\mathtt{c}^N$, which is not in L. This contradiction proves that L is not regular. ■■■

4.9.1 Al and Izzy Pump Strings

Two-player games are very helpful in understanding formulas with a large number of quantifiers, like the pumping theorem. (If you have not read Section 0.1 on quantifiers and two-player games, now might be a good time.) The first pumping theorem states that if L is a regular language, then

$\exists N$
$\forall z \in L$ such that $|z| \geq N$
$\exists u, v, w$ such that $uvw = z$, $|uv| \leq N$, and $|v| > 0$
$\forall i \geq 0$
$uv^i w \in L$.

This statement contains four quantifiers. When we consider the equivalent two-player game, restrictions on the quantifiers reappear as restrictions on the choices made by Izzy and Al. Select a regular language L. The game for L is

(i) Izzy chooses a natural number N.

(ii) Al chooses z such that $z \in L$ and $|z| \geq N$.

(iii) Izzy chooses u, v, and w such that $uvw = z$, $|uv| \leq N$, and $|v| > 0$.

(iv) Al chooses $i \geq 0$, trying to make $uv^i w \notin L$.

Let us present a strategy[3] by which Izzy can win the game. This amounts to restating the proof of the first pumping theorem in terms of games, which will not be difficult. Let L be accepted by a DFA P.

(i) Izzy picks $N = |Q|$, where Q is the set of control states of P.

(ii) Al picks a string z such that $|z| \geq N$ and $z \in L$. (If there is no such string, then Al loses. In this case, the second quantifier says that all elements of the empty set have a certain property, which is clearly true no matter what the property is.)

[3] The reader may have observed that in all of our examples the winning player, either Izzy or Al, has an algorithm by which to make his choices. We do not require that the players' strategies be computable. For example, in a game corresponding to the first pumping theorem, one might select a Turing machine program known to recognize a regular language L. Not knowing a finite machine program that recognizes L, Izzy might have great difficulty computing a pumping number N. However, such a number N still exists, and Izzy has a winning strategy available.

(iii) Izzy finds the computation of P that accepts z. (Such a computation exists because $z \in L$.) He notes the control state before and after reading each character of z. (Because $|z| \geq N$, there are at least $N+1$ of these control states. But Q contains only N states, so some state must be repeated, by the pigeonhole principle.) Let q be the first repeated control state. Izzy breaks the computation into three pieces determined by the first two configurations with control state q. The computation looks like

$$\begin{aligned} uvw &\overset{\alpha}{\longmapsto} (q_{\text{start}}, uvw) \\ &\overset{\Pi *}{\longmapsto} (q, vw) \\ &\overset{\Pi +}{\longmapsto} (q, w) \\ &\overset{\Pi *}{\longmapsto} (q_{\text{accept}}, \Lambda) \\ &\overset{\omega}{\longmapsto} \text{ACCEPT} \end{aligned}$$

where u is the string scanned before first reaching the control state q, v is the string scanned after that time but before returning to q, and w is scanned during the remainder of the computation. uvw is equal to the input string z, $|uv| \leq N$, and $|v| > 0$.) Izzy chooses u, v, and w as so determined.

(iv) Al picks any natural number i. The computation

$$\begin{aligned} uv^i w &\overset{\alpha}{\longmapsto} (q_{\text{start}}, uv^i w) \\ &\overset{\Pi *}{\longmapsto} (q, v^i w) \\ &\overset{(\Pi +)^i}{\longmapsto} (q, w) \\ &\overset{\Pi *}{\longmapsto} (q_{\text{accept}}, \Lambda) \\ &\overset{\omega}{\longmapsto} \text{ACCEPT} \end{aligned}$$

is an accepting computation of P on input $uv^i w$, so $uv^i w \in L$. Thus Al loses and Izzy wins.

Ordinarily the pumping theorems are applied to prove by contradiction that a language L is not regular. (It is a common mistake to try to prove that a language *is* regular via a pumping theorem.) An outside party selects the language L, which may or may not be regular, and play proceeds as above. Here again is the game for L:

(i) Izzy chooses a natural number N.

(ii) Al chooses z such that $z \in L$ and $|z| \geq N$.

(iii) Izzy chooses u, v, and w such that $uvw = z$, $|uv| \leq N$, and $|v| > 0$.

(iv) Al chooses $i \geq 0$, trying to make $uv^iw \notin L$.

If L is regular, then Izzy can use his general strategy to win the game. Thus Al can win with a particular L only if L is not regular. (Note that Al may have to lose anyway, even if L isn't regular. See Exercise 4.9-8(b).) Finding a winning strategy for Al in this game constitutes a proof that L is not regular. (However, finding a winning strategy for Izzy in this game proves nothing.) Now we present a slightly more general version of Example 4.51, this time using the game paradigm.

EXAMPLE 4.55. We prove that if the language L consists of an infinite set of prime numbers in monadic (base 1) notation, then L is not regular. Let S be an infinite set containing only prime numbers, and let $L = \{1^j : j \in S\}$. Here is a winning strategy for Al, no matter how Izzy plays.

(i) Izzy chooses a natural number N.

(ii) Al chooses a string $z = 1^p$ where $p \in S$ and $p > N$. (This is possible because S contains infinitely many primes. Since $p \in S$, $z \in L$.)

(iii) Izzy chooses u, v, and w such that $uvw = z$, $|uv| \leq N$, and $|v| > 0$.

(iv) Al chooses $i = p + 1$. Then

$$|uv^iw| = |uvw| + p|v| = p + p|v| = p(1 + |v|).$$

Since $p \geq 2$ and $1 + |v| \geq 2$, $p(1 + |v|)$ is not prime; i.e., $|uv^iw|$ is not prime. Therefore, $uv^iw \notin L$, so Al wins.

Because Al has a winning strategy no matter how Izzy plays, L must not be regular. ■■■

EXAMPLE 4.56. Let L consist of an infinite set of strings whose lengths are perfect squares. We prove that L is not regular by presenting a winning strategy for Al no matter how Izzy plays.

(i) Izzy chooses a natural number N.

(ii) Al chooses a string $z \in L$ where $|z| > N^2$. (This is possible because L is infinite.)

(iii) Izzy chooses u, v, and w such that $uvw = z$, $|uv| \leq N$, and $|v| > 0$.

(iv) Al chooses $i = 2$. Since $z \in L$, $|z| = m^2$ for some m. By Al's choice of z, $m > N$. We have $0 < |v| \leq N$. Let k denote $|v|$. Then

$$m^2 < m^2 + k = |uv^2w| \leq m^2 + N < m^2 + m < (m+1)^2.$$

The length of uv^2w falls between two consecutive squares; therefore $uv^2w \notin L$, so Al wins.

Because Al has a winning strategy no matter how Izzy plays, L must not be regular. In particular, $\{\mathtt{a}^n : n \text{ is the square of an integer}\}$ is not regular. ■ ■ ■

A general principle will remind you whether to identify with Al or with Izzy when working with theorems involving quantifiers: When *using* a theorem, you may specify values for the universally quantified variables, e.g., z for $(\forall z)$ and i for $(\forall i)$, but you must not specify values for the existentially quantified variables. In contrast, when *proving* a theorem you must specify values for the existentially quantified variables, but you may not specify values for the universally quantified variables. When *using* theorems you play Al's role; when *proving* theorems you play Izzy's role.

Exercises

4.9-1 Let L be the regular language $\{\mathtt{ab}\}$. Let $z = \mathtt{ab}$, which belongs to L. Note that z cannot be written as uvw where $v \neq \Lambda$ and $uv^*w \subseteq L$. Why does this not contradict the first pumping theorem?

Solution: The reason is that every DFR that recognizes L has at least three states. In the terminology of the first pumping theorem, $N = 3$. However $|z| = 2 < N$.

4.9-2 The proof of the first pumping theorem shows that the number of control states in a DFA that accepts L can be used as a pumping number for L.

(a) Prove that the number of control states in an NFA that accepts L is also a pumping number for L as in the first pumping theorem.

(b) Prove that 1 plus the length of a regular expression that generates L is also a pumping number for L as in the first pumping theorem.

4.9-3 Prove the following variant of the first pumping theorem. If L is regular, then there exists N such that for all strings z of length at least N

$$(\exists u, v, w)[v \neq \Lambda, |uv| \leq N, z = uvw, \text{ and } (\forall i \geq 0)[z \in L \iff uv^i w \in L]].$$

4.9-4 (a) Let L be a regular language. Prove that there is a positive integer N (depending on L) such that if $z_1, \ldots, z_N$ are nonempty strings with the concatenation $z_1 \cdots z_N \in L$, then there exist i and j with $0 \leq i < j \leq N$ satisfying

$$z_1 \cdots z_i (z_{i+1} \cdots z_j)^* z_{j+1} \cdots z_N \subseteq L.$$

(b) Use part (a) to prove Theorem 4.47.

4.9-5 Use the first pumping theorem to prove that the following languages are not regular:

(a) $\{\mathtt{a}^n : n \text{ is composite}\}$

(b) $\{w \in \{\mathtt{a}, \mathtt{b}, \mathtt{c}\}^* : w \text{ contains more } \mathtt{a}\text{'s than } \mathtt{b}\text{'s}\}$.

4.9-6 Use closure properties and/or the pumping theorems to prove that the following languages are not regular:

(a) $\{w : w \text{ is the decimal representation of an integer squared}\}$. Hint: Intersect with $1(00)^*2(00)^*1$.

*(b) $\{w : w \text{ is the decimal representation of a prime number}\}$

Solution: We will prove this for primes written in b-ary for any $b \geq 2$. The exercise is the special case $b = 10$. We will treat strings as equal to the b-ary number they represent. Here is Al's strategy:

i. Izzy chooses N.

ii. Al chooses z to be the b-ary representation, without leading zeroes, of a prime p greater than b such that z has at least N digits. (This is possible because there are infinitely many primes.)

iii. Izzy chooses u, v, and w such that $uvw = z$ and $|v| > 0$.

iv. Al chooses $i = p! + 1$. (The number $p!$ is the product $p(p-1)\cdots 1$.) We will show that $uv^{p!+1}w$ is an integer multiple of p. Since $uv^{p!+1}w > p$, $uv^{p!+1}w$ is not prime, and Al wins.

Now we prove that $uv^{p!+1}w$ is a multiple of p. Let $f_y(z) = zy \bmod p$. By b-ary arithmetic,

$$zy = z \cdot b^{|y|+1} + y,$$

where $\cdot$ denotes multiplication and $b^{|y|+1}$ denotes the number b raised to the $(|y| + 1)$st power. Therefore by modular arithmetic, if $z_1 \equiv z_2 \bmod p$, then $z_1 w \equiv z_2 w \bmod p$. Furthermore, because p is prime, the mapping f_y is one-one on $\{0, \ldots, p-1\}$, so it is a permutation of $\{0, \ldots, p-1\}$. Hence $f_y^{(p!)}$, where $f^{(m)}$ denotes m-fold composition, is equal to the identity function. Therefore $f_v^{(p!+1)}(uv) \equiv uv \bmod p$, i.e.,

$$\begin{aligned} uv^{p!+1} &\equiv uv \bmod p, \\ uv^{p!+1}w &\equiv uvw \bmod p. \end{aligned}$$

(Here $v^{p!+1}$ denotes the concatenation of $p! + 1$ copies of v.) Since $uvw = z = p$, $uv^{p!+1}w$ is divisible by p, as promised.

(c) $\{w \in \{\mathtt{a}, \mathtt{b}, \mathtt{c}\}^* : w$ contains more a's than b's after the last c$\}$.

(d) $\{w : w$ is the decimal representation of a composite number$\}$.

4.9-7 Let $L = \{\mathtt{a}^i\mathtt{b}^j\mathtt{c}^k : j = k \text{ or } i = 0\}$. Design a single finite transduction $\mathcal{T}$ such that $L\mathcal{T} = \{\mathtt{a}^n\mathtt{b}^n : n \geq 0\}$.

4.9-8 (a) **Pumping theorem partial converse.** Let L be a subset of 0^*. Prove that L is regular iff L has a pumping number as in the first pumping theorem. Thus the converse of the first pumping theorem is true for L a subset of a 1-character alphabet.

(b) Let $L = \{x_1y_1 \cdots x_ny_n : n$ is composite and $(\forall i \leq n)$ $[(x_i \in \mathtt{a}^+)$ and $(y_i \in \mathtt{b}^+)]\}$. (Less formally, L is the set of all strings of the form $(\mathtt{a}^+\mathtt{b}^+)^n$ such that n is composite). Prove that L is not regular, but that strings in L can be pumped even in the middle. That is, show that L has a pumping number N as in the second pumping theorem. Do not forget the case $i = 0$, which permits pumping down. Conclude that the converse of the second pumping theorem is not true for general L.

4.9-9 Call a language an n-state language if it is recognized by an n-state DFR. Find functions f and g such that the following are true:

(a) An n-state language is empty if and only if it contains no strings of length $\leq f(n)$. Make f as small as possible.

(b) An n-state language is infinite if and only if it contains a string of length $\geq g(n)$. Make g as small as possible.

4.10 CHAPTER SUMMARY

In this chapter we proved the equivalence of regular expressions, NFAs, and DFRs; i.e., the regular languages, the NFA languages, and the DFR languages are all the same class; we also gave algorithms for converting from one representation of regular languages to another. Then we proved that any DFR that recognizes a language L has at least as many states as L has prefix equivalence classes; this idea is used in proofs of nonregularity and in a minimization algorithm for DFRs. The regular languages are closed under Boolean operations, regular operations, quotient by any language, and finite transductions. Closure properties are useful for direct proofs of regularity and for indirect proofs (by contradiction) of nonregularity. Furthermore, we proved that many machine-based language classes are closed under finite transductions. Finally, we proved pumping theorems, which are very useful tools for proving that certain languages are nonregular.

Exercises

4.10-1 Suppose that you are given a DFR P that you wish to simulate efficiently on a real computer in a high-level programming language. Each step of P should be simulated by a small fixed number of steps in the high-level program. Describe informally how to do this simulation. (To simplify your job, you may assume that the input to your program is in fact a string over P's alphabet, rather than having your high-level program handle input characters that would be invalid for P.)

Solution: First, eliminate null instructions, EOF, and blocking from P. Initialize an array NextState in the high-level program so that for every control state q and character c, NextState$[q, c]$ is the unique control state r such that $(q \to r, \text{SCAN}c)$ is an instruction in P, i.e.,

$$\text{NextState}[q, c] := qt_c.$$

Initialize an array Accepting to indicate whether each state is accepting, i.e.,

$$\text{Accepting}[q] := \begin{cases} \text{true} & \text{if } q \text{ is an accepting state,} \\ \text{false} & \text{otherwise.} \end{cases}$$

The high-level program will do the following:

```
state := q_start;
while not eof do begin
      read(ch);
      state := NewState[state, ch];
end;
if Accepting[state] then write('accept') else write('reject').
```

4.10-2 Let p be a fixed string of length n. Let P be a minimal DFR that recognizes $\{x : p \text{ is a substring of } x\}$. How many states does P have?

4.10-3 (a) We define FIRST-HALF(x) as follows: If x is a string of even length, let $x = uv$ where $|u| = |v|$, and let FIRST-HALF$(x) = u$; if x has odd length, then FIRST-HALF(x) is undefined. We extend FIRST-HALF() to languages in the ordinary way:

$$\text{FIRST-HALF}(L) = \{\text{FIRST-HALF}(x) : x \in L \text{ and FIRST-HALF}(x) \text{ is defined}\}.$$

Prove that if R is regular then FIRST-HALF(R) is regular.

(b) Define SECOND-HALF() by analogy to part (a) and prove that if R is regular then SECOND-HALF(R) is regular.

(c) We define MIDDLE-THIRD(x) as follows: If x is a string whose length is a multiple of 3, let $x = uvw$ where $|u| = |v| = |w|$, and let MIDDLE-THIRD$(x) = v$; if the length of x is not a multiple of 3 then MIDDLE-THIRD(x) is undefined. Extend MIDDLE-THIRD() to languages in the ordinary way. Prove that if R is regular, then MIDDLE-THIRD(R) is regular.

4.10-4 Let $x = x_1 \cdots x_n$. We say that a string y is a *subsequence* of x if there exist $i_1 < i_2 < \cdots < i_k$ such that $y = x_{i_1} x_{i_2} \cdots x_{i_k}$. Define

$$\begin{aligned} \text{SUBSEQ}(x) &= \{y : y \text{ is a subsequence of } x\}, \\ \text{SUBSEQ}(L) &= \bigcup_{x \in L} \text{SUBSEQ}(x), \end{aligned}$$

i.e., SUBSEQ(L) consists of all subsequences of all strings in L. For example, SUBSEQ(bab) $= \{\Lambda, \texttt{a}, \texttt{b}, \texttt{ba}, \texttt{ab}, \texttt{bb}, \texttt{bab}\}$, SUBSEQ(aa) $= \{\Lambda, \texttt{a}, \texttt{aa}\}$, and SUBSEQ($\{\texttt{bab}, \texttt{aa}\}$) $= \{\Lambda, \texttt{a}, \texttt{b}, \texttt{aa}, \texttt{ba}, \texttt{ab}, \texttt{bb}, \texttt{bab}\}$. Is the class of the regular languages closed under SUBSEQ()?

Solution: Yes. We define a nondeterministic finite transduction $\mathcal{T}$ that maps each string x to each subsequence of x by scanning characters and nondeterministically deciding whether to write them. Its unique control state is 0 (unique starting and accepting state as well). Its instructions consist of $(0 \to 0, \text{SCAN}c, \text{WRITE}c)$ and $(0 \to 0, \text{SCAN}c, \text{NOOP})$ for each c in Σ. Then $L\mathcal{T} = \text{SUBSEQ}(L)$. Since the class of regular languages is closed under finite transductions, it is closed under SUBSEQ().

*4.10-5 Let L be any language and let $A = \text{SUBSEQ}(L)$. In this exercise you will prove that A is regular.

(a) Let us write $x \leq y$ if x is a subsequence of y. We say that a string x is a minimal element of a set S if (1) $x \in S$ and (2) for all $y \in S$, if $y \leq x$ then $y = x$. Let M be the set of all minimal elements of $\overline{A}$. Prove that $y \in \overline{A}$ if and only if there exists $x \in M$ such that x is a subsequence of y.

(b) If x is any string, prove that $\{y : x \leq y\}$ is regular.

(c) Call two strings x and y *incomparable* if $x \not\leq y$ and $y \not\leq x$. Prove that if x and y are distinct strings in M, then x and y are incomparable.

(d) Let S be a language over $\{\texttt{a}, \texttt{b}\}$. Prove that if all strings in S are incomparable, then S is finite. Hint: Let x be any string and let $\ell = |x|$. Prove that $x \leq (\texttt{ba})^\ell$. Next, prove that if x and y are incomparable, then $(\texttt{ba})^\ell \not\leq y$. Let $L_{2k} = (\texttt{a}^*\texttt{b}^*)^k$ and $L_{2k+1} = L_{2k}\texttt{a}^*$. Prove that if x and y are incomparable, then $y \in L_{2\ell}$. Finally, prove, by induction on k, that if $z \in L_k$, $S \subseteq L_k$, and all strings in S are incomparable, then S contains only finitely many strings y such that $z \not\leq y$.

(e) Let S be any language. Prove that if all strings in S are incomparable, then S is finite.

(f) Prove that M is finite.

(g) Prove that $\overline{A}$ is regular.
(h) Prove that A is regular.

4.10-6 Define

$$\text{HALF-SUBSEQ}(x) = \{y : y \text{ is a subsequence of } x \text{ and } |y| = \tfrac{1}{2}|x|\},$$

i.e., y is obtained by deleting exactly half of the characters from x, and

$$\text{HALF-SUBSEQ}(L) = \bigcup_{x \in L} \text{HALF-SUBSEQ}(x).$$

Is the class of regular languages closed under HALF-SUBSEQ()?

4.10-7 Prove that the following languages are regular:
(a) the set of all strings representing decimal numbers that neither contain the digit 7 nor are divisible by the number 7
(b) $\{xyx^R : x, y \in \Sigma^*\}$
(c) $\{x : |x| \equiv 0 \pmod 3\}$
(d) $\{x : \texttt{abba} \text{ is not a subsequence of } x\}$

4.10-8 If x is a string, then a *rotation* of x is a string zy such that $yz = x$. Let rotation(x) be the set consisting of all rotations of x and let rotation(L) be the set consisting of all rotations of strings in L, i.e.,

$$\text{rotation}(L) = \{zy : (\exists x \in L)[yz = x]\}.$$

For example,

$$\text{rotation}(\{\texttt{abc}, \texttt{abab}\}) = \{\texttt{abc}, \texttt{bca}, \texttt{cab}, \texttt{abab}, \texttt{baba}\}.$$

Is the class of regular languages closed under rotation( )?

*4.10-9 Let S be any subset of $\texttt{a}^*$. Prove that S^* is regular. Hint: Find a positive integer d and a finite set F such that $S^* = (\texttt{a}^d)^* - F$.

4.10-10 **ω-FMs and ω-regular ω-languages.** An *infinite* input device holds an infinite sequence of characters belonging to an alphabet Σ. (In practical applications, the infinite input is provided by some external source as needed, rather than stored.) An ω-language is a set of infinite sequences. (The last letter of the Greek alphabet, ω, means infinite in this context. Try not to confuse it with a terminator.)

An ω-FM is a machine [control, infinite input]. A program for an ω-FM has a unique initial control state and an instruction set that does not contain any null instructions. We need to define acceptance specially for ω-FM programs because they never halt. Two definitions are in general use:

An ω-NFA has a set of accepting control states; it accepts an infinite sequence x iff it has an infinite trace on input x in which infinitely many of the configurations contain an accepting control state. (Historically ω-NFAs have been called Büchi automata.)

An ω-DFA has a set A of sets of accepting control states, i.e., $A \subseteq 2^Q$; it accepts an infinite sequence x iff it has an infinite trace (which must be unique by determinism) in which the set of control states reached infinitely often is an element of A. (Historically ω-DFAs have been called Muller automata.)

Recall that a language is a set of *finite* strings. If L is a language, we define L^ω to be the set of infinite sequences obtained by concatenating infinitely many elements of L. We define ω-regular ω-languages:

L is ω-regular if and only if there exist regular languages $U_1, \ldots, U_k$ and nonempty regular languages $V_1, \ldots, V_k$ such that

$$L = \bigcup_{1 \leq i \leq k} U_i V_i^{\omega}.$$

(a) Prove that an ω-NFA P accepts an infinite sequence x iff P has an accepting control state q and an infinite trace on input x in which infinitely many of the configurations contain control state q.

(b) Prove that every ω-NFA ω-language is ω-regular.

(c) Prove that the class of ω-NFA ω-languages is closed under union and intersection. Hint: Use a pairing construction.

(d) Prove that every ω-regular ω-language is an ω-NFA ω-language.

(e) Prove that every ω-DFA ω-language is an ω-NFA ω-language.

**(f) Prove that every ω-NFA ω-language is an ω-DFA ω-language. Conclude that the class of ω-NFA ω-languages, the class of ω-DFA ω-languages, and the class of ω-regular ω-languages are equal.

(g) Prove that the class of ω-regular ω-languages is closed under complementation.

(h) Prove that if R is a regular language and S is an ω-regular ω-language, then RS is ω-regular.

(i) We define *projection* as follows. Fix the alphabet $\Sigma = \{0, 1\}^k$. If $c = (c_1, \ldots, c_{k-1}, c_k) \in \Sigma$, then $\text{PROJ}(c) = (c_1, \ldots, c_{k-1})$. If $x = \langle\langle x_1, x_2, \ldots \rangle\rangle$, an infinite sequence over Σ, then $\text{PROJ}(x) = \langle\langle \text{PROJ}(x_1), \text{PROJ}(x_2), \ldots \rangle\rangle$. If L is an ω-language over Σ, then $\text{PROJ}(L) = \{\text{PROJ}(x) : x \in L\}$. If L is an ω-regular ω-language over $\{0, 1\}^k$, prove that $\text{PROJ}(L)$ is an ω-regular ω-language over $\{0, 1\}^{k-1}$.

(j) Give an algorithm to determine whether an ω-NFA accepts $\emptyset$.

(k) State and prove a pumping theorem for ω-regular ω-languages.

(l) Prove that $\{\texttt{a}^n\texttt{b}^n\texttt{c}^\omega : n \geq 0\}$ is not ω-regular.

5

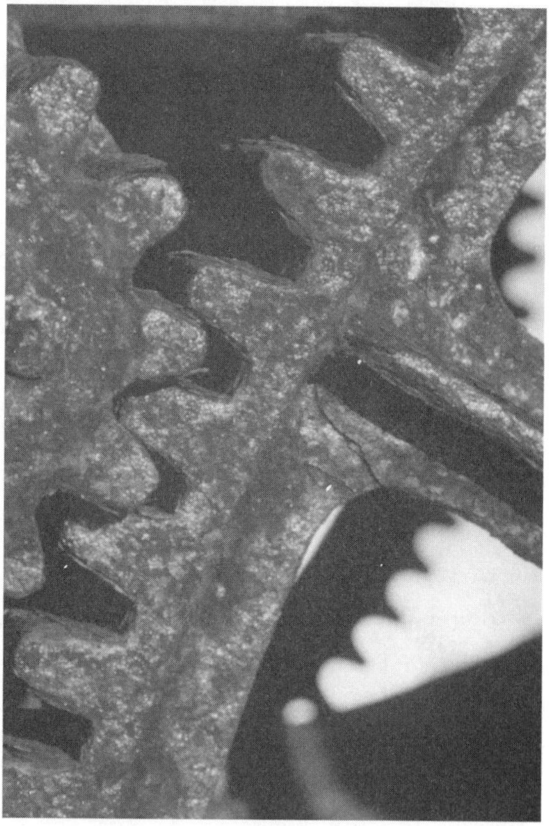

Context-Free Languages

IN THIS CHAPTER we introduce context-free grammars, which are used in describing programming languages as well as certain aspects of natural human languages. Context-free grammars (CFGs) can express languages that are not expressed by any regular expression. In this chapter we prove the equivalence of CFGs and NSAs, define key properties like ambiguity, and investigate closure properties. We also present several CFG standardizations and algorithms that are useful in constructing compilers. In particular, there is an algorithm to test membership in context-free languages.

5.1 DEFINING LANGUAGES AS SOLUTIONS TO EQUATIONS

We saw in Chapter 4 that some languages may be defined by a formula built up from individual characters by the regular operations union, concatenation, and Kleene-closure, as in

$$(\mathtt{1} \cup \mathtt{10})^*,$$

i.e, by regular expressions. There are languages that cannot be defined by regular expressions but can be defined implicitly by an equation where the name of the language itself appears in the defining expression, as in

$$X \;=\; \mathtt{\#} \cup \mathtt{a}X\mathtt{a} \cup \mathtt{b}X\mathtt{b}.$$

(This is similar to a recursive definition.) We call such equations, which allow union and concatenation on the right-hand side, *regular equations*.[1] The name of the unknown language being solved for is called a *variable*. Suppose that $X = L$ is a solution of the equation above. The equation says that the language L contains the string # and all strings of the form axa and bxb where x is itself a string in L. If we call the members of L "pals," then L's defining equation can be paraphrased: A pal is #, or a followed by a pal followed by a, or b followed by a pal followed by b. From this definition, we can find pals by a simple iteration:

Length 1: # is a pal.

Length 3: a#a and b#b are pals.

[1] Since we do not allow Kleene-closure (*) in our regular equations, a more precise name might be "starless regular equations." The class of languages definable via regular equations including Kleene-closure is the same as the class of languages definable using starless regular equations (Exercise 5.2-7(c)). Our convention of disallowing Kleene-closure follows the classical treatment of context-free grammars.

Length 5: aa#aa, ba#ab, ab#ba, and bb#bb are pals.

Length 7: aaa#aaa, baa#aab, . . . , and bbb#bbb are pals. (And so on.)

If we specify that the pals must be the least language satisfying the equation, then a straightforward structural induction shows that the pals consist of all symmetrical strings of a's, b's, and #'s with exactly one #, so "pal" is a synonym for "palindrome with central marker." An application of the first pumping theorem with $z = \mathtt{a}^N\#\mathtt{a}^N$ shows that L is not a regular language, so regular equations can define languages that regular expressions cannot define.

We can go a step further and define several languages by simultaneous regular equations. Usually one of these is the language that we really want to define, and the others are useful auxiliary languages, like the set of noun phrases or predicates in English grammar. In Figure 5.1, we give a vastly oversimplified system of equations for English. For another example, we present in Figure 5.2 a simplified system of equations that define statements in the Pascal programming language.

Below we present a system of equations defining a part of conventional mathematical notation, arithmetic expressions like a×(b+a)×c×b+c; these expressions often arise in programming languages. In these equations, V, F, T, and E denote languages over the alphabet $\{\mathtt{a}, \mathtt{b}, \mathtt{c}, +, \times, (,)\}$.

$$\begin{aligned} V &= \mathtt{a} \cup \mathtt{b} \cup \mathtt{c} \\ F &= V \cup (E) \\ T &= F \cup T{\times}F \\ E &= T \cup E{+}T \end{aligned}$$

Paraphrasing, *V(ariables)* are a, b, and c; *F(actors)* are variables and expressions with parentheses around them; *T(erms)* are factors and terms multiplied by factors; *E(xpressions)* are terms and expressions added to terms. (Although this is not the simplest system of equations for defining arithmetic expressions, it has the usual precedence rules built in, in a sense.)

Let $V = L_V$, $F = L_F$, $T = L_T$, and $E = L_E$ be a solution of the equations, assuming a solution exists. From the defining equations, we can deduce that certain strings belong to L_V, L_F, L_T, or L_E, i.e., that they are

$$
\begin{aligned}
\langle \textit{Sentence} \rangle &= \langle \textit{Subject} \rangle \; \langle \textit{Predicate} \rangle \\
\langle \textit{Subject} \rangle &= \langle \textit{Pronoun1} \rangle \cup \langle \textit{Noun-Phrase} \rangle \\
\langle \textit{Pronoun1} \rangle &= \{\texttt{I}, \texttt{we}, \texttt{you}, \texttt{he}, \texttt{she}, \texttt{it}, \texttt{they}\} \\
\langle \textit{Noun-Phrase} \rangle &= (\Lambda \cup \langle \textit{Article} \rangle) \; \langle \textit{Simple-Noun-Phrase} \rangle \\
\langle \textit{Article} \rangle &= \{\texttt{a}, \texttt{an}, \texttt{the}\} \\
\langle \textit{Simple-Noun-Phrase} \rangle &= \langle \textit{Noun} \rangle \cup \langle \textit{Adjective} \rangle \; \langle \textit{Simple-Noun-Phrase} \rangle \\
\langle \textit{Predicate} \rangle &= \langle \textit{Verb} \rangle \; (\Lambda \cup \langle \textit{Object} \rangle) \\
\langle \textit{Object} \rangle &= \langle \textit{Pronoun2} \rangle \cup \langle \textit{Noun-Phrase} \rangle \\
\langle \textit{Pronoun2} \rangle &= \{\texttt{me}, \texttt{us}, \texttt{you}, \texttt{him}, \texttt{her}, \texttt{it}, \texttt{them}\}
\end{aligned}
$$

FIGURE 5.1: A vastly oversimplified system of regular equations for English. Words in angle brackets denote variables. We have omitted the equations for ⟨*Noun*⟩, ⟨*Verb*⟩, and ⟨*Adjective*⟩ in order to save space. More seriously, we have omitted any notion of noun–verb agreement, tense, capitalization, or punctuation. Most seriously, we have omitted huge classes of interesting sentences.

This system allows sentences like "She drives a shiny black convertible car," as well as silly sentences like "The elven mug flew a huge blue tasty stapler." Furthermore, it doesn't allow more complicated sentences like "When the van, driven by a passed-out drunk, went careening in the direction of her sports car, she skillfully steered out of its path."

Designing an adequate syntax for English is an important unsolved problem. Part of the difficulty is that a lot real-world knowledge appears necessary in order to resolve common ambiguities that people handle easily. For a classic example, compare the sentence "Time flies like an arrow" with "Fruit flies like a banana."

variables, factors, terms, or expressions. For example,

$$
\begin{aligned}
\mathsf{a}, \mathsf{b}, \mathsf{c} \in L_V \subseteq L_V \cup (L_E) &= L_F \subseteq L_F \cup L_T{\times}L_F \\
&= L_T \subseteq L_T \cup L_E{+}L_T = L_E,
\end{aligned}
$$

so a, b, and c are variables, factors, terms, and expressions. In addition, we have

$$
\mathsf{a}{\times}\mathsf{b} \in L_T{\times}L_F \subseteq L_F \cup L_T{\times}L_F = L_T \subseteq L_T \cup L_E{+}L_T = L_E,
$$

$$
\begin{aligned}
\langle \textit{Statement} \rangle &= \Lambda \cup \langle \textit{Simple-Statement} \rangle \cup \langle \textit{Compound-Statement} \rangle \\
&\quad \cup \langle \textit{If-Statement} \rangle \cup \langle \textit{While-Statement} \rangle \\
&\quad \cup \langle \textit{Repeat-Statement} \rangle \cup \langle \textit{For-Statement} \rangle \\
\langle \textit{Simple-Statement} \rangle &= \langle \textit{Procedure-Call} \rangle \cup \langle \textit{Assignment-Statement} \rangle \\
\langle \textit{Compound-Statement} \rangle &= \texttt{begin}\ \langle \textit{Statement-List} \rangle\ \texttt{end} \\
\langle \textit{Statement-List} \rangle &= \langle \textit{Statement} \rangle\ (\Lambda \cup \texttt{;}\langle \textit{Statement-List} \rangle) \\
\langle \textit{If-Statement} \rangle &= \texttt{if}\ \langle \textit{Condition} \rangle\ \texttt{then}\ \langle \textit{Statement} \rangle \\
&\quad (\Lambda \cup \texttt{else}\ \langle \textit{Statement} \rangle) \\
\langle \textit{While-Statement} \rangle &= \texttt{while}\ \langle \textit{Condition} \rangle\ \texttt{do}\ \langle \textit{Statement} \rangle \\
\langle \textit{Repeat-Statement} \rangle &= \texttt{repeat}\ \langle \textit{Statement-List} \rangle\ \texttt{until}\ \langle \textit{Condition} \rangle \\
\langle \textit{For-Statement} \rangle &= \texttt{for}\ \langle \textit{Assignment-Statement} \rangle\ \texttt{to}\ \langle \textit{Expression} \rangle \\
&\quad \texttt{do}\ \langle \textit{Statement} \rangle
\end{aligned}
$$

FIGURE 5.2: A simplified system of regular equations for Pascal statements. The words in angle brackets denote variables. For simplicity, we have omitted defining equations for ⟨*Procedure-Call*⟩, ⟨*Assignment-Statement*⟩, ⟨*Condition*⟩, and ⟨*Expression*⟩. The observant reader may note that we have omitted some semantic restrictions on the for-loop index.

so

$$\texttt{a}\times\texttt{b}\times\texttt{c} \in L_T \times L_F \subseteq L_F \cup L_T \times L_F = L_T \subseteq L_T \cup L_E + L_T = L_E,$$

and so on; thus products of several variables are terms and expressions. Some further examples are as follows:

- $\texttt{a}\times\texttt{b+a}\times\texttt{b}\times\texttt{c} \in L_E + L_T \subseteq L_T \cup L_E + L_T = L_E.$
- $\texttt{a}\times\texttt{b+a}\times\texttt{b}\times\texttt{c+a} \in L_E + L_T \subseteq L_T \cup L_E + L_T = L_E.$
- $\texttt{(a}\times\texttt{b+a}\times\texttt{b}\times\texttt{c+a)} \in (L_E) \subseteq L_V \cup (L_E) = L_F \subseteq L_T.$
- $\texttt{(a}\times\texttt{b+a}\times\texttt{b}\times\texttt{c+a)}\times\texttt{b} \in L_T \times L_F \subseteq L_F \cup L_T \times L_F = L_T \subseteq L_E.$

By such reasoning, any conventional formula built up from a, b, and c by parenthesizing, multiplication, and addition can be shown to belong to L_E.

A powerful shorthand for expressing such reasoning is the *parse tree*. The tree

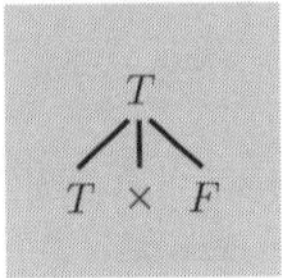

asserts that any string of the form $t{\times}f$, where t is a term and f is a factor, is itself a term. If we attach subtrees to the leaves labeled T and F, showing that $t \in L_T$ and $f \in L_F$, the resulting tree demonstrates that $t{\times}f \in L_T$. The parse tree in Figure 5.3 demonstrates that a×b×(a+b) is a term. Its subtrees show that a is a variable, a factor, and a term; b is a variable and a factor; a×b is a term; etc. We say that the string obtained by reading the parse tree's leaves left to right, in this example a×b×(a+b), is the *yield* of the parse tree. The process of finding a parse tree for a string is called *parsing*.

A subtree of a parse tree is called a *sub–parse tree*. If a sub–parse tree's root is a variable, then the yield of the sub–parse tree is called a *phrase*.[2] The strings a, b, a×b, a+b, (a+b), and a×b×(a+b) constitute all the phrases of the parse tree in Figure 5.3. Notice that b×(a+b) is not a phrase of that parse tree, although it could be a phrase in a parse tree for another expression.

Observe that if two sub–parse trees overlap, then one must be contained in the other. Thus any two phrases in a parse tree are either disjoint or nested. For example, in Figure 5.3 the phrases a×b and a+b are disjoint; the phrases a+b and (a+b) are nested.

Normally, defining equations will be designed so that the phrases in a parse tree constitute some kind of meaningful parts of the string yielded by the tree. The phrase structure of the parse tree in Figure 5.3 implies that a×b is meaningful in the string, while b×(a+b) is not; that is, the first b is multiplied by the a on its left, not by the (a+b) on its right. Because

[2] It would be logically simpler to say that the yield of any sub–parse tree is a phrase. Although this would have little effect on the theory, we would be uncomfortable calling "(" a phrase.

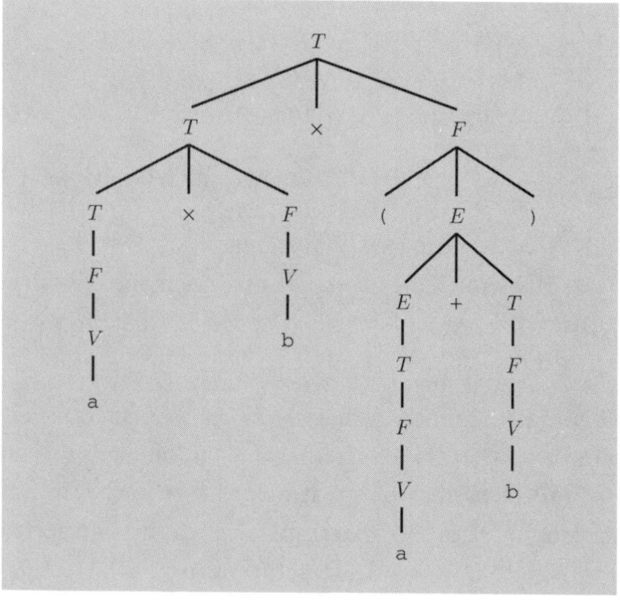

FIGURE 5.3: A parse tree for a×b×(a+b). It is in fact unique (Exercise 5.9-1).

the parse tree for a×b×(a+b) happens to be unique, there is no ambiguity about which parts are added or multiplied together.

EXAMPLE 5.1. Let us consider the language defined by solving the following equations for S:

$$\begin{aligned} S &= AB \cup BA \\ A &= \mathtt{a} \cup CAC \\ B &= \mathtt{b} \cup CBC \\ C &= \mathtt{a} \cup \mathtt{b}. \end{aligned}$$

Let $S = L_S$, $A = L_A$, $B = L_B$, $C = L_C$ be a solution of the equations, assuming that a solution exists. Clearly $L_C = \{\mathtt{a}, \mathtt{b}\}$. Then L_A contains the set of all strings of the form $\{\mathtt{a}, \mathtt{b}\}^i\mathtt{a}\{\mathtt{a}, \mathtt{b}\}^i$ for $i \geq 0$, and L_B contains the set of all strings of the form $\{\mathtt{a}, \mathtt{b}\}^j\mathtt{b}\{\mathtt{a}, \mathtt{b}\}^j$ for $j \geq 0$. Therefore L_S

contains the set of all strings of the form

$$\{\mathtt{a},\mathtt{b}\}^i\mathtt{a}\{\mathtt{a},\mathtt{b}\}^{i+j}\mathtt{b}\{\mathtt{a},\mathtt{b}\}^j \quad \text{or} \quad \{\mathtt{a},\mathtt{b}\}^i\mathtt{b}\{\mathtt{a},\mathtt{b}\}^{i+j}\mathtt{a}\{\mathtt{a},\mathtt{b}\}^j$$

where $i, j \geq 0$. Equivalently, L_S contains the set of all strings of the form

$$\{\mathtt{a},\mathtt{b}\}^i\mathtt{a}\{\mathtt{a},\mathtt{b}\}^j\{\mathtt{a},\mathtt{b}\}^i\mathtt{b}\{\mathtt{a},\mathtt{b}\}^j \quad \text{or} \quad \{\mathtt{a},\mathtt{b}\}^i\mathtt{b}\{\mathtt{a},\mathtt{b}\}^j\{\mathtt{a},\mathtt{b}\}^i\mathtt{a}\{\mathtt{a},\mathtt{b}\}^j$$

where $i, j \geq 0$. If we require that $S = L_S, A = L_A, B = L_B, C = L_C$ be the least solution of the simultaneous equations, then the containments above become equalities. In particular, L_S is the set of all strings of the form wx where $|w| = |x|$ and $w \neq x$. ■ ■ ■

If we are going to define languages via systems of equations, then it is important to know whether a system has a unique solution. If we place no restrictions on the system of equations, then the system may have zero solutions or several solutions. For example, there is no solution to $X \cup \mathtt{a} = \emptyset$, and every language containing $\mathtt{a}$ is a solution to $X = X \cup \mathtt{a}$.

The following restrictions will lead to the existence of at least one solution:

- The left-hand side of each equation consists of a single variable.
- Each variable appears exactly once as the left-hand side of an equation.

Henceforth we consider only systems of regular equations satisfying those two restrictions. In Section 5.2, we will show that any system of regular equations has a unique least solution. In Section 5.3, we will show how to standardize a system of regular equations; a particularly important standardized form is called a context-free grammar. In Section 5.4, we will prove that the least solution to a system of regular equations consists of all strings that have parse trees. It is customary to take this least solution to be the defined language. Because of the usefulness of parse trees in compiling (translating) programming languages, the languages defined by systems of regular equations have substantial importance. (In order to save time or avoid abstraction, the reader may wish to skip Sections 5.2 and 5.4, stipulating instead that the language defined by a system of regular equations is the set of strings that have parse trees.)

Exercises

5.1-1 In English, quotations are surrounded by double quotation marks, as in

> I say "hello."

Nested quotations are surrounded by single quotation marks, as in

> The Beatles sang, "You say 'goodbye,' and I say 'hello.' "

When quotations are nested more deeply than that, single and double quotation marks alternate, as in

> My textbook says, "The Beatles sang, 'You say "goodbye," and I say "hello." ' "

In parts (a–c) below, assume that opening and closing quotation marks are represented by distinct characters, as in the examples above, so there are four distinct characters in all. For simplicity, assume that apostrophes are represented by yet another character.

(a) Let L be the set of all sequences of single quotation and double quotation marks in correctly punctuated English sentences. Prove that L is a DCA language.

(b) Prove that L is not a regular language.

(c) Prove that the set of English sentences is not a regular language in this representation.

In parts (d–f), assume that opening and closing quotation marks are represented by the same character, as on a typewriter, e.g.,

```
The Beatles sang, "You say 'goodbye,' and I say 'hello.'"
```

Still assume that apostrophes are represented by yet another character.

(d) Let L' be the set of all sequences of single and double quotation marks in correctly punctuated English sentences, where opening and closing quotation marks are represented by the same character. Prove that L' is a DCA language.

(e) Prove that L' is not a regular language.

(f) Prove that the set of English sentences is not a regular language in this representation.

5.1-2 Pascal does not permit a semicolon before the word "else" in if-then-else statements. Modify the defining equations in Figure 5.2 in order to permit an optional semicolon before the word "else" in if-then-else statements.

5.1-3 Consider the language L_S defined in Example 5.1. Which strings in L_S have exactly one parse tree?

*5.2 EXISTENCE OF UNIQUE MINIMAL SOLUTIONS

In this section we will prove that every system of regular equations has a unique least solution. We begin by proving that a *single* regular equation has a unique least solution. In the proof of this special case, let us write $\bigwedge$ to denote $\bigcap$, and $\prec$ to denote $\subseteq$; also, let us fix an alphabet Σ, write $\mathcal{D}$ to denote the set of all languages over Σ, and write $\mathcal{U}$ to denote Σ^*. (The operation $\bigwedge$ is called *meet* or *greatest lower bound*. The relation $\prec$ is called *precedes*. The language $\mathcal{U}$ is called an upper bound, because every language precedes it in the ordering $\prec$.) Later in this section we will redefine $\bigwedge$, $\prec$, $\mathcal{D}$, and $\mathcal{U}$ so as to obtain a proof of the general case. For the sake of generality, we will call languages *sets*. By convention, we call a set of sets a *class* of sets. (This section can be safely skipped, as discussed at the end of Section 5.1.)

We state some basic facts of set theory in terms of $\bigwedge$ and $\prec$.

PROPOSITION 5.2

(*i*) ***Transitivity:*** *If $V \prec W$ and $W \prec X$, then $V \prec X$.*

(*ii*) ***Antisymmetry:*** *If $V \prec W$ and $W \prec V$, then $V = W$.*

(*iii*) ***Maximum element:*** *For all $V \in \mathcal{D}$, $V \prec \mathcal{U}$.*

PROPOSITION 5.3 (Completeness). *For any nonempty class $\mathcal{T}$ of sets, let $\bigwedge \mathcal{T}$ denote $\bigwedge_{W \in \mathcal{T}} W$. (If $\mathcal{T}$ is empty, let $\bigwedge \mathcal{T} = \mathcal{U}$.) Then*

(*i*) $(\forall V \in \mathcal{T})[\bigwedge \mathcal{T} \prec V]$. *(The intersection of all the sets in a class is a subset of every set in that class.)*

(*ii*) $((\forall W \in \mathcal{T})[V \prec W]) \Rightarrow V \prec \bigwedge \mathcal{T}$. *(If V is a subset of every set in a class, then V is a subset of the intersection of all sets in that class.)* ∎

For example, if $\mathcal{T}$ consists of the three sets $\{\mathtt{a}^i\mathtt{b}^i\mathtt{c}^j\mathtt{d}^k : i, j, k \geq 0\}$, $\{\mathtt{a}^i\mathtt{b}^j\mathtt{c}^j\mathtt{d}^k : i, j, k \geq 0\}$, and $\{\mathtt{a}^i\mathtt{b}^j\mathtt{c}^k\mathtt{d}^k : i, j, k \geq 0\}$, then $\bigwedge \mathcal{T}$ is equal to $\{\mathtt{a}^n\mathtt{b}^n\mathtt{c}^n\mathtt{d}^n : n \geq 0\}$.

We say that a function f from sets to sets is *monotone* if $V \prec W$ implies $f(V) \prec f(W)$.

EXAMPLE 5.4. Let min (X) denote the least element of X if X is nonempty, and define the function

$$f(X) = \begin{cases} X - \{\min(X)\} & \text{if } X \text{ has a least element,} \\ X & \text{otherwise.} \end{cases}$$

The function f is monotone. ∎∎∎

If f and g are monotone, then each of the functions called h below is also monotone:

- $h(X) = \emptyset$
- $h(X) = \{\Lambda\}$
- $h(X) = \{c\}$, for some character c
- $h(X) = X$
- $h(X) = f(g(X))$
- $h(X) = f(X) \cup g(X)$
- $h(X) = f(X) \otimes g(X)$
- $h(X) = f(X)^*$

The verification of these properties is left as an exercise. We summarize the last three properties by saying that regular operations preserve monotonicity.

Suppose that we are looking for a solution to a single regular equation,

$$X = f(X).$$

Then the function f is monotone. If f maps P to itself, i.e., if $P = f(P)$, we say that P is a *fixed point* of f. Thus solutions to $X = f(X)$ are exactly the same as fixed points of f.

Now we prove a special case of a classic theorem of mathematical logic, the Tarski–Knaster fixed-point theorem. Recall that $\mathcal{D}$ is the class of all languages over Σ.

THEOREM 5.5 (Tarski–Knaster Theorem). *If f is a monotone function from $\mathcal{D}$ to $\mathcal{D}$, then the inequality $f(X) \prec X$ has a unique least solution P. Furthermore, this P is also the unique least solution to the equality $f(X) = X$; i.e., P is the unique least fixed point of f.*

Proof: We say that C is a *contractor* (of f) if $f(C) \prec C$. To prove that there is a least contractor, we will exhibit L satisfying the following two properties:

(1) L is a contractor.

(2) If C is a contractor, then $L \prec C$.

To prove uniqueness, we will show that if L' also satisfies those two properties, then $L' = L$. Finally, we will prove that $f(L) = L$, so L is in fact a fixed point.

By Proposition 5.2(iii) $f(\mathcal{U}) \prec \mathcal{U}$, so $\mathcal{U}$ is a contractor. Let L be the meet of all contractors, i.e.,

$$L = \bigwedge\{C : C \text{ is a contractor}\}.$$

Let C be any contractor. Then $L \prec C$ by Proposition 5.3(i), so (2) is satisfied. Since $L \prec C$, monotonicity implies that $f(L) \prec f(C) \prec C$ (the second inequality follows because C is a contractor). Since $f(L) \prec C$ for every contractor C, it follows from Proposition 5.3(ii) that

$$f(L) \prec \bigwedge\{C : C \text{ is a contractor}\} = L,$$

so (1) is satisfied. Thus L is a contractor; since L precedes every contractor, L must be a least contractor.

Suppose that L' is also a least contractor. Since L' is a contractor and L is a least contractor, $L \prec L'$. Similarly, $L' \prec L$. Therefore $L' = L$ by Proposition 5.2(ii).

Since $f(L) \prec L$, monotonicity implies that $f(f(L)) \prec f(L)$, so $f(L)$ is also a contractor. Since L is the least contractor, it is necessary that $L \prec f(L)$. Combining the two inequalities, we obtain $f(L) = L$ by Proposition 5.2(ii); i.e., L is a fixed point of f. Any fixed point of f must also be a contractor; since L precedes any contractor of f, it precedes any fixed point, so it must also be the unique least fixed point of f. ■

Recalling the definitions of $\prec$ and $\mathcal{D}$, we obtain the following corollary:

COROLLARY 5.6. *If $X = f(X)$ is a regular equation, then it has a unique least solution, which is also the unique least solution of $X \supseteq f(X)$.* ■

We have seen that, when f is a monotone function on $\mathcal{D}$, the equation $X = f(X)$ has a unique least solution, called the least fixed point of f. We say that a function f from $\mathcal{D} \times \mathcal{D}$ to $\mathcal{D}$ is monotone if

$$(X_1 \subseteq X_2 \text{ and } Y_1 \subseteq Y_2) \Rightarrow f(X_1, Y_1) \subseteq f(X_2, Y_2).$$

When we have simultaneous equations, all with monotone right sides,

$$\left.\begin{array}{rcl} Y & = & g(Y,Z) \\ Z & = & h(Y,Z) \end{array}\right\} \qquad (5.1)$$

we again find a unique least solution. An easy way to see this is to transform (5.1) into a single equation $X = f(X)$ where X is the ordered pair (Y, Z), and we define $(Y, Z) \prec (Y', Z')$ to mean $Y \subseteq Y'$ and $Z \subseteq Z'$.

Define the two projection functions p_1 and p_2 by

$$\begin{array}{rcl} p_1(Y,Z) & = & Y, \\ p_2(Y,Z) & = & Z. \end{array}$$

It is easily verified that p_1 and p_2 are monotone. Suppose that we are looking for a solution $Y = A, Z = B$ to (5.1). Let C denote (A, B). Let

$$f(C) = (g(A,B), h(A,B)) = (g(p_1(C), p_2(C)), h(p_1(C), p_2(C))).$$

Since f is a composition of monotone functions, f is monotone. Furthermore, (A, B) is a solution of (5.1) if and only if C is a solution of $X = f(X)$. We have already redefined $\prec$ as it applies to ordered pairs. We redefine $\bigwedge$, $\mathcal{D}$, and $\mathcal{U}$ analogously. Let

$$\bigwedge \mathcal{T} = \left(\bigcap_{(X,Y)\in\mathcal{T}} X, \bigcap_{(X,Y)\in\mathcal{T}} Y \right),$$

let $\mathcal{D}$ be the set of ordered pairs of languages over Σ, and let $\mathcal{U} = \Sigma^* \times \Sigma^*$. The reader may easily verify that Propositions 5.2 and 5.3 remain true for these definitions. Thus the Tarski–Knaster theorem applies to ordered pairs of languages as well. That is, there is a least solution to $X = f(X)$; call it $C = (A, B)$. Then $Y = A, Z = B$ is the least simultaneous solution of (5.1).

The reader may easily extend this technique to k-tuples of languages and prove the following:

COROLLARY 5.7. *Every system of regular equations has a unique least solution.* ■

Hence we are justified in the following definition:

DEFINITION 5.8. The *sequence of languages defined by a system of regular equations* is the least fixed point of the system. If a particular variable X in the system is distinguished, then the least solution for X is the *language defined by the system*.

Exercises

5.2-1 Construct systems of simultaneous regular equations that define the following languages:

(a) $\{\mathtt{a}^i\mathtt{b}^j : j = i\}$
(b) $\{\mathtt{a}^i\mathtt{b}^j : j = 2i\}$
(c) $\{\mathtt{a}^i\mathtt{b}^j : j = i \text{ or } j = 2i\}$
(d) $\{\mathtt{a}^i\mathtt{b}^j : j \neq i\}$
(e) $\{\mathtt{a}^i\mathtt{b}^j : j < i \text{ or } j > 2i\}$

(f) $\{a^i b^j : i \leq j \leq 2i\}$
(g) $\{a^i b^j c^k : i = j \text{ or } j = k \text{ or } k = i\}$
(h) $\{xy : |x| = |y| \text{ and } y \neq x\}$
(i) $\{xy : |x| = |y| \text{ and } y \neq x^R\}$
(j) the set of all balanced strings of parentheses and brackets, $L_{()[]}$ (recall the definition from Example 1.11)
(k) $\{x\#y : y = x^R\}$
(l) $\{x\#y : y \neq x^R\}$
(m) $\{b^i c^i : i \geq 0\} \cup \{ab^i c^{2i} : i \geq 0\}$

5.2-2 (a) Prove Proposition 5.2.
(b) Prove Proposition 5.3.

5.2-3 Prove that the following functions of one or two sets are monotone:
(a) union
(b) intersection
(c) concatenation
(d) Kleene-closure
(e) shuffle
(f) perfect shuffle

5.2-4 Prove that monotonicity is preserved under composition.

5.2-5 Let f represent a system of equations using union, concatenation, Kleene-closure, and intersection, in which the left side of each equation is a single variable, and each variable occurs as the left side of exactly one equation. Prove that f has a least fixed point.

+5.2-6 Prove that if L_1 and L_2 are defined by systems of regular equations, then so are $L_1 \cup L_2$ and $L_1 L_2$.

+5.2-7 (a) Let A be any fixed language. Prove that $X = L$ is a solution of the equation

$$X = \Lambda \cup X \cup AX \tag{5.2}$$

if and only if there exists L_0 such that $L = A^* \cup A^* L_0$. What is the least solution of (5.2)? Hint: One direction is easy. For the other direction, show that if $X = L$ is a solution of (5.2), then $L = A^* \cup A^* L$.

(b) Using part (a), prove that if L is defined by a system of regular equations, then so is L^*.

*(c) Using part (a), prove that if L is defined by a system of simultaneous equations using all the regular operations, including Kleene-closure, then L can be defined by a set of simultaneous equations using only the operations union and concatenation.

5.2-8 An equation is *right-linear* if it is of the form $X_i = \emptyset$, $X_i = \Lambda$, or $X_i = s_1X_1 \cup \cdots \cup s_kX_k$, where $s_1, \ldots, s_k$ are strings and $X_1, \ldots, X_k$ are variables. Prove that L is regular if and only if L can be defined by a system of right-linear equations.

5.2-9 An equation is *left-linear* if it is of the form $X_i = \emptyset$, $X_i = \Lambda$, or $X_i = X_1s_1 \cup \cdots \cup X_ks_k$, where $s_1, \ldots, s_k$ are strings and $X_1, \ldots, X_k$ are variables. Prove that L is regular if and only if L can be defined by a system of left-linear equations.

5.2-10 Recall that a partial order is a relation that satisfies Proposition 5.2(i, ii). A *complete lower semilattice* $(S, \prec, \bigwedge)$ is a set S together with a partial order $\prec$ and a meet operation $\bigwedge$ satisfying Proposition 5.3. A partial order is called *complete* if it satisfies Proposition 5.2(iii) as well. A complete lower semilattice with a complete partial order is called a *TK-semilattice.*

(a) Prove that the Tarski–Knaster theorem applies to every TK-semilattice.

(b) Let $\succ$ denote the converse of $\prec$; i.e., $x \succ y$ iff $y \prec x$. We say that $(S, \prec, \bigwedge, \bigvee)$ is a *complete lattice* if $(S, \prec, \bigwedge)$ and $(S, \succ, \bigvee)$ are complete lower semilattices. (The $\bigvee$ operation is called *join* or *least upper bound*.) If $(S, \prec, \bigwedge, \bigvee)$ is a complete lattice, prove that $(S, \prec, \bigwedge)$ is a TK-semilattice.

(c) Let $[a, b]$ denote $\{x \in \mathsf{R} : a \leq x \leq b\}$. Let $x \min y$ denote the lesser of x and y, and let $x \max y$ denote the greater of x and y. Prove that $([a, b], \leq, \min, \max)$ is a complete lattice.

Solution: Every closed interval contains the least upper bound and greatest lower bound of every one of its subsets.

(d) We say that a function on the reals is *monotone* if $x \leq y \Rightarrow f(x) \leq f(y)$. Let f be a monotone function on $[0, 1]$. Prove that f has a fixed point.

(e) Construct a monotone function f on $[0, 1)$ that does not have a fixed point. Which property of TK-semilattices is violated?

Solution: Let $f(x) = \frac{1}{2}(x + 1)$. $[0, 1)$ has no universal element $\mathcal{U}$.

(f) Construct a monotone function f on $(0, 1]$ that does not have a fixed point. Which property of TK-semilattices is violated?

(g) Let $(S, \prec, \bigwedge)$ be a complete lower semilattice. For $\mathcal{T} \subseteq S$, let $f(\mathcal{T})$ denote $\{f(x) : x \in \mathcal{T}\}$. We say that a function on S is *continuous from above* if $f(\bigwedge \mathcal{T}) = \bigwedge f(\mathcal{T})$ for all $T \subseteq S$. Construct a function on $[0, 1]$ that is monotone but not continuous from above.

Solution: Let $f(x) = 0$ if $x = 0$, 1 if $x \in (0, 1]$. Then f is monotone. However, f is not continuous from above because $f(\bigwedge (0, 1]) = f(0) = 0$, but $\bigwedge f((0, 1]) = \bigwedge \{1\} = 1$.

5.3 CFGS AND THEIR STANDARDIZATIONS

In this section we present a scheme to standardize systems of regular equations to a form we call context-free grammars. We continue standardizing to obtain a normal form due to Chomsky, which was used in the first efficient parsing algorithms. Our goal is to have a system of equations, each of which is in a particularly simple form.

Distribute. Because concatenation distributes over union, the right side of a regular equation can be written as a union of concatenations. For example, consider the regular equation

$$L = \Lambda \cup \texttt{a}(\Lambda \cup L\texttt{a}) \cup \texttt{b}(\Lambda \cup L\texttt{b}),$$

which defines the language of palindromes over $\{\texttt{a}, \texttt{b}\}$. By distributivity, the equation can be rewritten as

$$L = \Lambda \cup \texttt{a} \cup \texttt{a}L\texttt{a} \cup \texttt{b} \cup \texttt{b}L\texttt{b}.$$

Replace = by ⊇. By the Tarski–Knaster theorem, least solutions are the same as least contractors, so we are justified in replacing $=$ by $\supseteq$. Continuing the example, we get

$$L \supseteq \Lambda \cup \mathtt{a} \cup \mathtt{a}L\mathtt{a} \cup \mathtt{b} \cup \mathtt{b}L\mathtt{b}.$$

Eliminate unions. To eliminate unions, we replace $V \supseteq f \cup g$ by two containments, $V \supseteq f$ and $V \supseteq g$, and iterate as needed. Continuing the example, we obtain the following:

$$\begin{aligned} L &\supseteq \Lambda \\ L &\supseteq \mathtt{a} \\ L &\supseteq \mathtt{a}L\mathtt{a} \\ L &\supseteq \mathtt{b} \\ L &\supseteq \mathtt{b}L\mathtt{b}. \end{aligned}$$

A system of regular containments in such a restricted form is called a *context-free grammar* (CFG) for L. We will typically be interested in solving a system of regular containments for only one of its variables, say S. This variable is called the *start* variable for the set of regular containments. In general, if G is a context-free grammar with start variable S, then we write $L(G)$ to denote $L(S)$. $L(G)$ is called the language *generated* by G. Strings in $L(G)$ are called *sentences*. If L is generated by a CFG, then we call L a *context-free language* (CFL). The class of CFLs is closed under regular operations (Exercises 5.2-6 and 5.2-7). When describing context-free grammars, containments are usually denoted by right arrows and called productions because we think of the variable on the left side of the containment as producing everything on the right side.

EXAMPLE 5.9. The following is a CFG for the set of all palindromes over $\{\mathtt{a}, \mathtt{b}\}$:

$$\begin{aligned} L &\rightarrow \Lambda \\ L &\rightarrow \mathtt{a} \\ L &\rightarrow \mathtt{b} \\ L &\rightarrow \mathtt{a}L\mathtt{a} \\ L &\rightarrow \mathtt{b}L\mathtt{b}. \end{aligned}$$

■■■

The variable that appears to the left of the arrow is called the *left side* of the production. The string of variables and characters that appears to the right of the arrow is called the *right side* of the production. Productions of the form $X \rightarrow Y$ where Y is a variable are called *unit* productions, and productions of the form $X \rightarrow \Lambda$ are called Λ-*productions*.

The remainder of this section is devoted to converting context-free grammars to a form called Chomsky normal form, which we will define later. The next standardization introduces new variables but does not affect the solutions for the old variables.

Make the right side of each production either a character or a concatenation of variables. For each character c, introduce a new variable V_c and the production $V_c \rightarrow c$. In each of the other productions, replace c by V_c. Except for the new variables, this system has the same solutions as the original. Continuing the example, we obtain the following:

$$\begin{aligned} L &\rightarrow \Lambda \\ L &\rightarrow A \\ L &\rightarrow ALA \\ L &\rightarrow B \\ L &\rightarrow BLB \\ A &\rightarrow \texttt{a} \\ B &\rightarrow \texttt{b}. \end{aligned}$$

Eliminate long right sides. Replace each production of the form $X \rightarrow Y_1 Y_2 \cdots Y_k$, where $k \geq 3$, by the following productions:

$$\begin{aligned} X &\rightarrow Y_1 N_1 \\ N_1 &\rightarrow Y_2 N_2 \\ &\vdots \\ N_{k-3} &\rightarrow Y_{k-2} N_{k-2} \\ N_{k-2} &\rightarrow Y_{k-1} Y_k, \end{aligned}$$

where $N_1, \ldots, N_{k-2}$ are new variables. Except for the new variables, this system has the same solutions as the original. Every production is now of the form $X \to \Lambda$, $X \to c$, $X \to Y$, or $X \to YZ$. Continuing the example, we obtain the following:

$$\begin{aligned}
L &\to \Lambda \\
L &\to A \\
L &\to AN_1 \\
N_1 &\to LA \\
L &\to B \\
L &\to BN_2 \\
N_2 &\to LB \\
A &\to \texttt{a} \\
B &\to \texttt{b}.
\end{aligned}$$

Eliminate Λ as much as possible. For each variable X we introduce two new variables:

- X_+ stands for the set of nonempty strings in X, i.e., $X - \{\Lambda\}$.
- X_Λ stands for the set of empty strings in X, i.e., $X \cap \{\Lambda\}$. (That is, X_Λ is equal to $\{\Lambda\}$ if X contains Λ; $\emptyset$ otherwise.)

We also introduce the productions $X \to X_+$ and $X \to X_\Lambda$.

Replace each production of the form $X \to c$ by $X_+ \to c$. Replace each production of the form $X \to \Lambda$ by $X_\Lambda \to \Lambda$. Replace each production of the form $X \to Y$ by $X_+ \to Y_+$ and $X_\Lambda \to Y_\Lambda$.

Replace each production of the form $X \to YZ$ by the following four productions:

- $X_+ \to Y_+Z_+$
- $X_+ \to Y_+Z_\Lambda$
- $X_+ \to Y_\Lambda Z_+$
- $X_\Lambda \to Y_\Lambda Z_\Lambda$.

Except for the new variables, the system constructed so far has the same solutions as the original system. Let $L(V)$ denote the least solution for variable V. It is not hard to see the following for all X:

- $L(X) = L(X_+) \cup L(X_\Lambda)$.
- $L(X_+)$ cannot contain Λ.
- $L(X_\Lambda)$ cannot contain any nonempty string.

Therefore $L(X_\Lambda) = L(X) \cap \{\Lambda\}$ and $L(X_+) = L(X) - \{\Lambda\}$.

Delete all of the original variables X except the start variable S. The only productions involving S are $S \to S_+$ and $S \to S_\Lambda$.

For each variable determine, by an algorithm that we will specify, whether $L(X_\Lambda)$ is equal to $\{\Lambda\}$ or $\emptyset$. If $L(X_\Lambda) = \{\Lambda\}$, then replace X_Λ by Λ on the right side of all productions; otherwise replace X_Λ by $\emptyset$ on the right side of all productions. Delete all productions that have X_Λ on the left side. This system has the same solutions as the original, but Λ does not appear except for possibly the production $S \to \Lambda$. Furthermore, S does not appear on the right side of any production.

Continuing the example, we find the minimal solutions $L(L_\Lambda) = \Lambda$, $L(N_{1\Lambda}) = \emptyset$, $L(N_{2\Lambda}) = \emptyset$, $L(A_\Lambda) = \emptyset$, and $L(B_\Lambda) = \emptyset$, and we substitute the corresponding values for these variables into the productions. For example, $N_2 \to LB$ becomes four productions,

$$
\begin{aligned}
N_{2+} &\to L_+B_+ \\
N_{2+} &\to L_+B_\Lambda \\
N_{2+} &\to L_\Lambda B_+ \\
N_{2+} &\to L_\Lambda B_\Lambda,
\end{aligned}
$$

which, upon substituting the values above, become

$$
\begin{aligned}
N_{2+} &\to L_+B_+ \\
N_{2+} &\to B_+.
\end{aligned}
$$

The other two productions are deleted because their right sides are $\emptyset$.

The full grammar is given below:

$$
\begin{aligned}
L &\rightarrow \Lambda \\
L &\rightarrow L_+ \\
L_+ &\rightarrow A_+ \\
L_+ &\rightarrow A_+N_{1+} \\
N_{1+} &\rightarrow L_+A_+ \\
N_{1+} &\rightarrow A_+ \\
L_+ &\rightarrow B_+ \\
L_+ &\rightarrow B_+N_{2+} \\
N_{2+} &\rightarrow L_+B_+ \\
N_{2+} &\rightarrow B_+ \\
A_+ &\rightarrow \texttt{a} \\
B_+ &\rightarrow \texttt{b}.
\end{aligned}
$$

As promised, we present an algorithm to determine for every X whether $L(X_\Lambda)$ is equal to $\emptyset$ or $\{\Lambda\}$. Consider the productions that involve only variables of the form X_Λ. We will find all solutions to these productions. Try both possible values for every X_Λ (2^k total possibilities, where k is the number of such variables), and see which ones satisfy the system. If there is a solution with $X_\Lambda = \emptyset$, then $L(X_\Lambda) = \emptyset$; otherwise $L(X_\Lambda) = \{\Lambda\}$. A faster algorithm is described in Exercise 5.3-3.

Eliminate unit productions. Recall that productions of the form $A \rightarrow B$ where B is a variable are called *unit* productions.

Say that a variable A *leads to* a variable C if $A = C$ or there exist productions $A \rightarrow B_1, B_1 \rightarrow B_2, \ldots, B_{k-1} \rightarrow B_k$, where $B_k = C$. Determine for all X_0, X_1 whether X_0 leads to X_1. (An algorithm for this is discussed in Exercise 5.3-5.)

For each production of the form $X \rightarrow c$ and each X_0 such that X_0 leads to X, introduce the production $X_0 \rightarrow c$.

For each production of the form $X \rightarrow YZ$, each X_0 such that X_0 leads to X, each Y_1 such that Y leads to Y_1, and each Z_1 such that Z leads to Z_1, introduce the production $X_0 \rightarrow Y_1Z_1$. That, is we work backward from X

using a sequence of unit productions, and we work forward from Y and Z using a sequence of unit productions.

For example, the production $L_+ \to A_+N_{1+}$ yields the following four productions:

$$\begin{aligned}
L_+ &\to A_+N_{1+} \\
L_+ &\to A_+A_+ \\
L &\to A_+N_{1+} \\
L &\to A_+A_+.
\end{aligned}$$

Finally, we delete all unit productions. This transformation does not affect the solution to the system. The resulting grammar for our example follows:

$$\begin{aligned}
L &\to \Lambda \\
L_+ &\to A_+N_{1+} \\
L_+ &\to A_+A_+ \\
L &\to A_+N_{1+} \\
L &\to A_+A_+ \\
N_{1+} &\to L_+A_+ \\
N_{1+} &\to A_+A_+ \\
N_{1+} &\to B_+A_+ \\
L_+ &\to B_+N_{2+} \\
L_+ &\to B_+B_+ \\
L &\to B_+N_{2+} \\
L &\to B_+B_+ \\
N_{2+} &\to L_+B_+ \\
N_{2+} &\to A_+B_+ \\
N_{2+} &\to B_+B_+ \\
A_+ &\to \mathtt{a} \\
L &\to \mathtt{a} \\
L_+ &\to \mathtt{a} \\
N_{1+} &\to \mathtt{a}
\end{aligned}$$

$$
\begin{aligned}
B_+ &\rightarrow \mathtt{b} \\
L &\rightarrow \mathtt{b} \\
L_+ &\rightarrow \mathtt{b} \\
N_{2+} &\rightarrow \mathtt{b}.
\end{aligned}
$$

Now each production has the form $X \rightarrow c$, $X \rightarrow YZ$, or $S \rightarrow \Lambda$, where S is the start variable and S does not appear on the right side of any production. If $L(S)$ does not contain Λ, then each production has the form $X \rightarrow c$ or $X \rightarrow YZ$. This normal form for grammars is called *Chomsky* normal form (CNF). The *size* of a context-free grammar (denoted $|G|$) is the total number of characters in all of its productions. When we convert a context-free grammar G to a CNF grammar G' as described above, the resulting grammar is not much larger; i.e., $|G'| = O(|G|)$.

Exercises

5.3-1 Construct CFGs for the languages in Exercise 5.2-1.

5.3-2 Construct a context-free grammar G such that $L(G)$ consists of all regular expressions over the alphabet $\{\mathtt{a}, \mathtt{b}\}$.

Solution: We work directly from the recursive definition. G's alphabet consists of a and b, and the symbols ∪, *, (, and). G's only variable (and start symbol) is R.

$$
\begin{aligned}
R &\rightarrow \emptyset \\
R &\rightarrow \mathbf{\Lambda} \\
R &\rightarrow \mathtt{a} \\
R &\rightarrow \mathtt{b} \\
R &\rightarrow (R)\cup(R) \\
R &\rightarrow (R)\,(R) \\
R &\rightarrow (R)^{*}.
\end{aligned}
$$

+5.3-3 Design an algorithm to determine, for all variables V in a CFG, whether $\Lambda \in L(V)$. The running time of your algorithm should be linear in the size of the CFG.

Solution: First we will sketch a solution; then we will present a detailed algorithm. A production depends on all the variables on its right side. A variable X depends on all of the productions of the form $X \rightarrow Y_1 \cdots Y_k$. A production is ready when all of the variables it depends on are ready; in particular, a production of the form $X \rightarrow \Lambda$ is ready immediately. A variable is ready when at least one of the productions it depends on is ready. An object is a variable or a production. We say that a production $X \rightarrow Y_1 \cdots Y_k$ needs k objects. We say that a variable X needs only one object. When an object α becomes ready for the first time, we see what objects depend on α; their needs are reduced by 1 and α becomes done. If a variable is done, then it derives Λ. By processing this information in the right order, we avoid processing any variable or production twice.

For each object α, let dependents$[\alpha]$ contain a list of all objects that depend on α. The array dependents[ ] can easily be computed in time linear in the size of the grammar. The remainder of the algorithm is shown in Figure 5.4. A variable X derives Λ if and only if $X \in$ done.

Notes: It is helpful to think of the objects as the nodes in a directed graph. There is an edge from α to β if β depends on α. Label variables "OR," label null productions "TRUE," and label all other productions "AND." The graph models a monotone circuit that may contain cycles. Assume that all AND- and OR-gates start in the state FALSE. The algorithm above determines the stable state attained by each gate. The algorithm can be extended to monotone circuits containing threshold gates that test whether at least t of their inputs are TRUE (by initializing NEEDS to t) or to general monotone threshold gates that test whether $\sum_i w_i x_i \geq t$ (by subtracting w_i from NEEDS when x_i is processed).

```
readyset := ∅;
done := ∅;
for all variables X do NEEDS[X] := 1;
for all productions P do begin
    NEEDS[P] := the length of the right side of P;
    if NEEDS[P] ≤ 0 then (* P is of the form X → Λ *)
        insert P in readyset;
end;
while readyset ≠ ∅ do begin
    remove an object (* variable or production *) α from readyset;
    if α ∉ done then begin
        insert α in done;
        for each object β in dependents[α] do begin
            NEEDS[β] := NEEDS[β] − 1;
            if NEEDS[β] ≤ 0 then insert β in readyset;
        end;
    end;
end;
```

FIGURE 5.4: An algorithm for testing which variables in a CFG derive Λ.

5.3-4 Design an algorithm to determine, for context-free grammars G, whether $L(G) = \emptyset$. Hint: Use Exercise 5.3-3.

Solution: Construct a new grammar G' by replacing all characters by Λ in all of G's productions. Then $L(G) \neq \emptyset$ if and only if $\Lambda \in L(G)$; an algorithm to answer the latter question is provided by Exercise 5.3-3.

5.3-5 (a) Present an algorithm for determining the reflexive, transitive closure of a relation. Hint: A relation R can be represented as a directed graph in which there is an edge from X to Y if and only if $(X, Y) \in R$. Use the algorithm associated with Kleene's theorem in Section 4.4.

(b) Present an algorithm for determining which variables in a CFG lead to which.

*5.4 PARSE TREES

In Section 5.2 we proved that every system of regular equations has a least solution. We also asserted that this least solution is equal to the set of strings that have parse trees. In this section we prove that assertion. (If you skipped Section 5.2, then skip this section as well.)

We give a recursive definition of parse trees.

DEFINITION 5.10 (Parse Trees). Let G be a context-free grammar. If $A \rightarrow B_1 \cdots B_k$ is a production in G, then there is a parse tree whose root is A and whose subtrees are $T_1, \ldots, T_k$ (in that order) where

- T_i consists of a single node labeled B_i, if B_i is a character.
- T_i is a parse tree whose root is B_i, if B_i is a variable.

(See Figure 5.5.)

Observe that a parse tree's leaves are always labeled with characters, and its internal nodes are always labeled with variables.

THEOREM 5.11. *The least fixed point of a set of regular equations is equal to the set of strings that have parse trees in the corresponding grammar.*

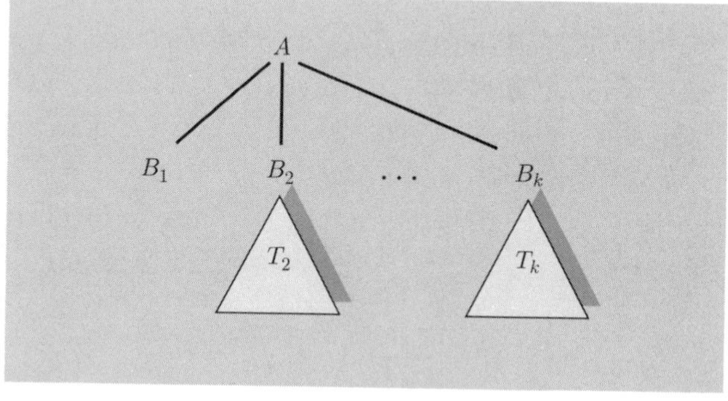

FIGURE 5.5: A parse tree starting with $A \rightarrow B_1 \cdots B_k$. In this example, B_1 is a character; $B_2, \ldots, B_k$ are variables.

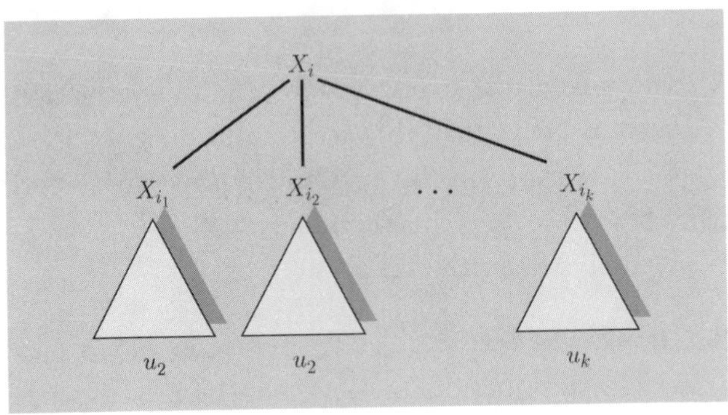

FIGURE 5.6: A parse tree for $u = u_1u_2 \cdots u_k$.

Proof: Let the system of regular equations be $X_i = f_i(X_1, \ldots, X_n)$ for $i = 1, \ldots, n$. Let $f(\vec{X}) = \langle\langle f_1(\vec{X}), \ldots, f_n(\vec{X})\rangle\rangle$, where $\vec{X}$ denotes $\langle\langle X_1, \ldots, X_n\rangle\rangle$. Form the associated grammar, and standardize it by eliminating null and unit productions. This does not alter the set of strings having parse trees.

Let $P(V)$ denote the set of strings for which there is a parse tree rooted at V. We will show that $\langle\langle P(X_1), \ldots, P(X_n)\rangle\rangle$ is the least contractor of f; by Theorem 5.5, it is also the least fixed point.

We will prove by induction on the length of u that if $u \in f_i(P(X_1), \ldots, P(X_n))$, then $u \in P(X_i)$. Suppose $u \in f_i(P(X_1), \ldots, P(X_n))$. Then there exists a production $X_i \to X_{i_1} \cdots X_{i_k}$ such that $u \in P(X_{i_1}) \cdots P(X_{i_k})$. Then Figure 5.6 is a parse tree for u rooted at X_i, so $u \in P(X_i)$. Thus, $f_i(P(X_1), \ldots, P(X_n)) \subseteq P(X_i)$, and this is true for every i. Therefore $f(P(X_1), \ldots, P(X_n)) \prec \langle\langle P(X_1), \ldots, P(X_n)\rangle\rangle$, so $\langle\langle P(X_1), \ldots, P(X_n)\rangle\rangle$ is a contractor of f.

Now we will prove that $\langle\langle P(X_1), \ldots, P(X_n)\rangle\rangle$ is a least contractor of f. If $u \in P(X_i)$, then, roughly speaking, a parse tree for u embodies a proof that $u \in C_i$ for every contractor $\langle\langle C_1, \ldots, C_n\rangle\rangle$ of f. To be precise, we will prove for every string u, every variable X_i, and every contractor $\langle\langle C_1, \ldots, C_n\rangle\rangle$ that $u \in P(X_i) \Rightarrow u \in C_i$. The proof is by induction on the size of u's parse tree.

Let u be any string in $P(X_i)$. Let $\langle\langle C_1, \ldots, C_n\rangle\rangle$ be any contractor of f. Suppose, inductively, that $v \in C_j$ for all v and j such that v is the yield of a parse tree rooted at X_j that is smaller than u's parse tree. Since $u \in P(X_i)$, there is a parse tree with root X_i whose yield is u. Let the children of the root be $X_{i_1}, \ldots, X_{i_k}$, and let the yields of their subtrees be $u_1, \ldots, u_k$, respectively, again as in Figure 5.6. The strings $u_1, \ldots, u_k$ are the yields of parse trees that are smaller than u's parse tree (because they are subtrees of u's parse trees). Therefore, by the inductive hypothesis, $u_j \in C_{i_j}$ for $j = 1, \ldots, k$. Now it follows that $u = u_1 \cdots u_k \in C_{i_1} \cdots C_{i_k}$. From the parse tree for u we know that there is a production $X_i \to X_{i_1} \cdots X_{i_k}$, so $C_{i_1} \cdots C_{i_k} \subseteq f_i(C_1, \ldots, C_n)$. Therefore,

$$u \in C_{i_1} \cdots C_{i_k} \subseteq f_i(C_1, \ldots, C_n) \subseteq C_i$$

because $\langle\langle C_1, \ldots, C_n \rangle\rangle$ is a contractor of f. Since $u \in C_i$ for every $u \in P(X_i)$, we have shown that $P(X_i) \subseteq C_i$. Therefore $\langle\langle P(X_1), \ldots, P(X_n) \rangle\rangle \prec \langle\langle C_1, \ldots, C_n \rangle\rangle$ for every contractor $\langle\langle C_1, \ldots, C_n \rangle\rangle$. Thus $\langle\langle P(X_1), \ldots, P(X_n) \rangle\rangle$ is a least contractor of f, as asserted.

By Theorem 5.5, the least contractor is unique and is equal to the least fixed point. Thus $\langle\langle P(X_1), \ldots, P(X_n) \rangle\rangle$ is the least fixed point of f. ■

Exercises

5.4-1 (a) In a fixed grammar, can there be infinitely many different parse trees with root A and yield x?

(b) Can you standardize each grammar so that for every A and x there are only finitely many different parse trees with root A and yield x?

5.4-2 Let G be a CNF grammar and let x be a string in $L(G)$.

(a) Prove that in every parse tree for x each node has either one terminal or two nonterminal characters as children.

(b) Prove that every parse tree for x in G has exactly $2|x| - 1$ internal nodes.

(c) Prove that every parse tree for x in G has height at least $\lceil \log_2(|x|) \rceil + 1$.

5.4-3 Let G be any grammar without Λ-productions or unit productions, and let x be a string in $L(G)$.

(a) Prove that every parse tree for x in G has at most $2|x| - 1$ internal nodes.
(b) Construct a grammar in which a single string has unboundedly large parse trees.

5.5 DERIVATIONS

Consider a system of regular containments using alphabet Σ and variable set V; these are called defining containments. As much as possible, we use capital letters to denote variables, early lowercase letters (such as a, b, and c) to denote characters, late lowercase letters (such as x, y, and z) to denote strings over Σ, and lowercase Greek letters to denote strings over $V \cup \Sigma$. For example, the right side of the production $B \rightarrow aBC$ is aBC, a string over $V \cup \Sigma$ that we might denote β.

Although the statement $\alpha \supseteq \beta$ has only one mathematical meaning, it has three nuances in the study of grammars. We have three different symbols to denote these nuances. A defining containment $B \supseteq \beta$ is denoted by the production $B \rightarrow \beta$, as we have already seen. An immediate consequence of that defining containment is that $\alpha B \gamma \supseteq \alpha \beta \gamma$ for any α, γ; in this case, we say that $\alpha B \gamma$ *immediately derives* $\alpha \beta \gamma$, which is denoted $\alpha B \gamma \Rightarrow \alpha \beta \gamma$. We say that the production $B \rightarrow \beta$ is *applied* to the variable B in $\alpha B \gamma$ and that the variable B is *rewritten*.

The reflexive transitive closure of $\Rightarrow$ is denoted $\stackrel{*}{\Rightarrow}$; if $\alpha \Rightarrow \beta \Rightarrow \cdots \Rightarrow \zeta$, we say that α *derives* ζ. If $A \stackrel{*}{\Rightarrow} u$, then we can conclude $A \supseteq \{u\}$, so the string $u \in L(A)$ whenever $A = L(A)$ is part of a solution to the set of defining containments; in particular, u belongs to the least solution for A.

We summarize the notation as follows:

- $A \rightarrow \beta$ denotes the defining containment $A \supseteq \beta$.
- $\alpha \Rightarrow \beta$ denotes that α immediately derives β.
- $\alpha \stackrel{*}{\Rightarrow} \beta$ denotes that α derives β.

Given an immediate derivation, if we know which variable was rewritten we can determine from context which production was applied. However, we may not always be able to determine which variable was rewritten.

EXAMPLE 5.12. Consider the following grammar:

$$\begin{aligned} E &\rightarrow \texttt{1} \\ E &\rightarrow E\texttt{-}E \\ E &\rightarrow E\texttt{+}E. \end{aligned}$$

In this grammar,

$$E \Rightarrow E\texttt{-}E \Rightarrow E\texttt{-}E\texttt{-}E \Rightarrow \texttt{1-}E\texttt{-}E \Rightarrow \texttt{1-1-}E \Rightarrow \texttt{1-1-1},$$

so $E \stackrel{*}{\Rightarrow}$ `1-1-1`. We cannot tell whether the first E or the second E was rewritten at the second step. If the first, we would interpret the derived string to mean $(1-1)-1=-1$. If the second, we would interpret it to mean $1-(1-1)=1$. ■ ■ ■

A *derivation* of ζ from α consists of a sequence $\alpha \Rightarrow \beta \Rightarrow \cdots \Rightarrow \zeta$, together with an indication of which variable was rewritten at each step. Typically the rewritten variable is underlined, e.g.,

$$\underline{E} \Rightarrow \underline{E}\texttt{-}E \Rightarrow \underline{E}\texttt{-}E\texttt{-}E \Rightarrow \texttt{1-}\underline{E}\texttt{-}E \Rightarrow \texttt{1-1-}\underline{E} \Rightarrow \texttt{1-1-1}.$$

A derivation that starts with a variable and ends with a string over Σ is called a *complete* derivation. A derivation in which the leftmost variable is rewritten at every step is called a *leftmost* derivation. (If we are told that the derivation is leftmost, then there is no real need to mark which variable is rewritten.) For example, the derivation above is complete and leftmost. The derivation below is neither complete nor leftmost:

$$\underline{E} \Rightarrow E\texttt{-}\underline{E} \Rightarrow E\texttt{-}E\texttt{-}E.$$

Each step in a derivation rewrites a variable as a string of variables and characters. Because characters cannot be rewritten, they are called *terminal characters* or *terminals*. Because variables appear in strings, they are called *nonterminal characters* or *nonterminals*.

If $\beta\gamma\cdots\zeta \Rightarrow \alpha'$, then the rewritten variable occurs in one of the strings β, γ, ..., or ζ. In the first case, $\alpha' = \beta'\gamma\cdots\zeta$, where $\beta \Rightarrow \beta'$; in the second case, $\alpha' = \beta\gamma'\cdots\zeta$, where $\gamma \Rightarrow \gamma'$; in the last case, $\alpha' = \beta\gamma\ldots\zeta'$, where $\zeta \Rightarrow \zeta'$. In any case, there exist $\beta', \gamma', \ldots, \zeta'$ (all but one of them equal to the corresponding unprimed string) such that $\alpha' = \beta'\gamma' \cdots \zeta'$, $\beta \stackrel{*}{\Rightarrow} \beta', \gamma \stackrel{*}{\Rightarrow} \gamma', \ldots$, and $\zeta \stackrel{*}{\Rightarrow} \zeta'$, where each derivation takes one step or zero. By a simple induction, we obtain the following lemma:

LEMMA 5.13 (Decomposition). *Let $\alpha_0 = \beta_0\gamma_0 \cdots \zeta_0$. If*

$$\alpha_0 \Rightarrow \alpha_1 \Rightarrow \cdots \Rightarrow \alpha_n,$$

then, for every i, there exist $\beta_i, \gamma_i, \ldots, \zeta_i$ with $\alpha_i = \beta_i\gamma_i \cdots \zeta_i$ such that

$$\begin{array}{ccccccc}
\beta_0 & \stackrel{*}{\Rightarrow} & \beta_1 & \stackrel{*}{\Rightarrow} & \cdots & \stackrel{*}{\Rightarrow} & \beta_n \\
\gamma_0 & \stackrel{*}{\Rightarrow} & \gamma_1 & \stackrel{*}{\Rightarrow} & \cdots & \stackrel{*}{\Rightarrow} & \gamma_n \\
\vdots & \vdots & \vdots & \vdots & \vdots & \vdots & \vdots \\
\zeta_0 & \stackrel{*}{\Rightarrow} & \zeta_1 & \stackrel{*}{\Rightarrow} & \cdots & \stackrel{*}{\Rightarrow} & \zeta_n,
\end{array}$$

where each derivation takes one step or zero. In particular, if $\beta_0\gamma_0 \ldots \zeta_0 \Rightarrow x$ then $x = \beta_n\gamma_n \ldots \zeta_n$ where $\beta_0 \stackrel{*}{\Rightarrow} \beta_n$, $\gamma_0 \stackrel{*}{\Rightarrow} \gamma_n$, and $\zeta_0 \stackrel{*}{\Rightarrow} \zeta_n$. ∎

Now we are ready to prove the equivalence of derivations and parse trees.

THEOREM 5.14

(i) For every derivation $A \stackrel{*}{\Rightarrow} x$, there is a parse tree whose root is A and yield is x.

(ii) There is a one-one correspondence from parse trees with root A and yield x to leftmost derivations of $A \stackrel{*}{\Rightarrow} x$.

Proof: (i) Our proof is by strong induction on the length of a derivation. Consider any derivation of $A \stackrel{*}{\Rightarrow} x$. The derivation must begin by applying a production to A, i.e., $A \Rightarrow \beta_1 \cdots \beta_k$, where each β_i is either a character or a variable. By the decomposition lemma, because $\beta_1 \ldots \beta_k \stackrel{*}{\Rightarrow} x$, we can write $x = x_1 \cdots x_k$ where $\beta_1 \stackrel{*}{\Rightarrow} x_1, \ldots, \beta_k \stackrel{*}{\Rightarrow} x_k$. We make a tree whose root is A and whose children are $\beta_1, \ldots, \beta_k$, in that order (see Figure 5.7).

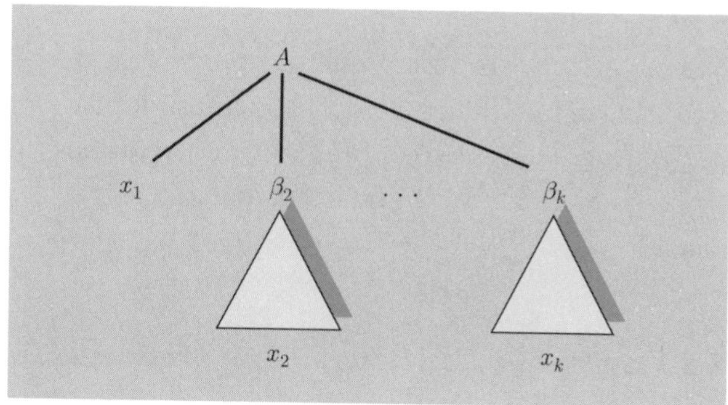

FIGURE 5.7: The parse tree corresponding to a derivation $A \Rightarrow \beta_1 \cdots \beta_k \overset{*}{\Rightarrow} x_1 \cdots x_k$. In this example $\beta_1 = x_1$.

If $\beta_i \in \Sigma$, then $\beta_i = x_i$. Otherwise β_i is a variable and there is a derivation of $\beta_i \overset{*}{\Rightarrow} x_i$; this derivation is shorter than the derivation of $A \overset{*}{\Rightarrow} x$. By the inductive hypothesis, there is a parse tree with root β_i and yield x_i. Combine these trees to produce a parse tree with root A and yield x (Figure 5.7).

(ii) The one-one correspondence is defined recursively. Consider any parse tree with root A and yield x. Let the children of A be $\beta_1, \ldots, \beta_k$, where each β_i is either a character or a variable (Figure 5.7). Either β_i is a character x_i, or β_i is the root of a sub–parse tree whose yield is some string x_i. Then $x_1 \cdots x_k$ is the yield of A, so $x_1 \cdots x_k = x$.

The leftmost derivation begins $A \Rightarrow \beta_1 \cdots \beta_k$. If the string $\beta_1 \cdots \beta_k$ contains any variables, let β_ℓ be the leftmost variable in the string. Then $\beta_1 \cdots \beta_k = x_1 \cdots x_{\ell-1}\beta_\ell\beta_{\ell+1} \cdots \beta_k$. Recursively find a leftmost derivation of $\beta_\ell \overset{*}{\Rightarrow} x_\ell$, so we have

$$\underline{A} \Rightarrow x_1 \cdots x_{\ell-1}\underline{\beta_\ell}\beta_{\ell+1} \cdots \beta_k \overset{*}{\Rightarrow} x_1 \cdots x_{\ell-1}x_\ell\beta_{\ell+1} \cdots \beta_k.$$

As long as there are any variables left in that string, repeat the process of deriving, in leftmost fashion, a substring of x from the leftmost variable.

The algorithm we just presented provides a mapping f from parse trees with root A and yield x to leftmost derivations of $A \stackrel{*}{\Rightarrow} x$. In part (i), we presented a mapping g from derivations to parse trees, which happens to be the right inverse of f; i.e., $f \circ g = I$, so f is one-one. ■

COROLLARY 5.15. *The least fixed point of a set of regular equations is equal to the set of strings that have derivations in the corresponding grammar.*

Note that parse trees avoid many repetitions found in derivations. Therefore they are superior to derivations as a data structure for representing the meaning of English sentences or real computer programs.

Exercises

5.5-1 Let $\alpha_0 = \beta_0\gamma_0 \cdots \zeta_0$. Prove that if

$$\alpha_0 \stackrel{*}{\Rightarrow} \alpha_1 \stackrel{*}{\Rightarrow} \cdots \stackrel{*}{\Rightarrow} \alpha_n,$$

then, for every i, there exist $\beta_i, \gamma_i, \ldots, \zeta_i$ with $\alpha_i = \beta_i\gamma_i \cdots \zeta_i$ such that

$$\begin{array}{ccccccc} \beta_0 & \stackrel{*}{\Rightarrow} & \beta_1 & \stackrel{*}{\Rightarrow} & \cdots & \stackrel{*}{\Rightarrow} & \beta_n \\ \gamma_0 & \stackrel{*}{\Rightarrow} & \gamma_1 & \stackrel{*}{\Rightarrow} & \cdots & \stackrel{*}{\Rightarrow} & \gamma_n \\ \vdots & \vdots & \vdots & \vdots & \vdots & \vdots & \vdots \\ \zeta_0 & \stackrel{*}{\Rightarrow} & \zeta_1 & \stackrel{*}{\Rightarrow} & \cdots & \stackrel{*}{\Rightarrow} & \zeta_n. \end{array}$$

5.5-2 (a) Let G be a CNF grammar and let x be a string in $L(G)$. Prove that every derivation of x in G takes exactly $2|x| - 1$ steps.

(b) Let G be any grammar without Λ-productions or unit productions, and let x be a string in $L(G)$. Prove that every derivation of x in G takes at most $2|x| - 1$ steps.

5.6 CFLS ARE THE SAME AS NSA LANGUAGES

In this section we show that every CFL is accepted by a nondeterministic stack acceptor (NSA). Then we show that the set of computations of an NSA is a CFL and that every NSA language is itself a CFL. Thus the class of NSA languages is equal to the class of context-free languages.

THEOREM 5.16. *Every CFL is an NSA language.*

Proof: Let L be a CFL over an alphabet Σ. Then L is generated by a context-free grammar G whose set of variables is N and whose start variable is S. Each production has the form $X \to Y_1 \cdots Y_k$, where each Y_i is either a character or a variable. We will design a program P for a machine [control, stack, input]. (We list the stack before the input, because the stack is the more important device in this proof.) P's control set consists of a start state q_{start}, an accepting state q_{accept}, and all prefixes of right sides of productions. P's stack alphabet is $\Sigma \cup N$, the set of all characters and variables in the grammar G.

The first instruction performed by P is $(q_{\text{start}} \to \Lambda, \text{PUSH}S, \text{NOOP})$.

The production $X \to Y_1 \cdots Y_k$ is simulated by the instructions

$$(\Lambda \to Y_1 \cdots Y_k \quad , \text{POP}X \quad , \text{NOOP})$$

and

$$\begin{array}{lll}(Y_1 \cdots Y_k \to Y_1 \cdots Y_{k-1} & , \text{PUSH}\,Y_k & , \text{NOOP}) \\ (Y_1 \cdots Y_{k-1} \to Y_1 \cdots Y_{k-2}, & \text{PUSH}\,Y_{k-1}, & \text{NOOP}) \\ \quad\vdots & \quad\vdots & \quad\vdots \\ (Y_1 \to \Lambda & , \text{PUSH}\,Y_1 & , \text{NOOP}),\end{array}$$

which remove X from the stack and replace it by $Y_k \cdots Y_1$.

The generation of characters is simulated by the NSA instructions $(\Lambda \to \Lambda, \text{POP}c, \text{SCAN}c)$ for each $c \in \Sigma$; the accepting state can be reached by the instruction $(\Lambda \to q_{\text{accept}}, \text{EMPTY}, \text{EOF})$. The details of a correctness proof are left to the reader. ∎

It is worth noting that the number of control states in the NSA constructed above is essentially equal to the size of the grammar. As an example

$$
\begin{aligned}
A &\rightarrow \mathtt{a}A \\
A &\rightarrow \mathtt{a}E \\
A &\rightarrow \mathtt{b}AA \\
E &\rightarrow \Lambda \\
E &\rightarrow \mathtt{a}E\mathtt{b} \\
E &\rightarrow EE.
\end{aligned}
$$

FIGURE 5.8: A context-free grammar.

of applying the construction, we convert the grammar shown in Figure 5.8 to an equivalent NSA, which is shown in Figure 5.9.

As a corollary to the next theorem, we will show that every NSA language is a CFL. We have already seen how to standardize a nondeterministic program so that it does not use the EOF test (Section 4.1). We have also seen how to standardize a stack machine program so that it never uses the empty test (Section 3.3.3).

THEOREM 5.17. *Let P be an NSA that does not use the* EOF *test or the* EMPTY *test and that empties the stack before accepting. The set of accepting computations of P is a CFL.*

Proof: Let P be an NSA with control set Q, start state 0, final state f, and input alphabet Σ. Let P run on a machine [control, stack, input]. Assume that P does not use the EOF test or the EMPTY test and that P empties the stack before accepting.

Consider any sequence of input operations used by P. Since P does not use the EOF test, that sequence contains only SCANs and NOOPs. Therefore the sequence of input operations is executable on one input string, namely $c_1 \cdots c_n$, where the sequence of SCAN operations is SCAN$c_1, \ldots,$ SCANc_n.

Consider any sequence $o_1, \ldots, o_k$ of stack operations used by P that maps Λ to Λ, i.e.,

$$\Lambda o_1 \cdots o_k = \Lambda.$$

We will show that $o_1 \cdots o_k$ has the same effect on the stack as a NOOP. Since P does not use the EMPTY test, the sequence $o_1, \ldots, o_k$ contains only

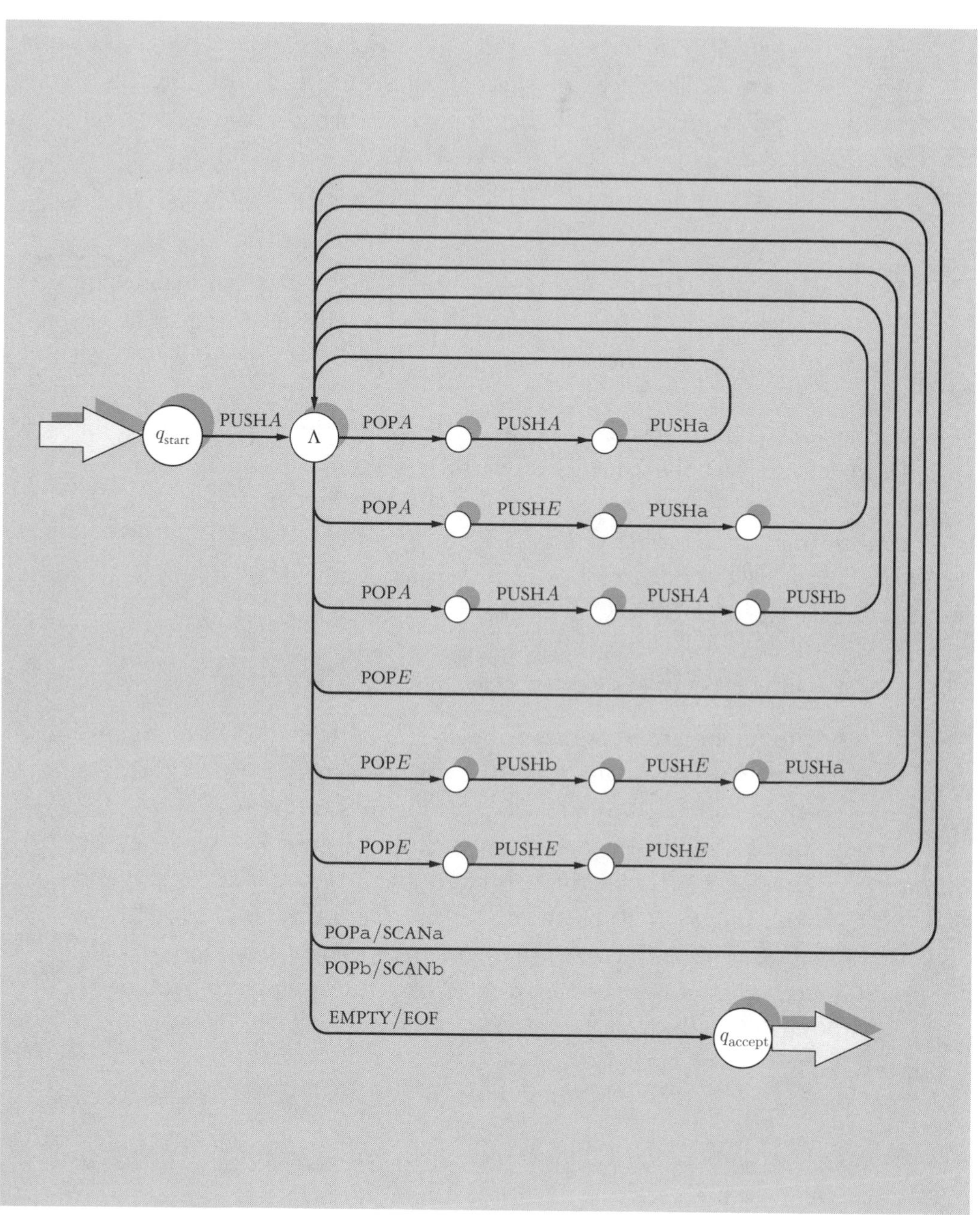

FIGURE 5.9: An NSA equivalent to the CFG in Figure 5.8.

PUSHes, POPs, and NOOPs. If we apply that sequence of operations to a stack that initially holds a nonempty string s, then the original top character cannot be popped off, for otherwise the sequence of operations would block when applied to Λ. Therefore the effect of that sequence of stack operations does not depend on the original stack contents. Therefore, the sequence of stack operations maps each stack string s to s, i.e.,

$$so_1 \cdots o_k = s.$$

Thus we have shown that any sequence of stack operations that maps Λ to Λ is equivalent to NOOP (the identity relation) on the stack. In particular, the sequence of stack operations in any computation of P is equivalent to NOOP.

For each pair of control states i and j, let $L_{i,j}$ be the set of computation fragments in which the sequence of control operations is equivalent to $i \rightarrow j$ and the sequence of stack operations is equivalent to NOOP. Then the set of accepting computations of P is $L_{0,f}$, so $L_{0,f}$ will be the start variable of the grammar we construct. Any computation fragment belonging to $L_{i,m}$ must have one of the following forms:

- The computation fragment may be Λ if $i = m$.
- The computation fragment may begin with a PUSH, which must be matched by a POP of the same character. Suppose that the corresponding PUSH and POP instructions are $(i \rightarrow j, \text{PUSH}c, f_{\text{in}})$ and $(k \rightarrow \ell, \text{POP}c, g_{\text{in}})$. Those instructions must be separated by a sequence of instructions that goes from control state j to k while performing NOOP on the stack, and they must be followed by a sequence of instructions that goes from control state ℓ to m while performing NOOP on the stack. That is, the computation fragment must have the form

$$(i \rightarrow j, \text{PUSH}c, f_{\text{in}})\, L_{j,k}\, (k \rightarrow \ell, \text{POP}c, g_{\text{in}})\, L_{\ell,m}.$$

- The computation fragment may begin with an instruction that does not use the stack, in which case it is of the form

$$(i \rightarrow j, \text{NOOP}, f_{\text{in}})\, L_{j,m}.$$

No computation fragment in $L_{i,m}$ may begin with a POP because the composition of the sequence of stack operations would then be a strictly partial function instead of being NOOP. Thus we obtain the following context-free grammar:

$$
\begin{array}{lll}
L_{i,i} & \rightarrow & \Lambda \qquad \text{for each control state } i \\
L_{i,m} & \rightarrow & (i \rightarrow j, \text{PUSH}c, f_{\text{in}})\, L_{j,k}\, (k \rightarrow \ell, \text{POP}c, g_{\text{in}})\, L_{\ell,m} \\
 & & \text{for each } i, j, k, \ell, m, c, f_{\text{in}}, g_{\text{in}} \\
 & & \text{such that the instructions on the right side occur in } P \\
L_{i,m} & \rightarrow & (i \rightarrow j, \text{NOOP}, f_{\text{in}})\, L_{j,m} \\
 & & \text{for each } i, j, m, f_{\text{in}} \\
 & & \text{such that the instruction on the right side occurs in } P.
\end{array}
$$

The details of a correctness proof are left to the reader. ■

COROLLARY 5.18. *Every NSA language is a CFL.*

Proof: Modify the grammar constructed in the preceding proof as follows: Replace each instruction by the character that it scans or by Λ if the instruction does not scan anything, i.e., if the instruction performs a NOOP on the input device. Instead of generating each computation, as in the preceding proof, this grammar generates the string scanned during each computation. ■

The size of the CFG constructed above is $O(n^3)$, where n is the number of instructions in the NSA.

EXAMPLE 5.19. Figure 2.3 shows an NSA program that accepts palindromes with central marker. We construct a CFG for the set of computations of that NSA. (Note that the order of the input and stack devices has been unreversed.) The start variable is $L_{1,2}$.

$$
\begin{array}{lll}
L_{1,1} & \rightarrow & \Lambda \\
L_{2,2} & \rightarrow & \Lambda \\
L_{1,1} & \rightarrow & (1 \rightarrow 1, \text{SCAN}\mathtt{a}, \text{PUSH}\mathtt{a})\, L_{1,2}\, (2 \rightarrow 2, \text{SCAN}\mathtt{a}, \text{POP}\mathtt{a})\, L_{2,1}
\end{array}
$$

$$\begin{aligned}
L_{1,1} &\to (1 \to 1, \text{SCAN}\mathtt{b}, \text{PUSH}\mathtt{b})\, L_{1,2}\, (2 \to 2, \text{SCAN}\mathtt{b}, \text{POP}\mathtt{b})\, L_{2,1} \\
L_{1,2} &\to (1 \to 1, \text{SCAN}\mathtt{a}, \text{PUSH}\mathtt{a})\, L_{1,2}\, (2 \to 2, \text{SCAN}\mathtt{a}, \text{POP}\mathtt{a})\, L_{2,2} \\
L_{1,2} &\to (1 \to 1, \text{SCAN}\mathtt{b}, \text{PUSH}\mathtt{b})\, L_{1,2}\, (2 \to 2, \text{SCAN}\mathtt{b}, \text{POP}\mathtt{b})\, L_{2,2} \\
L_{1,2} &\to (1 \to 2, \text{SCAN}\#, \text{NOOP})\, L_{2,2}.
\end{aligned}$$

We convert the grammar for the set of accepting computations into a grammar for the accepted language:

$$\begin{aligned}
L_{1,1} &\to \Lambda \\
L_{2,2} &\to \Lambda \\
L_{1,1} &\to \mathtt{a}L_{1,2}\mathtt{a}L_{2,1} \\
L_{1,1} &\to \mathtt{b}L_{1,2}\mathtt{b}L_{2,1} \\
L_{1,2} &\to \mathtt{a}L_{1,2}\mathtt{a}L_{2,2} \\
L_{1,2} &\to \mathtt{b}L_{1,2}\mathtt{b}L_{2,2} \\
L_{1,2} &\to \#L_{2,2}.
\end{aligned}$$

Since $L_{1,1}$ cannot be a descendant of $L_{1,2}$ in any parse tree, we may eliminate $L_{1,1}$'s productions from the grammar. Since $L_{2,2}$ generates only Λ, we may replace $L_{2,2}$ by Λ everywhere. Thus we obtain the following simplified grammar, which should already be familiar:

$$\begin{aligned}
L_{1,2} &\to \mathtt{a}L_{1,2}\mathtt{a} \\
L_{1,2} &\to \mathtt{b}L_{1,2}\mathtt{b} \\
L_{1,2} &\to \#.
\end{aligned}$$

Beware: In many other examples the grammar does not turn out to be so simple. ■■■

EXAMPLE 5.20. We can also use Corollary 5.18 to prove that certain languages are context-free without actually constructing the grammar. For example, let

$$L = \{w : w \text{ contains an equal number of } \mathtt{a}\text{'s and } \mathtt{b}\text{'s}\}.$$

A signed counter can keep track of the number of a's minus the number of b's in w, so L is accepted by a program for a machine [control, input, signed counter]. Such a program is shown in Figure 1.12. A signed counter can be simulated by an unsigned counter, which can be simulated by a stack, so L is an NSA language. By Corollary 5.18, L is a CFL. ■■■

We have shown that L is a CFL if and only if L is accepted by an NSA. If a CFL L is in fact accepted by a DSA, then L is called *deterministic*. The deterministic CFLs are called DCFLs for short. The syntax for most programming languages is essentially a DCFL (ignoring the customary syntactic requirement to declare identifiers before using them).

Exercises

5.6-1 Construct an NSA that is equivalent to the following grammar:

$$\begin{aligned} A &\to BC \\ B &\to CA \\ C &\to AB \\ A &\to \texttt{a} \\ B &\to \texttt{b} \\ C &\to \texttt{c}. \end{aligned}$$

5.6-2 Construct a CFG that is equivalent to the NSA in Figure 1.13.

5.6-3 (a) Prove that every DCFL is generated by a grammar in which all productions have one of the following forms—

- $A \to \Lambda$
- $A \to b\gamma$

—and for each variable A and character b there is at most one production of the second form.

(b) Prove that the set of even-length palindromes over $\{\texttt{a}, \texttt{b}\}$ is generated by a grammar of the form described in part (a). (In Section 6.4 we will prove that the set of palindromes over $\{\texttt{a}, \texttt{b}\}$ is not a DCFL.)

**(c) Define a class of grammars that generate exactly the DCFLs.

Solution: The LR(1) grammars are such a class of grammars. We will not define them in this book. To learn about them, refer to a textbook on compiler design.

5.6-4 (a) Give a constructive proof that the class of regular languages is closed under quotient with context-free languages.

(b) Give a constructive proof that the class of regular languages is closed under derivative by context-free languages. (See Exercise 4.8-5 for a definition.)

*5.7 THE CHOMSKY HIERARCHY

In Section 5.6, we saw that CFGs generate exactly the languages accepted by NSAs. There is a hierarchy of grammars that is related to the hierarchy of machines, although the correspondence is not exact. In this section we describe that hierarchy briefly.

Special cases of context-free grammars are the right-linear grammars and the left-linear grammars. A grammar is *right-linear* if every production is of the form $V \to \Lambda$ or $V \to sW$, where s is a string of terminal characters and W is a nonterminal. A grammar is *left-linear* if every production is of the form $V \to \Lambda$ or $V \to Ws$, where s is a string of terminal characters and W is a nonterminal. The right-linear grammars generate exactly the regular languages (Exercise 5.2-8) and so do the left-linear grammars (Exercise 5.2-9). For this reason right-linear grammars and left-linear grammars are called *regular grammars*. Regular grammars generate exactly the languages accepted by NFAs.

The context-free grammars are so-called because the rules for rewriting a symbol B, such as $B \to \beta$, do not depend on the characters surrounding the variable B (its context). Context-sensitive grammars (CSGs) are a generalization of CFGs that allow a variable to be rewritten according to its context.

In general, a production of the form $\alpha \to \beta$, where α and β are strings of terminals and nonterminals, means that the string α can be replaced by the string β in derivations. A *context-sensitive grammar* (CSG) is a system of productions of the form $\alpha \to \beta$ where $|\beta| \geq |\alpha|$, e.g., $ABA \to ACA$ and $ABA \to CCCC$ are allowable productions in a CSG but $ABA \to AA$ is not.

The production $S \to \Lambda$ is also allowed under the restrictions that S is the start variable and S does not appear on the right side of any production. The name "context-sensitive" comes from a normal form in which all productions have the form

$$\alpha B\gamma \to \alpha\beta\gamma,$$

where β is nonempty. The languages generated by CSGs are called *context-sensitive languages* (CSLs); they are exactly the same as the languages that are accepted by nondeterministic Turing acceptors that use at most $n+1$ squares on each tape, where n is the length of the input. (For more information on space-bounded Turing machines, see Exercise 9.1-5.)

Unrestricted grammars may contain any production of the form $\alpha \to \beta$. These unrestricted grammars, also called semi-Thuë systems, are discussed extensively in Section 7.10. Unrestricted grammars generate exactly the languages accepted by NTAs.

Right-linear grammars, context-free grammars, context-sensitive grammars, and unrestricted grammars form what is called *Chomsky's hierarchy*. In this hierarchy, unrestricted grammars are called type 0; context-sensitive, type 1; context-free, type 2; and right-linear, type 3. The Chomsky hierarchy is strict, meaning that there exist languages of each type that do not belong to the next higher type (cf. Exercise 9.2-3(c), Example 5.22, and Example 4.26).

Exercises

5.7-1 Show how to convert any right-linear grammar to one in which every production has the form $V \to \Lambda$ or $V \to cW$, where c is a terminal character and W is a nonterminal.

5.7-2 Construct a right-linear grammar that generates the set of all strings over $\{\mathtt{a}, \mathtt{b}\}$ with an odd number of a's.

5.7-3 (a) Prove that every CSL is accepted by an NTA in which the tape heads do not leave the first $|x|+1$ tape squares on input x. Hint: The NTA may copy x to the tape, then apply productions in reverse, nondeterministically guessing which production and where to use it. The tape string stays the same length or gets shorter each time a production is applied.

*(b) Prove the converse of part (a). Hint: Without loss of generality, we assume that the NTA begins by copying the input x to one of its tapes. By using a larger alphabet, we may assume that the NTA has only one tape (cf. Section 7.1.1). Standardize it so that it halts in a fixed final state q_{accept} with empty tape. Represent a configuration of the NTA by the string t_1qt_2, where q is the control state, t_1 is the string to the left of the tape head, and t_2 is the string to the right of the tape head. The behavior of the NTA at each step depends only on q and the characters next to the tape head; design a corresponding production.

*5.7-4 Show how to convert every context-sensitive grammar to a normal form in which every production has the form $\alpha B\gamma \to \alpha\beta\gamma$, where $\beta \neq \Lambda$.

5.8 PUMPING THEOREMS FOR CFLS

In Chapter 4 we proved several pumping theorems for regular languages. Let us say that a language L is *1-pumpable* if there is a number N such that for every string $x \in L$ having length at least N, there exist u, v, and w such that $v \neq \Lambda$ and, for all $i \geq 0$, $uv^iw \in L$. Recall that our simplest pumping theorem says that all regular languages are 1-pumpable. We are able to prove that certain languages are not regular by proving that they are not 1-pumpable.

A similar theorem is desirable for context-free languages, so we can prove that certain languages are not context-free. We cannot hope that exactly the same pumping theorem applies to context-free languages, because we showed in Chapter 4 that several context-free languages, like $\{\mathtt{a}^i\mathtt{b}^i : i \geq 0\}$, are not 1-pumpable. Instead, we will define a pumping condition that allows a string to be pumped up in two places simultaneously.

In this section we will prove three pumping theorems for context-free languages. The first of these is the weakest but the easiest to prove. The second theorem is a generalization of the first, and its proof builds on the proof of the first. The third theorem is a simple corollary of the second. On an initial reading, we recommend that the reader try to understand the proof of the first theorem and the applications of the third theorem.

THEOREM 5.21 (First Pumping Theorem for CFLs). *Let L be a context-free language. There exists a natural number N (depending on L) such that, for all $z \in L$ with $|z| \geq N$, there exist strings u, v, w, x, y satisfying the following conditions:*

- $z = uvwxy$
- $v \neq \Lambda$ *or* $x \neq \Lambda$
- $|vwx| \leq N$
- *for all* $i \geq 0$, $uv^iwx^iy \in L$

Proof: Let $L - \{\Lambda\}$ be generated by a context-free grammar G without null productions or unit productions. Let G's variable set be V and G's terminal alphabet be Σ. Let r be the length of the longest right side of any production in G. If $r < 2$, let $r = 2$. Define $N_0 = r^{|V|} + 1$ and $N = r^{|V|+1}$. Let z be any string generated by G such that $|z| \geq N \geq N_0$.

We will work with a parse tree for z. Recall that the height of a node A, denoted $\text{height}(A)$, is the distance from A to its deepest descendant. We define the *weight* of a node A, denoted $\text{weight}(A)$, to be the number of leaves that are A's descendants; i.e., the weight of a node is the length of the string it yields in the parse tree.

Since r is the length of the longest right side of any production, each node in the parse tree has at most r children. By an easy induction, every node A in the parse tree satisfies $\text{weight}(A) \leq r^{\text{height}(A)}$. Because $|z| \geq N_0 > r^{|V|}$, the height of the root must be greater than $|V|$, so the height of the root is at least $|V| + 1$. Therefore there is a path from the root to a leaf that contains at least $|V| + 1$ edges and consequently at least $|V| + 1$ internal nodes.

We will be concerned only with the lowest $|V| + 1$ internal nodes on that path. By the pigeonhole principle, two of these nodes must be labeled with the same variable, say A. The situation is shown in Figure 5.10.

Let w denote the yield of the lower A. The yield of the upper A must include w as a substring, so let the yield of the upper A be vwx. The string

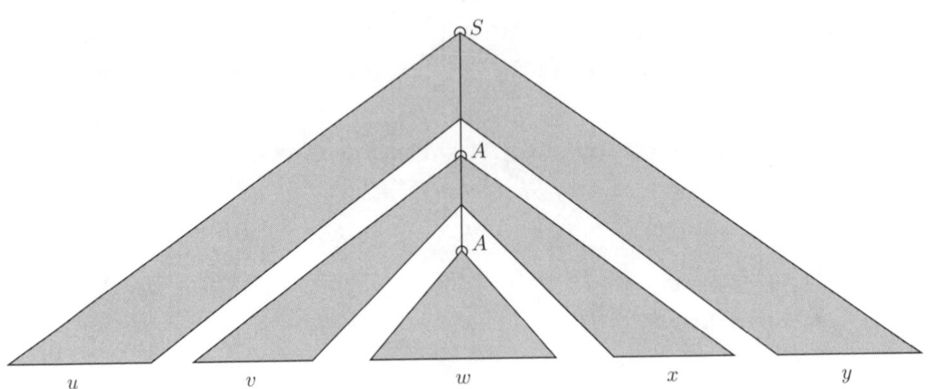

FIGURE 5.10: A path with two A's lets us decompose z into $uvwxy$.

vwx must be a substring of z, so let $z = uvwxy$. Then we have the following derivations in G:

Derivation (1): $S \stackrel{*}{\Rightarrow} uAy$

Derivation (2): $A \stackrel{*}{\Rightarrow} vAx$

Derivation (3): $A \stackrel{*}{\Rightarrow} w$

Since G contains no null productions or unit productions, v and x cannot both be the empty string (Exercise 5.8-5). Since the height of the upper A is at most $|V| + 1$, its weight is at most $r^{|V|+1}$, so $|vwx| \leq r^{|V|+1} = N$.

By applying derivation (1) once, then derivation (2) i times where $i \geq 0$, and finally derivation (3) once, we obtain

$$S \stackrel{*}{\Rightarrow} uAy \stackrel{*}{\Rightarrow} uv^iAx^iy \stackrel{*}{\Rightarrow} uv^iwx^iy.$$ ■

We restate the first pumping theorem to highlight the sequence of quantifiers. Let L be a CFL.

$\exists N$
$\forall z \in L$ such that $|z| \geq N$
$\exists u, v, w, x, y$ such that $uvwxy = z$, $|vwx| \leq N$, and $|vx| > 0$
$\forall i \geq 0$
$uv^iwx^iy \in L$.

The Al–Izzy game can be played much as with regular languages (cf. Section 0.1 and Section 4.9.1). Let L be a language. The game is played as follows:

- Izzy picks a natural number N.
- Al picks $z \in L$ such that $|z| \geq N$.
- Izzy picks u, v, w, x, y such that $z = uvwxy$, $|vwx| \leq N$, and v or x is nonempty.
- Al picks i.

If Al successfully picks i such that $uv^iwx^iy \notin L$, then Al wins. If Al can always win no matter how Izzy plays, then L is not context-free. If Al loses, sometimes or always, nothing can be validly deduced about L.

EXAMPLE 5.22. Let $L = \{\mathtt{a}^n\mathtt{b}^n\mathtt{c}^n : n \geq 0\}$. We will use the first pumping theorem for CFLs to prove that L is not a CFL.

For the sake of contradiction, suppose that L is a CFL. Let N be as in the first pumping theorem for CFLs, and let $z = \mathtt{a}^N\mathtt{b}^N\mathtt{c}^N$. Then there exist strings u, v, w, x, y such that $z = uvwxy$, v or x is nonempty, and $uv^iwx^iy \in L$ for every $i \geq 0$. If v contains a positive number of a's and a positive number of b's, then uv^2wx^2y contains a b followed by an a, so $uv^2wx^2y \notin \mathtt{a}^*\mathtt{b}^*\mathtt{c}^*$ and $uv^2wx^2y \notin L$. (See Figure 5.11.) We obtain a similar contradiction if v contains any other pair of distinct characters or if x contains a pair of distinct characters. Therefore v and x each belong to $\mathtt{a}^*$, $\mathtt{b}^*$, or $\mathtt{c}^*$. Recall that v and x are not both empty. If $v \in \mathtt{a}^+$ and $x \in \mathtt{b}^*$, then uv^2wx^2y

$$z = uvwxy = \underbrace{\mathtt{aa}\cdots\mathtt{a}}_{u}\underbrace{\mathtt{aab}}_{v}\underbrace{\mathtt{b}\cdots\mathtt{bbbc}}_{w}\underbrace{\mathtt{c}\cdots}_{x}\underbrace{\mathtt{ccc}}_{y}$$

$$\text{pumped } z = uv^2wx^2y = \underbrace{\mathtt{aa}\cdots\mathtt{a}}_{u}\underbrace{\mathtt{aab}}_{v}\underbrace{\mathtt{aab}}_{v}\underbrace{\mathtt{b}\cdots\mathtt{bbbc}}_{w}\underbrace{\mathtt{c}\cdots}_{x}\underbrace{\mathtt{c}\cdots}_{x}\underbrace{\mathtt{ccc}}_{y}$$

FIGURE 5.11: If v contains a positive number of a's and a positive number of b's, then $uv^2wx^2y \notin \mathtt{a}^*\mathtt{b}^*\mathtt{c}^*$, so $uv^2wx^2y \notin L$.

$$z = uvwxy = \underbrace{\texttt{aa}}_{u}\underbrace{\cdots\texttt{aa}}_{v}\underbrace{\texttt{abb}\cdots}_{w}\underbrace{\texttt{bb}}_{x}\underbrace{\texttt{bcc}\cdots\texttt{ccc}}_{y}$$

$$\text{pumped } z = uv^2wx^2y = \underbrace{\texttt{aa}}_{u}\underbrace{\cdots\texttt{aa}}_{v}\underbrace{\cdots\texttt{aa}}_{v}\underbrace{\texttt{abb}\cdots}_{w}\underbrace{\texttt{bb}}_{x}\underbrace{\texttt{bb}}_{x}\underbrace{\texttt{bcc}\cdots\texttt{ccc}}_{y}$$

FIGURE 5.12: If $v \in \texttt{a}^+$ and $x \in \texttt{b}^*$, then uv^2wx^2y contains more a's than c's, so $uv^2wx^2y \notin L$.

contains more a's than c's, so $uv^2wx^2y \notin L$. (See Figure 5.12.) We obtain a similar contradiction no matter how v and x are chosen: Because vx contains at least one occurrence of a character d and possibly a second character e but no occurrence of the remaining character f, uv^2wx^2y must contain more d's than f's and thus not belong to L. ■ ■ ■

EXAMPLE 5.23. Let $L = \{\texttt{a}^i\texttt{b}^j\texttt{c}^i\texttt{d}^j : i, j \geq 0\}$. We show that L is not a CFL. Suppose, for the sake of contradiction, that L is a CFL. Let N be a pumping number for L as in the first pumping theorem for CFLs, and let $z = \texttt{a}^N\texttt{b}^N\texttt{c}^N\texttt{d}^N$. By the first pumping theorem for CFLs, there exist u, v, w, x, y such that $z = uvwxy$, $|vwx| \leq N$, v or x is nonempty, and $uv^iwx^iy \in L$ for all $i \geq 0$. Because $|vwx| \leq N$, vwx must be of the form $\texttt{a}^*\texttt{b}^*$, $\texttt{b}^*\texttt{c}^*$, or $\texttt{c}^*\texttt{d}^*$. In any of these cases, pumping down results in a string not in L. (For example, if $vwx \in \texttt{a}^*\texttt{b}^*$, then uwy contains fewer a's and b's than c's and d's.) This contradiction proves that L is not a CFL. ■ ■ ■

EXAMPLE 5.24. Let $L = \{\texttt{a}^i\texttt{b}^j\texttt{c}^k : i \leq j \leq k\}$. We show that L is not a CFL. For the sake of contradiction, assume that L is context-free. Let N be as in the first pumping theorem for CFLs, and let $z = \texttt{a}^N\texttt{b}^N\texttt{c}^N$. Then there exist strings u, v, w, x, y such that $z = uvwxy$, v or x is nonempty, and $uv^iwx^iy \in L$ for all $i \geq 0$. Then v and x must each belong to one of $\texttt{a}^*$, $\texttt{b}^*$, or $\texttt{c}^*$, for otherwise uv^2wx^2y would not belong to $\texttt{a}^*\texttt{b}^*\texttt{c}^*$ and therefore not to L. Therefore vx cannot contain an a, a b, and also a c. If vx contains at least one a but no b's, then uv^2wx^2y contains more a's than b's, a contradiction. If vx contains at least one b but no a's, then uwy contains more a's than b's, a contradiction. We obtain a similar contradiction in the other four cases, because if vx contains at least one d but no e's, then uv^2wx^2y

contains more d's than e's and uwy contains more e's than d's, so they cannot both belong to L. ■■■

The first pumping theorem for CFLs differs in several ways from the pumping theorems for regular languages that we proved in Chapter 4. The most important difference is that strings in CFLs are pumped in two places, whereas strings in regular languages are pumped in only one place. As noted at the start of this section, that difference is inevitable and in fact desirable. If the same pumping theorem applied to regular languages and CFLs, then we could not have used it to prove that any CFLs were nonregular.

A second difference is that some of the pumping theorems for regular languages allow us to localize part of a string for pumping. The first pumping theorem for CFLs does not localize the pumping at all; v and x could be located anywhere in the string z, subject to $|vwx| \leq N$. We will partially rectify that situation now.

Ogden's pumping theorem lets us mark characters in a string. If z is a string in L that contains at least N marked characters, then z is pumpable and one of the pumped substrings, v or x, contains a marked character.

We *mark* characters in a string by specifying their positions. For example, let $z = \texttt{aabbaa}$. We can mark the first two a's and the second b in z by specifying positions 1, 2, and 4. The weight of a substring of z is the number of marked characters it contains (think of the characters as marked with heavy paint). For example, the weight of z is 3. If we write $z = vwx$ where $v = \texttt{aa}$, $w = \texttt{bb}$, and $x = \texttt{aa}$, then the weight of v is 2, the weight of w is 1, and the weight of x is 0. Keep in mind that the weight of a substring depends on where it appears in z; that is why v and x have different weights.

Although our current motivation is to obtain a better pumping theorem for CFLs, we will state Ogden's pumping lemma for arbitrary CFGs, as he originally stated it. Because this lemma applies directly to derivations in any context-free grammar, Ogden was able to use it in proving that a certain CFL is inherently ambiguous; i.e., all of its grammars are ambiguous. We will do the same in the next section.

LEMMA 5.25 (Ogden's Derivation-Pumping Lemma for CFGs). *Let G be a CFG. There exists a natural number N (depending on G) such that for all*

$z \in L(G)$, if z is marked so that $\text{weight}(z) \geq N$*, then there exist a variable A and terminal strings u, v, w, x, y satisfying the following conditions:*

- $z = uvwxy$
- $\text{weight}(v) \geq 1$ *or* $\text{weight}(x) \geq 1$
- $\text{weight}(vwx) \leq N$
- $S \stackrel{*}{\Rightarrow}_G uAy$
- $A \stackrel{*}{\Rightarrow}_G vAx$
- $A \stackrel{*}{\Rightarrow}_G w$
- *for all* $i \geq 0$, $A \stackrel{*}{\Rightarrow}_G v^i w x^i$

Proof: Let L be generated by a context-free grammar G. Let G's variable set be V. Let r be the length of the longest right side of any production in G. If $r < 2$, let $r = 2$. Define $N_0 = r^{|V|} + 1$ and $N = r^{|V|+1}$. Let z be any string generated by G such that $\text{weight}(z) \geq N \geq N_0$.

We will work with a parse tree for z. We define the weight of a node A to be the number of leaves below A that are labeled with marked characters; i.e., $\text{weight}(A)$ is the weight of the string that A yields in the parse tree.

We define the *weight-branching height* of a node A, denoted $\text{wb-height}(A)$, as though nodes of weight 0 were not present in the parse tree and as though an only child were identical to its parent. More precisely, $\text{wb-height}(A) =$

$$\begin{cases} 0 & \text{if } A \text{ is a leaf,} \\ 1 + \max\limits_{C \text{ is a child of } A} \text{wb-height}(C) & \text{if } A \text{ has more than one child with positive weight,} \\ \max\limits_{C \text{ is a child of } A} \text{wb-height}(C) & \text{otherwise.} \end{cases}$$

In particular, since the weight of an internal node is the sum of the weights of its children, an internal node A has the same wb-height as one of its children C if and only if A has the same weight as C; otherwise A's wb-height is 1 greater than the maximum wb-height of any of its children.

Since r is the length of the longest right side of any production, each node in the parse tree has at most r children. By an easy induction, every node A

in the parse tree satisfies $\text{weight}(A) \leq r^{\text{wb-height}(A)}$. Consequently, because $\text{weight}(z) \geq N_0 > r^{|V|}$, the weight-branching height of the root must be greater than $|V|$, so the weight-branching height of the root is at least $|V|+1$. Each node with positive weight-branching height has a descendant whose weight-branching height is exactly one smaller. Therefore there is a path from the root to a leaf that contains internal nodes whose weight-branching heights are wb-height(root), wb-height(root) $- 1, \ldots, 1$.

We will be concerned with the nodes on that path having weight-branching height $|V| + 1, |V|, \ldots, 1$. By the pigeonhole principle, two of those $|V| + 1$ nodes must be labeled with the same variable, say A. The situation is essentially the same as in Figure 5.10.

We define u, v, w, x, y as in the preceding proof. Because the upper A has greater weight-branching height than the lower A, $\text{weight}(vwx) > \text{weight}(w)$. Therefore $\text{weight}(v) \geq 1$ or $\text{weight}(x) \geq 1$. Since the weight-branching height of the upper A is at most $|V| + 1$, its weight is at most $r^{|V|+1}$, so $\text{weight}(vwx) \leq r^{|V|+1} = N$.

By the same reasoning as in the preceding proof, $S \overset{*}{\Rightarrow}_G uAy$, $A \overset{*}{\Rightarrow}_G vAx$, $A \overset{*}{\Rightarrow}_G w$, and $A \overset{*}{\Rightarrow}_G v^i w x^i$ for all $i \geq 0$. ∎

We have an immediate corollary for CFLs.

THEOREM 5.26 (Ogden's Pumping Theorem for CFLs). *Let L be a CFL. There exists a natural number N (depending on L) such that for all $z \in L$, if z is marked so that* $\text{weight}(z) \geq N$, *there exist strings u, v, w, x, y satisfying the following conditions:*

- $z = uvwxy$
- $\text{weight}(v) \geq 1$ *or* $\text{weight}(x) \geq 1$
- $\text{weight}(vwx) \leq N$
- *for all $i \geq 0$, $uv^iwx^iy \in L$* ∎

Observe that the first pumping theorem for CFLs is the special case of Ogden's pumping theorem in which every character of z is marked.

EXAMPLE 5.27. Let $L = \{\mathtt{a}^i\mathtt{b}^j\mathtt{c}^k : i \neq j \text{ and } j = k\}$. The first pumping theorem for CFLs is not strong enough to prove that L is not a CFL (Exercise 5.8-6). Instead, we use Ogden's pumping theorem for CFLs.

For the sake of contradiction, assume that L is a CFL. Let N be as in Ogden's pumping theorem for CFLs. Let $z = \mathtt{a}^{N+N!}\mathtt{b}^N\mathtt{c}^N$. Mark all the b's, so z has weight N. Then there exist strings u, v, w, x, y such that $z = uvwxy$, weight$(v) \geq 1$ or weight$(x) \geq 1$, and $uv^iwx^iy \in L$ for all $i \geq 0$.

v and x must each belong to $\mathtt{a}^*$, $\mathtt{b}^*$, or $\mathtt{c}^*$, for otherwise $uv^2wx^2y \notin \mathtt{a}^*\mathtt{b}^*\mathtt{c}^*$. Because only the b's are marked, either v or x must be equal to $\mathtt{b}^m$ for some m between 1 and N. The other of v or x must be equal to $\mathtt{c}^m$, or else uv^2wx^2y would contain different numbers of b's and c's, a contradiction. Therefore $v = \mathtt{b}^m$ and $x = \mathtt{c}^m$. Let $i = N!/m + 1$ (pump up $N!/m$ times). Then

$$uv^iwx^iy = uvv^{N!/m}wxx^{N!/m}y = uv\mathtt{b}^{N!}w\mathtt{c}^{N!}y = \mathtt{a}^{N+N!}\mathtt{b}^{N+N!}\mathtt{c}^{N+N!},$$

which has the same number of a's as b's, a contradiction. ■ ■ ■

In many applications of Ogden's pumping theorem, the marked characters are consecutive; i.e., they form a substring of z. A very useful corollary of Ogden's pumping theorem lets us pump a substring of the marked substring. Recall that the first pumping theorem for CFLs gave us a bound on the length of vwx but no other control over the location of v or x inside z. The third pumping theorem, proved below, is a useful companion to the first pumping theorem. It will let us locate v or x inside a particular N-character substring of z but without any bound on $|vwx|$. For most applications, either the first pumping theorem or the third pumping theorem for CFLs will suffice. Ogden's pumping theorem for CFLs is rarely needed.

COROLLARY 5.28 (Third Pumping Theorem for CFLs). *Let L be a CFL. There exists a natural number N (depending on L) such that for all $z \in L$, if $z = z_1z_2z_3$ where $|z_2| \geq N$, there exist strings u, v, w, x, y satisfying the following conditions:*

- $z = uvwxy$
- *v or x is a nonempty substring of z_2*
- *for all $i \geq 0$, $uv^iwx^iy \in L$*

Proof: (If we mark each character in z_2, Theorem 5.26 gives us u, v, w, x, y such that $z = uvwxy$, v or x overlaps z_2, and $(\forall i \geq 0)[uv^iwx^iy \in L]$. A clever trick will guarantee that v or x is actually a substring of z_2.)

Let # be a new character that does not belong to L's alphabet. Let $\hat{L}$ consist of all strings in L with exactly two #'s inserted anywhere; i.e., $\hat{L} = L \clubsuit \{\#\#\}$, the shuffle of L and $\{\#\#\}$. Given an NSA that accepts L, we can construct an NSA that accepts $\hat{L}$ by using an extra control to count #'s. Thus $\hat{L}$ is a CFL. (In fact, we will see that the class of CFLs is closed under shuffle with regular languages by Exercise 6.1-5.)

Let N be a pumping number for $\hat{L}$, as in Ogden's pumping theorem. Suppose that $z = z_1 z_2 z_3 \in L$ where $|z_2| \geq N$. Let $\hat{z} = z_1 \# z_2 \# z_3$, which belongs to $\hat{L}$. Mark all characters in z_2. By Ogden's pumping theorem, there exist $\hat{u}, \hat{v}, \hat{w}, \hat{x}, \hat{y}$ satisfying the following conditions:

- $\hat{z} = \hat{u}\hat{v}\hat{w}\hat{x}\hat{y}$
- weight$(\hat{v}) \geq 1$ or weight$(\hat{x}) \geq 1$
- weight$(\hat{v}\hat{w}\hat{x}) \leq N$
- for all $i \geq 0$, $\hat{u}\hat{v}^i\hat{w}\hat{x}^i\hat{y} \in L$

Neither $\hat{v}$ nor $\hat{x}$ can contain a #, because then, pumping down, $\hat{u}\hat{w}\hat{y}$ would contain fewer than two #'s. Furthermore, $\hat{v}$ or $\hat{x}$ must contain a marked character and therefore must be a nonempty substring of z_2. Obtain u, v, w, x, y by deleting all #'s from $\hat{u}, \hat{v}, \hat{w}, \hat{x}, \hat{y}$, respectively. Then the following conditions are satisfied:

- $z = uvwxy$
- v or x is a nonempty substring of z_2
- for all $i \geq 0$, $uv^iwx^iy \in L$ ∎

In the next example, we could use either Ogden's pumping theorem or the third pumping theorem to prove that a language is not context free. We use the latter because it is easier to apply. (For an example where Ogden's pumping theorem cannot be applied directly but the third pumping theorem can be, see Exercise 5.8-8.)

EXAMPLE 5.29. Let us apply this corollary to show that the language $L = \{\mathtt{a}^i\mathtt{b}^j\mathtt{c}^k : i \neq j \text{ and } j \neq k\}$ is not a CFL. Suppose, for the sake of contradiction, that L is a CFL. Let N be the number from Corollary 5.28, and let $z = \mathtt{a}^{N+N!}\mathtt{b}^N\mathtt{c}^{N+N!}$. Then $z = z_1z_2z_3$ where $z_1 = \mathtt{a}^{N+N!}$, $z_2 = \mathtt{b}^N$, and $z_3 = \mathtt{c}^{N+N!}$. By Corollary 5.28 there exist strings u, v, w, x, y such that $z = uvwxy$, v or x is a nonempty string of b's, and $uv^iwx^iy \in L$ for all $i \geq 0$. If v contains a b, then x cannot contain any a's; if x contains a b, then v cannot contain any c's. Let m be the total number of b's contained by v and x. Then $1 \leq m \leq N$, so $r = N!/m$ is an integer. Then $uv^{r+1}wx^{r+1}y$ contains exactly $N + N!$ b's, but it must also contain exactly $N + N!$ a's or $N + N!$ c's, so it does not belong to L. This contradiction proves that L is not a CFL. ∎

Exercises

5.8-1 (a) Prove that the first pumping theorem for CFLs remains true if we require that v be nonempty instead of just requiring that v or x be nonempty.

(b) Does Ogden's pumping theorem for CFLs remain true if we require that v contain a marked character instead of just requiring that v or x contain one?

5.8-2 Redo Example 5.29 using Ogden's pumping theorem for CFLs.

5.8-3 Prove that the following are not CFLs:

(a) $\{\mathtt{a}^i\mathtt{b}^j\mathtt{c}^k : i < j < k\}$

(b) $\{\mathtt{a}^i\mathtt{b}^j\mathtt{c}^k : j < i = k\}$

(c) $\{\mathtt{a}^{i^2} : i \geq 0\}$

(d) $\{\mathtt{a}^i : i \text{ is composite}\}$. Hint: Let p be the least prime number that is greater than $(N! + 1)! + 1$, and show that in fact $p > (N!+1)!+N!+1$. Let $i = p-N!$ and apply Theorem 5.21.

*(e) $\{w : w$ is the decimal representation of an integer squared$\}$

*(f) $\{w : w$ is the decimal representation of an integer cubed$\}$

*(g) $\{w : w$ is the decimal representation of a prime number$\}$

*(h) $\{w : w$ is the decimal representation of a composite number$\}$

5.8-4 Let L be the set of syntactically correct Pascal programs (if you do not know Pascal, consider some other block-structured programming language in which variables must be declared before they are used). Prove that L is not a CFL.

5.8-5 Let G be a CFG without null productions or unit productions. Prove that if $A \stackrel{*}{\Rightarrow} \alpha$, then α is either a single terminal character or else $|\alpha| > 1$. If B is a nonterminal, conclude that it is not possible for A to derive B by a nonempty sequence of productions.

5.8-6 Let $L = \{\mathtt{a}^i\mathtt{b}^j\mathtt{c}^k : i \neq j \text{ and } j = k\}$. Although L is not a CFL by Example 5.27, in this exercise you will prove that L satisfies the conclusions of Theorem 5.21.

(a) Let $N \geq 2$. Let $z = \mathtt{a}^{N+N!}\mathtt{b}^N\mathtt{c}^N$. Find u, v, w, x, y such that $z = uvwxy$, $|v| \geq 1$ or $|x| \geq 1$, $|vwx| \leq N$, and, for all $i \geq 0$, $uv^iwx^iy \in L$.

Solution: Let $v = \mathtt{a}$, $y = \mathtt{a}^{N+N!-1}\mathtt{b}^N\mathtt{c}^N$, and $u = w = x = \Lambda$.

(b) Let $N = 8$. Let z be any string in L such that $|z| \geq N$. Show how to find u, v, w, x, y such that $z = uvwxy$, $|v| \geq 1$ or $|x| \geq 1$, $|vwx| \leq N$, and, for all $i \geq 0$, $uv^iwx^iy \in L$.

Solution: Let $z = \mathtt{a}^i\mathtt{b}^j\mathtt{c}^j$. We take three cases.

- If $i = j + 1$ or $i = j - 1$, let $v = \mathtt{aa}$, $y = \mathtt{a}^{i-2}\mathtt{b}^j\mathtt{c}^j$, and $u = w = x = \Lambda$.
- If $i \geq j+2$, let $v = \mathtt{a}$, $y = \mathtt{a}^{i-1}\mathtt{b}^j\mathtt{c}^j$, and $u = w = x = \Lambda$.
- If $i \leq j - 2$, let $v = \mathtt{b}$, $x = \mathtt{c}$, $u = \mathtt{a}^i\mathtt{b}^{j-1}$, $w = \Lambda$, and $y = \mathtt{c}^{j-1}$.

5.8-7 Let $L = \{\mathtt{a}^i\mathtt{b}^j\mathtt{c}^i\mathtt{d}^j : i, j \geq 0\}$. Although L is not a CFL by Example 5.23, prove that L satisfies the conclusions of Corollary 5.28.

5.8-8 Let $L = \{\mathtt{a}^i\mathtt{bcbd}^i\mathtt{bcbe}^i : i \geq 0\} \cup \{\mathtt{a}^i\mathtt{cd}^j\mathtt{bcbe}^k : i, j, k \geq 0\} \cup \{\mathtt{a}^i\mathtt{bcbd}^j\mathtt{ce}^k : i, j, k \geq 0\} \cup \{x \in \{\mathtt{a}, \mathtt{b}, \mathtt{c}, \mathtt{d}, \mathtt{e}\}^* : x \text{ contains at least six } \mathtt{b}\text{'s}\}$.

(a) Prove that L satisfies the conclusions of Theorem 5.26.

(b) Use Corollary 5.28 directly to prove that L is not a CFL.

Solution: Assume, for the sake of contradiction, that L is a CFL. Let N be a pumping number for L as in Corollary 5.28, and let $z = \mathtt{a}^N\mathtt{bcbd}^N\mathtt{bcbe}^N$. Then $z = z_1z_2z_3$ where $z_1 = \Lambda$,

$z_2 = \mathtt{a}^N$, and $z_3 = \mathtt{bcbd}^N\mathtt{bcbe}^N$. Apply Corollary 5.28 to obtain u, v, w, x, y where v or x is a nonempty string of a's.

Case 1: v is a nonempty string of a's. If x contains a c, then pumping down we obtain uwy, which contains at most one c and at most four b's, so $uwy \notin L$. Therefore x contains no c's. x cannot contain three or more b's, because then x would contain a c. If x contains two b's, then $x = \mathtt{bd}^N\mathtt{b}$; therefore uwy contains only two b's and no occurrence of the pattern bcb, so $uwy \notin L$. Therefore x does not contain two b's. If x contains one b, then uwy contains exactly three b's, so $uwy \notin L$. Therefore x does not contain one b. Consequently, x is a substring of $\mathtt{a}^N$, $\mathtt{d}^N$, or $\mathtt{e}^N$, so $uwy \in \mathtt{a}^*\mathtt{bcbd}^*\mathtt{bcbe}^*$. If x is a substring of $\mathtt{a}^N$, then uwy contains more d's than a's, so $uwy \notin L$; if x is a substring of $\mathtt{d}^N$, then uwy contains more e's than d's, so $uwy \notin L$; if x is a substring of $\mathtt{e}^N$, then uwy contains more a's than e's, so $uwy \notin L$. Thus any choice of x contradicts Corollary 5.28.

Case 2: x is a nonempty string of a's. Then v is a substring of $\mathtt{a}^N$. Pumping down, we obtain $uwy = \mathtt{a}^m\mathtt{bcbd}^N\mathtt{bcbe}^N$, where $m < N$, so $uwy \notin L$, contradicting Corollary 5.28.

In either case, we obtain a contradiction, so L must not be a CFL.

5.8-9 In this exercise, you will prove an extension of Ogden's pumping theorem for CFLs. We mark a *substring* of z by specifying its first and last position. For example, to mark the second and third occurrences of abb in abbaabbaaabbb, we would specify the pairs $(5, 7)$ and $(10, 12)$. Let L be a CFL. Prove that there exists N (depending on L) such that for all $z \in L$, if at least N nonoverlapping substrings of z are marked, then there exist u, v, w, x, y satisfying the following conditions:

- $z = uvwxy$
- v or x contains at least one marked substring
- vwx overlaps with at most N marked substrings
- for all $i \geq 0$, $uv^iwx^iy \in L$

5.9 AMBIGUITY

In typical applications of CFGs, sentences and phrases have meanings. Often the meaning of a sentence or phrase is determined from the meaning of its constituent phrases. If there is exactly one way to parse a string, i.e., exactly one parse tree, then its meaning is uniquely determined. If there is more than one parse tree, a string might not have a unique meaning. For example, the arithmetic expression $7 - 3 - 2$ could mean $(7 - 3) - 2$ or $7 - (3 - 2)$, which have different numerical values.

A string that can be parsed in more than one way—i.e., a string that is yielded by more than one parse tree—is called *ambiguous*. Equivalently, by Theorem 5.14(ii), a string is ambiguous if and only if it has more than one leftmost derivation. (However, an unambiguous string will usually have several derivations that are not leftmost.)

If a grammar provides multiple parse trees for some strings, the grammar itself is called *ambiguous*. If all grammars defining a particular language are ambiguous, so that no grammar provides a satisfactory framework for assigning unique meanings to strings, the language is called *inherently* ambiguous. A CFG is called *unambiguous* if it is not ambiguous; a CFL is called *unambiguous* if it is not inherently ambiguous.

EXAMPLE 5.30. It is important that real programming languages be unambiguous so that programs will have unique meanings. Consider the grammar G given below:

$$\begin{aligned} S &\rightarrow \texttt{if } C \texttt{ then } S \\ S &\rightarrow \texttt{if } C \texttt{ then } S \texttt{ else } S \\ S &\rightarrow \texttt{statement} \\ C &\rightarrow \texttt{condition}. \end{aligned}$$

(The words `if`, `then`, `else`, `statement`, and `condition` are terminals in this grammar. In a real programming language, `condition` and `statement` might generate a variety of meaningful conditions and statements.) G is ambiguous because the string

```
if condition then if condition then statement else statement
```

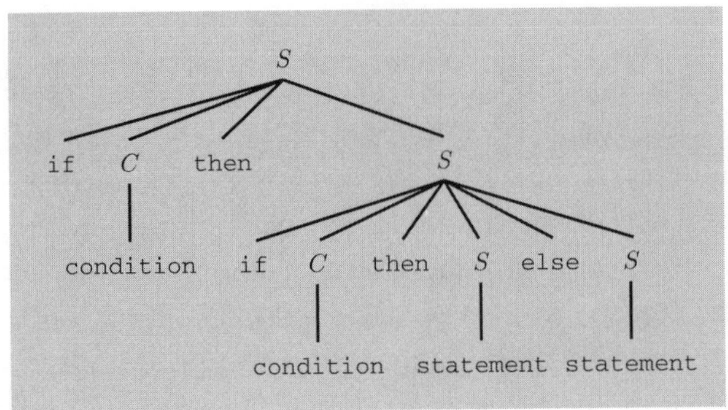

FIGURE 5.13: One way to parse

`if condition then if condition then statement else statement`

in the ambiguous grammar G.

can be parsed as in Figure 5.30, meaning

```
if condition then
    if condition then
        statement
    else
        statement
```

but it can also be parsed as in Figure 5.30, meaning

```
if condition then
    if condition then
        statement
else
    statement
```

Note that the first interpretation of the program is equivalent to

`if condition then statement,`

whereas the second is equivalent to `statement`. This ambiguity, called

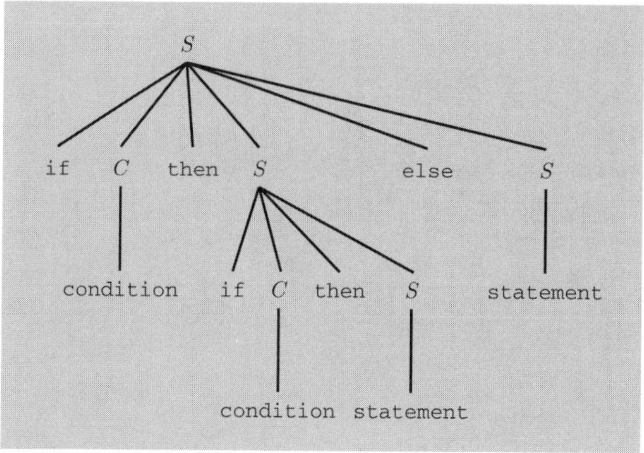

FIGURE 5.14: Another way to parse

`if condition then if condition then statement else statement`

in the ambiguous grammar G.

the *dangling else*, was present in the original specification for the Algol60 language.

This particular ambiguous grammar can be converted to an unambiguous CFG G' for the same language:

$$\begin{aligned} T &\rightarrow \texttt{statement} \\ T &\rightarrow \texttt{if}\ C\ \texttt{then}\ T\ \texttt{else}\ S \\ S &\rightarrow T \\ S &\rightarrow \texttt{if}\ C\ \texttt{then}\ S \\ C &\rightarrow \texttt{condition}. \end{aligned}$$

The new variable T generates plain statements and if-then-else statements but not if-then statements. In G' the string

`if condition then if condition then statement else statement`

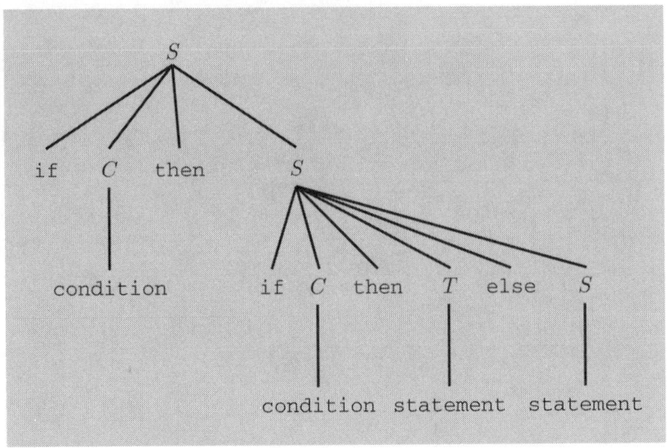

FIGURE 5.15: The only way to parse

`if condition then if condition then statement else statement`

in the unambiguous grammar G'.

can only be parsed as in Figure 5.30, meaning

```
if condition then
    if condition then
        statement
    else
        statement
```

■■■

A substantial amount of effort goes into disambiguating CFGs for real programming languages, i.e., converting them to unambiguous grammars for the same language. Not only does this guarantee that programs have well-defined meanings, but it also permits faster parsing (cf. Section 5.12).

Unfortunately, some grammars cannot be disambiguated:

THEOREM 5.31. *There exists an inherently ambiguous context-free language.*

Proof: Such a language is

$$L = \{\mathtt{a}^i\mathtt{b}^j\mathtt{c}^k : i = j \text{ or } j = k\}.$$

We will show that, no matter which grammar we use to generate L, there is a string of the form $\mathtt{a}^m\mathtt{b}^m\mathtt{c}^m$ that can be parsed in two different ways.

Let G be any CFG for L, and let N be a pumping number for G as in Ogden's lemma. Without loss of generality, assume that $N > 1$. Let $z = \mathtt{a}^N\mathtt{b}^N\mathtt{c}^{N+N!}$. Mark all the b's. By Ogden's lemma, the grammar G contains a variable A such that the following conditions hold:

- $S \stackrel{*}{\Rightarrow} uAy$
- for all $i \geq 0$, $A \stackrel{*}{\Rightarrow} v^i w x^i$

The only way to pump is for $z = uvwxy$ where $v = \mathtt{a}^k$, $x = \mathtt{b}^k$, and $1 \leq k \leq N$. (Why? Each string v and x must contain only one character, possibly repeated, for otherwise pumping up produces a string that is not in $\mathtt{a}^*\mathtt{b}^*\mathtt{c}^*$. The string v must contain the same number of a's as x contains b's, for otherwise pumping down produces a string with all different numbers of a's, b's, and c's.)

Letting $i = N!/k + 1$, we see that $A \stackrel{*}{\Rightarrow} \mathtt{a}^{N!+k}w\mathtt{b}^{N!+k}$, so

$$\begin{aligned} S &\stackrel{*}{\Rightarrow} uAy \\ &\stackrel{*}{\Rightarrow} u\mathtt{a}^{N!+k}w\mathtt{b}^{N!+k}y \\ &= u\mathtt{a}^{N!}vw\mathtt{b}^{N!}xy \\ &= \mathtt{a}^{N+N!}\mathtt{b}^{N+N!}\mathtt{c}^{N+N!}. \end{aligned}$$

In particular, there is a derivation of $\mathtt{a}^{N+N!}\mathtt{b}^{N+N!}\mathtt{c}^{N+N!}$ in which $\mathtt{a}^{N!+k}w\mathtt{b}^{N!+k}$ is a phrase.

Now apply the same argument to $z = \mathtt{a}^{N+N!}\mathtt{b}^N\mathtt{c}^N$ to find a derivation of $\mathtt{a}^{N+N!}\mathtt{b}^{N+N!}\mathtt{c}^{N+N!}$ in which $\mathtt{b}^{N!+k'}w'\mathtt{c}^{N!+k'}$ is a phrase.

Each of the two phrases, $\mathtt{a}^{N!+k}w\mathtt{b}^{N!+k}$ and $\mathtt{b}^{N!+k'}w'\mathtt{c}^{N!+k'}$, contains at least $N! + 1$ b's, but the string derived contains only $N! + N$ b's. Since $N! + 1 > \frac{1}{2}(N! + N)$, each phrase contains more than half of all the b's that are derived. Therefore the two phrases overlap.

The first phrase contains some a's but no c's, and the second phrase contains some c's but no a's. Therefore neither phrase is a substring of the other.

We know that two phrases in the same parse tree must be either disjoint or nested. Therefore the two phrases $\mathtt{a}^{N!+k}w\mathtt{b}^{N!+k}$ and $\mathtt{b}^{N!+k'}w'\mathtt{c}^{N!+k'}$ belong to different parse trees for the string $\mathtt{a}^{N+N!}\mathtt{b}^{N+N!}\mathtt{c}^{N+N!}$, so $\mathtt{a}^{N+N!}\mathtt{b}^{N+N!}\mathtt{c}^{N+N!}$ is ambiguous. Therefore G is ambiguous. Since the argument above applies to every grammar for L, the language L is inherently ambiguous. ■

Exercises

5.9-1 Prove that the grammar for arithmetical expressions given in Section 5.1 is unambiguous.

5.9-2 (a) Prove that the CFG constructed in the proof of Theorem 5.17 has exactly one parse tree per computation of the NSA.

(b) Prove that the CFG constructed in the proof of Corollary 5.18 has exactly one parse tree yielding x per computation of the NSA accepting x.

(c) Prove that the NSA constructed in the proof of Theorem 5.16 has exactly one computation on input x per parse tree of the CFG yielding x.

5.9-3 Prove that $\{\mathtt{a}^i\mathtt{b}^j\mathtt{a}^k\mathtt{b}^\ell : i = j \text{ or } k = \ell\}$ is an unambiguous CFL.

Solution: We give an unambiguous grammar in which E generates $\{\mathtt{a}^i\mathtt{b}^j : i = j\}$, U generates $\{\mathtt{a}^i\mathtt{b}^j : i \neq j\}$, L generates $\{\mathtt{a}^i\mathtt{b}^j : i < j\}$, and G generates $\{\mathtt{a}^i\mathtt{b}^j : i > j\}$:

$$
\begin{aligned}
S &\rightarrow EE \cup EU \cup UE \\
E &\rightarrow \Lambda \cup \mathtt{a}E\mathtt{b} \\
U &\rightarrow G \cup L \\
G &\rightarrow \mathtt{a}E \cup \mathtt{a}G \\
L &\rightarrow E\mathtt{b} \cup L\mathtt{b}.
\end{aligned}
$$

*5.9-4 Prove that $\{\mathtt{a}^i\mathtt{b}^j\mathtt{c}^k : i = j \text{ or } i = k\}$ is inherently ambiguous.

*5.9-5 A CFG G is *unboundedly ambiguous* if for every m there is a string that can be parsed at least m different ways in G. A CFL L is *inherently* unboundedly ambiguous if every CFG for L is unboundedly ambiguous. Let L be the set of all strings of the form $\mathtt{a}^i\mathtt{c}\{\mathtt{a},\mathtt{b}\}^*\mathtt{b}\mathtt{a}^i\mathtt{b}\{\mathtt{a},\mathtt{b}\}^*$, i.e.,

$$L = \{\mathtt{a}^i\mathtt{c}x\mathtt{b}\mathtt{a}^i\mathtt{b}y : x, y \in \{\mathtt{a},\mathtt{b}\}^* \text{ and } i \geq 0\}.$$

Prove that L is inherently unboundedly ambiguous.

*5.10 GREIBACH NORMAL FORM

A grammar is in *Greibach normal form* (GNF) if every production is of the form $X \to cY_1 \cdots Y_k$ where c is a character, $k \geq 0$, and $Y_1, \ldots, Y_k$ are variables. In the early 1960s Kuno and Oettinger developed a parsing program called the Predictive Analyzer to assist with experiments on natural language; their program required a GNF grammar as input. Sheila Greibach first showed how to convert arbitrary context-free grammars into this form. The normal form is also useful because any GNF grammar can be readily converted to a real-time NSA for the same language. However, GNF is not needed for the parsing algorithms we will present in Sections 5.11 and 5.12.

If L is a CFL that does not contain Λ, then we will construct a GNF grammar for L. (If L does contain Λ, then this is clearly impossible, because no GNF grammar generates a language containing Λ. However, see Exercise 5.10-1(a) for an extension of GNF that applies to every CFL.)

We begin by eliminating Λ-productions and unit productions. A simple, efficient way to accomplish this is by converting G to CNF.[3] Henceforth, assume that G is in CNF, so all of its productions are of the form $A \to BC$ or $A \to a$.

Let V be the set of variables in G. We define a new grammar G' that involves V and some new variables. For each pair X, Y of variables in G, we define a new variable that we denote formally as $[X, Y]$. It is our intention that $[X, Y]$ denote the set of strings u such that $X \overset{*}{\Rightarrow} Yu$; i.e., we want

$$L([X, Y]) = \{u : X \overset{*}{\Rightarrow} Yu\}.$$

[3] In eliminating Λ-productions and unit productions, it would be sufficient to omit the first two steps of the CNF conversion; however, the last two steps run in time that is exponential in the length of the right side of the longest production. Therefore, efficiency dictates that we perform the first two steps as well.

First, assume that $X \rightarrow YZ$ is a production of G. If $W \stackrel{*}{\Rightarrow} Xu$, then $W \stackrel{*}{\Rightarrow} YZu$, so we need to ensure that

$$L([W,Y]) \supseteq ZL([W,X]).$$

Therefore we make $[W,Y] \rightarrow Z[W,X]$ a production in G'.

Second, note that $X \stackrel{*}{\Rightarrow} X = X\Lambda$, so we want

$$L([X,X]) \supseteq \Lambda.$$

Therefore we make $[X,X] \rightarrow \Lambda$ a production in G'.

Third, assume that $X \rightarrow c$ is a production of G. If $W \stackrel{*}{\Rightarrow} Xu$, then $W \stackrel{*}{\Rightarrow} cu$, so we want

$$L(W) \supseteq cL([W,X]).$$

Therefore we make $W \rightarrow c[W,X]$ a production in G'.

To summarize, we define G' to be a grammar whose variables are $V \cup \{[X,Y] : X \in V \text{ and } Y \in V\}$; for each production in G, the corresponding productions in G' are shown in the table below.

Production in G	*Productions in G′*	
(1) $X \rightarrow YZ$	$[W,Y] \rightarrow Z[W,X]$	for all $W \in V$
(2) $X \rightarrow c$	$W \rightarrow c[W,X]$	for all $W \in V$
(3)	$[X,X] \rightarrow \Lambda$	for all $X \in V$

It will not be hard to convert G' to GNF. First, let us show that G' generates the same language as G.

Assertion 1: If $X \stackrel{*}{\Rightarrow}_G u$ where u is a string of characters, then $X \stackrel{*}{\Rightarrow}_{G'} u$. We prove this assertion by strong induction on the length of u. Suppose that $X \stackrel{*}{\Rightarrow}_G u$. Assume that the assertion is true for all variables X and for all strings shorter than u.

Because G contains no Λ-productions, u must be nonempty. A leftmost derivation of $X \stackrel{*}{\Rightarrow}_G u$ begins by applying productions to the first variable

Derivation in G		*Derivation in G′*	
String	*Production*	*String*	*Production*
X		X	
	$X \to Y_1Z_1$		$X \to c[X, Y_4]$
Y_1Z_1		$c[X, Y_4]$	
	$Y_1 \to Y_2Z_2$		$[X, Y_4] \to Z_4[X, Y_3]$
$Y_2Z_2Z_1$		$cZ_4[X, Y_3]$	
	$Y_2 \to Y_3Z_3$		$[X, Y_3] \to Z_3[X, Y_2]$
$Y_3Z_3Z_2Z_1$		$cZ_4Z_3[X, Y_2]$	
	$Y_3 \to Y_4Z_4$		$[X, Y_2] \to Z_2[X, Y_1]$
$Y_4Z_4Z_3Z_2Z_1$		$cZ_4Z_3Z_2[X, Y_1]$	
	$Y_4 \to c$		$[X, Y_1] \to Z_1[X, X]$
$cZ_4Z_3Z_2Z_1$		$cZ_4Z_3Z_2Z_1[X, X]$	
			$[X, X] \to \Lambda$
		$cZ_4Z_3Z_2Z_1$	

TABLE 5.1: On the left side, we show the process of rewriting the first variable (five times) until it is finally replaced by a terminal character. This is a derivation of $X \stackrel{*}{\Rightarrow}_G cZ_4Z_3Z_2Z_1$. On the right side, we show a corresponding derivation of $X \stackrel{*}{\Rightarrow}_{G'} cZ_4Z_3Z_2Z_1$. Whereas the derivation in G is leftmost, this portion of the derivation in G' is rightmost. The 1st production on the left corresponds to the 5th production on the right; the 2nd production on the left corresponds to the 4th production on the right; and so on.

(at least once) until it is a character. This initial portion of the leftmost derivation is a derivation of

$$X \stackrel{*}{\Rightarrow}_G cZ_kZ_{k-1} \cdots Z_2Z_1$$

for some $k \geq 0$. For concreteness assume that $k = 4$; this is illustrative of the general case. This initial portion of the derivation is shown on the left side of Table 5.1. The corresponding derivation in G' starts out rightmost. The

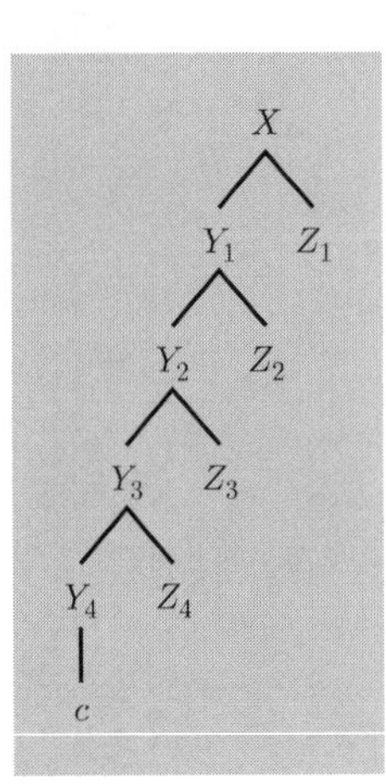

FIGURE 5.16: $X \stackrel{*}{\Rightarrow}_G cZ_4Z_3Z_2Z_1$.

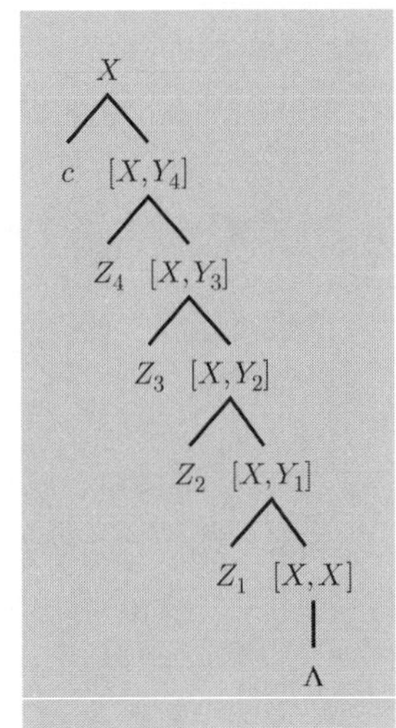

FIGURE 5.17: $X \stackrel{*}{\Rightarrow}_{G'} cZ_4Z_3Z_2Z_1$

corresponding initial portion of that derivation is shown on the right side of Table 5.1, demonstrating that $X \stackrel{*}{\Rightarrow}_{G'} cZ_4Z_3Z_2Z_1$. (The corresponding parse trees are shown in Figures 5.16 and 5.17.) In the general case,

$$X \stackrel{*}{\Rightarrow}_{G'} cZ_kZ_{k-1} \cdots Z_2Z_1.$$

By the decomposition lemma, there exist strings u_k, u_{k-1}, ..., u_2, and u_1, such that $u = cu_ku_{k-1} \cdots u_2u_1$ and $Z_k \stackrel{*}{\Rightarrow}_G u_k$, $Z_{k-1} \stackrel{*}{\Rightarrow}_G u_{k-1}$, ..., $Z_2 \stackrel{*}{\Rightarrow}_G u_2$, and $Z_1 \stackrel{*}{\Rightarrow}_G u_1$. By the inductive hypothesis, $Z_k \stackrel{*}{\Rightarrow}_{G'} u_k$, $Z_{k-1} \stackrel{*}{\Rightarrow}_{G'} u_{k-1}$, ..., $Z_2 \stackrel{*}{\Rightarrow}_{G'} u_2$, and $Z_1 \stackrel{*}{\Rightarrow}_{G'} u_1$. Therefore, $X \stackrel{*}{\Rightarrow}_{G'} u$, completing the induction. This proves assertion 1. ∎

We digress momentarily from the proof because the conversion from G to G' may seem a bit mysterious. By repeatedly rewriting leftmost variables in the derivation $X \stackrel{*}{\Rightarrow}_G cZ_4Z_3Z_2Z_1$, we obtain a parse tree in G that branches to the left (Figure 5.16). By repeatedly rewriting rightmost variables in the corresponding derivation $X \stackrel{*}{\Rightarrow}_{G'} cZ_4Z_3Z_2Z_1$, we obtain a parse tree in G' that branches to the right (Figure 5.17). For this reason, the conversion from G to G' converts left-branching parse trees to right-branching parse trees. The net effect is that a derivation of $X \stackrel{*}{\Rightarrow} cZ_4Z_3Z_2Z_1$ in G that *ends* by rewriting a variable as a character is converted to a derivation of $X \stackrel{*}{\Rightarrow} cZ_4Z_3Z_2Z_1$ in G' that *begins* by rewriting a variable as a character followed by another variable. This is important because we want the right side of each production to begin with a character.

Assertion 2: If $X \stackrel{*}{\Rightarrow}_{G'} u$ where u is a string of characters, then $X \stackrel{*}{\Rightarrow}_{G} u$. Assume that $X \stackrel{*}{\Rightarrow}_{G'} u$. Then the derivation must begin with a production from line (2) in the table on page 376, and by rewriting the rightmost variable until it is no longer a pair of the form $[X, Y_i]$, we get a derivation of

$$X \stackrel{*}{\Rightarrow}_{G'} cZ_kZ_{k-1} \cdots Z_2Z_1.$$

Again, the case $k = 4$ is illustrative of the general case. This is shown in Table 5.2. The productions in G' that we used in rewriting the rightmost variable imply the existence of corresponding productions in G, shown in the third column of Table 5.2. By those productions, X derives the same string in G (for details see Table 5.1). In general,

$$X \stackrel{*}{\Rightarrow}_{G} cZ_kZ_{k-1} \cdots Z_2Z_1.$$

Using the decomposition lemma and strong induction as in the proof of assertion 1, we may conclude that $X \stackrel{*}{\Rightarrow}_{G} u$. This proves assertion 2. ■

By assertions 1 and 2, for every variable X and string u, $X \stackrel{*}{\Rightarrow}_{G} u$ if and only if $X \stackrel{*}{\Rightarrow}_{G'} u$. In particular, $S \stackrel{*}{\Rightarrow}_{G} u$ if and only if $S \stackrel{*}{\Rightarrow}_{G'} u$, so G and G' generate the same language.

We have now finished the hard part of the construction. Two easy manipulations will complete the conversion to GNF. We eliminate the Λ-productions $[X, X] \rightarrow \Lambda$ from G'. Concretely, we combine the production $[X, Y] \rightarrow Z[X, X]$ with $[X, X] \rightarrow \Lambda$ to form $[X, Y] \rightarrow Z$, and we combine

String	*Production in G′*	*From Production in G*
X		
	$X \to c[X, Y_4]$	$Y_4 \to c$
$c[X, Y_4]$		
	$[X, Y_4] \to Z_4[X, Y_3]$	$Y_3 \to Y_4Z_4$
$cZ_4[X, Y_3]$		
	$[X, Y_3] \to Z_3[X, Y_2]$	$Y_2 \to Y_3Z_3$
$cZ_4Z_3[X, Y_2]$		
	$[X, Y_2] \to Z_2[X, Y_1]$	$Y_1 \to Y_2Z_2$
$cZ_4Z_3Z_2[X, Y_1]$		
	$[X, Y_1] \to Z_1[X, X]$	$X \to Y_1Z_1$
$cZ_4Z_3Z_2Z_1[X, X]$		
	$[X, X] \to \Lambda$	
$cZ_4Z_3Z_2Z_1$		

TABLE 5.2: In the first two columns, we show the process of rewriting the last variable four times, until it is finally replaced by a variable in V. This is a derivation of $X \overset{*}{\Rightarrow}_{G'} cZ_4Z_3Z_2Z_1$. In the third column, we show the corresponding productions in G.

$X \to c[X, X]$ with $[X, X] \to \Lambda$ to form $X \to c$. Hence we obtain a grammar G'' with the following productions.

Production in G		*Productions in G″*	
(1)	$X \to YZ$	$[W, Y] \to Z[W, X]$	for all $W \in V$
(1′)	$X \to YZ$	$[X, Y] \to Z$	
(2)	$X \to c$	$W \to c[W, X]$	for all $W \in V$
(2′)	$X \to c$	$X \to c$	

Now the right side of any production of G'' starts either with a character or with a variable Z in V. By substituting for Z, we obtain an equivalent grammar, again by the decomposition lemma.

	Productions in G''		Productions in G'''
(1*a*)	$[W, Y] \to Z[W, X]$	$Z \to c$	$[W, Y] \to c[W, X]$
(1*b*)	$[W, Y] \to Z[W, X]$	$Z \to c[Z, W']$	$[W, Y] \to c[Z, W'][W, X]$
(1′*a*)	$[X, Y] \to Z$	$Z \to c$	$[X, Y] \to c$
(1′*b*)	$[X, Y] \to Z$	$Z \to c[Z, W']$	$[X, Y] \to c[Z, W']$
(2)	$W \to c[W, X]$		$W \to c[W, X]$
(2′)	$X \to c$		$X \to c$

This grammar G''' is in GNF. Thus we have proved the following theorem:

THEOREM 5.32. *Every CFL that does not contain Λ is generated by a GNF grammar.* ■

Table 5.3 combines the separate steps in the GNF conversion. It shows how to convert G directly to GNF.

	Productions in G		Productions in G'''	
(1*a*)	$X \to YZ$	$Z \to c$	$[W, Y] \to c[W, X]$	for all $W \in V$
(1*b*)	$X \to YZ$	$W' \to c$	$[W, Y] \to c[Z, W'][W, X]$	for all $W \in V$
(1′*a*)	$X \to YZ$	$Z \to c$	$[X, Y] \to c$	
(1′*b*)	$X \to YZ$	$W' \to c$	$[X, Y] \to c[Z, W']$	
(2)	$X \to c$		$W \to c[W, X]$	for all $W \in V$
(2′)	$X \to c$		$X \to c$	

TABLE 5.3: Converting a grammar directly to GNF. In each line, one or two productions of G are replaced by one or $|V|$ productions in G'''.

Productions in G			*Productions in G‴*
(1*a*)	$B \to CA$	$A \to \mathtt{a}$	$[A,C] \to \mathtt{a}[A,B]$
			$[B,C] \to \mathtt{a}[B,B]$
			$[C,C] \to \mathtt{a}[C,B]$
	$C \to AB$	$B \to \mathtt{b}$	$[A,A] \to \mathtt{b}[A,C]$
			$[B,A] \to \mathtt{b}[B,C]$
			$[C,A] \to \mathtt{b}[C,C]$
(1*b*)	$A \to BC$	$A \to \mathtt{a}$	$[A,B] \to \mathtt{a}[C,A][A,A]$
			$[B,B] \to \mathtt{a}[C,A][B,A]$
			$[C,B] \to \mathtt{a}[C,A][C,A]$
	$A \to BC$	$B \to \mathtt{b}$	$[A,B] \to \mathtt{b}[C,B][A,A]$
			$[B,B] \to \mathtt{b}[C,B][B,A]$
			$[C,B] \to \mathtt{b}[C,B][C,A]$
	$B \to CA$	$A \to \mathtt{a}$	$[A,C] \to \mathtt{a}[A,A][A,B]$
			$[B,C] \to \mathtt{a}[A,A][B,B]$
			$[C,C] \to \mathtt{a}[A,A][C,B]$
	$B \to CA$	$B \to \mathtt{b}$	$[A,C] \to \mathtt{b}[A,B][A,B]$
			$[B,C] \to \mathtt{b}[A,B][B,B]$
			$[C,C] \to \mathtt{b}[A,B][C,B]$
	$C \to AB$	$A \to \mathtt{a}$	$[A,A] \to \mathtt{a}[B,A][A,C]$
			$[B,A] \to \mathtt{a}[B,A][B,C]$
			$[C,A] \to \mathtt{a}[B,A][C,C]$
	$C \to AB$	$B \to \mathtt{b}$	$[A,A] \to \mathtt{b}[B,B][A,C]$
			$[B,A] \to \mathtt{b}[B,B][B,C]$
			$[C,A] \to \mathtt{b}[B,B][C,C]$

TABLE 5.4: Converting the grammar $A \to BC$, $B \to CA$, $C \to AB$, $A \to \mathtt{a}$, $B \to \mathtt{b}$ to GNF.

	Productions in G		*Productions in G'''*
(1'a)	$B \to CA$	$A \to$ a	$[B,C] \to$ a
	$C \to AB$	$B \to$ b	$[C,A] \to$ b
(1'b)	$A \to BC$	$A \to$ a	$[A,B] \to$ a$[C,A]$
	$A \to BC$	$B \to$ b	$[A,B] \to$ b$[C,B]$
	$B \to CA$	$A \to$ a	$[B,C] \to$ a$[A,A]$
	$B \to CA$	$B \to$ b	$[B,C] \to$ b$[A,B]$
	$C \to AB$	$A \to$ a	$[C,A] \to$ a$[B,A]$
	$C \to AB$	$B \to$ b	$[C,A] \to$ b$[B,B]$
(2)	$A \to$ a		$A \to$ a$[A,A]$
			$B \to$ a$[B,A]$
			$C \to$ a$[C,A]$
	$B \to$ b		$A \to$ b$[A,B]$
			$B \to$ b$[B,B]$
			$C \to$ b$[C,B]$
(2')	$A \to$ a		$A \to$ a
	$B \to$ b		$B \to$ b

TABLE 5.4: (continued)

EXAMPLE 5.33. Let us convert the following grammar to GNF:

$$\begin{aligned} A &\to BC \\ B &\to CA \\ C &\to AB \\ A &\to \texttt{a} \\ B &\to \texttt{b}. \end{aligned}$$

We apply the rules from Table 5.3 and present the resulting grammar in Table 5.4. ■■■

A program is called *real-time* if there is a bound on the number of consecutive instructions it can perform without scanning a character. If we convert a GNF grammar, constructed as above, to an equivalent NSA by the technique of Section 5.6, we obtain an NSA that performs one POP and at most two PUSHes between consecutive SCANs.

COROLLARY 5.34. *Every CFL that does not contain Λ is accepted by a real-time NSA. In fact, every CFL that does not contain Λ is accepted by an NSA that scans a character among every three stack operations.*

Proof: Let L be a CFL. Construct a GNF grammar for L as described in this section. Observe that all productions are of the form $X \to c$, $X \to cY$, or $X \to cYZ$. An NSA can simulate such a production by popping an X, pushing zero, one, or two variables, depending on the right side of the production, and then scanning a c. ∎

By handling Λ as a special case, an extension to general CFLs is possible. The proof is left as Exercise 5.10-1(b).

COROLLARY 5.35. *Every CFL is accepted by a real-time NSA. In fact, every CFL is accepted by an NSA that scans a character among every three stack operations.* ∎

The conversion from G to G' was the crucial step in constructing the GNF grammar. Because this transformation can seem mysterious, we describe an alternative transformation. This method may be easier to remember, because it corresponds to a natural transformation on NSAs.

Recalling that G is in Chomsky normal form, let us convert G to an equivalent NSA program P, essentially as in Theorem 5.16 except that we convert productions of the form $X \to c$ directly to a POPX followed by a SCANc (see Figure 5.18). We call the control state Λ the *base state.* We assume, by modifying ω, that the only accepting configuration of P occurs when the control state is Λ, the input device is empty, and the stack is empty. Thus there is no need to use the operations EOF or EMPTY. It is also convenient to assume, by modifying α, that the start variable is initially on the stack rather than being explicitly pushed onto it.

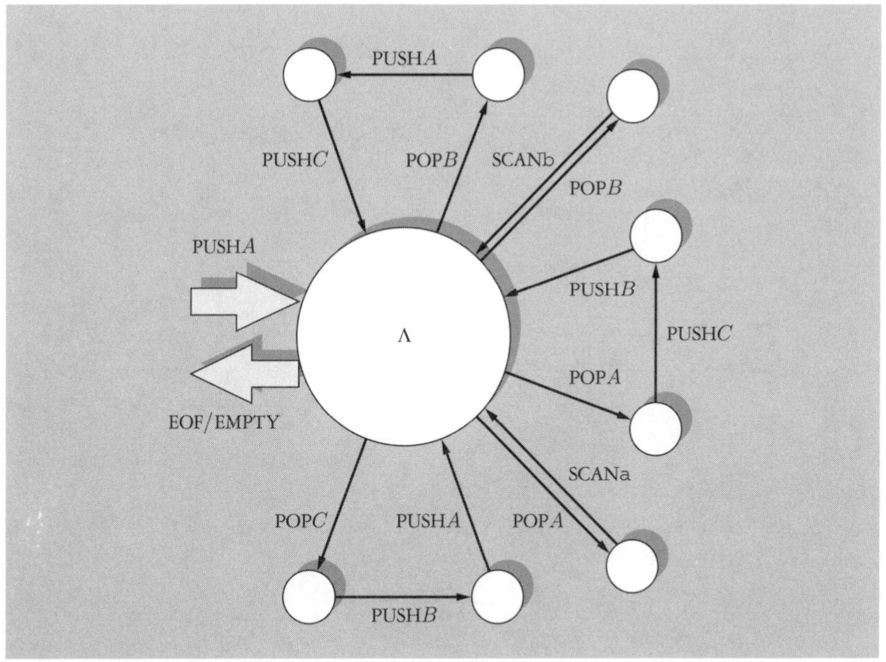

FIGURE 5.18: An NSA constructed from the CNF grammar $A \to BC$, $B \to CA$, $C \to AB$, $A \to \mathsf{a}$, $B \to \mathsf{b}$ (with start variable A).

This NSA program P has two useful properties:

- Every instruction that goes from the base state is a POP instruction, and every POP instruction goes from the base state.
- Every instruction going to the base state is either a PUSH instruction or a SCAN instruction.

A PUSH instruction immediately followed by a POP instruction is called an *adjacent* PUSH–POP pair. (Note that the intermediate state must be the base state.) We merge adjacent PUSH–POP pairs, forming null instructions that bypass the base state, and we eliminate all PUSH instructions going to the base state. Now the only instructions going to the base state are SCAN

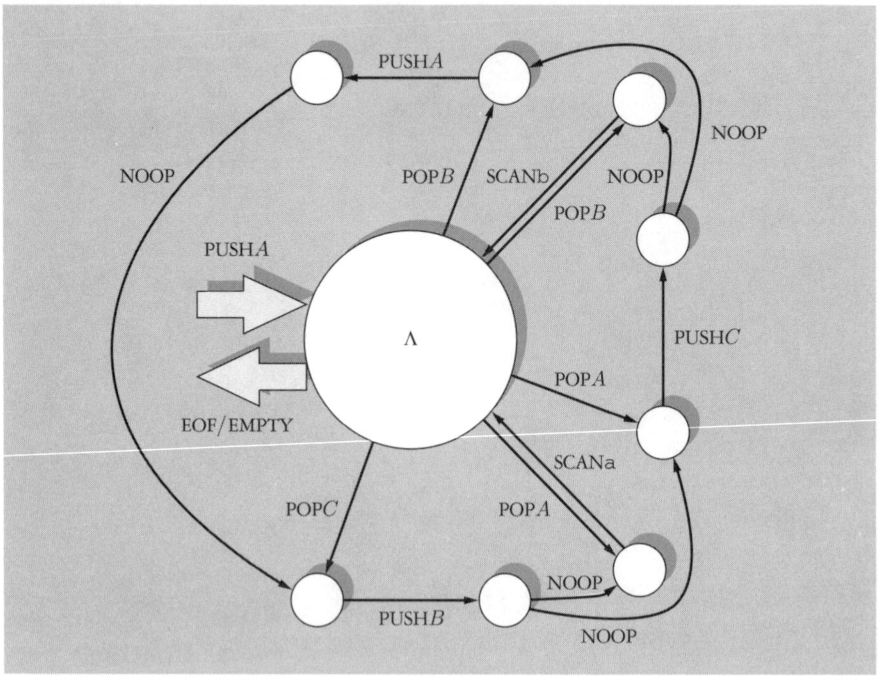

FIGURE 5.19: The result of eliminating adjacent PUSH–POP pairs from Figure 5.18.

instructions, and the only instructions going from the base state are POP instructions (Figure 5.19). Call this new program P'.

Since the base state is the unique start state and the unique accepting state of P', each computation consists of a sequence of fragments that begin and end at the base state. Each such fragment consists of (a) an instruction of the form $(\Lambda \rightarrow q, \text{POP}c, \text{NOOP})$, followed by (b) a sequence of PUSH instructions, and then (c) an instruction of the form $(r \rightarrow \Lambda, \text{NOOP}, \text{SCAN}d)$.

For a particular q and r above, let $L(q, r)$ denote the set of strings of variables that could be pushed in part (b). The language $L(q, r)$ is regular; in fact, the productions of G' on line (1) of Table 5.1 make up right-linear grammars for these regular languages. (See Exercise 5.2-8 for a definition of "right-linear.") Alternatively, if we determine regular expressions for these sets, we can write down a system of regular containments (allowing

Kleene-closure) directly from the program P'. We obtain

$$\begin{aligned} A &\to (\mathtt{a} \cup \mathtt{b}C)(BAC)^* \\ B &\to (\mathtt{a}BA \cup \mathtt{b})(CBA)^* \\ C &\to (\mathtt{a}B \cup \mathtt{b}CB)(ACB)^*. \end{aligned}$$

We introduce new formal variables $[BAC*]$, $[CBA*]$, and $[ACB*]$ corresponding to the starred expressions, along with productions

$$\begin{aligned} [BAC*] &\to \Lambda \cup BAC[BAC*] \\ [CBA*] &\to \Lambda \cup CBA[CBA*] \\ [ACB*] &\to \Lambda \cup ACB[ACB*], \end{aligned}$$

and we modify the original productions to use the new variables:

$$\begin{aligned} A &\to (\mathtt{a} \cup \mathtt{b}C)[BAC*] \\ B &\to (\mathtt{a}BA \cup \mathtt{b})[CBA*] \\ C &\to (\mathtt{a}B \cup \mathtt{b}CB)[ACB*]. \end{aligned}$$

We substitute these productions into the leftmost occurrences of each variable on the right side of the productions for $[BAC*]$, $[CBA*]$, and $[ACB*]$, obtaining the following:

$$\begin{aligned} [BAC*] &\to \Lambda \cup (\mathtt{a}BA \cup \mathtt{b})[CBA*]AC[BAC*] \\ [CBA*] &\to \Lambda \cup (\mathtt{a}B \cup \mathtt{b}CB)[ACB*]BA[CBA*] \\ [ACB*] &\to \Lambda \cup (\mathtt{a} \cup \mathtt{b}C)[BAC*]CB[ACB*]. \end{aligned}$$

Next we eliminate Λ-productions as in Section 5.3. In that section, we wrote V_+ to denote the set of nonempty strings in $L(V)$. For simplicity, we will write $[BAC+]$ for $[BAC*]_+$, $[CBA+]$ for $[CBA*]_+$, and $[ACB+]$ for $[ACB*]_+$; we will also retain the names A, B, and C for A_+, B_+, and C_+, respectively. Eliminating Λ-productions results in the following productions:

$$\begin{aligned}
A &\rightarrow (\mathtt{a} \cup \mathtt{b}C)(\Lambda \cup [BAC+]) \\
B &\rightarrow (\mathtt{a}BA \cup \mathtt{b})(\Lambda \cup [CBA+]) \\
C &\rightarrow (\mathtt{a}B \cup \mathtt{b}CB)(\Lambda \cup [ACB+]) \\
[BAC+] &\rightarrow (\mathtt{a}BA \cup \mathtt{b})(\Lambda \cup [CBA+])AC(\Lambda \cup [BAC+]) \\
[CBA+] &\rightarrow (\mathtt{a}B \cup \mathtt{b}CB)(\Lambda \cup [ACB+])BA(\Lambda \cup [CBA+]) \\
[ACB+] &\rightarrow (\mathtt{a} \cup \mathtt{b}C)(\Lambda \cup [BAC+])CB(\Lambda \cup [ACB+]).
\end{aligned}$$

We expand the right sides by the distributive law, obtaining

$$\begin{aligned}
A &\rightarrow \mathtt{a} \cup \mathtt{b}C \cup \mathtt{a}[BAC+] \cup \mathtt{b}C[BAC+] \\
B &\rightarrow \mathtt{a}BA \cup \mathtt{b} \cup \mathtt{a}BA[CBA+] \cup \mathtt{b}[CBA+] \\
C &\rightarrow \mathtt{a}B \cup \mathtt{b}CB \cup \mathtt{a}B[ACB+] \cup \mathtt{b}CB[ACB+] \\
[BAC+] &\rightarrow \mathtt{a}BABA \cup \mathtt{a}BA[ACB+]BA \cup \mathtt{a}BABA[CBA+] \cup \\
&\qquad \mathtt{a}BA[ACB+]BA[CBA+] \cup \mathtt{b}BA \cup \mathtt{b}[ACB+]BA \cup \\
&\qquad \mathtt{b}BA[CBA+] \cup \mathtt{b}[ACB+]BA[CBA+] \\
[CBA+] &\rightarrow \mathtt{a}BBA \cup \mathtt{a}B[ACB+]BA \cup \mathtt{a}BBA[CBA+] \cup \\
&\qquad \mathtt{a}B[ACB+]BA[CBA+] \cup \mathtt{b}CBBA \cup \mathtt{b}CB[ACB+]BA \cup \\
&\qquad \mathtt{b}CBBA[CBA+] \cup \mathtt{b}CB[ACB+]BA[CBA+] \\
[ACB+] &\rightarrow \mathtt{a}CB \cup \mathtt{a}[BAC+]CB \cup \mathtt{a}CB[ACB+] \cup \\
&\qquad \mathtt{a}[BAC+]CB[ACB+] \cup \mathtt{b}CCB \cup \mathtt{b}C[BAC+]CB \cup \\
&\qquad \mathtt{b}CCB[ACB+] \cup \mathtt{b}C[BAC+]CB[ACB+].
\end{aligned}$$

Finally, eliminate unions to obtain a GNF grammar.

Exercises

+5.10-1 (a) If L is any CFL, show that L is generated by a grammar in which all productions are of the form $S \rightarrow \Lambda$ or $X \rightarrow cY_1 \cdots Y_k$, where S does not occur on the right side of any production.

(b) Prove that every CFL is accepted by a real-time NSA.
(c) Present an algorithm for testing membership in a CFL. Hint: Consider all possible computations of a real-time NSA on input x.

5.11 CYK PARSING ALGORITHM

In Exercise 5.10-1(c), we saw how to test whether a string s belongs to a CFL L by searching for a computation of a real-time NSA for L. Because we must try exponentially many possibilities, that algorithm is very slow. In this section we will present a more efficient algorithm called the CYK algorithm.[4] This algorithm can be readily modified to produce parse trees for strings in the language (Exercise 5.11-2).

We can test whether a CFL contains Λ as in Exercise 5.3-3. Without loss of generality, we assume that the CFL does not contain Λ, so we can put its grammar G into Chomsky normal form. Let $s = s_1 \cdots s_n$ be a string of length n, and let s_{ik} denote $s_i \cdots s_k$. The algorithm will determine for each i, k with $0 < i \le k \le n$ and each variable X whether X derives s_{ik}. We denote the answer to the question by $T[i, k, X]$. First consider the case when $i = k$, so $s_{ik} = s_{ii} = c$, a one-character string; then $T[i, k, X]$ is true if and only if $X \to c$ is a production in G. Next assume that $k > i$, so that $|s_{ik}| \ge 2$. Then $T[i, k, X]$ is true if and only if there is a production $X \to YZ$, where Y derives some prefix of s and Z derives the remaining suffix of s. Formally, $T[i, k, X]$ is true if and only if there exists a production $X \to YZ$ and an integer j with $i \le j < k$ such that Y derives s_{ij} and Z derives $s_{j+1,k}$. This leads to the following recurrence:

$$T[i,k,X] = \begin{cases} \text{true} & \text{if } i = k \text{ and there exists a production } X \to s_{ii}, \\ \text{true} & \text{if } i < k \text{ and there exists a production } X \to YZ \\ & \quad \text{such that } (\exists j)[i \le j < k,\ T[i,j,Y], \\ & \qquad\qquad \text{and } T[j+1,k,Z]], \\ \text{false} & \text{otherwise.} \end{cases}$$

[4] CYK is an acronym of Cocke, Younger, and Kasami, who independently invented variants of the algorithm.

```
n := |s|; (* initialization *)
for every variable X do begin
    for i := 1 to n do
        for k := i to n do
            T[i, k, X] := false;
    for i := 1 to n do
        if X → s_ii is a production then
            T[i, i, X] := true;
end;

for k := 2 to n do
    for i := k − 1 down to 1 do
        for all productions of the form X → YZ do
            for j := i to k − 1 do
                if T[i, j, Y] and T[j + 1, k, Z] then
                    T[i, k, X] := true;
```

FIGURE 5.20: The CYK algorithm. The string s belongs to $L(G)$ if and only if $T[1, n, S] = \text{true}$, where $n = |s|$ and S is G's start variable.

This recurrence may be easily solved by using recursion. However, for efficiency, we will use the dynamic programming technique of Section 4.4.1. We store the values of T in an array that is initialized to false everywhere. We need to go through the array in such an order that $T[i, j, Y]$ and $T[j + 1, k, Z]$ are evaluated before $T[i, k, X]$ for $i \leq j < k$. One way to accomplish this is to go through the array for increasing values of k and, subject to that, decreasing values of i, as shown in Figure 5.20.

Thus we have proved the following theorem:

THEOREM 5.36. *There is an algorithm to test membership in CFLs in time* $O(n^3)$.

■

COROLLARY 5.37. *There is an algorithm to determine whether a nondeterministic stack machine program halts on a particular input.*

Proof: Modify the NSM program P as follows: First, remove any output device, if present. Second, change all final states to accepting states. The resulting program P' is an NSA that accepts x if and only if P halts on x. Convert P' to an equivalent CFG G, and use the CYK algorithm to test whether $x \in L(G)$. ∎

The CYK algorithm takes a grammar G and a string s as input, and it determines whether $s \in L(G)$. While we do not mean to say that there is a different algorithm for each grammar G, it may be instructive to see how the CYK algorithm works for a particular fixed grammar G like

$$\begin{aligned} A &\rightarrow BC \\ B &\rightarrow CA \\ C &\rightarrow AB \\ A &\rightarrow \texttt{a} \\ B &\rightarrow \texttt{b} \end{aligned}$$

with start symbol A. With this particular grammar, the CYK algorithm specializes to the program in Figure 5.21.

Exercises

5.11-1 If $s = s_1 \cdots s_n$, let us define $s_{ij} = s_{i+1} \cdots s_j$, for $j \geq i - 1$. (By convention $s_{i+1} \cdots s_i = \Lambda$, so $s_{ii} = \Lambda$.) Though not the most obvious notation, this is usually the most convenient, because, for example, $s_{ij}s_{jk} = s_{ik}$. Restate the CYK algorithm in this notation.

5.11-2 (a) Modify the CYK algorithm so that it produces a derivation of x if $x \in L(G)$.
(b) Modify the CYK algorithm so that it produces a parse tree for x if $x \in L(G)$.

*5.12 EARLEY'S PARSING ALGORITHM

In this section we present the most practical known algorithm for testing membership in general context-free languages. The CYK algorithm

```
n := |s|; (* initialization *)
for i := 1 to n do
        for k := i to n do
                T[i, k, A] := T[i, k, B] := T[i, k, C] := false;
for i := 1 to n do begin
        if s_ii = a then T[i, i, A] := true;
        if s_ii = b then T[i, i, B] := true;
end;

for k := 2 to n do
        for i := k − 1 down to 1 do
                for j := i to k − 1 do begin
                        if T[i, j, B] and T[j + 1, k, C] then T[i, k, A] := true;
                        if T[i, j, C] and T[j + 1, k, A] then T[i, k, B] := true;
                        if T[i, j, A] and T[j + 1, k, B] then T[i, k, C] := true;
                end;
```

FIGURE 5.21: A special case of the CYK algorithm in which the grammar is $A \rightarrow BC$, $B \rightarrow CA$, $C \rightarrow AB$, $A \rightarrow$ a, $B \rightarrow$ b. The string s belongs to $L(G)$ if and only if $T[1, n, A] =$ true, where $n = |s|$.

attempts, in a bottom–up fashion, to parse every substring of the input. In contrast, Earley's algorithm uses a top–down approach to generate goals; it only tries to parse those substrings that are potentially phrases in a derivation of the entire input. If there is a production $A \rightarrow BC$, the CYK algorithm will attempt to derive from C a string that could start anywhere in the input. However, Earley's algorithm will try to derive from C a string that starts only where a string derived from B ends.

Unlike the CYK algorithm, Earley's algorithm does not require the grammar to be in Chomsky normal form, only that Λ-productions and unit productions be eliminated. Earley's algorithm and CYK both run in time $O(n^3)$ on general grammars. However, Earley's algorithm does much better on grammars of practical interest. Although we will not prove it, Earley's algorithm runs in time $O(n^2)$ on unambiguous grammars and in time $O(n)$ on LR(1) grammars. (We will not define LR(1) grammars, but they are equivalent to DCFLs. Furthermore, the syntax of almost every programming language is essentially an LR(1) grammar. For more information, see a textbook on compiler design.) In contrast, the CYK algorithm always takes time bounded above and below by multiples of n^3, regardless of the grammar.

Let G be a grammar with start variable S. Suppose we want to determine whether the input string x belongs to $L(G)$. For convenience in describing the algorithm, let $x[i]$ denote x's ith character and $x[i..j]$ the substring consisting of characters i through j. The input string will actually be read only once from left to right and need not be stored.

The algorithm will produce records of the form (i, j, P, α, β), where i and j are integers and $P \to \alpha\beta$ is a production in the grammar G. The record embodies an assertion and a goal. The assertion is that $x[i+1..j]$ is derivable from α, i.e, $\alpha \stackrel{*}{\Rightarrow} x[i+1..j]$. The goal is to find all k such that $\beta \stackrel{*}{\Rightarrow} x[j+1..k]$. (We think of the assertion as ending at position j and the goal as beginning at position $j+1$.) If we find such a k, then $P \stackrel{*}{\Rightarrow} x[i+1..k]$, which is potentially a phrase in a complete derivation of x.

For each j, the set RECORD[j] will hold all records produced by the algorithm of the form (i, j, P, α, β).

(Efficiency notes: The second field (j) of each record need not be stored, because it is equal to the index into the array called RECORD. The string α need not be stored because it is not used by the algorithm. The string β need not be copied into the record; a pointer to the beginning of β is sufficient because the algorithm processes β from left to right.)

We can test whether a CFL contains Λ as in Exercise 5.3-3. Henceforth, assume that $\Lambda \notin L(G)$ and, without loss of generality, that G has been standardized so it contains no unit productions or null productions. Assume that G's start variable is S.

Step 1: Initialization. (Establish goals to find each prefix of x derivable from S. We really only want to find a derivation of the entire string x; the extra information is a by-product of the algorithm.) Let

$$\text{RECORD}[0] = \{(0, 0, S, \Lambda, \beta) : S \to \beta \text{ is a production in } G\}.$$

Let RECORD[j] $= \emptyset$ for $j = 1, \ldots, n$. Let $j = 0$.

Step 2: Closure. (Each goal that starts at position $j+1$ is given its chance to contribute subgoals to RECORD[j].) For each record

$(i, j, P, \alpha, Q\gamma)$ in RECORD[j] and each production $Q \rightarrow \delta$, create the record $(j, j, Q, \Lambda, \delta)$ and insert it in RECORD[j]. (Note that RECORD[j] is a set, so it does not contain duplicates.) This step must also be applied to entries that are newly inserted in RECORD[j] during this step. (If the elements of RECORD[j] are stored in a queue, it is easy to run through all of them, even while more are being inserted. Additional data structures are needed, though, to support the set operations.)

Step 3: Advance. (Update assertions and goals based on the next input character. This is the only step where $x[j+1]$ is examined.) For each record $(i, j, P, \alpha, c\gamma)$ in RECORD[j], where c is a terminal character and $c = x[j+1]$ (that is, c is equal to the next input character), create the record $(i, j+1, P, \alpha c, \gamma)$ and insert it in RECORD[$j+1$]. Let $j = j+1$.

Step 4: Completion. (A record of the form $(i, j, P, \alpha, \Lambda)$ asserts a complete derivation of $x[i+1..j]$ from P. Update other records that have that derivation as a subgoal.) For each pair of records of the form $(i, j, P, \alpha, \Lambda)$ in RECORD[j] and $(h, i, R, \gamma, P\delta)$ in RECORD[i], create the new record $(h, j, R, \gamma P, \delta)$ and insert it in RECORD[j]. Notice that if $\delta = \Lambda$, then the new record also asserts a complete derivation, so it must be processed in this step as well.

Step 5. If $j < n$, go to step 2.

Step 6. ($j = n$, so the entire input has been processed.) If a record of the form $(0, n, S, \alpha, \Lambda)$ is present in RECORD[n] then accept x, else reject.

Correctness proof for Earley's algorithm: Because each record is constructed only if the derivation it asserts is known to be true, the algorithm can only accept strings that are derivable in the grammar G. To show that the algorithm accepts every string in the language $L(G)$, we must show that if a string x has a parse tree, then Earley's algorithm accepts x. We will sketch a proof by structural induction on sub–parse trees.

Inductive hypothesis: Suppose that a parse tree for x contains a sub–parse tree whose root is Y and yield is $x[a+1..d]$. Suppose also that the records $(a, a, Y, \Lambda, \beta)$, for all β such that $Y \rightarrow \beta$, are produced by the algorithm. Then a record of the form $(a, d, Y, \beta, \Lambda)$ will eventually be produced; i.e., the algorithm will produce the assertion $Y \stackrel{*}{\Rightarrow} x[a+1..d]$.

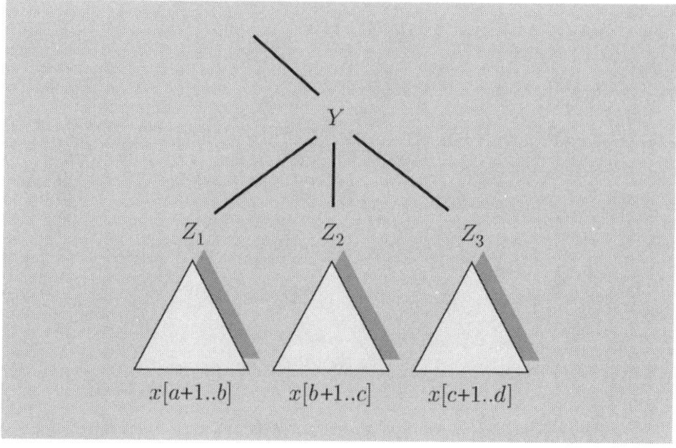

FIGURE 5.22: A sub–parse tree in a parse tree for x.

Proof: Assume that the inductive hypothesis is true for all proper sub–parse trees of the sub–parse tree rooted at Y. For concreteness, let Y's children be variables Z_1, Z_2, Z_3, as in Figure 5.22. (The general case is not significantly different. In particular, the case when some of Y's children are characters is left as an exercise.) Let $x[a+1..b], x[b+1..c], x[c+1..d]$ be the respective yields of Z_1, Z_2, Z_3; each of these strings is nonempty because we eliminated null productions.

The closure step, when $j = a$, creates the record $(a, a, Z_1, \Lambda, \beta)$ for every β such that $Z_1 \rightarrow \beta$. By the inductive hypothesis, a record of the form $(a, b, Z_1, \beta, \Lambda)$ will be produced; i.e., the algorithm will produce the assertion $Z_1 \overset{*}{\Rightarrow} x[a+1..b]$. The completion step, when $j = b$, combines this with $(a, a, Y, \Lambda, Z_1Z_2Z_3)$ to produce (a, b, Y, Z_1, Z_2Z_3).

The closure step, when $j = b$, creates $(b, b, Z_2, \Lambda, \beta)$ for every β such that $Z_2 \rightarrow \beta$. By the inductive hypothesis, a record of the form $(b, c, Z_2, \beta, \Lambda)$ will be produced. The completion step, when $j = c$, creates (a, c, Y, Z_1Z_2, Z_3).

The closure step, when $j = c$, creates $(c, c, Z_3, \Lambda, \beta)$ for all β such that $Z_3 \rightarrow \beta$. By the inductive hypothesis, a record of the form

$(c, d, Z_3, \beta, \Lambda)$ will be produced. The completion step, when $j = d$, creates $(a, d, Y, Z_1Z_2Z_3, \Lambda)$. This completes the proof of the inductive hypothesis. ■

Step 1 of Earley's algorithm produces the records $(0, 0, S, \Lambda, \beta)$ for every β such that $S \rightarrow \beta$. Assume that x is in $L(G)$ so there is a parse tree for x. This tree is a sub–parse tree of itself. Applying the inductive hypothesis to the entire tree, we deduce that the algorithm will produce a record of the form $(0, n, S, \beta, \Lambda)$. Therefore, x will be accepted in step 6. ■

A noninductive proof may be more motivating.

Alternative correctness proof in terms of fixed points: Fix a grammar G with variables $A_1, \ldots, A_k$, but do not fix a start variable. Recall that $L(A)$ denotes the set of strings derivable from A in G. We identify G with the corresponding system of regular containments. Recall that $\langle\!\langle L(A_1), \ldots, L(A_k) \rangle\!\rangle$ is the least contractor.

Let $E(A)$ denote the set of strings accepted by Earley's algorithm when A is the start variable. Because each record is constructed only if the derivation it asserts is known to be true, $E(A)$ contains only strings that are derivable from A; i.e., $E(A) \subseteq L(A)$. Since that is true for every variable, $\langle\!\langle E(A_1), \ldots, E(A_k) \rangle\!\rangle \prec \langle\!\langle L(A_1), \ldots, L(A_k) \rangle\!\rangle$; i.e., $\langle\!\langle E(A_1), \ldots, E(A_k) \rangle\!\rangle$ is contained in the least contractor. To complete the correctness proof, we will show that $\langle\!\langle E(A_1), \ldots, E(A_k) \rangle\!\rangle$ satisfies all the containments in G; i.e., $\langle\!\langle E(A_1), \ldots, E(A_k) \rangle\!\rangle$ is a contractor, so it must be the least contractor. Then $E(A) = L(A)$ for every A.

Let y be a string and let Y be a variable. Observe that Earley's algorithm parses substrings in the same way it parses entire strings. By inspection of the algorithm, we find that the following conditions are equivalent:

- $y \in E(Y)$.
- If y is the input string and the algorithm creates the records $(0, 0, Y, \Lambda, \beta)$ for all β such that $Y \rightarrow \beta$ is a production, then the algorithm will create a record of the form $(0, |y|, Y, \beta, \Lambda)$.
- If y is a prefix of the input string and the algorithm creates the records $(0, 0, Y, \Lambda, \beta)$ for all β such that $Y \rightarrow \beta$ is a production, then the algorithm will create a record of the form $(0, |y|, Y, \beta, \Lambda)$.

- If x is the input string, $y = x[i+1..i+|y|]$, and the algorithm creates the records $(i, i, Y, \Lambda, \beta)$ for all β such that $Y \rightarrow \beta$ is a production, then the algorithm will create a record of the form $(i, i+|y|, Y, \beta, \Lambda)$.

For simplicity, we will give the proof for the special case that G is in CNF; i.e., every production has the form $X \rightarrow YZ$ or $X \rightarrow c$. The general case is not very different. Consider any production in G.

Case 1: The production is of the form $X \rightarrow YZ$. We wish to show that $E(X) \supseteq E(Y)E(Z)$. Let y be any string in $E(Y)$, let z be any string in $E(Z)$, and let $x = yz$. We must show that $x \in E(X)$. Consider the behavior of Earley's algorithm with input string x and start variable X. The initialization step creates the record $(0, 0, X, \Lambda, YZ)$. The closure step, when $j = 0$, creates $(0, 0, Y, \Lambda, \beta)$ for every β such that $Y \rightarrow \beta$ is one of G's productions. Because $y \in E(Y)$ and y is a prefix of x, the algorithm will create a record of the form $(0, |y|, Y, \beta, \Lambda)$. The completion step, when $j = |y|$, combines this record with $(0, 0, X, \Lambda, YZ)$ to create $(0, |y|, X, Y, Z)$.

The closure step, when $j = |y|$, creates $(|y|, |y|, Z, \Lambda, \beta)$ for every β such that $Z \rightarrow \beta$ is a production. Because $z \in E(Z)$ and $z = x[|y|+1..|x|]$, the algorithm will create a record of the form $(|y|, |x|, Z, \beta, \Lambda)$. The completion step, when $j = |x|$, combines this record with $(0, |y|, X, Y, Z)$ to create $(0, |x|, X, YZ, \Lambda)$. Therefore the algorithm accepts, so $x \in E(X)$.

Case 2: The production is of the form $X \rightarrow c$. We wish to show that $E(X) \supseteq \{c\}$, i.e., that $c \in E(X)$. Consider the behavior of Earley's algorithm with input string c and start variable X. The initialization step creates the record $(0, 0, X, \Lambda, c)$. The advance step, with $j = 0$, creates $(0, 1, X, c, \Lambda)$. Therefore the algorithm accepts, so $c \in E(X)$.

Thus $\langle\langle E(A_1), \ldots, E(A_k)\rangle\rangle$ satisfies every one of the containments in G, completing the proof. ∎

Let G be the grammar

$$\begin{aligned} S &\rightarrow T \cup S\texttt{+}T \\ T &\rightarrow F \cup T\texttt{*}F \\ F &\rightarrow \texttt{a} \cup \texttt{b} \cup \texttt{(}S\texttt{)}. \end{aligned}$$

j	$x[j]$	*Advance*	*Initialization, Closure, and Completion*
0			$S \to .T$, 0 $S \to .S{+}T$, 0 $T \to .F$, 0 $T \to .T{*}F$, 0 $F \to .\mathrm{a}$, 0 $F \to .\mathrm{b}$, 0 $F \to .(S)$, 0
1	a	$F \to \mathrm{a}.$, 0	$T \to F.$, 0 $S \to T.$, 0 $T \to T.{*}F$, 0 $S \to S.{+}T$, 0
2	+	$S \to S{+}.T$, 0	$T \to .F$, 2 $T \to .T{*}F$, 2 $F \to .\mathrm{a}$, 2 $F \to .\mathrm{b}$, 2 $F \to .(S)$, 2
3	b	$F \to \mathrm{b}.$, 2	$T \to F.$, 2 $S \to S{+}T.$, 0 $T \to T.{*}F$, 2
4	*	$T \to T{*}.F$, 2	$F \to .\mathrm{a}$, 4 $F \to .\mathrm{b}$, 4 $F \to .(S)$, 4
5	(	$F \to (.S)$, 4	$S \to .T$, 5 $S \to .S{+}T$, 5 $T \to .F$, 5 $T \to .T{*}F$, 5 $F \to .\mathrm{a}$, 5 $F \to .\mathrm{b}$, 5 $F \to .(S)$, 5
6	a	$F \to \mathrm{a}.$, 5	$T \to F.$, 5 $S \to T.$, 5 $T \to T.{*}F$, 5 $S \to S.{+}T$, 5
7	+	$S \to S{+}.T$, 5	$T \to .F$, 7 $T \to .T{*}F$, 7 $F \to .\mathrm{a}$, 7 $F \to .\mathrm{b}$, 7 $F \to .(S)$, 7
8	b	$F \to \mathrm{b}.$, 7	$T \to F.$, 7 $T \to T.{*}F$, 7 $S \to S{+}T.$, 5 $F \to (S.)$, 4 $S \to S.{+}T$, 5
9	)	$F \to (S).$, 4	$T \to T{*}F.$, 2 $S \to S{+}T.$, 0 $T \to T.{*}F$, 2

TABLE 5.5: The records produced by Earley's algorithm when parsing the string a+b*(a+b) for the grammar $S \to T \cup S{+}T$, $T \to F \cup T{*}F$, $F \to \mathrm{a} \cup \mathrm{b} \cup (S)$. The third and fourth columns show the sets RECORD[j] produced by Earley's algorithm. The results of step 3 (Advance) are shown in the third column, and the results of steps 1, 2, and 4 are shown in the fourth column.

We present an example using Earley's algorithm to parse the string a+b*(a+b). When working examples by hand, it is often convenient to write $P \to \alpha.\beta$, i to represent the record (i, j, P, α, β). The period can be thought of as a pointer to the current position in processing the production $P \to \alpha\beta$. Table 5.5 displays the behavior of Earley's algorithm on this example.

Because the record $S \to S{+}T.$, 0 is in RECORD[9], the algorithm correctly accepts the input string. Each advance step produces only one

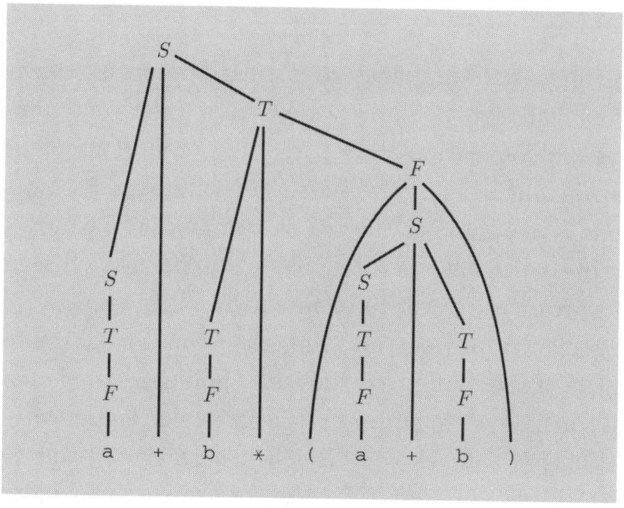

FIGURE 5.23: A parse tree for `a+b*(a+b)`.

record because the grammar G is unambiguous. Notice that the algorithm can complete goals that it does not subsequently make use of. In particular, the record $S \rightarrow S\text{+}T., 0$ in RECORD[3] asserts that $S \stackrel{*}{\Rightarrow} x[1..3]$, which is not part of any derivation of x. All other completed goals do, however, contribute to the complete derivation. A parse tree corresponding to this derivation is shown in Figure 5.23.

Exercises

5.12-1 In showing the correctness of Earley's algorithm, fill in the proof for the case when Z_1, Z_2, or Z_3 is a character.

5.12-2 (a) Modify Earley's algorithm so that it produces a derivation of x if $x \in L(G)$.

(b) Modify Earley's algorithm so that it produces a parse tree for x if $x \in L(G)$.

5.13 CHAPTER SUMMARY

We defined context-free languages as least fixed points of systems of regular equations, which are equivalent to systems of regular containments. These containments are conventionally written as productions, and systems of them are called context-free grammars. The language defined by a system of productions is the same as the set of strings that have parse trees and the set of strings that have derivations. A useful normal form for CFGs is Chomsky normal form (CNF). Context-free languages are the same as NSA languages. We proved pumping theorems for CFLs; they provide useful techniques for proving that particular languages are not context-free. Pumping also helped us to prove that a particular language is inherently ambiguous. Then we developed Greibach normal form for CFLs, which is mainly of historical interest. Finally, we presented two algorithms for testing membership in CFLs. CYK is the simpler algorithm, although Earley's algorithm is faster on grammars that arise in practice.

Exercises

5.13-1 Given a CFG that generates a language L and a finite transducer computing a transduction τ show how to construct a CFG that generates $L\tau$.

5.13-2 Assume that we are given a CFG G for a language L.

(a) Given an NFA for a language R, show how to construct a CFG for $L \cap R$. Your goal is to construct a small grammar.

(b) Let s be a string. Using the method of part (a), construct a CFG G' for $L \cap \{s\}$. How large is your grammar G'? Would a particular normal form for G make the size of G' more manageable?

(c) By testing whether the grammar G' of part (b) generates a nonempty language, we determine whether $s \in L$. Compare this algorithm to the CYK algorithm.

6

Stack and Counter Machines

A STACK MACHINE consists of a control, a stack, and possibly input and output. A counter machine consists of a control, a counter, and possibly input and output. To review our notational conventions, stack machines are called SMs and counter machines are called CMs. Nondeterministic acceptors that run on these machines are called NSAs and NCAs; deterministic acceptors are called DSAs and DCAs; recognizers (necessarily deterministic) are called DSRs and DCRs.

Counter machines are more powerful than finite machines, and stack machines are more powerful than counter machines. Although even stack machines are not as powerful as Turing machines, they are important because the NSA languages are exactly the same as the context-free languages (cf. Section 5.6). In this sense, stack machines are to context-free languages as finite machines are to regular languages.

In this chapter we will develop closure properties of CFLs based on their characterization as NSAs. We will also compare the computing power of nondeterministic and deterministic stack and counter machines and consider the computing power of 2-counter machines. Surprisingly, two counters can simulate any number of counters and stacks. This fact will be very useful when we analyze the capabilities of more powerful machines in Chapter 7.

6.1 CLOSURE PROPERTIES

Recall that closure properties are a very important tool in the study of languages. By using them directly, we can show that a language is accepted or recognized by some program for a certain machine type. By using them indirectly (in proofs by contradiction), we can show that a language is not accepted or recognized by any program for a certain machine type.

From Theorem 4.38, it follows that the class of languages accepted by nondeterministic programs for any reasonable kind of machine is closed under finite transductions. In particular, we have

COROLLARY 6.1

(i) The class of CFLs is closed under finite transductions.

(ii) The class of NCA languages is closed under finite transductions.

Proof: The CFLs are the same as the NSA languages. Apply Theorem 4.38(i) to a machine [control, input, stack] for part (i) and to a machine [control, input, unsigned counter] for part (ii). ∎

Later we will see that the class of CFLs and the class of NCA languages are not closed under complementation. We summarize some important closure properties for CFLs:

THEOREM 6.2. *The class of context-free languages and the class of NCA languages are both closed under the following operations:*

- *regular operations (union, concatenation, and Kleene-closure)*
- *reversal*
- *finite transductions*
- *intersection with a regular language*
- *quotient by a regular language*

Proof: We prove the theorem for NSA languages. The proof for NCA languages is similar. The theorem follows immediately for CFLs because the class of NSA languages is equal to the class of CFLs.

Suppose we are given an NSA. Standardize the program so that it empties the stack before accepting (Section 3.4.5) and does not use the EOF test (Section 3.4.2). Then closure under regular operations is obtained as in the proof of Lemma 4.16. Closure under reversal is obtained by replacing each non-input operation by its converse, i.e., by reversing the direction of each edge in the program's digraph and interchanging PUSHc with POPc. Closure under finite transductions is Corollary 6.1. Closure under intersection with regular languages follows from Corollary 4.40(i). Closure under quotient by a regular language follows because quotient by a regular language is a finite transduction, as shown in Figure 4.36. ∎

Closure properties can be useful for proving that certain languages are not CFLs.

EXAMPLE 6.3. Let $L = \{\mathtt{a}^n\mathtt{b}\mathtt{a}^n\mathtt{b}\mathtt{a}^n : n \geq 0\}$. We prove that L is not a CFL. Suppose, for the sake of contradiction, that L is a CFL. It is easy to construct a finite transducer that will scan a group of a's while writing a's, then scan a b while writing nothing, then scan a second group of a's while writing b's, then scan a second b while writing nothing, and finally scan a third group of a's while writing c's. The finite transducer is depicted in Figure 6.1. Let $\mathcal{T}$ be that finite transducer's transfer relation. Then $L\mathcal{T} = \{\mathtt{a}^n\mathtt{b}^n\mathtt{c}^n : n \geq 0\}$, which must be a CFL, contradicting Example 5.22. ∎∎∎

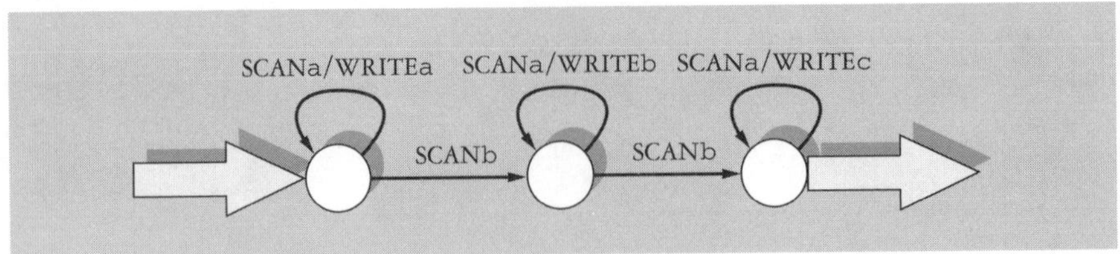

FIGURE 6.1: A finite transducer that maps strings of the form $\mathtt{a}^i\mathtt{ba}^j\mathtt{ba}^k$ to $\mathtt{a}^i\mathtt{b}^j\mathtt{c}^k$ (and does not accept any other strings).

THEOREM 6.4. *The class of DSR languages and the class of DCR languages are both closed under the following operations:*

(i) complementation

(ii) the converse of any deterministic finite transduction

(iii) intersection with a regular language

(iv) union with a regular language

Proof: We prove the theorem only for DSRs. The proof for DCRs is similar. Closure under complementation is obtained by interchanging accepting and rejecting states. Closure under the converses of deterministic finite transductions follows from Theorem 4.38(iii). Let L be a DSR language. If R is a regular language, then R is recognized by a DFR. By replacing each SCANc operation by SCANc/WRITEc in that DFR, we construct a deterministic finite transducer whose transfer relation τ is the partial identity function I_R (such a program is called a *filter* for R). Since τ is a partial identity function, τ is symmetric, so $\tau = \tau^{-1}$. Thus $L \cap R = L\tau = L\tau^{-1}$, which is a DSR language by (ii). By De Morgan's laws we have $L \cup R = \overline{\overline{L} \cap \overline{R}}$, which is a DSR language by (i) and (iii). ■

We can use these closure properties to prove that certain languages are DSR languages.

EXAMPLE 6.5. Recall that the set of palindromes with central marker is a DSR language. The complement of that language is therefore a DSR language. Intersect with the regular language $\mathtt{a}^*\mathtt{b}^*\#\mathtt{b}^*\mathtt{a}^*$ to obtain the set of all strings of the form $\mathtt{a}^i\mathtt{b}^j\#\mathtt{b}^k\mathtt{a}^\ell$ such that $i \neq \ell$ or $j \neq k$, a DSR language. Let τ be a deterministic finite transduction that copies characters until a c is scanned, writes #b, and then replaces the remaining c's with b's and all d's with a's. Applying τ^{-1} to the previous DSR language, we obtain the set of all strings of the form $\mathtt{a}^i\mathtt{b}^j\mathtt{c}^k\mathtt{d}^\ell$ such that $k > 0$ and $(i \neq \ell$ or $j \neq k)$, also a DSR language. ■■■

Additional closure properties for DSR languages will be proved in Section 6.4. These include closure under quotient by a regular language and under concatenation on the right with a regular language.

Exercises

6.1-1 Use the pairing construction (Section 3.2.1) to give alternate proofs that the class of DSR languages is closed under intersection with a regular language and under union with a regular language.

6.1-2 Prove that the following are NCA languages:

(a) $\{\mathtt{a}^i\mathtt{b}^j : j = i \text{ or } j = 2i\}$

(b) $\{\mathtt{a}^i\mathtt{b}^j : j < i \text{ or } j > 2i\}$

(c) $\{\mathtt{a}^i\mathtt{b}^j : i \leq j \leq 2i\}$

(d) $\{\mathtt{a}^i\mathtt{b}^j\mathtt{c}^k : i = j \text{ or } j = k \text{ or } k = i\}$

(e) $\{xy : |x| = |y| \text{ and } y \neq x\}$

(f) $\{xy : |x| = |y| \text{ and } y \neq x^R\}$

6.1-3 Prove that the following language over alphabet $\{\mathtt{a}, \mathtt{b}\}$ is an NCA language and a DSR language: $\{x\#y : y \neq x^R\}$.

6.1-4 Prove that the following is a DCA language: $\{\mathtt{b}^i\mathtt{c}^i : i \geq 0\} \cup \{\mathtt{a}\mathtt{b}^i\mathtt{c}^{2i} : i \geq 0\}$.

6.1-5 Prove that the class of CFLs is closed under shuffle with a regular language (see Exercise 4.8-9 for a definition).

6.1-6 Prove that the class of CFLs is closed under SUBSEQ$(\cdot)$. (See Exercise 4.10-4 for a definition. Do not use Exercise 4.10-5.)

6.1-7 Use closure properties to prove that the following languages are not CFLs:

(a) $\{\mathtt{a}^i\mathtt{b}\mathtt{a}^j\mathtt{b}\mathtt{a}^i\mathtt{b}\mathtt{a}^j : i, j \geq 0\}$

(b) $\{ww : w \in \{\mathtt{a}, \mathtt{b}\}^*\}$

(c) the set of all strings x with $\#_\mathtt{a}(x) = \#_\mathtt{b}(x)$ and $\#_\mathtt{c}(x) = \#_\mathtt{d}(x)$. (Recall that $\#_e(x)$ is the number of e's in the string x.)

6.1-8 See Exercise 4.8-13 for the definition of $\text{PERM}(\cdot)$.

(a) Prove that none of the following classes is closed under $\text{PERM}(\cdot)$: regular languages, DCA languages, NCA languages, DSR languages, and context-free languages. Hint: Find a single regular language L such that $\text{PERM}(L)$ is not a CFL.

Solution: Let $L = (\mathtt{abc})^*$, which is regular. $\text{PERM}(L)$ consists of all strings with equal numbers of a's, b's, and c's.

$$\text{PERM}(L) \cap \mathtt{a}^*\mathtt{b}^*\mathtt{c}^* = \{\mathtt{a}^i\mathtt{b}^i\mathtt{c}^i : i \geq 0\},$$

which is not a CFL. Because the class of CFLs is closed under intersection with regular languages, $\text{PERM}(L)$ must not be a CFL either.

*(b) If L is a regular language over a 2-character alphabet, prove that $\text{PERM}(L)$ is an NCA language and therefore a CFL.

6.1-9 Let $L = \{\mathtt{a}^i\mathtt{bcbd}^i\mathtt{bcbe}^i : i \geq 0\} \cup \{\mathtt{a}^i\mathtt{cd}^j\mathtt{bcbe}^k : i, j, k \geq 0\} \cup \{\mathtt{a}^i\mathtt{bcbd}^j\mathtt{ce}^k : i, j, k \geq 0\} \cup \{x \in \{\mathtt{a}, \mathtt{b}, \mathtt{c}, \mathtt{d}, \mathtt{e}\}^* : x$ contains at least 6 b's$\}$. Use closure properties to prove that L is not a CFL (cf. Exercise 5.8-8).

Solution: Assume for the sake of contradiction that L is a CFL. Construct a finite transducer that scans a group of a's while writing a's, scans bcb while writing nothing, scans a group of d's while writing b's, scans bcb while writing nothing, and finally scans a group of e's while writing c's. Let τ be the transfer relation of this finite transducer. Then $L\tau = \{\mathtt{a}^i\mathtt{b}^i\mathtt{c}^i : i \geq 0\}$, which must therefore be a CFL. However, by Example 5.22, that language is not a CFL. This contradiction proves that L is not a CFL.

*6.2 DSA LANGUAGES ARE DSR LANGUAGES

A general problem in the theory of computing is to convert deterministic acceptors to recognizers for the same language. For example, we have seen how to convert DFAs to DFRs. Two standardizations are necessary for such a conversion: eliminating blocking and eliminating infinite computations. Blocking is easy to eliminate, as shown in Section 3.4.5. Infinite computations are not as easy to eliminate. In Section 6.2.2 we will show how to eliminate infinite computations from DSAs; thus we will be able to convert them to DSRs. Consequently, every DCFL is recognized by a DSR. In contrast, it is not possible to convert DTAs to DTRs, as we shall see in Chapter 7.

6.2.1 Eliminating PUSH–POP Pairs from DSAs

As a major step towards eliminating infinite computations, we will remove from the DSA certain instructions whose effects are always cancelled out. Consider a DSA that is in factored form, so that every non-null instruction operates on either the stack or the input but not both. Suppose that the program, in one of its computations, performs a PUSH*c* that is followed by a POP*c* without any intervening stack or input operations; i.e., the PUSH*c* is followed immediately by the matching POP*c* or is separated from it only by null instructions. Such a pair of instructions is called a PUSH–POP pair. A program fragment containing a PUSH–POP pair is shown in the left half of Figure 6.2. Since the program is deterministic, that PUSHa must always be followed by the POPa. The PUSHa operation is therefore unnecessary, because it will always be undone by the next non-null instruction. Hence we can combine the PUSHa and POPa instructions into a null instruction and delete the PUSHa (but not the POPa). The result of the transformation is shown in the right half of Figure 6.2.

To eliminate all PUSH–POP pairs from a DSA, we eliminate them one at a time until there are none left. If desired, we can eliminate null instructions after *all* of the PUSH–POP pairs have been eliminated.

It is not obvious that this standardization process will ever finish, because when we eliminate a PUSH–POP pair, we may create additional PUSH–POP pairs (see Figure 6.3). Thus it might appear that no progress is made. Fortunately, because the number of PUSH instructions in the DSA does

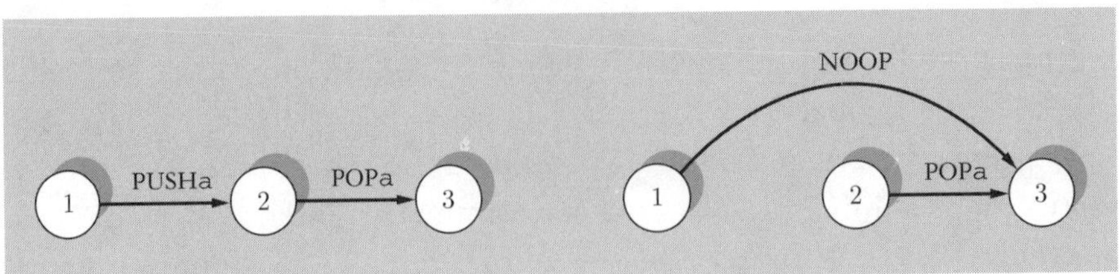

FIGURE 6.2: Eliminating a PUSH–POP pair. (Imagine that there are additional instructions going to control states 1 through 3 as well as going from control states 2 and 3.) The instructions on the left, (1 → 2, NOOP, PUSHa) and (2 → 3, NOOP, POPa), are combined into a single null instruction on the right, (1 → 3, NOOP, NOOP). The PUSHa instruction can be deleted, because it must always be followed by the POPa instruction in any deterministic program. The POPa instruction is retained, however, because other instructions (not shown) might go to control state 2; thus the POPa would not necessarily be used only in conjunction with the PUSHa that was deleted.

decrease, we can prove that the process finishes by an easy induction on the number of PUSH instructions (Exercise 6.2-2).

Thus we can standardize DSAs so that no PUSHc is immediately followed by a POPc in any computation. We also note that similar techniques can be used in order to eliminate INC–DEC pairs from a DCA (Exercise 6.2-3).

Exercises

6.2-1 Eliminate PUSH–POP pairs from the deterministic program fragment shown below:

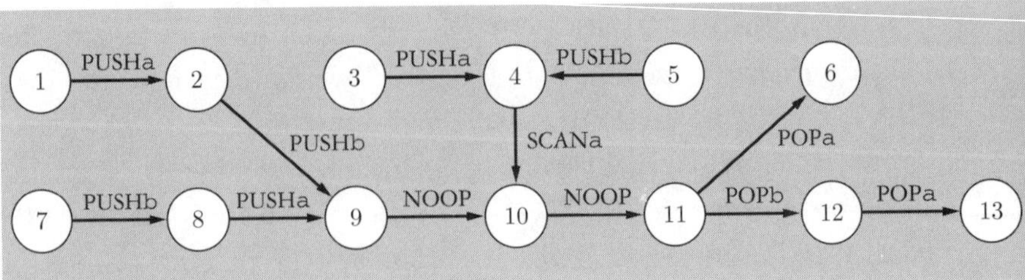

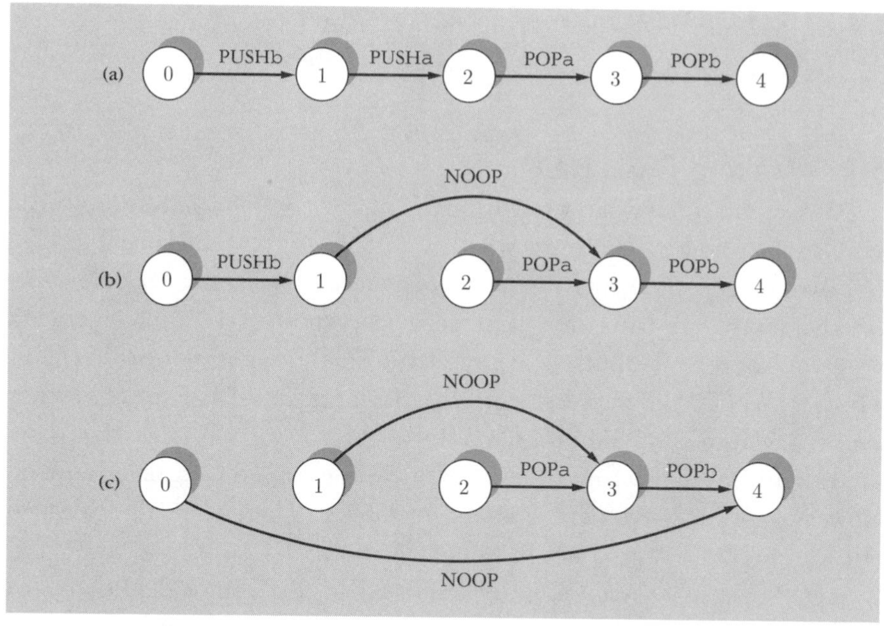

FIGURE 6.3: Eliminating nested PUSH–POP pairs. The program fragment in part (a) contains a PUSH–POP pair. (Imagine that there are additional instructions going to control states 0 through 4 as well as going from control states 2 through 4.) In part (b) the PUSH–POP pair has been eliminated. This results in another PUSH–POP pair that surrounds the newly created null instruction. In part (c) that PUSH–POP pair has been eliminated.

6.2-2 Prove that this section's process for eliminating PUSH–POP pairs is guaranteed to finish.

Solution: For the base case, a DSA with zero PUSH instructions has no PUSH–POP pairs, so the process finishes immediately. Let us assume, for some particular n, that the standardization process always finishes when started with a DSA that has exactly n PUSH instructions. Now consider a DSA with $n + 1$ PUSH instructions. If it has no PUSH–POP pairs, then the process finishes immediately. Otherwise, a PUSH–POP pair is eliminated and the process continues with a program that has exactly n PUSH instructions. By the inductive hypothesis, the process finishes.

6.2-3 Define INC–DEC pairs by analogy to PUSH–POP pairs. Show how to eliminate INC–DEC pairs from a DCA. (Assume that the counter is unsigned.)

6.2.2 Making DSAs Halt

In this section, we show how to eliminate infinite computations from DSAs. We also show how to determine whether a DSM program halts on all inputs.

Two general problems in the theory of computing are to determine whether a program halts on a particular input and to determine whether a program halts on all inputs. By Corollary 5.37, there is an algorithm to test whether an NSM program halts on a particular input. The same algorithm works, of course, for DSM programs. In Chapter 7, we will prove that there is no algorithm to determine whether an NSM program halts on all inputs. However, we can solve that problem for DSMs: There is an algorithm to test whether a DSM program halts on all inputs.

Let P be a DSA. We begin by standardizing P. Factor P so that each non-null instruction operates on the stack or the input but not both. Eliminate dead states, so there is a path from each control state to an accepting state. Standardize the input so that P performs at most one EOF test. The control can also remember whether the most recent stack operation was an EMPTY test; thus we may standardize P so that it never performs two consecutive EMPTY tests. Eliminate PUSH–POP pairs and then eliminate null instructions; thus P never performs a PUSHc that is immediately followed by a POPc.

Since the input has been standardized, P can perform at most $|x|$ SCANs on input x, followed by at most one EOF, i.e., at most $|x|+1$ input operations.

The input instructions partition a computation (finite or infinite) into at most $|x|+2$ *fragments*: one fragment before the first input instruction, at most $|x|$ fragments between successive input instructions, and one fragment (possibly infinite) after the last input instruction. Since P has no null instructions, the only instructions that take place in a fragment are stack instructions.

What can the sequence of stack operations in a fragment look like? In any program, a PUSHc cannot be followed immediately by POPc' for any $c' \neq c$. Because we eliminated PUSH–POP pairs, PUSHc cannot be followed immediately by POPc either. Therefore all the POPs in the fragment must occur before all the PUSHes. In any program, an EMPTY cannot occur immediately after a PUSH or before a POP. Therefore if there are any EMPTY tests in the fragment, then they must occur after the sequence of POPs and before the sequence of PUSHes. Because we standardized the stack, there cannot be two consecutive EMPTY tests. Thus each fragment consists of a sequence of POPs, followed by at most one EMPTY, followed by a sequence of PUSHes.

Let Q denote the set of control states in P. We assert that there are fewer than $|Q|$ consecutive PUSHes in any partial computation of P. Why? Suppose, by way of contradiction, that there were $|Q|$ consecutive pushes in some partial computation. During $|Q|$ instructions, P must enter $|Q| + 1$ control states (possibly repeated). Since P has only $|Q|$ control states, one of them is *necessarily* repeated, by the pigeonhole principle; call that state q. Thus there is a nonempty sequence of PUSHes that leads from q back to q (which we call a PUSH-loop); since PUSHc is a total function and P is deterministic, there can be no instructions going out of this loop (Figure 6.4). No state entered by the PUSH-loop can be final, because P is deterministic. Therefore there is no path from q to a final state, so q is a dead state. But P has no dead states, so this is a contradiction, establishing the assertion.

We have shown that there are at most $|Q| - 1$ PUSHes in any fragment. Therefore, there are at most $(|x| + 2)(|Q| - 1)$ PUSHes in any partial computation on input x. The number of POPs cannot exceed the number of PUSHes in any partial computation, so it is at most $(|x| + 2)(|Q| - 1)$ also. There is at most one EMPTY per fragment, so the number of EMPTY's is at most $|x| + 2$. Therefore, the total number of instructions in any partial computation is bounded by $(|x| + 1) + (|x| + 2) + 2(|x| + 2)(|Q| - 1) = 2(|x| + 2)|Q| - 1$. Therefore, P has no infinite computations.

We have shown that P has no infinite computations. By eliminating blocking, we convert P to a recognizer for L. Thus we have proved that every DSA language is a DSR language.

THEOREM 6.6. *The class of DCFLs is equal to the class of DSR languages.*

Proof: Every DCFL is a DSA language, which we just proved must be a DSR language. By changing rejecting states to nonfinal states, we see that every DSR language is a DSA language, which is a DCFL by definition. ■

COROLLARY 6.7. *The class of DCFLs is closed under complementation.*

Proof: If L is a DCFL, then L is a DSR language by Theorem 6.6. We may interchange accepting and rejecting states in order to obtain a recognizer for $\overline{L}$. Consequently, $\overline{L}$ is a DSR language and therefore a DCFL by Theorem 6.6. ∎

COROLLARY 6.8. *There is an algorithm to determine whether a DSM program halts on all inputs.*

Proof: Let P be a DSM program and let L be the set of strings that P halts on. We remove P's output device, if any, and replace all final states by

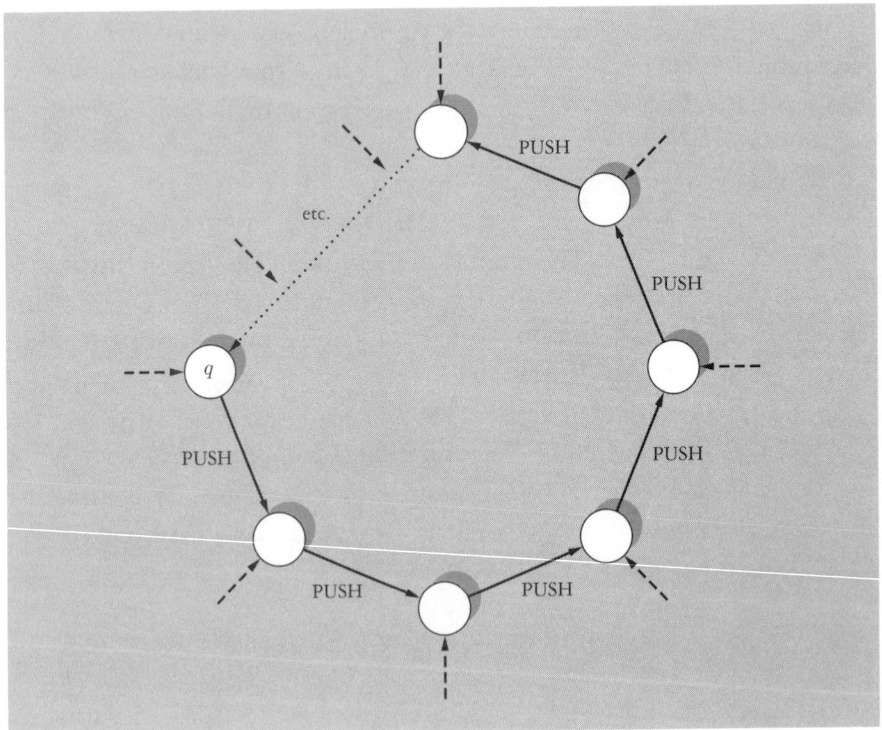

FIGURE 6.4: In a deterministic program, no edge can leave a PUSH-loop.

accepting states to produce a DSA P' that accepts L. Using the construction implicit in the proof of Corollary 6.7, we convert P' to a DSA P'' that accepts $\overline{L}$. Then, we convert P'' to a CFG G for $\overline{L}$ and test whether $L(G) = \emptyset$. ■

COROLLARY 6.9. *There is an algorithm to determine whether a stack machine program is a DSR.*

Proof: Given a program P for a machine [control, input, stack], we first check whether it is deterministic. If so, we eliminate infinite computations as above; this converts infinite computations to blocked computations. Call the resulting program P'. Finally, we check whether P' is nonblocking. P is a DSR if and only if P is deterministic and P' is nonblocking. ■

Similar standardizations are possible for DCM programs; i.e., we can eliminate infinite computations, convert DCAs to DCRs, determine whether a DCM program halts on all inputs, and determine whether a CM program is a DCR (see Exercise 6.2-5).

Exercises

6.2-4 Design a DCA that accepts $\{\texttt{a}, \texttt{b}\}^* - \{\texttt{a}^n\texttt{b}^n : n \geq 1\}$.

6.2-5 (a) Show how to eliminate infinite computations from a program for a machine [control, input, unsigned counter].

(b) Prove that the class of DCA languages is equal to the class of DCR languages.

(c) Prove that the class of DCA languages is closed under complementation.

(d) Give an algorithm to determine whether a DCM program halts on all inputs.

(e) Give an algorithm to determine whether a program for a machine [control, input, unsigned counter] is a DCR.

*6.3 UNAMBIGUOUS PROGRAMS

An important property of deterministic programs is that there is at most one computation for each argument. This property is shared by certain nondeterministic programs.

A program P is *ambiguous* if there exist x, y such that P has two or more computations with argument x and result y. A program P is *unambiguous* if P is not ambiguous, that is, if for every x, y there is at most one computation of P with argument x and result y. As a special case, an acceptor P is unambiguous if for every x there is at most one computation of P with argument x; i.e., if $x \in L$, then P has exactly one accepting computation on input x, and if $x \notin L$, then P has no accepting computations on input x.

The issue of unambiguity arises in the study of natural languages and computer programming languages, as we observed in Section 5.9.

When we convert an NSA to a CFG as in the proof of Corollary 5.18, each accepting computation of the NSA on input x is converted to exactly one parse tree of the CFG that yields x. When we convert a CFG to an NSA as in the proof of Theorem 5.16, each parse tree of the CFG that yields x is converted to exactly one computation of the NSA on input x. (See Exercise 5.9-2.) Thus unambiguous NSAs are equivalent to unambiguous CFGs.

THEOREM 6.10. *L is generated by an unambiguous CFG if and only if L is accepted by an unambiguous NSA.* ∎

Unambiguous programs are a useful tool for studying unambiguous grammars. For example, because every deterministic program is unambiguous, every deterministic CFL is an unambiguous CFL. However, the set of palindromes is an unambiguous CFL (the obvious NSA is unambiguous) but not a deterministic CFL, as we will show in Section 6.4. Thus, every deterministic CFL is an unambiguous CFL, but not conversely.

We complete this section by proving some useful closure properties for unambiguous languages.

THEOREM 6.11. *Let τ_1 be the transfer relation of an unambiguous program P_1 for a machine* [output, d_1], *and let τ_2 be the transfer relation of an unambiguous program P_2 for a machine* [input, d_2]. *Assume that P_1 has a well-behaved terminator, i.e.,* *that we can test whether d_1 is in an accepting state. Assume either that τ_1 is a partial function or that τ_2 is one-one. Then $\tau_1 \circ \tau_2$ is the transfer relation of an unambiguous program P for a machine* [control, d_1, d_2].

Proof: As in the proof of Lemma 4.44, we construct a program P for a machine [control, d_1, d_2] whose transfer relation is $\tau_1 \circ \tau_2$. For each computation of P_1 that outputs some string y and each computation of P_2 that inputs the same string y, there is exactly one computation of P. Suppose that $x \overset{\tau_1\tau_2}{\mapsto} z$.

If τ_1 is a partial function, there is a unique y such that $x \overset{\tau_1}{\mapsto} y$. If τ_2 is one-one there is a unique y such that $y \overset{\tau_2}{\mapsto} z$. In either case, there is a unique y such that $x \overset{\tau_1}{\mapsto} y \overset{\tau_2}{\mapsto} z$.

Because P_1 is unambiguous, there is a unique computation C_1 of P_1 that maps x to y. Because P_2 is unambiguous, there is a unique computation C_2 of P_2 that maps y to z. By the construction of P, there is a unique computation of P that maps x to z. Therefore P is unambiguous. ∎

Theorem 6.11 is particularly useful when the first program is a finite transducer and the second is an NSA.

COROLLARY 6.12. *Let L be an unambiguous CFL and τ be an unambiguous finite transduction.*

(i) *If τ is a partial function, then $L\tau^{-1}$ is an unambiguous CFL.*

(ii) *If τ is one-one then $L\tau$ is an unambiguous CFL.*

Proof: Let P be an unambiguous NSA that accepts L, and let τ_L be the transfer relation of P.

(i) By Theorem 6.11, there is an unambiguous stack machine program whose transfer relation is $\tau \circ \tau_L$; as in the proof of Theorem 4.38, that program accepts $L\tau^{-1}$. Therefore $L\tau^{-1}$ is an unambiguous CFL.

(ii) We assert that τ^{-1} is an unambiguous finite transduction. (Proof of assertion: Eliminate EOF from the finite transducer that computes τ and then interchange SCAN and WRITE operations.) Because τ

is one-one, τ^{-1} is a partial function. $L\tau = L(\tau^{-1})^{-1}$, which is an unambiguous CFL by part (i). ∎

A proof based on generators may be more intuitive.

Alternative proof of part (ii): Given an unambiguous NSA that accepts L, we replace each SCANc by a WRITEc to obtain an unambiguous generator for L, i.e., a stack machine program that writes each string belonging to L (one per computation). Let τ_L be the transfer relation of that generator. By Theorem 6.11, $\tau_L \circ \tau$ is the transfer relation of an unambiguous stack machine program. That program generates $L\tau$. By replacing each WRITEc by SCANc in that program, we construct an unambiguous NSA that accepts $L\tau$, so $L\tau$ is an unambiguous CFL. ∎

Because deterministic programs are unambiguous and compute partial functions, the class of unambiguous CFLs is closed under the converse of deterministic finite transductions.

COROLLARY 6.13. *Let L be an unambiguous CFL and τ be a deterministic finite transduction.*

(i) $L\tau^{-1}$ is an unambiguous CFL.

(ii) If τ is one-one, then $L\tau$ is an unambiguous CFL as well.

Proof

(i) Because τ is deterministic, τ is unambiguous and a partial function. The conclusion follows from Corollary 6.12(i).

(ii) Because τ is deterministic, τ is unambiguous. By assumption, τ is one-one. The conclusion follows from Corollary 6.12(ii). ∎

EXAMPLE 6.14. Let $L = \{\mathtt{a}^i\mathtt{b}^j\mathtt{c}^k : i = 2j \text{ or } k = 3j\}$. We will prove that L is inherently ambiguous. Clearly L is a CFL. Suppose, for the sake of contradiction, that L is an unambiguous CFL. Let τ be a deterministic finite transduction that replaces each aa by a, each b by b, and each ccc by c. $x\tau$ is undefined (i.e., the transducer rejects) if the a's do not come in pairs or

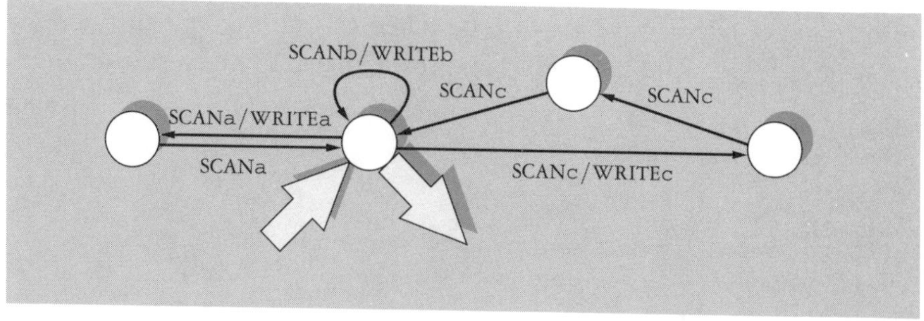

FIGURE 6.5: A deterministic finite transducer that replaces aa by a, replaces b by b, and replaces ccc by c. (It rejects strings in which the a's do not come in pairs or the c's do not come in triples.) In particular, it maps $\mathtt{a}^{2i}\mathtt{b}^j\mathtt{c}^{3k}$ to $\mathtt{a}^i\mathtt{b}^j\mathtt{c}^k$.

the c's do not come in triples. (The deterministic finite transducer is shown in Figure 6.5.) For example, $\mathtt{aaaabccc}\,\tau = \mathtt{aabc}$ and $\mathtt{aaaaabccc}\,\tau$ is undefined.

Observe that τ is one-one. The language $L\tau$ is $\{\mathtt{a}^i\mathtt{b}^j\mathtt{c}^k : i = j \text{ or } j = k\}$, which must be unambiguous by Corollary 6.13(ii) but was shown to be inherently ambiguous in the proof of Theorem 5.31. This contradiction proves that L is inherently ambiguous. ■ ■ ■

EXAMPLE 6.15. Let S be any nonempty language, let # be any character other than a, b, or c, and let

$$L = \{\mathtt{a}^i\mathtt{b}^j\mathtt{c}^k\#s : (i = j \text{ or } j = k) \text{ and } s \in S\}.$$

We will prove that L is inherently ambiguous. Suppose, for the sake of contradiction, that L is an unambiguous CFL. A deterministic finite transduction that discards the # and everything after it would map L to $\{\mathtt{a}^i\mathtt{b}^j\mathtt{c}^k : i = j \text{ or } j = k\}$; however, we have to be careful to obtain a transduction that is one-one. Let s be a fixed string belonging to S. Let τ be a deterministic finite transduction that copies characters until it scans a #, does not copy the #, and then accepts if the rest of the input is equal to s. Then τ maps $\mathtt{a}^i\mathtt{b}^j\mathtt{c}^k\#s$ to $\mathtt{a}^i\mathtt{b}^j\mathtt{c}^k$ and is undefined on all inputs that are not of that form, so

$$L\tau = \{\mathtt{a}^i\mathtt{b}^j\mathtt{c}^k : i = j \text{ or } j = k\}.$$

Furthermore τ is one-one. By Corollary 6.13(ii), that language must be unambiguous, but it was shown to be inherently ambiguous in the proof of Theorem 5.31. This contradiction proves that L is inherently ambiguous. ■■■

Exercises

6.3-1 Prove that $\{\mathtt{a}^i\mathtt{b}^j\mathtt{c}^k\mathtt{d}^\ell : i = j \text{ or } k = \ell\}$ is an unambiguous CFL.

6.3-2 Let L be any language. Using Corollary 6.13(ii), prove that the following languages are inherently ambiguous:

(a) $\{\mathtt{d}\mathtt{a}^i\mathtt{b}^j\mathtt{c}^k : i = j \text{ or } j = k\} \cup \mathtt{e}L$

(b) $\{\mathtt{d}^h\mathtt{a}^i\mathtt{b}^j\mathtt{c}^k : h \geq 0 \text{ and } (i = j \text{ or } j = k)\} \cup \mathtt{e}L$

6.3-3 Let L be the set of all strings of the form $\mathtt{a}^i\mathtt{b}\{\mathtt{a},\mathtt{b}\}^*\mathtt{b}\mathtt{a}^i\mathtt{b}\{\mathtt{a},\mathtt{b}\}^*$, i.e.,

$$L = \{\mathtt{a}^i\mathtt{b}x\mathtt{b}\mathtt{a}^i\mathtt{b}y : x, y \in \{\mathtt{a},\mathtt{b}\}^* \text{ and } i \geq 0\}.$$

Prove that L is inherently unboundedly ambiguous (defined in Exercise 5.9-5). Hint: Use the result of that exercise.

*6.4 ON-LINE RECOGNITION

Although every CFL is an NSA language, in this section we develop a useful technique for proving that certain CFLs are not DSR languages, i.e., not DCFLs. In particular, we prove that the set of palindromes is not a DCFL.

Consider a DSR P that has a well-behaved terminator and never uses the EOF test, and let L be the language recognized by P. We perform the following two standardizations: Because P's terminator is well-behaved, it can test whether its devices are in accepting or rejecting states; thus, we can modify its terminator so that it accepts if and only if the input is empty and the control state is accepting. In addition we factor P, so each control state is dedicated to a single device.

Suppose that after scanning a prefix w of the input string x, P is in a control state q that is dedicated to the input device. Since P does not use the EOF test, P must terminate in control state q on input w. Therefore q is an accepting control state if and only if w belongs to L. Thus we may determine which prefixes of x belong to L by looking at the control states dedicated to the input device that are entered during P's computation on input x. Intuitively, P determines which prefixes of x belong to L as its computation proceeds, so we say that P recognizes L *on line* and that P is an *on-line* program.

In this section we show how to eliminate the EOF test from a DSR. Then we use the fact that DSR languages can be recognized on line in order to prove that certain CFLs are not DSR languages.

In the following lemma, we consider an NSM program P that has no input device, but instead starts with the argument held in its stack. P is in an accepting configuration if and only if the stack is empty and the control is in an accepting state. Every regular language is accepted by such an NSM program, because SCANc can be simulated by POPc, EOF can be simulated by EMPTY, and the class of regular languages is closed under reversal. Surprisingly, the converse is true as well.

LEMMA 6.16. *Let P be a program for a machine* [control, stack] *such that* $\alpha_{\text{stack}} = I_{\Sigma^*}$ *and* $\omega_{\text{stack}} = \{(\Lambda, \text{ACCEPT})\}$. *Then P accepts a regular language. Furthermore, if P has p states, then $L(P)$ is accepted by a p-state NFA.*

Proof: Without loss of generality, assume that null instructions have been eliminated from P, and let L be the language accepted by P. We construct an NFA P' that accepts L^R. The control states and the initial state of P' are the same as those of P. We construct the instructions of P and accepting states of P below.

Let q be any control state of P and let c be any stack character. Suppose that P is in state q and that the stack holds xc for some string x. The possible behaviors of P up to and including the moment that c is removed from the stack depend only on q and c, but not on x, because the program cannot look at x without removing c from the stack first.

The instructions of P' are determined by the following rule:

Rule 1: If there is a sequence of instructions such that

- the composition of those instructions is $(q \rightarrow q_1, \text{POP}c)$—i.e., the sequence of instructions goes from q to q_1 and has the same net effect on the stack as popping the c that is on top of the stack—and

- the last instruction in the sequence performs POPc,

then let $(q \to q_1, \text{SCAN}c)$ be an instruction of P'.

The accepting states of P' are determined by the following rule:

Rule 2: If there is a sequence of instructions such that

- the composition of those instructions is $(q \to q_1, \text{NOOP})$—i.e., the sequence of instructions goes from q to q_1 and has no net effect on the stack—
- and q_1 is an accepting state of P,

then let q be an accepting state of P'. In particular, every accepting state of P is an accepting state of the NFA P'.

Now we prove informally that P' simulates P. Call a configuration of P a *milestone* if its stack height is lower than any previous stack height. Any computation of P can be decomposed at its milestones. Suppose that two consecutive milestones are (q, sc) and (q_1, s). The behavior between those two milestones is simulated by the instruction $(q \to q_1, \text{SCAN}c)$, which belongs to the NFA P' by rule 1. Let the last milestone be (q, Λ). The remaining instructions in the computation go from q to an accepting state; by rule 2, q is an accepting state in P'.

Conversely, given a computation of P', we can replace each instruction by a sequence of instructions of P according to rule 1. Concatenate these sequences and then the sequence given by rule 2 to obtain a computation of P.

Because the characters are popped off the stack in the reverse of their natural order, P' accepts L^R, so L^R is regular. Because the class of regular languages is closed under reversal, L is regular. ■

The preceding proof is nonconstructive because we did not give an algorithm for applying rules 1 and 2; however, the proof can be made constructive (Exercise 6.4-1).

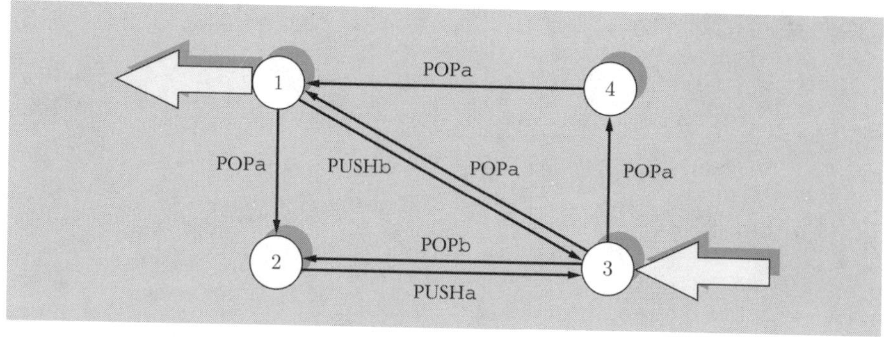

FIGURE 6.6: An NSM program for L that starts with the argument on the stack.

EXAMPLE 6.17. In Figure 6.6 we show an NSM program that starts with its argument in the stack, and in Figure 6.17 we show an NFA that accepts the reverse of the NSM program's language. ■■■

THEOREM 6.18. *If L is a DSR language then L is recognized by an on-line DSR.*

Proof: Suppose that L is recognized by a deterministic program P for a machine [control, input, stack]. Without loss of generality, let the control set of P be $Q = \{1, \ldots, |Q|\}$. For each q in Q, we define a regular language R_q to be the set of strings x such that P contains a sequence of instructions that lead from the configuration (q, Λ, x) to an accepting configuration. By Lemma 6.16, R_q is a regular language (apply the lemma to a program that is identical to P except that its starting control state is q). In fact, close analysis of the proof of Lemma 6.16 plus the subset construction shows that R_q is recognized by a DFR D_q whose control set is 2^Q and whose start state is $\{q\}$.

We define a DSR P' that simulates P while at the same time simulating the behavior of D_q, for each q, on the stack contents. In order to do so, P' will store $(|Q| + 1)$-tuples on the stack. For $i \leq |Q|$, the ith element of the tuple is the control state of D_q upon scanning the stack contents of P;

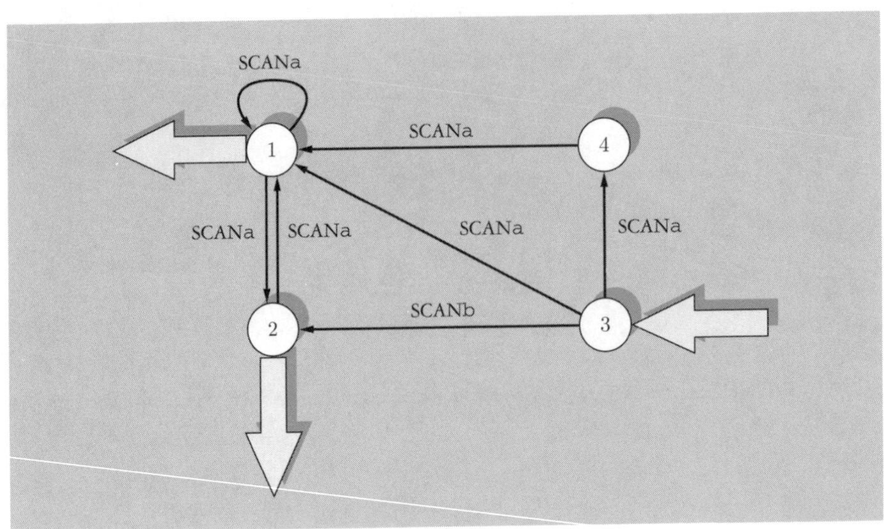

FIGURE 6.7: An NFA that accepts L^R. The edge ($2 \to 1$, SCANa) in the NFA comes from ($2 \to 3$, PUSHa) ($3 \to 4$, POPa) ($4 \to 1$, POPa) in the NSM program. The edge ($1 \to 1$, SCANa) in the NFA comes from ($1 \to 3$, PUSHb) ($3 \to 2$, POPb) ($2 \to 3$, PUSHa) ($3 \to 4$, POPa) ($4 \to 1$, POPa) in the NSM program. Each of the remaining edges labeled SCANc in the NFA comes from the corresponding edges labeled POPc in the NSM program. Control state 2 is an accepting state in the NFA because of the instruction sequence ($2 \to 3$, PUSHa) ($3 \to 1$, POPa).

the last element of the tuple is the character at the top of P's stack or a z to indicate that P's stack is empty. The details of the simulation follow.

Suppose that P has start state q_{start}. Then let P' have control set $Q \cup \{\nu_{\text{start}}\}$, where ν_{start} is a new state, and let its start state be ν_{start}. P' immediately executes the instruction $(\nu_{\text{start}} \to q_{\text{start}}, \text{PUSH}(1, \ldots, |Q|, \texttt{z}))$. Then the top of the stack indicates that each of the programs D_q is in its start state q and that P's stack is empty.

For each character c in P's stack alphabet, let t_c be the function such that $q_1 t_c$ is the unique state q_2 such that $(q_1 \to q_2, \text{SCAN}c)$ is an instruction of D_q. (Since each program D_q has the same instruction set, t_c does not depend on q. Since D_q is a recognizer, t_c is a total function.) We convert instructions of P into instructions of P' according to the following table, where each q_i ranges over all elements of Q and c ranges over all elements of Γ:

Instruction of P	*Instruction(s) of P′*
$(r \to s,\ f_{\text{in}},\ \text{PUSH}d)$	$(r \to \nu,\ f_{\text{in}},\ \text{TOP}(q_1, \ldots, q_{\lvert Q\rvert}, c))$ $(\nu \to s,\ \text{NOOP},\ \text{PUSH}(q_1 t_d, \ldots q_{\lvert Q\rvert} t_d, d))$
$(r \to s,\ f_{\text{in}},\ \text{POP}d)$	$(r \to s,\ f_{\text{in}},\ \text{POP}(q_1, \ldots, q_{\lvert Q\rvert}, d))$
$(r \to s,\ f_{\text{in}},\ \text{NOOP})$	$(r \to s,\ f_{\text{in}},\ \text{NOOP})$

A configuration of P' is accepting if the input is empty, the control is in an accepting state q of P, and the qth element of the tuple on the top of the stack is an accepting state of D_q.

Finally, so that the terminator will depend only on the control and not the top stack character, we keep the top stack character in a separate buffer that is absorbed into the control. ∎

An on-line program for a language L must determine, for each prefix of the input string, whether that prefix belongs to L. We can modify such a program to accept iff the string *and* a certain prefix both belong to L. Often the language recognized in this way will not be a CFL and hence not a DCFL; then we may conclude that the original language L must not be a DCFL.

By making an on-line program check a string and a particular prefix for membership in L, we make it do "double duty." This is formalized as a closure property. Let

$$\text{Double-Duty}(L) = \{x\#y : x \in L \text{ and } xy \in L\},$$

where # is a fixed character that does not belong to L's alphabet. For example,

$$\text{Double-Duty}(\{\texttt{a}, \texttt{ab}, \texttt{bb}\}) = \{\texttt{a\#b}, \texttt{a\#}, \texttt{ab\#}, \texttt{bb\#}\}.$$

COROLLARY 6.19 (Double-Duty Corollary). *If L is a DCFL, then Double-Duty(L) is a DCFL.*

Proof: Let L be a DCFL. Then there is an on-line DSR P that recognizes L. We construct a program P' that recognizes Double-Duty(L) as follows: Simulate P on input $x\#y$ until the # is scanned. If P rejects the string x scanned so far, then reject; otherwise continue simulating P on input xy. If P accepts xy as well, then accept; otherwise reject. ∎

The Double-Duty corollary can be applied to prove that many CFLs are not DCFLs.

EXAMPLE 6.20. We prove that the set of palindromes over $\{\texttt{a}, \texttt{b}\}$ is not a DCFL. Let L be the set of palindromes over $\{\texttt{a}, \texttt{b}\}$, and assume, for the sake of contradiction, that L is a DCFL. Then Double-Duty(L) must be a DCFL as well. Let

$$L' = \text{Double-Duty}(L) \cap (\texttt{a}^*\texttt{ba}^*\texttt{\#ba}^*),$$

which must be a DCFL, because the class of DCFLs is closed under intersection with regular languages. But $\texttt{a}^i\texttt{ba}^j\texttt{\#ba}^k$ belongs to L' if and only if $j = i$ and $k = i$. Therefore,

$$L' = \{\texttt{a}^i\texttt{ba}^i\texttt{\#ba}^i : i \geq 0\}.$$

which is not even a CFL, much less a DCFL. This contradiction proves that the set of palindromes over $\{\texttt{a}, \texttt{b}\}$ is not a DCFL. ∎∎∎

THEOREM 6.21. *The class of deterministic CFLs is a proper subset of the class of unambiguous CFLs.*

Proof: By Example 6.20, the set of palindromes over $\{\texttt{a}, \texttt{b}\}$ is not a DCFL. However, the grammar

$$S \rightarrow \Lambda \cup \texttt{a} \cup \texttt{b} \cup \texttt{a}S\texttt{a} \cup \texttt{b}S\texttt{b}$$

is an unambiguous grammar for the language. ∎

EXAMPLE 6.22. We show that $L = \{\mathtt{a}^i\mathtt{b}^j : j = i \text{ or } j = 2i\}$ is not a DCFL. Suppose it is. Then Double-Duty(L) must be a DCFL. Let

$$L' = \text{Double-Duty}(L) \cap (\mathtt{a}^+\mathtt{b}^+\mathtt{\#b}^+),$$

which must be a DCFL because the class of DCFLs is closed under intersection with regular languages. If i, j, and k are greater than 0, then $\mathtt{a}^i\mathtt{b}^j\mathtt{\#b}^k$ belongs to L' if and only if $j = i$ and $j + k = 2i$. Therefore

$$L' = \{\mathtt{a}^i\mathtt{b}^i\mathtt{\#b}^i : i \geq 1\},$$

which is not even a CFL. This contradiction proves that L is not a DCFL. ■ ■ ■

Exercises

6.4-1 Present an algorithm to determine the instruction set and accepting states of the NFA P' in the proof of Lemma 6.16. You may assume that the stack alphabet is $\{\mathtt{a}, \mathtt{b}\}$. Hint: First, determine the regular set of paths from state i to state j. Ignoring everything but the stack operations, we obtain a regular expression R over $\{\text{PUSH}\mathtt{a}, \text{PUSH}\mathtt{b}, \text{POP}\mathtt{a}, \text{POP}\mathtt{b}\}$. Construct a CFG G that generates the set of all sequences of stack operations whose composition is NOOP. Consider the CFLs $R \cap L(G)$, $R \cap (L(G) \otimes \text{POP}\mathtt{a})$, and $R \cap (L(G) \otimes \text{POP}\mathtt{b})$.

6.4-2 Prove that the following are not DCFLs:

(a) $\{ww^R : w \in \{\mathtt{a}, \mathtt{b}\}^*\}$
(b) $\{\mathtt{a}^i\mathtt{b}^j : 2i = 3j \text{ or } 3i = 2j\}$
(c) $\{\mathtt{a}^i\mathtt{b}^j : j \leq i \text{ or } j \geq 2i\}$
(d) $\{\mathtt{a}^i\mathtt{b}^j : j \neq i \text{ and } j \neq 2i\}$
(e) $\overline{L}$, where $L = \{ww : w \in \{\mathtt{a}, \mathtt{b}\}^*\}$
(f) $\overline{L}$, where $L = \{(w\mathtt{\#})^i : w \in \{\mathtt{a}, \mathtt{b}\}^i\}$

6.4-3 Find a language L such that L and $\overline{L}$ are CFLs but L is not a DCFL.

Solution: Let L be the set of palindromes over $\{\mathtt{a}, \mathtt{b}\}$.

6.4-4 Find a regular language R and a DCR language L such that RL is not a DSR language. Conclude that the class of DCR languages and the class of DSR languages are not closed under concatenation.

6.4-5 Prove that the class of DCR languages and the class of DSR languages are not closed under reversal.

6.4-6 Prove that the class of DCR languages and the class of DSR languages are not closed under Kleene-closure.

*6.4-7 Let S be a DCFL and let R be a regular language.

(a) Prove that $\text{PREFIX}(S)$ is a DCFL.

Solution: Let P be a DSA that recognizes S. Let L be the set of strings s such that the program P, when started with s on the stack, accepts at least one input string y. We assert that L is regular. Proof: L is accepted by an NSM program that starts with its input string s on the stack, nondeterministically guesses y character by character, and simulates P as though y were read. By Lemma 6.16, L is regular.
$\text{PREFIX}(S)$ is accepted by a DSA P' that simulates P on input x and accepts x iff the final stack contents belong to L. The latter can be checked as explained before Lemma 6.16.

(b) Prove that S/R is a DCFL; i.e., the class of DCFLs is closed under quotient with a regular language. Hint: Use Lemma 6.16.

(c) Let $\text{MAX}(L)$ be the set of strings x in L such that x is not a proper prefix of any other string in L, i.e.,

$$\text{MAX}(L) = L - L/\Sigma^{+}.$$

For example,

$$\text{MAX}(\{\texttt{a}, \texttt{ab}, \texttt{b}\}) = \{\texttt{ab}, \texttt{b}\}.$$

Prove that $\text{MAX}(S)$ is a DCFL. Hint: Prove that $S - S/R$ is a DCFL.

6.4-8 Fix an alphabet Σ. Let S be a DCFL. Let F be a finite set of strings. Let R be a regular language.

(a) Define $\text{DEJAVU}(L)$ to be the set of strings x in L such that some proper prefix of x is also in L, i.e.,

$$\text{DEJAVU}(L) = L \cap L\Sigma^{+}.$$

For example,

$$\text{DEJAVU}(\{\texttt{a}, \texttt{ab}, \texttt{bb}\}) = \{\texttt{ab}\}.$$

Prove that DEJAVU(S) is a DCFL.

Solution: Let P be an on-line DSR that recognizes S. Modify P to remember by means of an extra control whether a proper prefix of the input belongs to S. If one does and the entire string belongs to S, then accept; otherwise reject.

(b) Let MIN(L) be the set of strings x in L such that no proper prefix of x is also in L, i.e.,

$$\text{MIN}(L) = L - (L\Sigma^+).$$

For example,

$$\text{MIN}(\{\texttt{a}, \texttt{ab}, \texttt{bb}\}) = \{\texttt{a}, \texttt{bb}\}.$$

Prove that MIN(S) is a DCFL.

(c) Prove that SF is a DCFL.

(d) Prove that SR is a DCFL, i.e., the class of DCFLs is closed under concatenation on the right with a regular language.

(e) Prove that FS need not be a DCFL.

(f) Prove that S^R need not be a DCFL.

6.4-9 Prove that every DCR language is recognized by an on-line DCR. Hint: Use Exercise 4.4-8.

6.5 TWO COUNTERS SIMULATE A STACK

Although counters may appear qualitatively much less powerful than stacks, two counters are actually more powerful than a stack. For now, we will show that two counters can at least simulate a stack. This simulation will be important when we characterize the power of Turing machines in terms of stacks and counters in Chapter 7.

For simplicity we assume the stack alphabet is $\{1, 2\}$; however, the same techniques work for an arbitrary alphabet. The idea behind the simulation is to view the stack string as a dyadic numeral. Stack operations correspond to fairly simple arithmetic operations on this number. One counter will hold the number; the other counter will provide temporary storage in order to assist with operations on the number. (We have chosen dyadic numerals over binary because every number has a unique dyadic representation, whereas every number has infinitely many binary representations because of leading zeroes.)

Let P be a program for a machine [control, stack, other], where the stack alphabet is $\{1, 2\}$. Assume that α initializes the stack to be empty, i.e., $\alpha_{\text{stack}} = X \times \{\Lambda\}$, where X is the set of possible arguments. Without loss of generality, assume that P is in factored form (cf. Section 3.4.1).

We will simulate P by a program P' for a machine [control, $K1$, $K2$, other], where $K1$ and $K2$ are unsigned counters. Let $\alpha_{K1} = \alpha_{K2} = X \times \{0\}$; i.e., the counters are initialized to 0. In constructing P', we will ensure that if P has certain desirable properties like determinism, nonblocking, and the absence of infinite computations, then P' has those properties as well.

Each configuration (q, s, x) of P is represented by the configuration $(q, \text{dyadic}(s), 0, x)$ of P' where dyadic(s) is the natural number whose dyadic representation is the string s. The dyadic numerals are convenient because appending 1 or 2 to such a numeral corresponds to a simple arithmetic operation—doubling and adding 1 or 2—on the represented number. To double the value in the first counter, we repeatedly subtract 1 from it while adding 2 to the second counter; then we copy the result from the second counter back to the first. The following algorithm, started with $K1 = n$ and $K2 = b$, finishes with $K1 = 2n + b$ and $K2 = 0$:

while $K1 > 0$ do
 $K1 := K1 - 1; K2 := K2 + 2;$
(* Now $K1 = 0$ and $K2 = 2n + b$. *)
while $K2 > 0$ do
 $K1 := K1 + 1; K2 := K2 - 1;$
(* Now $K1 = 2n + b$ and $K2 = 0$. *)

Observe that we can add 2 to a counter by performing two INCs. Now we are ready to simulate PUSH operations using $K1$ and $K2$. Suppose that

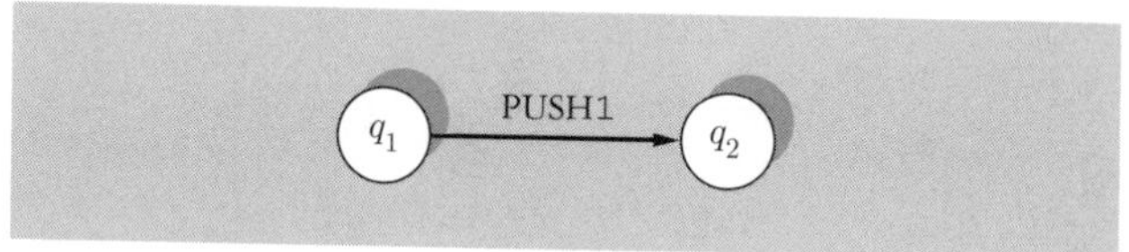

FIGURE 6.8: An instruction that uses the PUSH1 operation.

P contains the instruction $\pi = (q_1 \rightarrow q_2, \text{PUSH}1, \text{NOOP})$, as shown in Figure 6.8. (The operation PUSH2 can be handled analogously.)

Then $(q_1, s, x) \overset{\pi}{\mapsto} (q_2, s1, x)$. Let $n = \text{dyadic}(s)$; then $2n + 1 = \text{dyadic}(s1)$. Correspondingly, we want histories of P' to go, via a subprogram, from $(q_1, n, 0, x)$ to $(q_2, 2n + 1, 0, x)$. The subprogram corresponding to π is shown in Figure 6.9. Computations of this subprogram have the following form:

$$\begin{array}{rcl} (q_1, n, 0, x) & \overset{\Pi'}{\longmapsto} & (\nu_1, n, 1, x) \\ & \overset{(\Pi')^{2n}}{\longmapsto} & (\nu_1, 0, 2n+1, x) \\ & \overset{\Pi'}{\longmapsto} & (\nu_3, 0, 2n+1, x) \\ & \overset{(\Pi')^{2n+1}}{\longmapsto} & (\nu_3, 2n+1, 0, x) \\ & \overset{\Pi'}{\longmapsto} & (q_2, 2n+1, 0, x). \end{array}$$

A subprogram that simulates the instruction $(q_1 \rightarrow q_2, \text{PUSH}2, \text{NOOP})$ is shown in Figure 6.10. This subprogram works by adding 2 to the second counter, then adding $2n$, and finally copying the number $2n + 2$ back to the first counter. Computations of this subprogram have the form:

$$\begin{array}{rcl} (q_1, n, 0, x) & \overset{\Pi'}{\longmapsto} & (\nu_0, n, 1, x) \\ & \overset{\Pi'}{\longmapsto} & (\nu_1, n, 2, x) \\ & \overset{(\Pi')^{2n}}{\longmapsto} & (\nu_1, 0, 2n+2, x) \\ & \overset{\Pi'}{\longmapsto} & (\nu_3, 0, 2n+2, x) \\ & \overset{(\Pi')^{2n+2}}{\longmapsto} & (\nu_3, 2n+2, 0, x) \\ & \overset{\Pi'}{\longmapsto} & (q_2, 2n+2, 0, x). \end{array}$$

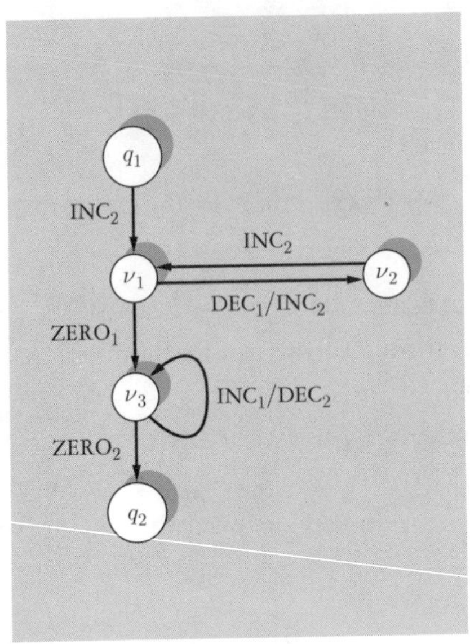

FIGURE 6.9: Simulating the stack operation PUSH1 with two counters.

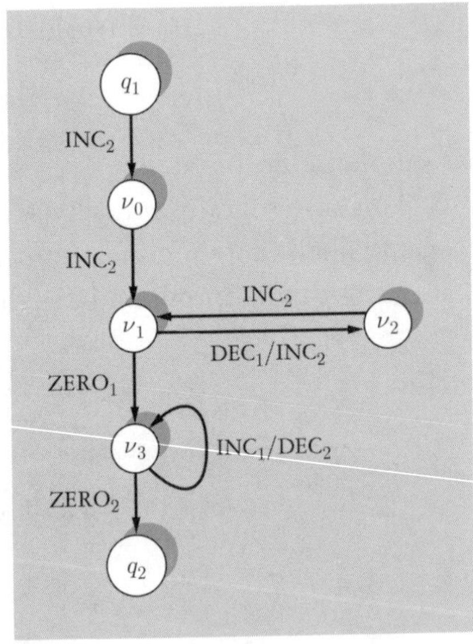

FIGURE 6.10: Simulating the stack operation PUSH2 with two counters.

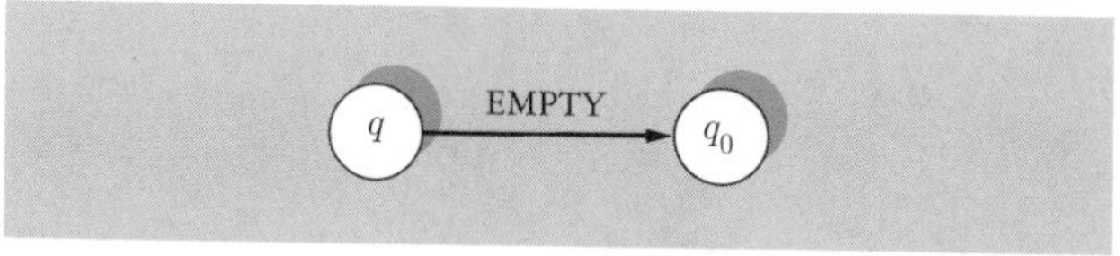

FIGURE 6.11: An instruction that uses the EMPTY operation.

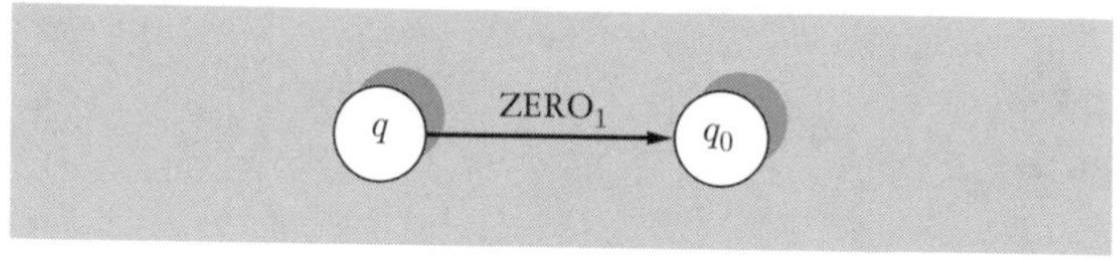

FIGURE 6.12: Simulating the stack operation EMPTY with two counters.

Since Λ denotes the number 0 in dyadic notation, simulating the stack's EMPTY operation is easy: We test whether $K1 = 0$. Suppose that P contains the instruction $(q \to q_0, \text{EMPTY}, \text{NOOP})$, as shown in Figure 6.11. Correspondingly, the program P' contains the instruction $(q \to q_0, \text{ZERO}, \text{NOOP}, \text{NOOP})$, as shown in Figure 6.12.

We have simulated pushing a digit on the stack by doubling the value of $K1$ and adding the digit. Correspondingly, popping a digit may be simulated by subtracting the digit from $K1$ and dividing by 2, where the digit must be chosen to make the division exact. In order to preserve determinism, we simulate both operations POP1 and POP2 via a single subprogram that determines which of them is applicable. Suppose that P contains the instructions

$$(q \to q_1, \text{POP1}, \text{NOOP})$$

$$(q \to q_2, \text{POP2}, \text{NOOP})$$

as shown in Figure 6.13.

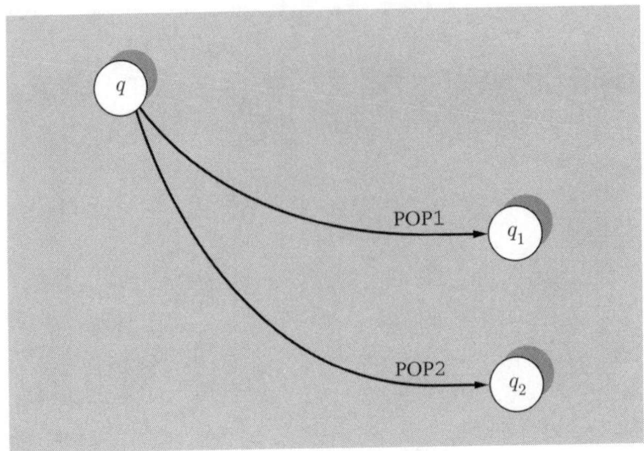

FIGURE 6.13: A single control state with a POP1 and a POP2 going from it.

Correspondingly, P' contains the instructions shown in Figure 6.14, which operate on configurations as follows:

$$\begin{aligned}(q, 2n+1, 0, x) &\overset{\Pi'}{\longmapsto} (\nu_1, 2n, 0, x)\\ &\overset{(\Pi')^{2n}}{\longmapsto} (\nu_1, 0, n, x)\\ &\overset{\Pi'}{\longmapsto} (\nu_2, 0, n, x)\\ &\overset{(\Pi')^{n}}{\longmapsto} (\nu_2, n, 0, x)\\ &\overset{\Pi'}{\longmapsto} (q_1, n, 0, x),\end{aligned}$$

and similarly

$$\begin{aligned}(q, 2n+2, 0, x) &\overset{\Pi'}{\longmapsto} (\nu_1, 2n+1, 0, x)\\ &\overset{(\Pi')^{2n}}{\longmapsto} (\nu_1, 1, n, x)\\ &\overset{\Pi'}{\longmapsto} (\nu_3, 0, n, x)\\ &\overset{\Pi'}{\longmapsto} (\nu_4, 0, n, x)\\ &\overset{(\Pi')^{n}}{\longmapsto} (\nu_4, n, 0, x)\\ &\overset{\Pi'}{\longmapsto} (q_2, n, 0, x).\end{aligned}$$

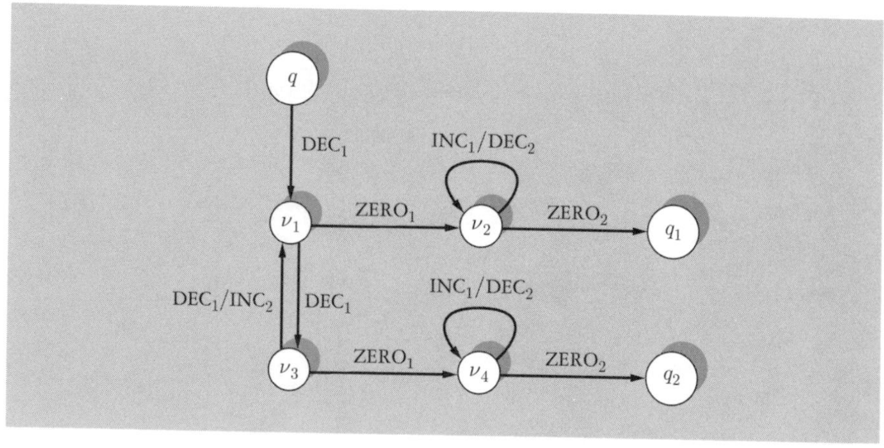

FIGURE 6.14: Simulating the stack operations POP1 and POP2 with two counters.

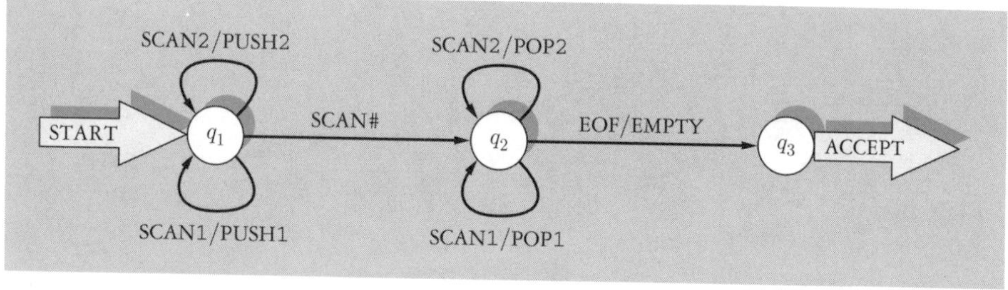

FIGURE 6.15: A DSA that accepts palindromes over $\{1,2\}$ with central marker.

It will be observed that this simulation requires many steps of P' in order to simulate one step of P.

EXAMPLE 6.23. Let P be the program shown in Figure 6.15, which accepts palindromes of the form $z\#z^R$ where $z \in \{1, 2\}^*$. The simulating program P' is shown in Figure 6.16 (we did not factor P although this is usually necessary in order to preserve determinism). Note that P is deterministic and has no infinite computations, but blocks on some inputs; P' also is deterministic and has no infinite computations, but blocks on exactly the same inputs as P.

■ ■ ■

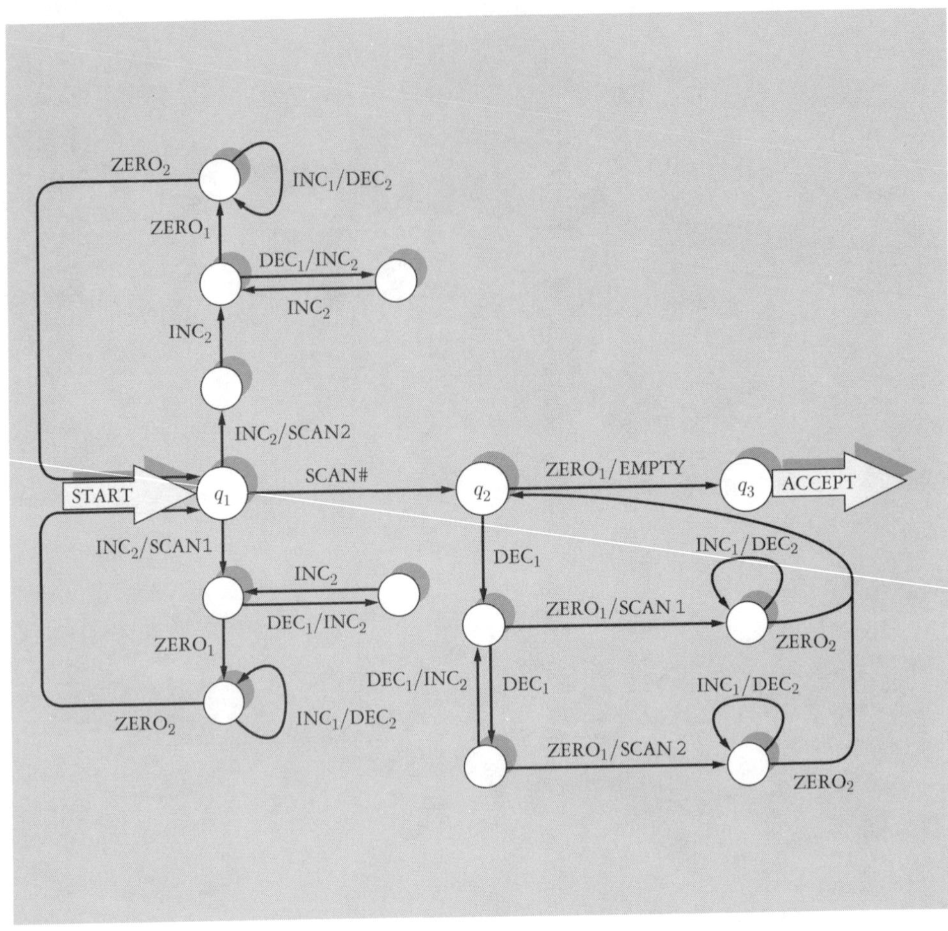

FIGURE 6.16: A deterministic 2-counter acceptor that accepts palindromes over $\{1,2\}$ with central marker.

Exercises

6.5-1 Informally show how two counters can simulate a stack with a k-character alphabet.

6.5-2 In each part of this exercise, refer to the simulation in this section of an SM via a 2-UCM, and use the same relation of representation.

(a) Construct a single subprogram with five control states that simulates both of the following instructions:

$$(q_1 \rightarrow q_1, \text{SCAN1}, \text{PUSH1})$$

$$(q_1 \rightarrow q_1, \text{SCAN2}, \text{PUSH2}).$$

(b) Using (a), simplify the program in Figure 6.16.

(c) Construct a single subprogram with seven control states that simulates both of the following instructions:

$$(q_1 \rightarrow q_3, \text{SCAN1}, \text{PUSH1})$$

$$(q_2 \rightarrow q_3, \text{SCAN2}, \text{PUSH2}).$$

Hint: The subprogram must have two initial control states.

6.5-3 Show how to simulate two stacks directly using three counters.

6.6 TWO COUNTERS SIMULATE ANY NUMBER OF COUNTERS

In the previous section we showed that two counters can simulate a stack. Consequently, $2k$ counters can simulate k stacks. In this section we show that two counters can simulate any number of counters. Consequently, two counters can simulate any number of stacks. In Chapter 7 we will show that two stacks can simulate a RAM, so two counters can simulate a RAM. Thus a pair of counters is extremely powerful.

We begin by showing how two counters can simulate three counters. Because we have seen that unsigned counters have the same computing power as signed counters, it suffices to prove the simulation for unsigned counters. Our treatment of simulation in this section will be fairly informal.

Let P be a program for a machine $[K1, K2, K3, \text{other}]$, where $K1$, $K2$, and $K3$ are unsigned counters. We will simulate P by a program P' for a machine $[\text{control}, C, \text{temp}, \text{other}]$, where C and temp are two unsigned counters. We describe the simulation informally. The values of $K1$, $K2$, and $K3$ will be encoded in the value of C; that is, the configuration (k_1, k_2, k_3, s)

of P is represented by the configuration $(0,\ 2^{k_1}3^{k_2}5^{k_3},\ 0,\ s)$ of P'. The operations on $K1$, $K2$, and $K3$ are simulated by multiplying or dividing C by 2, 3, or 5, using techniques we developed in the preceding section.

Below we present subprograms to perform each operation on each counter. The value in the counter called temp will be 0 at the beginning and end of each subprogram.

Increment $K1$: Multiply C by 2 as follows:

```
while C > 0 do begin
        C := C − 1; temp := temp + 2;
end;
while temp > 0 do begin
        C := C + 1; temp := temp − 1;
end;
```

Increment $K2$: Multiply C by 3 in similar fashion.
Increment $K3$: Multiply C by 5 in similar fashion.
Test whether $K1 = 0$: Test whether C is not divisible by 2 as follows:

```
even := true;
while C > 0 do begin
        C := C − 1; temp := temp + 1;
        if C = 0 then
                even := false
        else begin
                C := C − 1; temp := temp + 1;
        end;
end;
while temp > 0 do begin
        C := C + 1; temp := temp − 1;
end;
```

If the variable even is true, then the test fails; otherwise it succeeds.

Test whether $K2 = 0$: Test whether C is not divisible by 3 in similar fashion.

Test whether $K3 = 0$: Test whether C is not divisible by 5 in similar fashion.

Decrement $K1$: Divide C by 2 as follows:

```
test whether C is even as above;
if C is even then begin
    while C > 0 do begin
        C := C − 2; temp := temp + 1;
    end;
    while temp > 0 do begin
        C := C + 1; temp := temp − 1;
    end;
end;
```

If C is not even, then $K1$ is 0, so $K1$ cannot be decremented.

Decrement $K2$: Divide C by 3 in similar fashion.

Decrement $K3$: Divide C by 5 in similar fashion.

This completes the simulation of three counters by two counters. It will be observed that this simulation requires many steps of P' in order to simulate one step of P.

We have shown that two counters can simulate three counters. Therefore i counters can simulate $i+1$ counters for any $i \geq 2$. Thus, two counters can simulate three counters, which can simulate four counters, and so on for any positive integer k. By transitivity, two counters can simulate k counters.

Exercises

6.6-1 Show how two counters can directly simulate k counters. Hint: There are infinitely many prime numbers.

*6.7 COUNTER LANGUAGES AND PREFIX EQUIVALENCE

In Chapter 4 we applied the idea of prefix equivalence classes in order to show that certain languages are not regular. In this section we develop similar tools, which we apply to show that certain languages are not NCA languages. This is a hard section. We begin with some properties of stack machines, which include counter machines as a special case.

LEMMA 6.24. *Let P be a program for a machine* [stack] *that starts with an empty stack. We say that P* generates *a string s if P terminates in a final state with s on the stack. Then P generates a regular language. Furthermore, if P has p states, then L(P) is accepted by a p-state NFA.*

Proof: Let L be the language generated by P. Replacing each stack operation by its converse, we convert P to an NSM program that accepts L^R in the sense of Lemma 6.16. By that lemma, L^R is regular. Since the class of regular languages is closed under reversal, $(L^R)^R$ is regular, but that language is in fact L. ∎

LEMMA 6.25. *Let P be a program for a machine* [input, stack] *that starts with an empty stack. Define $x\ \rho\ s$ if there is a computation of P on input x that terminates in a final state with s on the stack. Then the class of regular languages is closed under ρ. Furthermore, if P has p states and R is accepted by an r-state NFA, then $R\rho$ is accepted by an $O(rp)$-state NFA.*

Proof: Let R be a regular language. Compose a nondeterministic finite generator for R with the NSM program P according to the construction implicit in Theorem 4.45. Use a pairing construction to merge controls; this multiplies the buffer size (a constant) and the number of control states in the two programs. The resulting NSM program generates $R\rho$, which must be regular by Lemma 6.24. ∎

Note that ρ is not necessarily a finite transduction because ρ could map $a^i b^j$ to c^{i-j}.

LEMMA 6.26. *Let P be an NSA. Define $x\ \rho\ s$ if there exist y and an accepting computation of P on input xy that includes a configuration in which the input holds y and the stack holds s. Then the class of regular languages is closed under ρ. Furthermore, if P has p states and R is accepted by an r-state NFA, then $R\rho$ is accepted by an $O(rp^2)$-state NFA.*

Proof: Let P's input alphabet be Σ, stack alphabet be Γ, control set be Q, start state be q_{start}, unique accepting state be q_{accept}, and sequel relation be Π. Define a relation σ from Σ^* to Γ^*Q by

$$x \; \sigma \; sq \iff (q_{\text{start}}, x, \Lambda) \overset{\Pi^*}{\mapsto} (q, \Lambda, s).$$

Let

$$S = \{sq : (\exists y)[(q, y, s) \overset{\Pi^*}{\mapsto} (q_{\text{accept}}, \Lambda, \Lambda)]\}.$$

Then $R\rho = (R\sigma \cap S)/Q$.

The relation σ is computed by an NSM program that holds the result on the stack; it simulates P until the input is empty, pushes P's control state on the stack, and then goes to a new accepting state. This NSM program has $p + 1$ control states. By Lemma 6.25, $R\sigma$ is an $O(rp)$-state NFA language.

The language S is accepted by an NSM program that holds its argument on the stack; it starts in a new control state, pops one character to determine a control state of P, and then simulates P by guessing its input y. This NSM program has $p + 1$ control states. By Lemma 6.16 S is a $(p + 1)$-state NFA language.

By the pairing construction, $R\sigma \cap S$ is an $O(rp^2)$-state NFA language. Since $R\rho = (R\sigma \cap S)/Q$, it is accepted by an NFA with the same number of control states. ∎

DEFINITION 6.27 (Strong Prefix Equivalence). With respect to a language L, we say that strings x and y are *strongly prefix inequivalent* if (a) x and y belong to PREFIX(L) and (b) every string z that witnesses that x or y is in PREFIX(L) also witnesses that x and y are prefix inequivalent, i.e., if both of the following conditions hold:

- $(\exists z_1)[xz_1 \in L]$ and $(\exists z_2)[yz_2 \in L]$
- $(\forall z)[xz \notin L$ or $yz \notin L]$

DEFINITION 6.28 (Internal Description). An *internal description* of a machine consists of the states of all devices except input and output; in other words it is a configuration minus the states of the input and output devices.

THEOREM 6.29. *If L is an NCA language, then the number of strings of length n or less that are strongly prefix inequivalent with respect to L is $O(n)$.*

Proof: A counter can be simulated by a stack with a 1-character alphabet. Therefore L is accepted by an NSA P with a 1-character stack alphabet. Let Q be the control set of P. As in Lemma 6.26, define $x \ \rho \ s$ iff there exists y such that there is an accepting computation of P on input xy that includes a configuration in which the input holds y and the stack holds s.

Let x be a string of length n or less belonging to PREFIX(L), and let $R = \{x\}$. Then R is accepted by a DFA with $n + 1$ states. By Lemma 6.26, $R\rho$ is accepted by an m-state NFA where $m = O(n|Q|^2)$. Since x is a prefix of a string in L, $R\rho$ is not empty, so $R\rho$ contains an element whose length is less than m by Exercise 4.4-7.

Now let $M = m|Q| + 1$, and assume that there are M strongly prefix-inequivalent strings $x_1, \ldots, x_M$ of length n or less. By the preceding paragraph, for each x_i, there exists y_i so that on input $x_i y_i$ the program P has an accepting computation that reaches a configuration where the input device stores y_i and the stack stores a string whose length is less than m. Since the stack has a 1-character alphabet, there are at most $m|Q|$ internal descriptions corresponding to such configurations. By the pigeonhole principle, there exist strings $x_i y_i$ and $x_j y_j$ in L that lead thus to identical internal descriptions after x_i or x_j has been read. Then $x_i y_j$ is in L, so x_i and x_j are not strongly prefix inequivalent. Therefore the number of strongly prefix-inequivalent strings of length n is at most $M - 1 = O(n|Q|^3) = O(n)$. ■

COROLLARY 6.30. $\{\mathtt{a}^i\mathtt{b}^j\mathtt{c}^j\mathtt{d}^i : i, j \geq 0\}$ *is not an NCA language.*

Proof: Let $L = \{\mathtt{a}^i\mathtt{b}^j\mathtt{c}^j\mathtt{d}^i : i, j \geq 0\}$. All strings of the form $\mathtt{a}^i\mathtt{b}^j$ are strongly prefix inequivalent with respect to L. There are at least $n^2/4$ such strings of length n or less. Therefore, by Theorem 6.29, L is not an NCA language. ■

Exercises

6.7-1 Prove that $L_{()[]}$ is not an NCA language.

6.7-2 Prove that the set of palindromes over $\{\mathtt{a}, \mathtt{b}\}$ with central marker is not an NCA language. Thus we have a language L such that L is a DSR language and $\overline{L}$ is an NCA language, but L is not an NCA language.

6.7-3 Prove that $\{\mathtt{a}^i\mathtt{b}^j\mathtt{c}^k\mathtt{d}^\ell\mathtt{e}^m\mathtt{f}^n : i \neq n \text{ and } j \neq m \text{ and } k \neq \ell\}$ is not an NCA language.

*6.7-4 Is $\{\mathtt{a}^i\mathtt{b}^j\mathtt{c}^k\mathtt{d}^\ell : i \neq \ell \text{ and } j \neq k\}$ an NCA language?

*6.7-5 Prove or disprove: If L is a DSR language and L and $\overline{L}$ are NCA languages, then L is a DCR language.

6.7-6 Prove that if L is a DCA language, then the number of strings of length n or less that are prefix inequivalent with respect to L is $O(n)$.

6.7-7
(a) Show how to compose nondeterministic programs as in Lemma 4.44 but without using an extra control.
(b) Improve Lemma 6.25 by showing that $R\rho$ is accepted by an rp-state NFA.
(c) Improve Lemma 6.26 by showing that $R\rho$ is accepted by an $r(p+1)^2$-state NFA.

6.8 CHAPTER SUMMARY

In this chapter, we proved that the class of CFLs is closed under finite transductions; this provides useful techniques for proving that certain languages are CFLs and that certain other languages are not CFLs. Next we showed how to determine whether a DSM program halts on all inputs, how to tell whether an SM program is a DSR, and how to convert a DSA to a DSR; the same applies to counter machines as well. We proved that every DCFL (DSA language) is recognized by a DSR and, in fact, is recognized by an on-line DSR. From that we deduced a variety of closure properties for DCFLs; we concluded that the set of palindromes, while an unambiguous CFL, is not a deterministic CFL. Therefore NSAs are more powerful than DSRs. Next we proved that two counters can simulate any number of stacks and counters. Finally, we generalized the notion of prefix equivalence and proved that NCAs are more powerful than DCRs, that NSAs are more powerful than NCAs, and that NCAs and DSRs have incomparable computing power.

Exercises

6.8-1 Let M be a machine [control, signed counter, input], where in addition to the ordinary operations of INC, DEC, ZERO, POS, and NEG, the signed counter is also equipped with the operation NONZERO, which tests whether the counter's value is different from zero. Let M' be a machine [control, signed counter, input], where the signed counter is not equipped with the operation NONZERO. Show informally how M' can simulate M.

6.8-2 Queues were defined in Exercise 1.1-1. Show informally how a machine [control, stack, stack, input] can simulate a machine [control, queue, input].

7

Computability

RECALL THAT A Turing machine has a control, a tape, and possibly input and output.[1] Turing defined his machines so as to model the capabilities of a human being working with pencil and

[1] Turing's original treatment differed in that he did not ever use separate devices for input or output as we do. Instead he used the tape for input and output as well as for memory.

paper. Turing modeled his tape after an endless supply of sheets of paper, upon which a mathematician can write formulas. The mathematician has a finite amount of internal memory (the mathematician's brain, which corresponds to the Turing machine's control). Assuming that the mathematician has limited perception, there is a limited number of distinguishable things that she could write on a single sheet of paper. Thus each sheet of paper holds a single character in a very large alphabet. The mathematician keeps the sheets of paper in order (say, left to right), and when she runs out, she buys more. Hence her supply of paper can be modeled as a sequence of characters extending arbitrarily far to the right, i.e., as an infinite tape. The tape head keeps track of which page the mathematician's head is currently looking at.

Recall that a RAM has a control, a random access memory, and input and output. We show that Turing machines have the same computational power as RAMs, as well as a number of other computational systems, such as rewriting systems and Herbrand–Gödel programs. In fact, it is generally believed that a Turing machine program can simulate *any* physically realizable computational process at all—including that of the most powerful digital computers or a human being. This belief is called *Church's thesis*.[2]

Informally, an *algorithm* is a "computational process" that takes a problem instance and in a finite amount of time produces a solution. In this book we have presented informal algorithms that solve numerous problems, e.g., converting a k-adic numeral to a decimal numeral, computing greatest common divisors, converting an NFA to a regular expression, converting an NFA to an equivalent DFA, minimizing a DFR, testing whether two DFRs recognize the same language, and testing whether a string belongs to a CFL. It is hard to make the definition of algorithm more precise except by saying that a computational process is anything that can be done by a program for a computing machine, and in that case one must accept that a human being with paper and pencil is a kind of computing machine. One interpretation

2 Church's thesis is not a mathematical theorem or axiom. Rather it is a generalization about the limitations of all known computing machines. Computer scientists believe Church's thesis in the same way that physicists believe in the conservation of energy. The development of real computers contradicting Church's thesis would be as startling as the development of perpetual motion machines.

of Church's thesis is that any algorithm at all can be implemented as a Turing machine program.

In order to understand the capabilities of real digital computers, we investigate the capabilities of Turing machines. It is notable that DTAs are equivalent to NTAs (Section 7.6); however, no efficient simulation of NTAs by DTAs is known (Chapter 9).

In order to understand the limitations of real digital computers, we investigate the limitations of Turing machines and we present certain languages that are provably not recognized by any Turing machine program. These languages formalize important problems that, assuming Church's thesis, cannot be solved by any algorithm. For example, there is no algorithm that determines which Turing machine programs halt or whether two Turing machine programs are equivalent; the same is true for computer programs in typical high-level languages, such as Pascal or LISP. There is no algorithm to determine whether a context-free grammar is ambiguous or whether two context-free languages are equal. There are also unsolvable problems outside of computer science. For example, there is no algorithm to determine whether a multivariate polynomial equation has an integer solution (Hilbert's tenth problem).

The study of computability also has applications to mathematical logic. By reasoning about computations, we will prove that there is no algorithm to determine whether a conclusion logically follows from a hypothesis in first-order logic.

7.1 TAPES AND TURING MACHINES

Tapes and Turing machines were introduced in Chapter 1. We begin this section with a review. Then we prove by several important simulations the equivalence of multitape, 1-tape, 2-stack, and 2-counter machines.

A tape holds a finite string and a read/write head that is located upon the character currently being examined. An operation on a tape consists of examining the character under the head, overwriting that character with a new character, moving the head left or right on the tape, or testing whether the head is at the leftmost end of the tape. It is not possible to move off the left end of the tape, but it is possible to extend the tape string by moving off the right end.

We write $\sqcup$ to denote a particular character that we think of as being blank, like "space" on a standard keyboard. The tape alphabet is assumed to contain the character $\sqcup$. When the head moves right from the right end of the tape, a blank is automatically concatenated to the right end of the tape string.

If Γ is the tape alphabet then we define a new alphabet

$$\boxed{\Gamma} = \left\{ \boxed{c} : c \in \Gamma \right\},$$

whose elements are assumed to be distinct from the elements of Γ. We write $\boxed{c}$ to denote a c that is under the tape head. Thus we write $x\boxed{c}y$ to denote that the tape holds the string xcy and that the c is under the head.

Formally, a tape with alphabet Γ (containing $\sqcup$) consists of the following:

realm: $\Gamma^*\boxed{\Gamma}\Gamma^*$

usual initial state: $\boxed{\sqcup}$

usual final states: $\Gamma^*\boxed{\Gamma}\Gamma^*$

repertory: $\{\text{SEE}c : c \in \Gamma\} \cup \{\text{PRINT}c : c \in \Gamma\} \cup$

$\{\text{MOVEL}, \text{MOVER}, \text{ATHOME}\}$

The tape operation SEEb is a test defined as follows (x and y denote strings over Γ, and a and b denote elements of Γ):

$$x\boxed{a}y\ \text{SEE}b \quad = \quad \begin{cases} x\boxed{a}y & \text{if } a = b \\ \text{undefined} & \text{otherwise.} \end{cases}$$

The tape operation PRINTb is defined as follows:

$$x\boxed{a}y\ \text{PRINT}b \quad = \quad x\boxed{b}y.$$

The tape operations MOVEL, MOVER, and ATHOME are defined as follows:

$$
\begin{array}{llll}
x\ a\ \boxed{b}\ y & \text{MOVEL} & = & x\ \boxed{a}\ b\ y, \\
\boxed{b}\ y & \text{MOVEL} & \text{is undefined.} & \\
x\ \boxed{a}\ b\ y & \text{MOVER} & = & x\ a\ \boxed{b}\ y, \\
x\ \boxed{a} & \text{MOVER} & = & x\ a\ \boxed{\sqcup}. \\
\boxed{b}\ y & \text{ATHOME} & = & \boxed{b}\ y.
\end{array}
$$

To simplify programs, it is customary to combine SEEa, PRINTb, and MOVED (where D indicates direction), in that order, into a single tape operation [SEEa, PRINTb, MOVED], i.e.,

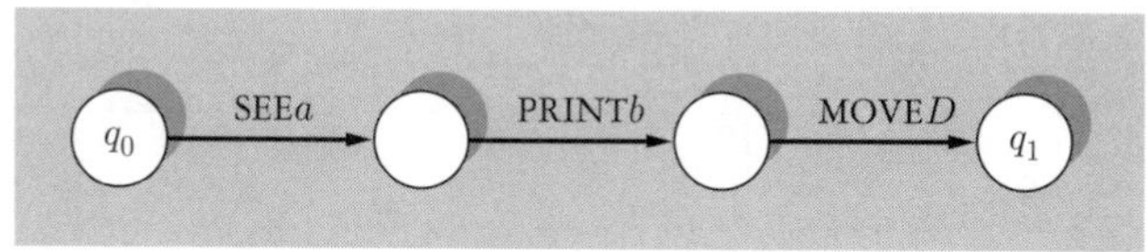

is abbreviated

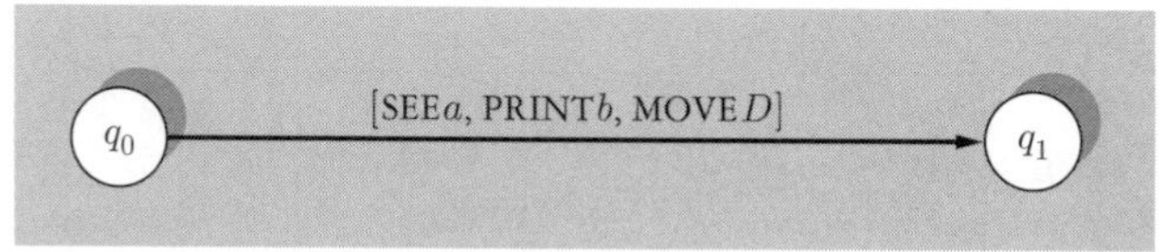

7.1.1 One Tape Simulates k Tapes

A machine with k tapes is called a *k-tape* Turing machine. We show that k tapes can be simulated by one tape.

Let P be a k-tape TM program. We may replace each tape alphabet by the union of all k of them, so, without loss of generality, let us assume that each tape of P has the same alphabet Γ. We will design a 1-tape TM program P' that simulates P. The tape alphabet of P' will be $\Gamma' = (\Gamma \cup \boxed{\Gamma})^k$. The nth character on the tape of P' represents all the nth characters, with or without a tape head, on every tape of P. The blank character in P' is $\sqcup^k$, and the tape of P' is initialized to contain $\boxed{\sqcup}^k$, representing the initially blank tapes of P with their heads on the home squares.

EXAMPLE 7.1. If P is a 4-tape TM with alphabet $\{\texttt{a}, \ldots, \texttt{z}, \sqcup\}$, then the contents of the four tapes in P might be:

a	b	c	$\boxed{\texttt{d}}$	e	f	g		

h	i	j	k	$\boxed{\texttt{l}}$	m	n	o	p

q	$\boxed{\texttt{r}}$	s	t	u	v	w		

x	y	z	$\boxed{\sqcup}$					

For clarity we have drawn a square around each character on each tape (two squares if the head is present). On tapes 1, 3, and 4, we have shown part of the blank area that is imagined to be to the right of the last character on a tape. It is convenient to depict the elements of Γ' vertically. The contents of P's four tapes are represented on a single tape in P' as follows:

a	b	c	$\boxed{\texttt{d}}$	e	f	g	$\sqcup$	$\sqcup$
h	i	j	k	$\boxed{\texttt{l}}$	m	n	o	p
q	$\boxed{\texttt{r}}$	s	t	u	v	w	$\sqcup$	$\sqcup$
x	y	z	$\boxed{\sqcup}$	$\sqcup$	$\sqcup$	$\sqcup$	$\sqcup$	$\sqcup$

For clarity, we have drawn a rectangle around each character on the single tape. The position of the tape head in P' is not shown. ■■■

To be precise, let P be a program for a machine [tape$_1$, ..., tape$_k$, other]. (The other device might incorporate a control, input, and output, for example.) Because we can factor P, we may assume that each instruction operates on at most one tape and possibly the other device. P will be simulated by a program P' for a machine [phase, tape, other], where phase is a control whose purpose we will describe shortly.

To simulate an instruction that uses tape i, we start at the left end of the tape in P' and move the head right in P' until we find the symbol corresponding to tape i's head in P. Then it is straightforward to simulate the instruction. To preserve determinism, the search for tape i's head is done simultaneously, using the same new states, for all instructions that use tape i. Finally, the tape head in P' is moved back to the home square, ready to simulate another instruction of P.

To be more precise, let $\pi = ([\text{SEE}a, \text{PRINT}b, \text{MOVE}D]_i, f)$, i.e., an instruction in P that performs the operation $[\text{SEE}a, \text{PRINT}b, \text{MOVE}D]$ on tape i and performs f on the other device. (The situation when π contains only zero, one, or two of the operations SEEa, PRINTb, MOVED is left as Exercise 7.1-4.) When we begin the simulation of an instruction, the tape head of P' is in the home position. π is simulated by moving the tape head right until we find a symbol on the tape that contains $\boxed{a}$ in the ith coordinate. That symbol is replaced by one with b in the ith coordinate, the head of P' moves in direction D, and the operation f is performed on the other device. After the head has moved, the symbol under the head is modified by replacing the character c in its ith coordinate by $\boxed{c}$, which represents P's new head position on tape i. Then the head of P' moves left to the home position, ready to simulate another instruction.

That informal simulation operates in three phases: finding P's head position, moving P's head position according to D, and returning home. We keep track of the phase by using the control called "phase," whose realm is {findhead, move, gohome}. The control called phase is initialized to findhead.

The detailed instructions for simulating $([\text{SEE}a, \text{PRINT}b, \text{MOVE}D]_i, f)$ are given below, where u takes on every value in $(\Gamma \cup \boxed{\Gamma})^{i-1}$, c takes on every value in Γ, and v takes on every value in $(\Gamma \cup \boxed{\Gamma})^{k-i}$.

$$\left\{\begin{array}{llll}(\text{findhead} \to \text{findhead} & , [\text{SEE}ucv, \text{MOVER}] & , \text{NOOP}), \\ (\text{findhead} \to \text{move} & , [\text{SEE}u\boxed{a}v, \text{PRINT}ubv, \text{MOVE}D] & , f \quad), \\ (\text{move} \to \text{gohome} & , [\text{SEE}ucv, \text{PRINT}u\boxed{c}v] & , \text{NOOP}), \\ (\text{gohome} \to \text{gohome} & , [\text{MOVEL}] & , \text{NOOP}), \\ (\text{gohome} \to \text{findhead} & , [\text{ATHOME}] & , \text{NOOP})\end{array}\right\}$$

That completes the simulation. The proof of correctness is left as an exercise. The simulation preserves determinacy. Although the simulation is not very efficient, observe that the number of steps spent in simulating a single instruction of P is bounded by twice the length of the tape string. We will use this fact when comparing the relative power of time-bounded machines in Chapter 9.

Because any positive number of tapes have the same computational power, usually k-tape Turing machines are simply called Turing machines or multitape Turing machines.

Exercises

7.1-1 Imagine that Turing's mathematician has no eraser, so she cannot overwrite symbols the way an ordinary tape head can. Define a write-once tape on which only blank characters can be overwritten. Prove that a write-once tape can simulate an ordinary tape.

7.1-2 When we factor a k-tape TM program so that each operation uses at most one tape, the resulting program may run k times slower than the original. Describe in words how to simulate an unfactored k-tape TM program directly by a 1-tape TM. Preserve determinism.

7.1-3 A two-way infinite tape is like a one-way infinite tape, but it extends infinitely far to the left and right, and it has no ATHOME instruction.
   (a) Define the realm and repertory of a two-way infinite tape.
   (b) Show how a two-way infinite tape can simulate a one-way infinite tape in lockstep.

(c) Show how a one-way infinite tape can simulate a two-way infinite tape in lockstep.

7.1-4 Refer to this section's simulation of k tapes by one tape.
(a) If π operates only on the other device, how can π be simulated in P'?
(b) How would you simulate $([\text{SEE}a]_i, f)$?
(c) How would you simulate $([\text{PRINT}b]_i, f)$?
(d) How would you simulate $([\text{MOVE}D]_i, f)$?

7.1-5 Prove the correctness of this section's simulation of k tapes by one tape.

7.1-6 A 2-*dimensional* tape (2-*D* tape) is a rectangular grid of tape squares extending infinitely far up and right. The operations SEEc and PRINTc are defined as usual. The ATLEFT and ATBOTTOM operations check that the tape head is on the left or bottom edge of the tape respectively. The MOVEL, MOVER, MOVEU, and MOVED operations move the tape head left, right, up, and down, respectively—except that it is not possible to move left or down past the edge of the tape.
(a) Formally define the realm and repertory of a 2-D tape. What is a reasonable initial state for a 2-D tape?
(b) Informally prove that a tape can simulate a 2-D tape.

7.1.2 Two Stacks Simulate a Tape

In this section we establish a fundamental relationship between stacks and tapes: Two stacks can simulate a tape. When we consider undecidability later in this chapter, this simulation will be the key to showing that many problems involving NSA languages, and consequently context-free languages, cannot be solved by any algorithm. As a corollary, we prove that two counters can simulate a tape. We will use this fact in proving the undecidability of some very important problems in mathematics and logic.

A tape will be simulated by two stacks and a control called "underhead." The first stack contains the string to the left of the tape head, underhead contains the character under the tape head, and the second stack contains the string to the right of the tape head but in reverse order.

EXAMPLE 7.2. The tape string `abc`[`d`]`efghij` is represented by (`abc`, `d`, `jihgfe`) on stack_1, underhead, and stack_2 (see the left half of

FIGURE 7.1: Two stacks and a control represent a tape. On the left the represented tape state is abc[d]efghij. On the right the represented tape state is the result of performing the operation MOVER, i.e., abcd[e]fghij. Observe that only the control state and the top character of each stack are modified.

Figure 7.1). The two characters adjacent to the tape head are stored at the tops of the two stacks so that characters can be transferred from one stack to the other while simulating the head's movement. ▪▪▪

The SEE operation is simulated by testing the value stored in the control called underhead. The PRINT operation is simulated by changing the value in underhead. The tape operation MOVER is simulated by pushing the value of underhead onto stack_1 and popping the top of stack_2 into underhead. Continuing the example above, when MOVER is performed the tape contents become abcd[e]fghij, which is represented by (abcd, e, jihgf), as depicted in the right half of Figure 7.1. The tape operation MOVEL is simulated by pushing the value of underhead onto stack_2 and popping the top of stack_1 into underhead. The tape operation ATHOME is simulated by testing whether the first stack is empty.

Let P be a program for a machine [tape, other] with tape alphabet Γ. We will simulate P by a program P' for a machine [stack_1, underhead, stack_2, other], where each stack alphabet is Γ and where underhead is a control whose realm is Γ. The stacks are initialized to Λ and underhead is initialized to ⊔. The details of the simulation are given in Table 7.1.

In Section 6.5 we showed that two counters can simulate a stack. Therefore four counters can simulate two stacks. We also showed how two counters can simulate four counters. Therefore two counters can simulate two stacks.

Instruction of P	*Instruction of P′*	*Remark*
(SEEa , f)	(NOOP , $a \to a$, NOOP , f)	
(PRINTa , f)	(NOOP , $c \to a$, NOOP , f)	for all $c \in \Gamma$
(MOVER , f)	(PUSHc , $c \to d$, POPd , f)	for all $c, d \in \Gamma$
(MOVEL , f)	(POPb , $c \to b$, PUSHc , f)	for all $b, c \in \Gamma$
(ATHOME , f)	(EMPTY , NOOP , NOOP , f)	

TABLE 7.1: Simulating a machine [tape, other] by a machine [stack, control, stack, other].

Since two stacks can simulate one tape, two counters can simulate one tape. Since one tape can simulate k tapes, two counters can simulate k tapes. Thus we have the following corollary:

COROLLARY 7.3. *Any multitape Turing machine can be simulated by a 2-counter machine.* ∎

Exercises

7.1-1 Let P be a nondeterministic 1-TM program with no input or output device. Construct an NCA that accepts all strings that are not traces of P.

7.1-2 Let P be a deterministic 1-TM program with no input or output device. Prove that the set of all strings that are not computations of P is not necessarily a CFL. Hint: For simplicity, encode each instruction of P as a single character.

7.2 PUTTING THE ARGUMENT ON A TAPE, STACK, OR COUNTER

A further standardization allows us to eliminate the input and output devices. This will simplify proofs later in this chapter and in Chapter 9, because it means fewer devices to simulate. To avoid encoding issues, assume that arguments and results are strings. We will describe how to eliminate I/O devices from 1-TMs, 2-SMs, 3-CMs, and 2-CMs.

1-TMs: We will simulate a 1-tape machine by a 1-tape machine without input or output. First we simulate the 1-tape machine by a 3-tape machine; then we combine these three tapes into one. Tape 1 simulates the original 1-TM's tape. Tape 2 is initialized to hold the argument, so SCANc is simulated by $[\text{SEE}c, \text{MOVER}]_2$, and EOF is simulated by $[\text{SEE}\sqcup]_2$. Tape 3 will hold the result; it is initialized to blank, and WRITEc is simulated by $[\text{PRINT}c, \text{MOVER}]_3$.

Now we simulate these three tapes using one tape. The start state for the simulating program will be ν_0. The argument starts on the tape. First, the program replaces each character c of the argument by the corresponding triple $(\sqcup, c, \sqcup)$. The instructions for this are $(\nu_0 \to \nu_0, [\text{SEE}c, \text{PRINT}(\sqcup, c, \sqcup), \text{MOVER}])$ for each nonblank character, $(\nu_0 \to \nu_1, [\text{SEE}\sqcup, \text{PRINT}(\sqcup, \sqcup, \sqcup)])$, $(\nu_1 \to \nu_1, [\text{MOVEL}])$, and $(\nu_1 \to q_{\text{start}}, \text{ATHOME})$. Then the program proceeds to simulate the 3-tape machine by a 1-tape machine as in Section 7.1.1. Once that part of the simulation is complete, the triples on the tape are replaced by the corresponding characters of the result in an analogous fashion, and the tape head is moved to the home square.

2-SMs: Now we simulate a machine [control, tape] that uses the tape to hold the argument and result by a machine [control, stack 1, underhead, stack 2]. The result will be held in reverse in stack 2. The argument $x_1 \cdots x_k$ starts on stack 1. First, the program moves the argument from stack 1 to stack 2 via the instructions $(\nu_{\text{start}} \to \nu_{\text{start}}, \text{POP}c, \text{NOOP}, \text{PUSH}c)$, reversing it in the process. Second, it pops the top character from stack 2 and stores it in a control called underhead. At this point the configuration is $(q_{\text{start}}, \Lambda, x_1, x_k \cdots x_2)$. Then the program proceeds to simulate the 1-tape machine by a 2-stack machine as in Section 7.1.2. Once that part of the simulation is complete, the configuration is $(q_{\text{accept}}, \Lambda, y_1, y_k \cdots y_2)$, where $y_1 \cdots y_k$ is the result. We finish the simulation by moving the character y_1 from the control underhead to the top of stack 2 via the instructions $(q_{\text{accept}} \rightarrow q_{\text{accept}}, \text{NOOP}, c \rightarrow \Lambda, \text{PUSH}c)$, so stack 2 holds $y_k \ldots y_1$.

3-CMs: We will show how to simulate a 1-TM by a 3-counter machine with no input or output device. Assume that the input and output alphabets of the TM have at most k characters, which may be renamed as $\{1, \ldots, k\}$. First, simulate the 1-TM by a 1-TM without input or output, as above.

Second, we will simulate that 1-TM by a machine [control, stack, tape] where the stack alphabet is $\{1\}$. The stack will initially hold $1^{k\text{-adic}(x)}$, where x is the argument. The stack will end up holding $1^{k\text{-adic}(y)}$, where y is the result. The program first copies the string from the stack to the tape; then, via some straightforward programming, it converts the value from monadic to k-adic. Now the input string is on the tape. The main part of the simulation is trivial, since the simulating machine has a tape. Once it is finished, the result is on the tape. The result is then converted from dyadic to monadic and moved to the stack.

The machine [control, stack, tape] can be converted to a 3-counter machine, because a counter can simulate a stack with a 1-character alphabet, and two counters can simulate a tape. The initial value of the first counter is the number $k\text{-adic}(x)$ and the final value is the number $k\text{-adic}(y)$.

2-CMs: Finally, we can simulate a 1-TM by a 2-CM without input or output; however, arguments and results are not represented in the way you might expect. First, simulate the 1-TM by a 3-CM without input or output as above. Recall from Section 6.6 that three counters can be simulated by two counters. In that simulation, the triple of counter values (c_1, c_2, c_3) is represented by the pair of counter values $(2^{c_1}3^{c_2}5^{c_3}, 0)$. Because c_1 holds the argument and result for the simulated machine, the first counter in the simulating machine is initialized to hold $2^{k\text{-adic}(x)}$, where x is the argument; it ends up holding $2^{k\text{-adic}(y)}$, where y is the result. Although this representation of arguments may seem inelegant, it is necessary. It is not possible to simulate a 1-TM by a 2-CM whose initializer is $x\alpha = (q_{\text{start}}, k\text{-adic}(x), 0)$.

Exercises

7.2-1 Show directly how a 1-TM program can be simulated by a 1-TM program that starts with its argument on the tape. Be informal.

7.2-2 Show directly how a 2-SM program can be simulated by a 2-SM program that starts with its argument on the first stack. Be informal.

*7.2-3 Prove that it is not possible to simulate a machine [control, input, output, tape] by a machine [control, output, unsigned counter, unsigned counter] whose initializer is $x\alpha = (q_{\text{start}}, \text{dyadic}(x), 0)$. (Hint: Prove that such a 2-CM cannot compute the function $f(x) = 2^x$.) Conclude that it is not possible to simulate a machine [control, input, output, tape] by a machine [control, unsigned counter, unsigned counter] whose initializer is $x\alpha = (q_{\text{start}}, \text{dyadic}(x), 0)$ and terminator is $(q_{\text{start}}, \text{dyadic}(y), 0)\omega = y$.

7.2-4 Let P be a DTR. Show how to construct an equivalent DTR P' that does not use the EOF test.

7.3 RANDOM ACCESS MEMORY

Recall that a RAM consists of a control, a random access memory, and possibly input and output devices. RAMs are like digital computers with limited repertories. We saw in Section 1.8 how to write RAM programs for some of the omitted operations like addition and multiplication. In fact, RAMs can be programmed to simulate any instruction currently available on digital computers. In this section, we prove that Turing machines can simulate RAMs; thus Turing machines are also as powerful as any real digital computer.

We show how a TM can simulate a RAM. The TM will have the following:

- several tapes, one to represent each of the RAM's registers
- one tape to represent the array MEM[ ]
- one "work" tape for intermediate calculations

Numbers will be represented on the tapes in binary.

The basic idea is to write Turing machine subroutines to simulate the RAM's register operations and to represent the RAM's memory as a list of ordered pairs $(i, \text{MEM}[i])$ stored sequentially. Then the Turing machine can access MEM[i] by searching for the pattern "$(i,$" on the tape. When MEM[i] changes, the ordered pairs to its right are copied over.

Register operations The register operations $+$, $-$, and halve can be performed by standard grade school algorithms using the work tape to hold the result, which is then copied to the destination register. The $\text{R}_a := 0$ operation is performed by overwriting R_a's tape with 0. The tests $\text{R}_a > \text{R}_b$ and $\text{R}_a = \text{R}_b$ are performed by subtracting and seeing whether the result is positive or zero respectively. R_a ODD and R_a EVEN are simulated by examining the low-order bit on R_a's tape.

Memory Location i in memory is represented as $(i, \text{MEM}[i])$, where the two numbers i and MEM[i] are written in dyadic. The entire memory array is represented as a sequence of such ordered pairs, one pair for each memory location in which a value has been written. The sequence of pairs can be written in any order, i.e,

$$(i_1, \text{MEM}[i_1])\,(i_2, \text{MEM}[i_2])\,\cdots\,(i_k, \text{MEM}[i_k]),$$

where $i_1, \ldots, i_k$ are distinct natural numbers.

$\text{R}_a := \text{MEM}[i]$ is implemented by moving the memory tape's head home; copying i to the work tape; looking for the pattern "$(i,$" on the memory tape; and, once a match is found, copying the next numeral to the tape representing R_a. Special case: If no match is found, then MEM[i] is uninitialized and so by convention is 0; therefore write $(i, 0)$ at the right end of the memory tape and overwrite 0 onto the tape representing R_a.

$\text{MEM}[i] := \text{R}_a$ is simulated by finding $(i, \text{MEM}[i]$ on the memory tape, copying the remainder of the memory tape to the work tape for safekeeping, overwriting $\text{MEM}[i]$ with the numeral on R_a's tape, and then copying the remainder of the memory tape back from the work tape. Special case: If no match is found, then write (i, R_a) at the end of the memory tape.

Thus, we have shown how a tape can simulate a random access memory. Using modern compilers, it is possible to mechanically translate programs written in high-level languages like Pascal, C, Fortran, or LISP into programs for a random access machine. (We will not give a formal proof of this fact.) Because it is tedious to write a TM or RAM program, we will henceforth describe algorithms using an informal high-level programming language. The reader will keep in mind that such informal algorithms can be translated by a competent programmer into high-level programs, which can in turn be simulated by TM programs.

7.4 UNIVERSAL TURING MACHINE PROGRAM

A *universal* Turing machine program is like a compiler or interpreter for deterministic Turing machine programs. It is a DTM program that solves the following problem:

Problem name: DTM emulation

Instance: a DTM program P and a string x

Answer: the result of running P on input x if P halts on input x, undefined otherwise

(Because a program has a fixed terminator, we actually need three different universal Turing machine programs: a universal DTR, a universal DTA, and a universal deterministic Turing transducer. The three programs are virtually identical, and they typically go by the same name. The construction below works equally well for all three.)

Here is the basic idea: We write a RAM program R that reads a DTM program P and a string x and then emulates the DTM program step by step on input x. Many such programs have been written in high-level languages, which can be mechanically translated into RAM programs by ordinary compilers, so we will just sketch a description of the RAM program R. Then we convert R to an equivalent 1-tape DTM program. For simplicity, we will emulate only 1-tape DTM programs.

As it scans its input, R stores the instructions of P in consecutive memory locations $1, \ldots, m$ and then stores the characters of x in consecutive memory locations $m+1, \ldots, n$. Register 1 is a pointer indicating the location of the next input character in memory; at the start of the emulation, this register holds the number $m+1$. Register 2 indicates the end of the input string in memory; it holds the number n. Memory locations $n+1$ and higher hold the sequence of characters on P's tape. Register 3 indicates the location of the tape head in memory. Register 4 holds P's control state.

Based on the information in its registers and memory, R can easily determine the control state, the next input character or end of input, the character under P's tape head, and whether the head is at the left end of the tape. To emulate a single instruction of P, R looks through the entire list of P's instructions for one that is applicable and then updates the control state, input pointer, tape character, and tape location accordingly. If that instruction produces output, then R writes the same character on its output device. If none of P's instructions is applicable, then R blocks (as does P). If P accepts or rejects, then R does likewise.

That completes the description of the RAM program R that emulates DTM programs. Because DTMs simulate RAMs, such an emulator can be converted to an equivalent DTM program, which is thus a universal TM program, which we will call U.

We have avoided one subtle issue in designing the universal TM program, namely, how to represent U's argument and result. The argument to U consists of a program P that has arbitrary input, tape, and output alphabets, as well as a string x over P's input alphabet. However, U's input alphabet, output alphabet, and tape alphabet are fixed. We resolve this issue by encoding P's characters, control states, and instructions as strings over $\{0, 1\}$. Each of these strings can be represented as a single binary number by the RAM program R.

Because control sets, input alphabets, output alphabets, and stack alphabets are finite, we can assign an arbitrary order to their elements. The ith element of one of these finite sets will be represented by $1^i 0$. The other letters that appear in instructions—parentheses, commas, arrows, and the letters that make up the operations' names—form a fixed finite set. We can encode those letters using any fixed-length binary code. For concreteness, we replace arrow (→) by underscore (_) and use the ASCII code, which represents every character on the typewriter keyboard by an 8-bit binary string. For example, $(3 \to 5, \text{SCAN}\,\texttt{c})$ is encoded as 00101000111001011111111100010-110001010011010000110100000101001110111000101001.

We represent a set of instructions as a sequence of codes for each instruction in the set. We represent a DTM program as the sequence of codes for its initial control state, its set of accepting control states, its set of rejecting control states, its set of nonfinal control states, and its instruction set.

As they are read, the strings over $\{0, 1\}$ that represent characters, control states, and instructions can easily be translated into numbers by the RAM program R that emulates DTM programs. It is these numbers that are stored in R's registers and memory locations.

The universal Turing machine program is used whenever an algorithm takes a DTM program P as input and then runs P. Because it is obvious that we can run programs, this use is typically implicit.

EXAMPLE 7.4. For example, let

$$K_{xy} = \{(x, y) : \text{DTM program } x \text{ halts on input } y\}.$$

We will construct a DTA that accepts K_{xy}. First, let us describe an informal algorithm that accepts K_{xy}:

> input (x, y);
> run DTM x on input y;
> accept;

The statement "input (x, y)" means "scan the entire input, which is assumed to represent the pair (x, y), and store the strings x and y someplace useful." Observe that the informal algorithm accepts if and only if x halts on input y.

We can convert that informal algorithm to a DTA that stores the strings x and y on a work tape and then uses a modified version of the universal TM that takes its input from an extra tape. In the rest of this chapter and in Chapter 8, we will describe algorithms in this informal style for the sake of readability. Such algorithms can readily be converted to TM programs if desired.

There is also a slick, unstructured way of producing a DTA that accepts K_{xy}. Start with the universal DTM program U. Produce a DTA P by converting all of U's final states to accepting states and removing U's output device. Then

$$P \text{ accepts } (x, y) \iff U \text{ halts on } (x, y) \iff x \text{ halts on } y \iff (x, y) \in K_{xy}.$$

∎∎∎

Exercises

7.4-1 Define and construct a universal NTM program.

*7.5 HERBRAND–GÖDEL COMPUTABILITY

Herbrand and Gödel[3] defined a recursive programming system. A Herbrand–Gödel program (HG program, for short) consists of a set of function symbols; a set of variables whose values are natural numbers; and a set of equations involving the function symbols, the variables, and natural numbers. Since strings can be encoded as natural numbers, HG programs may use strings; in particular, there is an HG program that concatenates a string x with a character c to form xc (see Exercise 7.5-4).

The number 0 and the successor function $s(n) = n + 1$ are predefined in every HG program. By repeated application of $s(\cdot)$, we obtain the positive integers $s(0) = 1$, $s(s(0)) = 2$, $s(s(s(0))) = 3$, and so on.

The letters u, v, w, x, y, z, possibly subscripted, denote variables. The letters f, g, h, possibly subscripted, denote function symbols. Words of two letters or more, possibly subscripted, denote functions as well. For example, pred and pred_c are function symbols. The number of arguments to a function is any fixed natural number. (A function of zero arguments

[3] Pronounced "GURD'l."

is a constant.) Henceforth we will use the terms "function" and "function symbol" interchangeably.

A variable x is a *formula*. If $e_1, \ldots, e_k$ are formulas and f is a function of k arguments, then $f(e_1, \ldots, e_k)$ is a formula.

If $e_1, \ldots, e_k$ and e are formulas and f is a function of k arguments, then $f(e_1, \ldots, e_k) = e$ is a *defining equation*. By substituting numbers for the variables in the expressions $e_1, \ldots, e_k$ and e, we may determine the value of f at one list of arguments.

EXAMPLE 7.5. Defining equations for addition are

$$\begin{aligned} \text{add}(x, 0) &= x \\ \text{add}(x, s(y)) &= s(\text{add}(x, y)). \end{aligned}$$

Substituting 3 for x in $\text{add}(x, 0) = x$, we find $\text{add}(3, 0) = 3$. Substituting 3 for x and 0 for y in $\text{add}(x, s(y)) = s(\text{add}(x, y))$, we find $\text{add}(3, 1) = s(\text{add}(3, 0)) = s(3) = 4$. It is not hard to see that $\text{add}(x, y) = x + y$ (Exercise 7.5-1(a)). Henceforth we are justified in writing $x + y$ to denote $\text{add}(x, y)$. ■■■

EXAMPLE 7.6. It is not hard to define the other arithmetic functions. Building on the previous example, we may write an HG program for multiplication. The additional defining equations are

$$\begin{aligned} \text{mult}(x, 0) &= 0 \\ \text{mult}(x, y + 1) &= \text{mult}(x, y) + x. \end{aligned}$$

Henceforth we write $x * y$ to denote $\text{mult}(x, y)$. The following equations define division (with truncation):

$$\begin{aligned} \text{divide}(x, x + y + 1) &= 0 \\ \text{divide}(x + y, y) &= \text{divide}(x, y) + 1. \end{aligned}$$

Substituting 3 for x and 2 for y in $\text{divide}(x + y, y) = \text{divide}(x, y) + 1$, we find $\text{divide}(5, 2) = \text{divide}(3, 2) + 1$. Substituting 1 for x and 2 for y in $\text{divide}(x + y, y) = \text{divide}(x, y) + 1$, we find $\text{divide}(3, 2) = \text{divide}(1, 2) + 1$. Substituting 1 for x and 0 for y in $\text{divide}(x, x + y + 1) = 0$, we find divide$(1, 2) = 0$. Therefore, divide$(3, 2) = 0 + 1 = 1$ and divide$(5, 2) = 1 + 1 = 2$.

The following equation defines subtraction:

$$\text{minus}(x + y, y) = x.$$

Note that minus(x, y) is undefined if $x < y$. The monus function extends subtraction to a total function that is 0 when $x < y$:

$$\begin{aligned} \text{monus}(x + y, y) &= x \\ \text{monus}(x, x + y) &= 0. \end{aligned}$$

■ ■ ■

HG programs compute the same partial functions as the most powerful realistic models of computations. (However, we do not not permit HG programs to compute multiple-valued functions, because expressions like monus$(f(x), f(x))$ become confusing when $f(x)$ is multiple-valued.)

THEOREM 7.7. *The Turing computable partial functions are the same as the Herbrand–Gödel computable partial functions.*

Proof: Part 1: We show that every Turing computable partial function is Herbrand–Gödel computable. Assume that f is a Turing computable partial function. Then f is computed by a deterministic 2-counter machine program P. For concreteness, let P be a deterministic transducer that runs on a machine [control, input, output, $K1$, $K2$] where $K1$ and $K2$ are counters. Standardize P so that each instruction operates on the input or exactly one of the counters, P has a unique accepting control state, and P cleans up before accepting. To be specific, we may assume that there is a unique accepting state q_{accept} such that P accepts if and only if its configuration has the form $(q_{\text{accept}}, \Lambda, y, 0, 0)$. For each state q of M, we will define a function f_q. Our goal is that $f_q(x, k_1, k_2)$ should be the result of running program P starting from the configuration $(q, x, \Lambda, k_1, k_2)$ rather than starting from the initial configuration determined by α.

To each instruction in P there corresponds an equation in our Herbrand–Gödel program H. Suppose, for example, that P contains the instruction $(q \rightarrow r, \text{SCAN}c, \text{NOOP}, \text{NOOP}, \text{NOOP})$. If P reaches the configuration (q, cx, y, k_1, k_2) in a partial computation, P must next reach the configuration (r, x, y, k_1, k_2), because P is deterministic and that instruction is

Instruction of P	*Equation in H*
$(q \to r, \text{SCAN}c, \text{NOOP}, \text{NOOP}, \text{NOOP})$	$f_q(cx, k_1, k_2) = f_r(x, k_1, k_2)$
$(q \to r, \text{EOF}, \text{NOOP}, \text{NOOP}, \text{NOOP})$	$f_q(\Lambda, k_1, k_2) = f_r(\Lambda, k_1, k_2)$
$(q \to r, \text{NOOP}, \text{WRITE}c, \text{NOOP}, \text{NOOP})$	$f_q(x, k_1, k_2) = cf_r(x, k_1, k_2)$
$(q \to r, \text{NOOP}, \text{NOOP}, \text{INC}, \text{NOOP})$	$f_q(x, k_1, k_2) = f_r(x, k_1 + 1, k_2)$
$(q \to r, \text{NOOP}, \text{NOOP}, \text{DEC}, \text{NOOP})$	$f_q(x, k_1 + 1, k_2) = f_r(x, k_1, k_2)$
$(q \to r, \text{NOOP}, \text{NOOP}, \text{ZERO}, \text{NOOP})$	$f_q(x, 0, k_2) = f_r(x, 0, k_2)$
$(q \to r, \text{NOOP}, \text{NOOP}, \text{NOOP}, \text{INC})$	$f_q(x, k_1, k_2) = f_r(x, k_1, k_2 + 1)$
$(q \to r, \text{NOOP}, \text{NOOP}, \text{NOOP}, \text{DEC})$	$f_q(x, k_1, k_2 + 1) = f_r(x, k_1, k_2)$
$(q \to r, \text{NOOP}, \text{NOOP}, \text{NOOP}, \text{ZERO})$	$f_q(x, k_1, 0) = f_r(x, k_1, 0)$

TABLE 7.2: Converting a deterministic 2-CM program P to a Herbrand–Gödel program H.

applicable. Therefore $f_q(cx, k_1, k_2) = f_r(x, k_1, k_2)$. This explains the first Herbrand–Gödel equation in Table 7.2. The rest are similar.

In addition we have an equation that corresponds to acceptance in P,

$$f_{q_{\text{accept}}}(\Lambda, 0, 0) = \Lambda,$$

and the result of H is given by

$$f(x) = f_{q_{\text{start}}}(x, 0, 0).$$

Suppose that there exists a computation fragment of P that starts in configuration (q, wx, y, k_1, k_2) and ends in configuration (r, x, yz, k_1', k_2'). We assert that the Herbrand–Gödel program H derives

$$f_q(wx, k_1, k_2) = zf_r(x, k_1', k_2').$$

This can be proved by induction on the length of the computation fragment (Exercise 7.5-6(a)). In particular, if there is a computation that starts in configuration $(q_{\text{start}}, w, \Lambda, 0, 0)$ and ends in configuration $(q_{\text{accept}}, \Lambda, z, 0, 0)$, then

$$f(w) = f_{q_{\text{start}}}(w, 0, 0) = zf_{q_{\text{accept}}}(\Lambda, 0, 0) = z\Lambda = z;$$

i.e., H derives $f(w) = z$.

Conversely, suppose that the Herbrand–Gödel program H derives

$$f_q(wx, k_1, k_2) = zf_r(x, k_1', k_2').$$

We assert that for every y there exists a computation fragment of P that starts in configuration (q, wx, y, k_1, k_2) and ends in configuration (r, x, yz, k_1', k_2'). This can be proved by induction on the length of the derivation (Exercise 7.5-6(b)). If $f(w) = z$, then, in particular,

$$f_{q_{\text{start}}}(w, 0, 0) = f(w) = z = zf_{q_{\text{accept}}}(\Lambda, 0, 0),$$

and so there is a computation of P that starts in the configuration $(q_{\text{start}}, w, \Lambda, 0, 0)$ and ends in configuration $(q_{\text{accept}}, \Lambda, z, 0, 0)$; i.e., P outputs z on input w.

Part 2: We show that every Herbrand–Gödel computable partial function is Turing computable. Let H be a Herbrand–Gödel program. It is easy to write a RAM program that tests whether a particular string is a derivation in H and whether the last line of the derivation is of the form $f(w) = z$ for given f and w. In other words, a RAM program may determine whether a string is a derivation of $f(w) = z$ in H. To evaluate $f(w)$, a nondeterministic RAM program may guess a string, halting with result z if that string is a derivation of $f(w) = z$ in H. That nondeterministic program can be simulated deterministically by trying all possible guess strings in order. Because TMs can simulate RAMs, there is a deterministic Turing machine program that computes f. ∎

Exercises

7.5-1 In each part, refer to the defining equations given in this section.

(a) Prove that the value of $\text{add}(x, y)$ is $x + y$.

(b) Prove that the value of $\text{mult}(x, y)$ is $x * y$.

(c) Prove that the value of divide(x, y) is $\lfloor x/y \rfloor$.

7.5-2 Write HG programs that compute the following functions:

(a) fact$(n) = n!$

(b) pow$(x, y) = x^y$

(c) modulo$(x, y) = x \bmod y$

7.5-3 Let the constants false and true denote two distinct natural numbers. Write HG programs for the following functions:

(a) greater$(x, y) =$ true if $x > y$, false otherwise.

(b) prime$(x) =$ true if x is a prime number, false otherwise.

7.5-4 **HG programs on strings.** We can represent strings over Σ as natural numbers written in $|\Sigma|$-adic.

(a) We define the total function $s_c(z) = zc$. Write an HG program that computes s_c.

(b) Let pred$_c$ be the partial function that removes a c from the end of the string x. Write an HG program that computes pred$_c$.

(c) Let concat$(x, y) = xy$, the concatenation of strings x and y. Write an HG program that computes concat.

7.5-5 By modifying the simulation of 2-counter machines, show directly how a Herbrand–Gödel program can simulate a deterministic 2-stack machine program.

7.5-6 (a) Refer to part 1 of the proof of Theorem 7.7. Suppose that there exists a computation fragment of P that starts in configuration (q, wx, y, k_1, k_2) and ends in configuration (r, x, yz, k_1', k_2'). Prove that the Herbrand–Gödel program H derives

$$f_q(wx, k_1, k_2) = zf_r(x, k_1', k_2').$$

Hint: Prove it for single instructions and use induction.

(b) Refer to part 2 of the proof of Theorem 7.7. Suppose that the Herbrand–Gödel program H derives

$$f_q(wx, k_1, k_2) = zf_r(x, k_1', k_2').$$

Prove that for every y there exists a computation fragment of P that starts in configuration (q, wx, y, k_1, k_2) and ends in configuration (r, x, yz, k_1', k_2').

7.6 RECURSIVE AND RECURSIVELY ENUMERABLE SETS

In the early to middle 1900s several researchers, with varied motivations, defined what are now known as the recursive or computable functions. Turing defined his functions to be the ones computable by Turing machines, and he called them *computable*. Herbrand and Gödel defined their functions in a recursive language, and they also called them *computable*. Kleene defined his functions in a functional language, and he called them *recursive*. Thuë defined his functions via rewriting systems. All of the definitions were shown to be equivalent, and the names "computable" and "recursive" continue to be used synonymously. Based on this evidence, Church hypothesized that the functions computable by algorithms are precisely those computable in the sense of Turing. This conjecture is known as *Church's thesis*.

We call a function or partial function *recursive* or *computable* if it is computed by a DTM. If a total function is recursive, it is customarily called a *total recursive function*, rather than the more logical "recursive total function." If a partial function is recursive, it is customarily called a *partial recursive function*; again, "recursive partial function" would be more logical, but historical usage prevails. The term *recursive function* is synonymous with "total recursive function"; however, we prefer the latter because it is more precise. Recall that every total function is a partial function, so every total recursive function is a partial recursive function.

DEFINITION 7.8 (Recursive Functions)

- A *partial recursive* function is a partial function computed by a DTM program.
- A *total recursive* function is a total function computed by a DTM program.

A language L is called *recursive* if L is recognized by a Turing machine or, equivalently, if L's characteristic function χ_L is total recursive. In referring to languages, the terms "recursive" and "decidable" are used interchangeably. Languages that are not recursive are called *nonrecursive* or *undecidable*. (The word "undecidable" has a different meaning in the field of mathematical logic. We will discuss mathematical logic and its connections to computability in Sections 7.12 and 8.3.)

A language L is called *recursively enumerable* (abbreviated r.e.) if L is accepted by an NTA or, equivalently, if L is the domain of a partial recursive function (recall that the domain of a partial function f is the set of inputs x for which $f(x)$ is defined). In this section, we will prove that NTAs are equivalent to DTAs, yielding another characterization of the r.e. languages.

We repeat the definitions of recursive and recursively enumerable languages below:

DEFINITION 7.9 (Recursive and Recursively Enumerable Languages). A language L is

- *recursive* if L is recognized by a DTR.
- *recursively enumerable* (*r.e.*) if L is accepted by an NTA.
- *co-r.e.* if $\overline{L}$ is accepted by an NTA or, equivalently, if $\overline{L}$ is r.e.

Equivalently, L is r.e. iff L is generated by an NTM program (see Exercise 2.10-4(a) for a definition of generators); this motivates the word "enumerable" in the name. The terms "recursive" and "r.e." are applicable to sets of objects other than strings if we represent objects as strings in the standard way (cf. Section 2.1). For example, we can talk about r.e. sets of DTM programs, recursive sets of natural numbers, recursive sets of integers, or recursive sets of ordered pairs of strings.

EXAMPLE 7.10. Examples of recursive languages include the set of prime numbers, the set of composite numbers and the set of 4-colorable graphs (suitably encoded as strings), because we can write programs in high-level languages to recognize them. Another example is any CFL, because it is recognized by the CYK algorithm or Earley's algorithm.

Examples of recursively enumerable languages include the transfer relation of any particular NTM program and the set of programs for a machine [control, tape] that have at least one complete computation. ■ ■ ■

EXAMPLE 7.11 (K_{xy} is r.e.). Recall that

$$K_{xy} = \{(x, y) : \text{DTM program } x \text{ halts on input } y\}.$$

By Example 7.4, K_{xy} is accepted by an NTA. Therefore K_{xy} is r.e. ∎∎∎

We end this section by proving five important properties of recursive and r.e. languages:

- L is r.e. if and only if L is accepted by a DTA; i.e., it does not matter whether we define recursive enumerability in terms of NTAs or DTAs.
- L is r.e. if and only if there exists a recursive language R such that

$$x \in L \iff (\exists y)[(x, y) \in R].$$

- L is recursive if and only if L is r.e. and $\overline{L}$ is r.e.
- Let L be a nonempty set. L is r.e. if and only if L is the range of a total recursive function.
- Let L be a nonempty set. L is recursive if and only if L is the range of a total recursive function that is nondecreasing. (Here we identify strings with natural numbers and use numerical order.)

We are about to study problems about programs and computations. In order to do so in our framework, we will need to represent programs and computations as strings. *A sequence of instructions is a string* in a sense that we will make precise. Fix a machine M, and fix the realms and repertories of all of M's devices. Since each device has a finite repertory, there are a finite number of possible instructions for M. Let Σ be this set of instructions. Any sequence of instructions for M is a string over Σ.

EXAMPLE 7.12. Let M be a machine [control, input] with input alphabet $\{\mathtt{a}, \mathtt{b}\}$ and control set $\{0, 1\}$. The set of all possible instructions for M is

$$\{0 \to 0, 0 \to 1, 1 \to 0, 1 \to 1\} \times \{\text{SCAN}\mathtt{a}, \text{SCAN}\mathtt{b}, \text{EOF}, \text{NOOP}\}$$

$$\begin{aligned}= \{&(0 \to 0, \text{SCAN}\mathtt{a}), (0 \to 0, \text{SCAN}\mathtt{b}), (0 \to 0, \text{EOF}), (0 \to 0, \text{NOOP}),\\ &(0 \to 1, \text{SCAN}\mathtt{a}), (0 \to 1, \text{SCAN}\mathtt{b}), (0 \to 1, \text{EOF}), (0 \to 1, \text{NOOP}),\\ &(1 \to 0, \text{SCAN}\mathtt{a}), (1 \to 0, \text{SCAN}\mathtt{b}), (1 \to 0, \text{EOF}), (1 \to 0, \text{NOOP}),\\ &(1 \to 1, \text{SCAN}\mathtt{a}), (1 \to 1, \text{SCAN}\mathtt{b}), (1 \to 1, \text{EOF}), (1 \to 1, \text{NOOP})\},\end{aligned}$$

a 16-element set that we call Σ. An example of a 2-character string over Σ is $(0 \to 0, \text{SCAN}\mathtt{a})(1 \to 1, \text{EOF})$. ■■■

Recall that a computation is a sequence of instructions that lead from an initial configuration to a final configuration. Thus the set of computations of a program P on input x is a language, which we denote $\mathcal{C}_P(x)$. For historical reasons, computations are also called *valid* computations.

EXAMPLE 7.13. Continuing the example above, we write a program P for M that accepts all even-length strings over $\{\mathtt{a}, \mathtt{b}\}$. The initial state is 0, and the final state is 0. The instruction set of P is

$$\{(0 \to 1, \text{SCAN}\mathtt{a}), (0 \to 1, \text{SCAN}\mathtt{b}), (1 \to 0, \text{SCAN}\mathtt{a}), (1 \to 0, \text{SCAN}\mathtt{b})\}.$$

One particular computation of P is

$$(0 \to 1, \text{SCAN}\mathtt{a})(1 \to 0, \text{SCAN}\mathtt{b})(0 \to 1, \text{SCAN}\mathtt{a})(1 \to 0, \text{SCAN}\mathtt{a}),$$

which is a 4-character string over Σ. ■■■

If P is a program, we write $\mathcal{C}(P)$ to denote the set of valid computations of P, i.e.,

$$\mathcal{C}(P) = \bigcup_x \mathcal{C}_P(x).$$

EXAMPLE 7.14. Then, continuing the preceding example, we have

$$\begin{aligned}\mathcal{C}(P) = \Big(&\big((0 \to 1, \text{SCAN}\mathtt{a}) \cup (0 \to 1, \text{SCAN}\mathtt{b})\big)\\ &\big((1 \to 0, \text{SCAN}\mathtt{a}) \cup (1 \to 0, \text{SCAN}\mathtt{b})\big)\Big)^*.\end{aligned}$$ ■■■

Next we show that if P is a suitably standardized program for a machine M, then the computations of P can be recognized by another program for M. This is useful because it implies that a nondeterministic program for M can guess a computation of P character by character and check its validity.

LEMMA 7.15. *Let M be a machine* $[\text{input}, \text{output}, d_1, \ldots, d_k]$ *where each* d_i *denotes a device other than input or output. Let P be a program for M whose input device has been standardized so that after* EOF *has been performed no instructions with input operations can be reached.*

(i) $\mathcal{C}(P)$ *is recognized by a program for a machine* $[\text{input}, d_1, \ldots, d_k]$.

(ii) If x is a string, then $\mathcal{C}_P(x)$ *is recognized by a program for a machine* $[\text{control}, \text{input}, d_1, \ldots, d_k]$.

Proof

(i) The computation can be checked step by step. Formally, we treat each instruction in a computation as a single character. Then $\mathcal{C}(P)$ is recognized by a program with the following instruction set: $\{(\text{SCAN}i, f_1, \ldots, f_k) : i = (f_{\text{in}}, f_{\text{out}}, f_1, \ldots, f_k)$ for some f_{in} and f_{out}, and i is an instruction in $P\}$. The initial and final states of each device are as in program P.

(ii) The set of all sequences of instructions whose SCAN operations spell out x is a regular set (depending on x). The intersection of $\mathcal{C}(P)$ with this regular set is recognized by a program for a machine [control, input, $d_1, \ldots, d_k$] by Corollary 4.40(iii). ∎

THEOREM 7.16

(i) Let P be an NTM program. The set of accepting computations of P is recursive.

(ii) Let P be an NTM program and let x be a string. The set of accepting computations of P on input x is recursive.

Proof: Change all nonaccepting final states of P to nonfinal states. The set of computations of the resulting program is exactly the set of accepting computations of P. Now the result follows by Lemma 7.15. ∎

As we just discussed, a sequence of instructions for a machine M is a string over a finite alphabet. If we number the characters in that alphabet 1 through k, then each string corresponds to a unique k-adic number. We say that this k-adic number *encodes* the sequence of instructions. Observe that digits can be obtained effectively by taking remainders modulo k. We will use this observation in proving the equivalence of NTAs and DTAs.

LEMMA 7.17. *L is r.e. iff L is accepted by a DTA.*

Proof: If L is r.e., then L is accepted by an NTA P. Testing whether P accepts x can be accomplished by searching for a sequence of instructions that happens to be an accepting computation of P with input x. We can try all such sequences by trying all nonnegative integers in increasing order, as follows:

```
i := 0;
while i does not encode an accepting computation of P on input x do
        i := i + 1;
accept;
```

By Theorem 7.16, we can determine whether a particular sequence of instructions is an accepting computation, so the algorithm above can be implemented as a deterministic RAM program, which can be simulated by a DTA.

Conversely, every DTA language is an NTA language and hence r.e. ∎

Furthermore, DTM programs compute the same partial functions as NTM programs (Exercise 7.6-1). The r.e. languages can be obtained from the recursive languages by applying an existential quantifier.

THEOREM 7.18. *L is r.e. if and only if there is a recursive language R such that for all x,*

$$x \in L \iff (\exists y)[(x, y) \in R].$$

(Geometrically, every r.e. set is obtained by projecting a recursive set in the x–y plane onto the x-axis.)

Proof: Let L be r.e., so there is an NTA P that accepts L. Let

$$R = \{(x, C) : C \text{ is an accepting computation of } P \text{ on input } x\}.$$

Then R is recursive by Theorem 7.16(ii), and $x \in L \iff (\exists y)[(x, y) \in R]$.

Conversely, suppose that $x \in L \iff (\exists y)[(x, y) \in R]$, where R is a recursive language. Here is an NTA that accepts L:

input x;[4]
guess y;[5]
if $(x, y) \in R$ then accept.

By definition, L is r.e. ∎

The string y in the statement of Theorem 7.18 is called a *certificate* or *witness* that $x \in L$, because once y is found one can convince someone that $x \in L$ by testing whether (x, y) belongs to the recursive language R. In this sense, y embodies a "proof" that $x \in L$.

THEOREM 7.19. *L is recursive if and only if L is r.e. and co-r.e.*

Proof: If L is recursive then $\overline{L}$ is recursive. Therefore L and $\overline{L}$ are r.e.

Conversely, suppose that L is r.e. and $\overline{L}$ is r.e. Then L is accepted by an NTA P_{yes} and $\overline{L}$ is accepted by an NTA P_{no}. Therefore L is recognized by the following algorithm, which tries all sequences of instructions until it finds a valid computation of P_{yes} or P_{no}.

$i := 0$;
while i does not encode an accepting computation of P_{yes} or P_{no} on input x do
    $i := i + 1$;
if i encodes an accepting computation of P_{yes} on input x
then accept, else reject.

(This algorithm is readily expressed as a DTM program.) Because $x \in L$ or $x \notin L$, either P_{yes} or P_{no} is guaranteed to have an accepting computation. Thus the while-loop in the algorithm above always finishes, and the resulting value of i encodes either a witness that $x \in L$ or a witness that $x \notin L$. ∎

---

[4] By "input x" we mean "scan the entire input string, store it on the tape, and call it x."

[5] By "guess y" we mean "nondeterministically write a sequence of characters on the tape and call the string y."

Alternate Proof: Since this is an important theorem, we present a second proof. Assume that L and $\overline{L}$ are r.e. By Lemma 7.17, L is accepted by a DTM program P_{yes} and $\overline{L}$ is accepted by a DTM program P_{no}. Because x belongs to L or $\overline{L}$, either P_{yes} or P_{no} must accept x; therefore the following algorithm terminates with either M_{yes} or M_{no} in an accepting configuration.

start M_{yes} in the initial configuration of P_{yes};
start M_{no} in the initial configuration of P_{no};
repeat
    run P_{yes} for one step on M_{yes};
    run P_{no} for one step on M_{no};
until M_{yes} or M_{no} is in an accepting configuration;
if M_{yes} is in an accepting configuration then accept, else reject. ∎

The algorithm above is analogous to running two programs or two processes at once on a modern time-sharing system. When this is done on a Turing machine, it is called *dovetailing*.

In the next theorem, we identify strings with natural numbers and use numerical order.

THEOREM 7.20. *Let L be a nonempty set of natural numbers.*

(i) L is r.e. iff L is the range of a total recursive function.

(ii) L is recursive iff L is the range of a total recursive function that is nondecreasing.

Proof: Let L be a nonempty set.

(i) Suppose that L is r.e. Since L is nonempty, we can let a be an arbitrary element of L. Let P be a Turing machine program that accepts L. Let $f(C)$ be the string scanned during the computation C if C is a computation of P, and let $f(C) = a$ if C is not a computation of P. Then f is a total recursive function whose range is L.

Conversely, suppose that L is the range of a total recursive function f. Then L is accepted by an NTA that behaves as follows:

input x;
guess y;
if $f(y) = x$, then accept;

Since L is accepted by an NTA, L is r.e.

(ii) Suppose that L is recursive. Let $f(0)$ be the least element of L. For $x > 0$, let $f(x) = x$ if $x \in L$, and let $f(x) = f(x-1)$ otherwise. Then f is a total recursive function that is nondecreasing, and L is the range of f.

Conversely, suppose that L is the range of a total recursive function f that is nondecreasing. We consider two cases:

Case 1: L is finite. Then L is recursive because every finite language is recursive.

Case 2: L is infinite. Then f takes on arbitrarily large values. The following algorithm tests membership in L:

input x;
$i := 0$;
while $f(i) < x$ do $i := i + 1$;
if $f(i) = x$ then accept else reject;

Note that the algorithm must halt because $f(i)$ is guaranteed to be at least x for some sufficiently large i. Since L is recognized by an algorithm, L is recursive. ∎

Note that the proof above is nonconstructive. In the proof of part (i), we did not say how to find some $a \in L$; we simply asserted that such an a exists, so there is some program that uses a correct value. In the proof of part (ii), we did not say how to find the least element of L; we simply asserted that the least element exists, so there is some program that uses the correct value. Also in the proof of part (ii), we did not say how to determine whether L is finite. If L is finite, we did not say how to determine which finite set L

is. We simply asserted that there is a program for each possibility, so some program handles the correct possibility.

Although only the reverse direction of part (i) is constructive as written, the reader may be reassured to know that the forward direction of parts (i) and (ii) can be made constructive (Exercise 7.6-8). Nonconstructive proofs are sometimes simpler; keep in mind that a nonconstructive proof is just as valid as any constructive proof. Furthermore, the reverse direction of part (ii) cannot be made constructive (Exercise 7.15-2); the nonconstructive proof is all there is.

Exercises

7.6-1 Let P be a nondeterministic program for a machine [control, input, output, tape]. If P computes a partial function, prove that P is simulated by a deterministic program for a machine [control, input, output, tape].

7.6-2 (a) Prove that χ_L is a total recursive function if and only if L is recognized by a DTR.
(b) Prove that L is the domain of a partial recursive function if and only if L is accepted by an NTA.

+7.6-3 Prove that every infinite recursive set is the range of a total recursive function that is strictly increasing.

7.6-4 Prove that every infinite r.e. language contains an infinite recursive subset.

7.6-5 Prove that L is r.e. if and only if there is a DTM program that runs forever, outputting a (possibly infinite) sequence consisting of the strings in L.

7.6-6 Prove that the class of r.e. languages is closed under the following operations:
(a) union
(b) concatenation
(c) intersection
(d) Kleene-closure

(e) shuffle
(f) perfect shuffle

7.6-7 Prove that the class of recursive languages is closed under the following operations:
(a) complementation
(b) union
(c) concatenation
(d) intersection
(e) Kleene-closure
(f) shuffle
(g) perfect shuffle

7.6-8 (a) Give a constructive proof of the forward direction of Theorem 7.20(i); i.e., present an algorithm that solves the following problem:

Instance: a DTA P that accepts a nonempty language

Answer: a DTM program P' such that $\tau_{P'}$ is a total function and $L(P) = \text{Range}(\tau_{P'})$

The algorithm may give an incorrect answer or fail to halt if P accepts the empty language.

(b) Give a constructive proof of the forward direction of Theorem 7.20(ii); i.e., present an algorithm that solves the following problem:

Instance: a DTR P that recognizes a nonempty language

Answer: a DTM program P' such that $\tau_{P'}$ is a nondecreasing function and $L(P) = \text{Range}(\tau_{P'})$

The algorithm may give an incorrect answer or fail to halt if P is not a DTR or if P accepts the empty language.

7.6-9 Assume that L_1 and L_2 are r.e., $L_1 \cup L_2$ is recursive, and $L_1 \cap L_2$ is recursive. Prove that L_1 and L_2 are recursive.

7.6-10 Professor Cindy Simd has received a huge grant to design a computer that can run a single program on infinitely many inputs. You will solve her problem with a mere Turing machine, although less quickly than she would like.

(a) Design a Turing machine program that will take a DTM program P and produce the results of running P on all inputs. Your program's output should be a (possibly infinite) sequence consisting of all pairs $(x, \tau_P(x))$ such that P halts on input x. Hint: Generalize the time-sharing/dovetailing idea.

(b) Modify your program from part (a) so that its output is sorted according to the number of steps that P runs on input x. Hint: You may assume that P scans its entire input, so P runs for at least s steps on inputs of length s.

7.7 THE HALTING PROBLEM

Recall that a program is said to halt on input x if it has a complete computation on input x. The *halting problem* is to determine whether a DTM program P halts on input x. We will see that this problem cannot be solved by any Turing machine program. By Church's thesis, the halting problem cannot be solved by any algorithm. In real life, this means that there is no general way to know whether a program is running forever or is merely taking a long time to finish. We will use the halting problem in later sections to prove that many important problems cannot be solved by any algorithm.

Problem name: the halting problem

Instance: a DTM program P and a string x

Question: Does P halt on input x?

In this section, assume that programs are represented as strings over $\{0, 1\}$ as in Section 7.4.

Our first and most important undecidability theorem says that there is no algorithm that solves the halting problem. The proof of this theorem uses Georg Cantor's diagonalization technique, which is illustrated by a variant of Bertrand Russell's *barber paradox*: The barber in a certain town has a sign on the wall saying, "I shave those men, and only those, who do not shave themselves." Let x denote an arbitrary man. According to the barber's sign

$$\text{the barber shaves } x \iff \neg(x \text{ shaves } x).$$

The barber cannot be equal to x, because one of them shaves x and the other one does not. Because that statement is true for every man x, the barber cannot be any man. Of course, the barber could be a woman or a robot, so the barber's paradox as stated above is not really paradoxical. Nonetheless, it is surprising that we can deduce that the barber is not a man from a seemingly innocuous sign. (See Exercise 7.8-11 for a more troublesome paradox.)

THEOREM 7.21. *There is no algorithm that determines, for every DTM program P and string x, whether P halts on input x.*

Proof: We encode programs as strings. An encoded program may be the input string to another program, just as real programs are input strings to compilers, interpreters, and editors on real computers. In particular, a copy of a program may be passed to itself as input. Suppose that there is an algorithm to solve the halting problem, and use it as a subroutine to perform the if-test in the following algorithm, which can be implemented as a DTM program P:

```
input x, which encodes a DTM program;
if program x halts on input x then
    loop forever
else
    halt;
```

Observe that

$$P \text{ halts on input } x \iff \neg(x \text{ halts on input } x).$$

Then P must be different from every DTM program x, but P is a DTM program by construction. This contradiction proves that there is no algorithm that solves the halting problem. ■

Observe that we have proved something slightly stronger than just Theorem 7.21: There is no algorithm that determines, for every program x, whether x halts on input x. In fact, such a statement is true for virtually every type of machine: There is no recognizer running on a machine of type M that determines, for all acceptors x running on machines of type M, whether x halts on input x (see Exercise 7.8-15).

DEFINITION 7.22

- $K_{xy} = \{(x, y) :$ DTM program x halts on input $y\}$
- $K_{diag} = \{x :$ DTM program x halts on input $x\}$
- $K_{pos} = \{x :$ DTM program x halts on at least one input$\}$
- $K_{inatt} = \{x :$ DTM program x with no input device halts$\}$
  (A Turing machine with no input device is called *inattentive*.)

By the proof above of Theorem 7.21, we actually have the following theorem.

THEOREM 7.23. *The languages K_{xy} and K_{diag} are nonrecursive.* ▪

Many other languages will be proved nonrecursive by a technique called reducing the halting problem. In particular, we will prove that K_{pos} and K_{inatt} are nonrecursive in Section 7.9.

Exercises

7.7-1 Is the universal Turing machine program used in the proof of Theorem 7.21? Justify your answer.

Solution: No. The universal Turing machine is used only by algorithms that scan a program x and then run that program x. The algorithm used in the proof of Theorem 7.21 does indeed scan a program x, but it never runs the program x; instead, it runs an algorithm that purportedly determines whether x halts on input x. That algorithm is not part of the input; rather, it is used as a subroutine.

7.8 DIAGONALIZATION

Let us look again at the proof that the halting problem is undecidable. We considered all DTM programs, and, assuming that K_{diag} was decidable, we constructed a DTM program that behaved differently from all of them. This contradiction—a DTM program that behaves differently from every DTM program, including itself—proved that K_{diag} must be undecidable.

Recall the correspondence between strings and natural numbers. Let us represent DTM programs and their inputs as natural numbers and envision a table whose entries indicate whether the DTM program x halts on input y. We will write $\downarrow$ to denote halting and $\uparrow$ to denote nonhalting. A portion of such a table is shown in Table 7.3.

In order for a sequence to differ from each row of the table, it is sufficient for it to differ from each row in just one place. It is particularly convenient to make it differ from the xth row in the xth position. That is, we construct a sequence that differs from the diagonal in every position. Thus, we write a program that halts on input 0, ..., halts on 900, runs forever on 901,

	$x \backslash y$	0	⋯	900	901	902	903	904	⋯
	0	$\uparrow$	⋯	$\uparrow$	$\uparrow$	$\uparrow$	$\uparrow$	$\uparrow$	⋯
	⋮	⋮	⋱	⋮	⋮	⋮	⋮	⋮	⋯
	900	$\uparrow$	⋯	$\uparrow$	$\uparrow$	$\uparrow$	$\downarrow$	$\uparrow$	⋯
x	901	$\downarrow$	⋯	$\downarrow$	$\downarrow$	$\downarrow$	$\downarrow$	$\downarrow$	⋯
	902	$\downarrow$	⋯	$\uparrow$	$\downarrow$	$\downarrow$	$\uparrow$	$\uparrow$	⋯
	903	$\uparrow$	⋯	$\uparrow$	$\downarrow$	$\downarrow$	$\downarrow$	$\downarrow$	⋯
	904	$\downarrow$	⋯	$\uparrow$	$\uparrow$	$\downarrow$	$\uparrow$	$\uparrow$	⋯
	⋮	⋮	⋮	⋮	⋮	⋮	⋮	⋮	⋱

TABLE 7.3: Does DTM program x halt on input y? For illustration, the entries have been filled in more or less at random.

runs forever on 902, runs forever on 903, halts on 904, and so on. If there is an algorithm to solve the halting problem, then this program can be implemented on a DTM, but this program behaves differently from every DTM program.

*7.8.1 The Real Numbers Are Uncountable

The nineteenth-century mathematician Georg Cantor first used the diagonalization technique in his study of the size, or cardinality, of infinite sets. He said that two sets A and B have the same *cardinality* if there is a one-one correspondence from A to B. (Recall that a one-one correspondence is a one-one, onto function.) Cantor's definition agrees with the usual definition of cardinality for finite sets. For example, $|\{1,2,3,4,5\}| = |\{5,10,50,100,101\}|$ and a one-one correspondence from $\{1,2,3,4,5\}$ to $\{5,10,50,100,101\}$ is

$$f(i) = \text{the } i\text{th smallest element of } \{5,10,50,100,101\}.$$

Cantor's definition has some surprising consequences. For example, even though N is a proper subset of Z, the sets N and Z have the same cardinality. A one-one correspondence from N to Z is

$$f(i) = \begin{cases} i/2 & \text{if } i \text{ is even,} \\ -(i+1)/2 & \text{if } i \text{ is odd.} \end{cases}$$

There are, therefore, exactly as many natural numbers as integers, even though there are infinitely many integers that are not natural numbers. An infinite set S is called *countable* if there is a one-one correspondence from N to S; an infinite set S is called *uncountable* otherwise. Because f is a one-one correspondence if and only if f^{-1} is a one-one correspondence, an infinite set S is countable if and only if there is a one-one correspondence from S to N.

For example, the language $\{1,2\}^*$ is countable because dyadic(x) is a one-one correspondence from $\{1,2\}^*$ to N. Thus there are exactly as many natural numbers as there are strings over $\{1,2\}$. The same is true for any alphabet (Exercise 7.8-5(a)). Because we can write rational numbers as strings, we make the surprising discovery that there are exactly as many natural numbers as rational numbers (Exercise 7.8-5(b)). Now we might start wondering if all infinite sets have the same cardinality, but in fact there are more real numbers than natural numbers.

THEOREM 7.24. *The set of real numbers is uncountable; i.e., if f is a mapping from* N *to* R*, then f is not onto.*

Proof: We will construct a real number x in $[0, 1)$ such that for all i, $f(i) \neq x$. For a real number r, let $d_i(r)$ denote the ith digit after the decimal point in the decimal representation of r (if r has two representations, choose the one that ends in all 0s, rather than in all 9s). For example, $d_2(\sqrt{2}) = d_2(1.4142\cdots) = 1$, $d_5(17.13579) = 9$, and $d_6(17.13579 = 0)$.

We define a function h that takes a digit and returns a different digit but never returns 0 or 9, so we do not have to worry about numbers with two representations:

$$h(n) = \begin{cases} 2 & \text{if } n = 1, \\ 1 & \text{if } n \in \{0, 2, 3, 4, 5, 6, 7, 8, 9\}. \end{cases}$$

We will define a real number x in $[0, 1)$ that is different from $f(i)$ for each $i \in \mathsf{N}$. Let the $(i+1)$st digit after the decimal point in x's decimal representation be $h(d_{i+1}(f(i)))$. Then x differs from $f(i)$ in the $(i+1)$st digit, so x has a different decimal representation from each of the numbers in the range of f. Since the decimal representation of x does not end in all 0s or all 9s, x has a unique decimal representation. Therefore x differs from every number in the range of f, so f is not onto. ■

An example of the diagonalization is depicted in Figure 7.2.

Exercises

7.8-1 Let A be any set. Prove that there is no one-one mapping from 2^A to A. (Recall that 2^A is the set of all subsets of A.)

+7.8-2 Let Σ be any alphabet.
(a) Prove that the set of all languages over Σ is uncountable.
(b) Prove that the set of all strings over Σ is countable.

$$
\begin{array}{lcccccccccc}
f(0) & = 0 & . & 9 & 9 & 9 & 9 & 9 & 9 & \cdots \\
f(1) & = 0 & . & 7 & \mathbf{0} & 7 & 1 & 0 & 6 & \cdots \\
f(2) & = 0 & . & 5 & 7 & \mathbf{7} & 3 & 5 & 0 & \cdots \\
f(3) & = 0 & . & 5 & 0 & 0 & \mathbf{0} & 0 & 0 & \cdots \\
f(4) & = 0 & . & 4 & 4 & 7 & 2 & \mathbf{1} & 3 & \cdots \\
f(5) & = 0 & . & 1 & 6 & 6 & 6 & 6 & \mathbf{6} & \cdots \\
\vdots & \vdots\ \vdots & \vdots & \vdots & \vdots & \vdots & \vdots & \vdots & \vdots & \ddots
\end{array}
$$

FIGURE 7.2: Using diagonalization to construct a real number that differs from $f(i)$ for all $i \in \mathsf{N}$. The diagonal number is $0.907016\cdots$. x is chosen to be $0.111121\cdots$, which differs from the diagonal number in every digit. Therefore x cannot be equal to $f(i)$ for any $i \in \mathsf{N}$.

(c) Prove that it is impossible to represent all languages over Σ by strings over any alphabet.

(d) Prove that the set of all recursive languages over Σ is countable and that the set of all nonrecursive languages over Σ is uncountable.

(e) Prove that the set of all r.e. languages over Σ is countable and that the set of all non-r.e. languages over Σ is uncountable.

(f) Prove that there is a language over Σ that is neither r.e. nor co-r.e.

7.8-3 Prove that there are exactly as many even integers as integers.

7.8-4 Construct a one-one correspondence from $\{0, 1\}^*$ to the set of positive integers.

Solution: Several solutions are possible. For example, let $h(x)$ be the finite transduction that replaces 1's by 2's and replaces 0's by 1's. The desired one-one correspondence is $f(x) = \text{dyadic}(h(x)) + 1$. A simpler solution is $f(x) = \text{binary}(1x)$.

7.8-5 In this exercise you will construct a one-one correspondence from the nonnegative rational numbers to the natural numbers.

(a) Let Σ be any alphabet. Prove that there are exactly as many strings over Σ as natural numbers.

Solution: Let $b = |\Sigma|$; then $b\text{-adic}(x)$ is a one-one correspondence from Σ^* to N.

(b) Prove that there are exactly as many nonnegative rational numbers as natural numbers.

Solution: We define a one-one mapping m from nonnegative rational numbers to strings over $\{1, 2, /\}$ as follows:

input r;

determine n and d such that $r = n/d$ and n and d are relatively prime;

output the string N/D where N is the dyadic representation of n and D is the dyadic representation of d.

Define a one-one correspondence g from $\{1, 2, /\}^*$ to N as in part (a). Let $h(r) = g(m(r))$, so h is a one-one mapping from the nonnegative rational numbers to N. Order the rational numbers according to $h(r)$. Let $f(r)$ be the rank of r in that ordering; i.e., $f(r)$ is the maximum value i such that there exist rational numbers $r_1, \ldots, r_i$ satisfying $h(r_1) < h(r_2) < \cdots < h(r_i) < h(r)$. f is the desired one-one correspondence.

7.8-6 A function f is monotone if $x \leq y \Rightarrow f(x) \leq f(y)$. Prove that there is no monotone one-one correspondence from the set of rational numbers to N.

7.8-7 A submarine travels under the Euclidean plane with constant velocity (speed and direction). Every hour on the hour it passes under a lattice point, and every hour on the hour you can drop a depth charge at any point in the plane, destroying the submarine if it is there. You cannot see the submarine and you do not know its initial position or its velocity. Is there a strategy you can follow that is certain to destroy the submarine eventually?

7.8-8 Use diagonalization to construct an irrational real number.

7.8-9 Present a one-one correspondence from $\mathsf{R} \times \mathsf{R}$ to R.

7.8-10 Assume that there is a one-one mapping from A to B and another one-one mapping from B to A.

(a) Assuming that A is countable, prove that there is a one-one correspondence from A to B.

*(b) **Schröder–Bernstein Theorem.** Without any extra assumptions, prove that there is a one-one correspondence from A to B. Hint: Let f be a one-one mapping from A to B, and let g be a one-one mapping from B to A. Rename elements so that A and B are disjoint. For x and y in $A \cup B$ we say that x is an ancestor of y if y is obtained from x by applying the functions f and/or g a finite number of times. For example, x is an ancestor of $f(g(f(x)))$. Define a mapping h from A to B as follows:

$$h(a) = \begin{cases} g^{-1}(a) & \text{if } a \text{ has an odd number of ancestors other than } a, \\ f(a) & \text{if } a \text{ has an even or infinite number of ancestors other than } a. \end{cases}$$

Prove that h is a one-one correspondence from A to B.

7.8-11 **Russell's paradox.** Prove that the following is not a set:

$$\{S : S \text{ is a set and } S \notin S\}.$$

7.8.2 Recursively Inseparable Sets

A common problem in computer science is to design programs that distinguish between two different kinds of objects. For example, an artificial intelligence program might assist in cancer therapy by distinguishing healthy cells from cancerous cells. Since cells may suffer from diseases other than cancer, this is not the same as recognizing healthy cells, nor is it the same as recognizing cancer cells. Another program might assist a banker by distinguishing high-risk loans from low-risk loans; the program might classify medium-risk loans arbitrarily.

If S_1 and S_2 are disjoint sets and P is a recognizer, then we say that P *distinguishes* S_1 from S_2 if P accepts all strings in S_1 and P rejects all strings in S_2. Sets S_1 and S_2 are *recursively separable* if there is a DTR P that distinguishes S_1 from S_2.

EXAMPLE 7.25. Let

$$\begin{aligned} S_1 &= \{P : P \text{ has an odd number of control states and } P \in K_{inatt}\}, \\ S_2 &= \{P : P \text{ has an even number of control states and } P \in K_{inatt}\}. \end{aligned}$$

S_1 and S_2 are nonrecursive (Exercise 7.9-1(a,b)), but they are recursively separable, because they are distinguished by a program that accepts P iff P has an odd number of control states. ■ ■ ■

Two sets S_1 and S_2 are *recursively inseparable* if S_1 and S_2 are disjoint and S_1 and S_2 are not recursively separable.

THEOREM 7.26. *There exist a pair of r.e. languages that are recursively inseparable.*

Proof: Recall that $\tau_P(x)$ is the result of program P on input x. Now define

$$\begin{aligned} K_{\text{ACCEPT}} &= \{P : P \text{ is a DTM program and } \tau_P(P) = \text{ACCEPT}\}, \\ K_{\text{REJECT}} &= \{P : P \text{ is a DTM program and } \tau_P(P) = \text{REJECT}\}; \end{aligned}$$

i.e., K_{ACCEPT} is the set of programs that accept themselves and K_{REJECT} is the set of programs that reject themselves.

K_{ACCEPT} is r.e. because it is accepted by a DTA that runs P on input P and accepts if that computation accepts. K_{REJECT} is r.e. for similar reasons.

We prove by contradiction that K_{ACCEPT} and K_{REJECT} are not recursively separable. Suppose that there is a DTR that distinguishes K_{ACCEPT} from K_{REJECT}. Interchange accepting and rejecting states to obtain a DTR P that accepts all strings in K_{REJECT} and rejects all strings in K_{ACCEPT}.

If P accepts P, then $P \in K_{\text{ACCEPT}}$, but P rejects all strings in K_{ACCEPT}, so P does not accept P. If P rejects P, then $P \in K_{\text{REJECT}}$, but P accepts all strings in K_{REJECT}, so P does not reject P. Thus P neither accepts P nor rejects P, so P cannot be a recognizer. This contradiction proves that K_{ACCEPT} and K_{REJECT} are recursively inseparable. ■

Exercises

7.8-12 Prove that S_1 and S_2 are recursively separable if and only if S_2 and S_1 are recursively separable.

7.8-13 Prove that S_1 and S_2 are recursively separable if and only if there exists a recursive language R such that $S_1 \subseteq R$ and $S_2 \subseteq \overline{R}$.

Solution: Suppose that S_1 and S_2 are recursively separable. Let P be a DTR that accepts all strings in S_1 and rejects all strings in S_2. Let $R = L(P)$. Then $S_1 \subseteq R$ and $S_2 \subseteq \overline{R}$.
Conversely, suppose that there exists a recursive language R such that $S_1 \subseteq R$ and $S_2 \subseteq \overline{R}$. Let P be a DTR that recognizes R. Then S_1 and S_2 are recursively separable via P.

7.8-14 In contrast to Theorem 7.26, prove that if S_1 and S_2 are disjoint *co-r.e.* languages, then S_1 and S_2 are recursively separable.

7.8-15 In this exercise you will prove that certain kinds of machines cannot solve their own halting problem.

(a) Prove that a DFR cannot distinguish $\{x : x \text{ is a DFA that halts on } x\}$ from $\{x : x \text{ is a DFA that does not halt on } x\}$.

Solution: The proof is by contradiction. Assume that P is a DFR that distinguishes $\{x : x \text{ is an DFA that halts on } x\}$ from $\{x : x \text{ is an DFA that does not halt on } x\}$. We construct a DFA P' that accepts whenever P rejects and that goes into an infinite loop whenever P accepts. This construction can be accomplished as follows: Let P' contain all of P's instructions and control states. Let P' contain a new control state ν as well and the instruction $(\nu \rightarrow \nu, \text{NOOP})$, which is an infinite loop. Let each of P's rejecting states be accepting in P', and let all other states of P' be nonfinal. For each accepting state q in P, include the instruction $(q \rightarrow \nu, \text{EOF})$ in P'. Let x be a DFA. Then P' halts on input x iff P rejects x iff x does not halt on input x. Therefore P' is different from every DFA. This contradiction proves that there is no DFR P that distinguishes $\{x : x \text{ is a DFA that halts on } x\}$ from $\{x : x \text{ is a DFA that does not halt on } x\}$.

(b) Prove that a DCR cannot distinguish $\{x : x \text{ is a DCA that halts on } x\}$ from $\{x : x \text{ is a DCA that does not halt on } x\}$.

(c) Prove that a DSR cannot distinguish $\{x : x \text{ is a DSA that halts on } x\}$ from $\{x : x \text{ is a DSA that does not halt on } x\}$.

*7.8.3 The Total Recursive Functions Cannot Be Enumerated Exactly

We say that a programming language "expresses" a function if it contains a program that computes that function. It would be very desirable to have a programming language that could express every total recursive function but not any partial functions. Programs written in such a language would be guaranteed to terminate. For comparison, most actual programming languages can express all partial recursive functions, not just the total ones. In this section we will show that it is impossible to find a programming language that expresses the total recursive functions and no partial functions.

A programming language is *allowable* if it satisfies the following practical restrictions:

Enumerability: The set of programs must be r.e.

Interpreter: There must be a DTM program that takes a program P and an input x and computes the result of P on input x, if it halts.

For example, the set of all DTM programs is recursive, and the set of all Pascal programs is recursive. Furthermore, there are interpreters for those two programming languages; those interpreters can be implemented as deterministic Turing machine programs.

If an allowable programming language expresses only total functions and S is the r.e. set of programs in that programming language, then we will construct a total recursive function that is not computed by any program in S.

THEOREM 7.27. *Let S be the set of programs in an allowable programming language. There exists a total recursive function f that is not computed by any of the programs in S, i.e,*

$$(\forall P \in S)[f \neq \tau_P].$$

Proof: If S is empty, then we can let f be any total recursive function. Henceforth, we may assume without loss of generality that S is nonempty. We represent programs as natural numbers and apply Theorem 7.20(i). Because S is a nonempty r.e. language, S is the range of a total recursive function g. We diagonalize by letting

$$f(x) = \tau_{g(x)}(x) + 1.$$

To compute f, we first compute $P = g(x)$, which is possible because g is totally recursive. Then, using the interpreter, we determine the result of program P on input x; this result exists because every program in S computes a total recursive function. Finally, we add one to the result. Thus f is total recursive.

However, for every x, f is different from $\tau_{g(x)}$, because those two functions differ on input x. Because the range of g is S, the function f is different from τ_P for every P in S. ∎

7.9 MANY-ONE REDUCTIONS

We say that a language A is *reducible* to a language B if A is recognized by an algorithm that uses the ability to test membership in B. If A is reducible to B and B is recursive, then it is clear that A is recursive. The contrapositive—if A is reducible to B and A is nonrecursive then B is nonrecursive—can be used in practice to prove that certain languages are nonrecursive.

It is all too easy to get the reduction principle backward. If A is reducible to B and B is nonrecursive, then we may conclude nothing of interest about A. Remember: Any fool can reduce an easy problem to a hard problem, but no one can reduce a hard problem to a truly easy problem.

So far we have not specified how an algorithm may use the "ability to test membership in B." Depending on how we specify this, we obtain different definitions of "reduction." The *many-one reduction*, defined below, is quite useful:

DEFINITION 7.28 (Many-one Reductions). A language A is *many-one reducible* to B (denoted $A \leq_m B$) if there is a total recursive function f (called a *many-one reduction* from A to B) such that[6]

$$x \in A \iff f(x) \in B.$$

If f is a many-one reduction from A to B, we may say that A is many-one reducible to B *via* f. The term "many-one reducible" is often abbreviated "m-reducible." If $A \leq_m B$, we think of B as being as *hard* as A or harder; A is as *easy* as B or easier.

As a trivial example, let A be the set of all even integers, and let B be the set of all integers that are divisible by 6. Then

$$x \in A \iff 3x \in B,$$

so $A \leq_m B$ via the reduction $f(x) = 3x$. We will see some nontrivial reductions soon in this section, but first we state some simple properties of many-one reductions.

PROPOSITION 7.29.

(i) **Reflexive.** $(\forall A)[A \leq_m A]$.

(ii) **Transitive.** *If* $A \leq_m B$ *and* $B \leq_m C$, *then* $A \leq_m C$.

(iii) *If* $A \leq_m B$ *and* B *is recursive, then* A *is recursive.*

(iv) *If* $A \leq_m B$ *and* B *is r.e., then* A *is r.e.*

Proof

(i) The identity function is a reduction from A to A: $x \in A \iff x \in A$.

(ii) Suppose that $A \leq_m B$ and $B \leq_m C$, so that for all x we have $x \in A \iff f(x) \in B$ and $x \in B \iff g(x) \in C$. Then for all x we have

$$x \in A \iff f(x) \in B \iff g(f(x)) \in C,$$

so $g \circ f$ is a reduction from A to C.

6 A is *one-one reducible* to B if there is a one-one total recursive function f such that $x \in A \iff f(x) \in B$. A many-one reduction need not be one-one, hence the name. We do not discuss one-one reductions further in this book.

(iii) Assume that for all x, $x \in A \iff f(x) \in B$ and that B is recognized by a DTR P_B. The following is a deterministic algorithm to test membership in A:

> input x;
> $y := f(x)$;
> run P_B on input y;
> if P_B accepts then accept, else reject.

(iv) Assume that for all x, $x \in A \iff f(x) \in B$ and that B is accepted by an NTA P_B. The following is a nondeterministic algorithm to test membership in A:

> input x;
> $y := f(x)$;
> run P_B on input y;
> if P_B accepts then accept. ■

Taking the contrapositive of part (iii), we have an important technique for proving undecidability:

COROLLARY 7.30 *If $A \leq_m B$ and A is nonrecursive, then B is nonrecursive.*

EXAMPLE 7.31 **($K_{diag} \leq_m K_{xy}$).** Recall that K_{xy} is the set of pairs (x, y) such that DTM program x halts on input y, and K_{diag} is the set of DTM programs that halt when given themselves as input. Let $f(x) = (x, x)$. Then

$$x \in K_{diag} \iff (x, x) \in K_{xy},$$

so $K_{diag} \leq_m K_{xy}$ via f. ■■■

EXAMPLE 7.32 **($K_{xy} \leq_m K_{inatt}$).** Recall that K_{inatt} is the set of DTM programs without input that halt. Let $f(x, y)$ be the inattentive program that runs program x on input y, i.e.,

$$f(x, y) = \text{"Run DTM program } x \text{ on input } y.\text{"}$$

(The program $f(x, y)$ is obtained by hard-coding the string y into the program x. If you were programming in a high-level language, you would take the program x and set an internal constant equal to y instead of having x read y. You can accomplish the same thing with Turing machines by initializing an extra control to hold y. The input operation SCANc is then simulated by the control operations $cz \to z$ for each of y's suffixes of the form cz. EOF is simulated by $\Lambda \to \Lambda$. Observe that the extra control always holds a suffix of y, so it has only $|y| + 1$ states, which is finite. The fact that you can hard-code a fixed input into a Turing machine program is quite useful. For historical reasons, this obvious programming principle is known by an arcane name: the *s-m-n* theorem.) Then

$$(x, y) \in K_{xy} \iff f(x, y) \in K_{inatt},$$

so $K_{xy} \leq_m K_{inatt}$ via f. ∎

EXAMPLE 7.33 ($K_{inatt} \leq_m K_{pos}$). Recall that K_{pos} is the set of DTM programs that halt on at least one input. Let $f(x)$ be the program that ignores its input and runs inattentive program x; i.e.,

$$f(x) = \text{"Input } z\text{; run inattentive DTM program } x.\text{"}$$

Then

$$\begin{aligned} x \in K_{inatt} &\Rightarrow f(x) \text{ halts on all inputs,} \\ x \notin K_{inatt} &\Rightarrow f(x) \text{ halts on no inputs,} \end{aligned}$$

so

$$x \in K_{inatt} \iff f(x) \text{ halts on at least one input} \iff f(x) \in K_{pos}.$$

Thus $K_{inatt} \leq_m K_{pos}$ via f. ∎

EXAMPLE 7.34 ($K_{pos} \leq_m K_{diag}$). Let $f(x)$ be the program that ignores its input and searches for a complete computation of program x; i.e., let $f(x)$ = the program below:

```
input z;
i := 0;
while i does not encode a computation of x do
      i := i + 1;
halt.
```

Then

$$
\begin{aligned}
x \text{ halts on at least one input} &\iff x \text{ has at least one complete computation} \\
&\iff f(x) \text{ halts on input } z \text{ for arbitrary } z \\
&\iff f(x) \text{ halts on input } f(x) \\
&\iff f(x) \in K_{diag},
\end{aligned}
$$

so $K_{pos} \leq_m K_{diag}$ via f. ■■■

THEOREM 7.35. *K_{inatt} and K_{pos} are nonrecursive.*

Proof: By Theorem 7.23, K_{xy} is nonrecursive. By Example 7.32, $K_{xy} \leq_m K_{inatt}$. Therefore, by Corollary 7.30, K_{inatt} is nonrecursive. By Example 7.33, $K_{inatt} \leq_m K_{pos}$. Therefore, by Corollary 7.30, K_{pos} is nonrecursive. ■

THEOREM 7.36. *Let K be any of the sets K_{xy}, K_{diag}, K_{pos}, and K_{inatt}.*

(i) K is r.e.

(ii) K is not recursive.

(iii) K is not co-r.e.

(iv) $\overline{K}$ is not r.e.

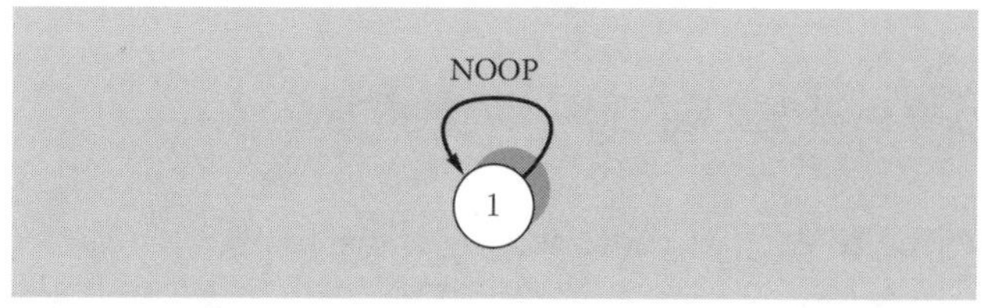

FIGURE 7.3: A (DTM) program that does not halt on any input.

Proof: (i) By Example 7.11, K_{xy} is r.e. By Examples 7.33, 7.34, and 7.31,

$$K_{inatt} \leq_m K_{pos} \leq_m K_{diag} \leq_m K_{xy},$$

so by transitivity each of those sets is m-reducible to K_{xy}. By Proposition 7.29(iv), each of those sets is r.e.

(ii) By Theorems 7.23 and 7.35, K is not recursive.

(iii) Since K is r.e. but not recursive, K must not be co-r.e. by Theorem 7.19.

(iv) Because K is not co-r.e., $\overline{K}$ is not r.e. ∎

We note that $\emptyset$ is reducible to K_{inatt} by setting $f(x) =$ the TM program in Figure 7.3, which does not halt on any input. Thus when $A \leq_m K_{inatt}$, we may not validly conclude that A is nonrecursive. In fact, every r.e. language (and, a fortiori, every recursive language) is m-reducible to K_{inatt}. The proper conclusion when $A \leq_m K_{inatt}$ is that A is as easy as the halting problem *or easier*.

THEOREM 7.37. *Let K denote K_{diag}, K_{xy}, K_{inatt}, or K_{pos}. A is r.e. if and only if $A \leq_m K$.*

Proof: Suppose that A is r.e. We prove that $A \leq_m K_{xy}$. Let P be a DTA that accepts A. Obtain P' by modifying P so that it goes into an infinite loop instead of ever blocking. Then P accepts x iff P' halts on input x. Therefore

$$x \in A \iff (P', x) \in K_{xy},$$

so $A \leq_m K_{xy}$ via $f(x) = (P', x)$. By Examples 7.32 through 7.34,

$$A \leq_m K_{xy} \leq_m K_{inatt} \leq_m K_{pos} \leq_m K_{diag},$$

so A is reducible to each of those sets by transitivity.

Conversely, suppose that $A \leq_m K$. Then $A \leq_m K_{xy}$ by Examples 7.33, 7.34, and 7.31. K_{xy} is r.e. by Example 7.11. Since $A \leq_m K_{xy}$, A is r.e. by Proposition 7.29(iv). ■

Since K is r.e. itself, K is thus a hardest r.e. language. If C is an r.e. language like K, such that every r.e. language is m-reducible to C, then C is called *complete*. In fact, K gets its name from the German word for "complete."

DEFINITION 7.38

- Let $K_{2\text{-}CM}$ be the set of deterministic 2-counter machine programs that halt on at least one input.
- Let $K_{2\text{-}SM}$ be the set of deterministic 2-stack machine programs that halt on at least one input.

THEOREM 7.39. *$K_{2\text{-}CM}$ and $K_{2\text{-}SM}$ are nonrecursive.*

Proof: By Corollary 7.3, a deterministic 2-CM program can simulate a DTM program. Because this simulation is effective, there is a total recursive function f that maps a DTM program x to an equivalent deterministic 2-CM program $f(x)$. Then $x \in K_{pos} \iff f(x) \in K_{2\text{-}CM}$, so $K_{pos} \leq_m K_{2\text{-}CM}$ via f. Because K_{pos} is nonrecursive, $K_{2\text{-}CM}$ must be nonrecursive. There is a trivial reduction from $K_{2\text{-}CM}$ to $K_{2\text{-}SM}$, so $K_{2\text{-}SM}$ is nonrecursive as well. ■

EXAMPLE 7.40. Many-one reductions can be used to prove that a language is not r.e. Let TOT be the set of DTM programs that halt on all inputs. We will show that $\overline{K}_{inatt}$ is m-reducible to TOT. If TOT were r.e., then $\overline{K}_{inatt}$ would be r.e. as well by Proposition 7.29(iv), contradicting Theorem 7.36; thus TOT must not be r.e.

Now we give the reduction. Let $f(P)$ be a program that behaves as follows:

input s; (* treat s as a natural number *)
if P halts within s steps then
    go into an infinite loop
else
    halt.

If P halts, then $f(P)$ doesn't halt for sufficiently large s, so $f(P) \notin$ TOT. If P does not halt, then $f(P)$ halts for all s, so $f(P) \in$ TOT. Thus

$$\overline{K}_{inatt} \leq_m \text{TOT},$$

as asserted. ■ ■ ■

Exercises

7.9-1 Prove that the following languages are nonrecursive:
(a) $\{P : P$ has an odd number of control states and $P \in K_{inatt}\}$
(b) $\{P : P$ has an even number of control states and $P \in K_{inatt}\}$
(c) $\{P : P$ is a DTM program that halts on an odd number of inputs$\}$
(d) $\{P : P$ is a DTM program that halts on an even number of inputs$\}$
(e) $\{P : P$ is a DTM program that halts on all inputs$\}$
(f) $\{P : P$ is a DTA that accepts a recursive language$\}$, i.e., there is a DTR that recognizes the language that P accepts

7.9-2 Which of the following languages are recursive? Which are r.e.?
(a) $\{P : P$ is a DTA that accepts a finite language$\}$
(b) $\{P : P$ is a DTA that accepts a regular language$\}$
(c) $\{P : P$ is a DTA that accepts an r.e. language$\}$
(d) $\{P : P$ is a DTA that accepts a co-r.e. language$\}$
(e) $\{P : P$ is a DTA that has at least 17 control states$\}$

(f) $\{P : P$ has at least 17 control states and $P \in K_{inatt}\}$
(g) $\{P : P$ is a DTA that has a computation of length 17 or less$\}$
(h) $\{P : P$ is a DTM program that halts on fewer than 17 inputs$\}$
(i) $\{P : P$ is a DTM program that halts on fewer inputs than P has control states$\}$

7.9-3 (a) Prove that $\{(P, Q) : P$ and Q are equivalent DTAs$\}$ is not r.e.
(b) Prove that there is no DTM program D that will take a pair of equivalent DTAs P and Q and produce a proof that they are equivalent. Make no assumption about D's behavior when its input consists of a pair of inequivalent DTAs. Hint: You may assume that there is an algorithm to verify proofs.

*7.10 REWRITING SYSTEMS AND WORD PROBLEMS

One theme in the theory of languages and machines is that language classes can either be defined in terms of grammars or in terms of programs. In Chapter 4 we saw that regular expressions are equivalent to NFAs. In Chapter 5 we saw that context-free grammars are equivalent to NSAs. We complete this motif by defining rewriting systems and proving that they are equivalent to NTAs.

Rewriting systems are a generalization of context-free grammars in which the left side of a production may contain more than one symbol. In this section we will consider semi-Thuë and Thuë[7] systems. A semi-Thuë system consists of productions (such as $\mathtt{a}S\mathtt{a} \to S$) that allow one string to be replaced with another string, much as a CFG's productions allow one variable to be replaced by a string. The word problem for a semi-Thuë system is to determine whether x derives y via its productions. We will see that the word problem for semi-Thuë systems is undecidable.

A Thuë system consists of a finite set of formal equalities between strings (such as $\mathtt{a}S\mathtt{a} = S$) that allow one string to be replaced by another and vice versa. The word problem for Thuë systems is to determine whether its equalities imply $x = y$. We will see that the word problem for Thuë systems is undecidable.

---

[7] Thuë's name is pronounced "two way," running the syllables together. This is a useful mnemonic because the productions in a Thuë system go in two directions, whereas the productions in a semi-Thuë system go only one way.

DEFINITION 7.41. A *semi-Thuë* system consists of an alphabet Σ and a finite set of *productions* of the form $x \longrightarrow y$ where x and y are strings over Σ^*. The set of ordered pairs $\{(x, y) : x \longrightarrow y\}$ is a relation, which we call G's *production relation* and denote by $\longrightarrow$ or R_G.

DEFINITION 7.42. Fix a semi-Thuë system G. Let s and t be strings over Σ.

- *s immediately derives t* (denoted $s \Rightarrow t$ or $s \Rightarrow_G t$) if there is a production $x \longrightarrow y$ in G such that

$$s = uxv \text{ and } t = uyv.$$

- The relation $\overset{*}{\Rightarrow}$ (pronounced *derives* and also denoted $\overset{*}{\Rightarrow}_G$) is the reflexive transitive closure of $\Rightarrow$. That is, $\overset{*}{\Rightarrow}$ is the least relation such that

$$s \overset{*}{\Rightarrow} t \text{ iff } s = t \vee (\exists r)[s \Rightarrow r \wedge r \overset{*}{\Rightarrow} t].$$

EXAMPLE 7.43. The context-free grammar

$$\begin{aligned} S &\longrightarrow \mathtt{a}S\mathtt{b} \\ S &\longrightarrow \Lambda \end{aligned}$$

is a semi-Thuë system with alphabet $\Sigma = \{\mathtt{a}, \mathtt{b}, S\}$. In fact, if G is any CFG in standard form, then the productions of G constitute a semi-Thuë system. There is no distinguished start symbol in a semi-Thuë system. Nor is there a distinction between terminal and nonterminal characters. However, for a nonterminal character V and a terminal string x, $V \overset{*}{\Rightarrow} x$ has the same meaning in a CFG as in the corresponding semi-Thuë system. ▪▪▪

EXAMPLE 7.44. Consider the semi-Thuë system with alphabet $\{\mathtt{a}, \mathtt{b}, \mathtt{c}, S\}$ and productions

$$\begin{aligned} S &\longrightarrow \mathtt{abc}S \\ S &\longrightarrow \Lambda \\ \mathtt{ba} &\longrightarrow \mathtt{ab} \\ \mathtt{cb} &\longrightarrow \mathtt{bc} \\ \mathtt{ca} &\longrightarrow \mathtt{ac}. \end{aligned}$$

In this semi-Thuë system we have

$$S \Rightarrow \texttt{abc}S \Rightarrow \texttt{abcabc}S \Rightarrow \texttt{abcabc} \Rightarrow \texttt{abacbc} \Rightarrow \texttt{aabcbc} \Rightarrow \texttt{aabbcc},$$

so $S \stackrel{*}{\Rightarrow} \texttt{aabbcc}$. In fact, S derives all strings in which each prefix contains at least as many a's as b's and at least as many b's as c's. ▪▪▪

A Thuë system is a symmetric version of a semi-Thuë system in which the right sides of productions can be replaced by the left sides as well.

DEFINITION 7.45. A *Thuë* system consists of an alphabet Σ and a set of *rules* of the form $x = y$ where x and y are strings over Σ^*.

Derivations are performed in Thuë systems by replacing strings with equal strings. The rule $x = y$ in a Thuë system G is equivalent to the pair of productions $x \longrightarrow y$ and $y \longrightarrow x$ in a semi-Thuë system. If R_G is symmetric, then G is equivalent to the Thuë system obtained by replacing $x \longrightarrow y$ and $y \longrightarrow x$ with $x = y$.

EXAMPLE 7.46. Consider the Thuë system with alphabet $\{\texttt{a}, \texttt{b}, S\}$ and rules

$$\begin{aligned} S &= \texttt{abc}S \\ S &= \Lambda \\ \texttt{ba} &= \texttt{ab} \\ \texttt{cb} &= \texttt{bc} \\ \texttt{ca} &= \texttt{ac}. \end{aligned}$$

In this rewriting system we have

$$S = \texttt{abc}S = \texttt{abc} = \texttt{bac} = \texttt{bca} = \texttt{cba}$$

because we can use the rule $\texttt{ba} = \texttt{ab}$ to replace ab by ba, and so on. Therefore $S = \texttt{cba}$. In fact, S is equal to every string consisting of equal numbers of a's, b's, and c's. ▪▪▪

DEFINITION 7.47. The *word problem* for a semi-Thuë system G is to determine whether $x \stackrel{*}{\Rightarrow}_G y$.

We will prove that semi-Thuë systems can simulate NTM programs. Then we will prove that the word problem for semi-Thuë systems is undecidable by reducing the halting problem to it.

THEOREM 7.48. *There is an algorithm to convert an NTM program N to a semi-Thuë system G such that*

(i) If N is a transducer with transfer relation τ, then

$$x\$ \stackrel{*}{\Rightarrow}_G \#y \qquad \text{iff} \qquad x \stackrel{\tau}{\mapsto} y.$$

(ii) If N is an acceptor, then

$$x\$ \stackrel{*}{\Rightarrow}_G \# \qquad \text{iff} \qquad N \text{ accepts } x.$$

(iii) If N is inattentive, then

$$\$ \stackrel{*}{\Rightarrow}_G \# \qquad \text{iff} \qquad N \text{ halts}.$$

In each part, # *and* \$ *are assumed to be characters that do not belong to N's input or output alphabet.*

Proof: Depending on whether N is a transducer, acceptor, or inattentive program, we proceed as in (i), (ii), or (iii) below.

(i) We can convert a k-tape transducer N to an equivalent program for a machine [stack, control, stack] such that the first stack is initialized to hold the argument and the second stack holds the reverse of the result (see Section 7.2). Factor the program and then eliminate null instructions so that each instruction operates on exactly one of the stacks. Eliminate the EMPTY test from each stack as in Section 3.3.3. By renaming symbols we may assume that the control set is disjoint from the stack alphabets and that none of these sets contains \$ or #. Let q_{start} be the initial control state, and let q_{accept} be the unique accepting control state. Call the resulting program P.

We will construct a semi-Thuë system G such that

$$xq_{\text{start}} \stackrel{*}{\Rightarrow}_G q_{\text{accept}}y \ \text{ iff } \ x\ \tau_P\ y^R \ \text{ iff } \ x\ \tau_N\ y.$$

Instruction in P	*Production in G*
(PUSHc , $q \to q'$, NOOP)	$q \to cq'$
(POPc , $q \to q'$, NOOP)	$cq \to q'$
(NOOP , $q \to q'$, PUSHd)	$q \to q'd$
(NOOP , $q \to q'$, POPd)	$qd \to q'$

TABLE 7.4: Converting an inattentive 2-SM program P to a semi-Thuë system G.

A configuration (s_1, q, s_2) of P will be represented by the string $s_1 q s_2^R$. Each instruction of P affects only q and one of the two stack characters adjacent to it in that string; each instruction of P will be simulated by a production of G that indicates the effect on q and those two stack characters, as shown in Table 7.4.

Referring to Table 7.4, we see that

$$(s_1, q, s_2) \overset{\Pi}{\mapsto} (s_1', q', s_2') \text{ iff } s_1 q s_2^R \Rightarrow_G s_1' q' (s_2')^R.$$

An easy induction shows that

$$(s_1, q, s_2) \overset{\Pi^*}{\mapsto} (s_1', q', s_2') \text{ iff } s_1 q s_2^R \overset{*}{\Rightarrow}_G s_1' q' (s_2')^R.$$

Therefore

$$x\ \tau_P\ y \text{ iff } (x, q_{\text{start}}, \Lambda) \overset{\Pi^*}{\mapsto} (\Lambda, q_{\text{accept}}, y) \text{ iff } x q_{\text{start}} \overset{*}{\Rightarrow}_G q_{\text{accept}} y^R.$$

Finally, replace q_{start} by \$ and replace q_{accept} by # everywhere in the semi-Thuë system G. Then

$$x\ \tau_N\ y \text{ iff } x\ \tau_P\ y^R \text{ iff } x q_{\text{start}} \overset{*}{\Rightarrow}_G q_{\text{accept}} y \text{ iff } x\$ \overset{*}{\Rightarrow}_G \#y.$$

(ii) Because no output device is used, we can standardize both stacks in a 2-SM so that they are empty in all final configurations. Other than that, the construction is the same as in part (i).

(iii) Because no input or output device is used, we can standardize both stacks in a 2-SM program so that they are empty in all initial and final configurations. Change all final states to accepting states as well, and then standardize so that the accepting state is unique. Other than that, the construction is the same as in part (i). ∎

COROLLARY 7.49. *The word problem for semi-Thuë systems is undecidable.*

Proof: Let f be the total recursive function that converts P to G in Theorem 7.48(iii). Then $P \in K_{inatt}$ iff $\$ \overset{*}{\Rightarrow}_{f(P)} \#$. Thus K_{inatt} is m-reducible to the word problem for semi-Thuë systems. ∎

We will show that a special case of the word problem, in which the derived string is Λ, is undecidable. Toward this end, we prove a version of Theorem 7.48(ii) without #'s.

THEOREM 7.50. *There is an algorithm to convert an NTA N to a semi-Thuë system G′ such that*

$$x\$ \overset{*}{\Rightarrow}_{G'} \Lambda \text{ iff } N \text{ accepts } x.$$

($ is assumed to be a character that does not belong to N's input alphabet.)

Proof: Construct the semi-Thuë system G as in the proof of Theorem 7.48. Include one additional production, $\# \rightarrow \Lambda$. Call the resulting semi-Thuë system G'. If N accepts x, then $x\$ \overset{*}{\Rightarrow}_G \#$, so

$$x\$ \overset{*}{\Rightarrow}_{G'} \# \overset{*}{\Rightarrow}_{G'} \Lambda.$$

Conversely, assume that $x\$ \overset{*}{\Rightarrow}_{G'} \Lambda$. The right side of every production in G is a nonempty string. Therefore the last production used in deriving Λ cannot be a production of G. Therefore the last production used in deriving Λ must be $\# \rightarrow \Lambda$. That production must have been applied to the string #. Therefore $x\$ \overset{*}{\Rightarrow}_{G'} \#$. If the production $\# \rightarrow \Lambda$ is used in a derivation $u \overset{*}{\Rightarrow}_{G'} v$, then v must contain fewer control states than u. Therefore the production $\# \rightarrow \Lambda$ could not be used in the derivation $x\$ \overset{*}{\Rightarrow}_{G'} \#$. Therefore $x\$ \overset{*}{\Rightarrow}_G \#$, so N accepts x. ∎

COROLLARY 7.51. *There is no algorithm to determine whether $x \stackrel{*}{\Rightarrow}_G \Lambda$ in a semi-Thuë system G.* ∎

The language generated by a semi-Thuë system G is defined by

$$L(G) = \{x : \Lambda \stackrel{*}{\Rightarrow}_G x\}.$$

COROLLARY 7.52. *The class of languages generated by semi-Thuë systems is equal to the class of r.e. languages.*

Proof: First, let G be a semi-Thuë system. We can test whether $x \in L(G)$ nondeterministically by guessing a derivation of $\Lambda \stackrel{*}{\Rightarrow}_G x$ and checking the derivation. Therefore $L(G)$ is r.e.

Conversely, let A be r.e. Then A is accepted by an NTA. By Theorem 7.50, there is a semi-Thuë system G such that

$$x \in A \ \text{ iff } \ x \stackrel{*}{\Rightarrow}_G \Lambda.$$

Reverse each production in G, i.e., replace $u \to v$ by $v \to u$, to obtain a semi-Thuë system G' such that

$$x \in A \ \text{ iff } \ \Lambda \stackrel{*}{\Rightarrow}_{G'} x.$$

Then $A = L(G')$. ∎

Next we will prove that Thuë systems are at least as powerful as deterministic TM programs, and the word problem for Thuë systems is undecidable as well.

THEOREM 7.53. *There is an algorithm to convert a DTM program D to a Thuë system G' such that*

(i) If D is a transducer with transfer relation τ, then

$$x\$ =_{G'} \#y \qquad \text{iff} \qquad x \stackrel{\tau}{\mapsto} y.$$

(ii) *If D is an acceptor, then*

$$x\$ =_{G'} \# \qquad \text{iff} \qquad D \text{ accepts } x.$$

(iii) *If D is inattentive, then*

$$\$ =_{G'} \# \qquad \text{iff} \qquad D \text{ halts.}$$

In each part, # and \$ are assumed to be characters that do not belong to D's input or output alphabet.

Proof: Construct P and the semi-Thuë system G as in the proof of Theorem 7.48. Note that P is deterministic. Let Π be P's sequel relation. Let R_G be G's production relation. Let G^{-1} be a semi-Thuë system with the same alphabet and with production relation R_G^{-1}, the converse of G's production relation. Let G' be a semi-Thuë system with the same alphabet and with production relation $R_G \cup R_G^{-1}$, the symmetric closure of G's production relation. Since its production relation is symmetric, G' is equivalent to a Thuë system.

For convenience of exposition, we identify \$ with q_{start} and # with q_{accept}. We will prove that $xq_{\text{start}} \overset{*}{\Rightarrow}_G q_{\text{accept}}y$ if and only if $xq_{\text{start}} \overset{*}{\Rightarrow}_{G'} q_{\text{accept}}y$. First, if $xq_{\text{start}} \overset{*}{\Rightarrow}_G q_{\text{accept}}y$, then it must also be true that $xq_{\text{start}} \overset{*}{\Rightarrow}_{G'} q_{\text{accept}}y$ because every production of G is a production of G'.

Conversely, suppose that $xq_{\text{start}} \overset{*}{\Rightarrow}_{G'} q_{\text{accept}}y$. Consider a shortest derivation in G' of $q_{\text{accept}}y$ from xq_{start}. By a simple induction, all strings derived from xq_{start} are of the form uqv where q is a control state and u and v are strings over P's stack alphabets. We assert that no step in this shortest derivation uses a production belonging to R_G^{-1}. The proof is by contradiction.

Consider the last step in the derivation to use a production in R_G^{-1}. If this step is the last step in the derivation, then it must have the form $uqv \Rightarrow_{G^{-1}} q_{\text{accept}}y$. By symmetry, $q_{\text{accept}}y \Rightarrow_G uqv$. Then $(\Lambda, q_{\text{accept}}, y^R) \overset{\Pi}{\mapsto} (u, q, v^R)$. Since (Λ, q, y^R) is an accepting configuration, this contradicts P's determinism.

Otherwise this step is not the last in the derivation, so it is followed by a step using a production in R_G. These two steps in the derivation have the form $z_0 \Rightarrow_{G^{-1}} z_1 \Rightarrow_G z_2$, so $z_1 \Rightarrow_G z_0$ and $z_1 \Rightarrow_G z_2$. Let $z_i = u_i q_i v_i$ for $i = 0, 1, 2$. Then $(u_1, q_1, v_1^R) \overset{\Pi}{\mapsto} (u_0, q_0, v_0^R)$ and $(u_1, q_1, v_1^R) \overset{\Pi}{\mapsto} (u_2, q_2, v_2^R)$.

Since P is deterministic, the configurations (u_0, q_0, v_0^R) and (u_2, q_2, v_2^R) must be equal. Therefore $z_2 = z_0$, so the derivation could be shortened by eliminating the superfluous steps $z_0 \Rightarrow_{G'} z_1 \Rightarrow_{G'} z_0$. But we chose a shortest derivation. This final contradiction proves that $xq_{\text{start}} \overset{*}{\Rightarrow}_G q_{\text{accept}}y$.

Thus $x \; \tau_P \; y$ iff $xq_{\text{start}} \overset{*}{\Rightarrow}_G q_{\text{accept}}y$ iff $xq_{\text{start}} \overset{*}{\Rightarrow}_{G'} q_{\text{accept}}y$. ∎

Because the halting problem for deterministic TM programs is undecidable, we have the following analogue to Corollary 7.49:

COROLLARY 7.54. *The word problem for Thuë systems is undecidable.* ∎

Exercises

7.10-1 Design a semi-Thuë system in which $x \overset{*}{\Rightarrow} y$ if and only if $x = y$ or x precedes y alphabetically. Use the alphabet $\{\mathtt{a}, \mathtt{b}, \mathtt{c}\}$.

7.10-2 Design a semi-Thuë system in which $S \overset{*}{\Rightarrow} x\#$ if and only if x is of the form $\mathtt{a}^i\mathtt{b}^i\mathtt{c}^i$.

Solution: We modify this section's example. The key point is to make sure that the string belongs to $\mathtt{a}^*\mathtt{b}^*\mathtt{c}^*$ before we put a # at the end of it. Imagine a special character 1 that can move right across a's, a special character 2 that can move right across b's, and a special character 3 that can move right across c's. A 1 can turn into a 2, a 2 can turn into a 3, and a 3 can turn into a # at any time. The special character starts as a 1 at the left end of the string. The only way it can get to the right end is if the string belongs to $\mathtt{a}^*\mathtt{b}^*\mathtt{c}^*$.

$$
\begin{aligned}
S &\rightarrow S\mathtt{abc} \\
S &\rightarrow 1 \\
\mathtt{ba} &\rightarrow \mathtt{ab} \\
\mathtt{cb} &\rightarrow \mathtt{bc} \\
\mathtt{ca} &\rightarrow \mathtt{ac} \\
\mathtt{1a} &\rightarrow \mathtt{a1} \\
1 &\rightarrow 2 \\
\mathtt{2b} &\rightarrow \mathtt{b2}
\end{aligned}
$$

$$2 \rightarrow 3$$
$$3c \rightarrow c3$$
$$3 \rightarrow \#.$$

7.10-3 Prove that there is no algorithm to decide whether $x = \Lambda$ in a Thuë system G. Hint: Reduce the word problem for Thuë systems. Suppose we want to determine whether $x =_G y$. Let G' contain all of G's equalities and also $[y] = \Lambda$, where [and] are new characters. Prove that

$$x =_G y \qquad \text{iff} \qquad [x] =_{G'} \Lambda.$$

7.10-4 A group can be represented as a Thuë system over an alphabet $\Sigma \cup \{a^{-1} : a \in \Sigma\}$ with the rules $aa^{-1} = \Lambda$ and $a^{-1}a = \Lambda$ for all characters a and possibly (usually) some other rules.

(a) Prove that the word problem ($x = y$?) for groups is m-reducible to the special case of determining whether $x = \Lambda$.

**(b) Prove that the word problem for groups is undecidable.

7.10-5 **(a) Prove that the word problem is undecidable for Thuë systems in which the right sides of all equalities are Λ.

**(b) Prove that there is no algorithm to decide whether $x = \Lambda$ in a Thuë system G, even if the right sides of all equalities are Λ. Hint: Use part (a).

7.10-6 Reduce K_{inatt} directly to the word problem for semi-Thuë systems. Do not use 2-stack machines. Hint: Represent the configuration $(q, x\boxed{c}y)$ of P by the string $xqcy\#$ where # is a new character.

7.10-7 (a) Define parse graphs for rewriting systems by analogy to parse trees for CFGs.

(b) Define leftmost derivations for rewriting systems.

(c) Is there a one-one correspondence between parse graphs and leftmost derivations?

(d) Define ambiguity for rewriting systems.

7.10-8 So far we have seen that regular expressions are equivalent to NFAs, CFGs are equivalent to NSAs, and rewriting systems are equivalent to NTAs. Design a class of grammars that are equivalent to NCAs. (Your class of grammars need not be as elegant and natural as regular expressions, CFGs, and rewriting systems.)

*7.11 THE POST CORRESPONDENCE PROBLEM

The Post correspondence problem (PCP) is usually described as follows: Given two lists, each containing the same number of strings, is some nontrivial concatenation of strings from the first list equal to the concatenation of the *corresponding* strings from the second list? Repetitions are allowed. More precisely, given strings $x_1, \ldots, x_n$ and $y_1, \ldots, y_n$, does there exist a nonempty sequence $\langle\langle i_1, \ldots, i_k \rangle\rangle$ of numbers in $\{1, \ldots, n\}$ such that

$$x_{i_1} \cdots x_{i_k} = y_{i_1} \cdots y_{i_k}?$$

To avoid double subscripts and to make our forthcoming reduction clearer, we treat the problem instance as a single set of ordered pairs rather than as two lists. The problem is stated below:

Problem name: Post correspondence problem

Instance: a set S of ordered pairs of strings

Question: Does there exist a nonempty sequence $\langle\langle (x_1, y_1), \ldots, (x_k, y_k) \rangle\rangle$ of pairs in S such that

$$x_1 \cdots x_k = y_1 \cdots y_k?$$

The sequence $\langle\langle (x_1, y_1), \ldots, (x_k, y_k) \rangle\rangle$ is called a *solution* to the PCP instance.

The Post correspondence problem is named after its inventor, logician Emil Post. We will prove that PCP is undecidable. Of all undecidable problems, it is perhaps the simplest to describe to a layperson, because it involves no explicit math or computation. Historically PCP was an important tool for proving the undecidability of problems involving context-free languages. PCP will not, however, be needed in our treatment of undecidability. Instead, in Section 7.13 we will reduce the halting problem for 2-stack machine programs to most of the important undecidable questions involving context-free languages. The undecidability of PCP is nonetheless an interesting application of rewriting systems.

EXAMPLE 7.55. Consider the following instance of PCP:

$$\{(\mathtt{ba}, \mathtt{b}), (\mathtt{na}, \mathtt{an}), (\mathtt{s}, \mathtt{as})\}.$$

It will be convenient to write the elements of an ordered pair one above the other. Thus we write the instance above as

$$\left\{ \frac{\mathtt{ba}}{\mathtt{b}}, \frac{\mathtt{na}}{\mathtt{an}}, \frac{\mathtt{s}}{\mathtt{as}} \right\}.$$

When we write a sequence of such pairs from left to right and omit the commas, the result has the appearance of concatenating the x's and the y's. Every sequence of the form

$$\frac{\mathtt{ba}}{\mathtt{b}} \left(\frac{\mathtt{na}}{\mathtt{an}} \right)^* \frac{\mathtt{s}}{\mathtt{as}}$$

is a solution, e.g.,

$$\frac{\mathtt{ba}}{\mathtt{b}}\frac{\mathtt{na}}{\mathtt{an}}\frac{\mathtt{na}}{\mathtt{an}}\frac{\mathtt{s}}{\mathtt{as}},$$

in which top and bottom spell out `bananas`. ▪▪▪

EXAMPLE 7.56. Consider another instance of PCP:

$$\left\{ \frac{\Lambda}{\mathtt{au}}, \frac{\mathtt{a}}{\mathtt{to}}, \frac{\mathtt{utom}}{\mathtt{ma}}, \frac{\mathtt{ton}}{\mathtt{n}} \right\}.$$

The sequence

$$\frac{\Lambda}{\mathtt{au}}\frac{\mathtt{a}}{\mathtt{to}}\frac{\mathtt{utom}}{\mathtt{ma}}\frac{\mathtt{a}}{\mathtt{to}}\frac{\mathtt{ton}}{\mathtt{n}}$$

is a solution, because top and bottom spell out `automaton`. (Naturally, there is no requirement that the solution to a PCP instance spell out a real English word.) ▪▪▪

Programs start in an initial configuration. Rewriting systems start with a given string. However, a solution to a PCP instance can start with any pair. If we are going to reduce a computational problem to PCP, it will be helpful if we can specify which pair comes first in a solution to the PCP instance. It will also be convenient to specify which pair comes last. Toward this end, we define a modified version of PCP.

Problem name: modified Post correspondence problem (MPCP)

Instance: a "starting" pair of strings $(x_{\text{start}}, y_{\text{start}})$, a "final" pair of strings $(x_{\text{final}}, y_{\text{final}})$, and a set S of "internal" pairs of strings

Question: Does there exist a sequence $\langle\langle (x_1, y_1), \ldots, (x_k, y_k) \rangle\rangle$ of pairs in S such that

$$x_{\text{start}} x_1 \cdots x_k x_{\text{final}} = y_{\text{start}} y_1 \cdots y_k y_{\text{final}}?$$

By analogy to PCP, the sequence $\langle\langle (x_{\text{start}}, y_{\text{start}}), (x_1, y_1), \ldots, (x_k, y_k), (x_{\text{final}}, y_{\text{final}}) \rangle\rangle$ is called a *solution* to the MPCP instance.

We will reduce MPCP to PCP; therefore, PCP is at least as hard as MPCP. Then we will reduce the problem of determining whether $x \stackrel{*}{\Rightarrow} \Lambda$ in a semi-Thuë system to MPCP. The former problem is undecidable by Corollary 7.51, so MPCP is undecidable. Therefore PCP is undecidable as well.

LEMMA 7.57. MPCP $\leq_m$ PCP.

Proof: If (x, y) is the first pair used in a solution to a PCP instance, then x is a prefix of y or y is a prefix of x; in particular, if x and y are nonempty, then x and y begin with the same character. If every pair of strings but one starts with different characters, then we know that that one must come first in any solution. Similarly, if every pair of strings but one ends with different characters, then we know that that one must come last in any solution. We will use these ideas in order to reduce MPCP to PCP.

Consider an instance of MPCP with starting pair $\frac{x_{\text{start}}}{y_{\text{start}}}$, final pair $\frac{x_{\text{final}}}{y_{\text{final}}}$, and set of internal pairs S. Let #, [, and] be new characters. In constructing our PCP instance, we will use [to mark the start pair and] to mark the final pair. In order to rule out trivial solutions to the PCP instance, we will interleave the characters in each pair with # but in a staggered fashion. If

$$\frac{x_{\text{start}}}{y_{\text{start}}} = \frac{a_1 \cdots a_p}{b_1 \cdots b_q},$$

let

$$\frac{x'_{\text{start}}}{y'_{\text{start}}} = \frac{[\#a_1\#a_2\# \cdots \#a_p}{[\#b_1\#b_2\# \cdots \#b_q\#}.$$

For each other pair $\frac{x}{y}$ in S, say

$$\frac{x}{y} = \frac{c_1 c_2 \cdots c_q}{d_1 d_2 \cdots d_r},$$

let

$$\frac{x'}{y'} = \frac{\#c_1\#c_2\# \cdots \#c_q}{d_1\#d_2\# \cdots \#d_r\#}.$$

If

$$\frac{x_{\text{final}}}{y_{\text{final}}} = \frac{e_1 \cdots e_p}{f_1 \cdots f_q},$$

let

$$\frac{x'_{\text{final}}}{y'_{\text{final}}} = \frac{\#e_1\#e_2\# \cdots \#e_p\#]}{f_1\#f_2\# \cdots \#f_q\#]}.$$

The PCP instance will consist of the pair $\frac{x'_{\text{start}}}{y'_{\text{start}}}$, the pair $\frac{x'_{\text{final}}}{y'_{\text{final}}}$, and all pairs $\frac{x'}{y'}$ such that $\frac{x}{y} \in S$. If

$$\frac{x_{\text{start}}}{y_{\text{start}}} \frac{x_1}{y_1} \cdots \frac{x_k}{y_k} \frac{x_{\text{final}}}{y_{\text{final}}}$$

is a solution to the MPCP instance, then it is easy to see that

$$\frac{x'_{\text{start}}}{y'_{\text{start}}} \frac{x'_1}{y'_1} \cdots \frac{x'_k}{y'_k} \frac{x'_{\text{final}}}{y'_{\text{final}}}$$

is a solution to the PCP instance.

Conversely, consider any solution to the PCP instance. The solution must start with the pair $\frac{x'_{\text{start}}}{y'_{\text{start}}}$ because this is the only pair in which both strings have the same first character. The solution must finish with the pair $\frac{x'_{\text{final}}}{y'_{\text{final}}}$ because this is the only pair in which both strings have the same last character. In particular, the solution must contain the pair $\frac{x'_{\text{final}}}{y'_{\text{final}}}$.

We assert that there cannot be a second occurrence of $\frac{x'_{\text{start}}}{y'_{\text{start}}}$ before the first occurrence of $\frac{x'_{\text{final}}}{y'_{\text{final}}}$. If there were, then the bottom string would contain the substring #[, but the top string can never contain this pattern. This proves the assertion.

Thus the solution must have the form

$$\frac{x'_{\text{start}}}{y'_{\text{start}}} \frac{x'_1}{y'_1} \cdots \frac{x'_k}{y'_k} \frac{x'_{\text{final}}}{y'_{\text{final}}} \cdots,$$

where more pairs may appear after the pair $\frac{x'_{\text{final}}}{y'_{\text{final}}}$. However, because the character] appears only in the pair $\frac{x'_{\text{final}}}{y'_{\text{final}}}$, the two]'s in that pair must line up. Therefore the prefix of that solution,

$$\frac{x'_{\text{start}}}{y'_{\text{start}}} \frac{x'_1}{y'_1} \cdots \frac{x'_k}{y'_k} \frac{x'_{\text{final}}}{y'_{\text{final}}},$$

is in fact a solution to the PCP instance. Consequently,

$$\frac{x_{\text{start}}}{y_{\text{start}}} \frac{x_1}{y_1} \cdots \frac{x_k}{y_k} \frac{x_{\text{final}}}{y_{\text{final}}}$$

is a solution to the MPCP instance.

Thus we have shown that the MPCP instance has a solution iff the PCP instance we constructed has a solution, so

$$\text{MPCP} \leq_m \text{PCP}.$$

■

Observe that in any solution

$$\frac{x_{\text{start}}}{y_{\text{start}}}\frac{x_1}{y_1}\cdots\frac{x_k}{y_k}\frac{x_{\text{final}}}{y_{\text{final}}}$$

to an instance of MPCP, it must be true for each i that one of the strings $x_{\text{start}}x_1\cdots x_i$ and $y_{\text{start}}y_1\cdots y_i$ is a prefix of the other. In our reduction to MPCP, it will always be the case that $x_{\text{start}}x_1\cdots x_i$ is a prefix of $y_{\text{start}}y_1\cdots y_i$. It is helpful to define the ith *underhang* of a sequence of pairs, denoted

$$\text{underhang}\left(\frac{x_{\text{start}}}{y_{\text{start}}}\frac{x_1}{y_1}\cdots\frac{x_i}{y_i}\right),$$

to be the unique string h such that

$$x_{\text{start}}x_1\cdots x_i h = y_{\text{start}}y_1\cdots y_i$$

if $x_{\text{start}}x_1\cdots x_i$ is a prefix of $y_{\text{start}}y_1\cdots y_i$; the underhang is undefined otherwise.

For example, take the PCP in Example 7.56, call $\frac{\Lambda}{\text{au}}$ the starting pair, and call $\frac{\texttt{ton}}{\texttt{n}}$ the final pair. Then

$$\text{underhang}\left(\frac{\Lambda}{\texttt{au}}\frac{\texttt{a}}{\texttt{to}}\right) = \texttt{uto},$$

and

$$\text{underhang}\left(\frac{\Lambda}{\texttt{au}}\frac{\texttt{a}}{\texttt{to}}\frac{\texttt{utom}}{\texttt{ma}}\right) = \texttt{a}.$$

If M is an MPCP instance, we define underhang(M) to be the set of all strings h such that h is the underhang of some sequence consisting of M's starting pair followed by some of M's internal pairs (the final pair is not allowed). If M is the MPCP above, then

$$\text{underhang}(M) = \{\texttt{au}, \texttt{uto}, \texttt{a}, \texttt{to}\}.$$

Overhangs can be defined analogously. When looking at solutions to an MPCP instance, it suffices to keep track of only the underhang or overhang, because all characters preceding the underhang or overhang are matched in the top and the bottom.

LEMMA 7.58. *MPCP is undecidable.*

Proof: Let G be a semi-Thuë system. Let s be a string. We reduce the problem of determining whether $s \stackrel{*}{\Rightarrow}_G \Lambda$.

We construct a corresponding instance of MPCP. Let # be a new character (distinct from the new characters used in reducing MPCP to PCP). The MPCP instance M will consist of the starting pair $\frac{\Lambda}{s\#}$, the final pair $\frac{\#}{\Lambda}$, and a set containing the following internal pairs:

$$\frac{u}{v} \qquad \text{for each production } u \rightarrow v \text{ in } G,$$

$$\frac{c}{c} \qquad \text{for each character } c \text{ in } G\text{'s alphabet},$$

$$\frac{\#}{\#}.$$

Let us explain informally why this is a reduction to MPCP. Concatenating the pair $\frac{u}{v}$ to a sequence of pairs has the effect of applying the production $u \rightarrow v$ at the left end of the underhang. The pairs $\frac{c}{c}$ and $\frac{\#}{\#}$ rotate the underhang so that v will be at the left end when we want to apply the next production. If we take a shortest solution to the MPCP instance and replace each # by $\stackrel{*}{\Rightarrow}$, the top and bottom strings will spell out a derivation of $s \stackrel{*}{\Rightarrow}_G \Lambda$. A formal correctness proof is given below.

Observe that every underhang of M contains exactly one #, because the starting pair has one # fewer on the top than on the bottom and each internal pair has the same number of #'s (0 or 1) on the top and bottom. We wish to prove that

$$s \stackrel{*}{\Rightarrow}_G t \text{ iff } t\# \in \text{underhang}(M).$$

The proof will be by induction, and it will be easier to prove something stronger. We assert that the following three statements are equivalent:

(*i*) $s \stackrel{*}{\Rightarrow}_G t$

(*ii*) $t\# \in \text{underhang}(M)$

(iii) $(\exists t_1, t_2)[t = t_1 t_2$ and $t_2 \# t_1 \in \text{underhang}(M)]$

The proof of the assertion is in three parts.

(i) $\Rightarrow$ (ii). Assume that $s \overset{*}{\Rightarrow}_G t$. We must prove that $t\# \in \text{underhang}(M)$. The proof is by induction on the length of the derivation $s \overset{*}{\Rightarrow}_G t$. If the derivation is 0 steps long, then $s = t$. Since

$$s\# = \text{underhang}\left(\frac{\Lambda}{s\#}\right),$$

the base case is established.

Now we assume it for derivations of length i and prove it for derivations of length $i+1$. Assume that $s \overset{*}{\Rightarrow}_G t$ by a derivation of length $i+1$. Then there is a string r such that

$$s \overset{*}{\Rightarrow}_G r \Rightarrow_G t$$

and $s \overset{*}{\Rightarrow}_G r$ by a derivation of length k. By the inductive hypothesis $r\# \in \text{underhang}(M)$. Let

$$r\# = \text{underhang}\left(\frac{\Lambda}{s\#}\frac{x_1}{y_1}\cdots\frac{x_i}{y_i}\right).$$

Let $u \rightarrow v$ be the production by which $r \Rightarrow_G t$. Then there exist strings r_1 and r_2 such that

$$r = r_1 u r_2 \quad \text{and} \quad t = r_1 v r_2.$$

Let $r_1 = c_1 \cdots c_m$ and $r_2 = c_{m+1} \cdots c_n$. Then

$$r = c_1 \cdots c_m u c_{m+1} \cdots c_n \quad \text{and} \quad t = c_1 \cdots c_m v c_{m+1} \cdots c_n.$$

Then

$$\begin{aligned} t\# &= \text{underhang}\left(\frac{\Lambda}{r\#}\frac{c_1}{c_1}\cdots\frac{c_m}{c_m}\frac{u}{v}\frac{c_{m+1}}{c_{m+1}}\cdots\frac{c_n}{c_n}\frac{\#}{\#}\right) \\ &= \text{underhang}\left(\frac{\Lambda}{s\#}\frac{x_1}{y_1}\cdots\frac{x_i}{y_i}\frac{c_1}{c_1}\cdots\frac{c_m}{c_m}\frac{u}{v}\frac{c_{m+1}}{c_{m+1}}\cdots\frac{c_n}{c_n}\frac{\#}{\#}\right), \end{aligned}$$

establishing the inductive case. This completes the inductive proof that (i) $\Rightarrow$ (ii).

(ii) $\Rightarrow$ (iii). Let $t_1 = \Lambda$ and $t_2 = t$. Then $t = t_1 t_2$ and $t_2\#t_1 = t\# \in$ underhang(M).

(iii) $\Rightarrow$ (i). Suppose that $t_2\#t_1 \in$ underhang(M). Then there is a sequence of pairs such that

$$t_2\#t_1 = \text{underhang}\left(\frac{\Lambda}{s\#}\frac{x_1}{y_1}\cdots\frac{x_i}{y_i}\right).$$

We must prove that $s \overset{*}{\Rightarrow}_G t_1 t_2$. The proof is by induction on i. If $i = 0$, then

$$t_2\#t_1 = \text{underhang}\left(\frac{\Lambda}{s\#}\right) = s\#,$$

so $t_2 = s$, $t_1 = \Lambda$, and $t = t_1 t_2 = s$. Since $s \overset{*}{\Rightarrow}_G s$, the base case is established. Now we assume that it is true for i, and we prove it for $i + 1$. Assume that

$$t_2\#t_1 = \text{underhang}\left(\frac{\Lambda}{s\#}\frac{x_1}{y_1}\cdots\frac{x_{i+1}}{y_{i+1}}\right).$$

Let

$$r_2\#r_1 = \text{underhang}\left(\frac{\Lambda}{s\#}\frac{x_1}{y_1}\cdots\frac{x_i}{y_i}\right).$$

Then, by the inductive hypothesis,

$$s \overset{*}{\Rightarrow}_G r_1 r_2.$$

By assumption,

$$\begin{aligned} t_2\#t_1 &= \text{underhang}\left(\frac{\Lambda}{s\#}\frac{x_1}{y_1}\cdots\frac{x_i}{y_i}\frac{x_{i+1}}{y_{i+1}}\right) \\ &= \text{underhang}\left(\frac{\Lambda}{r_2\#r_1}\frac{x_{i+1}}{y_{i+1}}\right). \end{aligned}$$

We consider three cases, depending on what kind of pair $\frac{x_{i+1}}{y_{i+1}}$ is.

Case 1: $\frac{x_{i+1}}{y_{i+1}} = \frac{u}{v}$ where $u \to v$ is a production in G. Then

$$t_2\#t_1 = \text{underhang}\left(\frac{\Lambda}{r_2\#r_1}\frac{u}{v}\right),$$

so $r_1v = t_1$ and thus $r_2 = ut_2$. Therefore

$$r_1r_2 = r_1ut_2 \Rightarrow_G r_1vt_2 = t_1t_2.$$

Since

$$s \overset{*}{\Rightarrow}_G r_1r_2 \Rightarrow_G t_1t_2,$$

that completes case 1.

Case 2: $\frac{x_{i+1}}{y_{i+1}} = \frac{c}{c}$ where c is a character in G's alphabet. Then

$$t_2\#t_1 = \text{underhang}\left(\frac{\Lambda}{r_2\#r_1}\frac{c}{c}\right),$$

so $r_1c = t_1$ and $r_2 = ct_2$. Therefore $r_1r_2 = r_1ct_2 = t_1t_2$. Since

$$s \overset{*}{\Rightarrow}_G r_1r_2 = t_1t_2,$$

that completes case 2.

Case 3: $\frac{x_{i+1}}{y_{i+1}} = \frac{\#}{\#}$. Then

$$t_2\#t_1 = \text{underhang}\left(\frac{\Lambda}{r_2\#r_1}\frac{\#}{\#}\right),$$

so $r_1 = t_2$ and $r_2 = t_1 = \Lambda$. Therefore $r_1r_2 = r_1 = t_2 = t_1t_2$. Since

$$s \overset{*}{\Rightarrow}_G r_1r_2 = t_1t_2,$$

that completes case 3.

Thus, in each of the three possible cases, the inductive step is established. This completes the proof by induction that (iii) $\Rightarrow$ (i). Because (i) $\Rightarrow$ (ii) $\Rightarrow$ (iii) $\Rightarrow$ (i), statements (i–iii) are equivalent. In particular,

$$s \overset{*}{\Rightarrow}_G \Lambda \quad \text{iff} \quad \# \in \text{underhang}(M).$$

Therefore, if $s \overset{*}{\Rightarrow}_G \Lambda$, there exists a sequence of pairs such that

$$\# = \text{underhang}\left(\frac{\Lambda}{s\#}\frac{x_1}{y_1}\cdots\frac{x_k}{y_k}\right),$$

so

$$\frac{\Lambda}{s\#}\frac{x_1}{y_1}\cdots\frac{x_k}{y_k}\frac{\#}{\Lambda}$$

is a solution to M.

Conversely, if

$$\frac{\Lambda}{s\#}\frac{x_1}{y_1}\cdots\frac{x_k}{y_k}\frac{\#}{\Lambda}$$

is a solution to M, then

$$\text{underhang}\left(\frac{\Lambda}{s\#}\frac{x_1}{y_1}\cdots\frac{x_k}{y_k}\right) = \#,$$

so $s \overset{*}{\Rightarrow}_G \Lambda$.

Thus $s \overset{*}{\Rightarrow}_G \Lambda$ if and only if the MPCP instance M has a solution, so we have reduced the problem of determining whether $s \overset{*}{\Rightarrow}_G \Lambda$ in a semi-Thuë system to MPCP. Because the former problem is undecidable, MPCP is undecidable as well. ∎

Because MPCP is both undecidable and m-reducible to PCP, PCP must be undecidable as well.

THEOREM 7.59. *PCP is undecidable.* ∎

Exercises

7.11-1 Prove that the following problem is undecidable:

Instance: a finite transducer with transfer relation τ

Question: Does there exist x such that $x\tau = x$?

7.11-2 Consider the following modified version of PCP.

Problem name: semimodified Post Correspondence Problem (SMPCP)

Instance: a "starting" pair of strings $(x_{\text{start}}, y_{\text{start}})$ and a set S of "other" pairs of strings

Question: Does there exist a sequence $\langle\langle(x_1, y_1), \ldots, (x_k, y_k)\rangle\rangle$ of pairs in S such that

$$x_{\text{start}} x_1 \cdots x_k = y_{\text{start}} y_1 \cdots y_k?$$

Prove that SMPCP is undecidable.

7.11-3 In parts (a) and (b) we will consider points $(x, y) \in \mathsf{N} \times \mathsf{N}$. An *affine transformation* on $\mathsf{N} \times \mathsf{N}$ is a function t such that

$$(x, y)\, t = (ax + by + c, dx + ey + f)$$

for some fixed natural numbers a, b, c, d, e, f.

(a) How would you represent an affine transformation?

(b) Prove that the following problem is undecidable:

Instance: a point $(x_0, y_0) \in \mathsf{N} \times \mathsf{N}$ and a finite set S of affine transformations on $\mathsf{N} \times \mathsf{N}$

Question: Is there a sequence of transformations in S that maps (x_0, y_0) to a point on the line $x = y$, i.e., do there exist a natural number x and a sequence of transformations $t_1, \ldots, t_k$ in S such that

$$(x_0, y_0) t_1 t_2 \cdots t_k = (x, x)?$$

Hint: Reduce SMPCP (Exercise 7.11-2). Represent each string by a k-adic numeral. Observe that $k\text{-adic}(ru) = k^{|u|} k\text{-adic}(r) + k\text{-adic}(u)$.

(c) Prove that the following problem is undecidable:

Instance: a point $(x_0, y_0, z_0) \in \mathsf{N}^3$ and a finite set S of 3×3 matrices over N

Question: Are there a sequence of matrices $M_1, \ldots, M_k$ in S and a point $(x, x, z) \in \mathsf{N}^3$ such that

$$(x_0, y_0, z_0) M_1 M_2 \cdots M_k = (x, x, z)?$$

(d) Prove that the following problem is undecidable:

Instance: a finite set S of 3×3 matrices over $\mathbb{N}$

Question: Is there a sequence of matrices $M_1, \ldots, M_k$ in S such that the product $M_1 M_2 \cdots M_k$ contains equal numbers in row 3, column 1 and in row 3, column 2?

(e) Prove that the following problem is undecidable:

Problem name: mortality

Instance: a finite set S of 3×3 matrices over $\mathbb{N}$ and a pair of natural numbers i, j between 1 and 3

Question: Is there a sequence of matrices $M_1, \ldots, M_k$ in S such that the product $M_1 M_2 \cdots M_k$ contains a 0 in row i, column j?

7.11-4 In this exercise, you will give another proof that MPCP is undecidable.

(a) Recall the definition of a queue from Exercise 1.1-1. Show how a queue can simulate a tape.

(b) Prove that the halting problem for queue machine programs is undecidable.

(c) Reduce the halting problem for queue machines to MPCP. You need only sketch a proof that your reduction is correct. Conclude that MPCP is undecidable. (Historically queue machines have been called Post machines.)

7.12 UNDECIDABILITY OF FIRST-ORDER LOGIC

A major goal of mathematics is to determine which statements are theorems. In any reasonable logic, the set of theorems is recursively enumerable. However, for any reasonably expressive logic the set of theorems is not recursive. In this section, we will prove an important special case, namely that there is no algorithm to determine which statements in first-order logic (defined below) are theorems.

We will prove the undecidability of first-order logic by reducing the halting problem. But first, in order to state the result, we will need to present a formal treatment of some aspects of logic. We will try not to be more formal than necessary.

First-order logic consists of statements that involve constants, variables, functions, and Boolean predicates as well as the usual logical symbols $\wedge$ (and), $\vee$ (or), $\neg$ (not), $\exists x$ (there exists x), and $\forall x$ (for all x), where x denotes a variable. Additional logical operations like implication ($\Rightarrow$) can be defined in terms of those operations, i.e., $x \Rightarrow y$ means $(\neg x) \vee y$. In this section we consider a subset of first-order logic in which each function has at most two arguments and the quantifiers $\exists$ and $\forall$ are not allowed. We call this logic *restricted first-order logic* (RFOL for short).

Rules of inference are the usual logical rules, e.g.,

- $a \vee \neg a$
- $a \Rightarrow a \vee b$
- $b \Rightarrow a \vee b$
- $a \wedge b \Rightarrow a$
- $a \wedge b \Rightarrow b$
- $(a \wedge (a \Rightarrow b)) \Rightarrow b,$

where a and b denote any logical expressions. The last rule above is called *modus ponens*; its right side b is called the logical consequence of its left side $a \wedge (a \Rightarrow b)$. A formal proof is a sequence of statements in which each statement is one of the following

- a rule of inference
- the conjunction (logical and) of some pair of preceding statements
- the logical consequence of the directly preceding statement

The last statement in a proof is called a *theorem*.

If a statement is a theorem in first-order logic, then it is true no matter how its variables, functions, predicates, and constants are interpreted. (This property is called *soundness*; its proof is beyond the scope of this book.)

EXAMPLE 7.60. Some examples of statements in RFOL include $p(f(x)) \wedge p(y) \Rightarrow p(f(x))$, $p(f(x)) \vee p(y) \Rightarrow p(f(x))$, and

$(p(z) \wedge (p(x) \Rightarrow p(f(x)))) \Rightarrow p(y)$ where x and y are variables, z is a constant, f is a function, and p is a Boolean predicate. Only the first of those three statements is a theorem; observe that it is true for all predicates p, all functions f, and all values of x and y. The second and third statements are easily seen to be false for particular interpretations of x, y, z, f, p. ■■■

Observe that the set of theorems is recursively enumerable because we can nondeterministically guess a proof and verify it line by line. However, we will see that the set of theorems in RFOL is nonrecursive, because we can reduce the halting problem for inattentive nondeterministic 2-counter machines to it.

Let P be a nondeterministic program for a machine [control, unsigned counter, unsigned counter]. By standardizations, we may assume that P has a unique final configuration $(q_{\text{accept}}, 0, 0)$ and that each instruction operates on exactly one of the counters. Let P's initial control state be q_{start}.

Let i and j be variables. For each control state $q \in Q$, let $f_q(\cdot, \cdot)$ be a predicate with two arguments. $f_q(i, j)$ will represent that (q, i, j) is a configuration belonging to a partial computation of P. Let $s(\cdot)$ be a function of one variable; $s(i)$ will represent $i + 1$. Let $\mathbf{z}$ be a constant; $\mathbf{z}$ will represent 0. Corresponding to P's initial configuration $(q_{\text{start}}, 0, 0)$ is the statement,

$$f_{q_{\text{start}}}(\mathbf{z}, \mathbf{z}).$$

Corresponding to each instruction π we define a statement ψ_π as in Table 7.5.

We define a statement H to be the conjunction of all these statements, i.e.,

$$H = f_{q_{\text{start}}}(\mathbf{z}, \mathbf{z}) \wedge \bigwedge_{\pi \in \mathcal{I}} \psi_\pi.$$

Corresponding to P's final relation is the statement

$$f_{q_{\text{accept}}}(\mathbf{z}, \mathbf{z}).$$

We assert that P halts if and only if the statement $H \Rightarrow f_{q_{\text{accept}}}(\mathbf{z}, \mathbf{z})$ is a theorem, i.e., iff there is a proof of the statement

$$\left(f_{q_{\text{start}}}(\mathbf{z}, \mathbf{z}) \wedge \bigwedge_{\pi \in \mathcal{I}} \psi_\pi \right) \Rightarrow f_{q_{\text{accept}}}(\mathbf{z}, \mathbf{z}).$$

Instruction π	*Statement* ψ_π
$(q \to r$, INC, NOOP$)$	$f_q(i,j) \Rightarrow f_r(s(i),j)$
$(q \to r$, DEC, NOOP$)$	$f_q(s(i),j) \Rightarrow f_r(i,j)$
$(q \to r$, ZERO, NOOP$)$	$f_q(\mathbf{z},j) \Rightarrow f_r(\mathbf{z},j)$
$(q \to r$, NOOP, INC$)$	$f_q(i,j) \Rightarrow f_r(i,s(j))$
$(q \to r$, NOOP, DEC$)$	$f_q(i,s(j)) \Rightarrow f_r(i,j)$
$(q \to r$, NOOP, ZERO$)$	$f_q(i,\mathbf{z}) \Rightarrow f_r(i,\mathbf{z})$

TABLE 7.5: Converting an inattentive 2-CM program to a statement in restricted first-order logic. Suppose, for example, that P contains the instruction $(q \to r, \text{INC}, \text{NOOP})$. If P reaches the configuration (q,i,j) in a partial computation, then P reaches the configuration $(r,i+1,j)$ in a partial computation that applies that instruction. Therefore $f_q(i,j) \Rightarrow f_r(s(i),j)$. This explains the first statement in the table. The rest are similar. (The reader will notice a similarity to the HG equations constructed in Section 7.5.)

First, let us assume that P halts. We assert that if $(q_{\text{start}},0,0) \overset{\Pi^k}{\longmapsto} (q,i,j)$, then there is a proof that $H \Rightarrow f_q(s^{(i)}(\mathbf{z}),s^{(j)}(\mathbf{z}))$ where $s^{(m)}$ denotes m-fold composition of s with itself. The proof is by induction on k. When $k=0$, $(q,i,j)=(q_{\text{start}},0,0)$, and $H \Rightarrow f_{q_{\text{start}}}(\mathbf{z},\mathbf{z})$ is a theorem by the fourth rule of inference, establishing the base case. Suppose that the assertion has been established for some $k \geq 0$. We establish it now for $k+1$. Assume that $(q_{\text{start}},0,0) \overset{\Pi^{k+1}}{\longmapsto} (q,i,j)$. Then there are a configuration (r,m,n) and an instruction π that precede (q,i,j) in such a partial computation so that

$$(q_{\text{start}},0,0) \overset{\Pi^k}{\longmapsto} (r,m,n) \overset{\pi}{\longmapsto} (q,i,j).$$

By the inductive hypothesis there is a proof that

$$H \Rightarrow f_r(s^{(m)}(\mathbf{z}),s^{(n)}(\mathbf{z})).$$

In addition, the statement

$$H \Rightarrow \psi_\pi$$

is a theorem by repeated application of the fourth and fifth rules of inference. Because of how ψ_π was defined, by substituting for its variables we can prove that

$$f_r(s^{(m)}(\mathbf{z}), s^{(n)}(\mathbf{z})) \Rightarrow f_q(s^{(i)}(\mathbf{z}), s^{(j)}(\mathbf{z})).$$

Combining these proofs, we have a proof that

$$H \Rightarrow f_q(s^{(i)}(\mathbf{z}), s^{(j)}(\mathbf{z})),$$

completing the induction.

If t is the number of steps in a halting computation of P, then

$$(q_{\text{start}}, 0, 0) \overset{\Pi^t}{\longmapsto} (q_{\text{accept}}, 0, 0).$$

By the preceding assertion, there is a proof that $H \Rightarrow f_{q_{\text{accept}}}(\mathbf{z}, \mathbf{z})$.

Conversely, suppose that there is a proof that $H \Rightarrow f_{q_{\text{accept}}}(\mathbf{z}, \mathbf{z})$. By the soundness of first-order logic, the statement must be true for every possible interpretation of the functions $f_q(\cdot, \cdot)$, the function $s(\cdot)$, and the constant $\mathbf{z}$. Interpret the statement $f_q(s^{(i)}(\mathbf{z}), s^{(j)}(\mathbf{z}))$ to mean that a partial computation of P reaches configuration (q, i, j), interpret $s(i)$ as $i + 1$, and interpret $\mathbf{z}$ as 0. All the statements in H are true in that interpretation, so any statement deduced from H must be true in that interpretation as well. In particular, $f_{q_{\text{accept}}}(\mathbf{z}, \mathbf{z})$ must be true in that interpretation, so there is a partial computation of P that reaches the configuration $(q_{\text{accept}}, 0, 0)$; i.e., P halts.

Thus we have reduced the halting problem to the problem of deciding which logical statements are theorems. Therefore the set of theorems in RFOL is undecidable. Consequently, the set of theorems in first-order logic is undecidable as well.

THEOREM 7.61. *The set of theorems in first-order logic is undecidable.*

EXAMPLE 7.62. Consider the partial function

$$\text{Collatz}(x) = \begin{cases} 0 & \text{if } x = 1, \\ \text{Collatz}(x/2) & \text{if } x \text{ is even}, \\ \text{Collatz}(3x + 1) & \text{otherwise.} \end{cases}$$

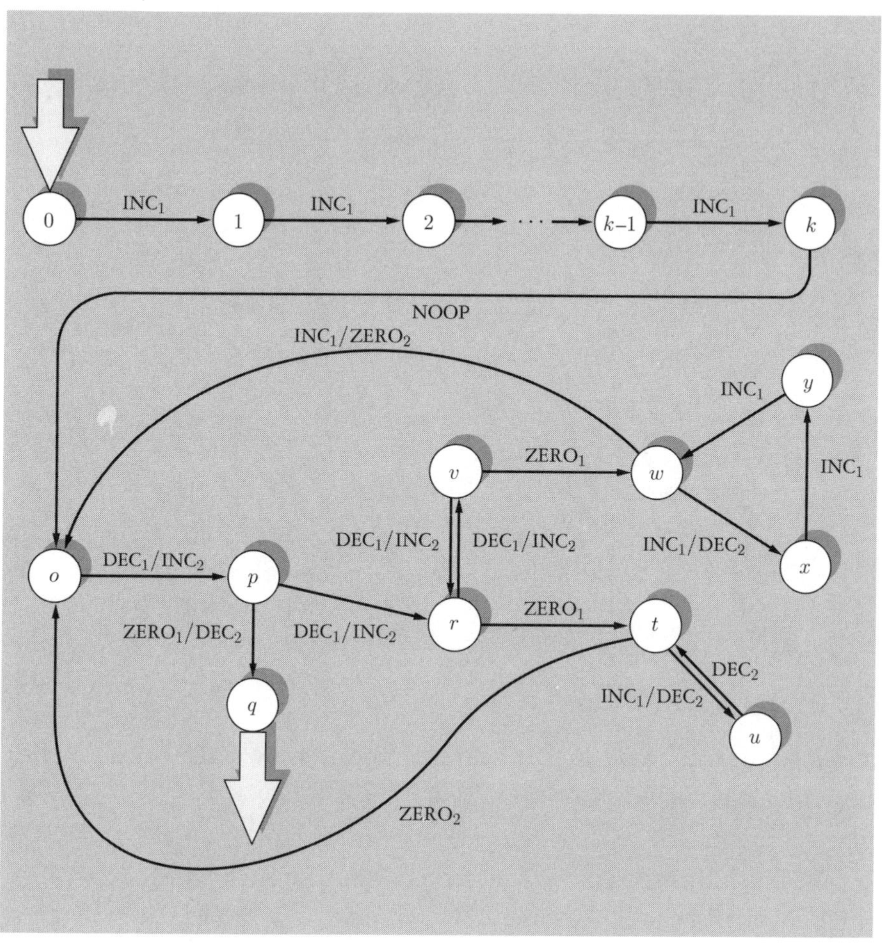

FIGURE 7.4: An inattentive 2-CM program that halts iff Collatz$(k) = 0$, where

$$\text{Collatz}(k) = \begin{cases} 0 & \text{if } k = 1, \\ \text{Collatz}(k/2) & \text{if } k \text{ is even}, \\ \text{Collatz}(3k+1) & \text{otherwise.} \end{cases}$$

Notice that Collatz(x) is either 0 or undefined. It is not known whether the Collatz function is total, although this question has generated a lot of interest. Let us fix a positive integer k. An inattentive 2-CM program

$$
\begin{aligned}
&\Big(f_0(\mathbf{z},\mathbf{z})\\
&\quad\wedge\ [f_0(i,j) \Rightarrow f_1(s(i),j)] \ \wedge\ [f_1(i,j) \Rightarrow f_2(s(i),j)]\\
&\quad\wedge\ \cdots\ \wedge\ [f_{k-1}(i,j) \Rightarrow f_k(s(i),j)]\\
&\quad\wedge\ [f_k(i,j) \Rightarrow f_o(i,j)] \ \wedge\ [f_o(s(i),j) \Rightarrow f_p(i,s(j))] \ \wedge\ [f_p(\mathbf{z},s(j)) \Rightarrow f_q(\mathbf{z},j)]\\
&\quad\wedge\ [f_p(s(i),j) \Rightarrow f_r(i,s(j))] \ \wedge\ [f_r(\mathbf{z},j) \Rightarrow f_t(\mathbf{z},j)] \ \wedge\ [f_t(i,s(j)) \Rightarrow f_u(s(i),j)]\\
&\quad\wedge\ [f_u(i,s(j)) \Rightarrow f_t(i,j)] \ \wedge\ [f_t(i,\mathbf{z}) \Rightarrow f_o(i,\mathbf{z})] \ \wedge\ [f_r(s(i),j) \Rightarrow f_v(i,s(j))]\\
&\quad\wedge\ [f_v(s(i),j) \Rightarrow f_r(i,s(j))] \ \wedge\ [f_v(\mathbf{z},j) \Rightarrow f_w(\mathbf{z},j)] \ \wedge\ [f_w(i,s(j)) \Rightarrow f_x(s(i),j)]\\
&\quad\wedge\ [f_x(i,j) \Rightarrow f_y(s(i),j)] \ \wedge\ [f_y(i,j) \Rightarrow f_w(s(i),j)] \ \wedge\ [f_w(i,\mathbf{z}) \Rightarrow f_o(s(i),\mathbf{z})]\Big)\\
&\quad\Rightarrow\ f_q(\mathbf{z},\mathbf{z}).
\end{aligned}
$$

FIGURE 7.5: The statement in first-order logic corresponding to the program in Figure 7.4. This statement is provable if and only if the 2-CM program halts, i.e., if and only if $\text{Collatz}(k) = 0$. Observe that it was not necessary to factor instructions or eliminate null instructions.

that halts iff $\text{Collatz}(k) = 0$ is shown in Figure 7.4. The corresponding first-order statement is shown in Figure 7.5. ■ ■ ■

We finish this section with a theorem due to Gödel, which we will not prove in this book. It is sometimes referred to as Gödel's completeness theorem.

THEOREM 7.63 (Completeness theorem for first-order logic). *A statement in first-order logic is provable if and only if it is true for all interpretations of its function symbols and constants.*

Statements that are true in all interpretations are called *valid*, so Gödel's completeness theorem can be restated as "provability is equivalent to validity in first-order logic." By Theorems 7.61 and 7.63, we have

COROLLARY 7.64. *The set of valid statements in first-order logic is undecidable.*

■

In contrast, in Section 8.3 we will examine Gödel's incompleteness theorem; it says that certain more complex systems of logic contain statements that are true for all interpretations of their function symbols and constants, but nonetheless are not provable.

Exercises

7.12-1 Suppose that we restrict RFOL further by allowing only one Boolean predicate, but we allow the predicate to have three arguments. Prove that the set of theorems in this logic is undecidable.

7.12-2 By modifying this section's construction, show directly how to m-reduce $K_{2\text{-}SM}$ to the problem of provability in RFOL. Do not reduce $K_{2\text{-}SM}$ to $K_{2\text{-}CM}$.

†7.12-3 Is the Collatz function total?

7.13 VALID AND INVALID COMPUTATIONS

Recall that a computation of a program may be represented as a string. Thus the set of computations of a program P is a language, which we denote $\mathcal{C}(P)$. For historical reasons, computations are also called *valid computations*. The complement of $\mathcal{C}(P)$, i.e., $\overline{\mathcal{C}(P)}$, is called the set of *invalid computations* of program P, even though many of its elements are not computations at all, nor even sequences of instructions.

Recall that $K_{2\text{-}CM}$ is the set of deterministic 2-counter machine programs that halt on at least one input. A program halts on input x if and only if it has a valid computation on input x. Thus

$$K_{2\text{-}CM} = \{P : P \text{ is a deterministic 2-CM program and } \mathcal{C}(P) \neq \emptyset\}.$$

Since $K_{2\text{-}CM}$ is undecidable, there is no algorithm to decide whether $\mathcal{C}(P)$ is empty for deterministic 2-counter machine programs P.

We will show that the set of valid computations of any particular 2-counter machine program is the intersection of two DCR languages. By closure properties, the set of invalid computations of any particular 2-CM program is an NCA language. These proofs are constructive; i.e., there is an algorithm that takes a nondeterministic 2-CM program P and produces the appropriate DCRs or NCA. Thus these two properties of $\mathcal{C}(P)$ will allow us to prove that many properties of NCAs are undecidable. Since every NCA can be trivially converted to an NSA, the same properties of NSAs are undecidable. Since NSAs can be effectively converted to equivalent CFGs, we conclude that the same properties of context-free grammars are undecidable.

The first problem we consider is whether the set of computations of a 2-CM program is empty. Recall:

DEFINITION 7.65. $\mathcal{C}(P)$ is the set of (valid) computations of the program P.

We show that the problem "Is $\mathcal{C}(P)$ empty?" is undecidable for 2-CM programs P.

THEOREM 7.66. *$\{P : P$ is a 2-CM program and $\mathcal{C}(P) = \emptyset\}$ is not recursive.*

Proof: Let $L = \{P : P \text{ is a 2-CM program and } \mathcal{C}(P) = \emptyset\}$. We reduce $K_{2\text{-}CM}$ to $\overline{L}$, deducing that $\overline{L}$ (and hence L) is not recursive. We have $P \in K_{2\text{-}CM}$ iff P is a deterministic 2-CM program and P halts on at least one input. The second conjunct is true iff P has at least one accepting computation, i.e., $\mathcal{C}(P) \neq \emptyset$. Let p be some program that never halts. Let

$$f(P) = \begin{cases} P & \text{if } P \text{ is deterministic,} \\ p & \text{otherwise.} \end{cases}$$

Then $P \in K_{2\text{-}CM} \iff f(P) \in \overline{L}$. ∎

Next we observe that the set of valid computations of a 2-CM program is the intersection of two DCR languages. In fact the proof is constructive, which is essential to obtaining certain further proofs of undecidability.

LEMMA 7.67. *There is an algorithm that takes a 2-CM program P and produces two DCR programs D_1 and D_2 such that $\mathcal{C}(P)$ is the intersection of the languages recognized by D_1 and D_2.*

Proof: This is similar to the proof of Lemma 7.15. Let P be a 2-CM program with instruction set $\mathcal{I}$. One may determine whether a string C is a computation of P by verifying that C is a sequence of instructions of P in which no SCAN follows an EOF and performing separately the sequence of control operations, the sequence of operations on the first counter, and the sequence of operations on the second counter. The set of sequences of instructions of P in which no SCAN follows an EOF is a regular language. One needs only device d in order to perform the sequence of operations on d starting in its initial state, accepting if d ends up in a final state and rejecting if the sequence of operations is not executable or if d ends up in a nonfinal state. Therefore verifying the last three conditions amounts to testing membership in a DFR language, a DCR language, and another DCR language. Therefore $\mathcal{C}(P)$ is the intersection of two regular languages and two DCR languages. Since the intersection of a regular language with a DCR language is itself a DCR language, $\mathcal{C}(P)$ is the intersection of two DCR languages. Let D_1 and D_2 be DCRs, readily constructed, that recognize those languages. ∎

Thus there is no algorithm to determine whether the intersection of two DCR languages is nonempty.

COROLLARY 7.68. *The set* $S = \{(D_1, D_2) : D_1$ *and* D_2 *are DCRs and* $L(D_1) \cap L(D_2) \neq \emptyset\}$ *is nonrecursive.*

Proof: We reduce the problem of determining whether $\mathcal{C}(P) \neq \emptyset$ to S. Since the former is undecidable, S must be undecidable. Let $f(P) = (D_1, D_2)$ as given by the preceding theorem. Then $\mathcal{C}(P) \neq \emptyset$ iff $L(D_1) \cap L(D_2) \neq \emptyset$ iff $f(P) \in S$. ∎

Conventionally we represent context-free languages by CFGs or NSAs; it doesn't matter which because we have an algorithm to convert CFGs to NSAs and vice versa. Similarly, we represent DCR languages, NCA languages, and DSR languages by the corresponding programs. We say that a property of context-free languages, DCR languages, NCA languages, or DSR languages is undecidable if it is undecidable for the conventional representation of them. By trivial reductions we have

COROLLARY 7.69. *It is undecidable whether the intersection of two CFLs, two DSR languages, two NCA languages, or two DCR languages is empty.*

Proof: By Corollary 7.68 it is undecidable whether the intersection of two DCR languages is nonempty; therefore it is undecidable whether their intersection is empty. Because a DCR can be converted to an NCA, DSR, or CFG for the same language, it is undecidable whether the intersection of two NCA languages, two DSR languages, or two CFLs is empty. ■

For the remainder of this section, let Σ denote an alphabet containing at least two characters. Next we show that it is undecidable whether an NCA language is equal to Σ^*.

COROLLARY 7.70. *The set* $\{N : N \text{ is an NCA program such that } L(N) \neq \Sigma^*\}$ *is nonrecursive.*

Proof: Given DCRs D_1 and D_2, interchange accepting and rejecting states to construct DCRs D_1' and D_2' that recognize $\overline{L(D_1)}$ and $\overline{L(D_2)}$, respectively. Then, as in the proof of closure under union, construct an NCA $N = f(D_1, D_2)$ such that

$$L(N) = L(D_1') \cup L(D_2') = \overline{L(D_1) \cap L(D_2)}.$$

Then $L(D_1) \cap L(D_2) = \emptyset$ iff $L(N) = \Sigma^*$. ■

In contrast to the preceding theorem, it is possible to test whether $L(N) = \emptyset$ when N is an NCA or even an NSA, because we can convert an NCA to an NSA, convert the NSA to a CFG G, and test whether $L(G) = \emptyset$ as in Exercise 5.3-4. It is also possible to test whether a particular string belongs to an NCA language or an NSA language by applying CYK or Earley's membership algorithm to the corresponding CFG. For another contrast, it is possible to test whether a regular language is equal to Σ^*.

Since there is no algorithm to decide whether an NCA language is Σ^*, there is no algorithm to solve the more general problem for NSA languages, i.e., CFLs.

COROLLARY 7.71. *It is undecidable whether a CFL is equal to* Σ^*. ■

As a consequence of Corollary 7.71, there is no algorithm that determines whether (a) two CFLs are equal or (b) whether a CFL and a regular language are equal—because testing for equality to Σ^* is a special case of those two problems. As a practical consideration, if two compilers use different grammars, there is no general way to verify that they really implement the same programming language. The moral is that compilers should use the published grammar for a language or else use a grammar obtained by transformations that are known to produce an equivalent grammar.

Ambiguous CFGs are troublesome because they do not assign unique meanings to strings. An early example is the Algol60 language, which did not assign a unique meaning to the "dangling else" described in Section 5.9. This led to a search for algorithms that would determine in general whether a CFG is ambiguous. However, we will prove that such an algorithm is an impossibility. The moral is that programming languages should be designed in such a way that we know they are unambiguous from the start; there is no general way to test for ambiguity after the fact.

COROLLARY 7.72. *It is undecidable whether*

(i) a CFG is ambiguous.

(ii) a CFL is inherently ambiguous.

Proof: Let L denote the set $\{(D_1, D_2) : D_1$ and D_2 are DSRs such that $L(D_1) \cap L(D_2) \neq \emptyset\}$.

(i) Let L_1 denote the set of ambiguous NSAs. We begin by reducing L to L_1. Let $f(D_1, D_2) = P$, where P is an NSA (constructed in the standard way) that accepts $L(D_1) \cup L(D_2)$. The number of accepting computations of P on input x is equal to the number of accepting computations of D_1 on input x plus the number of accepting computations of D_2 on input x. Since D_1 and D_2 are DSRs, each of them has at most one accepting computation per input. The program P will have exactly two accepting computations on each input belonging to $L(D_1) \cap L(D_2)$; program P will have zero or one accepting computation on each other input. Thus P is ambiguous if and only if $L(D_1) \cap L(D_2)$ is nonempty, so

$$(D_1, D_2) \in L \iff P \in L_1 \iff f(D_1, D_2) \in L_1.$$

Thus $L_1 \leq_m L$. Since L is known to be nonrecursive, the set of ambiguous NSAs is nonrecursive. Because NSAs can be effectively converted to CFGs while preserving ambiguity or unambiguity, the set of ambiguous CFGs is nonrecursive.

(ii) Recall that a CFL is inherently ambiguous iff every CFG that generates it is ambiguous iff every NSA that accepts it is ambiguous. We reduce L to the set of NSAs that accept inherently ambiguous CFLs. Let $f(D_1, D_2) = P$ where P is an NSA (constructed in the standard way) that accepts all strings of the form

$$\mathtt{a}^i\mathtt{b}^i\mathtt{c}^*\#L(D_1) \cup \mathtt{a}^*\mathtt{b}^i\mathtt{c}^i\#L(D_2).$$

If $L(D_1) \cap L(D_2) \neq \emptyset$, then there is some string s that belongs to $L(D_1) \cap L(D_2)$.

As in the proof of Theorem 5.31, it is readily verified that every grammar that generates $L(P)$ has two parse trees for $\mathtt{a}^{N+N!}\mathtt{b}^{N+N!}\mathtt{c}^{N+N!}\#s$ for all sufficiently large N, so $L(P)$ is inherently ambiguous. (Alternatively, we can use Corollary 6.13(i). Assume that $L(P)$ is unambiguous. Define a deterministic finite transduction τ such that $x\tau = x\#s$. Then

$$L(P)\tau^{-1} = \{\mathtt{a}^i\mathtt{b}^j\mathtt{c}^k : i = j \text{ or } j = k\},$$

which is inherently ambiguous. This contradicts Corollary 6.13(i), so $L(P)$ must be inherently ambiguous.)

On the other hand, if $L(D_1) \cap L(D_2) = \emptyset$, then P is unambiguous as in the proof of part (i), so the corresponding grammar for $L(P)$ is unambiguous. ∎

COROLLARY 7.73

(i) It is undecidable whether the intersection of two DCR languages is any of the following:

- *a CFL*
- *a DSR language*
- *a regular language*
- *a finite language*

(*ii*) *It is undecidable whether the intersection of two CFLs is*

- *a CFL*
- *a DSR language*
- *a regular language*
- *a finite language*

Proof

(i) Let L be the language $\{(D_1, D_2) : D_1$ and D_2 are DCRs such that $L(D_1) \cap L(D_2) = \emptyset\}$. Let $f(D_1, D_2) = (D_1', D_2')$ where D_1' is a DCR that accepts all strings of the form $\mathtt{a}^i\mathtt{b}^i\mathtt{c}^*\#L(D_1)$ and D_2' is a DCR that accepts all strings of the form $\mathtt{a}^*\mathtt{b}^i\mathtt{c}^i\#L(D_2)$. Then $L(D_1') \cap L(D_2')$ consists of all strings of the form $\mathtt{a}^i\mathtt{b}^i\mathtt{c}^i\#s$ where $s \in L(D_1) \cap L(D_2)$. Thus, if $L(D_1) \cap L(D_2)$ is empty, $L(D_1') \cap L(D_2')$ is also empty (hence a context-free language, a DSR language, a regular language, and a finite language). On the other hand, if $L(D_1) \cap L(D_2)$ is nonempty, then $L(D_1') \cap L(D_2')$ is not a CFL (hence not a DSR language, a regular language, or a finite language either). Thus f is a reduction from L to each of the following problems: determining whether the intersection of two DCR languages is a CFL, determining whether the intersection of two DCR languages is a DSR language, determining whether the intersection of two DCR languages is a regular language, and determining whether the intersection of two DCR languages is a finite language. Since L is nonrecursive, each of those problems must be undecidable.

(ii) Because every DCR can be converted to a context-free grammar for the same language, the corresponding problems for CFLs are undecidable as well. ∎

A language is a *co-CFL* if its complement is a CFL.

COROLLARY 7.74

(*i*) *It is undecidable whether an NCA language is any of the following:*

- *a co-CFL*
- *a DSR language*

- *a regular language*
- *a co-finite language*

(ii) It is undecidable whether a CFL is any of the following:

- *a co-CFL*
- *a DSR language*
- *a regular language*
- *a co-finite language*

Proof

(i) If D_1 and D_2 are DCRs, construct an NCA N that accepts the language $\overline{L(D_1)} \cup \overline{L(D_2)}$. (Interchange accepting and rejecting states in the DCRs and then use the standard union construction for nondeterministic programs.) Then, by De Morgan's law, $L(N) = \overline{L(D_1) \cap L(D_2)}$. Then $L(D_1) \cap L(D_2)$ is a CFL, a DSR language, a regular language, or a finite language if and only if $L(N)$ is a co-CFL, a DSR language, a regular language, or a co-finite language, respectively. Because it is undecidable whether the intersection of two DCR languages is any of the former, it is undecidable whether an NCA language is any of the latter.

(ii) Because we can convert an NCA to a CFG for the same language, the same problems are undecidable for CFLs. ■

EXAMPLE 7.75. We show that there is no algorithm to determine for an NSA N whether $L(N) = (\mathtt{aa} \cup \mathtt{bb})^*$. We reduce the problem of determining for an NSA P whether $L(P) = \{\mathtt{a}, \mathtt{b}\}^*$. Suppose that L is accepted by the NSA N. Let τ be a finite transduction that replaces a with aa and b with bb. Then $L\tau$ is an NSA language, for which we can construct an NSA. Let $f(N)$ be that NSA. Then

$$L(N) = \{\mathtt{a}, \mathtt{b}\}^* \iff L(f(N)) = (\mathtt{aa} \cup \mathtt{bb})^*,$$

completing the reduction. Consequently, there is no algorithm to determine whether an NSA accepts or a CFG generates $(\mathtt{aa} \cup \mathtt{bb})^*$. ■■■

In contrast, for any string x there is an algorithm to determine whether $L(G) = \{x\}$ (Exercise 7.13-1(f)).

Exercises

7.13-1 Which of the following problems are undecidable?

(a) **Instance:** CFGs G_1 and G_2

Question: Is $\text{PREFIX}(L(G_1)) = \text{PREFIX}(L(G_2))$?

Solution: Undecidable. We will reduce the problem of determining whether $L(H_1) = L(H_2)$ for CFGs H_1 and H_2. Let # be a character that does not belong to the terminal alphabet of H_1 or H_2. Let $L_1 = L(H_1)$ and $L_2 = L(H_2)$. Let G_1 be a grammar for $L_1\#$, and let G_2 be a grammar for $L_2\#$. We assert that $L_1 = L_2$ if and only if $\text{PREFIX}(L_1\#) = \text{PREFIX}(L_2\#)$. Proof of assertion: If $L_1 = L_2$, then $\text{PREFIX}(L_1\#) = \text{PREFIX}(L_2\#)$. Conversely, if $\text{PREFIX}(L_1\#) = \text{PREFIX}(L_2\#)$, then

$$L_1\# = \text{PREFIX}(L_1\#) \cap \Sigma^*\# = \text{PREFIX}(L_2\#) \cap \Sigma^*\# = L_2\#,$$

so $L_1 = L_2$.

(b) **Instance:** a CFG G and variables X and Y

Question: Is $L(X) = L(Y)$?

(c) **Instance:** a CFG G with terminal alphabet Σ and variable set V, and variables X and Y

Question: Is $\{u \in \Sigma^* : (\exists v \in V^*)[X \overset{*}{\Rightarrow} uv]\}$ equal to $\{u \in \Sigma^* : (\exists v \in V^*)[Y \overset{*}{\Rightarrow} uv]\}$?

Solution: Undecidable. We will reduce the problem of determining whether $\text{PREFIX}(L(G_1)) = \text{PREFIX}(L(G_2))$ for CFGs G_1 and G_2. Without loss of generality assume that G_1 and G_2 have disjoint variable sets, X is the start variable of G_1, and Y is the start variable of G_2. Standardize G_1 and G_2 so they are in CNF or GNF. A variable is *useless* if it derives no terminal strings or if it is unreachable from the start variable. Eliminate from G_1 and G_2 all useless variables and all productions involving them. Combine G_1 and G_2 into a new grammar G. Then for each variable Z in G,

$$\{u \in \Sigma^* : (\exists v \in V^*)[Z \overset{*}{\Rightarrow} uv]\} = \text{PREFIX}(L(Z)).$$

Therefore $\text{PREFIX}(L(G_1)) = \text{PREFIX}(L(G_2))$ if and only if $\text{PREFIX}(L(X)) = \text{PREFIX}(L(Y))$ if and only if $\{u \in \Sigma^* : (\exists v \in V^*)[X \overset{*}{\Rightarrow} uv]\} = \{u \in \Sigma^* : (\exists v \in V^*)[Y \overset{*}{\Rightarrow} uv]\}$.

(d) **Instance:** a CFG G

Question: Is $L(G)$ inherently unboundedly ambiguous?

(e) **Instance:** a CFG G

Question: Is $L(G) = \mathtt{a}^* \cup \mathtt{b}(\mathtt{a} \cup \mathtt{b})^*$?

(f) **Instance:** a CFG G and a string x

Question: Is $L(G) = \{x\}$?

Solution: Decidable.

$$L(G) = \{x\} \iff (L(G) - \{x\} = \emptyset) \land (L(G) \cap \{x\} \neq \emptyset).$$

CFGs for $L(G) - \{x\}$ and $L(G) \cap \{x\}$ may be readily constructed because $\{x\}$ is a regular language. Then those two languages can be tested for emptiness by Exercise 5.3-4.

(g) **Instance:** a CFG G

Question: Is $|L(G)| = 1$; i.e., does G generate exactly one string?

(h) **Instance:** a CFG G

Question: Is $L(G)$ finite?

Solution: Decidable. Compute a pumping number N for G as in the proof of the first pumping theorem for CFLs. We assert that $L(G)$ is infinite iff $L(G)$ contains a string whose length is between N and $2N - 1$. Proof: If $L(G)$ contains such a string, then the string is pumpable, so $L(G)$ is infinite. Conversely, if $L(G)$ is infinite, then let x be the shortest string

in $L(G)$ having length N or greater. $|x| < 2N$ because otherwise x could be pumped down yielding a shorter string in $L(G)$ having length N or greater.
The algorithm tests whether $L(G) \cap (\Sigma^N (\Lambda \cup \Sigma)^{N-1})$ is empty.

(i) **Instance:** a CFG with terminal alphabet $\{\mathtt{a}, \mathtt{b}\}$

Question: Is $L(G) \subseteq \mathtt{a}^*$?

Solution: Decidable. Test whether $L(G) - \mathtt{a}^*$ is empty.

(j) **Instance:** a CFG G

Question: Is $L(G) = \mathtt{a}^*$?

7.13-2 (a) We say that an NSA for L is minimal if it has the smallest possible number of control states. Prove that there is no algorithm to minimize NSAs.

(b) We say that a CFG for L is minimal if it has the smallest possible number of productions. Prove that there is no algorithm to minimize CFGs.

*7.14 DIOPHANTINE AND EXPONENTIAL DIOPHANTINE EQUATIONS

Diophantus, a third-century Greek mathematician, was very interested in finding integer solutions to equations. A *diophantine equation* is a polynomial equation involving more than one variable in which the coefficients are integers and for which nonnegative integral solutions are sought. Examples are $3x - 5y = 1$, which has the solution $x = 2, y = 1$, and one of Fermat's equations, $(x + 1)^3 + (y + 1)^3 = (z + 1)^3$, which has no solution. Difficult diophantine equations are not hard to concoct. For example, solving $(x + 2)(y + 2) = n$ is as hard as factoring the number n.

In 1900 the mathematician David Hilbert, in a now-famous address to the International Mathematical Congress, challenged mathematicians of his day and mathematicians yet to come to solve a list of 23 problems or to prove that no solution existed. All but a few of those problems have been solved since then. Hilbert's tenth problem was to find an algorithm to solve diophantine equations.

Mathematicians at that time realized that such an algorithm would in principle resolve many open questions. For example, to answer Fermat's question "Do there exist $x, y, z > 0$ such that $x^n + y^n = z^n$?" for a particular n, it suffices to solve

$$(\exists x, y, z)[(x+1)^n + (y+1)^n = (z+1)^n].$$

To fully answer Fermat's question, one must determine whether the equation above has a solution with $n > 2$. Thus it suffices to solve

$$(\exists x, y, z, n)[(x+1)^{n+3} + (y+1)^{n+3} = (z+1)^{n+3}],$$

which is not a diophantine equation but an exponential diophantine equation because it involves exponentiation with nonconstant exponents, as well as addition and multiplication. Mathematicians in the early 1900s expected that an algorithm would be found for solving diophantine equations. Hilbert's tenth problem remained open until 1970, when it was proved that no such algorithm exists. In 1993, Andrew Wiles proved that Fermat's equation has no solutions; his proof was being checked as this book went to press.

It is notable that the solution to Hilbert's tenth problem did not come from the mainstream of mathematics. Logic and computability theory were not considered serious avenues of mathematical thought at the time, but they provided the first major progress towards a solution. This work was performed by two logicians, Martin Davis and Julia Robinson, and a philosopher, Hillary Putnam. The proof was later completed, using number theory, by a mathematician, Yuri Matijasevič.

Although a complete proof of the undecidability of Hilbert's tenth problem is beyond the scope of this book, we will present one of the important steps in its solution. Namely, we will show that there is no algorithm to solve exponential diophantine equations.

DEFINITION 7.76 (Exponential Diophantine Equations)

(i) A function $f(x_1, \ldots, x_n)$, where the variables $x_1, \ldots, x_n$ range over the natural numbers, is an *exponential polynomial* if f is built up from these variables and natural number constants by the operations of addition, $g + h$; subtraction, $g - h$; multiplication, gh; and exponentiation, g^h.

(ii) An equation $f(x_1, \ldots, x_m) = 0$ is *exponential diophantine* if f is an exponential polynomial.

(iii) A set $A \subseteq \mathsf{N}^n$ is *exponential diophantine* if there exists an exponential polynomial f such that A satisfies

$$(a_1, \ldots, a_n) \in A \iff (\exists x_1, \ldots, x_m)[f(a_1, \ldots, a_n, x_1, \ldots, x_m) = 0].$$

If the operation of exponentiation is disallowed, then we obtain the ordinary *diophantine equations.*

THEOREM 7.77 (Davis–Putnam–Robinson Theorem). *Every r.e. subset of* N^n *is exponential diophantine.*

We will prove this shortly. The proof is in two parts. In Section 7.14.1 we show that certain simple relations are exponential diophantine. In Section 7.14.2 we show how to express an accepting history of a 3-counter machine program using the relations discussed in Section 7.14.1. (Although it would be possible to directly represent the history of a TM program by an exponential diophantine equation, it is much easier to work with a 3-counter machine program because counter operations involve only very simple arithmetic.) The program has an accepting history on input a if and only if the corresponding exponential diophantine equation has a solution.

COROLLARY 7.78. *There is no algorithm for determining whether an exponential diophantine equation has any solutions.*

Proof: Let A be any nonrecursive r.e. subset of N. By Theorem 7.77, there exists an exponential polynomial f such that

$$\begin{aligned} a \in A \quad &\iff \quad (\exists x_1, \ldots, x_m)[f(a, x_1, \ldots, x_m) = 0] \\ &\iff \quad (\exists x_1, \ldots, x_m)[g(x_1, \ldots, x_m) = 0], \end{aligned} \tag{7.1}$$

where $g(x_1, \ldots, x_m) = f(a, x_1, \ldots, x_m)$. The function f is fixed, depending only on the set A;[8] thus the exponential polynomial g may be written down by an algorithm given only a. This constitutes an m-reduction from A to the problem of determining whether an exponential diophantine equation has any solutions. Since A is undecidable, the latter must be undecidable as well. ∎

Exercises

7.14-1 Prove that the set of numbers that are not powers of 2 is a diophantine set.

7.14-2 Prove that the set of composite numbers is a diophantine set.

7.14-3 Suppose that

$$A = \{a : (\exists x_1, \ldots, x_n)[f(a, x_1, \ldots, x_n) = 0]\},$$

where f is a polynomial (or exponential polynomial). Construct a polynomial (or exponential polynomial) g such that A is the set of nonnegative values taken by g, i.e.,

$$A = \{g(x_1, \ldots, x_m) : g(x_1, \ldots, x_m) \geq 0\}.$$

7.14-4 In this exercise, we consider the relation between equations over Z and equations over N.

(a) Suppose that

$$A = \{a : (\exists x_1, \ldots, x_n \in \mathsf{Z})[f(a, x_1, \ldots, x_n) = 0]\},$$

where f is a polynomial (or exponential polynomial). Construct a polynomial (or exponential polynomial) g such that

$$A = \{a : (\exists x_1, \ldots, x_n \in \mathsf{N})[g(a, x_1, \ldots, x_n) = 0]\}.$$

[8] In fact, this step can be made constructive, since the proof of Theorem 7.77 is constructive.

(b) Suppose that

$$A = \{a : (\exists x_1, \ldots, x_n \in \mathsf{N})[f(a, x_1, \ldots, x_n) = 0]\},$$

where f is a polynomial (or exponential polynomial). Construct a polynomial (or exponential polynomial) g such that

$$A = \{a : (\exists x_1, \ldots, x_n \in \mathsf{Z})[g(a, x_1, \ldots, x_n) = 0]\}.$$

Hint: Use the fact from number theory that every nonnegative integer is the sum of four squares, i.e.,

$$(\forall x \in \mathsf{N})(\exists y_1, y_2, y_3, y_4 \in \mathsf{N})[x = y_1^2 + y_2^2 + y_3^2 + y_4^2].$$

(c) Prove that there is an algorithm for solving diophantine (or exponential diophantine) equations over N if and only if there is an algorithm for solving diophantine (or exponential diophantine) equations over Z.

7.14-5 Present an algorithm for solving diophantine equations in a single variable.

7.14-6 Diophantus was really interested in finding rational solutions to equations. However, he realized that it would be sufficient to find integer solutions.

(a) Reduce the problem of finding rational solutions to polynomial equations to the problem of finding integer solutions to polynomial equations.

†(b) Is there an algorithm to determine whether a polynomial equation has a rational solution?

7.14.1 Some Diophantine and Exponential Diophantine Relations

In this section we define some convenient notation and present some number theory needed for the proof of Theorem 7.77. All variables range over N.

Without loss of generality, we may allow exponential polynomials other than 0 on the right side of an equality because

$$R = S \iff R - S = 0.$$

This principle will make many of our diophantine and exponential diophantine relations easier to state.

A simple but important example of a diophantine relation is the less-than relation, $<$, on N:

$$a < b \iff (\exists x)[a + x + 1 = b].$$

Similarly,

$$a \leq b \iff (\exists x)[a + x = b].$$

The relation $\geq$ is diophantine as well because

$$a \geq b \iff b \leq a,$$

as is the exact integer division relation $a = b/c$ (with no remainder) for $c > 0$ because

$$a = b/c \iff ac = b.$$

A disjunction or conjunction of equations can be combined into a single equivalent equation using

$$\begin{aligned} R = 0 \text{ or } S = 0 \quad &\iff \quad RS = 0, \\ R = 0 \text{ and } S = 0 \quad &\iff \quad R^2 + S^2 = 0. \end{aligned}$$

The first of these principles can be used to show that arithmetic congruence is a diophantine relation:

$$a \equiv b \pmod{c} \iff (\exists x)[a = b + cx \text{ or } b = a + cx].$$

Next we show that the binomial coefficient relation, $m = \binom{n}{k}$, is exponential diophantine. The proof depends on the binomial theorem

$$(B + 1)^n = \sum_{0 \leq k \leq n} \binom{n}{k} B^k.$$

If B is larger than $\binom{n}{k}$ for every k (say we take $B > 2^n$), then the binomial coefficients are exactly the digits in the base B expansion of the number $(B+1)^n$. For example, take $B = 100$ and $n = 6$. The binomial coefficients $\binom{6}{0}, \ldots, \binom{6}{6}$ are 1, 6, 15, 20, 15, 6, and 1, and

$$101^6 = 1061520150601.$$

The *digit* relation, $d = \text{digit}(N, k, B)$, is defined to be true iff d is the kth digit of N in base B. The digit relation is exponential diophantine because

$$\begin{aligned} d &= \text{digit}(N, k, B) \\ &\iff (\exists c, e)[N = cB^{k+1} + dB^k + e \text{ and } d < B \text{ and } e < B^k]. \end{aligned}$$

It follows that the relation $m = \binom{n}{k}$ is exponential diophantine because

$$m = \binom{n}{k} \iff (\exists B)[B = 2^n + 1 \text{ and } m = \text{digit}((B+1)^n, k, B)].$$

Next we define the *bitwise less-than* relation, $\preceq$, on numbers written in binary.

DEFINITION 7.79. Let $a = \sum_{0 \le i \le n} a_i 2^i$ and $b = \sum_{0 \le i \le n} b_i 2^i$, where $0 \le a_i, b_i \le 1$ for all i. We define

$$a \preceq b \iff (\forall i)[a_i \le b_i].$$

A nice lemma reduces the $\preceq$-relation to the binomial coefficient relation.

LEMMA 7.80. $r \preceq s \iff \binom{s}{r} \equiv 1 \pmod 2$.

Proof: This follows immediately from Lucas's theorem (Exercise 7.14-11), which states that

$$\binom{s}{r} \equiv \binom{s_n}{r_n} \cdots \binom{s_0}{r_0} \pmod p,$$

where p is a prime number, $s_n \cdots s_0$ is the p-ary representation of s, and $r_n \cdots r_0$ is the p-ary representation of r. Take $p = 2$ and note that when $0 \le r_i, s_i \le 1$, we have $\binom{s_i}{r_i} = 1$ if $r_i \le s_i$, 0 otherwise. ∎

Exercises

7.14-7 Prove that the inequality relation, $a \neq b$, is a diophantine relation.

7.14-8 Prove that the remainder relation, $a = b \bmod c$, is a diophantine relation.

7.14-9 Prove the following properties of the bitwise less-than relation, $\preceq$.

$^+$(a) B is a power of 2 iff $B \preceq 2B - 1$.

(b) $a \preceq b \iff a \,\&\, b = a$, where $a \,\&\, b$ denotes the bitwise logical and of a and b, i.e., $a \,\&\, b = \sum_{0 \le i \le n} a_i b_i 2^i$.

(c) $a \,\&\, b = c \iff c \preceq b$ and $b \preceq a + b - c$.

(d) Let B be a power of 2 such that $a < B$ and $b < B$. Then

$$a \preceq b \text{ and } c \preceq d \iff a + cB \preceq b + dB.$$

7.14-10 (a) Prove that

$$\binom{p^k}{i} \equiv \begin{cases} 1 \pmod{p} & \text{if } i = 0 \text{ or } i = p^k, \\ 0 \pmod{p} & \text{otherwise.} \end{cases}$$

(b) Conclude that $(1 + x)^{p^i} = 1 + x^{p^i}$ as polynomials with coefficients reduced modulo p.

7.14-11 Prove Lucas's theorem that

$$\binom{s}{r} \equiv \binom{s_n}{r_n} \cdots \binom{s_0}{r_0} \pmod{p},$$

where p is a prime number, $s_n \cdots s_0$ is the p-ary representation of s, and $r_n \cdots r_0$ is the p-ary representation of r. Hint: Consider the coefficient of x^r in the polynomial $(1+x)^s$. Write $s = \sum_k s_k p^k$ where $0 \le s_k < p$, and use Exercise 7.14-10(b).

7.14-12 The degree of a term (product) in a polynomial is the sum of the degrees of the variables that appear in it. The degree of a polynomial is the maximum degree of all of its terms. For example, the degree of $xyz + x^2 + y^2 + 1$ is 3.

(a) Prove that there is an algorithm for solving diophantine equations over N if and only if there is an algorithm for solving fourth-degree diophantine equations over N.

Solution: If there is an algorithm for solving diophantine equations, then that algorithm works for fourth-degree diophantine equations as a special case. Conversely, we reduce the problem for general diophantine equations to the problem for fourth-degree diophantine equations.
Consider any polynomial. By the distributive law, this polynomial can be written as a sum of terms where each term is the product of a bag of variables. For each bag S of variables introduce a new variable x_S, and replace the corresponding product by the single variable x_S. This creates a polynomial p of degree 1; we have to make sure that $p(\cdots) = 0$ and that each new variable x_S is equal to the term that it represents. The least common multiple of all the terms is the product of a bag of variables, which we will call M. By a straightforward strong induction, it is enough that $x_{\{v\}} = v$ for each variable v and that $x_{S \uplus T} = x_S x_T$ whenever $S \uplus T \subseteq M$. Let r be equal to p^2 plus the following expressions:

$(x_{\{v\}} - v)^2$ for each variable v

$(x_{S \uplus T} - x_S x_T)^2$ for all bags S and T such that $S \uplus T \subseteq M$.

(b) A polynomial is called *homogeneous* if every term has the same degree. Prove that there is an algorithm for solving diophantine equations over N if and only if there is an algorithm for solving equations over N of the form $p(x_1, \ldots, x_n) = 1$ where p is homogeneous of degree 4.

Solution: If there is an algorithm for solving diophantine equations, then it works for the special case. Conversely, we reduce the general problem to the special case. Suppose we are given a polynomial $q(\cdots)$. Convert q to an equivalent fourth-degree polynomial as in part (a). By construction, this polynomial will always take nonnegative values. Let u be a new variable. If any term has the form $x_1 \cdots x_k$ where $k < 4$ then we replace it by $x_1 \cdots x_k u^{4-k}$. Call the resulting polynomial, which is homogeneous of degree 4, r. Now it suffices to guarantee that $r(\cdots) = 0$ and that $u = 1$. Because $r(\cdots)$ and u are nonnegative, this is ensured by the equation

$$2r(\cdots) + u^4 = 1.$$

Let $p = 2r + u^4$.

7.14.2 Arithmetization of 3-Counter Machine Programs

In this section we convert from programs to diophantine equations using the tools of the preceding section. By definition, every r.e. language is accepted by an NTA. In Section 7.2 we showed how to simulate an NTA by a 3-counter machine that initializes its first counter to hold the value $k\text{-adic}(x)$, where x is the argument. Thus, every r.e. set is accepted by a nondeterministic program for a machine [control, $K1$, $K2$, $K3$], where $K1$, $K2$, and $K3$ are three unsigned counters and $K1$ is initialized to hold the argument to the program. The counters $K2$ and $K3$ are initialized to 0. By standardizing this program, we may assume that it has a unique accepting configuration, in which all three counter values are 0.

Fix such a program for such a 3-counter machine. Let the control set be Q. Let *start* be the initial control state. Let *accept* be the unique accepting control state. Let the instruction set be $\mathcal{I}$.

Let x denote the argument, and let s be the number of steps in some computation on input x. We will use vectors of numbers $v_0, \ldots, v_s$ to encode the corresponding history. Using a number B as a base, where B is a sufficiently large power of 2, we can encode a vector into a single number

$$V = \sum_{0 \le t \le s} v_t B^t.$$

By Exercise 7.14-9(a), we can ensure that B is a power of 2 with

$$B \preceq 2B - 1. \tag{7.2}$$

It will be convenient to require

$$B \geq 4. \tag{7.3}$$

We will specify additional lower bounds on B as necessary via our equations.

Let $k_{w,t}$ denote the contents of Kw at time t for $w = 1, 2, 3$ and $t = 0, \ldots, s$. Let $q_{u,t}$ be 1 if the control state is u at time t and 0 otherwise for $u \in Q$ and $t = 0, \ldots, s$. (Note that we represent the value of a counter differently from the value of the control. This is because the value of a counter is numerically meaningful, whereas the value of a control has no arithmetic significance.) Let $i_{j,t}$ be 1 if the instruction j is performed at time t and 0 otherwise for $j \in \mathcal{I}$ and $t = 0, \ldots, s-1$. Let

$$K_w = \sum_{0 \le t \le s} k_{w,t} B^t \qquad \text{for } w = 1, 2, 3, \tag{7.4}$$

$$Q_u = \sum_{0 \le t \le s} q_{u,t} B^t \qquad \text{for } u \in Q, \tag{7.5}$$

$$I_j = \sum_{0 \le t \le s-1} i_{j,t} B^t \qquad \text{for } j \in \mathcal{I}, \tag{7.6}$$

$$\text{and all values } k_{w,t}, q_{u,t}, i_{j,t} < B. \tag{7.7}$$

Equations (7.4–7.6) are not exponential diophantine because they involve unbounded sums of quantities that are not even expressed by exponential polynomials themselves. Those equations tell us what we want K_w, Q_u, and I_j to represent. It is now necessary to write exponential diophantine equations or relations known to be exponential diophantine from the preceding section that force K_w, Q_u, and I_j to represent what we want them to represent. For the purpose of designing those equations, we think of $k_{w,t}$, $q_{u,t}$, and $i_{j,t}$ as being defined in terms of K_w, Q_u, $I_{j,t}$, and B rather than the other way around.

It will be convenient to have a number that encodes a vector of all 1s. Let $T = \sum_{0 \le t \le s} B^t$. By the formula for a geometric series,

$$1 + (B-1)T = B^{s+1}, \tag{7.8}$$

and T is uniquely specified by that equation.

Since $q_{u,t}$ is either 0 or 1 for every t, we must force Q_u to encode a vector of $s + 1$ 0s and 1s. Since B is a power of 2, this is accomplished by

$$Q_u \preceq T. \tag{7.9}$$

Similarly, we force I_j to encode a vector of s 0s and 1s:

$$I_j \preceq T - B^s. \tag{7.10}$$

Since the control must have exactly one state at each time $t \leq s$, we want to be sure that for every t there is exactly one u such that $q_{u,t} = 1$. This is accomplished by

$$\sum_{u \in Q} Q_u = T, \tag{7.11}$$

provided that there are no carries when the addition is performed in base B, so it suffices to require that

$$|Q| < B. \tag{7.12}$$

Since exactly one instruction is executed at each time t, we want to be sure that for every $t < s$ there is exactly one j such that $i_{j,t} = 1$. This is accomplished by

$$\sum_{j \in \mathcal{I}} I_j = T - B^s, \tag{7.13}$$

provided that there are no carries when the addition is performed in base B, so it suffices to require that

$$|\mathcal{I}| < B. \tag{7.14}$$

Now we write equations that enforce the initial and final relation on the control. Since the initial control state is *start*, we require that

$$1 \preceq Q_{start} \tag{7.15}$$

Since the final control state in an accepting computation is *accept*, we require that

$$B^s \preceq Q_{accept}. \tag{7.16}$$

It is not hard to write equations that enforce the sequel relation on the control. Suppose that instruction j specifies the control operation $u \rightarrow v$. If instruction j is performed at time t, then the control state at time t must be u. That is, $i_{j,t} = 1 \Rightarrow q_{u,t} = 1$. Because $i_{j,t}$ and $q_{u,t}$ are 0,1-valued, that is the same as $i_{j,t} \preceq q_{u,t}$, which can be enforced for all t by

$$I_j \preceq Q_u. \tag{7.17}$$

Similarly, if that instruction j is performed at time t, then the control state at time $t+1$ must be v. That is, $i_{j,t} = 1 \Rightarrow q_{v,t+1} = 1$. That is the same as $i_{j,t} \preceq q_{v,t+1}$, which can be enforced for all t by

$$BI_j \preceq Q_v. \tag{7.18}$$

It is a bit trickier to enforce the sequel relation on the counter. Suppose that instruction j specifies the counter operation ZERO on Kw. If instruction j is performed at time t, then Kw must hold the value 0 at time t. That is, $i_{j,t} = 1 \Rightarrow k_{w,t} = 0$. As long as $k_{w,t} \leq B/2$, that is equivalent to $(B/2)i_{j,t} \preceq (B/2) - k_{w,t}$. Instead of $k_{w,t} \leq B/2$, we will impose the stronger condition that $k_{w,t} < B/2$, which is equivalent to $k_{w,t} \preceq B/2 - 1$. Because the numbers on each side of the $\preceq$ are strictly less than B, that condition can be enforced for all t via

$$K_w \preceq (B/2 - 1)T. \tag{7.19}$$

Each side of the condition $(B/2)i_{j,t} \preceq (B/2) - k_{w,t}$ is also a number less than B. Hence it can be enforced for all t via

$$(B/2)I_j \preceq (B/2)T - K_w. \tag{7.20}$$

Suppose that instruction j specifies the counter operation DEC on Kw. If instruction j is performed at time t, then Kw must hold a positive value at time t. That is, $i_{j,t} = 1 \Rightarrow k_{w,t} > 0$. As long as $k_{w,t} \leq B/4$, that is equivalent to $(B/4)i_{j,t} \preceq B/2 - k_{w,t}$. Those two conditions are guaranteed for all t by these two equations:

$$K_w \preceq (B/4-1)T, \tag{7.21}$$

$$(B/4)I_j \preceq (B/2)T - K_w. \tag{7.22}$$

We still have to account for the actions of INC and DEC. Let INC(w) be the set of instructions that specify the INC operation on Kw. Let DEC(w) be the set of instructions that specify the DEC operation on Kw. Correct counter values are enforced by the equations

$$K_1 = BK_1 + \sum_{j \in \mathrm{INC}(1)} BI_j - \sum_{j \in \mathrm{DEC}(1)} BI_j + x, \tag{7.23}$$

$$K_w = BK_w + \sum_{j \in \mathrm{INC}(w)} BI_j - \sum_{j \in \mathrm{DEC}(w)} BI_j \qquad \text{for } w = 2, 3. \tag{7.24}$$

Note that equation (7.23) guarantees that the low-order digit of K_1 is x to correspond to $K1$'s initial value, and that the $(t+1)$st digit is computed from the tth according to the whether $K1$ is incremented, decremented, or neither at time t. K_2 and K_3 are similar except that their low-order digit is 0. It is important that the final value of each counter Kw be 0, for otherwise the number K_w would be infinite.

Given an accepting computation, we may determine the values of s, $k_{w,t}$, $q_{u,t}$, and $i_{j,t}$ for all w, u, j, t. Then we may choose B to be larger than $|\mathcal{I}|$ and larger than $k_{w,t}$ for all w, t. The values of K_w, Q_u, and I_j are given by equations (7.4–7.6). The values so determined satisfy the simultaneous equations (7.2–7.3,7.8–7.24).

Conversely, suppose we are given s, B, and K_w, Q_u, I_j (for all values of w, u, j) satisfying the simultaneous equations (7.2–7.3,7.8–7.24). Then we may determine the values of $k_{w,t}$, $q_{u,t}$, and $i_{j,t}$ for all t from (7.4–7.7). These values determine an accepting computation on input x.

The simultaneous equations (7.2–7.3,7.8–7.24) have a solution if and only if x is accepted. The conjunction of those equations can be expressed, via the techniques of the preceding section, as a single exponential diophantine equation, which has a solution iff x is accepted. This completes the proof of Theorem 7.77. ∎

LEMMA 7.81. *The relation $a = b^c$ is diophantine.*

The proof of that lemma is beyond the scope of this book.

THEOREM 7.82 (Matijasevič's Theorem). *Every r.e. subset of* N^n *is diophantine.*

Proof: By Theorem 7.77 every r.e. subset of N is exponential diophantine. The exponential equations may be replaced by diophantine equations by Lemma 7.81. ∎

COROLLARY 7.83. *There is no algorithm for determining whether a diophantine equation has a solution.* ∎

Exercises

7.14-13 Show that equations (7.15) and (7.16) can be expressed using arithmetic congruence instead of $\preceq$.

7.14-14 Prove that $2^{xy^2} \bmod (2^{xy} - x) = x^y$.
Hint: Use $2^{xy} \equiv x \pmod{2^{xy} - x}$.

7.14-15 An exponential diophantine equation is called *unary exponential diophantine* if the underlying exponential polynomial can be built up by addition, subtraction, and multiplication using only one-place exponentials, 2^x, rather than two-place exponentials, y^x. Prove that there is no algorithm for determining whether a unary exponential diophantine equation has a solution. Do not use Matijasevič's theorem. Hint: Use Exercise 7.14-14.

7.14-16 Using Matijasevič's theorem, prove that there exists a polynomial p such that $\{p(x_1, \ldots, x_n) : p(x_1, \ldots, x_n) > 0\}$ is equal to the set of prime numbers.

7.14-17 Use Matijasevič's theorem to prove that there is no algorithm to determine the minimum value taken on by a multivariate polynomial, i.e., $\min_{x_1,\ldots,x_n \in \mathsf{N}} p(x_1, \ldots, x_n)$.

7.14-18 (a) Using Matijasevič's theorem, prove that there is no algorithm to determine whether there exists a solution to a system of equations in which each equation has one of the following five forms:

$$\begin{aligned} x &= y \\ x &= yz \\ x &= y+z \\ x &= 0 \\ x &= 1, \end{aligned}$$

where x, y, z are variables denoting integers.

(b) Using part (a), prove that there is no algorithm to determine whether there exists a solution to a system of equations in which each equation has one of the following five forms:

$$\begin{aligned} X &= Y \cup Z \\ X &= Y \times Z \\ X &= Y \cap Z \\ |X| &< |Y| \\ |X| &= |Y|, \end{aligned}$$

where X, Y, Z are variables denoting finite sets.

Solution: We reduce the problem of part (a). For each integer variable x we introduce a set variable X. Corresponding to the equation $x = y$, we have the equation $|X| = |Y|$. Corresponding to the equation $x = yz$, we have the equation $|X| = |Y \times Z|$. We can express conditions like $|U| = |V \times W|$ as two equations: $|U| = |T|$ and $T = V \times W$. Such shortcuts will be implicit in our solution. We will need to express the condition that a set S is empty using the given types of set equations. Observe that $|S| = |S \times S|$ if and only if $|S|$ is 0 or 1. (By assumption, S is finite.) Thus we can express the condition that $S = \emptyset$ by the equations $|S| = |S \times S|$, $|T| = |T \times T|$, and $|S| < |T|$. As a bonus, we can express the condition that X is a singleton by the equation $|X| = |T|$.

Corresponding to the equation $x = y + z$, we have the equations $|X| = |Y' \cup Z'|$, $|Y'| = |Y|$, $|Z'| = |Z|$, and $\emptyset = Y' \cap Z'$. Corresponding to the equation $x = 0$, we have the equation $X = \emptyset$. Corresponding to the equation $x = 1$, we have the condition that X is a singleton.

7.15 CHAPTER SUMMARY

We proved that Turing machines are equivalent to RAMs and several other computational models. We introduced the recursive or decidable languages, which are the languages recognized by DTRs, and the r.e. languages, which are the languages accepted by NTAs or, equivalently, by DTAs. Completing the machine–grammar equivalence paradigm, we proved that the r.e. languages are the same as the languages generated by semi-Thuë systems. Using diagonalization we proved that the halting problem is not recursive. By reducing known nonrecursive languages to certain other languages, we proved that the other languages are not recursive either. In particular, the set of valid computations of a 2-CM program is nonrecursive. Applying this fact in Section 7.13, we proved the undecidability of a variety of formal language problems. As another application, we proved that the set of theorems in first-order logic is not recursive. A famous undecidable problem is Hilbert's tenth problem: Does a multivariate polynomial equation have a solution in integers? We finished the chapter by proving that a closely related problem is undecidable. For more information about undecidability, we recommend the *Handbook of Theoretical Computer Science* (Elsevier and MIT Press).

Exercises

7.15-1 A language L is *prefix-free* if, for all distinct x and y in L, x is not a prefix of y. Throughout this problem, let P denote a DTR whose input device does not use the EOF test and whose final relation does not depend on the input device (i.e., the input need not be empty for acceptance to occur).

(a) Prove that P recognizes a prefix-free language.

(b) Define $\Pr(x) = 2^{-|x|}$. Prove that if L is prefix-free, then $\sum_{x \in L} \Pr(x) \leq 1$.

(c) Let L denote the language accepted by P, and let $\gamma(P) = \sum_{x \in L} \Pr(x)$. Let r denote a rational number. Prove that $\{(P, r) : \gamma(P) > r\}$ is r.e.

(d) Is $\{(P, r) : \gamma(P) \geq r\}$ r.e?

(e) Let P be a particular program. Assume that $\{r : \gamma(P) > r\}$ is recursive. Prove that P accepts a recursive language.

7.15-2 By Theorem 7.20(ii), if L is the range of a total recursive function that is nondecreasing, then L is recursive. Prove that there is no constructive proof of this fact; i.e., there is no algorithm to solve the following problem:

Instance: a DTM program P that computes a total recursive function that is nondecreasing

Answer: a DTR that recognizes $\text{Range}(\tau_P)$

Solution: Proof by contradiction. Suppose there is an algorithm that takes a DTM program P which computes a nondecreasing total recursive function and outputs a DTR P' that recognizes $\text{Range}(\tau_P)$. We solve the halting problem as follows: On input z, construct the following program P:

```
input a natural number s;
if z halts in s or fewer steps on input z then
        write 1
else
        write 0.
```

The program P computes a total recursive function that is nondecreasing. Construct the program P' that recognizes $\text{Range}(\tau_P)$. P' accepts 1 if and only if $z \in K$.

7.15-3 (a) Given two finite sets of strings $U = \{u_1, \ldots, u_m\}$ and $V = \{v_1, \ldots, v_n\}$, construct an NCA that solves the following problem:

Instance: a string x

Question: Do there exist sequences of positive integers $i_1, \ldots, i_k$ and $j_1, \ldots, j_k$ such that $x = u_{i_1} \ldots u_{i_k} = v_{j_1} \cdots v_{j_k}$?

(b) Prove that the following problem is decidable:

Instance: two finite sets of strings $U = \{u_1, \ldots, u_m\}$ and $V = \{v_1, \ldots, v_n\}$

Question: Do there exist sequences of positive integers $i_1, \ldots, i_k$ and $j_1, \ldots, j_k$ such that $u_{i_1} \ldots u_{i_k} = v_{j_1} \cdots v_{j_k}$?

7.15-4 Consider a deterministic 1-TM program P whose argument is an infinite sequence of characters that the tape is initialized to hold. Suppose that P halts on every argument. Prove that P uses only a bounded portion of its tape; i.e., there is a natural number b such that P's head remains on the first b tape squares regardless of their initial contents. (Hint: Consider the infinite tree in which xc is a child of x for $x \in \Sigma^*$ and $c \in \Sigma$. Apply Exercise 0.6-29.) Conclude that there exists a finite set F of finite strings such that P accepts argument x if and only if $x \in F\Sigma^\omega$. (See Exercise 4.10.10 for a definition of Σ^ω.)

7.15-5 Is every r.e. language the intersection of two CFLs?

7.15-6 Is there an algorithm to determine whether an NSM program halts on all inputs, i.e., has at least one complete computation on each input?

8

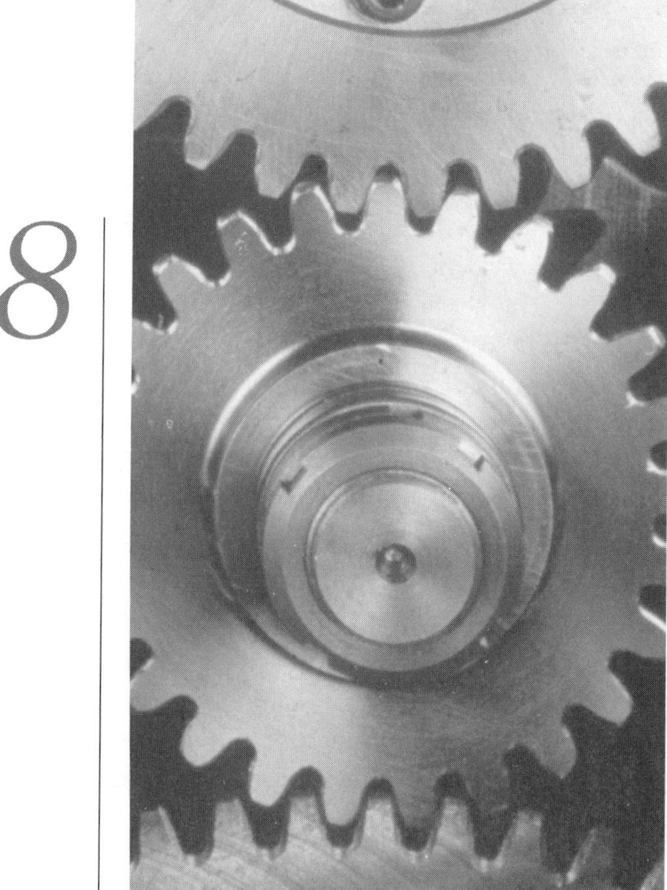

Recursion Theory

IN THE PRECEDING chapter we studied the recursive functions and the recursive and r.e. languages with the goal of proving that certain important problems were undecidable. In this chapter we also study the recursive functions and the recursive and r.e. languages, but our goal this time is to find interesting general properties rather than to classify particular problems.

We start by presenting Rice's theorem, which says that every nontrivial question about the partial function computed by a DTM program is undecidable. Then we present the fixed-point and recursion theorems. As an application of the recursion theorem we will construct an arithmetic statement that is neither provable nor disprovable unless the axioms of arithmetic are inconsistent; this is Gödel's celebrated incompleteness theorem. Finally, we define problems that are harder than the halting problem, and we examine the arithmetical hierarchy.

Because DTAs accept the same sets that NTAs accept, it is conventional to concentrate on deterministic programs. The transfer relation of a DTM program is a partial function called its *transfer* function. Although we have been using τ_P in general to denote P's transfer relation, the conventional notation for the transfer function of a DTM program P is φ_P.[1]

8.1 RICE'S THEOREM

One can ask infinitely many questions about the transfer function of a DTM program P, e.g., "Is φ_P total?", "Is $\mathrm{Dom}(\varphi_P)$ empty?", "Is $\mathrm{Dom}(\varphi_P)$ infinite?", "Is $\mathrm{Range}(\varphi_P)$ infinite?", "Is $\varphi_P(\mathtt{ab})$ defined?", or "Is $\varphi_P(\mathtt{a}) = \mathtt{b}$?" All of those questions are undecidable. In fact, every nontrivial question one can ask about the transfer function of DTM programs is undecidable.

A convenient way to formalize the notion that a question is about the transfer relation of a Turing machine program is in terms of index sets. A set S of DTM programs is a DTM-index set if every pair of equivalent DTM programs either both belong to S or both belong to $\overline{S}$. We make this definition formal below:

DEFINITION 8.1 (Index Sets). A set S of DTM programs is a *DTM-index set*[2] if

$$\varphi_P = \varphi_{P'} \;\Rightarrow\; \chi_S(P) = \chi_S(P').$$

---

[1] The letter φ, pronounced "fee," is Greek for f. Although $\varphi_P = \tau_P$, the use of the φ_P notation is intended to remind us through alliteration that the transfer relation of the DTM program P is a partial function.

[2] The word "index" generally means a number that indicates an element of a list; such indices are often denoted by subscripts. Historically, the DTM program P was represented by a natural number, which was considered an index for the partial function φ_P.

For brevity, we will call DTM-index sets simply index sets.

Suppose that S is an index set. If P and P' are equivalent programs, then either P and P' both belong to S or neither belongs to S. Thus P's membership in S depends only on φ_P. For this reason, membership of a program in S is considered a property of the program's transfer function. In particular, membership in S does not depend on the syntax of the program.

EXAMPLE 8.2. The following are index sets:

- $\{P : P$ accepts the string $\mathtt{10001}\}$
- $\{P : P$ accepts the empty language$\}$
- $\{P : \varphi_P$ is total$\}$
- $\{P : \varphi_P$ is one-one$\}$
- $\{P : \varphi_P$ is total or one-one$\}$
- $\{P : |\mathrm{Dom}(\varphi_P)| \geq 17\}$, i.e., the set of programs that halt on at least 17 inputs

The following are not index sets:

- $\{P : P$ has exactly four control states$\}$
- $\{P : P$ halts within $2|x|$ steps on every input $x\}$
- $\{P : P$ accepts more inputs than P has control states$\}$ ∎∎∎

DEFINITION 8.3. An index set S is *trivial* if S is empty or S consists of all DTM programs. A trivial index set corresponds to either of two trivial questions about DTM programs: "Is P a DTM program?" and "Is P not a DTM program?"

Throughout this chapter, let K denote K_{diag}.

THEOREM 8.4 (Rice's Theorem). *Let S be a nontrivial index set. Then either*

- *$K \leq_m S$ or*
- *$\overline{K} \leq_m S$.*

In any case, S is undecidable.

Proof: Let S be a nontrivial index set. Let D be a program that runs forever on every input.

Case 1: $D \notin S$. We will m-reduce K to S. Since $S \neq \emptyset$, we can let A be any element of S. For any DTM program P, we define (but do not *run*) a DTM program P' that does the following:

Step 1: run φ_P on input P;

Step 2: input x;

Step 3: run A on input x.

If $P \in K$, then step 1 runs to completion, so P' computes the same function that A computes, and therefore $P' \in S$. If $P \notin K$, then step 1 does not halt, so P' runs forever on every input; i.e., P' computes the same function that D computes and therefore $P' \notin S$. Thus

$$P \in K \iff P' \in S.$$

Since the program P' can be produced algorithmically from P, $K \leq_m S$ via the reduction $f(P) = P'$.

Case 2: $D \in S$. We will m-reduce $\overline{K}$ to S. Since S does not contain all DTM programs, we can let A be any DTM program that is not in S. For any DTM program P, we define a DTM program P' that does the following:

Step 1: run φ_P on input P;

Step 2: input x;

Step 3: run A on input x.

If $P \in K$, then step 1 runs to completion, so P' computes the same function that A computes and therefore $P' \notin S$. If $P \notin K$, then step 1 does not halt, so P' runs forever on every input; i.e., P' computes the same function that D computes and therefore $P' \in S$. Thus

$$P \notin K \iff P' \in S.$$

Since the program P' can be produced algorithmically from P, $\overline{K} \leq_m S$ via the reduction $f(P) = P'$.

Since K is undecidable, S must be undecidable. ∎

Exercises

8.1-1 Prove that the class of index sets is closed under complementation, union, and intersection.

8.1-2 Professor Latella has assigned the following problem to her students: Write a program that will convert a Pascal program P to an equivalent C program P'. Her TA would like some automatic grading software that will test the students' programs for correctness. Prove that no such automatic grading software can be implemented on real computers as we know them.

8.1-3 Prove that every nontrivial question about the transfer relation of NTM programs is undecidable.

*8.1-4 **Rice's theorem for r.e. DTA-index sets.** DTA-index sets are defined by analogy to DTM-index sets. A set S of DTAs is a *DTA-index* set if

$$L(P) = L(P') \Rightarrow \chi_S(P) = \chi_S(P').$$

Recall that $L(P)$ denotes the language accepted by program P.
Prove that a DTA-index set S is r.e. if and only if the following three statements are all true:

(a) If $P \in S$ and $L(P) \subseteq L(P')$, then $P' \in S$.
(b) If $P \in S$, then there exists $P' \in S$ such that $L(P') \subseteq L(P)$ and $L(P')$ is finite.

(c) Let us encode finite sets as strings. The following set is r.e.:

$$F = \{x : (\exists P)[L(P) \text{ is finite, } P \in S, \text{ and } x \text{ encodes } L(P)]\}.$$

Solution: Assume that S is r.e.
We show that condition (a) is necessary by contradiction. Suppose not. Then there exist P and P' such that $P \in S$, $L(P) \subseteq L(P')$, and $P' \notin S$. We reduce $\overline{K}$ to S as follows. Let z be a string whose membership in $\overline{K}$ is to be decided. Consider the following high-level algorithm, which can be implemented as a DTA $D(z)$:

Line 1: Input x.
Line 2: If P accepts x, then accept.
Line 3: Run z on input z.
Line 4: If P' accepts x, then accept.

If $z \notin K$, then line 4 is never reached, so $D(z)$ accepts $L(P)$. If $z \in K$, then $D(z)$ accepts $L(P) \cup L(P')$, which is equal to $L(P')$. Thus $z \in \overline{K} \iff D(z) \in S$. Thus, $\overline{K}$ is m-reducible to an r.e. set, so $\overline{K}$ is r.e., a contradiction.
We show that condition (b) is necessary by contradiction. Suppose not. Then there exists $P \in S$ such that, for all $P' \in S$, either $L(P') \not\subseteq L(P)$ or $L(P')$ is infinite. We reduce $\overline{K}$ to S as follows. Let z be a string whose membership in $\overline{K}$ is to be decided. Consider the following high-level algorithm, which can be implemented as a DTA $D(z)$:

Line 1: Input x.
Line 2: Run z on input z for x steps (interpreting x as a natural number). If z has a complete computation on input z of x steps or fewer, then reject; otherwise, continue to the next line.
Line 3: If P accepts x, then accept.

If $z \notin K$, then $D(z)$ accepts $L(P)$, so $D(z) \in S$. Otherwise, $D(z)$ accepts a finite subset of $L(P)$, so $D(z) \notin S$. Thus, $\overline{K}$ is m-reducible to S, so $\overline{K}$ is r.e., a contradiction.
We prove directly that condition (c) is necessary. Let $f(x)$ be the obvious program that accepts the finite set of strings encoded by x.

Then $x \in F \iff f(x) \in S$, so F is m-reducible to S. Therefore F is r.e.

Conversely, assume that the three conditions are satisfied. Then we can test whether $P \in S$ as follows: Guess x encoding a finite set $\{x_1, \ldots, x_k\}$; check that each of $x_1, \ldots, x_k$ belongs to $L(P)$; check that $x \in F$. Therefore S is r.e.

*8.1-5 **Rice's theorem for r.e. index sets.** Say that a partial function f *extends* a partial function g (denoted $f \supset g$) if $f(x) = g(x)$ whenever $g(x)$ is defined.

Prove that an index set S is r.e. if and only if the following three statements are all true:

(a) If $e \in S$ and $\varphi_i \supset \varphi_e$, then $i \in S$.

(b) If $e \in S$, then there exists $i \in S$ such that $\varphi_e \supset \varphi_i$ and $\mathrm{Dom}(\varphi_i)$ is finite.

(c) Let us encode functions with finite domain as strings: The following set is r.e.:

$$\{x : (\exists P)[\mathrm{Dom}(\varphi_P) \text{ is finite, } P \in S, \text{ and } x \text{ encodes } \varphi_P]\}.$$

Hint: One approach is to mimic the proof for DTA-index sets. An alternative approach is to convert a DTM program with transfer function τ to a DTA that accepts the set of all ordered pairs of the form $(x, \tau(x))$.

8.2 THE RECURSION THEOREM AND THE FIXED-POINT THEOREM

Recall that we can represent programs as strings. Suppose that we want to write a program P such that P accepts a string x if and only if $x = P$. Most practical programming languages and operating systems allow P to read itself from disk and compare itself to the input x, so in practice this problem is easily solved. In general, if h is a partial recursive function, then we may use this trick on most practical computers in order to write a program P that computes the function $g(x) = h(P, x)$.

It is not so clear, however, how to write such a program for a machine that does not have a built-in method to read its program. The recursion theorem says that Turing machine programs can nonetheless simulate this kind of self-reference. This theorem has a central role in the theory of computability and complexity.

The recursion theorem is equivalent to a fixed-point theorem[3] for recursive functions, which we will state below. This fixed-point theorem has its roots in mathematical logic, where similar ideas were first used to construct a self-referential arithmetic sentence that cannot be proved or disproved using the axioms of arithmetic (this is discussed further in Section 8.3).

THEOREM 8.5 (Fixed-Point Theorem). *Let f be a total recursive function that maps deterministic TM programs to deterministic TM programs. There exists a deterministic TM program P such that P and $f(P)$ compute the same partial recursive function.*

Before giving the proof of the fixed-point theorem, we will sketch the main ideas. Let us set the quixotic goal of finding P such that $f(P) = P$. Of course this is impossible even for very simple functions like $f(x) = x + 1$; nonetheless, we will learn something useful from our certain failure. Because the fixed-point theorem is equivalent to the recursion theorem, which involves self-reference, we may guess that the desired fixed point P is obtained by running some program V on itself, where the program V is yet to be determined. That is, let us guess that $P = \varphi_V(V)$. Recall that φ_e denotes the partial function computed by the deterministic TM program e. Define $D(e)$ to be the result of running program e on itself, i.e., $D(e) = \varphi_e(e)$, so $P = D(V)$. We desire

$$f(D(V)) = D(V) = \varphi_V(V).$$

Thus it suffices to take $\varphi_V = f \circ D$, i.e., let V be a program that computes the partial function $f \circ D$. Then $D(V)$ is the desired fixed point of f, provided that $D(V)$ is defined. Unfortunately, there is no reason to expect that V halts on input V, so $D(V)$ could be undefined. We can avoid this pitfall by defining $d(e)$ to be a *program* that emulates program e on input e rather than the *result* of that emulation. This idea is used below in the proof of the fixed-point theorem.

---

[3] In other treatments, the fixed-point theorem goes by the name "recursion theorem," and the recursion theorem itself is not formally stated.

Proof: First we will define the total recursive function d, called the *diagonal* function, which maps TM programs to TM programs so as to satisfy

$$\varphi_{d(e)} = \begin{cases} \varphi_{\varphi_e(e)} & \text{if } \varphi_e(e) \text{ is defined,} \\ \text{the everywhere undefined function} & \text{otherwise.} \end{cases}$$

More precisely, d maps a program e to the following program, which we write in a high-level language to avoid the cumbersome details of TM programming:

input x;
let z be the result of running e on input e;
run z on input x.

Note that this is the output of d, not the algorithm for evaluating d. An algorithm for evaluating d would be:

input e;
print "input x; let z be the result of running e on input e; run z on input x."

In particular, d is a total recursive function, although it can map e to a program for a strictly partial function.

Since f and d are total recursive functions, $f \circ d$ is a total recursive function. Let v be a deterministic TM program that computes $f \circ d$, i.e.,

$$\varphi_v = f \circ d.$$

Let $P = d(v)$. Then

$$\varphi_P = \varphi_{d(v)} = \varphi_{\varphi_v(v)}$$

by the definition of d, since φ_v is total. In fact, $\varphi_v(v) = (f \circ d)(v)$ by the definition of v, so

$$\varphi_{\varphi_v(v)} = \varphi_{(f \circ d)(v)}.$$

Furthermore,

$$\varphi_{(f \circ d)(v)} = \varphi_{f(d(v))} = \varphi_{f(P)}$$

by the definition of P. By transitivity,

$$\varphi_P = \varphi_{f(P)};$$

i.e., P and $f(P)$ compute the same partial recursive function. ■

EXAMPLE 8.6. A deterministic program P for an inattentive machine is called *self-actualized* if it writes itself, i.e., if the output of P is equal to P. We can use the fixed-point theorem to construct a self-actualized DTM program P. Let $f(e)$ be the inattentive program "output e." That is, the program $f(e)$ has no input and it writes the string e. By the fixed-point theorem, there exists a program P such that P and $f(P)$ are programs for the same partial recursive function. By construction $f(P)$ writes the string P. Therefore P writes the string P. ■ ■ ■

In the example above, we used the fixed-point theorem in order to give a program access to itself. This idea is generalized below by the recursion theorem.

COROLLARY 8.7 (Recursion Theorem). *Let $h(\cdot,\cdot)$ be a partial recursive function of two variables. Then there exists a deterministic TM program P that computes the partial function $h(P,\cdot)$, i.e., on input x the program P outputs $h(P,x)$.*

Proof: We will apply the fixed-point theorem to an appropriately defined mapping f. Let $f(e)$ be the following program: "input x; output $h(e,x)$." That is, on input x, the program $f(e)$ outputs $h(e,x)$. By the fixed-point theorem, there exists P such that P and $f(P)$ are programs for the same partial recursive function. By construction, $f(P)$ is a program for the partial function $h(P,x)$. Therefore P is a program for the partial function $h(P,x)$. ■

EXAMPLE 8.8. A recognizer P is called *self-aware* if it recognizes itself or, more precisely, if it recognizes the language $\{P\}$. We use the recursion theorem to construct a self-aware DTM program P. Let $h(P,x) =$ ACCEPT if $P = x$, REJECT otherwise. By the recursion theorem there is a DTM program P whose transfer function is $h(P,\cdot)$. Thus P recognizes $\{P\}$. ■ ■ ■

EXAMPLE 8.9. Let us give a different proof that the halting problem is undecidable. Assume, for the sake of contradiction, that there is an algorithm for solving the halting problem. Then by the recursion theorem there exists a program P with no input that does the following:

if P halts then go into an infinite loop, else halt.

Observe that P halts if and only if P does not halt. This contradiction proves that there cannot be an algorithm for solving the halting problem. ■ ■ ■

In Section 8.3 we will apply the recursion theorem to produce a statement that cannot be proved or disproved. For technical convenience we will want a version of the recursion theorem for 2-counter machines.

COROLLARY 8.10 (2-CM Recursion Theorem). *Let $h(\cdot,\cdot)$ be a partial recursive function of two variables. Then there exists a deterministic 2-counter machine program P that computes the partial function $h(P,\cdot)$, i.e., on input x the program P outputs $h(P,x)$.*

Proof: The proofs we gave for the fixed-point theorem and the recursion theorem work for any machine with the same power as a Turing machine. ■

Exercises

8.2-1 Prove that the following languages are nonrecursive:
   (a) the set of self-actualized DTM programs
   (b) the set of self-aware DTM programs
   (c) the set of DTM programs P such that P halts on the same number of inputs as P has control states

8.2-2 Dr. Lychenko purports to have written a DTM program P that solves the halting problem for inattentive DTM programs. Construct an input x on which P gives the wrong answer or doesn't halt.

8.2-3 In this exercise we identify programs with natural numbers in the usual way. A DTM program e is called the *minimal* program for a partial function f if

- $\varphi_e = f$ and
- $\varphi_i = f \Rightarrow e \leq i$.

(a) Let R be a recursive set that contains only minimal programs; i.e., if $e \in R$, then there is a partial function f such that e is the minimal program for f. Prove that R is finite.

Solution: The proof is by contradiction. Assume that R is an infinite recursive set. Then R is the range of a total recursive function h that is strictly increasing by Exercise 7.6-3. Let $g(x) = h(x+1)$. Then for all x, $g(x) > x$ and $g(x) \in R$. By the fixed-point theorem there exists n such that $\varphi_n = \varphi_{g(n)}$. But $g(n) > n$, so $g(n)$ cannot be a minimal index. That is a contradiction.

(b) Let R be an r.e. set that contains only minimal programs, i.e., if $e \in R$ then there is a partial function f such that e is the minimal program for f. Prove that R is finite.

Solution: Every infinite r.e. set contains an infinite recursive subset by Exercise 7.6-4. The assertion follows from part (a).

8.2-4 Let f be a partial recursive function that maps DTM programs to DTM programs. Prove that there exists P such that

$$\varphi_P = \begin{cases} \varphi_{f(P)} & \text{if } f(P) \text{ is defined,} \\ \text{the everywhere undefined function} & \text{otherwise.} \end{cases}$$

8.2-5 Let f be a total recursive function that maps NTM programs to NTM programs. Prove that there exists P such that P and $f(P)$ have the same transfer relation.

8.2-6 Use the recursion theorem to prove the fixed-point theorem.

8.2-7 **The uniform recursion theorem**

(a) Let $h_1(\cdot,\cdot,\cdot)$ and $h_2(\cdot,\cdot,\cdot)$ be total recursive functions whose first two arguments are programs. Prove that there exist programs P_1 and P_2 such that P_1 computes $h_1(P_1, P_2, \cdot)$ and P_2 computes $h_2(P_1, P_2, \cdot)$.

(b) Let $h_1, \ldots, h_k$ be $(k+1)$-place total recursive functions whose first k arguments are programs. Prove that there exist programs $P_1, \cdots, P_k$ such that P_i computes $h_i(P_1, \ldots, P_k, \cdot)$ for each i.

(c) Let h be a 3-place total recursive function whose first argument is a program. Prove that there exists a total recursive function u mapping natural numbers to deterministic TM programs such that, for all i, the program $u(i)$ computes $h(P, i, \cdot)$ where P is a program for u.

8.3 GÖDEL'S INCOMPLETENESS THEOREM

At one time mathematicians operated under the belief that every statement about the natural numbers or set theory is either provable or disprovable. (To avoid trivial counterexamples, statements with unquantified variables like $x + y = 3$ are not allowed. However $(\forall x)(\forall y)[x + y = 3]$ is a statement about the natural numbers. It can be disproved by observing that $1 + 1 \neq 3$.) Although no one had tried to prove that every statement is provable or disprovable, hardly anyone questioned the belief. Eventually self-contradictory sentences like "This statement is false" were pointed out. As a response, logic was formalized to make clear exactly what constituted a statement. Needless to say, explicitly self-referential sentences like "This statement is false" are not statements. Mathematicians went back to thinking that every statement is either provable or disprovable.

In 1931 all that changed. Kurt Gödel astounded the mathematical world (including himself) by constructing a true statement about the natural numbers that cannot be proved from the axioms of arithmetic[4] unless those axioms are inconsistent.

Gödel's statement expresses the idea "There is no proof that this statement is true." Because it is self-referential, it is not obvious how to state it in terms of arithmetic. Gödel invented a version of the recursion theorem that

[4] More precisely, for each sound axiomatization AX of arithmetic, Gödel constructed a true statement ψ that cannot be proved from AX. It is necessary to fix AX once and for all before constructing ψ, for otherwise ψ could be made an axiom, and then ψ would be provable.

allowed him to implicitly make such a self-referential statement. The recursion theorem and the fixed-point theorem that we saw in the preceding section were discovered later by Kleene, who carefully examined Gödel's work.

Let us define some terms from logic. We will assume that the reader has a sufficient, though possibly imprecise, understanding of the terms "true," "axiom," "statement," and "rule of inference."

DEFINITION 8.11

(i) A *theory* is a set of axioms.

(ii) A *proof* (in a specified theory) is a sequence of statements, each of which either is an axiom or else follows from some of the preceding statements by a rule of inference.

(iii) A statement ψ is *a theorem* (in a specified theory) if there is a proof (in that theory) whose last statement is ψ.

(iv) $\neg\psi$ stands for the logical negation of the statement ψ.

(v) A theory is *consistent* if there is no statement ψ such that ψ is a theorem and $\neg\psi$ is also a theorem.

(vi) A theory is *sound* if all theorems are true.

(vii) A theory is *complete* if, for every statement ψ, ψ is a theorem or $\neg\psi$ is a theorem.

By "the axioms of arithmetic," we mean any fixed recursive set of axioms for arithmetic with which the reader is comfortable, such as the Peano axioms. No matter which axioms you use, we prove that the axioms of arithmetic are either unsound or incomplete.

THEOREM 8.12 (Gödel's Incompleteness Theorem). *Assume that the axioms of arithmetic are sound. Then there is an arithmetic statement ψ such that*

- *ψ is true,*
- *ψ is not a theorem, and*
- *$\neg\psi$ is not a theorem.*

Proof: Because the axioms constitute a recursive set and the rules of inference constitute a finite set, it is possible to check each statement in a proof mechanically, by checking each to see if it is an axiom or if it follows from preceding statements by one of the rules of inference. Thus an algorithm may determine whether a sequence of statements constitutes a proof, so 2-counter machines can verify proofs. Recall as well that the natural numbers can be used to encode all strings and hence all sequences of statements. Using the recursion theorem for 2-counter machines, we define a 2-CM program P that behaves as follows:

> for $i := 0$ to ∞ do
>
> if i encodes a proof that P does not halt, then halt.

Let ψ be the statement "P does not halt." Because P is a 2-counter machine program, ψ can be written as a statement in the language of arithmetic, as in the proof of Theorem 7.61. By construction, P halts iff there is a proof that P does not halt. Therefore

$$\neg\psi \iff \text{there is a proof of } \psi. \tag{8.1}$$

If ψ is false, then by (8.1) there is a proof of ψ, which violates the soundness of arithmetic. Therefore ψ is true. Since $\neg\psi$ is false, by soundness there must not be a proof of $\neg\psi$. Since $\neg\psi$ is false, by (8.1) there must not be a proof of ψ. ■

Soundness is a much stronger assumption than consistency. By modifying Gödel's construction, we can show that mere consistency implies incompleteness.

THEOREM 8.13 (Rosser's Version of Gödel's Incompleteness Theorem) *Assume that the axioms of arithmetic are consistent. Then there is an arithmetic statement ψ such that*

- *ψ is true,*
- *ψ is not a theorem, and*
- *$\neg\psi$ is not a theorem.*

Proof: Using the recursion theorem for 2-counter machines, we define a 2-CM program P that behaves as follows:

```
for i := 1 to ∞ do begin
    if i encodes a proof that P halts, then go into an infinite loop;
    if i encodes a proof that P does not halt, then halt;
end.
```

By construction P halts if and only if there is a proof i that P does not halt such that i is less than any proof that P does halt. Let ψ be the statement "P does not halt." Therefore

$$\neg\psi \iff \text{there is a proof of } \psi \text{ that is less than any proof of } \neg\psi. \quad (8.2)$$

Assume for the sake of contradiction that there is a proof of ψ or a proof of $\neg\psi$. Let the minimum such proof be i. We consider two cases.

Case 1: i is a proof of ψ. Because i is minimal, $0, \ldots, i-1$ are not proofs of $\neg\psi$. By definition of proof, i cannot prove more than one statement, so i is not a proof of $\neg\psi$. We can prove $\neg\psi$ from (8.2) by mechanically verifying that i is a proof of ψ and that $0, \ldots, i$ are not proofs of $\neg\psi$. But then $\neg\psi$ is provable, contradicting consistency.

Case 2: i is a proof of $\neg\psi$. Because i is minimal, $0, \ldots, i-1$ are not proofs of ψ. We can prove ψ from (8.2) by mechanically verifying that i is a proof of $\neg\psi$ and that $0, \ldots, i-1$ are not proofs of ψ. But then ψ is provable, contradicting consistency.

In either case, we obtain a contradiction. Therefore there is no proof of ψ and there is no proof of $\neg\psi$. Since there is no proof of ψ, by (8.2) ψ must be true. ∎

Let *Con* be the statement that the axioms of arithmetic are consistent. It is not obvious how to express *Con* as an arithmetic statement, but it is possible (Exercise 8.3-5). Although the true but unprovable statements constructed for Theorems 8.12 and 8.13 were ad hoc, *Con* is a statement of natural interest. *Con* is the first example of a natural statement that is true if and only if it cannot be proved.

COROLLARY 8.14. *Con is true if and only if Con is not a theorem.*

Proof: First we will prove by contradiction that $Con \Rightarrow Con$ is not a theorem. Assume that Con is true and Con is a theorem. Let ψ be as in Theorem 8.13. By Theorem 8.13, because Con is true, ψ is not a theorem. By Theorem 8.13, $Con \Rightarrow \psi$. Therefore, because Con is a theorem, ψ is a theorem. This contradiction completes the proof.

For the converse, assume that Con is false. Then arithmetic is inconsistent, so all statements are theorems by Exercise 8.3-2. ■

The proofs in this section really apply to any theory that is capable of expressing arithmetic statements. Thus, the preceding corollary means that in any consistent theory $\mathcal{T}$ that is at least as expressive as arithmetic, there is no proof that $\mathcal{T}$ is consistent.

Exercises

8.3-1 Let ψ be as in Theorem 8.12. Let x be any TM program. Prove the following:

(a) If x halts, then there is a proof in arithmetic that x halts.

Solution: Convert x to an equivalent 2-CM program x'. If x halts then there is a computation of x'. The step-by-step verification of this computation can be written as a sequence of arithmetic statements, which constitute a proof that x' halts and therefore x halts.

(b) If arithmetic is consistent, then ψ is true.

Solution: Assume for the sake of contradiction that ψ is false. Then P halts. By (a) there is a proof that P halts. But by the construction of P there is a proof that P does not halt. This contradicts consistency, so ψ must be true.

(c) If arithmetic is consistent, then there is no proof in arithmetic of ψ.

Solution: By (b) ψ is true. By (8.1), there is no proof in arithmetic of ψ.

8.3-2 Prove that a nonempty theory is consistent if and only if at least one statement is unprovable.

Solution: First, assume the theory is consistent. Let ψ be any statement. One of the statements ψ and $\neg\psi$ is unprovable.
For the converse, assume the theory is inconsistent. Then there is a statement ψ such that ψ and $\neg\psi$ are both provable. Let y be any statement. Because "$(\psi \wedge \neg\psi) \Rightarrow y$" is a logical tautology, y is provable. Thus we have shown that every statement is provable.

8.3-3 A theory is *ω-consistent* if there is no predicate $Q(\cdot)$ such that there exists a proof of $(\exists x)[Q(x)]$ as well as proofs of $\neg Q(c)$ for each constant c. (For example, a theory of arithmetic is ω-consistent iff there is no predicate $Q(\cdot)$ such that there exists a proof of $(\exists x)[Q(x)]$ as well as proofs of $\neg Q(0), \neg Q(1), \neg Q(2), \ldots$.)

(a) Prove that if a theory is sound, then it is ω-consistent.

(b) Prove that if a theory is ω-consistent, then it is consistent.

8.3-4 Let ψ be as in Theorem 8.12. Assume that arithmetic is ω-consistent and prove the following: There is no proof in arithmetic of $\neg\psi$.

8.3-5 Let ψ be as in the proof of Theorem 8.13. Prove

$$\mathit{Con} \iff \psi \text{ is not a theorem.}$$

How could you phrase *Con* as a statement in arithmetic?

8.4 ORACLES AND TURING REDUCTIONS

In this section we introduce new and powerful devices called oracles. The definition of these devices is motivated by the mythological Delphic oracle and by special purpose chips that can be installed as add-ons to real computers.

The mythological Delphic oracle[5] could answer any question. The oracles we define will be limited in their omniscience. Let B be a language over an alphabet Γ. An oracle for B can hold a string, called the *query* string,

[5] According to Greek mythology, an oracle resided in the city of Delphi. The oracle would answer any question truthfully, but her answer could be ambiguous or even misleading, depending on the will of the gods or how well she was paid.

and tell whether the query string belongs to the language B. The oracle for B has realm Γ^*. Its initial state is Λ. Its operations are APPENDc, which appends a c to the query string; INB, which tests whether the query string belongs to B and then clears the query string; and NOT-INB, which tests whether the query string belongs to $\overline{B}$ and then clears the query string. We define the operations formally below: For all strings s,

- s APPEND$c = sc$.
- s IN$B = \Lambda$ if $s \in B$ but is undefined otherwise.
- s NOT-IN$B = \Lambda$ if $s \in \overline{B}$ but is undefined otherwise.

An oracle for B may also be called simply an "oracle B."

An oracle for B is like a read-only database that can answer membership queries for the language B. As an exercise, the reader may define oracles for functions; these are analogous to add-on chips that perform floating point or graphics calculations.

A Turing machine with oracle B is a machine with a control, some number of tapes, and an oracle for the language B; as usual, it may have input and output as well. A program can ask the oracle whether a string s belongs to B by copying s to the oracle string (using repeated APPENDs) and then performing either the INB or NOT-INB operation (whichever is applicable). When the program asks the oracle whether some string belongs to B, we call this *querying* the oracle. If $s \in B$, then the edge labeled INB is followed and we say that the oracle answers yes; if $s \notin B$, then the edge labeled NOT-INB is followed and we say that the oracle answers no. For example, it is an easy matter for a program for a TM with oracle B to recognize the language B by querying the oracle about the input string, as in Figure 8.1.

EXAMPLE 8.15. If $A \leq_m B$, then a TM with oracle B can recognize A by making a single query, as shown below. Let f be a reduction from A to B.

```
input x;
y := f(x);
if y ∈ B then accept, else reject.
```

■■■

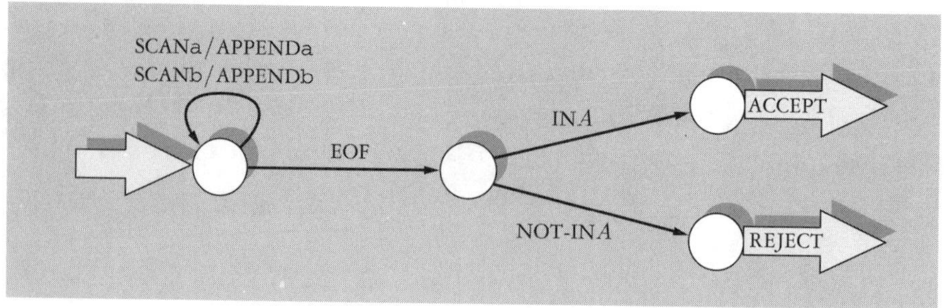

FIGURE 8.1: A program running on a TM with oracle B that recognizes B.

EXAMPLE 8.16. Let us now consider an example using an oracle for K_{pos}. A program for a Turing machine with an oracle for K_{pos} can recognize the following language: $\{P : P \text{ halts on exactly one input}\}$, as we will show. Let $K_{\geq 2}$ be the set of DTM programs P that halt on at least two inputs. $K_{\geq 2}$ is r.e., because we can guess two strings and check that P halts on both of them. Then, by Theorem 7.37, $K_{\geq 2} \leq_m K_{pos}$. Let f be a reduction from $K_{\geq 2}$ to K_{pos}. The following algorithm determines whether program P halts on exactly one input:

> input P;
> if $P \notin K_{pos}$ then reject; (∗ P halts on zero inputs ∗)
> $y := f(P)$;
> if $y \in K_{pos}$ then reject; (∗ P halts on two or more inputs ∗)
> accept.

■■■

DEFINITION 8.17 (Turing reductions)

(i) A partial function f is *Turing-reducible* to B (denoted $f \leq_T B$) if f is computed by a program P for a DTM with oracle B. (P is called a *Turing* reduction from f to B.)

(ii) A language A is *Turing-reducible* to B (denoted $A \leq_T B$) if A is recognized by a DTR P with oracle B. (P is called a *Turing* reduction from A to B.)

By Example 8.15, if $A \leq_m B$, then $A \leq_T B$. By Example 8.16, $\{P : P$ halts on exactly one input$\}$ is Turing-reducible to K_{pos}.

Exercises

8.4-1 Prove that the following sets and partial functions are Turing-reducible to K_{pos}:

(a) $A = \{P : P \text{ halts on exactly 17 inputs}\}$

(b) $A = \{P : P \text{ halts on between 1 and 100 inputs}\}$

(c) $A = \{P : |\mathcal{C}(P)| \leq 100 \text{ and } |\mathcal{C}(P)| \text{ is odd}\}$

(d) $f(P) = \begin{cases} \text{the least } x \text{ such } P \text{ halts on } x & \text{if } P \in K_{pos}, \\ \text{undefined} & \text{otherwise.} \end{cases}$

(Identify input strings with natural numbers and use numerical order.)

8.4-2 (a) Prove that $\leq_T$ is reflexive and transitive.

(b) Is $\leq_T$ symmetric?

(c) Prove that $A \leq_T \emptyset$ if and only if A is recursive.

(d) Prove that if $A \leq_T B$ and B is recursive, then A is recursive.

8.4-3 In this section, we defined an oracle for a set B. How would you define an oracle for a function f? For a relation ρ?

8.4-4 Recall that K is the halting problem. Prove that there is a function $f \leq_T K$ such that f has no fixed points, i.e.,

$$(\forall e)[\varphi_{f(e)} \neq \varphi_e].$$

8.4.1 Representational Issues

A subtlety arises when we represent programs for a DTM with oracle B. Because it is not possible to represent the language B as a string (see Exercise 7.8-2(c)), we cannot represent the oracle operations INB and NOT-INB as such. Instead, we represent the oracle operations INB and NOT-INB as IN and NOT-IN, respectively. Because such programs can be run on a TM with any oracle, they are called *oracle TM programs*; the behavior of the program depends on which oracle the machine has. If P is an oracle TM program, we write P^B to denote program P running on a TM with oracle B. It is important to define determinism syntactically: An oracle TM program is *deterministic* if it is deterministic for every oracle.

8.4.2 Relativization

As a rule of thumb, most true statements about programs for a TM have true analogues about programs for a TM with oracle B. Because the analogy is an informal one, we describe it informally.

EXAMPLE 8.18. Consider the statement (1) "Every language accepted by an NTA is accepted by a DTA." An analogous statement (1^B) is obtained by adding an oracle for B to all Turing machines in the original statement: "Every language accepted by an NTA with oracle B is accepted by a DTA with oracle B." That transformation on statements about Turing machines is called *relativization*. In addition to relativizing theorems about TMs, we can relativize their proofs. Typically the relativized proof is, in fact, a proof of the relativized theorem. We illustrate this with statement (1) and the relativized statement (1^B).

Proof of statement (1): Let L be accepted by an NTA P. The following DTA accepts L:

```
input x;
for i := 1 to ∞ do
    if i encodes an accepting computation of P on input x, then accept;
```

Observe that a DTR can run a computation of an NTA step by step, verifying that x is the string scanned and that the computation accepts, so it can check whether i encodes an accepting computation of P on input x. ■

Proof of statement (1^B): Let L be accepted by an NTA P with oracle B. The following DTA with oracle B accepts L:

input x;
for $i := 1$ to ∞ do
  if i encodes an accepting computation of P on input x, then accept;

Observe that a DTR with oracle B can run a computation of an NTA with oracle B step by step, verifying that x is the string scanned and that the computation accepts, so it can check whether i encodes an accepting computation of P on input x. ∎

It is convenient to relativize the definitions of "recursive" and "r.e." We say that A is *recursive in* B if A is recognized by a DTR with oracle B. We say that A is r.e. in B if A is accepted by an NTA with oracle B. We say that a function f is *recursive in* B if f is computed by a DTM program with oracle B.

EXAMPLE 8.19. As shown above, A is r.e. in B if and only if A is accepted by a DTA with oracle B. By relativizing the proofs for ordinary TM programs, we can prove many analogous theorems about oracle TM programs. For example:

- There is a universal oracle TM program P such that, on input (x, y), P^B emulates DTM program x on input y with oracle B.
- L is recursive in B if and only if L and $\overline{L}$ are r.e. in B.
- L is r.e. in B if and only if there exists a set R recursive in B such that $x \in L \iff (\exists y)[(x, y) \in R]$.
- Let L be a nonempty set. L is r.e. in B if and only if L is the range of a total function that is recursive in B.
- Let L be a nonempty set. L is recursive in B if and only if L is the range of a nondecreasing, total function that is recursive in B.
- If $S \leq_m T$ and T is recursive in B, then S is recursive in B.
- If $S \leq_m T$ and T is r.e. in B, then S is r.e. in B.

Because the proofs reiterate previous ideas, they are left as exercises. ■ ■ ■

Caveat: Only statements about machines can be relativized. We are able to relativize statements about r.e. languages, for example, because they are defined in terms of NTAs. We can relativize problems like the halting problem because it is a problem about Turing machines. However, *it is not possible to relativize statements about particular problems* without first restating those problems in terms of machines.

EXAMPLE 8.20. There is no natural way to relativize a rewriting system. The statement "No DTR can solve the word problem for semi-Thuë systems" is true, but the statement "No DTR with oracle K can solve the word problem for semi-Thuë systems" is *false*. ■ ■ ■

Exercises

8.4-5 Prove each of the following statements by relativizing the corresponding statement for ordinary TMs:

(a) L is recursive in B if and only if L and $\overline{L}$ are r.e. in B.

(b) L is r.e. in B if and only if there exists a set R recursive in B such that $x \in L \iff (\exists y)[(x, y) \in R]$.

(c) Let L be a nonempty set. L is r.e. in B if and only if L is the range of a total function that is recursive in B.

(d) Let L be a nonempty set. L is recursive in B if and only if L is the range of a nondecreasing, total function that is recursive in B.

(e) If $S \leq_m T$ and T is recursive in B, then S is recursive in B.

(f) If $S \leq_m T$ and T is r.e. in B, then S is r.e. in B.

8.4.3 Jumps

Some undecidable problems are harder, i.e., more undecidable, than others. Recall that in Chapter 7 we proved that no DTR can solve the halting problem for DTM programs. A similar theorem is true for oracle TMs: No DTR with oracle B can solve the halting problem for DTM programs with oracle B. In particular, although a DTR with oracle K can solve the halting problem for ordinary DTM programs, it cannot solve the halting problem for DTM programs with oracle K.

DEFINITION 8.21 (Jumps). The *halting problem for DTM programs with oracle B* (denoted K^B or B') is the following language:

$$\{P : P \text{ is an oracle DTM program and } P^B \text{ halts on input } P\}.$$

As the halting problem is undecidable, similarly K^B is harder than B.

THEOREM 8.22

(i) *A is r.e. in B if and only if $A \leq_m K^B$.*

(ii) *K^B is not recursive in B.*

Proof

(i) Relativize the proof of Theorem 7.37.

(ii) Relativize the proof of Theorem 7.21. ∎

Thus, in particular, K^K is not recursive in K.

Because K^B is strictly harder than B, K^B is called the *jump* of B. Using the jump operator, we can define a sequence of problems, each of which is more undecidable than the one before:

$$K, K^K, K^{K^K}, K^{K^{K^K}}, \ldots.$$

We adopt the following notation: $A^{(0)} = A$, $A^{(1)} = A' = K^A$, $A^{(2)} = A'' = K^{K^A}$, and $A^{(3)} = A''' = K^{K^{K^A}}$. In general, $A^{(i+1)} = K^{A^{(i)}}$. For example, $\emptyset^{(3)} = K^{K^{K^\emptyset}}$.

Exercises

8.4-1 (a) Prove that $K^{(i)} \leq_m \emptyset^{(i+1)}$.
(b) Prove that $\emptyset^{(i+1)} \leq_m K^{(i)}$.

8.5 ARITHMETICAL HIERARCHY

Not only are some problems more undecidable than others, but there is an infinite hierarchy of more and more undecidable problems. In this section we describe a hierarchy of languages, with the recursive languages at the bottom, the r.e. and co-r.e. languages at the next level, and more highly undecidable languages at each higher level. Many natural problems about Turing machines fit neatly into this hierarchy.

Recall that the r.e. languages are obtained by applying an existential quantifier to the recursive languages. Similarly, the co-r.e. languages can be obtained by applying a universal quantifier to the recursive languages. We generalize these ideas. Let $\mathcal{C}$ be a class of languages. We define two classes of languages, $\Sigma\mathcal{C}$ and $\Pi\mathcal{C}$, as follows:

- $L \in \Sigma\mathcal{C}$ if and only if there exists $R \in \mathcal{C}$ such that

$$x \in L \iff (\exists y)[(x, y) \in R].$$

- $L \in \Pi\mathcal{C}$ if and only if there exists $R \in \mathcal{C}$ such that

$$x \in L \iff (\forall y)[(x, y) \in R].$$

(In this section, we will work with ordered pairs, n-tuples, and sequences. All of them will be represented as strings in the usual way.)

For example, if $\mathcal{C}$ is the class of recursive languages, then $\Sigma\mathcal{C}$ is the class of r.e. languages by Theorem 7.18 and $\Pi\mathcal{C}$ is the class of co-r.e. languages. By alternately applying the Σ and Π operators, we obtain larger classes of languages.

DEFINITION 8.23 (Arithmetical Hierarchy). We define the language classes Σ_i, Π_i, and Δ_i recursively.

- $\Sigma_0 = \Pi_0 =$ the class of recursive languages.
- $\Pi_{i+1} = \Pi\Sigma_i$.
- $\Sigma_{i+1} = \Sigma\Pi_i$.
- $\Delta_i = \Sigma_i \cap \Pi_i$.

The *arithmetical hierarchy* consists of the classes $\Sigma_i, \Pi_i, \Delta_i$ for all $i \geq 0$.[6] A language L is called *arithmetical* if L belongs to one of the classes in the arithmetical hierarchy, i.e., if $L \in \bigcup_{i \geq 0} (\Sigma_i \cup \Pi_i)$.

Observe that Σ_1 is the class of r.e. languages and Π_1 is the class of co-r.e. languages. Many important properties of the arithmetical hierarchy follow from simple quantifier manipulation. We begin with a normal form.

LEMMA 8.24 (Normal Form)

(i) *Let i be even. $A \in \Sigma_i$ if and only if there exists a recursive language R such that*

$$x \in A \iff (\exists y_1)(\forall y_2)\cdots(\exists y_{i-1})(\forall y_i)[(x, y_1, \ldots, y_i) \in R].$$

(ii) *Let i be odd. $A \in \Sigma_i$ if and only if there exists a recursive language R such that*

$$x \in A \iff (\exists y_1)(\forall y_2)\cdots(\forall y_{i-1})(\exists y_i)[(x, y_1, \ldots, y_i) \in R].$$

(iii) *Let i be even. $A \in \Pi_i$ if and only if there exists a recursive language R such that*

$$x \in A \iff (\forall y_1)(\exists y_2)\cdots(\forall y_{i-1})(\exists y_i)[(x, y_1, \ldots, y_i) \in R].$$

(iv) *Let i be odd. $A \in \Pi_i$ if and only if there exists a recursive language R such that*

$$x \in A \iff (\forall y_1)(\exists y_2)\cdots(\exists y_{i-1})(\forall y_i)[(x, y_1, \ldots, y_i) \in R].$$

Proof: We prove all parts simultaneously by induction on i. $A \in \Sigma_0 \iff A \in \Pi_0 \iff A$ is recursive, so the base case is established. Now assume that the lemma is true for $i - 1$. We will prove it for i. Part (i) will follow from the inductive hypothesis for part (iv). Part (ii) will follow from the

6 These classes are sometimes denoted $\Sigma_i^0, \Pi_i^0, \Delta_i^0$ in order to distinguish them from the *analytic hierarchy*, in which the quantified variables are functions rather than strings.

inductive hypothesis for part (iii). Part (iii) will follow from the inductive hypothesis for part (ii). Part (iv) will follow from the inductive hypothesis for part (i). We give the proof only for part (i), where i is even and A is in Σ_i. The other three parts are proved similarly.

Because $A \in \Sigma_i$, there exists $B \in \Pi_{i-1}$ such that $x \in A \iff (\exists y)[(x, y) \in B]$. By the inductive hypothesis in part (iv), there exists a recursive language S such that

$$(x, y) \in B \iff (\forall y_1)(\exists y_2) \cdots (\exists y_{i-2})(\forall y_{i-1})[((x, y), y_1, \ldots, y_{i-1}) \in S].$$

Therefore

$$x \in A \iff (\exists y)(\forall y_1)(\exists y_2) \cdots (\exists y_{i-2})(\forall y_{i-1})[((x, y), y_1, \ldots, y_{i-1}) \in S].$$

By renaming variables,

$$\begin{aligned} x \in A &\iff (\exists y_1)(\forall y_2)(\exists y_3) \cdots (\exists y_{i-1})(\forall y_i)[((x, y_1), y_2, \ldots, y_i) \in S] \\ &\iff (\exists y_1)(\forall y_2)(\exists y_3) \cdots (\exists y_{i-1})(\forall y_i)[(x, y_1, \ldots, y_i) \in R], \end{aligned}$$

where R is the recursive language $\{(x, y_1, \ldots, y_i) : ((x, y_1), y_2, \ldots, y_i) \in S\}$.

Conversely, let R be a recursive language, and assume that

$$x \in A \iff (\exists y_1)(\forall y_2)(\exists y_3) \cdots (\exists y_{i-1})(\forall y_i)[(x, y_1, \ldots, y_i) \in R)].$$

Let

$$B = \{(x, y_1) : (\forall y_2)(\exists y_3) \cdots (\exists y_{i-1})(\forall y_i)[(x, y_1, \ldots, y_i) \in R]\},$$

and let $S = \{((x, y_1), y_2, \ldots, y_i) : (x, y_1, \ldots, y_i) \in R\}$. Then

$$B = \{(x, y_1) : (\forall y_2)(\exists y_3) \cdots (\exists y_{i-1})(\forall y_i)[((x, y_1), y_2 \ldots, y_i) \in S]\},$$

so $B \in \Pi_{i-1}$ by the inductive hypothesis in part (iv). Since $x \in A \Leftrightarrow (\exists y_1)[(x, y_1) \in B]$, therefore $A \in \Sigma_i$. This establishes part (i) of the inductive hypothesis. The remaining parts are similar. ∎

We state the normal forms more succinctly by using a symbol Q to denote the last quantifier.

- $A \in \Sigma_i$ if and only if there exists a recursive language R such that
$$x \in A \iff (\exists y_1)(\forall y_2)\cdots(Qy_i)[(x, y_1, \ldots, y_i) \in R],$$
where Q is $\forall$ if i is even, and Q is $\exists$ if i is odd.
- $A \in \Pi_i$ if and only if there exists a recursive language R such that
$$x \in A \iff (\forall y_1)(\exists y_2)\cdots(Qy_i)[(x, y_1, \ldots, y_i) \in R],$$
where Q is $\exists$ if i is even, and Q is $\forall$ if i is odd.

From this normal form it follows that $L \in \Sigma_i$ if and only if $\overline{L} \in \Pi_i$. (Recall that co-$\mathcal{C}$ is the class of all languages whose complements belong to $\mathcal{C}$.)

COROLLARY 8.25. $\Sigma_i = \text{co-}\Pi_i$.

Proof: Let $A \in \Sigma_i$. By the normal form lemma, there exists a recursive language R such that

$$x \in A \iff (\exists y_1)(\forall y_2)\cdots(Qy_i)[(x, y_1, \ldots, y_i) \in R].$$

Therefore

$$\begin{aligned} x \in \overline{A} &\iff \neg(\exists y_1)(\forall y_2)\cdots(Q\,y_i)[(x, y_1, \ldots, y_i) \in R] \\ &\iff (\forall y_1)(\exists y_2)\cdots(Q'y_i)[(x, y_1, \ldots, y_i) \in \overline{R}] \end{aligned}$$

(where Q' is the opposite quantifier from Q, i.e., Q' is $\exists$ if Q is $\forall$, and Q' is $\forall$ if Q is $\exists$). Therefore $\overline{A} \in \Pi_i$, so $A \in \text{co-}\Pi_i$.

Conversely, let $A \in \text{co-}\Pi_i$. Then $\overline{A} \in \Pi_i$, so there exists a recursive language R such that

$$x \in \overline{A} \iff (\forall y_1)(\exists y_2)\cdots(Qy_i)[(x, y_1, \ldots, y_i) \in R].$$

Therefore

$$\begin{aligned} x \in A &\iff \neg(\forall y_1)(\exists y_2)\cdots(Q\,y_i)[(x, y_1, \ldots, y_i) \in R] \\ &\iff (\exists y_1)(\forall y_2)\cdots(Q'y_i)[(x, y_1, \ldots, y_i) \in \overline{R}]. \end{aligned}$$

Therefore $A \in \Sigma_i$. ∎

Many proofs will be simpler if we work with recursive predicates rather than recursive languages.

DEFINITION 8.26. $P(\cdot)$ is a *recursive* predicate if $\{x : P(x)\}$ is a recursive language.

Recursive languages and recursive predicates are virtually interchangeable. We restate the normal form lemma in terms of recursive predicates (the proof is left as Exercise 8.5-1):

- $A \in \Sigma_i$ if and only if there exists a recursive predicate R such that

  $$x \in A \iff (\exists y_1)(\forall y_2)\cdots(Qy_i)[R(x, y_1, \ldots, y_i)],$$

  where Q is $\forall$ if i is even, and Q is $\exists$ if i is odd.

- $A \in \Pi_i$ if and only if there exists a recursive predicate R such that

  $$x \in A \iff (\forall y_1)(\exists y_2)\cdots(Qy_i)[R(x, y_1, \ldots, y_i)],$$

  where Q is $\exists$ if i is even, and Q is $\forall$ if i is odd.

This normal form usually shortens proofs because in the last step we can simply note that the predicate in square brackets is recursive, without having to give it a name or convert it to a set of i-tuples. Let us use this normal form to prove that Σ_i and Π_i are closed under m-reductions.

COROLLARY 8.27

(i) If $A \leq_m B$ and $B \in \Sigma_i$, then $A \in \Sigma_i$.

(ii) If $A \leq_m B$ and $B \in \Pi_i$, then $A \in \Pi_i$.

Proof: We prove only part (i). The proof of part (ii) is similar. Let $B \in \Sigma_i$. By the normal form lemma, there exists a recursive language R such that

$$x \in B \iff (\exists y_1)(\forall y_2)\cdots(Qy_i)[(x, y_1, \ldots, y_i) \in R].$$

Since $A \leq_m B$, there is a total recursive function f such that $x \in A \iff f(x) \in B$. Thus

$$x \in A \iff (\exists y_1)(\forall y_2)\cdots(Qy_i)[(f(x), y_1, \ldots, y_i) \in R].$$

Because $(f(x), y_1, \ldots, y_i) \in R$ is a recursive predicate, $A \in \Sigma_i$. ∎

The next lemma says that applying a quantifier to a class in the arithmetical hierarchy yields a class that is at least as large. The reason for this is that we need never refer to the extra quantified variable.

LEMMA 8.28. $\Sigma_i \subseteq \Sigma\Sigma_i$, $\Sigma_i \subseteq \Pi\Sigma_i$, $\Pi_i \subseteq \Sigma\Pi_i$, *and* $\Pi_i \subseteq \Pi\Pi_i$.

Proof: We prove only $\Sigma_i \subseteq \Sigma\Sigma_i$. The other parts have similar proofs.

Let $A \in \Sigma_i$. By the normal form lemma, there is a recursive set R such that

$$\begin{aligned} x \in A &\iff (\exists y_1)(\forall y_2)\cdots(Qy_i)[(x, y_1, \ldots, y_i) \in R] \\ &\iff (\exists y)(\exists y_1)(\forall y_2)\cdots(Qy_i)[(x, y_1, \ldots, y_i) \in R]. \end{aligned}$$

Thus $x \in A \iff (\exists y)[(x, y) \in B]$, where

$$B = \{(x, y) : (\exists y_1)(\forall y_2)\cdots(Qy_i)[(x, y_1, \ldots, y_i) \in R]\}.$$

Since $(x, y_1, \ldots, y_i) \in R$ is a recursive predicate, $B \in \Sigma_i$, so $A \in \Sigma\Sigma_i$. Because we have proved this for every $A \in \Sigma_i$, it follows that $\Sigma_i \subseteq \Sigma\Sigma_i$. ∎

COROLLARY 8.29. $\Sigma_i \subseteq \Pi_{i+1}$ *and* $\Pi_i \subseteq \Sigma_{i+1}$.

Proof: By Lemma 8.28, $\Sigma_i \subseteq \Pi\Sigma_i = \Pi_{i+1}$ and $\Pi_i \subseteq \Sigma\Pi_i = \Sigma_{i+1}$. ∎

Next we show that classes at the $(i+1)$st level of the arithmetical hierarchy are at least as large as classes at the ith level. Later in this section we will prove that they are strictly larger.

THEOREM 8.30. $\Sigma_i \subseteq \Sigma_{i+1} \cap \Pi_{i+1}$ *and* $\Pi_i \subseteq \Sigma_{i+1} \cap \Pi_{i+1}$.

Proof: By Corollary 8.29, $\Sigma_i \subseteq \Pi_{i+1}$ and $\Pi_i \subseteq \Sigma_{i+1}$. Thus it suffices to show that $\Sigma_i \subseteq \Sigma_{i+1}$ and $\Pi_i \subseteq \Pi_{i+1}$. We prove only $\Sigma_i \subseteq \Sigma_{i+1}$; the proof that $\Pi_i \subseteq \Pi_{i+1}$ is similar.

Let $A \in \Sigma_i$. By the normal form lemma, there is a recursive language R such that

$$\begin{aligned} x \in A &\iff (\exists y_1)(\forall y_2)\cdots(Qy_i)[(x, y_1, \ldots, y_i) \in R] \\ &\iff (\exists y_1)(\forall y_2)\cdots(Qy_i)(Q'y_{i+1})[(x, y_1, \ldots, y_i) \in R], \end{aligned}$$

where Q' is the opposite quantifier from Q. Because $(x, y_1, \ldots, y_i) \in R$ is a recursive predicate, $A \in \Sigma_{i+1}$. ∎

The next lemma says that we can combine two adjacent $\exists$ quantifiers or two adjacent $\forall$ quantifiers.

LEMMA 8.31 (Quantifier Contraction). *Let* $i \geq 1$.

(i) $\Sigma\Sigma_i = \Sigma_i$.

(ii) $\Pi\Pi_i = \Pi_i$.

Proof: We prove only part (i). Part (ii) is similar.

By Lemma 8.28, $\Sigma_i \subseteq \Sigma\Sigma_i$. Now we prove that $\Sigma\Sigma_i \subseteq \Sigma_i$. Let $A \in \Sigma\Sigma_i$. Then there exists $B \in \Sigma_i$ such that $x \in A \iff (\exists y)[(x, y) \in B]$. Because $B \in \Sigma_i$, there exists a recursive language R such that

$$(x, y) \in B \iff (\exists y_1)(\forall y_2) \cdots (Qy_i)[((x, y), y_1, \ldots, y_i) \in R].$$

Therefore

$$\begin{aligned} x \in A \quad &\iff \quad (\exists y)(\exists y_1)(\forall y_2) \cdots (Qy_i)[((x, y), y_1, \ldots, y_i) \in R] \\ &\iff \quad (\exists (y, y_1))(\forall y_2) \cdots (Qy_i)[((x, y), y_1, \ldots, y_i) \in R], \end{aligned}$$

Because $((x, y), y_1, \ldots, y_i) \in R$ is a recursive predicate, $A \in \Sigma_i$. Because we have proved this fact for every $A \in \Sigma\Sigma_i$, it follows that $\Sigma\Sigma_i \subseteq \Sigma_i$. ∎

By definition, $\Sigma\Pi_i = \Sigma_{i+1}$ and $\Pi\Sigma_i = \Pi_{i+1}$. However, when the first quantified variable is restricted to a finite set, we obtain just Π_i and Σ_i, which is one level lower in the hierarchy than one might have expected.

LEMMA 8.32 (Bounded Quantification). *Let $f(x)$ be a total recursive function.*

(i) Let $A \in \Sigma_i$ and let $B = \{x : (\forall k \leq f(x))[(x, k) \in A]\}$. (Here we identify strings with natural numbers and use numerical order.) Then $B \in \Sigma_i$.

(ii) Let $A \in \Pi_i$ and let $B = \{x : (\exists k \leq f(x))[(x, k) \in A]\}$. Then $B \in \Pi_i$.

Proof: We prove only part (i); the proof of part (ii) is similar. When $i = 0$, A is a recursive language, so B is a recursive language; i.e., B is in Σ_0. Henceforth assume $i \geq 1$.

Let $A \in \Sigma_i$ and let $B = \{x : (\forall k \leq f(x))[(x, k) \in A]\}$. By the definition of Σ_i, there exists a set $R \in \Pi_{i-1}$ such that $x \in A \iff (\exists y)[(x, y) \in R]$.

$$\begin{aligned} x \in B &\iff (\forall k \leq f(x))(\exists y)[((x, k), y) \in R] \\ &\iff (\exists y)[((x, 0), y) \in R] \wedge \cdots \wedge (\exists y)[((x, f(x)), y) \in R]. \end{aligned}$$

By renaming variables,

$$\begin{aligned} x \in B &\iff (\exists y_0)[((x, 0), y_0) \in R] \wedge \cdots \wedge \\ &\qquad (\exists y_{f(x)})[((x, f(x)), y_{f(x)}) \in R] \\ &\iff (\exists y_0) \cdots (\exists y_{f(x)})[((x, 0), y_0) \in R \wedge \cdots \wedge \\ &\qquad\qquad ((x, f(x)), y_{f(x)}) \in R] \\ &\iff (\exists \langle\langle y_0, \ldots, y_{f(x)} \rangle\rangle)(\forall k \leq f(x))[((x, k), y_k) \in R]. \end{aligned}$$

If $i = 0$, then R is recursive so the predicate $(\forall k \leq f(x))[((x, k), y_k) \in R]$ is recursive and therefore $B \in \Sigma_1$. If $i \geq 1$, then $B \in \Sigma_i$ by quantifier contraction on $(\forall k \leq f(x))$ and R's first quantifier. ∎

COROLLARY 8.33. *Σ_i and Π_i are closed under union and intersection.*

Proof: We prove only that Σ_i is closed under intersection. The other three parts are proved similarly. Let A and B belong to Σ_i. By the normal form lemma, there exist recursive languages R and S such that the following conditions hold:

$$\begin{aligned} x \in A &\iff (\exists y_1)(\forall y_2) \cdots (Q y_i)[(x, y_1, y_2, \ldots, y_i) \in R]. \\ x \in B &\iff (\exists y'_1)(\forall y'_2) \cdots (Q y'_i)[(x, y'_1, y'_2, \ldots, y'_i) \in S]. \end{aligned}$$

Therefore

$$\begin{aligned} x \in A \cap B &\iff x \in A \ \wedge \ x \in B \\ &\iff (\exists y_1)(\forall y_2) \cdots (Q y_i)[(x, y_1, y_2, \ldots, y_i) \in R] \\ &\qquad \wedge \ (\exists y'_1)(\forall y'_2) \cdots (Q y'_i)[(x, y'_1, y'_2, \ldots, y'_i) \in S] \\ &\iff (\exists y_1)(\exists y'_1)(\forall y_2)(\forall y'_2) \cdots (Q y_i)(Q y'_i) \\ &\qquad [(x, y_1, y_2, \ldots, y_i) \in R \ \wedge \ (x, y'_1, y'_2, \ldots, y'_i) \in S]. \end{aligned}$$

Because R and S are recursive languages,

$$(x, y_1, y_2, \ldots, y_i) \in R \ \wedge \ (x, y_1', y_2', \ldots, y_i') \in S$$

is a recursive predicate. By quantifier contraction, $A \cap B \in \Sigma_i$. ■

Next we look at hardest languages in each level of the arithmetical hierarchy. We say that a language L is *hard* for a class of languages $\mathcal{C}$ if every language $A \in \mathcal{C}$ is m-reducible to L. We say that L is *complete* for $\mathcal{C}$ (or $\mathcal{C}$-complete) if $L \in \mathcal{C}$ and L is hard for $\mathcal{C}$. For example, a language is complete (defined in Section 7.9) if and only if it is complete for the class of r.e. languages.

By iterating the jump operator, we obtain complete languages for each Σ_i. (Some fairly natural examples of complete languages are known for Σ_i when i is small. Later in this section, we will present natural examples of complete languages for Σ_2.) Recall that $\emptyset^{(i)}$ is the language obtained by applying the jump operator i times to $\emptyset$.

THEOREM 8.34. *For all $i \geq 1$, $\emptyset^{(i)}$ is complete for Σ_i.*

Proof: The proof is by induction on i. For the base case, take $i = 1$. $\emptyset^{(1)} = K^{\emptyset}$. It is easy to see that $K^{\emptyset}$ is r.e. and $K \leq_m K^{\emptyset}$, so $K^{\emptyset}$ is complete, hence complete for Σ_1.

Now assume that the theorem has been proved for some $i \geq 1$. First we prove that $\emptyset^{(i+1)}$ is in Σ_{i+1}. Let $B = \emptyset^{(i)}$. Let x be an oracle TM program. The program x belongs to K^B iff there is a complete history H of program x with oracle B on input x. Furthermore, if y is a query string for which the oracle answers yes during that history H, then $y \in B$; if n is a query string for which the oracle answers no during that history H, then $n \in \overline{B}$. Thus $x \in K^B$ if and only if there exist $H, y_1, \ldots, y_k, n_1, \ldots, n_j$ such that

(1) H is a complete history of program x with some oracle on input x.

(2) $y_1, \ldots, y_k$ are the query strings for which the oracle answers yes during the history H.

(3) $n_1, \ldots, n_j$ are the query strings for which the oracle answers no during the history H.

(4) $y_1, \ldots, y_k$ belong to B.

(5) $n_1, \ldots, n_j$ belong to $\overline{B}$.

Conditions (2–5) guarantee that H is in fact a history of x with oracle B. For $m = 1, \ldots, 5$, let R_m be the set of all tuples $(x, H, y_1, \ldots, y_k, n_1, \ldots, n_j)$ satisfying condition (m) above. Let $R = R_1 \cap \cdots \cap R_5$. We will show that each R_m is in Σ_{i+1}. R_1 is recursive because a history can be mechanically checked except for oracle answers; we also examine the oracle answers to make sure that each query is answered the same way each time it is asked. R_2 and R_3 are recursive, because the queries can be compared to those made in the history H. By the inductive hypothesis, $B \in \Sigma_i$, so $R_4 \in \Sigma_i$ by bounded quantification. Since $B \in \Sigma_i$, $\overline{B} \in \Pi_i$; therefore $R_5 \in \Pi_i$ by quantifier contraction. Thus each R_m is in Σ_{i+1}.

Therefore R is in Σ_{i+1} because Σ_{i+1} is closed under intersection. Then $\emptyset^{(i+1)} K^B \in \Sigma\Sigma_{i+1} = \Sigma_{i+1}$ by quantifier contraction.

Now we show that $\emptyset^{(i+1)}$ is hard for Σ_{i+1}. Let $A \in \Sigma_{i+1}$. Then there is a set $B \in \Pi_i$ such that $x \in A \iff (\exists y)[(x, y) \in B]$. Since $B \in \Pi_i$, $\overline{B} \in \Sigma_i$. By the inductive hypothesis $\overline{B} \leq_m \emptyset^{(i)}$. Let f be an m-reduction from $\overline{B}$ to $\emptyset^{(i)}$. Then

$$x \in A \iff (\exists y)[(x, y) \notin \overline{B}] \iff (\exists y)[f(x, y) \notin \emptyset^{(i)}].$$

Then A is accepted by an NTA with oracle $\emptyset^{(i)}$ as follows: Guess y; if $f(x, y) \notin \emptyset^{(i)}$ then accept. Therefore A is r.e. in $\emptyset^{(i)}$; by Theorem 8.22(i), $A \leq_m K^{\emptyset^{(i)}} = \emptyset^{(i+1)}$. ∎

In general, Δ_{i+1} is equal to the class of languages that are recursive in languages belonging to Σ_i.

THEOREM 8.35

$$A \in \Delta_{i+1} \iff (\exists B \in \Sigma_i)[A \leq_T B] \iff (\exists B \in \Pi_i)[A \leq_T B].$$

Proof: First note that $A \leq_T B$ if and only if $A \leq_T \overline{B}$, so the last two conditions above are equivalent by Corollary 8.25. It remains to show that $A \in \Delta_{i+1} \iff (\exists B \in \Sigma_i)[A \leq_T B]$.

Suppose that $A \in \Delta_{i+1} = \Sigma_{i+1} \cap \Pi_{i+1} = \Sigma_{i+1} \cap \text{co-}\Sigma_{i+1}$. Then A and $\overline{A}$ are m-reducible to $\emptyset^{(i+1)}$, which is equal to $K^{\emptyset^{(i)}}$. Therefore, by Theorem 8.22, A and $\overline{A}$ are both r.e. in $\emptyset^{(i)}$. By relativizing the proof of Theorem 7.19, it follows that A is recursive in $\emptyset^{(i)}$, which belongs to Σ_i.

Conversely, assume that $A \leq_T B$, where $B \in \Sigma_i$. Then $A \leq_T \emptyset^{(i)}$ because $\emptyset^{(i)}$ is complete for Σ_i, so A is r.e. in $\emptyset^{(i)}$ and $\overline{A}$ is r.e. in $\emptyset^{(i)}$. Therefore $A \leq_m K^{\emptyset^{(i)}} = \emptyset^{(i+1)}$ and $\overline{A} \leq_m K^{\emptyset^{(i)}} = \emptyset^{(i+1)}$, so $A \in \Sigma_{i+1}$ and $\overline{A} \in \Sigma_{i+1}$. The latter implies $A \in \Pi_{i+1}$, so $A \in \Sigma_{i+1} \cap \Pi_{i+1} = \Delta_{i+1}$. ▪

Because $\emptyset^{(i+1)}$ is harder than $\emptyset^{(i)}$, we will prove that the classes in the arithmetical hierarchy are distinct. In the proof we will use an important operation that combines two sets into a set that is just as hard as both sets put together.

$$A \oplus B = \{(x, 0) : x \in A\} \cup \{(x, 1) : x \in B\}.$$

$A \oplus B$ is called the *join* of A and B.

LEMMA 8.36. *A and B are both m-reducible to $A \oplus B$.*

Proof: $x \in A \iff (x, 0) \in A \oplus B$, so $A \leq_m A \oplus B$ via the m-reduction $f(x) = (x, 0)$. Similarly, $B \leq_m A \oplus B$ via the m-reduction $f(x) = (x, 1)$. ▪

In a sense, $A \oplus B$ is an easiest set that A and B are both m-reducible to (Exercise 8.5-3(a)).

COROLLARY 8.37

(i) For all $i \geq 1$, $\Sigma_i \neq \Pi_i$.

(ii) For all $i \geq 1$, $\Sigma_i \cup \Pi_i \subset \Delta_{i+1}$.

(iii) For all $i \geq 1$, $\Delta_i \subset \Sigma_i$ and $\Delta_i \subset \Pi_i$.

Proof

(i) Proof by contradiction. Assume $\Sigma_i = \Pi_i$. Then $\Sigma_i = \Delta_i$, so every language in Σ_i is recursive in a language belonging to Σ_{i-1}. Therefore $\emptyset^{(i)}$ is recursive in a language belonging to Σ_{i-1}. Because $\emptyset^{(i-1)}$ is complete for Σ_{i-1}, it follows that $\emptyset^{(i)} \leq_T \emptyset^{(i-1)}$, contradicting Theorem 8.22(ii).

(ii) By Theorem 8.30, Σ_i and Π_i are subsets of Σ_{i+1} and Π_{i+1}, so $\Sigma_i \cup \Pi_i \subseteq \Sigma_{i+1} \cap \Pi_{i+1} = \Delta_{i+1}$. Let $A = \emptyset^{(i)} \oplus \overline{\emptyset^{(i)}}$, i.e.,

$$A = \{(x, 0) : x \in \emptyset^{(i)}\} \cup \{(x, 1) : x \notin \emptyset^{(i)}\}.$$

Then A is recursive in $\emptyset^{(i)}$, so $A \in \Delta_{i+1}$. We assert that A does not belong to Σ_i or Π_i. Why? Observe that $\emptyset^{(i)}$ and $\overline{\emptyset^{(i)}}$ are both m-reducible to A. If $A \in \Sigma_i$, then we have $\overline{\emptyset^{(i)}} \in \Sigma_i$; if $A \in \Pi_i$, then $\emptyset^{(i)} \in \Pi_i$. In either case we would have $\Sigma_i = \Pi_i$, because $\emptyset^{(i)}$ is complete for Σ_i, and that would contradict part (i).

(iii) By definition, $\Delta_i = \Sigma_i \cap \Pi_i$, which is a subset of Σ_i and of Π_i. Why are both containments proper? If $\Sigma_i = \Sigma_i \cap \Pi_i$, then we have $\Sigma_i \subseteq \Pi_i = \text{co-}\Sigma_i$, so $\Sigma_i = \text{co-}\Sigma_i = \Pi_i$, contradicting part (i). We obtain a similar contradiction if $\Pi_i = \Sigma_i \cap \Pi_i$. ■

Figure 8.2 depicts the relationships among the classes in the arithmetical hierarchy.

We can use the techniques developed in this section to pinpoint the exact location in the arithmetical hierarchy of certain particular languages. Recall that $\text{Dom}(\varphi_P)$ is the set of inputs for which DTM program P has a complete computation, i.e., the set of inputs on which P halts.

DEFINITION 8.38

- $\text{FIN} = \{P : \text{Dom}(\varphi_P) \text{ is finite}\}$.
- $\text{INF} = \{P : \text{Dom}(\varphi_P) \text{ is infinite}\}$.
- $\text{TOT} = \{P : \varphi_P \text{ is total}\}$.

THEOREM 8.39. TOT *is complete for* Π_2.

Proof: First we show that $\text{TOT} \in \Pi_2$.

$$\begin{aligned} x \in \text{TOT} &\iff (\forall y)[x \text{ halts on input } y] \\ &\iff (\forall y)[(x, y) \in K_{xy}]. \end{aligned}$$

Because K_{xy} is r.e., $\text{TOT} \in \Pi\Sigma_1 = \Pi_2$.

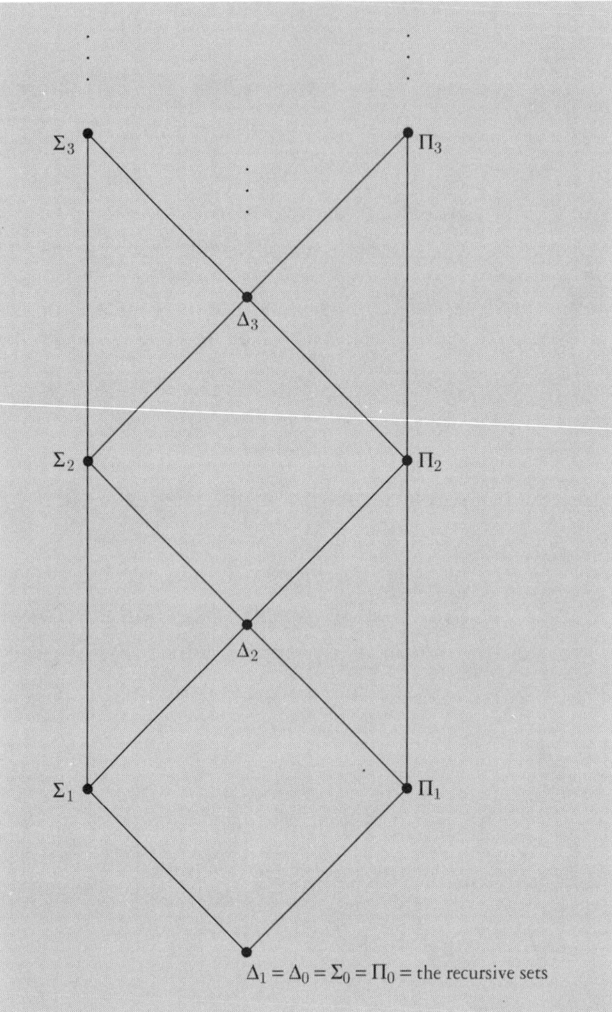

FIGURE 8.2: The relationships among the classes in the arithmetical hierarchy. If two classes are on the same level horizontally, then neither is a subset of the other; i.e., they are incomparable under $\subseteq$. If one class is vertically lower than another, then the lower class is a proper subset of the higher one. Edges are drawn between classes at adjacent levels to indicate the proper containment.

Let A be any language in Π_2. We m-reduce A to TOT. Since $A \in \Pi_2$, there exists a recursive language R such that

$$x \in A \iff (\forall y)(\exists z)[(x, y, z) \in R].$$

Let $f(x)$ be the following DTM program:

```
input y;
for z := 1 to ∞ do
    if (x, y, z) ∈ R then halt;
```

Then $x \in A \iff (\forall y)(\exists z)[(x, y, z) \in R] \iff f(x) \in \text{TOT}$, so $A \leq_m \text{TOT}$. ■

COROLLARY 8.40. INF *is complete for* Π_2 *and* FIN *is complete for* Σ_2.

Proof: First we show that INF $\in \Pi_2$:

$$\begin{aligned} x \in \text{INF} &\iff (\forall y)(\exists z)[z > y \text{ and } x \text{ halts on input } z] \\ &\iff (\forall y)(\exists z)[(x, y, z) \in S], \end{aligned}$$

where $S = \{(x, y, z) : z > y \text{ and } x \text{ halts on input } z\}$. Since S is r.e., INF $\in \Pi\Sigma\Sigma_1 = \Pi_2$.

We reduce TOT to INF. Let $f(x)$ be the following DTM program:

```
input y;
for z := 1 to y do
    emulate program x on input z;
```

If $x \in \text{TOT}$, then $f(x) \in \text{TOT} \subseteq \text{INF}$. If $x \notin \text{TOT}$, then there exists z such that x does not halt on z; the program $f(x)$ will not halt on any $y \geq z$, so $f(x) \notin \text{INF}$. Therefore $x \in \text{TOT} \iff f(x) \in \text{INF}$, so $\text{TOT} \leq_m \text{INF}$. Hence INF is Π_2-complete.

Because FIN $= \overline{\text{INF}}$, FIN is complete for co-$\Pi_2 = \Sigma_2$. ■

Exercises

8.5-1 (a) Let $Q_1, \ldots, Q_i$ be any sequence of existential and universal quantifiers. Prove that there is a recursive language R such that

$$(Q_1 x_1) \cdots (Q_i x_i)[(x_1, \ldots, x_i) \in R]$$

if and only if there is a recursive predicate R' such that

$$(Q_1 x_1) \cdots (Q_i x_i)[R'(x_1, \ldots, x_i)].$$

(b) Prove that $A \in \Sigma_i$ if and only if there exists a recursive predicate R such that

$$x \in A \iff (\exists y_1)(\forall y_2) \cdots (Q y_i)[R(x, y_1, \ldots, y_i)],$$

where Q is $\forall$ if i is even, and Q is $\exists$ if i is odd.

(c) Prove that $A \in \Pi_i$ if and only if there exists a recursive predicate R such that

$$x \in A \iff (\forall y_1)(\exists y_2) \cdots (Q y_i)[R(x, y_1, \ldots, y_i)],$$

where Q is $\exists$ if i is even, and Q is $\forall$ if i is odd.

8.5-2 Let AH be the class of all arithmetical languages, i.e., AH $= \bigcup_{i \geq 0} \Sigma_i$.

(a) Prove that AH is closed under m-reductions.

(b) Prove that there is no complete language for AH.

(c) Prove that the set of nonarithmetical languages is uncountable.

(d) Let $\emptyset^{(\omega)} = \{(x, i) : x \in \emptyset^{(i)}\}$. Prove that $\emptyset^{(\omega)}$ is not arithmetical.

*(e) Let L be the set of inattentive NTM programs that have an infinite computation that enters an accepting control state infinitely often. Prove that $\emptyset^{(\omega)} \leq_m L$ and therefore L is not arithmetical. Hint: To reduce $\emptyset^{(i)}$ to L, write an NTM program that guesses a complete computation of a program with oracle $\emptyset^{(i-1)}$, verifies the yes answers using nonaccepting

states, and dovetails the no answers using accepting states and halting if any no answer actually halts.

8.5-3 (a) Let C be any set such that $A \leq_m C$ and $B \leq_m C$. Prove that $A \oplus B \leq_m C$.
(b) Prove that Σ_i and Π_i are closed under join.

8.5-4 Prove that $\{(x,y) : \varphi_x = \varphi_y\}$ is Π_2-complete.

8.5-5 Prove that $\{(x,y) : \mathrm{Dom}(\varphi_x) = \mathrm{Dom}(\varphi_y)\}$ is Π_2-complete.

8.5-6 Let L be the set of inattentive NTM programs that have at least one infinite computation. Prove that L is complete for Π_1. Hint: Use König's lemma (Exercise 0.6-29).

8.5-7 (a) Let $\mathrm{COF} = \{P : \mathrm{Dom}(\varphi_P) \text{ is co-finite}\}$. Prove that $\mathrm{COF} \in \Sigma_3$.
*(b) Prove that COF is Σ_3-complete.
(c) Let $\mathrm{REC} = \{P : \mathrm{Dom}(\varphi_P) \text{ is a recursive language}\}$. Prove that $\mathrm{REC} \in \Sigma_3$.
(d) Prove that REC is Σ_3-complete. Hint: Reduce COF.

Solution: We m-reduce COF to REC. Given a program P, we construct a program P' that does the following:

```
input (x, y);
if x ≥ y then halt;
for i := 0 to ∞ do begin
      if i encodes a computation of x on input x then halt;
      if i encodes a computation of P on input y then halt;
end;
```

If $P \in \mathrm{COF}$, then P halts for all $y >$ some y_0. Then P' halts whenever $y > y_0$ or $x \geq y_0$ so $P' \in \mathrm{COF} \subseteq \mathrm{REC}$.
If $P \notin \mathrm{COF}$, then we assert that

$$x \in K \iff (\forall y)[(x,y) \in \mathrm{Dom}(\varphi_{P'})].$$

Why? If $x \in K$, then clearly P' halts for all pairs (x,y). If $x \notin K$, then choose $y > x$ such that P does not halt on y (such a y exists because $P \notin \mathrm{COF}$). Then P' does not halt on input

(x, y). Thus we have proved that K is co-r.e. in $\text{Dom}(\varphi_{P'})$. If $\text{Dom}(\varphi_{P'})$ were recursive, then K would be co-r.e., which it is not. Therefore $\text{Dom}(\varphi_{P'})$ is not recursive, so $P' \notin \text{REC}$.
Thus we have shown that $P \in \text{COF} \iff P' \in \text{REC}$, so $\text{COF} \leq_m \text{REC}$ via $f(P) = P'$. COF is Σ_3-complete by part (b), so REC is Σ_3-hard. $\text{REC} \in \Sigma_3$ by part (c), so REC is Σ_3-complete.

(e) Let f and g denote partial functions. We say that f *extends* g if $f(x) = g(x)$ for all $x \in \text{Dom}(g)$. Let

$$\text{EXT} = \{x : (\exists y)[\varphi_y \text{ is total and } \varphi_y \text{ extends } \varphi_x]\}.$$

Prove that $\text{EXT} \in \Sigma_3$.

*(f) Prove that EXT is Σ_3-complete.

(g) Let $\text{SEP} = \{(x, y) : \text{Dom}(\varphi_x) \text{ and } \text{Dom}(\varphi_y) \text{ are recursively separable}\}$ (cf. Section 7.8.2). Prove that $\text{SEP} \in \Sigma_3$.

*(h) Prove that SEP is Σ_3-complete.

(i) Recall that a set is complete iff it is complete for Σ_1 under many-one reductions. Let

$$\text{MCOMP} = \{x : \text{Dom}(\varphi_x) \text{ is complete}\}.$$

Prove that MCOMP is in Σ_3.

*(j) Prove that MCOMP is Σ_3-complete.

(k) A language is called *Turing-complete* if it is complete for Σ_1 under Turing reductions. Let

$$\text{COMP} = \{x : \text{Dom}(\varphi_x) \text{ is Turing-complete}\}.$$

Prove that COMP is in Σ_4.

(l) Prove that COMP is Σ_3-hard.

**(m) Prove that COMP is Σ_4-complete.

8.6 CHAPTER SUMMARY

In this chapter we proved several important general theorems about recursive functions, recursive languages, and r.e. languages. The first of these is Rice's theorem, which states that every nontrivial property of a DTM program's transfer function is undecidable. The recursion theorem says that programs for partial recursive functions can be self-referential, i.e., a program can read its own code. The recursion theorem is the key to a constructive proof of Gödel's incompleteness theorem: Using self-reference, we constructed a particular true statement that is neither provable nor disprovable. Next we defined oracles, computation relative to an oracle, and Turing reductions, which are the most general computable reductions between problems. Because virtually every proof in recursion theory is independent of the precise machine model, virtually every theorem "about" Turing machines applies as well to oracle Turing machines (however, see the caveat at the end of Section 8.4.2). Next we defined the jump of a set A, which is the halting problem relative to A. Jumps provide an infinite hierarchy of successively harder problems, each being more undecidable than its predecessors. Finally, we defined the arithmetical hierarchy by applying quantifiers to recursive languages or, equivalently, to recursive predicates. This hierarchy helps us to classify undecidable problems, because many natural problems concerning Turing machines are complete for some class in the arithmetical hierarchy. For more information about recursion theory we recommend Rogers' *Theory of Recursive Functions and Effective Computability*, Soare's *Recursively Enumerable Sets and Degrees*, or the *Handbook of Theoretical Computer Science* (Elsevier and MIT Press).

Exercises

8.6-1 Professors Curly, Moe, and Larry report discovering an algorithm with the following marvelous property: On input of a deterministic TM program P, it outputs a deterministic TM program P' such that P and P' are guaranteed to compute different partial functions. Duplicate their feat, or prove that it is impossible.

9

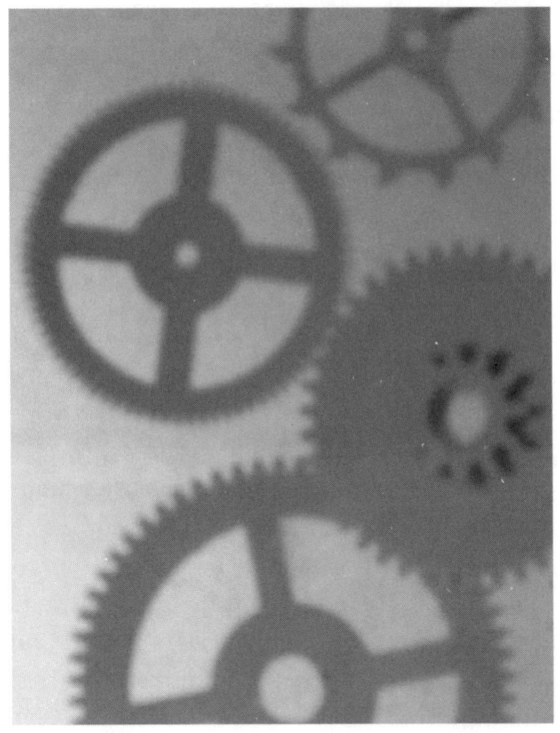

Feasible and Infeasible Problems

THE AMOUNT OF time it takes a program to run to completion can be of the utmost importance in real-world applications. Most banks run programs to process checks and update accounts; these programs must finish overnight. Some investors run programs to detect inconsistent pricing in the market, e.g., in currency exchange rates; these programs must run fast enough so that the investor can correct or exploit these pricing anomalies before someone else does. Some automobiles contain programs that control automatic braking systems; these programs must run virtually instantaneously.

9.1 TIME-BOUNDED COMPUTATION: P AND NP

In this section we define a formal measure of the running time for programs. The *length* of a computation $\langle\langle \pi_1, \ldots, \pi_t \rangle\rangle$ is t, the length of the sequence of instructions; this is also referred to as the number of steps in the computation. Nondeterministic programs may have zero, one, or more than one computation with the same input. We define the *running time* of a program P on input x to be the length of its shortest computation with input x; the running time on x is undefined if there is no computation of P with input x. In particular, if P is deterministic and always halts, then the running time of P on input x is the length of P's unique computation with input x.

Because we expect programs to take more time on longer inputs, the running time of a program is described as a function of the input length. We usually reserve x to denote the input and n to denote $|x|$, the length of the input. We say that a program P runs in time bounded by $t(n)$ if for every x the running time of P on input x is defined and is less than or equal to $t(|x|)$. We say that P runs in time $O(t(n))$ if there exists a function f such that P runs in time bounded by $f(n)$, where $f(n) = O(t(n))$. (If you have not read Section 0.5 on the $O(\cdot)$ notation, now might be a good time to do so.) Observe that $t(\cdot)$ is a function of input length rather than of the argument; for this reason, the method of encoding arguments can have a significant effect on running time. By convention, numbers will be encoded in binary without leading zeroes unless otherwise specified.

As a rule of thumb, most real-world RAM programs that are practical for long inputs, e.g., programs for sorting and matrix multiplication, run in time bounded by $10n^{1.5}$. However, there are many problems for which no practical solution is known for long inputs; for most such problems the best available algorithms take $2^{\sqrt{n}}$ steps or more on inputs of length n (for example, the traveling salesman problem and the equipartition problem). For purposes of comparison, suppose n is 10^4. Current computers typically perform between one million and one billion instructions per second. At a conservative rate of one million steps per second, $10n^{1.5}$ (10^7) instructions could be executed within 10 seconds but, even at a currently unattainable rate of one trillion steps per second, $2^{\sqrt{n}}$ (more than 10^{30}) instructions would require over 10^{18} seconds, which is greater than the age of the universe.

Theoretical computer scientists often draw the line between efficient programs and inefficient programs according to a criterion called polynomial time. We say that a program P runs in *polynomial time* if there exists a positive integer k such that P runs in time $O(n^k)$. Equivalently, P runs in polynomial time if and only if there exists a polynomial p such that P runs in time bounded by $p(n)$ (Exercise 9.1-3). Although a program with a running time of $100n^{17}$ would not be considered fast in practice, empirically most problems that can be solved in polynomial time at all can be solved in time an^k for small values of a and k. It is also worth noting that for modest values of n, like one million, $100n^{17}$ is much smaller than $2^{\sqrt{n}}$.

Polynomial time is a theoretically attractive criterion of feasibility because its definition is rather robust with respect to the model of computation. If a program P runs in polynomial time on a RAM, a 1-TM, a k-TM, or a 2-SM, then P can be simulated by a program that runs in polynomial time on any of those machines (Exercise 9.1-1). In particular, a problem can be solved in polynomial time on a Turing machine if and only if it can be solved in polynomial time on a RAM. Informally, that means that polynomial time on a Turing machine is the same as polynomial time on any general-purpose computer currently in use. (However, there exist certain problems that are solvable in polynomial time on a deterministic TM but not on a deterministic 2-CM. See Exercise 9.1-4.)

We define three important classes of languages in terms of programs that run in time bounded by a polynomial in the input length.

DEFINITION 9.1 (P and NP)

- P is the class of languages that are recognized by DTM programs running in polynomial time.
- NP is the class of languages that are accepted by NTM programs running in polynomial time.
- co-NP is the class of languages L such that $\overline{L}$ belongs to NP, i.e., co-NP consists of the complements of all NP languages.

By the previous remarks, P is also equal to the class of languages that are recognized by deterministic RAM programs running in polynomial time, and NP is also equal to the class of languages that are accepted by nondeterministic RAM programs running in polynomial time.

For example, all context-free languages belong to P, because the CYK algorithm runs in time $O(n^3)$. The next two problems belong to NP; it is not known whether they belong to P.

EXAMPLE 9.2

Problem name: subset sum[1]

Instance: a bag S of positive integers and a positive integer g (bags are discussed in Section 0.2.5)

Question: Does there exist a sub-bag of S whose elements add up to g?

The subset sum problem is in NP because in polynomial time we can nondeterministically guess a sub-bag of S, compute its sum, and accept if this sum is equal to g. It is not known whether subset sum is in P. ■■■

EXAMPLE 9.3

Problem name: compositeness

Instance: a positive integer k

Question: Does there exist an integer i such that $1 < i < k$ and k is divisible by i?

The compositeness problem is in NP because in polynomial time we can guess a number i between 2 and $k - 1$, divide k by i, and accept if the remainder is 0.

However, it is not known whether the set of composite numbers written in binary is in P. (Recall the representation conventions from Section 2.1.) The obvious algorithm is

```
input x; (* the binary representation of the argument k *)
for i := 2 to √k do
    if k is divisible by i then accept and halt;
reject.
```

[1] It would be logical to call this problem sub-bag sum, but historical usage prevails.

Clearly the algorithm runs for more than $\sqrt{k}$ steps when k is prime. But the input length is at most $\log k + 1$.[2] Thus $t(n) > 2^{\frac{1}{2}(n-1)}$, which is not polynomial bounded. However, if the argument is represented in monadic, then the obvious algorithm becomes

> input x; (* the monadic representation of the argument k *)
> compute the binary representation of k;
> for $i := 2$ to $\sqrt{k}$ do
>   if k is divisible by i then accept and halt;
> reject.

The conversion to binary can be performed in $O(k)$ steps and so can the for-loop. Now the input length is k, so the running time is $O(n)$. Typically numbers will be represented in base 2; thus the set of composite numbers, as typically represented, is not known to belong to P. ■ ■ ■

Although it is usually impractical, we can solve any problem in NP by brute force in exponential time.

THEOREM 9.4. *If $L \in$ NP, then L can be recognized deterministically in time $2^{n^{O(1)}}$.*

Proof: Suppose that $L \in$ NP. Then L is accepted by an NTA N that runs in time an^k for some a and k. Let x have length n. Then there are at most an^k configurations in any computation of N on input x. We can check every string of length an^k ($|\mathcal{I}|^{an^k}$ in all) to see if it is an accepting computation of N on input x. Each potential computation can be checked in polynomial time, so the total running time is a polynomial times $|\mathcal{I}|^{an^k}$, which is $2^{n^{O(1)}}$. ■

The class P is the polynomial-time-bounded analogue of the class of recursive languages. The class NP is the polynomial-time-bounded analogue of the class of r.e. languages. The class co-NP is the polynomial-time-bounded analogue of the class of co-r.e. languages. The following theorem is analogous to Theorem 7.18 for unbounded time computation.

---

[2] In this chapter all logarithms use the base 2.

THEOREM 9.5. *L belongs to* NP *if and only if there exist a language R in* P *and a polynomial p such that, for all strings x,*

$$x \in L \iff (\exists y)[|y| \leq p(|x|) \text{ and } (x, y) \in R].$$

That is, elements of L have short witnesses.

Proof: Assume that $L \in$ NP, so L is accepted by an NTA N running in time $p(n)$ for some polynomial p. Because N has a fixed instruction set, each instruction can be encoded as a single character in the alphabet $\mathcal{I}$. Let

$$R = \{(x, C) : C \text{ is an accepting computation of } N \text{ on input } x\}.$$

Because computations may be checked step by step, R is in P. If $x \in L$, then N has an accepting computation that consists of at most $p(|x|)$ instructions, i.e., $(\exists C)[|C| \leq p(|x|) \text{ and } (x, C) \in R]$. If $x \notin L$, then no accepting computation of any length exists, i.e., $\neg(\exists C)[(x, C) \in R]$. Therefore,

$$x \in L \iff (\exists C)[|C| \leq p(|x|) \text{ and } (x, C) \in R].$$

Conversely, let R be any language in P, and let p be a polynomial. Assume that

$$x \in L \iff (\exists y)[|y| \leq p(|x|) \text{ and } (x, y) \in R].$$

Then the following high-level nondeterministic program accepts L:

> input x;
> guess a string y having length $p(|x|)$ or less;
> if $(x, y) \in R$ then accept.

This program runs in polynomial time and can be readily implemented on an NTA; therefore $L \in$ NP. ∎

Exercises

9.1-1 In each part, make sure that your simulations preserve determinism.
(a) Let P be a RAM program that runs in time bounded by $t(n)$.

Recall that RAMs have built-in addition and subtraction operations but not multiplication or division. Prove that, on arguments of length n, P uses at most $t(n)$ different memory locations and stores no value larger than $2^{t(n)-1}$ into memory. Prove that P can be simulated by a multitape machine program that runs in time $O((t(n))^3)$.

(b) Let P be a multitape machine program that runs in time bounded by $t(n)$. Prove that on arguments of length n, P's tape head never leaves the leftmost $t(n)$ tape squares. Prove that P can be simulated by a 1-tape machine program that runs in time $O((t(n))^2)$.

(c) Let P be a 1-tape machine program that runs in time bounded by $t(n)$. Prove that P can be simulated by a 2-stack machine program that runs in time $t(n)$.

(d) Let P be a RAM program that runs in time bounded by $t(n)$. Prove that P can be simulated by a 1-tape machine program that runs in time $O((t(n))^6)$. Prove that P can be simulated by a 2-stack machine program that runs in time $O((t(n))^6)$.

(e) Let P be a 2-stack machine program that runs in time bounded by $t(n)$. Prove that P can be simulated by a RAM program that runs in time $O(t(n))$.

9.1-2 You will show that the simulation in Exercise 9.1-1(b) is essentially as fast as possible.

(a) Prove that the set of palindromes is recognized by a deterministic 2-TM program that runs in time $O(n)$.

*(b) Let P be a deterministic 1-TM program that recognizes the set of palindromes and runs in time $t(n)$. Prove that there exist a rational number c and an integer N_0 (depending on P) such that $t(n) \geq cn^2$ for all $n \geq N_0$.

9.1-3 Recall the definition of polynomial from Exercise 0.5-1. Prove that a program P runs in polynomial time if and only if there is a polynomial p such that P runs in time bounded by $p(n)$.

Solution: If P runs in polynomial time, then there exists some positive integer k such that P runs in time $O(n^k)$; i.e., there exists $t(n)$ such that P runs in time bounded by $t(n)$ and $t(n) = O(n^k)$. Then there exists $c > 0$ such that $t(n) \leq cn^k + c$. Therefore P runs in time bounded by $cn^k + c$, which is a polynomial.

Conversely, suppose P runs in time bounded by $p(n)$ for some polynomial p. By Exercise 0.5-1(a), there exists k such that $p(n) = O(n^k)$, so P runs in polynomial time.

9.1-4 Let $L = \{w\#w^R : w \in \{\mathtt{a}, \mathtt{b}\}^*\}$.

(a) Prove that there is a multitape DTM program that recognizes L in time n.

(b) An *internal description* (id) consists of the states of all devices except for the input. Let P be any deterministic program that recognizes L. For every n, prove that there are at least 2^n different id's that are reached on arguments of length $2n + 1$.

(c) Let P be a deterministic k-counter machine program with control set Q that recognizes L. Prove that in t steps at most $(t+1)^k|Q|$ distinct id's can be reached by the k-CM program.

(d) Let P be a deterministic multicounter machine program that recognizes L. Prove that there are constants a and b such that the running time of P is at least $2^{n/a}/b$.

(e) Let P be a nondeterministic multicounter machine program that accepts L. Prove that there are constants a and b such that the running time of P is at least $2^{n/a}/b$.

+9.1-5 Let P be a program for a machine whose devices are some number of inputs, outputs, controls, stacks, and tapes. Define the *space* used by a computation C of P to be the length of the longest string stored on a stack or tape in any configuration of C. We define the *space* used by program P on argument x to be the least space used by any computation of P with argument x.

Define the *space* used by a RAM computation to be the larger of the following two values:

- the number of different memory addresses accessed during the computation
- $\lceil \log (v+1) \rceil$, where v is the largest value stored in any memory location during the computation.

Define the *space* used by a RAM program P on argument x to be the least space used by any of P's computations with argument x. We say that a simulating program uses a *polynomially related* amount of space if there is a polynomial p such that, whenever the simulated program uses space bounded by s, the simulating program uses space bounded by $p(s)$.

(a) Prove that every program for a RAM is simulated by a program for a k-tape Turing machine that uses a polynomially related amount of space.

(b) Prove that every program for a k-tape machine is simulated by a program for a 1-tape machine that uses the same amount of space.

(c) Prove that every program for a 1-tape machine is simulated by a program for a 2-stack machine that uses the same amount of space.

(d) Let P be a program for a k-tape or k-stack machine. Prove that if P runs in time t on argument x, then P runs in space t on argument x.

(e) Let P be a program for a k-tape or k-stack machine. Find a constant c (depending on P) such that for all x, if P runs in space s on argument x, then P runs in time c^{s+1} on argument x.

(f) Let $s(x)$ be a total recursive function and let P be a deterministic TM program such that for every x and every partial computation with argument x, the tape head remains in the leftmost $s(x)$ squares. Prove that P accepts a recursive language.

*+9.1-6 (a) The reachability problem for a directed graph G and vertices s and t is to determine whether there is a directed path from s to t in G. Show how to solve the reachability problem using space $O((\log n)^2)$.

(b) **Savitch's theorem.** Let DSPACE$(s(n))$ be the set of languages recognized by a DTR using space $O(s(n))$. Let NSPACE$(s(n))$ be the set of languages accepted by an NTA using space $O(s(n))$. Prove that NSPACE$(s(n)) \subseteq$ DSPACE$((s(n))^2)$. Hint: Let N be an NTA using space $s(n)$. Call N's sequel relation Π. Consider a directed graph whose nodes are all possible configurations of N. Make an edge from C_1 to C_2 iff $C_1 \ \Pi \ C_2$. Because this graph has size $2^{O(s(n))}$, do not store it explicitly. Show how to solve the reachability problem in this graph deterministically using space $O((s(n))^2)$.

(c) Let PSPACE be the set of languages recognized by a DTR

using polynomial space. Let NPSPACE be the set of languages accepted by an NTA using polynomial space. Prove that PSPACE = NPSPACE.

9.1-7 Recall that a context-sensitive language is generated by a rewriting system in which the right side of each production is at least as long as the left side.

(a) Prove that if L is a CSL, then L is accepted by an NTA using space $O(n)$.

*(b) Prove that if L is accepted by an NTA using space $O(n)$, then L is a CSL.

(c) **Immerman–Szelepcsényi theorem. Prove that L is a CSL if and only if $\overline{L}$ is a CSL. Hint: Let N be an NTA that accepts L. Fix a string x. Consider a graph G whose vertices are configurations of N. There is an edge from C to C' iff $C \overset{\Pi}{\mapsto} C'$. Don't actually store G in memory because it contains $2^{O(n)}$ vertices; recompute edges as they are needed. N accepts x iff there is a path from the initial configuration C_0 to an accepting configuration in G. Find a nondeterministic linear space algorithm to test whether there is a path of length d from C_0 to C. Let $f(d)$ be the number of configurations at distance d from C_0. Give a nondeterministic recursive algorithm to compute $f(d)$. One can then prove that there is no path of length d from C_0 to C by finding $f(d)$ other configurations at distance d from C_0.

9.1-8 Let PRIMES denote the set of positive prime numbers written in binary. Prove that PRIMES $\in$ co-NP.

*9.1-9 **Pratt's theorem:** PRIMES $\in$ NP. Let Z_p^* denote the group $\{1, \ldots, p-1\}$ under multiplication modulo p. An element a has order m in a group if $a^m = 1$ and, for every j such that $0 < j < m$, $a^j \neq 1$.

(a) Prove that p is prime iff Z_p^* contains an element whose order is $p - 1$.

(b) Prove that a has order m in Z_p^* iff $a^m = 1$ and for every j such that $0 < j < m$ and j is a divisor of m, $a^j \neq 1$.

(c) Prove that a has order m in Z_p^* iff $a^m = 1$ and for every prime q such that q divides m, $a^{m/q} \neq 1$.

(d) Prove that PRIMES $\in$ NP. Hint: Recursively guess and check the prime factorization of $p - 1$.

9.1-10 Suppose that we define the running time of a nondeterministic program to be the length of the longest computation, and we define NP accordingly. Prove that we obtain the same class NP as in Definition 9.1.

9.2 NP-COMPLETENESS

A traveling salesman tries to find a short route that visits each city in his territory exactly once and then returns him to his home. Before heading out, the salesman tries to pack his odd-sized merchandise into a small number of suitcases. While on the road, he is robbed of his merchandise by a pair of highwaymen who then try to divide their booty into two piles having equal value.

The problems solved by the salesman and the highwaymen have two things in common: First, all of those problems have short solutions that can be verified efficiently; i.e., the salesman may check that a proposed route visits every city exactly once and that the route's length is less than or equal to some particular number; he may also verify that a proposed packing fits his merchandise into his suitcases and that the total number of suitcases is less than or equal to some particular number; the highwaymen may verify that two piles of booty have the same value. Second, despite decades of study by mathematicians, computer scientists, operations researchers, businessmen, and economists, no one has discovered an efficient way to find a solution to any of those problems. Decision problems closely related to those three problems belong to NP, but no one knows whether those decision problems are in P. We state the three decision problems below:

Problem name: traveling salesman problem

Instance: a graph $G = (V, E)$ with nonnegative integral edge weights, and an integer C

Question: Does G contain a cycle that has weighted length C or less and includes each vertex in V exactly once?

Problem name: bin packing

Instance: a bag S of positive integers, a positive integer B, and a positive integer k (this might be a good moment to review Section 0.2.5 on bags)

Question: Is it possible to partition S into k bags such that the elements of each bag add up to at most B?

Problem name: partition

Instance: a bag S of positive integers

Question: Is it possible to partition S into two bags such that the elements of the first bag add up to the same total as the elements of the second bag?

As we said, the problems above are in NP but not known to be in P. Those problems and thousands (yes, thousands) like them have a third thing in common: They are, in a sense that we will formalize below, among the hardest problems in NP.

In Section 7.9 we introduced m-reducibility in order to prove that certain problems are undecidable. Now we introduce a time-bounded version of m-reducibility in order to prove that certain decidable problems are hard.

DEFINITION 9.6 (Polynomial-Time Reductions)

- A language A is *polynomial-time m-reducible* to a language B (denoted $A \leq_m^p B$ and abbreviated $\leq_m^p$-reducible) if there is a polynomial-time computable function f such that for all x

$$x \in A \iff f(x) \in B.$$

Such a function f is called a *polynomial-time m-reduction* from A to B.

- A function f is *polynomial-time Turing-reducible* to a language B (denoted $f \le_T^p B$ and abbreviated $\le_T^p$-reducible) if there is a Turing reduction from f to B that runs in polynomial time (recall Definition 8.17).
- A language A is *polynomial-time Turing-reducible* to a language B (denoted $A \le_T^p B$ and abbreviated $\le_T^p$-reducible) if there is a Turing reduction from A to B that runs in polynomial time. Such a reduction is called a *polynomial-time Turing reduction* from A to B.

Informally, if $A \le_m^p B$ or $A \le_T^p B$, then A is "about" as easy to solve as B or easier, where the word "about" allows for a polynomial expansion of running time. Of these two types of reduction, polynomial-time m-reductions are the most commonly used. In fact, there are very few interesting problems A and B in NP for which we know a $\le_T^p$-reduction from A to B but don't know an $\le_m^p$-reduction from A to B. Two useful facts about $\le_m^p$-reducibility follow:

PROPOSITION 9.7

(i) If $A \le_m^p B$ and $B \in \mathrm{P}$, then $A \in \mathrm{P}$.

(ii) If $A \le_m^p B$ and $A \notin \mathrm{P}$, then $B \notin \mathrm{P}$.

Observe that part (i) of this proposition is analogous to Proposition 7.29(iii).

Proof: Assume that $A \le_m^p B$.

(i) If $B \in \mathrm{P}$, then the following polynomial-time algorithm tests membership in A:

```
input x;
y := f(x);
if y ∈ B then accept else reject;
```

The algorithm is correct because f is an m-reduction. Suppose that f is computable in time $p(n)$ and membership in B can be tested deterministically in time $q(n)$ where p and q are polynomials.

Then the running time of the algorithm above is bounded by n steps to scan the input, plus $p(n)$ steps to compute y, plus $q(p(n))$ steps to test whether $y \in B$, because the length of y is bounded by the number of steps to compute y. Thus the running time of the algorithm is at most $n + p(n) + q(p(n))$, which is a polynomial.

(ii) Let $A \notin$ P. For the sake of contradiction, assume that $B \in$ P. Then $A \in$ P by part (i), a contradiction. ■

The reader may verify that $\leq_m^p$-reducibility, like m-reducibility, is reflexive and transitive (Exercise 9.2-4).

Next we define what it means to be a hardest language in a class of languages.

DEFINITION 9.8

(i) A language B is $\leq_m^p$*-hard* for a class $\mathcal{C}$ if every language $A \in \mathcal{C}$ satisfies $A \leq_m^p B$.

(ii) A language B is $\leq_m^p$*-complete* for a class $\mathcal{C}$ if $B \in \mathcal{C}$ and B is $\leq_m^p$-hard for $\mathcal{C}$.[3]

A language L is called NP-*hard* if L is $\leq_m^p$-hard for the class NP. A language L is called NP-*complete* if L is $\leq_m^p$-complete for the class NP.[4] The following proposition, which is analogous to Corollary 7.30, follows from the definition of NP-hardness and the transitivity of $\leq_m^p$-reducibility.

PROPOSITION 9.9. *If $A \leq_m^p B$ and A is* NP*-hard, then B is* NP*-hard.* ■

All NP-complete problems have virtually the same difficulty in the sense that if one NP-complete problem is in P, then they all are. Since no one has ever found a polynomial-time (or even subexponential-time) algorithm to solve any NP-complete problem despite decades of effort, many people believe that no NP-complete problem is in P, i.e., that P $\neq$ NP (see Exercise 9.2-2).

---

[3] Different notions of hardness and completeness correspond to different reductions, e.g., $\leq_T^p$-hardness and $\leq_T^p$-completeness. See Exercise 9.2-5.

[4] Some authors define NP-hardness in terms of polynomial-time Turing reductions, but everyone defines NP-completeness in terms of polynomial-time m-reductions.

When we know a problem is in NP, we know it can be solved in exponential time. If we prove that it is NP-complete, we make it plausible that the problem cannot be solved in less than exponential time; i.e., a problem's NP-completeness is circumstantial evidence that it cannot be solved efficiently. This evidence is not as satisfying as an undecidability proof or even as satisfying as a proof that the language is not in P. However, when your employer asks you to write an efficient program to solve an NP-complete problem, it is unlikely that you will be able to comply. You can, however, point out that brilliant minds have worked for decades on equivalent problems without finding efficient algorithms. If you are clever, you will reconsider the real-world problem facing your company. Perhaps an approximate solution is sufficient in practice. Perhaps the real-world problem is only a special case of the originally posed NP-complete problem; then you can look for an efficient algorithm to solve the special case. The study of general algorithms and approximation algorithms is, however, beyond the scope of this book.

In Section 9.3 we examine the connection among optimization, search, and decision problems. Sections 9.4 through 9.9 are devoted to techniques for proving that specific problems are NP-complete.

Exercises

9.2-1 Prove that every language in NP is recursive.

9.2-2 Prove that the following three statements are equivalent:

- P = NP
- at least one NP-complete language is in P
- every NP-complete language is in P

9.2-3 (a) If L is recognized by a DTR that runs in time bounded by $t(n)$, prove that there are infinitely many DTRs that recognize L and run in time bounded by $t(n)$.

(b) Construct a language that is not in P but is recognized by a DTR that runs in time bounded by 2^n. Hint: Use diagonalization. Design a DTR that does the following on input x: Spend $2^{|x|}$ steps total using the universal Turing machine to emulate DTR program x on input x; accept if and only if the emulation finishes within the allotted time and program x rejects input x. You may assume that there is a polynomial p such that the universal Turing machine can emulate the first s steps of a DTM program within $O(p(s))$ steps. You may also use Exercise 0.5-1(b).

(c) Construct a recursive language that is not in PSPACE. (See Exercises 9.1-5 and 9.1-6 for definitions.)

(d) Let EXP denote the class of languages that are recognized by a DTM program in time 2^{n^k} for some positive integer k. What does it mean for a set to be $\leq_m^p$-hard for EXP? Prove that if A is $\leq_m^p$-hard for EXP, then A is not in P.

9.2-4 Prove that $\leq_m^p$ is reflexive and transitive. Is $\leq_m^p$ symmetric?

9.2-5 B is $\leq_T^p$-hard for $\mathcal{C}$ if every language $A \in \mathcal{C}$ satisfies $A \leq_T^p B$. B is $\leq_T^p$-complete for $\mathcal{C}$ if $B \in \mathcal{C}$ and B is $\leq_T^p$-hard for $\mathcal{C}$.

(a) Prove that $\leq_T^p$ is reflexive and transitive.

(b) Is $\leq_T^p$ symmetric?

(c) Prove that $A \leq_T^p \emptyset$ if and only if $A \in$ P.

(d) Prove that if $A \leq_T^p B$ and $B \in$ P, then $A \in$ P.

(e) Prove that if A is $\leq_m^p$-hard for $\mathcal{C}$, then A is $\leq_T^p$-hard for $\mathcal{C}$.

(f) Prove that if A is $\leq_m^p$-hard for co-NP, then A is $\leq_T^p$-hard for NP.

9.3 SEARCH AND OPTIMIZATION VS. DECISION

We are not usually satisfied in knowing that a solution exists; we want to find it. For example, recall that the traveling salesman problem is to determine whether a weighted graph contains a cycle whose weighted length is C or less and which includes each vertex exactly once. In practice, one typically wants to determine the minimum such C and find a cycle that has this minimum weighted length. For clarity, let us call the traveling salesman problem the "TSP decision" problem; the other two versions are called "TSP cost" and "TSP search." All three are stated formally below:

Problem name: TSP decision

Instance: a graph $G = (V, E)$ with nonnegative integral edge weights and an integer C

Question: Does G contain a cycle that has weighted length C or less and includes each vertex in V exactly once?

Problem name: TSP cost

Instance: a graph $G = (V, E)$ with nonnegative integral edge weights

Answer: the minimum number C such that G contains a cycle that has weighted length C and includes each vertex in V exactly once, or ∞ if no cycle includes each vertex exactly once

Problem name: TSP search

Instance: a graph $G = (V, E)$ with nonnegative integral edge weights

Answer: a cycle that has minimum weighted length and includes each vertex in V exactly once, or Λ if no cycle includes each vertex exactly once

If we can solve the TSP search problem, then by performing a simple addition we can solve the TSP cost problem. If we can solve the TSP cost problem, then by performing a simple comparison we can solve the TSP decision problem. Thus TSP search is at least as hard as TSP cost, which is at least as hard as TSP decision. In fact, the reverse is true as well.

In Figure 9.1, we show how to reduce TSP cost to TSP decision in polynomial time by performing a binary search. We use a polynomial-time Turing reduction; i.e., we query several instances of TSP decision in order to solve one instance of TSP cost.

In Figure 9.2, we show how to reduce TSP search to TSP cost and TSP decision in polynomial time by a judicious process of elimination. We use a polynomial-time Turing reduction; i.e., we query several instances of TSP cost and TSP decision in order to solve one instance of TSP search.

```
input G;
let U be the sum of all edge weights in G; (* an upper bound *)
let L := 0; (* a lower bound *)
if TSP-decision(G, U) = no then
    output ∞ (* no solution *)
else begin
    repeat
        let M := ⌊½(U + L)⌋; (* the average *)
        if TSP-decision(G, M) = yes then
            let U := M
        else
            let L := M + 1
    until U = L;
    output L;
end;
```

FIGURE 9.1: Using binary search to Turing-reduce TSP cost to TSP decision in polynomial time. TSP-decision$(\cdot,\cdot)$ is an oracle for the TSP decision problem.

We have seen that the optimization, search, and decision versions of the traveling salesman problem are all polynomial-time interreducible. The phenomenon of optimization, search, and decision being equally difficult is a common one. Additional examples are discussed in the exercises. In fact, this phenomenon is seen for a very general class of NP-complete optimization problems (Exercise 9.3-3).

Exercises

9.3-1 (a) Define decision, cost, and search versions of bin packing.

(b) Give a polynomial-time Turing reduction from bin-packing cost to bin-packing decision.

(c) Give a polynomial-time Turing reduction from bin-packing search to bin-packing cost and bin-packing decision.

```
input G;
let C = TSP-cost(G);
if C = ∞ then
    output Λ (* no solution *)
else begin
    for each edge e in G do begin
        delete e from G;
        if TSP-decision(G, C) = no then
            replace e in G; (* e is needed for the min-cost cycle *)
    end;
    output G; (* all unneeded edges have been deleted *)
end;
```

FIGURE 9.2: Using a judicious process of elimination to Turing-reduce TSP search to TSP cost and TSP decision in polynomial time. TSP-cost$(\cdot)$ and TSP-decision$(\cdot,\cdot)$ are oracles for the TSP cost and decision problems, respectively.

*9.3-2 The graph-coloring problem is to assign the minimum number of colors to the graph's vertices in such a way that adjacent vertices have different colors. Repeat Exercise 9.3-1 for the graph-coloring problem.

9.3-3 For most optimization problems, we can define a two-place valuation function v that takes a problem instance and a solution and assigns a value to that solution. Let p be a polynomial, and let v be a polynomial-time computable partial function from $\Sigma^* \times \Sigma^*$ to N such that $v(x, y)$ is defined if and only if $|y| \leq p(|x|)$. Based on the valuation function v, we define three problems: v-Decision, v-Cost, and v-Search. v-Decision is the problem of deciding whether there is a solution to instance x having cost $\leq c$. v-Cost outputs the minimum cost of a solution for x. v-Search outputs any solution for x having minimum cost. More precisely,

- v-Decision $= \{(x, c) : (\exists y)[v(x, y) \leq c]\}$.
- v-Cost$(x) = \min_y v(x, y)$.

- v-Search(x) = any y such that $v(x, y) = v$-Cost(x).

(a) Prove that v-Cost $\leq_T^p$ v-Decision.
(b) Prove that v-Search $\leq_T^p$ v-Cost.
(c) Prove that v-Decision $\leq_T^p$ v-Search.

9.3-4 Consider the reduction we presented from TSP cost to TSP decision. Let s denote the sum of the edge weights in G. Let C denote the actual TSP cost. The reduction queries $\lceil \log(s+1) \rceil + 1$ instances of TSP decision in the worst case, e.g., when $C = 0$.

(a) Describe a reduction that queries only one instance of TSP decision when $C = \infty$, two instances when $C = 0$, and $2\lceil \log(C+1) \rceil + 1$ instances when $0 < C < \infty$. Hint: Start by determining c such that $c \leq C < 2c$.

Solution: First query TSP-decision(G, s) to determine whether there is any Hamiltonian path at all; then perform the following doubling search:

```
c := 1
while C ≥ c do
      c := 2c;
```

(Note that $C \geq c$ iff TSP-decision$(G, C - 1)$ = false.) If $C = 0$, the search determines that fact with one additional query. If $C > 0$, the search determines c such that $c/2 \leq C < c$ while making $\lceil \log(C+1) \rceil + 1$ queries. Finally, the exact value of C can be determined via binary search on the interval $[c/2, c)$ by querying an additional $\log(c/2) = \lceil \log(C+1) \rceil - 1$ instances.

(b) Describe a reduction that queries only $\log C + O(\log\log C)$ instances of TSP decision when C is finite. Hint: Use the method of part (a) to determine $\lfloor \log C \rfloor$ with $O(\log\log C)$ queries. Then use binary search to determine C exactly.

(c) Describe a reduction that queries only $\log C + \log\log C + O(\log\log\log C)$ instances of TSP decision when C is finite. Hint: Use the method of part (b) to determine $\lfloor \log C \rfloor$; then use binary search.

(d) Generalize.

9.3-5 Consider variants of the traveling salesman problem in which the graph G has rational edge weights. Call them rational TSP decision, rational TSP cost, and rational TSP search.

(a) How would you represent the edge weights?

(b) Prove that rational TSP decision is in NP.

(c) Prove that TSP decision is $\leq_m^p$-reducible to rational TSP decision.

(d) Give a polynomial-time reduction from rational TSP search to rational TSP cost.

(e) Give a polynomial-time reduction from rational TSP cost to rational TSP decision.

9.4 CANONICAL NP-COMPLETE PROBLEMS

We can prove a problem is NP-complete by showing how to efficiently reduce each individual NP language to it. This kind of reduction is called a *generic* reduction. In this section we define two *canonical* NP-complete languages, which essentially encode the problem "Does NP program P accept input string x?" (They are analogous to the halting problem K_{xy}, which is at least as hard as any r.e. set.) Provided that the encoding is polynomial-time computable, the NP-completeness of such languages follows immediately from the definition.

Generic reductions are not typical NP-completeness proofs. Once we have proved that some languages are NP-complete, we can prove that a language L in NP is NP-complete by reducing a known NP-complete language to L, thanks to Proposition 9.9. (This is analogous to the way we proved a language L nonrecursive in Chapter 7 by reducing a known nonrecursive language to L.)

In the next section, we will prove that a language called SSS is NP-complete by reducing a canonical NP-complete language to SSS. For technical reasons, this is substantially easier than reducing every NP language to SSS. In later sections we will prove that various problems of practical interest are NP-complete, in some cases by reducing SSS to them.

In defining a canonical NP-complete language and proving that it is NP-complete, we have to deal with two technical issues:

- The canonical language must be accepted in a fixed polynomial running time, but it must encode the acceptance problem for arbitrary NP programs, whose running time may be a much larger polynomial. We will deal with this by padding input strings with trailing zeros. Since this increases input length without substantially affecting running time, the running time becomes a smaller function of input length.
- The canonical language must be over a fixed alphabet, but it must encode the acceptance problem for arbitrary NP programs, whose devices may use arbitrarily large alphabets. We will deal with this by encoding inputs and programs as strings over $\{0, 1\}$.

We encode programs as strings over $\{0, 1\}$ as described in Section 7.4. Let

$$K_{1,\mathrm{NP}} = \{P\#x\#0^s : P \text{ is an NTM program, } x \in \{0,1\}^*, \text{ and } P \text{ has an accepting computation } s \text{ steps or shorter on input } x\}.$$

$K_{1,\mathrm{NP}}$ is a time-bounded analogue to K_{xy}. $K_{1,\mathrm{NP}}$ is as hard as any set in NP for much the same reason that K_{xy} is as hard as any r.e. set.

THEOREM 9.10. *$K_{1,\mathrm{NP}}$ is NP-complete.*

Proof: $K_{1,\mathrm{NP}} \in$ NP because we may decode the program P character by character, nondeterministically guess an accepting computation of P having length s or less, and check that computation step by step in time that is polynomial in s, $|x|$, and $|P|$.

Let A be any language over $\{0, 1\}$ belonging to NP. We give a generic reduction from A to $K_{1,\mathrm{NP}}$. The language A is accepted by an NTM program that runs in polynomial time. Let P encode that program, and let $p(n)$ bound its running time. Then

$$x \in A \iff P\#x\#0^{p(|x|)} \in K_{1,\mathrm{NP}},$$

so $A \leq_m^p K_{1,\mathrm{NP}}$. The proof is complete except for one detail.

Let Σ be any alphabet $\{c_1, \ldots, c_k\}$, and let $\sigma(c_i) = 1^i0$. We extend σ to strings: If x is a string $x_1 \cdots x_n$ over Σ, let $\sigma(x) = \sigma(x_1) \cdots \sigma(x_n)$, which is computable in polynomial time. (For example, if $\Sigma = \{\mathtt{a}, \mathtt{b}, \mathtt{c}, \mathtt{d}\}$, then $\sigma(\mathtt{abcba}) = \mathtt{10110111011010}$.) Extending this operation to languages over Σ, we define $\sigma(B) = \{\sigma(x) : x \in B\}$, and we have $x \in B \iff \sigma(x) \in \sigma(B)$. Thus $B \leq_m^p \sigma(B)$ via σ. Similarly, $\sigma(B) \leq_m^p B$ via σ^{-1}.

Assume $B \in$ NP. Then $\sigma(B) \in$ NP. Since $\sigma(B) \subseteq \{0,1\}^*$, $\sigma(B) \leq_m^p K_{1,\mathrm{NP}}$, as shown above. By transitivity, $B \leq_m^p K_{1,\mathrm{NP}}$. Since this is true for every $B \in$ NP, the language $K_{1,\mathrm{NP}}$ is NP-complete. ■

A closely related language is

$$\begin{aligned} K_{2,\mathrm{NP}} = \{&P\#x\#0^s : P \text{ is an NTM program, } x \in \{0,1\}^*, \text{ and} \\ &P \text{ has an accepting computation exactly } s \text{ steps long} \\ &\text{on input } x\}. \end{aligned}$$

By a simple reduction from $K_{1,\mathrm{NP}}$, we see that $K_{2,\mathrm{NP}}$ is NP-complete as well.

THEOREM 9.11. *$K_{2,\mathrm{NP}}$ is NP-complete.*

Proof: $K_{2,\mathrm{NP}} \in$ NP because we can guess an accepting computation exactly s steps long and check it in time polynomial in s, $|x|$, and $|P|$. If P is any NTM program, we construct a program P' by adding null instructions that loop from each accepting state back to itself. Then P accepts x in s steps or fewer if and only if P' accepts x in exactly s steps. Therefore,

$$P\#x\#0^s \in K_{1,\mathrm{NP}} \iff P'\#x\#0^s \in K_{2,\mathrm{NP}}.$$

Since P' is computable from P in polynomial time,

$$K_{1,\mathrm{NP}} \leq_m^p K_{2,\mathrm{NP}}.$$

Since $K_{1,\mathrm{NP}}$ is NP-complete, $K_{2,\mathrm{NP}}$ is NP-complete as well. ■

Exercises

9.4-1 Representing the ith character in an alphabet by 1^i0 is not very efficient. Describe more compact binary representations of characters. Be sure that you can decode strings represented in your code.

9.4-2 Construct a PSPACE-complete language. (See Exercise 9.1-6 for a definition of PSPACE.)

9.5 SYMBOL SYSTEMS

In this section we define an important NP-complete problem that does not explicitly involve Turing machines. We present an example before proceeding to the formal definition.

Consider the system of inequalities involving the variables x, y, z, and w shown in Figure 9.3. Each inequality is called a *constraint*. Observe that each constraint involves at most three of the variables; we call 3 the *locality* of the system. We allow each variable to take on the value 0, 1, or 2. The set $\{0, 1, 2\}$ is called the system's alphabet.

Consider the function $A : \{x, y, z, w\} \to \{0, 1, 2\}$ defined by $A(x) = 1$, $A(y) = 1$, $A(z) = 2$, $A(w) = 1$. The function A is called an assignment to the variables. Observe that $2 > 1$, $1 \neq 0$, and $1 + 1 \geq 2$. Because

$$\begin{aligned} z &> w, \\ w &\neq 0, \\ x + y &\geq z. \end{aligned}$$

FIGURE 9.3: A symbol system with alphabet $\Gamma = \{0, 1, 2\}$, locality 3, variable set $V = \{x, y, z, w\}$, and three constraints. In expressing the constraints, $+$, $>$, and $\geq$ denote the usual operations on natural numbers. The symbol system has six distinct satisfying assignments. One of them is $A(x) = 1$, $A(y) = 1$, $A(z) = 2$, $A(w) = 1$.

the assignment A to the variables satisfies all of the constraints, we call A a *satisfying* assignment.

Now we present the formal definition of symbol systems. Let Γ denote an alphabet and k a positive integer. A (k, Γ)-*symbol system* consists of a finite set V of variables over Γ and a set of local constraints on the variables. A *local constraint* is a predicate on a set consisting of k or fewer elements of V. For that reason, k is called the *locality* of the system. The set of variables in a constraint is called a *constrained set*. We typically denote variables by w, x, y, or z, possibly with subscripts. We typically denote their values by a, b, or c, possibly subscripted.

In the preceding example, we have the alphabet $\Gamma = \{0, 1, 2\}$, the variable set $V = \{w, x, y, z\}$, and the locality $k = 3$. One of the local constraints is $x + y \geq z$; its constrained set is $\{x, y, z\}$.

A mapping $A : V \to \Gamma$ is called an *assignment*. An example of an assignment is

$$A'(w) = 1, A'(x) = 0, A'(y) = 0, A'(z) = 2.$$

We say that an assignment A *satisfies a constraint* $C(x_1, \ldots, x_i)$ if $C(A(x_1), \ldots, A(x_i)) =$ true. For example, the assignment A' given above satisfies the constraint $w \neq 0$ because "$1 \neq 0$" is a true statement. However, the assignment A' does not satisfy the constraint $x + y \geq z$, because "$0 + 0 \geq 2$" is not a true statement.

We say that an assignment *satisfies a symbol system* if it satisfies all the constraints. Such assignments are called *satisfying assignments*. The assignment A defined on page 624 is a satisfying assignment for the symbol system in our example, but the assignment A' is not a satisfying assignment.

A mapping from a constrained set to Γ is called a *local assignment* to the constraint. Observe that a local assignment does not specify values for all variables, but only for the variables involved in the specific constraint. A local assignment A *satisfies* a constraint $C(x_1, \ldots, x_i)$ if $C(A(x_1), \ldots, A(x_i)) =$ true.

In proofs and informal discussions, we write constraints in whatever form is convenient and clear to humans. However, inputs to programs must be represented in a fixed language. For that reason, we represent a constraint as the constrained subset, followed by the set of local assignments that satisfy the constraint. The number of distinct local assignments is at most $|\Gamma|^k$, and each can be represented by a string of length k or less over Γ. Thus a constraint can be represented by a string of length $k(|\Gamma|^k + 1)$ or less over $V \cup \Gamma$. Although this formula is exponential in k, recall that k is a constant independent of the size of the problem instance, so the length of constraints is bounded by a constant. In the example shown in Figure 9.3, the local constraint $z > w$ is represented as $\langle\langle wz, \texttt{01}, \texttt{02}, \texttt{12}\rangle\rangle$, and the local constraint $w \neq 0$ is represented as $\langle\langle w, \texttt{1}, \texttt{2}\rangle\rangle$.

We can check deterministically in polynomial time whether a *particular* assignment satisfies a given symbol system, because we can easily check whether the assignment satisfies each constraint. No one has found a deterministic polynomial-time algorithm for determining whether *there exists* an assignment that satisfies a given symbol system. We call this the (k, Γ)-symbol-system satisfiability problem, or (k, Γ)-SSS for short (or simply SSS, when k and Γ are understood).

Problem name: (k, Γ)-SSS

Instance: a finite set of variables over Γ and a finite set of constraints having locality k

Question: Is there an assignment that satisfies all the constraints?

Another symbol system example is given in Figure 9.4.

Because solutions may be verified in polynomial time, (k, Γ)-SSS is in NP. Because there are $|\Gamma|^{|V|}$ possible assignments to $|V|$ variables, the obvious brute force, deterministic approach to finding a satisfying assignment

$$(w \neq z) \vee (x \neq \texttt{a} \wedge y \neq \texttt{b}),$$

$$wxy = xyz.$$

FIGURE 9.4: A symbol system with alphabet $\Gamma = \{\texttt{a}, \texttt{b}, \texttt{c}\}$, locality 4, variable set $V = \{x, y, z, w\}$, and two constraints. In expressing the first constraint, we used the logical operations AND ($\wedge$) and OR ($\vee$). In expressing the second constraint we used concatenation. The symbol system has exactly one satisfying assignment: $A(x) = \texttt{c}$, $A(y) = \texttt{c}$, $A(z) = \texttt{c}$, $A(w) = \texttt{c}$.

takes exponential time; furthermore, no one knows how to solve the symbol-system satisfiability problem in less than exponential time. We show that this is no accident.

LEMMA 9.12. *If L is a language in* NP, *then there exist k and Γ such that* $L \leq_m^p (k, \Gamma)$-SSS.

Proof: Since $L \in \text{NP}$, there is an NTM program P that accepts L. Let Γ_0 denote P's tape alphabet, let Q denote P's control set, and let q_{start} denote P's initial control state. Let $p(n)$ be a polynomial upper bound on P's running time. Without loss of generality, we make the following assumptions:

- $p(n) \geq n$.
- The tape of P is initialized to hold the argument x padded to length $p(|x|)$, i.e., the string $x\sqcup^{p(|x|)-|x|}$. (The NTM does not have an input device.)
- P has a unique accepting state, with a null instruction looping back to it, so that if P accepts at time t, then P accepts at all times greater than t.

Let $k = 8$ and $\Gamma = \Gamma_0 \cup \boxed{\Gamma_0} \cup Q$. Let V consist of the variables $m_{i,t}$, and q_t for $0 \leq i \leq p(n) + 1$ and $0 \leq t \leq p(n)$. The variable $m_{i,t}$ represents the ith character on the tape at time t, and q_t represents the control state at time t. These variables suffice to represent an entire trace (sequence of configurations) of P (cf. Figures 9.5 and 9.6).

Next we define the local constraints. Some constraints correspond to the initial relation of P with input $x_1 \cdots x_n$. These are

$$\begin{aligned} q_0 &= q_{\text{start}} \\ m_{1,0} &= \boxed{x_1} \\ m_{i,0} &= x_i && \text{for } 2 \leq i \leq n \\ m_{i,0} &= \sqcup && \text{for } n < i \leq p(n). \end{aligned}$$

Other constraints enforce convenient boundary conditions:

$$\begin{aligned} m_{0,t} &= \sqcup && \text{for } 0 \leq t \leq p(n) \\ m_{p(n)+1,t} &= \sqcup && \text{for } 0 \leq t \leq p(n). \end{aligned}$$

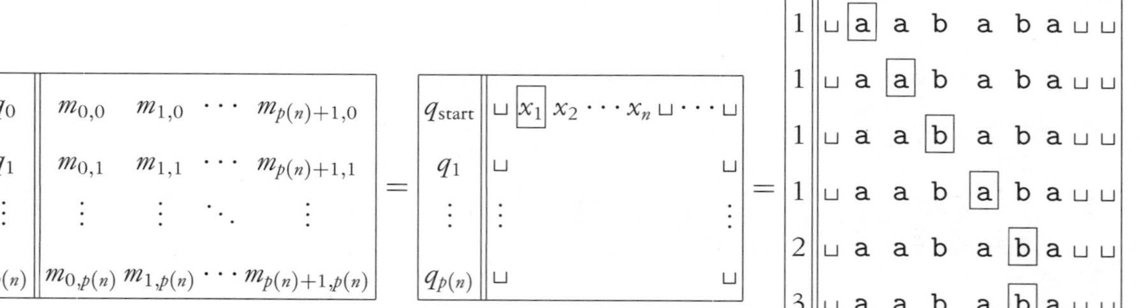

FIGURE 9.5: When representing an accepting trace via Boolean variables, it is convenient to arrange the variables in the rows of a tableau. The ith row in each tableau represents the configuration at time i. The first two tableaus depict the general case. The third tableau depicts an accepting trace of the fairly trivial NTA program in Figure 9.6 on input aababa.

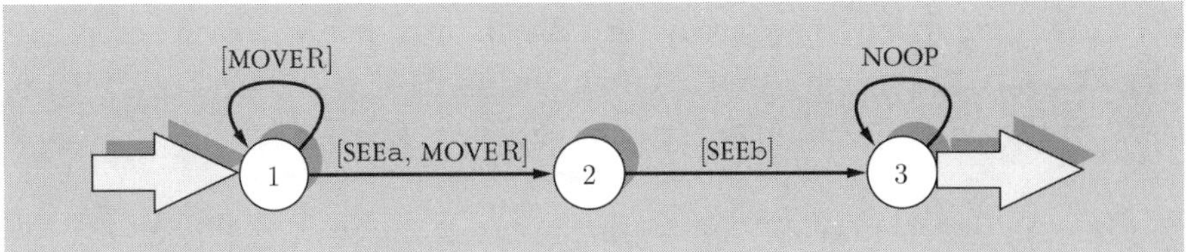

FIGURE 9.6: An NTA that accepts $\Sigma^*\texttt{ab}\Sigma^*$.

Additional constraints ensure that the control state and the tape contents change at time t in accordance with an instruction of P. Because the tape head moves only one character at a time, individual constraints need only involve three adjacent tape squares and the control. (This locality of a TM's reference to its tape is crucial to the proof.) The first set of these constraints represent the fact that tape squares do not change except near the head:

$$m_{i-1,t}m_{i,t}m_{i+1,t} \in \Gamma_0^3 \Rightarrow m_{i,t} = m_{i,t+1} \qquad \text{for } 1 \leq i \leq p(n), 0 \leq t < p(n).$$

The next set of constraints represent the fact that the behavior near the tape head is governed by an instruction of P:

$$m_{i-1,t}m_{i,t}m_{i+1,t} \in \Gamma_0 \boxed{\Gamma_0} \Gamma_0 \Rightarrow$$
$$\left(q_t, m_{i-1,t}m_{i,t}m_{i+1,t}\right) \overset{\Pi}{\mapsto} \left(q_{t+1}, m_{i-1,t+1}m_{i,t+1}m_{i+1,t+1}\right),$$

for $1 \leq i \leq p(n), 0 \leq t < p(n)$.

A final constraint ensures that the program accepts:

$$q_{p(n)} = q_{\text{accept}}.$$

All of these constraints can be written down in polynomial time using simple iteration, i.e., for-loops. It remains to show that they form a reduction from L to (k, Γ)-SSS.

If P accepts x, then it has an accepting trace (the sequence of configurations reached during an accepting computation). Then the symbol system above has a satisfying assignment in which q_t is the control state in that trace at time t and $m_{i,t}$ is the ith tape character at time t. Conversely, if the symbol system above has a satisfying assignment, then P has an accepting trace $\langle\langle C_0, \ldots, C_{p(n)} \rangle\rangle$ on input x in which $C_t = (q_t, m_{1,t} \cdots m_{p(|x|),t})$. Thus $x \in L$ iff the symbol system constructed above is satisfiable. ■

Observe that Lemma 9.12 does not by itself say that (k, Γ)-SSS is NP-complete for any particular k and Γ, because it leaves open the possibility that a different k and Γ are required for each L in NP. However, this defect is easily rectified.

THEOREM 9.13. *There exist k and Γ such that (k, Γ)-SSS is NP-complete.*

Proof: Recall that $K_{1,\mathrm{NP}}$ is NP-complete by Theorem 9.10. By Lemma 9.12, there exist k and Γ such that $K_{1,\mathrm{NP}} \leq^p_m (k, \Gamma)$-SSS. By Proposition 9.9, (k, Γ)-SSS must be NP-hard. Because (k, Γ)-SSS is also in NP, (k, Γ)-SSS is NP-complete. ■

Because we have shown that (k, Γ)-SSS is NP-complete for at least one choice of k and Γ, if we want to prove that a language L is NP-complete, it is certainly sufficient to reduce (k, Γ)-SSS to L for all k and Γ. Many reductions from symbol-system satisfiability will take this general form.

Other reductions will use restricted versions of symbol-system satisfiability that we will introduce and prove NP-complete in the next section. Although the constraints in the proof of Lemma 9.12 are easy to state, they involve up to eight symbols each and are written in a fairly general form. Some improvements are mentioned in the exercises. Moreover, in the next section we will see that a special form of constraint, involving only three variables over a 2-character alphabet, is sufficient.

Exercises

9.5-1 (a) Show how to simulate an input device initialized to hold the argument x by using a stack initialized to hold x^R.

(b) Working directly with machines that have three stacks, where one of the stacks holds the argument but there is no input device per se, give another proof of Lemma 9.12.

9.5-2 Is it possible to prove Lemma 9.12 by working directly with nondeterministic 2-counter machines and using our simulation of Turing machines by 2-counter machines?

Solution: No. 2-CM programs may require exponential time to simulate polynomial-time Turing machine programs.

9.5-3 Show how to decrease the number of constraints in the proof of Lemma 9.12 by approximately a factor of 2.

9.5-4 Give a polynomial-time m-reduction from (k, Γ)-SSS to $(2, \Gamma^k)$-SSS. Conclude that there exists Γ such that $(2, \Gamma)$-SSS is NP-complete.

9.5-5 In the proof of Lemma 9.12 we always have $k = 8$. Why did we need to prove Theorem 9.13 separately?

Solution: Because, in the proof of Lemma 9.12, Γ is not fixed but depends on the program that accepts L.

9.6 BOOLEAN FORMULA SATISFIABILITY

Variables whose values are either true or false are called *Boolean*. Consider a constraint like

$$u \vee \overline{v} \vee w,$$

which is the logical-or of some variables (u, w) and negations of some variables (v). Such a constraint is called a clause. An assignment satisfies this particular clause if and only if it assigns true to u or w or assigns false to v. A system of clauses, such as

$$u \vee \overline{v} \vee w$$

$$w \vee \overline{x}$$

$$u \vee v \vee x$$

can be expressed in a single formula as

$$(u \vee \overline{v} \vee w) \ \wedge \ (w \vee \overline{x}) \ \wedge \ (u \vee v \vee x),$$

where $\wedge$ denotes logical-and. An assignment satisfies such a formula if and only if it satisfies each clause.

Formally, let $V = \{x_1, \ldots, x_n\}$ be a set of variables over $\{\text{true}, \text{false}\}$. The *literals* are x_i and $\overline{x}_i$, where $\overline{x}_i$ denotes the logical negation of x_i for $i = 1, \ldots, n$. Recall that "disjunction" means "logical-or." A *clause* is a disjunction of literals, e.g.,

$$x_1 \vee \overline{x}_3 \vee x_8.$$

A *local assignment* is a mapping from the variables in a clause to $\{\text{true}, \text{false}\}$. A clause is true iff at least one of its literals is true, so a clause rules out exactly one local assignment (the one that makes all of its literals false).

The word "conjunction" means "logical-and." A *conjunctive-normal-form formula* (CNF formula) $F(x_1, \ldots, x_n)$ is a conjunction of clauses, e.g.,

$$(x_1 \vee x_2 \vee \overline{x}_5) \wedge x_5 \wedge (x_2 \vee \overline{x}_5) \wedge (\overline{x}_1 \vee \overline{x}_2).$$

A conjunction is true iff all of its clauses are true, so a conjunction rules out many assignments (any that make one of its clauses false).

An *assignment* to the variables of a Boolean formula is a function from $\{x_1, \ldots, x_n\}$ to $\{\text{true}, \text{false}\}$. An assignment A *satisfies* a formula F if $F(A(x_1), \ldots, A(x_n)) = \text{true}$. For example, the assignment

$$A(x_1) = \text{false}, A(x_2) = \text{true}, A(x_3) = \text{true}, A(x_4) = \text{true}, A(x_5) = \text{true}$$

satisfies the formula F given above. The *CNF-satisfiability* problem is to determine for a CNF formula whether there exists an assignment that satisfies it. This problem is commonly called SAT. Next we will reduce SSS to SAT.

THEOREM 9.14 (Cook–Levin Theorem). SAT *is* NP-*complete.*

Proof: SAT is in NP because we can guess an assignment and easily verify (in polynomial time) that it satisfies F.

Let k be a positive integer and Γ be an alphabet. We reduce SSS to SAT. Let S be a (k, Γ)-symbol system with variable set V. We will construct a CNF formula F whose variables are $[A(x){=}c]$ for each $x \in V$ and each $c \in \Gamma$.

The variable $[A(x){=}c]$ in F will represent the condition that x is assigned the value c in S. The clauses of F are of two kinds.

First, we write a conjunction of $|V|$ clauses that ensure, for each x, that x is assigned a value, i.e., that at least one of the Boolean variables $[A(x){=}c]$ is true:

$$\bigwedge_{x\in V}\left(\bigvee_{c\in\Gamma}[A(x){=}c]\right).$$

An assignment to these Boolean variables yields, in the obvious way, an assignment A to the variables of S (if $[A(x){=}c_1]$ and $[A(x){=}c_2]$ are both true, then we can choose either of those two values for $A(x)$).

Second, we write a conjunction of clauses that ensure that the assignment A so determined does not violate any of the constraints in S. For each constraint C let $V(C)$ denote the constrained set of C, and let invalid(C) denote the set of local assignments that do not satisfy C. The constraint C is logically equivalent to

$$\bigwedge_{I\in\text{invalid}(C)}\left(\bigvee_{x\in V(C)}(A(x)\neq I(x))\right),$$

which is equivalent to a conjunction of $|\text{invalid}(C)|$ clauses:

$$\bigwedge_{I\in\text{invalid}(C)}\left(\bigvee_{x\in V(C)}\overline{[A(x){=}I(x)]}\right).$$

(Observe that if there are distinct c_1 and c_2 such that $[A(x){=}c_1]$ and $[A(x){=}c_2]$ are both true, this only makes it more likely that one of these clauses is unsatisfied. For this reason we do not need separate constraints to ensure for each x that at most one variable of the form $[A(x){=}c]$ is true.)

Thus the symbol system S is equivalent to

$$\bigwedge_{\substack{C\text{ is a constraint}\\ I\in\text{ invalid}(C)}}\left(\bigvee_{x\in V(C)}\overline{[A(x){=}I(x)]}\right)\wedge\bigwedge_{x\in V}\left(\bigvee_{c\in\Gamma}[A(x){=}c]\right),$$

which is a conjunction of clauses, i.e., a CNF formula. The symbol system S is satisfiable if and only if the formula F is satisfiable, so SSS $\leq_m^p$ SAT. Since SSS is NP-complete, SAT is NP-complete as well. ∎

We demonstrate this reduction in Figure 9.7.

Although the satisfiability problem for formulas in conjunctive normal form is NP-complete, the satisfiability problem for formulas in disjunctive normal form is in P (Exercise 9.6-4).

Next we define a special form of CNF formula in which the clauses involve only a bounded number of variables. Such formulas are special cases of symbol systems in which clauses are local constraints and the alphabet is $\{\text{true}, \text{false}\}$. We say that a CNF formula is in k-CNF if each clause involves exactly k literals. The *k-satisfiability* problem (k-SAT) is to determine whether a given k-CNF formula is satisfiable.

THEOREM 9.15. 3-SAT *is* NP-*complete.*

Proof: 3-SAT is in NP because we can guess an assignment and verify it in polynomial time.

We reduce SAT to 3-SAT. Let F be a CNF formula, and let $C = \ell_1 \vee \cdots \vee \ell_k$ be any of its clauses with three or more literals. First, we define a formula F' that is satisfiable if and only if F is satisfiable, and in which every clause contains three literals or fewer. Corresponding to C, it contains the conjunction C' defined as follows:

$$C' = (\ell_1 \vee y_1) \wedge (\overline{y}_1 \vee \ell_2 \vee y_2) \wedge \cdots \wedge (\overline{y}_{k-2} \vee \ell_{k-1} \vee y_{k-1}) \wedge (\overline{y}_{k-1} \vee \ell_k),$$

where $y_1, \ldots, y_{k-1}$ are new variables and we use a different set of new variables for each clause. (For motivation, think of y_i as the logical-or of all the literals with indices greater than i.) We define F' to be the conjunction of all the conjunctions C', so F' is indeed a CNF formula with at most three literals per clause, which can easily be produced in polynomial time. Now we show that F' is satisfiable if and only if F is satisfiable.

If A is an assignment to the variables, extend A by defining $A(\overline{x}) = \neg A(x)$, so A is defined on all literals. Suppose that A satisfies F. Then A satisfies every clause C in F. Let $C = \ell_1 \vee \cdots \vee \ell_k$. We will define an extension A' that satisfies every clause of C': Let $A'(\ell_i) = A(\ell_i)$ for all i, and let

$$A'(y_i) = A(\ell_{i+1}) \vee \cdots \vee A(\ell_k).$$

$$
\begin{aligned}
&([A(x)=0] \vee [A(x)=1] \vee [A(x)=2]) \;\wedge \\
&([A(y)=0] \vee [A(y)=1] \vee [A(y)=2]) \;\wedge \\
&([A(z)=0] \vee [A(z)=1] \vee [A(z)=2]) \;\wedge \\
&([A(w)=0] \vee [A(w)=1] \vee [A(w)=2]) \;\wedge \\
&(\overline{[A(z)=0]} \vee \overline{[A(w)=0]}) \;\wedge \\
&(\overline{[A(z)=0]} \vee \overline{[A(w)=1]}) \;\wedge \\
&(\overline{[A(z)=0]} \vee \overline{[A(w)=2]}) \;\wedge \\
&(\overline{[A(z)=1]} \vee \overline{[A(w)=1]}) \;\wedge \\
&(\overline{[A(z)=1]} \vee \overline{[A(w)=2]}) \;\wedge \\
&(\overline{[A(z)=2]} \vee \overline{[A(w)=2]}) \;\wedge \\
&(\overline{[A(w)=1]}) \;\wedge \\
&(\overline{[A(w)=2]}) \;\wedge \\
&(\overline{[A(x)=0]} \vee \overline{[A(y)=0]} \vee \overline{[A(z)=1]}) \;\wedge \\
&(\overline{[A(x)=0]} \vee \overline{[A(y)=0]} \vee \overline{[A(z)=2]}) \;\wedge \\
&(\overline{[A(x)=0]} \vee \overline{[A(y)=1]} \vee \overline{[A(z)=2]}) \;\wedge \\
&(\overline{[A(x)=1]} \vee \overline{[A(y)=0]} \vee \overline{[A(z)=2]}).
\end{aligned}
$$

FIGURE 9.7: An example of reducing SSS to SAT: a Boolean formula that is satisfiable if and only if the symbol system

$$
\begin{aligned}
z &> w \\
w &\neq 0 \\
x + y &\geq z
\end{aligned}
$$

is satisfiable. The Boolean formula's 12 variables are $[A(x)=0]$, $[A(x)=1]$, $[A(x)=2]$, $[A(y)=0]$, $[A(y)=1]$, $[A(y)=2]$, $[A(z)=0]$, $[A(z)=1]$, $[A(z)=2]$, $[A(w)=0]$, $[A(w)=1]$, and $[A(w)=2]$.

A' satisfies $\ell_1 \vee y$ because A satisfies C; A' satisfies the other clauses by logical tautologies. Thus A' satisfies C'. Since the y_i's are different for each clause, if A satisfies all clauses C of F, then we can define A' on all the y_i's so all clauses C' of F' are satisfied.

Conversely, suppose that some assignment A' satisfies F'. Then A' satisfies every C'. We prove by contradiction that there exists i such that $A'(\ell_i) = \text{true}$. Assume not. Then $A'(\ell_i) = \text{false}$ for all i. We assert that $A'(y_i) = \text{true}$ for all i. The proof is by induction. The base case ($i = 1$) is established because the clause $\ell_1 \vee y_1$ is satisfied and $A'(\ell_1) = \text{false}$. Assume the assertion is true for some i. Since $A'(y_i) = \text{true}$, $A'(\ell_{i+1}) = \text{false}$, and A' satisfies $\overline{y}_i \vee \ell_{i+1} \vee y_{i+1}$, it is necessary that $A'(y_{i+1}) = \text{true}$. This completes the inductive proof. In particular, $A'(y_{k-1}) = \text{true}$. Since A' satisfies the clause $\overline{y}_{k-1} \vee \ell_k$ and $A'(\ell_k) = \text{false}$, it is necessary that $A'(y_{k-1}) = \text{false}$. This contradiction implies that there must exist i such that $A'(\ell_i) = \text{true}$. Let A be the restriction of A' to the literals of F, i.e., let $A(\ell_i) = A'(\ell_i)$. Then A satisfies C. Since this is true for every C, A satisfies F.

Thus we have shown that F' is satisfiable if and only if F is satisfiable. Next we convert F' to an equivalent formula F'' containing exactly three literals per clause. Let z_1, z_2, and z_3 be three new variables. The following conjunction of six clauses ensures that z_1 and z_2 are both assigned the value false in any satisfying assignment:

$$(\overline{z}_1 \vee \overline{z}_2 \vee \overline{z}_3) \wedge (\overline{z}_1 \vee \overline{z}_2 \vee z_3) \wedge (\overline{z}_1 \vee z_2 \vee \overline{z}_3) \wedge (z_1 \vee \overline{z}_2 \vee \overline{z}_3)$$
$$\wedge (z_1 \vee \overline{z}_2 \vee z_3) \wedge (\overline{z}_1 \vee z_2 \vee z_3).$$

(The reader may easily verify this by noting which local assignment is ruled out by each clause.) We conjoin those six clauses to F'; additionally, we replace any clause of the form ℓ by $\ell \vee z_1 \vee z_2$, and we replace any clause of the form $\ell_1 \vee \ell_2$ by $\ell_1 \vee \ell_2 \vee z_1$. Clearly F' is satisfiable if and only if F'' is satisfiable. Furthermore, F'' can be written down in polynomial time.

Since F'' is in 3-CNF and can be constructed in polynomial time, SAT $\leq_m^p$ 3-SAT. Therefore 3-SAT is NP-complete. ■

EXAMPLE 9.16. Consider the CNF formula

$$(u \vee v \vee w \vee x) \wedge (u \vee \overline{v} \vee w \vee \overline{x}).$$

An equivalent 3-CNF formula is

$$\begin{aligned}&(u \vee y_1 \vee z_1) \wedge (\overline{y}_1 \vee v \vee y_2) \wedge (\overline{y}_2 \vee w \vee y_3) \wedge (\overline{y}_3 \vee x \vee z_1)\\ \wedge\ &(u \vee y_4 \vee z_1) \wedge (\overline{y}_4 \vee \overline{v} \vee y_5) \wedge (\overline{y}_5 \vee w \vee y_6) \wedge (\overline{y}_6 \vee \overline{x} \vee z_1)\\ \wedge\ &(\overline{z}_1 \vee \overline{z}_2 \vee \overline{z}_3) \wedge (\overline{z}_1 \vee \overline{z}_2 \vee z_3) \wedge (\overline{z}_1 \vee z_2 \vee \overline{z}_3) \wedge (z_1 \vee \overline{z}_2 \vee \overline{z}_3)\\ \wedge\ &(z_1 \vee \overline{z}_2 \vee z_3) \wedge (\overline{z}_1 \vee z_2 \vee z_3).\end{aligned}$$

The assignment $A(u)$ = false, $A(v)$ = true, $A(w)$ = false, $A(x)$ = false satisfies the original formula. The corresponding assignment $A'(u)$ = false, $A'(v)$ = true, $A'(w)$ = false, $A'(x)$ = false, $A'(y_1)$ = true, $A'(y_2)$ = false, $A'(y_3)$ = false, $A'(y_4)$ = true, $A'(y_5)$ = true, $A'(y_6)$ = true, $A'(z_1)$ = false, $A'(z_2)$ = false, $A'(z_3)$ = false satisfies the 3-CNF formula produced by the reduction. ■■■

COROLLARY 9.17. *$(3, \{\mathtt{a}, \mathtt{b}\})$-SSS is* NP*-complete.*

Proof: Let a denote true and b denote false. Then every 3-CNF formula is a $(3, \{\mathtt{a}, \mathtt{b}\})$-symbol system. ■

One may wonder if the last two results can be improved. The 2-satisfiability problem is in P (Exercise 9.6-6), so 2-SAT is not NP-complete unless P = NP. $(2, \{\mathtt{a}, \mathtt{b}\})$-SSS is in P as well (Exercise 9.6-7) by reduction to 2-SAT. On the other hand, $(2, \{\mathtt{a}, \mathtt{b}, \mathtt{c}\})$-SSS is NP-complete (Exercise 9.6-8(c)). This is dual to the fact that $(3, \{\mathtt{a}, \mathtt{b}\})$-SSS is NP-complete. If $k = 1$ or $|\Gamma| = 1$, then (k, Γ)-SSS is in P for trivial reasons. Therefore (k, Γ)-SSS is in P if $k = 1$, if $|\Gamma| = 1$, or if $k = |\Gamma| = 2$; and (k, Γ)-SSS is NP-complete otherwise.

Exercises

9.6-1 In the proof of Theorem 9.14 we did not need to guarantee that for every x at most one variable of the form $[A(x){=}c]$ is true. But we could have guaranteed this if we wanted to. Write clauses that do so.

Solution

$$\bigwedge_{x \in V} \bigwedge_{c_1 \neq c_2} \left(\overline{[A(x) = c_1]} \vee \overline{[A(x) = c_2]} \right)$$

9.6-2 Let $k \geq 3$. Prove that k-SAT is NP-complete.

9.6-3 A reduction between two problems is called *parsimonious*[5] if it preserves the number of solutions.

(a) Prove that parsimonious $\leq_m^p$-reducibility is transitive.

(b) Find a parsimonious $\leq_m^p$-reduction from SAT to $(3, \{\text{true}, \text{false}\})$-SSS.

Solution: Modify the reduction from SAT to 3-SAT to use the constraint $y_i = (\ell_{i+1} \vee y_{i+1})$ in place of the clause $\overline{y}_i \vee \ell_{i+1} \vee y_{i+1}$ and the constraint $y_k = \ell_k$ in place of $\overline{y}_{k-1} \vee \ell_k$. The values of $y_1, \ldots, y_{k-1}$ in a satisfying assignment are then completely determined by the values of $\ell_1, \ldots, \ell_k$. Do not use z_1, z_2, z_3. Then the number of satisfying assignments is preserved.

(c) Find a parsimonious $\leq_m^p$-reduction from $(3, \{\text{true}, \text{false}\})$-SSS to 3-SAT.

(d) Find a parsimonious $\leq_m^p$-reduction from $(k, \{\text{true}, \text{false}\})$-SSS to k-SAT.

9.6-4 A formula is in *disjunctive normal form* (DNF) if it is an OR of ANDs, i.e., disjunction of conjunctions. For example, the formula

$$(x \wedge y \wedge z) \vee (\overline{w} \wedge \overline{x} \wedge z) \vee (x \wedge \overline{y} \wedge z) \vee (\overline{w} \wedge y \wedge z)$$

is in disjunctive normal form.

(a) Prove that the set of satisfiable DNF formulas is in P.

(b) A symbol system or Boolean formula is called *tautological* or a *tautology* if all assignments satisfy it. Prove that the set of tautological (k, Γ)-symbol systems is in P.

(c) Prove that the set of tautological CNF formulas is in P.

(d) Prove that the set of tautological DNF formulas is co-NP-complete.

---

[5] The dictionary meaning of "parsimonious" is "miserly."

9.6-5 A clause is called *monotone* if it consists entirely of variables or entirely of the negations of variables. For example, $x \vee y \vee z$ is monotone and $\overline{x} \vee \overline{y} \vee \overline{z}$ is monotone, but $x \vee \overline{y} \vee z$ is not monotone.

(a) MONOTONE-SAT is the set of satisfiable CNF formulas in which every clause is monotone. Prove that MONOTONE-SAT is NP-complete. Hint: Look carefully at the reduction from SAT to 3-SAT. Alternative hint: Replace $\overline{x}$ by x'. Introduce two new clauses $(x \vee x')$ and $(\overline{x} \vee \overline{x'})$.

(b) MONOTONE-3-SAT is the set of satisfiable 3-CNF formulas in which every clause is monotone. Prove that MONOTONE-3-SAT is NP-complete.

9.6-6 Prove that 2-SAT is in P. Hint: Let F be a formula with literals $\ell_1, \ldots, \ell_m$. Rewrite each clause $\ell_i \vee \ell_j$ as the logically equivalent implications $\overline{\ell}_i \Rightarrow \ell_j$ and $\overline{\ell}_j \Rightarrow \ell_i$. Prove that F is unsatisfiable if and only if there is a literal ℓ and a sequence of implications such that $\ell \Rightarrow \cdots \Rightarrow \overline{\ell} \Rightarrow \cdots \Rightarrow \ell$. Represent implications as edges in a directed graph.

9.6-7 Prove that $(2, \{\mathtt{a}, \mathtt{b}\})$-SSS is in P. Hint: Reduce to 2-SAT.

9.6-8 (a) Prove that if Γ is an 8-character alphabet, then $(2, \Gamma)$-SSS is NP-complete. Hint: Reduce 3-SAT, letting each variable in the symbol system represent three variables of the 3-CNF formula.

(b) Prove that if Γ is a 4-character alphabet, then $(2, \Gamma)$-SSS is NP-complete.

*(c) Prove that if Γ is a 3-character alphabet, then $(2, \Gamma)$-SSS is NP-complete.

9.6-9 Give a generic reduction to prove that SAT is NP-complete.

9.7 NP-COMPLETE GRAPH PROBLEMS

Some of the most important problems facing computer scientists, operations researchers, and managers can be modeled in terms of graphs. Recall from Section 0.4 that a directed graph (V, E) consists of a vertex set V and an edge relation $E \subseteq V \times V$. An *undirected* graph is a digraph in which E is symmetric. Graphs can be represented in three different ways, as described in Section 2.1. Some representations will permit faster algorithms than others. However, it is possible to convert among these representations in polynomial time, so for the purposes of this chapter it does not matter which representation is used. We proceed to consider some specific graph problems.

A *clique* is a set of vertices $K \subseteq V$ such that every vertex in K is connected by an edge to every other vertex in K, i.e.,

$$(v_1 \in K \wedge v_2 \in K \wedge v_1 \neq v_2) \Rightarrow (v_1, v_2) \in E.$$

For example, let V be the set of students at a particular school. Let E be the "like each other" relation, i.e., $(v_1, v_2) \in E$ if v_1 likes v_2 and v_2 likes v_1. A clique in this graph is a set of students at the school all of whom like each other.

A k-clique is a clique consisting of exactly k vertices. The clique problem is to determine for a given undirected graph G and a given number k whether G contains a k-clique.

Problem name: clique
Instance: an undirected graph G and a positive integer k
Question: Does G contain a clique of size k?

Observe that a clique of size k contains cliques of size $1, 2, \ldots, k-1$; therefore a graph containing a clique of size k also contains cliques of all smaller sizes.

In time $O\left(\binom{k}{2}\binom{|V|}{k}\right)$ we can try every set of k vertices, so we can test whether a graph has a clique of size k. This is polynomial bounded if k is fixed but not if k grows as a function of n. In fact if $k = |V|/2$, then this time bound is bigger than $2^{|V|}$. This is no accident.

THEOREM 9.18. *Clique is* NP-*complete.*

Proof: We will reduce SSS to CLIQUE. Let $k \geq 1$, let Γ be an alphabet, and let S be a (k, Γ)-symbol system with c constraints in all. Recall that if $\{x_1, \ldots, x_k\}$ is a constrained subset in the symbol system, then a mapping $A : \{x_1, \ldots, x_k\} \rightarrow \Gamma$ is called a *local assignment*. A is called a *satisfying local assignment* to C if $\{x_1, \ldots, x_k\}$ is the subset constrained by C and

$C(A(x_1), \ldots, A(x_k)) = \text{true}$. We will construct an undirected graph (V, E) that contains a c-clique if and only if S is satisfiable.

For each constraint C in S and each satisfying local assignment A to the constrained variables of C, we place a vertex $[C, A]$ in G. Since there are at most $|\Gamma|^k$ local assignments to a single constrained subset, $|V| \leq c|\Gamma|^k$. Each vertex can be constructed in polynomial time; the total number of vertices is linear because $|\Gamma|$ and k are constants.

We say that two local assignments A_1 and A_2 to constraints are *consistent* if $A_1(x) = A_2(x)$ for all x on which A_1 and A_2 are both defined. (Note that distinct local assignments to a single constrained subset cannot be consistent.) Let E consist of all pairs of vertices corresponding to consistent satisfying local assignments. Each edge can be constructed in polynomial time; the total number of edges is $O(n^2)$ because the number of vertices is $O(n)$. This completes the reduction.

We assert that S is satisfiable if and only if the graph (V, E) contains a clique of size c. Suppose first that S is satisfiable. Let A be a satisfying assignment to the variables of S. Restricting A to the individual constraints in S, we obtain consistent satisfying local assignments to each constraint. The corresponding vertices in G form a clique of size c. Conversely, suppose that G contains a clique of size c. As noted above, all vertices in this clique must correspond to consistent satisfying local assignments to distinct constraints. Since there are c vertices in the clique, these vertices correspond to consistent satisfying local assignments to all constraints of S. By combining these local assignments, we obtain a satisfying assignment to S. ■

EXAMPLE 9.19. Consider the following $(3, \{\mathsf{a}, \mathsf{b}\})$-symbol system with variable set $\{w, x, y, z\}$:

$$z \neq x \quad \wedge \quad z \neq y \qquad (C_1)$$

$$z = w \quad \vee \quad z = x \qquad (C_2)$$

$$z = \mathsf{a} \quad \Rightarrow \quad w = \mathsf{b}. \qquad (C_3)$$

For compactness, let us represent a local assignment A by the string $A(w)A(x)A(y)A(z)$, where we write `X` to denote that $A(v)$ is undefined.

The satisfying local assignments to C_1 are `Xaab` and `Xbba`. The satisfying local assignments to C_2 are `aaXa`, `abXa`, `abXb`, `baXa`, `baXb`, and

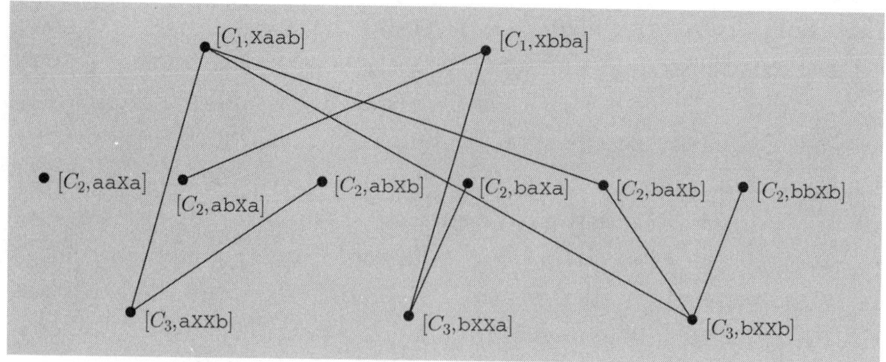

FIGURE 9.8: An instance of the clique problem corresponding to the symbol system

$$z \neq x \quad \wedge \quad z \neq y \qquad (C_1)$$

$$z = w \quad \vee \quad z = x \qquad (C_2)$$

$$z = \mathtt{a} \quad \Rightarrow \quad w = \mathtt{b}. \qquad (C_3)$$

The symbol system's unique satisfying assignment baab corresponds to the graph's unique 3-clique (triangle) [C_1, Xaab]-[C_2, baXb]-[C_3, bXXb].

bbXb. The satisfying local assignments to C_3 are aXXb, bXXa, and bXXb. The corresponding undirected graph is shown in Figure 9.8. ■ ■ ■

A *Hamiltonian path* in a directed graph G is a path that includes each vertex exactly once. A *Hamiltonian cycle* in a directed graph G is a path that starts and ends at some vertex v (i.e., a cycle) and includes every other vertex exactly once.

Problem name: Hamiltonian cycle

Instance: a directed graph G

Question: Does G contain a Hamiltonian cycle?

THEOREM 9.20. *Hamiltonian cycle is* NP-*complete.*

Proof: We reduce 3-SAT to Hamiltonian cycle. Let F be a CNF formula with variables $x_1, \ldots, x_n$. Call the clauses $C_1, \ldots, C_k$. We construct a corresponding graph G. The graph is organized into parts called gadgets that we describe below:

Variable gadget: For each variable x, G contains a gadget that we call x's gadget. The gadget for variable x contains $4k + 2$ vertices, which are labeled and connected as in Figure 9.9.

Clause gadget: For each clause C, G contains a gadget that we call C's gadget. Let C contain the literals u, v, and w, i.e., $C = (u \vee v \vee w)$. The gadget for clause C contains six vertices, which are labeled and connected as in Figure 9.10.

In addition to the edges that stay entirely inside a gadget, there are edges that connect vertices in distinct gadgets.

Variable–clause edges: For each clause C, for each literal ℓ in C, there is an edge from vertex $[\ell \text{ to } C]$ to $\langle \ell \text{ to } C \rangle$ and an edge from $[C \text{ to } \ell]$ to $\langle C \text{ to } \ell \rangle$. (These edges are indicated by the dashed lines in Figure 9.11.)

Variable–variable edges: For $1 \leq i \leq n-1$ there is an edge from gadget vertex $[x_i \text{ out}]$ to gadget vertex $[x_{i+1} \text{ in}]$. There is also an edge from $[x_n \text{ out}]$ to $[x_1 \text{ in}]$, as shown in Figure 9.11.

This completes the reduction. Now we prove that G contains a Hamiltonian path if and only if F is satisfiable. First, assume that G contains a Hamiltonian cycle, which we will call H. We will show that H travels from $[x_1 \text{ in}]$ through x_1's gadget, then x_2's gadget, ..., then x_n's gadget, and back to $[x_1 \text{ in}]$, visiting each clause's gadget at least once along the way. We will construct a satisfying assignment based on H's behavior in each variable's gadget.

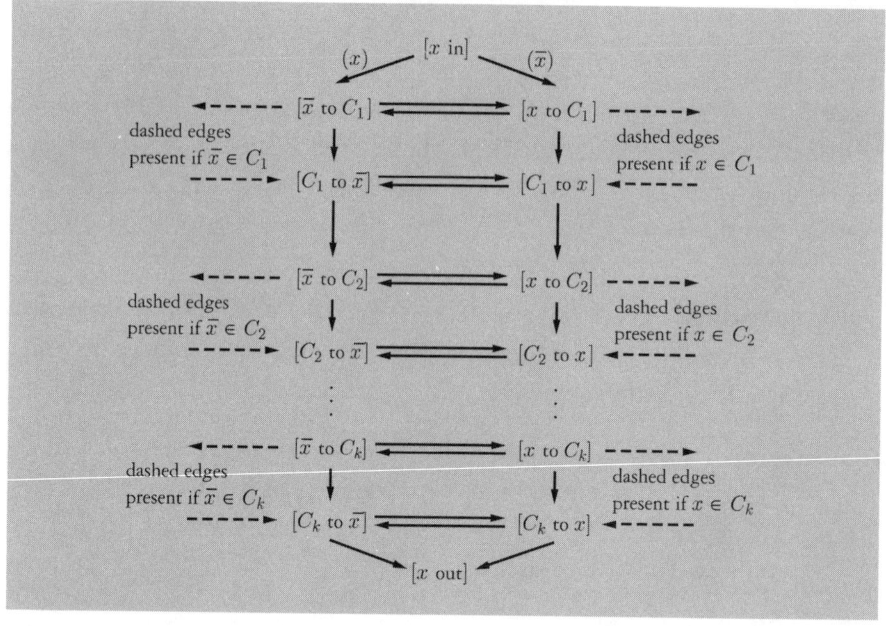

FIGURE 9.9: A gadget for the variable x.

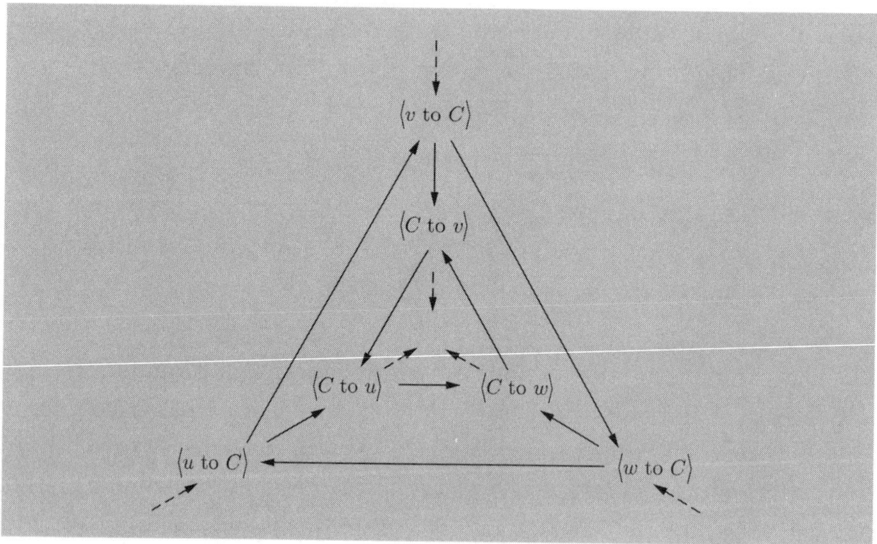

FIGURE 9.10: A gadget for the clause C, where $C = (u \vee v \vee w)$.

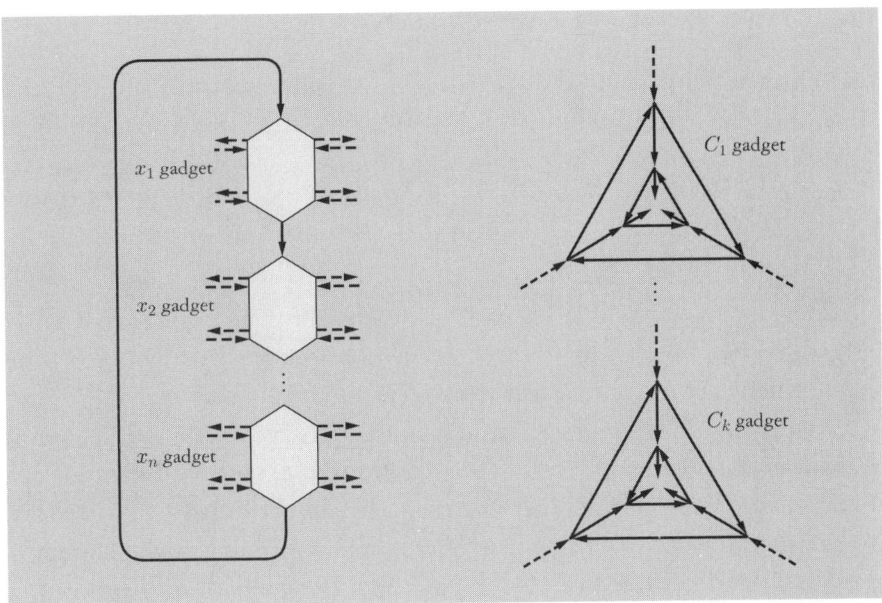

FIGURE 9.11: The reduction from SAT to Hamiltonian cycle. x_1's gadget, x_2's gadget, . . . , and x_n's gadget are arranged in a directed cycle. In addition, for each variable in a clause, there is a pair of directed edges between the corresponding variable gadget and clause gadget. Let ℓ denote a literal, either x or $\overline{x}$ for some variable x. If ℓ is a literal in the clause C, then there is an edge from the vertex labeled $[\ell \text{ to } C]$ (in x's gadget) to the vertex labeled $\langle \ell \text{ to } C \rangle$ (in C's gadget), as well as an edge going back from $\langle C \text{ to } \ell \rangle$ to $[C \text{ to } \ell]$. Details of the vertex and clause gadgets are shown in Figures 9.9 and 9.10.

Call vertex u a *predecessor* of vertex v and v a *successor* of u if there is an edge from u to v in G. If we cut a Hamiltonian cycle by removing the edge from u to v, then we obtain a Hamiltonian *path* that starts at v and ends at u. Consider any Hamiltonian path, recalling that it visits each vertex exactly once. Because the path is directed, we may think of the vertices as being visited in temporal order. Three simple principles will help us to pin down H's behavior.

No-choice principle: If v is the only successor of u that is not visited before u, then v must be visited immediately after u.

Last-chance principle: If u is the last of v's predecessors to be visited and v is not visited before u, then v must be visited immediately after u.

Dead-end principle: If all of u's successors are visited before u, then u must be the last vertex on the Hamiltonian path.

Consider any particular clause C. The Hamiltonian cycle H may enter C's gadget one, two, or three times. Let us consider the behavior of H from a time when it enters C's gadget until it next exits C's gadget.

Assertion: If H enters a clause gadget at the vertex $\langle \ell \text{ to } C \rangle$, then it next leaves that gadget at vertex $\langle C \text{ to } \ell \rangle$. **Proof of assertion:** By symmetry, we may assume that $\ell = u$, i.e., that the path enters C's gadget at $\langle u \text{ to } C \rangle$. By cutting H before $\langle u \text{ to } C \rangle$, we obtain a Hamiltonian path that starts at $\langle u \text{ to } C \rangle$ and ends at $[u \text{ to } C]$. From $\langle u \text{ to } C \rangle$, the path may proceed to $\langle v \text{ to } C \rangle$ or $\langle C \text{ to } u \rangle$. If the latter, it must leave C's gadget in order to avoid dead-ending $\langle w \text{ to } C \rangle$. If the former, it may proceed to $\langle w \text{ to } C \rangle$ or $\langle C \text{ to } v \rangle$. If the latter, it must proceed to $\langle C \text{ to } u \rangle$ by the last-chance principle and then leave C's gadget in order to avoid dead-ending $\langle w \text{ to } C \rangle$. If the former, then it must proceed to $\langle C \text{ to } w \rangle$ by the no-choice principle. From there it must proceed to $\langle C \text{ to } v \rangle$ and then $\langle C \text{ to } u \rangle$ by two applications of the last-chance principle. Finally, it must exit C's gadget from $\langle C \text{ to } u \rangle$ by the no-choice principle. ∎

Let ℓ denote the literal x or $\overline{x}$. The portion of a path that goes from a vertex $[\ell \text{ to } C]$ in x's gadget, travels inside C's gadget, and then returns to $[C \text{ to } \ell]$ in x's gadget is called a *side trip* from ℓ to C.

For any particular variable x, let us consider the behavior of H from the time it enters x's gadget at $[x \text{ in}]$ until it exits x's gadget from $[x \text{ out}]$. Cut H to obtain a Hamiltonian path that starts at $[x \text{ in}]$. From the vertex $[x \text{ in}]$ the path must go either left or right. For concreteness, assume it goes left to the vertex $[\overline{x} \text{ to } C_1]$. The next edge must go right, to $[x \text{ to } C_1]$, by the last-chance principle.

There is now a choice between going directly down to $[C_1 \text{ to } x]$ or (if x is a literal in C_1) making a side trip from x to C_1, which finishes at $[C_1 \text{ to } x]$ by the assertion. In either case, the path reaches $[C_1 \text{ to } x]$. In principle, the vertex $[C_1 \text{ to } \overline{x}]$ could be reached later at the end of a side trip from $\overline{x}$ to C_1; however, by the assertion, that side trip would have to start at $[\overline{x} \text{ to } C]$, which has already been visited. Therefore, if $[C_1 \text{ to } \overline{x}]$ is to ever be reached, the path must proceed immediately to it.

Next the path must proceed to $[\overline{x} \text{ to } C_2]$ by the no-choice principle and then to $[x \text{ to } C_2]$ by the last-chance principle. Then there may be an optional side trip from x to C_2; whether or not the side trip is taken, the path then proceeds to $[C_2 \text{ to } x]$. From there the same kind of pattern repeats, snaking down x's gadget, with optional side trips only to clauses containing x.

Observe that if the first edge had gone right, then by symmetry the path would snake down x's gadget with optional side trips only to clauses containing $\overline{x}$.

Now we construct a satisfying assignment for the formula F. For each variable x, let $A(x) =$ true if the Hamiltonian cycle H takes the edge labeled (x) in the x gadget and false otherwise. Because H visits every vertex, every clause gadget C is visited on a side trip from x's gadget for some x. If the path through x's gadget starts leftward, then C contains the literal x and $A(x) =$ true, so C is satisfied. If the path through the x gadget starts rightward, then C contains the literal $\overline{x}$ and $A(x) =$ false, so C is satisfied. Thus A satisfies every clause.

Conversely, suppose that A is a satisfying assignment for F. We construct a Hamiltonian cycle in G. The cycle traverses x_1's gadget, then x_2's gadget, and so on, then x_n's gadget, finally returning to $[x_1 \text{ in}]$. For each variable x, if $A(x) =$ true then we start the path through x's gadget leftward; otherwise we start it rightward. This completely determines the snakelike path that visits each of the variable gadget's vertices—except for side trips to clause gadgets. From each clause C, choose the first literal ℓ such that $A(\ell) =$ true and take a side trip from ℓ to C (this is possible because of how the topmost edge in each variable gadget was selected), visiting all the vertices in C's gadget. Thus every clause vertex is visited exactly once, so the cycle constructed in this way is Hamiltonian. ■

COROLLARY 9.21. *The traveling salesman problem is* NP-*complete.*

Proof: Observe that the traveling salesman problem is to determine whether a graph has a Hamiltonian cycle whose cost is c or less. We reduce Hamiltonian cycle to traveling salesman. Given a graph G, we construct a complete graph G' with the same vertex set. An edge e is given weight 0 in G' if e is an edge in G; otherwise e is given weight 1 in G'. There is a Hamiltonian cycle in G if and only if there is a Hamiltonian cycle in G' whose cost is 0 or less. ■

Exercises

*9.7-1 Modify the reduction from 3-SAT to Hamiltonian cycle as follows: First delete all clauses in F that contain both literals x and $\overline{x}$ for any variable x. In addition, replace each clause gadget with a single vertex. Prove that F is satisfiable if and only if the resulting graph contains a Hamiltonian cycle.

*9.7-2 Find a parsimonious reduction from 3-SAT to Hamiltonian cycle.

9.7-3 Let $G_1 = (V_1, E_1)$ and $G_2 = (V_2, E_2)$. G_1 is *isomorphic* to G_2 if there exists a one-one, onto mapping g from V_1 to V_2 such that $(u, v) \in E_1$ if and only if $(g(u), g(v)) \in E_2$. Such a function g is called an *isomorphism* from G_1 to G_2.

(a) Give a polynomial-time Turing reduction from the problem of finding an isomorphism from one graph to another to the problem of determining whether two graphs are isomorphic. (It is not known whether the graph isomorphism problem is NP-complete.)

(b) A graph $G_1 = (V_1, E_1)$ is a *subgraph* of a graph $G_2 = (V_2, E_2)$ if $V_1 \subseteq V_2$ and $E_1 \subseteq E_2$. Prove that the following problem is NP-complete.

Problem name: subgraph isomorphism

Instance: undirected graphs G and H

Question: Does G contain a subgraph isomorphic to H?

9.7-4 A weighted graph satisfies the *triangle inequality* if for every three vertices u, v, w the weight of the edge (u, w) is less than or equal to the weight of (u, v) plus the weight of (v, w). Prove that the following problem is NP-complete:

Problem name: TSP with triangle inequality
Instance: a weighted graph G and a natural number c
Question: Does G satisfy the triangle inequality and also have a Hamiltonian cycle whose weighted path length is c or less.

9.7-5 An *independent set* in an undirected graph is a set of vertices, no two of which are connected by an edge. In other words, I is an independent set in $G = (V, E)$ if $I \subseteq V$ and $(I \times I) \cap E = \emptyset$. Prove that the following problem is NP-complete.

Problem name: independent set
Instance: an undirected graph G and a positive integer k
Question: Does there exist an independent set in G consisting of k vertices?

9.7-6 A *vertex cover* in an undirected graph is a set C of vertices that contains at least one endpoint from each edge. (Think of C as a set of vertices that covers the edges of the graph.) In other words, C is a vertex cover for $G = (V, E)$ if $C \subseteq V$ and, for all edges (u, v) in E, $u \in C$ or $v \in C$.

(a) Let $G = (V, E)$. Prove that C is a vertex cover for G if and only if $V - C$ is an independent set in G.

(b) Consider the following problem:

Problem name: vertex cover
Instance: an undirected graph G and a positive integer k
Question: Does there exist a vertex cover for G consisting of k vertices?

Show how to solve the vertex cover problem in time $O(|E| + k|V|^{k+1})$.

(c) How large is $O(|E|+k|V|^{k+1})$ as a function of the input length?

Solution: The number k can be represented by $O(\log k)$ bits. Therefore, in principle k could be as large as 2^n, where n is the input length. Thus

$$|E| + k|V|^{k+1} = O(n + 2^n n^{2^n}) = O(2^n n^{2^n}).$$

In practice, the size of a vertex cover is at most $|V|$, and we could modify the algorithm to immediately output yes if $k > |V|$. The modified algorithm runs in time $O(n^{n+2})$.

(d) Suppose that we restrict the allowable values of k in the vertex cover problem. For what values of k is $O(|E| + k|V|^{k+1})$ a polynomial-bounded function of the input length?

(e) Surprisingly, it is possible to solve the vertex cover problem in time $O\left(|E| + |V| + k^2\binom{k^2}{k}\right)$. Give an algorithm to do so. Hint: Prove that if G has a vertex cover consisting of k vertices, then that cover must contain every vertex having degree $k+1$ or higher.

(f) How large is $O\left(|E| + |V| + k^2\binom{k^2}{k}\right)$ as a function of the input length?

(g) Suppose that we restrict the allowable values of k in the vertex cover problem. For what values of k is $O\left(|E| + |V| + k^2\binom{k^2}{k}\right)$ a polynomial-bounded function of the input length?

(h) Prove that the vertex cover problem is NP-complete.

9.7-7 A *dominating set* in an undirected graph is a set D of vertices such that each of the graph's vertices belongs to D or is adjacent to a vertex in D. In other words, D is a dominating set for $G = (V, E)$ if $D \subseteq V$ and, for all v in V,

$$v \in D \text{ or } (\exists u \in D)[(u, v) \in E].$$

(a) Prove that the following problem is NP-complete:

Problem name: dominating set

Instance: an undirected graph G and a positive integer k

Question: Does there exist a dominating set for G consisting of k vertices?

Hint: Reduce SAT or vertex cover.

(b) An undirected graph (V, E) is called *bipartite* if there exists a partition of V into sets T and U such that all edges in E go between T and U. In other words (V, E) is bipartite if there exist T and U such that $T \cap U = \emptyset$, $T \cup U = V$, and $(x, y) \in E \Rightarrow (x \in T \iff y \in U)$.
Prove that a graph G is bipartite if and only if every cycle in G has even length.

(c) Prove that the following problem is NP-complete:

Problem name: bipartite dominating set

Instance: an undirected bipartite graph G and a positive integer k

Question: Does there exist a dominating set for G consisting of k vertices?

9.7-8 Reduce SAT directly to clique.

9.7-9 Prove that the following problems are NP-complete:

(a) **Problem name:** Hamiltonian path

Instance: a directed graph G

Question: Does G contain a Hamiltonian path?
Hint: Reduce Hamiltonian cycle. Pick an arbitrary vertex v in G and replace it by a pair of vertices v_{in} and v_{out}.

(b) **Problem name:** Hamiltonian s–t path

Instance: a directed graph G and distinct vertices s and t

Question: Does G contain a Hamiltonian path that starts at s and ends at t?

(c) **Problem name:** undirected Hamiltonian cycle

Instance: an undirected graph G

Question: Does G contain a Hamiltonian cycle?
Hint: Reduce (directed) Hamiltonian cycle. Replace each vertex v by three vertices v_{in}, v_{mid}, and v_{out} connected by a pair of edges as shown below:

v_{in} ———— v_{mid} ———— v_{out}

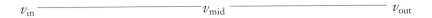

9.7-10 A k-coloring of an undirected graph G is a mapping c from V (the vertices) to $\{1, \ldots, k\}$ (the set of colors) such that

$$(u, v) \in E \Rightarrow c(u) \neq c(v),$$

i.e., adjacent vertices are given distinct colors. Consider the following problem:

Problem name: k-colorability
Instance: an undirected graph $G = (V, E)$
Question: Is there a k-coloring of G?

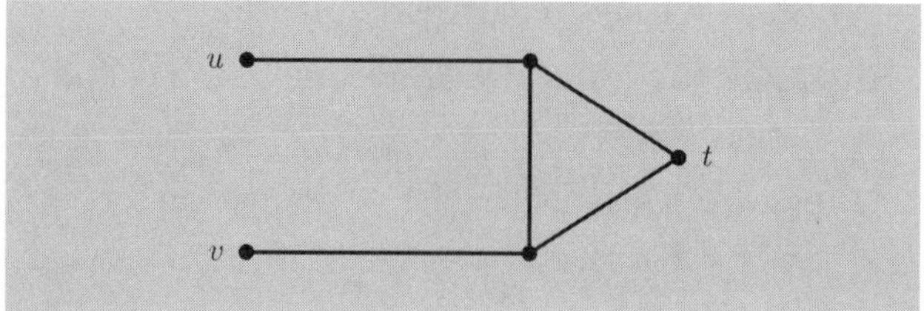

FIGURE 9.12: A gadget that ensures that if $c(u) = c(v)$, then $c(t) = c(u) = c(v)$ in any 3-coloring, while not excluding any other possible colorings for t, u, and v.

In this exercise, you will prove that 3-colorability is NP-complete. Let F be a 3-CNF formula with variables $x_1, \ldots, x_n$.

(a) Consider the graph in Figure 9.12. Prove that, in any 3-coloring c of this graph, if $c(u) = c(v)$ then $c(t) = c(u) = c(v)$; i.e., if u and v are colored the same, then t, u, and v are all colored the same.

(b) Consider the graph in Figure 9.12. Suppose that u and v are given distinct colors and t is given an arbitrary color. Show how to color the remaining two vertices using exactly three colors in all.

(c) By parts (a) and (b), the graph in Figure 9.12 ensures that $c(u) = c(v) \Rightarrow c(t) = c(u) = c(v)$, but it does not rule out any other possibilities for $c(t)$, $c(u)$, and $c(v)$. Construct a graph that ensures that if u, v, and w are colored the same, then t, u, v, and w are all colored the same, while not excluding any other possible colorings for t, u, v, and w.

(d) Construct a graph with vertices named True, False, Other; $x_1, \ldots, x_n$; and $\overline{x}_1, \ldots, \overline{x}_n$. Your graph should ensure the following while not excluding any other possible colorings.

- True, False, and Other are all colored differently.
- For each i, either x_i is colored $c(\text{True})$ and $\overline{x}_i$ is colored $c(\text{False})$, or else x_i is colored $c(\text{False})$ and $\overline{x}_i$ is colored $c(\text{True})$.

Each coloring of the graph you construct will correspond to an assignment, where

$$A(x) = \text{true} \iff c(x) = c(\text{True}) \iff c(\overline{x}) = c(\text{False}),$$

$$A(x) = \text{false} \iff c(x) = c(\text{False}) \iff c(\overline{x}) = c(\text{True}).$$

(e) Consider three literals ℓ_1, ℓ_2, and ℓ_3. Using part (c), construct a graph that ensures that ℓ_1, ℓ_2, and ℓ_3 are not all colored $c(\text{False})$.

(f) Combining the graph from part (d) and the graphs from part (e), one for each clause, construct a graph that is 3-colorable if and only if F is satisfiable.

9.7-11 Let $k > 3$. Prove that k-colorability is NP-complete.

Solution: k-colorability is in NP because we may guess a k-coloring and verify its correctness in polynomial time. We reduce 3-colorability. Let G be an instance of 3-colorability. Construct G' by inserting a clique of $k - 3$ new nodes into G and connecting each of these new nodes to every node in G. Then G is 3-colorable if and only if G' is k-colorable.

9.8 NP-COMPLETE PROBLEMS INVOLVING SETS, VECTORS, AND NUMBERS

In this section we consider the set cover, vector sum, and subset sum problems. The subset sum problem models a kind of change-making problem: Given a bag of coins, does it contain a sub-bag whose sum is a desired total? (This would be a good time to review Section 0.2.5 on bags.) By reducing subset sum, it can be shown that several important problems in operations research are NP-complete (Exercises 9.8-2 and 9.8-3). Recall that by convention numbers are represented in binary.

In principle, we could prove that the subset sum problem is NP-complete by reducing SAT to it directly, but this would be complicated. Instead, we introduce set cover and vector sum in order to divide the proof into manageable pieces. This makes it easier to isolate and understand the key steps.

Consider the following problem:

Problem name: set cover

Instance: a set S, subsets $S_1, \ldots, S_m$ of S, and a natural number k

Question: Do there exist k natural numbers $i_1, \ldots, i_k$ such that

$$S = S_{i_1} \cup \cdots \cup S_{i_k}?$$

THEOREM 9.22. *The set cover problem is* NP*-complete.*

Proof: The set cover problem is in NP because we may guess $i_1, \ldots, i_k$ and verify in polynomial time that $S = S_{i_1} \cup \cdots \cup S_{i_k}$. We reduce SAT to set cover.

Let F be a Boolean formula with variables $x_1, \ldots, x_k$. Let

$$S = \{C : C \text{ is a clause of } F\} \cup \{x_1, \ldots, x_k\}.$$

Let $m = 2k$, and for $j = 1, \ldots, k$ let

$$\begin{aligned} S_{2j-1} &= \{C : C \text{ is a clause of } F \text{ containing the literal } x_j\} \cup \{x_j\} \\ S_{2j} &= \{C : C \text{ is a clause of } F \text{ containing the literal } \overline{x}_j\} \cup \{x_j\}. \end{aligned}$$

The number k and the sets $S, S_1, \ldots, S_m$ can be written down easily in polynomial time. We complete the proof that set cover is NP-complete by showing that F is satisfiable if and only if there exist $i_1, \ldots, i_k$ such that $S = S_{i_1} \cup \cdots \cup S_{i_k}$.

Assume that F is satisfiable via an assignment A. Let

$$i_j = \begin{cases} 2j - 1 & \text{if } A(x_j) = \text{true}, \\ 2j & \text{otherwise.} \end{cases}$$

Let C be any clause of F. Because A satisfies C, $A(\ell)$ must be true for some literal ℓ appearing in C. If $\ell = x_j$, then $C \in S_{2j-1} = S_{i_j}$; if $\ell = \overline{x}_j$, then $C \in S_{2j} = S_{i_j}$.

Let x_j be any variable of F. Then $x_j \in S_{2j-1}$ and $x_j \in S_{2j}$, so $x_j \in S_{i_j}$.

Since every clause C of F is contained in $S_{i_1} \cup \cdots \cup S_{i_k}$, and every variable x_j of F is contained in $S_{i_1} \cup \cdots \cup S_{i_k}$,

$$S \subseteq S_{i_1} \cup \cdots \cup S_{i_k}.$$

But $S_i \subseteq S$ for every i, so

$$S_{i_1} \cup \cdots \cup S_{i_k} \subseteq S.$$

Therefore

$$S = S_{i_1} \cup \cdots \cup S_{i_k}.$$

Conversely, suppose that there exist $i_1 < i_2 < \cdots < i_k$ such that $S = S_{i_1} \cup \cdots \cup S_{i_k}$. Since $x_j \in S$, $2j - 1$ or $2j$ must belong to the set $\{i_1, \ldots, i_k\}$ for $j = 1, \ldots, k$. This observation accounts for k elements of the set $\{i_1, \ldots, i_k\}$. The numbers $2j - 1$ and $2j$ cannot both belong to $\{i_1, \ldots, i_k\}$, because then $\{i_1, \ldots, i_k\}$ would contain at least $k+1$ elements. Therefore i_j is equal to $2j - 1$ or $2j$. Let

$$A(x_j) = \begin{cases} \text{true} & \text{if } i_j = 2j - 1, \\ \text{false} & \text{otherwise.} \end{cases}$$

Let C be any clause of F. Because $C \in S = S_{i_1} \cup \cdots \cup S_{i_k}$, C must belong to S_{i_j} for some j. If $i_j = 2j - 1$, then x_j is a literal of C and $A(x_j) = \text{true}$; if $i_j = 2j$, then $\overline{x}_j$ is a literal of C and $A(x_j) = \text{false}$. In either case A satisfies C. Since that is true for every C, A satisfies F. ∎

EXAMPLE 9.23. To illustrate the reduction from SAT to set cover, consider the Boolean formula F with clauses

$$\begin{aligned} C_1 &= x_1 \vee x_2 \vee x_3 \\ C_2 &= \overline{x}_1 \vee x_2 \vee x_3 \\ C_3 &= x_1 \vee \overline{x}_2 \vee \overline{x}_3 \\ C_4 &= \overline{x}_2 \vee x_3. \end{aligned}$$

The reduction maps F to the following instance of set cover:

$$\begin{aligned}
k &= 3 \\
S &= \{C_1, C_2, C_3, C_4, x_1, x_2, x_3\} \\
S_1 &= \{C_1, C_3, x_1\} \\
S_2 &= \{C_2, x_1\} \\
S_3 &= \{C_1, C_2, x_2\} \\
S_4 &= \{C_3, C_4, x_2\} \\
S_5 &= \{C_1, C_2, C_4, x_3\} \\
S_6 &= \{C_3, x_3\}.
\end{aligned}$$

A satisfying assignment of F is $A(x_1) = \text{false}$, $A(x_2) = \text{false}$, $A(x_3) = \text{true}$. In correspondence, we have

$$S = S_2 \cup S_4 \cup S_5.$$

■■■

Next we consider an NP-complete problem involving vectors. A *vector* over N is a finite sequence of elements of N. The sum of two equal-length vectors is defined by extending the addition operation from components to vectors, i.e.,

$$\langle\langle x_1, \ldots, x_k \rangle\rangle + \langle\langle y_1, \ldots, y_k \rangle\rangle = \langle\langle x_1 + y_1, \ldots, x_k + y_k \rangle\rangle.$$

For example, $\langle\langle 1, 2, 3 \rangle\rangle + \langle\langle 4, 5, 6 \rangle\rangle = \langle\langle 5, 7, 9 \rangle\rangle$.

Consider the following problem:

Problem name: vector sum

Instance: a bag V of "resource" vectors over N and a "goal" vector $\vec{g}$ over N

Question: Does there exists a sub-bag of resource vectors whose sum is $\vec{g}$, i.e.,

$$(\exists U \subseteq V) \left[\sum_{\vec{u} \in U} \vec{u} = \vec{g} \right] ?$$

The *0,1-valued* vector sum problem is a special case of the vector sum problem in which all components of all vectors in V must be 0 or 1. (No restriction is placed on the goal vector $\vec{g}$.)

THEOREM 9.24. *The 0,1-valued vector sum problem is* NP*-complete.*

Proof: The 0,1-valued vector sum problem is in NP because it is easy to guess a bag of resource vectors and verify that their sum is $\vec{g}$ in polynomial time. We reduce set cover to 0,1-valued vector sum.

Let $S, S_1, \ldots, S_m, k$ be an instance of the set cover problem with $S = \{x_1, \ldots, x_t\}$.

Let $\vec{g}$ be the vector whose first t components are $k+1$ and whose $(t+1)$st component is k, i.e.,

$$\vec{g} = \langle\langle k+1, \ldots, k+1, k\rangle\rangle.$$

For $i = 1, \ldots, m$ let

$$\vec{v}_i = \langle\langle \chi_{S_i}(x_1), \ldots, \chi_{S_i}(x_t), 1\rangle\rangle.$$

That is, the jth component of $\vec{v}_i$ is 1 if $x_j \in S_i$ and 0 otherwise for $i = 1, \ldots, t$; the $(t+1)$st component of $\vec{v}_i$ is 1. Observe that $S = S_{i_1} \cup \cdots \cup S_{i_k}$ if and only if $S \subseteq S_{i_1} \cup \cdots \cup S_{i_k}$ if and only if the vector $\vec{v}_{i_1} + \cdots + \vec{v}_{i_k}$ is at least one in each of the first t components. For $j = 1, \ldots, t$ let $\vec{p}_j$ be a vector of length $t+1$ with a 1 in the jth component and 0s elsewhere.

Let V be the bag containing one copy of the vector $\vec{v}_i$ for $i = 1, \ldots, m$ and k copies of the vector p_j for $j = 1, \ldots, t$. We will show that the set cover instance $(S, \langle\langle S_1, \ldots, S_m\rangle\rangle, k)$ has a solution if and only if the vector sum instance $(V, \vec{g})$ has a solution.

Assume that $S = S_{i_1} \cup \cdots \cup S_{i_k}$. Let $W = \{\vec{v}_{i_1}, \ldots, \vec{v}_{i_k}\}$, and let $\vec{w} = \vec{v}_{i_1} + \cdots + \vec{v}_{i_k}$. Let w_j be the jth component of $\vec{w}$ for $j = 1, \ldots, t$. Because $S = S_{i_1} \cup \cdots \cup S_{i_k}$, we have $w_j \geq 1$ for $j = 1, \ldots, t$. Because the $(t+1)$st component of each v_i is 1, $w_{t+1} = k$. Let P be the bag containing $k - w_j + 1$ copies of the vector $\vec{p}_j$ for $j = 1, \ldots, t$. Let $U = W \uplus P$. Then

$$\sum_{\vec{u} \in U} \vec{u} = \vec{g}.$$

Conversely, suppose that there exists $U \subseteq V$ such that $\sum_{\vec{u} \in U} \vec{u} = \vec{g}$. Since the last component of $\vec{g}$ is k, the set U must contain exactly k of the $\vec{v}_i$'s; call them $\vec{v}_{i_1}, \ldots, \vec{v}_{i_k}$. The set U may contain some of the $\vec{p}_j$'s, but their sum is at most k in each component, so $\vec{v}_{i_1} + \cdots + \vec{v}_{i_k}$ must be at least 1 in each of the first t components. Therefore $S \subseteq S_{i_1} \cup \cdots \cup S_{i_k}$. ■

EXAMPLE 9.25. To illustrate the reduction from set cover to vector sum, consider the following instance of the set cover problem:

$$
\begin{aligned}
S &= \{A, B, C, D, E, F, G\} \\
S_1 &= \{A, C, E\} \\
S_2 &= \{B, E\} \\
S_3 &= \{A, B, F\} \\
S_4 &= \{C, D, F\} \\
S_5 &= \{A, B, D, G\} \\
S_6 &= \{C, G\} \\
k &= 3
\end{aligned}
$$

The reduction maps this to the following instance of vector sum where V contains one copy of $\vec{v}_i$ for $i = 1, \ldots, 6$ and three copies of $\vec{p}_j$ for $j = 1, \ldots, 7$ (we have omitted punctuation in vectors for the sake of readability)

$$
\begin{aligned}
\vec{v}_1 &= 1\ 0\ 1\ 0\ 1\ 0\ 0\ 1 \\
\vec{v}_2 &= 0\ 1\ 0\ 0\ 1\ 0\ 0\ 1 \\
\vec{v}_3 &= 1\ 1\ 0\ 0\ 0\ 1\ 0\ 1 \\
\vec{v}_4 &= 0\ 0\ 1\ 1\ 0\ 1\ 0\ 1 \\
\vec{v}_5 &= 1\ 1\ 0\ 1\ 0\ 0\ 1\ 1 \\
\vec{v}_6 &= 0\ 0\ 1\ 0\ 0\ 0\ 1\ 1 \\
\vec{p}_1 &= 1\ 0\ 0\ 0\ 0\ 0\ 0\ 0 \\
\vec{p}_2 &= 0\ 1\ 0\ 0\ 0\ 0\ 0\ 0 \\
\vec{p}_3 &= 0\ 0\ 1\ 0\ 0\ 0\ 0\ 0 \\
\vec{p}_4 &= 0\ 0\ 0\ 1\ 0\ 0\ 0\ 0 \\
\vec{p}_5 &= 0\ 0\ 0\ 0\ 1\ 0\ 0\ 0 \\
\vec{p}_6 &= 0\ 0\ 0\ 0\ 0\ 1\ 0\ 0 \\
\vec{p}_7 &= 0\ 0\ 0\ 0\ 0\ 0\ 1\ 0 \\
\vec{g} &= 4\ 4\ 4\ 4\ 4\ 4\ 4\ 3
\end{aligned}
$$

A solution to the instance of set cover is

$$S = S_2 \cup S_4 \cup S_5.$$

A corresponding solution to the instance of 0,1-valued vector sum is

$$\vec{g} = \vec{v}_2 + \vec{v}_4 + \vec{v}_5 + 3\vec{p}_1 + 2\vec{p}_2 + 3\vec{p}_3 + 2\vec{p}_4 + 3\vec{p}_5 + 3\vec{p}_6 + 3\vec{p}_7.$$ ∎∎∎

Recall the subset sum problem:

Problem name: subset sum

Instance: a bag S of positive integers and a positive integer g

Question: Does there exist a sub-bag of S whose elements add up to g, i.e.,

$$(\exists U \subseteq S)\left[\sum_{u \in U} u = g\right]?$$

THEOREM 9.26. *The subset sum problem is* NP-*complete.*

Proof: The subset sum problem is in NP because we can easily guess a sub-bag U of S and verify in polynomial time that $\sum_{u \in U} u = g$. We reduce 0,1-valued vector sum to subset sum.

Let $(V, \vec{g})$ be an instance of the 0,1-valued vector sum problem. Let $B = |V| + 1$. Each vector $\vec{v}$ can be treated as a number x in base B by treating the jth component of $\vec{v}$ as the jth digit of x. Let x_i be the number corresponding to $\vec{v}_i$. Let $S = \{x_i : \vec{v}_i \in V\}$. Let g be the binary number corresponding to $\vec{g}$. This reduction can easily be carried out in polynomial time.

Furthermore, the base B was chosen large enough so that there are no carries when adding elements of S. Therefore

$$\sum_i \vec{v}_i = \vec{g} \iff \sum_i x_i = g.$$ ∎

EXAMPLE 9.27. To illustrate the reduction from 0,1-valued vector sum to subset sum, consider the following instance of the 0,1-valued vector sum problem:

$$
\begin{aligned}
\vec{v}_1 &= 1\ 0\ 1\ 0\ 1\ 0\ 0\ 1 \\
\vec{v}_2 &= 0\ 1\ 0\ 0\ 1\ 0\ 0\ 1 \\
\vec{v}_3 &= 1\ 1\ 0\ 0\ 0\ 1\ 0\ 1 \\
\vec{v}_4 &= 0\ 0\ 1\ 1\ 0\ 1\ 0\ 1 \\
\vec{v}_5 &= 1\ 1\ 0\ 1\ 0\ 0\ 1\ 1 \\
\vec{v}_6 &= 0\ 0\ 1\ 0\ 0\ 0\ 1\ 1 \\
\vec{v}_7 &= 0\ 0\ 1\ 0\ 1\ 0\ 1\ 0 \\
\vec{v}_8 &= 1\ 1\ 1\ 1\ 1\ 0\ 1\ 0 \\
\vec{v}_9 &= 1\ 0\ 1\ 0\ 1\ 0\ 1\ 0 \\
\vec{g} &= 1\ 2\ 1\ 2\ 1\ 1\ 1\ 3
\end{aligned}
$$

The reduction maps this to the following instance of subset sum, where we have written the numbers in base 10:

$$
\begin{aligned}
x_1 &= 10101001 \\
x_2 &= 1001001 \\
x_3 &= 11000101 \\
x_4 &= 110101 \\
x_5 &= 11010011 \\
x_6 &= 100011 \\
x_7 &= 101010 \\
x_8 &= 11111010 \\
x_9 &= 10101010 \\
g &= 12121113
\end{aligned}
$$

A solution to the instance of 0,1-valued vector sum is

$$\vec{g} = \vec{v}_2 + \vec{v}_4 + \vec{v}_5.$$

The corresponding solution to the instance of subset sum is

$$g = x_2 + x_4 + x_5.$$ ■■■

Exercises

9.8-1 **Problem name:** equipartition[6]
Instance: a bag S of positive integers
Question: Do there exist bags T and U such that $T \uplus U = S$ and

$$\sum_{x \in T} x = \sum_{x \in U} x?$$

Prove that equipartition is NP-complete.

Solution: Obviously equipartition is in NP. We reduce subset sum. Consider an instance (S, g) of the subset sum problem. Let $s = \sum_{x \in S} x$. Let $S' = S \cup \{s - 2g\}$. This reduction can be performed in polynomial time. We prove that the reduction is correct. Note that $\sum_{x \in S'} x = s + (s - 2g) = 2s - 2g$.

Suppose that there is a solution to the subset sum instance (S, g), i.e., there exists $T \subseteq S$ such that $\sum_{x \in T} x = g$. Let $T' = T \uplus \{s - 2g\}$. Then $T' \subseteq S$ and

$$\sum_{x \in T'} x = s - 2g + \sum_{x \in T} x = s - g = \frac{1}{2} \sum_{x \in S'} x.$$

Let $U' = S' - T'$, so T' and U' form an equipartition of S'.

Conversely, suppose that T' and U' form an equipartition of S'.

[6] The equipartition problem is also known as the partition problem.

Then T' or U' contains $s - 2g$; without loss of generality, assume that $s - 2g \in T'$. Let $T = T' - \{s - 2g\}$. Then

$$\begin{aligned}\sum_{x \in T} x &= \sum_{x \in T'} x - (s - 2g) = \frac{1}{2} \sum_{x \in S'} x - (s - 2g) \\ &= \frac{1}{2}(2s - 2g) - (s - 2g) = g,\end{aligned}$$

so T is a solution to the subset sum instance (S, g).

9.8-2 **Problem name:** bin packing

Instance: a bag of positive integers S (the sizes of the items to be packed), a positive integer B (a bin size), and a positive integer k (a number of bins)

Question: Do there exist bags $S_1, \ldots, S_k$ such that $S_1 \uplus \cdots \uplus S_k = S$ and $\sum_{x \in S_i} x \leq B$ for $i = 1, \ldots, k$? (Is it possible to pack all the items whose sizes are given by S into k bins of size B?)

Prove that bin packing is NP-complete.

9.8-3 **Problem name:** knapsack

Instance: a bag S of ordered pairs (v_i, w_i) of positive integers (interpreted as the value and weight, respectively, of the ith object), a positive integer c (the capacity of the knapsack), and a positive integer g (the goal).

Question: Does there exist $T \subseteq S$ such that the sum of the weights of the objects in T is at most c and the sum of the values of the objects in T is at least g?

Prove that knapsack is NP-complete.

9.8-4 Reduce the vector sum problem for vectors over N to the subset sum problem. (Do not use the fact that subset sum is NP-complete.)

9.8-5 (a) Prove that the vector sum problem is NP-complete even if the elements of the goal vector g are represented in monadic notation (base 1).

(b) A string x is an *anagram* of a string y if $x \in \text{PERM}(y)$, i.e., if x can be obtained by permuting the characters of y. Prove that the following problem is NP-complete.

Instance: a bag of strings B and a goal string g

Question: Does there exist a sub-bag $\{s_1, \ldots, s_m\} \subseteq B$ such that $s_1 \cdots s_m$ is an anagram of g?

9.8-6 **(a) Prove that the bin-packing problem remains NP-complete even if the sizes of the objects and bins are represented in monadic (base 1).

(b) Prove that the following problem is NP-complete.

Instance: a bag of strings B and a goal string g

Question: Does there exist an ordering $\langle\langle s_1, \ldots, s_m \rangle\rangle$ such that $\{s_1, \ldots, s_m\} = B$ and $s_1 \cdots s_m = g$?

*9.8-7 The 3-dimensional matching problem is a kind of marriage problem for species with three genders, which we will call δ-male, ϵ-male, and ϕ-male. Suppose that a set X consists of k δ-males, Y consists of k ϵ-males, and Z consists of k ϕ-males. A set C consists of all triples (x, y, z) such that x, y, and z are compatible for marriage. Informally, the 3-dimensional matching problem amounts to finding k compatible triples that do not overlap so that each creature is involved in exactly one three-way marriage.

Formally, if we are given three sets X, Y, and Z such that $|X| = |Y| = |Z| = k$ and a fourth set $C \subseteq X \times Y \times Z$, a *3-dimensional matching* for X, Y, Z, C is a set $M \subseteq C$ such that $|M| = k$ and distinct elements of M disagree coordinatewise, i.e.,

$$(x_1, y_1, z_1) \in M \text{ and } (x_2, y_2, z_2) \in M \Rightarrow x_1 \neq x_2, y_1 \neq y_2, \text{ and } z_1 \neq z_2.$$

Prove that the following problem is NP-complete:

Problem name: 3-dimensional matching

Instance: three sets X, Y, and Z such that $|X| = |Y| = |Z|$ and a fourth set $C \subseteq X \times Y \times Z$

Question: Does there exist a 3-dimensional matching for X, Y, Z, C?

Hint: Reduce set cover.

9.8-8 In the proof of Theorem 9.24 the set V has cardinality $m+tk$. Modify the proof to use a set V having cardinality $m+t\lceil \log (k+1) \rceil$. Hint: Use powers of 2 in defining the $\vec{p}$'s.

*9.9 AN NP-COMPLETE PROBLEM ABOUT DFRS

In this section we apply the theory of NP-completeness to the study of finite machines. We consider the problem of constructing a small DFR whose transfer relation is consistent with some given data. The problem originally arose in learning theory. Suppose that a student is trying to learn a language. A teacher presents a finite set S of positive examples, i.e., strings that belong to the language, and a finite set T of negative examples, i.e., strings that do not belong to the language. The student tries to find some kind of simple rule that is consistent with the examples, hoping that it will be consistent with further examples. To be concrete, assume that the language to be learned is regular. A rule may be expressed as a DFR, and one measure of a DFR's simplicity is the number of states. Thus the student tries to solve the following optimization problem:

Problem name: minimum separation by DFRs

Instance: two finite sets of strings S and T

Answer: the least k such that there is a k-state DFR that accepts all strings in S and rejects all strings in T (it may accept or reject strings in $\overline{S \cup T}$)

The corresponding decision problem is

Problem name: separation by DFRs

Instance: two finite sets of strings S and T and a natural number k

Question: Does there exist a k-state DFR that accepts all strings in S and rejects all strings in T (it may accept or reject strings in $\overline{S \cup T}$)?

The language recognized by the sought-after DFR is said to *separate* S from T.

THEOREM 9.28. *Separation by DFRs is* NP-*complete.*

Proof: We see that separation by DFRs is in NP, because in polynomial time we may easily guess a k-state DFA and then check that it accepts each string in S and rejects each string in T.

We reduce SAT to separation by DFRs. Let F be a Boolean formula with m clauses and v variables. Call F's clauses $C_0, \ldots, C_{m-1}$, and call F's variables $x_0, \ldots, x_{v-1}$. For convenience, let the literals $x_0, \ldots, x_{v-1}, \overline{x}_0, \ldots, \overline{x}_{v-1}$ be denoted by $\ell_0, \ldots, \ell_{2v-1}$, respectively. Let $k = m + 2v$, i.e., the number of clauses plus literals.

We will construct sets S and T such that any k-state DFR P that accepts all strings in S and rejects all strings in T must encode a satisfying assignment to F.

We begin by specifying subsets $S_1 \subseteq S$ and $T_1 \subseteq T$ that will ensure that the control states of P form a cycle connected by edges labeled a. Let

$$\begin{aligned} S_1 &= \{\Lambda, \mathtt{a}^k\} \\ T_1 &= \{\mathtt{a}^i : 0 < i < k\}. \end{aligned}$$

Assume that P is a k-state DFR that accepts all strings in S_1 and rejects all strings in T_1. We will give convenient names to the control states of P. For $i = 0, \ldots, k-1$, let q_i denote the state of program P after scanning the input string $\mathtt{a}^i$. If $0 \leq i < j < k$, then states q_i and q_j are distinguished (cf. Section 4.7) by $\mathtt{a}^{k-j}$, so $q_i \neq q_j$. Since P has only k control states, $q_0, \ldots, q_{k-1}$ comprise all the states of P, and q_0 is P's unique accepting state. For convenience, we will label states $q_0, \ldots, q_{k-1}$ by $C_0, \ldots, C_{m-1}, x_0, \ldots, x_{v-1}, \overline{x}_0, \ldots, \overline{x}_{v-1}$, respectively (Figure 9.13). In this notation, C_0 is P's unique accepting state; all other states are rejecting states.

Next we construct a subset $T_2 \subseteq T$ that will ensure that the edge labeled b that goes from C_i goes to a literal of C_i. Let

$$T_2 = \{\mathtt{a}^i\mathtt{b}\mathtt{a}^j : 0 \leq i < m \text{ and } 0 \leq j < k\} - \{\mathtt{a}^i\mathtt{b}\mathtt{a}^{2v-j} : \ell_j \text{ is a literal of } C_i\}.$$

Assume that P rejects all strings in T_2 as well. If the edge from C_i labeled b goes to ℓ_j, then there is a path from C_0 to ℓ_j labeled $\mathtt{a}^i\mathtt{b}$. There is also a path from ℓ_j to C_0 labeled $\mathtt{a}^{2v-j}$, so $\mathtt{a}^i\mathtt{b}\mathtt{a}^{2v-j}$ is accepted. Therefore ℓ_j is a literal of C_0, as promised.

We ensure that the edge labeled b that goes from ℓ_j goes to either $\overline{x}_0$ or C_0 by constructing the following set $T_3 \subseteq T$. Let

$$T_3 = \{\mathtt{a}^{m+j}\mathtt{b}\mathtt{a}^h : 0 \leq j < 2v, 0 < h < k, \text{ and } h \neq v)\}.$$

For convenience, we will label the state C_0 by true and the state $\overline{x}_0$ by false.

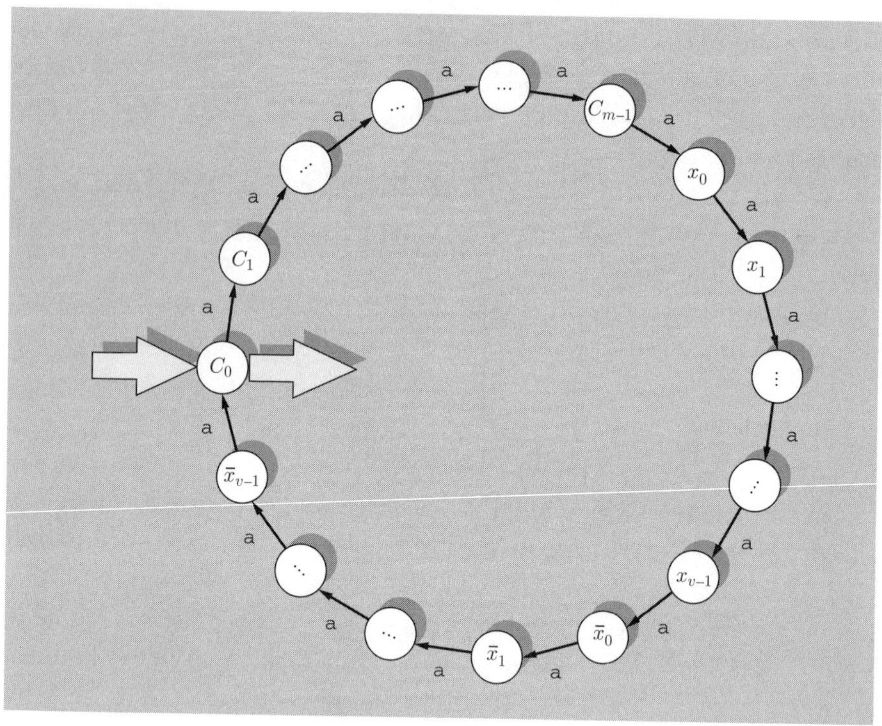

FIGURE 9.13: States and edges necessary in any k-state DFR that separates S_1 from T_1. All states except C_0 are rejecting.

Say that ℓ_j is "vrai" (from the French for "true") if there is an edge labeled b from ℓ_j to C_0. Next we construct a subset $T_4 \subseteq T$ that will ensure that x_j and $\overline{x}_j$ are not both vrai. Let

$$T_4 = \{\mathtt{a}^{m+j}\mathtt{b}\mathtt{a}^{m+v+j}\mathtt{b} : 0 \leq j < v\}.$$

Finally, by constructing $S_5 \subseteq S$, we ensure that the edge labeled b that goes from C_i goes to a vrai variable. Let

$$S_5 = \{\mathtt{a}^i\mathtt{bb} : 0 \leq i < m\}.$$

Let $S = S_1 \cup S_5$, and let $T = T_1 \cup T_2 \cup T_3 \cup T_4$.

If P is indeed a k-state DFR that accepts all strings in S and rejects all strings in T, then we construct a satisfying assignment A that assigns true to the vrai literals, i.e.,

$$A(x_j) = \begin{cases} \text{true} & \text{if } (x_j \to \text{true}, \text{SCAN}\,\mathtt{b}) \in \mathcal{I}, \\ \text{false} & \text{otherwise}, \end{cases}$$

where $\mathcal{I}$ denotes the instruction set of P.

Conversely, assume that A is a satisfying assignment of F. Let $w(C_i)$ denote the first literal ℓ in C_i such that $A(\ell) = \text{true}$. We construct a DFR P with the control set, start state, and accepting state named above. P's instruction set is

$$\begin{array}{ll} (q_i \to q_{(i+1)\bmod k}, \text{SCAN}\,\mathtt{a}) & \text{for } 0 \le i < k \\ (C_i \to w(C_i) \quad, \text{SCAN}\,\mathtt{b}) & \text{for } 0 \le i < m \\ (\ell_j \to A(\ell_j) \quad, \text{SCAN}\,\mathtt{b}) & \text{for } 0 \le j < 2v. \end{array}$$

It is easily verified that P accepts all strings in S and rejects all strings in T.

Thus we have shown that F is satisfiable if and only if there exists a k-state DFR that accepts all strings in S and rejects all strings in T. (In fact, more careful analysis of our construction shows that F is satisfiable if and only if there exists a k-state NFA that accepts all strings in S and accepts no strings in T. See Exercise 9.9-2.)

Because k, S, and T can easily be constructed in polynomial time, SAT is $\le_m^p$-reducible to separation by DFRs, as asserted. Therefore separation by DFRs is NP-complete. ■

EXAMPLE 9.29. Let us demonstrate the reduction on the Boolean formula F with five variables $x_0, \ldots, x_4$ and the following six clauses:

$$\begin{aligned} C_0 &= x_0 \vee x_2 \vee x_3 \\ C_1 &= x_1 \vee \overline{x}_3 \vee \overline{x}_4 \\ C_2 &= x_0 \vee \overline{x}_1 \vee x_4 \\ C_3 &= \overline{x}_1 \vee \overline{x}_2 \vee \overline{x}_4 \\ C_4 &= x_2 \vee x_3 \vee \overline{x}_4 \\ C_5 &= \overline{x}_0 \vee \overline{x}_1 \vee x_2. \end{aligned}$$

Then $m = 6$ and $v = 5$, so $k = m + 2v = 16$. $S = S_1 \cup S_5$ and $T = T_1 \cup T_2 \cup T_3 \cup T_4$, where

$$
\begin{aligned}
S_1 &= \{\Lambda, \mathtt{a}^{16}\} \\
T_1 &= \{\mathtt{a}, \mathtt{a}^2, \ldots, \mathtt{a}^{15}\} \\
T_2 &= \quad \{\ \mathtt{ba}^j : j = 0, 1, 2, 3, 4, 5, 6, \quad 9, \quad 11, 12, 13, 14, 15\} \\
&\quad \cup \{\ \mathtt{aba}^j : j = 0, \quad 3, 4, 5, 6, 7, 8, \quad 10, 11, 12, 13, 14, 15\} \\
&\quad \cup \{\mathtt{a}^2\mathtt{ba}^j : j = 0\ 1, 2, 3, \quad 5, \quad 7, 8, 9, \quad 11, 12, 13, 14, 15\} \\
&\quad \cup \{\mathtt{a}^3\mathtt{ba}^j : j = 0, \quad 2, \quad 5, 6, 7, 8, 9, 10, 11, 12, 13, 14, 15\} \\
&\quad \cup \{\mathtt{a}^4\mathtt{ba}^j : j = 0, \quad 2, 3, 4, 5, 6, \quad 9, 10, 11, 12, 13, 14, 15\} \\
&\quad \cup \{\mathtt{a}^5\mathtt{ba}^j : j = 0, 1, 2, 3, \quad 6, 7, \quad 9, 10, 11, 12, 13, 14, 15\} \\
T_3 &= \{\mathtt{a}^j\mathtt{ba}^h : j = 6, \ldots, 15 \text{ and } h = 1, \ldots, 4, 6, \ldots, 15\} \\
T_4 &= \{\mathtt{a}^6\mathtt{ba}^{11}\mathtt{b}, \mathtt{a}^7\mathtt{ba}^{12}\mathtt{b}, \mathtt{a}^8\mathtt{ba}^{13}\mathtt{b}, \mathtt{a}^9\mathtt{ba}^{14}\mathtt{b}, \mathtt{a}^{10}\mathtt{ba}^{15}\mathtt{b}\} \\
S_5 &= \{\mathtt{bb}, \mathtt{abb}, \mathtt{a}^2\mathtt{bb}, \mathtt{a}^3\mathtt{bb}, \mathtt{a}^4\mathtt{bb}, \mathtt{a}^5\mathtt{bb}\}.
\end{aligned}
$$

A satisfying assignment for F is

$$
\begin{aligned}
A(x_0) &= \text{false} \\
A(x_1) &= \text{true} \\
A(x_2) &= \text{false} \\
A(x_3) &= \text{true} \\
A(x_4) &= \text{true.}
\end{aligned}
$$

The corresponding DFR is presented in Figure 9.14. ■■■

Exercises

9.9-1 Verify that the program P constructed in the proof of Theorem 9.28 rejects all strings in T_4.

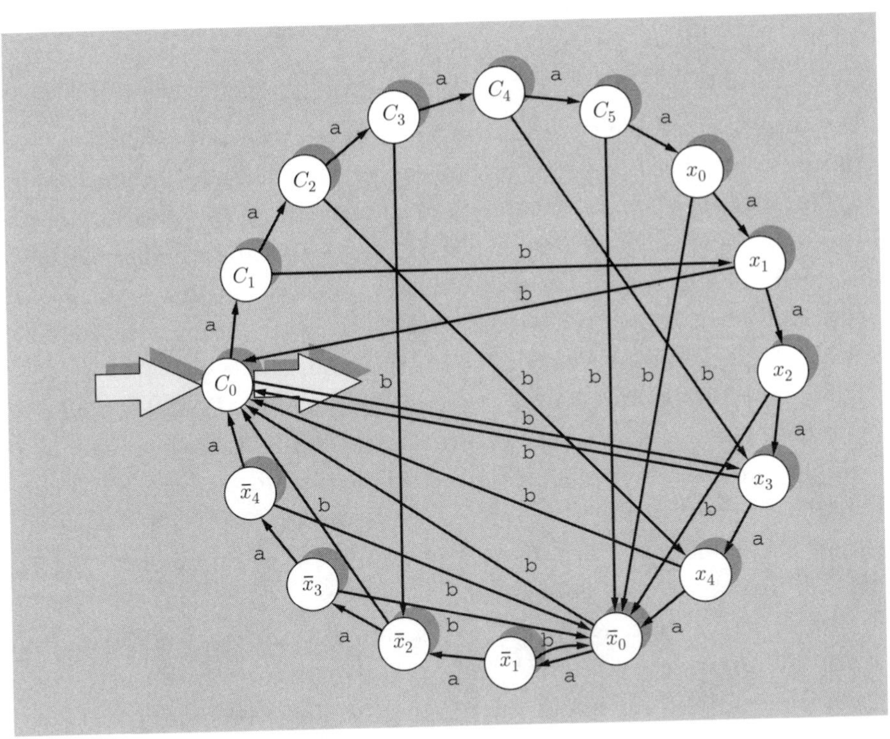

FIGURE 9.14: The DFR corresponding to a satisfying assignment. All states except C_0 are rejecting.

9.9-2 (a) By analyzing our construction more carefully, show that if there exists a k-state NFA that accepts all strings in S and accepts no strings in T, then F is satisfiable.

(b) Prove that the problem of determining whether there is a k-state NFA that accepts all strings in S and accepts no strings in T is NP-complete.

9.9-3 The reduction from SAT to separation by DFRs does not guarantee that at least one of x_j and $\overline{x}_j$ is vrai if F is satisfiable. Why was this property not needed in proving that separation by DFRs is NP-complete?

*9.10 COMPLEXITY OF SOME PROBLEMS INVOLVING REGULAR LANGUAGES

Two important problems are testing membership in a language and determining whether two languages are equal. The membership problem for regular languages and even context-free languages is in P. However, we saw in Section 7.13 that there is no algorithm at all for testing whether two CFLs are equal. In this section we will consider the time and space complexity of testing whether two regular languages are equal. (See Exercises 9.1-5 and 9.1-6 for definitions and important theorems about space.)

Suppose that we are given a string x and a DFA P, and we wish to determine whether x is accepted by P. Using a RAM, we could simulate a single step of P by table lookup in time $O(\log |P|)$, where $|P|$ denotes the length of the string that represents the program P. Thus we could simulate P on input x in time $O(|P| + |x| \log |P|)$, so this problem is solvable deterministically in polynomial time.

In particular, every DFA language is in P. Because every NFA language is a DFA language, every NFA language is in P as well. However, that statement says nothing about the running time of a program that takes a string x *and an NFA program* P as input and determines whether P accepts x. It is not efficient to convert P to a DFA using the subset construction (see Chapter 3), because the conversion takes time that is exponential in the size of the program P; the total time for conversion plus simulation is $O(2^{|P|} + |x||P|)$.

Fortunately, there is a more efficient way to test whether x is accepted by an NFA P. We use the idea behind the subset construction, but we do not construct a DFA. We simulate P by keeping track of the set of possible control states of P. Thus simulating a single step takes time $O(|P| \log |P|)$, so the total time for the simulation is $O(|x||P| \log |P|)$, which is bounded by a polynomial.

Now suppose that we are given a string x and a regular expression r, and we wish to determine whether x is generated by r. We can efficiently convert r to an NFA program P whose size is $O(r)$. Then we use the same algorithm as in the preceding paragraph, so this problem is in P as well.

Thus we have proved the following result:

PROPOSITION 9.30. *Let us represent regular languages by DFAs, NFAs, or* *regular expressions. There is a deterministic algorithm for testing whether a string x belongs to a regular language L that runs in time bounded by a polynomial in the length of x and the length of L's representation.* ■

Next we consider the equivalence problem for regular languages, i.e., "How hard is it to determine whether two regular languages are equal?" Unlike the membership problem, the difficulty of this problem seems to depend strongly on how the regular languages are represented.

If the regular languages are given by DFRs, then the equivalence problem is in P via the algorithm of Theorem 4.32. However, if the regular languages are given by regular expressions, then the equivalence problem is $\leq_m^p$-complete for PSPACE (defined in Exercise 9.1-6). Before proving that, we will consider a restricted kind of regular expression for which the equivalence problem is co-NP-complete. (Recall that a language is co-NP-complete if and only if its complement is NP-complete.)

Two regular expressions are called *equivalent* if they generate the same language and *inequivalent* if they generate different languages. A regular expression is called *star-free* if it does not contain the Kleene-closure (*) operation. The problem of determining whether two star-free regular expressions are inequivalent is called the *inequivalence problem* for star-free regular languages.

Problem name: inequivalence of star-free regular languages

Instance: two star-free regular expressions r_1 and r_2

Question: Is $L(r_1) \neq L(r_2)$?

The problem is the same as testing membership in the language

$$\{(r_1, r_2) : r_1 \text{ and } r_2 \text{ are star-free regular expressions and } L(r_1) \neq L(r_2)\}.$$

Observe that a star-free regular expression cannot generate strings that are longer than it is; thus every star-free regular expression generates a finite language. Although not as general as the equivalence problem for general regular expressions, the equivalence problem for star-free regular expressions appears quite hard.

A seemingly simpler problem, stated formally below, is to determine whether $L(r) \neq \{0, 1\}^n$. This is a special case of the inequivalence problem for star-free regular expressions taking $r_1 = r$ and $r_2 = (0 \cup 1)^n$.

Problem name: nonuniversality of star-free regular expressions

Instance: a star-free regular expression r and a natural number n

Question: Is $L(r) \neq \{0, 1\}^n$?

THEOREM 9.31. *Nonuniversality of star-free regular expressions is* NP*-complete.*

Proof: First we show that nonuniversality of star-free regular expressions is in NP. Note that a star-free regular expression r cannot generate any string x such that $|x| > |r|$. We present a nondeterministic algorithm to test whether r generates a language different from Σ^n: If $|r| < n$ then accept; otherwise guess a string x such that $|x| = n$; if x does not belong to $L(r)$, then accept; next guess a string x such that $|x| \leq |r|$ and $|x| \neq n$; if x belongs to $L(r)$, then accept. Thus nonuniversality of star-free regular expressions is in NP.

Next we reduce SAT to nonuniversality of regular expressions. Let F be a CNF formula with variables $x_1, \ldots, x_n$ and clauses $C_1, \ldots, C_k$. For each clause C_i we write a star-free regular expression $R_i = y_{i1} \cdots y_{in}$, where

$$y_{ij} = \begin{cases} 0 & \text{if } x_j \text{ belongs to } C_i, \\ 1 & \text{if } \overline{x}_j \text{ belongs to } C_i, \\ (0 \cup 1) & \text{otherwise.} \end{cases}$$

Note that an assignment A fails to satisfy C_i if and only if $A(x_1) \cdots A(x_n) \in L(R_i)$. An assignment fails to satisfy a formula if and only if it fails to satisfy one of the clauses; therefore A fails to satisfy F if and only if $A(x_1) \cdots A(x_n) \in L(R_1 \cup \cdots \cup R_k)$. Let $r = R_1 \cup \cdots \cup R_k$. F is satisfiable if and only if $L(r) \neq \{0, 1\}^n$. ∎

COROLLARY 9.32. *Inequivalence of star-free regular expressions is* NP*-complete.*

Proof: We show that inequivalence of star-free regular expressions is in NP. Note that a star-free regular expression r cannot generate any string x such that $|x| > |r|$. We present a nondeterministic algorithm to test whether r_1 and r_2 are inequivalent: Guess a string x such that $|x| \leq \max(|r_1|, |r_2|)$; determine whether x belongs to $L(r_1)$, and determine whether x belongs to $L(r_2)$; if x belongs to exactly one of them, then accept. Thus inequivalence of star-free regular expressions is in NP.

Nonuniversality of star-free regular expressions is $\leq_m^p$-reducible to inequivalence of star-free regular expressions by the reduction $f(r, n) = (r, (0 \cup 1)^n)$ if $|r| \geq n$, $(0, 1)$ otherwise. Since the nonuniversality problem is NP-complete by Theorem 9.31, the inequivalence problem is NP-complete as well. ■

EXAMPLE 9.33. To illustrate the reduction from SAT to nonuniversality of star-free regular-expressions, consider the Boolean formula F with clauses

$$\begin{aligned} C_1 &= x_1 \vee x_2 \vee x_3 \\ C_2 &= \overline{x}_1 \vee x_2 \vee x_3 \\ C_3 &= x_1 \vee \overline{x}_2 \vee \overline{x}_3 \\ C_4 &= \overline{x}_2 \vee x_3. \end{aligned}$$

The reduction maps the Boolean formula F to the star-free regular-expression $r = 000 \cup 100 \cup 011 \cup (0 \cup 1)10$. A satisfying assignment of F is $A(x_1) = \text{false}$, $A(x_2) = \text{false}$, $A(x_3) = \text{true}$. Correspondingly, r does not generate the string 001. ■■■

Having seen that the inequivalence problem for star-free regular expressions is NP-complete, let us now consider general regular expressions, which may include the Kleene-closure operation. Their inequivalence problem is apparently harder.

THEOREM 9.34. *The problem of determining whether a regular expression generates a language different from* $\{0, 1\}^*$ *is PSPACE-complete.*

Proof: Let Σ be the regular expression $(0 \cup 1)$ and let

$$A = \{R : R \text{ is a regular expression and } L(R) \neq \Sigma^*\}.$$

The nondeterministic polynomial-space algorithm given below recognizes A by mimicking the subset construction (Section 4.6):[7]

```
convert R to an equivalent NFA P;
eliminate null instructions from P and call the new program P';
let q_start be the start state of P' and I the instruction set of P';
S := {q_start}; (* x := Λ *)
while S contains an accepting state do begin (* while x is accepted by P' *)
    nondeterministically choose a character c in Σ;
    S' := {q' : (∃q)[q ∈ S ∧ (q → q', SCANc) ∈ I]}; (* S' := St_c *)
    S := S'; (* x := xc *)
end;
accept; (* because x was not accepted by P' *)
```

This program uses only a linear amount of space in order to store S and S' plus a negligible amount for other variables. Thus L is accepted by an NTM program using space n. By Savitch's theorem (Exercise 9.1-6) L is recognized by a DTM program using space $O(n^2)$, so $L \in$ PSPACE.

We will prove that A is PSPACE-complete by a generic reduction. The set of *invalid* traces of a TM program is the complement of the set of accepting traces. Our key idea is that the set of invalid traces of a polynomial space-bounded Turing machine program on input x is generated by a regular expression whose length is bounded by a polynomial in x. We will show how to determine such a regular expression in polynomial time.

Let $B = n^k$ and let P be a DTM program that uses space bounded by B. Without loss of generality, assume that P has no input; instead, the input is initially stored on P's tape. Thus P is a program for a machine [control, tape]. Let the control set be Q, the tape alphabet be Γ, and the instruction set be

---

[7] The polynomial-space-bounded NTA we construct for A does not halt if the input is not in A. But a space-bounded algorithm can be made time bounded as well, if we wish, by Exercise 9.1-5. In either case, Savitch's theorem (Exercise 9.1-6) is applicable.

$\mathcal{I}$. Let x be a string of length n. A trace of M can be represented as

$$\#q_0 \sqcup s_0 \# \cdots \# q_m \sqcup s_m \#$$

for some $m \geq 0$, where q_t is the control state at time t and s_t is the tape state at time t, padded with blanks so that $|s_t| = B + 1$ for all t. In this representation, we assert that the set of invalid traces of P on input x is a regular set. In fact we will show that it is generated by a regular expression that we can write down in polynomial time.

Let $T = \Gamma \cup \boxed{\Gamma}$, and let $\Sigma = Q \cup T \cup \{\#\}$. A string C over Σ represents a valid trace of M on input x if and only if all of the following conditions are true. For each condition, we write regular expressions that generate all strings C which *do not* satisfy the condition.

(i) C must end with #.

The set of strings that do not satisfy this condition is R_0, where

$$R_0 = \Sigma^*(Q \cup T).$$

(ii) C must have exactly $B + 3$ characters between consecutive #s.

The set of strings that do not satisfy this condition is $R_1 \cup R_2$, where

$$R_1 = \Sigma^* \#(Q \cup T \cup \Lambda)^{B+2} \# \Sigma^* \text{ and } R_2 = \Sigma^*(Q \cup T)^{B+4}\Sigma^*.$$

(iii) The second character in C after a # must be a $\sqcup$ (or nonexistent).

The set of strings that do not satisfy this condition is R_3, where

$$R_3 = \bigcup_{c \neq \sqcup} \Sigma^* \# \Sigma c \Sigma^*.$$

(iv) Let $x = x_1 \cdots x_n$. Let $z = \#q_0 \sqcup \boxed{x_1} x_2 \cdots x_n \sqcup^{B+1-n}$. The string z must be a prefix of C.

Define z_i by $z_1 \cdots z_{B+4} = z$. The set of strings that do not satisfy this condition is R_4, where

$$R_4 = \bigcup_{1 \leq i \leq |z|} \bigcup_{c \neq z_i} \Sigma^{i-1}(\Lambda \cup c\Sigma^*).$$

(v) If the tape head is not on one of three adjacent squares at time t, then it must not be on the middle one at time $t+1$ and the middle one must not change between time t and $t+1$.

The set of strings that do not satisfy this condition is R_5, where

$$R_5 = \bigcup_{a,b,c \in \Gamma} \bigcup_{d \neq b} \Sigma^* abc \Sigma^{B+4} adc \Sigma^*.$$

(vi) If the tape head is on square j at time t, then the surrounding squares and the control state must be updated according to an instruction of P at time $t+1$.

The set of strings that do not satisfy this condition is R_6, where

$$R_6 = \bigcup_{\substack{0 \le i \le B-3 \\ b \in \boxed{\Gamma}}} \bigcup_{\neg[(q,abc) \overset{\Pi}{\mapsto} (q',a'b'c')]} \Sigma^* \# q \sqcup \Sigma^i abc \Sigma^{B-i-2} \# q' \sqcup \Sigma^i a'b'c' \Sigma^*.$$

(vii) q_m must be an accepting control state.

The set of strings that do not satisfy this condition is R_7, where

$$R_7 = \bigcup_{q \text{ a nonaccepting control state}} \Sigma^* q \Sigma^{B+3}.$$

Let $R = R_0 \cup \cdots \cup R_7$. Then $L(R)$ is the set of invalid traces of P on input x. P accepts x if and only if $L(R) \neq \Sigma^*$. ∎

Exercises

9.10-1 In each of the exercises below, state the problem formally in terms of languages and prove that the problem is in P, is NP-complete, is co-NP-complete, or is PSPACE-complete.

(a) Determine for DFRs P_1 and P_2 whether $L(P_1) \subseteq L(P_2)$.

Solution: Let $L = \{(P_1, P_2) : P_1$ and P_2 are DFRs such that $L(P_1) \subseteq L(P_2)\}$. L is in P. Let P_3 be a DFR for $L(P_1) \cup L(P_2)$ (obtained by the pairing construction), and test in polynomial time whether $L(P_2) = L(P_3)$.

(b) Determine for DFRs P_1 and P_2 whether $L(P_1) \subset L(P_2)$.

(c) Determine for star-free regular expressions r_1 and r_2 whether $L(r_1) \subseteq L(r_2)$.

Solution: Let $L = \{(r_1, r_2) : r_1$ and r_2 are star-free regular expressions such that $L(r_1) \subseteq L(r_2)\}$. L is co-NP-complete. We can nondeterministically test membership in $\overline{L}$ by guessing a string x with $|x| \leq |r_1|$ and checking in polynomial time that x is in $L(r_1)$ but not in $L(r_2)$. Thus $\overline{L} \in$ NP, so $L \in$ co-NP.

L is co-NP-hard because the special case with $r_1 = \Sigma^n$ is co-NP-hard by Theorem 9.31.

(d) Determine for regular expressions r_1 and r_2 whether $L(r_1) \subseteq L(r_2)$.

Solution: Let $L = \{(r_1, r_2) : r_1$ and r_2 are regular expressions such that $L(r_1) \subseteq L(r_2)\}$. L is PSPACE-complete. L is in PSPACE by the following algorithm: Let $r_3 = r_1 \cup r_2$, and test whether $L(r_2) = L(r_3)$. L is PSPACE-hard because the special case with $r_1 = \Sigma^*$ is PSPACE-hard.

(e) Determine for regular expressions r_1 and r_2 whether $L(r_1) \subset L(r_2)$.

9.10-2 Let $L = \{(r_1, r_2) : r_1$ and r_2 are star-free regular expressions such that $L(r_1) \subset L(r_2)\}$. Prove that L is NP-hard and co-NP-hard.

Solution: L is NP-hard because the special case with $r_2 = \Sigma^n$ is NP-hard. To see that L is co-NP-hard, note that determining whether $L(r_1) \subseteq L(r_2)$ is co-NP-complete by Exercise 9.10-1(c). For the reduction, note that $L(r_1) \subseteq L(r_2)$ if and only if $L(r_1) \subset L(r_2 \cup \#)$ where # is some character that does not belong to the alphabet of r_1.

9.10-3 Say that control states q_1 and q_2 are *equivalent* in an FM program P if P accepts the same strings when started in state q_1 as when started in state q_2. How hard is it to determine for an FM program P and control states q_1, q_2 whether q_1 and q_2 are equivalent in P?

(a) Assume that P is a DFR.

(b) Assume that P is an NFA.

9.10-4 We say that an NFA is an *acyclic* NFA if its state graph is acyclic (contains no cycles).

(a) Prove that L is generated by a star-free regular expression if and only if L is accepted by an acyclic NFA.

(b) How hard is it to determine whether two acyclic NFAs accept different languages?

9.10-5 (a) Is there a deterministic polynomial-time algorithm for determining whether a string x is generated by a CNF grammar G?

(b) Using part (a), present a deterministic polynomial-time algorithm for determining whether a string x is accepted by an NFA P. Do not use the algorithm presented in this section.

Solution: Eliminate null instructions and the EOF test from P. We construct a right-linear grammar G that generates the language accepted by P. The variables of G are the states of P. The start variable of G is the start state of P. For each instruction $(i \longrightarrow j, \text{SCAN}c)$, G contains the production $i \longrightarrow cj$. For each accepting state q and each instruction $(i \longrightarrow q, \text{SCAN}c)$ in P, G also contains the production $i \longrightarrow c$. The right-linear grammar G is converted to CNF by introducing new variables V_c for each character c as in Section 5.3. Then we apply part (a).

(c) Using part (b), present a deterministic polynomial-time algorithm for determining whether a string x is generated by a regular expression r. Do not use the algorithm presented in this section.

9.10-6 Suppose that we represent regular languages by Turing machine programs that accept them. If we use this representation, how hard is it to test whether a string x belongs to a regular language L?

Solution: Undecidable. We reduce from K. Given a string z, we construct a program P_z that does the following on input x: If $z \in K$, then accept, else reject. P_z accepts a language $L(P_z)$, which is either

$\emptyset$ or Σ^*, and hence regular. Any string x belongs to $L(P_z)$ if and only if z belongs to K.

9.10-7 Consider the problem of determining whether two CFGs generate the same language.

(a) Prove that the problem is NP-hard.

Solution: Reduce the halting problem, which is NP-hard and more.

(b) Is the problem NP-complete?

Solution: No. It is not in NP because it is undecidable.

9.10-8 (a) Let P be a space-bounded Turing machine program. Prove that the set of invalid traces of P is a regular set.

(b) Let P be a space-bounded Turing machine program. Prove that the set of valid traces of P is a regular set.

(c) Let P be a time-bounded Turing machine program. Prove that the set of invalid traces of P is a regular set.

9.11 CHAPTER SUMMARY

Polynomial time (P) is the class of decision problems that are efficiently solvable from a theoretical point of view. Nondeterministic polynomial time (NP) is an apparently larger class, to which a frustratingly large number of important decision problems are known to belong. We defined $\leq_m^p$-reductions, a polynomial-time-bounded version of Chapter 7's m-reductions. The hardest problems in NP, under $\leq_m^p$-reductions, are called NP-complete. P $=$ NP iff all NP-complete problems are in P iff at least one NP-complete problem is in P. Although we cannot say for sure whether NP-complete problems can be solved efficiently, it is safe to say that they cannot be solved efficiently by currently available techniques.

We can prove that many particular problems are NP-complete by reducing any known NP-complete problems to them. For such reductions, the most important NP-complete problem is 3-SAT, which is a special case of Boolean satisfiability, which in turn is a special case of symbol-system satisfiability. We proved many problems to be NP-complete in the text.

More are presented as exercises. Certain among them, like clique, vertex cover, Hamiltonian cycle, k-colorability, and equipartition, are widely used in reductions to other problems. For a more extensive treatment of NP-completeness, the reader should refer to the classic *Computers and Intractability* by Garey and Johnson.

To learn efficient deterministic methods for solving specific problems, the reader should refer to any textbook on the design and analysis of algorithms. The theory of probabilistic algorithms is also very important; e.g., primality can be solved probabilistically in polynomial time.

10 Appendix

10.1 GREEK SYMBOLS

We summarize the most important usages for various Greek letters.

α **(alpha)** The initializer of a program (Chapters 2–4, 6, 7). A string of characters and variables in a CFG (Chapter 5).

α_d **(alpha-sub-d)** The initializer of the device d (Chapters 2–4, 6).

β **(beta)** A string of characters and variables in a CFG (Chapter 5).

γ **(gamma)** A string of characters and variables in a CFG (Chapter 5).

Γ **(Gamma)** The alphabet of a non-I/O device (Chapters 2, 3, 6). The alphabet for a symbol system (Chapter 9).

Δ **(Delta)** The output alphabet (Chapter 2).

Δ_i **(Delta-sub-i)** One of the classes in the *i*th level of the arithmetical hierarchy (Chapter 8).

ζ **(zeta)** A string of characters and variables in a CFG (Chapter 5).

Λ **(empty string)** The empty string (Chapters 0–9). Not called by its Greek name, lambda.

ν **(nu)** A new control state in a simulation via subprograms (Chapter 3).

π **(pi)** An instruction (Chapters 2, 3, 7, 9).

Π **(Pi)** The sequel relation of a program (Chapters 2–4, 7, 9). An operator used in defining the arithmetical hierarchy (Chapter 8).

Π_i **(Pi-sub-i)** One of the classes in the *i*th level of the arithmetical hierarchy (Chapter 8).

ρ **(rho)** An arbitrary relation (Chapters 0, 6). A relation of representation (Chapter 3).

σ **(sigma)** An arbitrary relation (Chapter 0).

Σ **(Sigma)** An alphabet, especially the input alphabet (Chapters 0–8). An operator used in defining the arithmetical hierarchy (Chapter 8).

Σ_i **(Sigma-sub-i)** One of the classes in the *i*th level of the arithmetical hierarchy (Chapter 8).

τ **(tau)** The transfer relation of a program (Chapters 2–8).

φ_P **(phi-sub-P)** The transfer function of the deterministic program P (Chapter 8).

χ_A **(chi-sub-A)** The characteristic function of the set or bag A (Chapters 0, 7–9).

ω **(omega)** The terminator of a program (Chapters 2–4, 6, 7).

ω_d **(omega-sub-d)** The terminator of the device d (Chapters 2–4, 6).

10.2 GLOSSARY

We summarize some important definitions. Historical names for similar, but not necessarily identical, concepts are given in parentheses.

Block To enter a configuration to which no instruction is applicable.

Co-Finite S is a co-finite set if and only if $\overline{S}$ is a finite set.

Computation The sequence of instructions executed by a program when it is run to completion.

Configuration The states of all of a machine's devices.

Counter machine A machine with a control, a counter, and possibly input and/or output. The counter may be signed or unsigned, but is usually unsigned.

Deterministic A program is deterministic if there is at most one instruction that can be applied to each configuration and no instruction that can be applied to a final configuration. This condition must hold for all configurations, whether actually entered on some input or not.

Final configuration A configuration in which all states are final, i.e., a configuration that is in the domain of the terminator.

Finite machine A machine with a control and possibly input and/or output. (Historically, a finite automaton.)

Finite transducer A transducer running on a machine [control, input, output]. (Historically, a gsm.)

Finite transduction The relation computed by a finite transducer, usually treated as a multiple-valued function. (Historically, a gsm map.)

Halt To enter a final configuration and stay there.

History The argument, initializer, sequence of configurations entered and instructions performed, terminator, and result of a program when it is run to completion.

Inattentive Having no input device.

Initial configuration The configuration a program starts in.

Initializer A partial function that maps an argument to a program's initial configuration or a device's initial state.

Instruction A tuple consisting of an operation for each device. By applying an instruction to a configuration of a machine, we obtain a new configuration of the machine.

Machine A tuple of devices.

Nondeterministic Not necessarily deterministic. Permitted to choose among instructions at each step and to choose between halting and continuing execution.

Operation A partial function on the realm of a device. By applying an operation to a device's state, we obtain a new state for the device.

Program An initializer, terminator, and set of instructions.

Reachable A control state is reachable if there is a path from the initial control state to it in the program's digraph. It need not actually be entered when the program is run on any argument.

Realm The set of states that a device can hold.

Recursive Computed or recognized by a deterministic Turing machine program.

Recursively enumerable Accepted by a nondeterministic Turing acceptor.

Repertory The set of operations that a device is capable of performing.

Sequel relation For a particular program, this is the relation that maps a configuration to a next configuration.

Stack machine A machine with a control, a stack, and possibly input and/or output. (Historically, a pushdown automaton.)

Tape machine A machine with a control, a tape, and possibly input and/or output.

Terminator A partial function that maps a final configuration of a program to the result. A relation that maps a state of a device to a result.

Trace The sequence of configurations entered by a program when it is run to completion.

Transfer function A transfer relation that happens to be a partial function.

Transfer relation The relation that maps a program's argument to a result.

Turing machine A machine with a control, one or more tapes, and possibly input and/or output.

2-Counter machine A machine with a control, two counters, and possibly input and/or output. The counters may be signed or unsigned but are usually unsigned.

2-Stack machine A machine with a control, two stacks, and possibly input and/or output.

***k*-Tape machine** A machine with a control, k tapes, and possibly input and/or output.

10.3 COMMON ACRONYMS

In this section we list the most important acronyms. Historical names for similar, but not necessarily identical, objects are given in parentheses.

CFG Context-Free Grammar. A grammar consisting of a start variable and a set of productions of the form $A \to \beta$, where A is a variable and β is a string of variables and terminal characters.

CFL Context-Free Language. A language generated by a CFG.

CM Counter Machine. A machine with a control, a counter, and possibly input and/or output.

CNF Chomsky Normal Form. A normal form for CFGs in which every production has the form $A \to c$ or $A \to BC$ where A, B, and C denote variables and c denotes a terminal character.

co-NP co-Nondeterministic Polynomial time. The class of all languages whose complement belongs to NP.

$$\text{co-NP} = \{L : \overline{L} \in \text{NP}\}.$$

co-r.e. language co-recursively enumerable language. A language whose complement is recursively enumerable. L is co-r.e. if and only if $\overline{L}$ is r.e.

CYK Cocke–Younger–Kasami. A particular algorithm, using dynamic programming, that tests membership in CFLs.

DCA Deterministic Counter Acceptor. A deterministic acceptor running on a counter machine. The counter may be signed or unsigned. Assume that the counter is unsigned if not specified.

DCFL Deterministic Context-Free Language. A language accepted by a DSA.

DCM program Deterministic Counter Machine program. A deterministic program for a counter machine.

DCR Deterministic Counter Recognizer. A recognizer running on a machine [control, input, counter]. The counter may be signed or unsigned. Assume that the counter is unsigned if not specified.

DFA Deterministic Finite Acceptor. A deterministic acceptor running on a machine [control, input].

DFM program Deterministic Finite Machine program. A deterministic program for a finite machine.

DFR Deterministic Finite Recognizer. A recognizer running on a machine [control, input]. (Historically, a DFA.)

DSA Deterministic Stack Acceptor. A deterministic acceptor running on a machine [control, input, stack]. (Historically, a DPDA.)

DSM program Deterministic Stack Machine program. A deterministic program for a stack machine.

DSR Deterministic Stack Recognizer. A recognizer running on a machine [control, input, stack]. (Historically, a DPDA.)

DTA Deterministic Tape Acceptor or Deterministic Turing Acceptor. A deterministic acceptor running on a machine [control, input, tape].

DTM program Deterministic Turing Machine program. A deterministic program for a machine with a control, one or more tapes, and possibly input and/or output.

DTR Deterministic Turing Recognizer. A recognizer running on a machine consisting of a control, an input, and one or more tapes.

FM Finite Machine. A machine with a control and possibly input and/or output.

GNF Greibach Normal Form. A normal form for CFGs in which every production has the form $A \to b\gamma$ where A is a variable, b is a terminal character, and γ is a string of terminal characters and variables.

NCA Nondeterministic Counter Acceptor. A nondeterministic acceptor running on a machine [control, input, counter]. The counter may be signed or unsigned. Assume that the counter is unsigned if not specified.

NCM program Nondeterministic Counter Machine program. A nondeterministic program for a counter machine.

NFA Nondeterministic Finite Acceptor. A nondeterministic acceptor running on a machine [control, input].

NFM program Nondeterministic Finite Machine program. A nondeterministic program for a finite machine.

NP Nondeterministic Polynomial time. The class of languages accepted by NTAs in polynomial time.

NSA Nondeterministic Stack Acceptor. A nondeterministic acceptor running on a machine [control, input, stack]. (Historically, a PDA.)

NSM program Nondeterministic Stack Machine program. A nondeterministic program for a stack machine.

NTA Nondeterministic Turing Acceptor. A nondeterministic acceptor running on a machine consisting of a control, an input, and one or more tapes.

NTM program Nondeterministic Turing Machine program. A nondeterministic program for a machine with a control, one or more tapes, and possibly input and/or output.

P Polynomial time. The class of languages recognized by DTRs in polynomial time.

RAM Random Access Memory or Random Access Machine. (1) A device consisting of a finite number of registers and an unbounded random access memory array. (2) A machine with a control, a random access memory, and possibly input and/or output.

r.e. language recursively enumerable language. A language accepted by an NTA.

SM Stack Machine. A machine with a control, a tape, and possibly input and/or output.

TM Turing Machine. A machine with a control, one or more tapes, and possibly input and/or output.

10.4 PROGRAM AND GRAMMAR EQUIVALENCES

In the first column of the table, we list the most important kinds of programs for testing membership in languages, in approximately increasing order of their computational power. There is one exception: DSAs and DSRs cannot in general simulate NCAs, nor can NCAs simulate DSAs and DSRs. In order to save space, we have used some atypical abbreviations: DRR, DRA, and NRA refer to programs for a machine [control, input, RAM]; 2-DCR, 2-DCA, 2-NCA, 2-DSR, 2-DSA, and 2-NSA refer to two-counter and two-stack machine programs. Programs with equivalent computing power are grouped together; order within a group is not important. Note, however, that 2-CM programs require exponential time in order to simulate the other programs in their group.

In the second column we list grammars and other models that are equivalent to the programs in the first column. Order within a group is not important. In the third column we give the typical name for the class of languages accepted or recognized by programs in the first column.

Program	*Grammar*	*Language*
DFR DFA NFA	regular expression left-linear grammar right-linear grammar	regular language
DCA DCR		DCR language
NCA*		NCA language
DSA* DSR*	LR(1) grammar	deterministic context-free language (DCFL)
NSA	context-free grammar	context-free language (CFL)
2-DCR† 2-DSR DTR DRR		recursive language
2-DCA† 2-NCA† 2-DSA 2-NSA DTA NTA DRA NRA	semi-Thuë system Thuë system HG-program	recursively enumerable (r.e.) language

*Starred programs in different groups have incomparable computing power.

†These programs require exponential time to simulate the others in their group.

10.5 HIERARCHY OF PARTIAL FUNCTIONS

In the first column of the table, we list the most important kinds of programs for computing partial functions and functions. To save space, we use atypical notation. The letter "T" in DFT, NFT, etc., stands for "transducer"; 2-DCT, 2-NCT, 2-DST, and 2-NST refer to two-counter and two-stack transducers.

Note that nondeterministic programs are not guaranteed to compute partial functions; however, we have included them in the table with the understanding that only partial functions are allowed. Programs with equivalent computing power are grouped together. Note that 2-CM programs require exponential time in order to simulate the other programs in their group. As much as possible, the programs increase in computational power from top to bottom in the table. However, NFTs and DSTs have incomparable computing power (Exercise 4.6-2); NFTs and DCTs also have incomparable computing power, as do NCTs and DSTs.

In the second column we list grammars and other models equivalent to the programs in the first column. Order within a group is unimportant. In the third column we give the typical name for functions or partial functions computed by the programs in the first column. Note that finite transductions may in general be multiple-valued. Note also that none of these programs is guaranteed to compute a total function.

Program	*Grammar*	*Partial Function*
DFT		deterministic finite transduction
NFT*		finite transduction
DCT*		
NCT*		
DST*		
NST		
2-DCT† 2-NCT† 2-DST 2-NST DTT NTT DRT NRT	semi-Thuë system Thuë system HG-program	partial recursive function recursive function

*Some of these programs have incomparable computing power.
†These programs require exponential time to simulate the others in their group.

10.6 HIERARCHY OF RELATIONS

In the first column of the table, we list the most important kinds of programs for computing relations. To save space, we use atypical notation. The letter "T" in NFT, NCT, etc., stands for "transducer"; 2-NCT and 2-NST refer to nondeterministic two-counter and two-stack transducers, respectively. Programs with equivalent computing power are grouped together. Note that 2-CM programs require exponential time in order to simulate the other programs in their group. The programs increase in computational power from top to bottom in the table.

In the second column we list grammars and other models equivalent to the programs in the first column. In the third column we give the typical name for relations computed by the programs in the first column.

Program	*Grammar*	*Relation*
NFT		finite transduction
NCT		
NST		
2-NCT† 2-NST NTT NRT	semi-Thuë system	

†This program requires exponential time to simulate the others in its group.

10.7 CLOSURE PROPERTIES FOR LANGUAGE CLASSES

In the table below we list important closure properties for important language classes. Many other closure properties are considered in the text. We mention only the most significant here. L, L_1, and L_2 represent languages in the class. $\mathcal{T}$ represents any finite transduction. Observe that finite transductions include many closure properties: intersection with arbitrary regular languages, shuffle with arbitrary regular languages, perfect-shuffle with arbitrary regular languages, and quotient by arbitrary regular languages.

Language/Operation	$L_1 \cup L_2$	$L_1 \cap L_2$	$\overline{L}$	L_1L_2	L^*	L^R	$L\mathcal{T}$
regular	yes	yes	yes	yes	yes	yes	yes
DCFL	no	no	yes	no	no	no	no
CFL	yes	no	no	yes	yes	yes	yes
recursive	yes	yes	yes	yes	yes	yes	no
r.e.	yes	yes	no	yes	yes	yes	yes

10.8 DECISION PROBLEMS FOR LANGUAGE CLASSES

In the table below we indicate whether certain important decision problems are solvable for important classes of languages. Many other decision problems are considered in the text; we mention only the most significant here. L, L_1, and L_2 denote languages in the class. Σ denotes an alphabet with at least two characters.

Language/Problem	$x \in L$	$L = \emptyset$	$L = \Sigma^*$	$L_1 = L_2$	$L_1 \cap L_2 = \emptyset$
regular	yes	yes	yes	yes	yes
DCFL	yes	yes	yes	unknown	no
CFL	yes	yes	no	no	no
recursive	yes	no	no	no	no
r.e.	no	no	no	no	no

INDEX

ACCEPT, 142
accept a language, 143
accept a string, 69, 134
  by AFM program, 257
  by nondeterministic program, 101, 134–135, 143
accepting computation, 135
accepting control state, 69
accepting history, 134
accepting trace, 135
acceptor, 73, 143, 150
acyclic NFA, 678
adjacent nodes in a tree, 63
adjacent PUSH–POP pair, 385
agree in a position (two strings), 104
Algol60, 531
alphabet, 30
alternating finite machine program, 256–257
ambiguous GFG, 369–372
ambiguous program, 414
ambiguous string, 369
anagram, 292, 662
analytic hierarchy, 583
answer, 112
antisymmetric relation, 24
apply an instruction, 119–120
apply a production, 342
arithmetical hierarchy, 582–597
assignment, 625
  Boolean, 632
associative operation, 12
at least as powerful, 155

bag, 16–18
balanced parentheses, 84–86
balanced parentheses and brackets, 88
barber paradox, 478–479
base state, 384–386
beginning-of-line, 226–227
binary notation, 34
binary tree, 64–65
bin packing problem, 612, 662
bipartite dominating set problem, 651
bipartite graph, 650
bit-vector representation, 113
bitwise less-than relation, 543
blocked configuration, 135, 141
blocked program, 74
blocking program, 141
Boolean variable, 631
Büchi automaton, 311
buffer, 200–203

canonical NP-complete problem, 621–623, 630
cardinality
  of bags, 17
  of sets, 7
  infinite, 482–486
Cartesian product, 7, 167
catenation, 229
certificate
  for membership in an NP language, 606
  for membership in an r.e. language, 473
CFG (*see* context-free grammar)
CFL (*see* context-free language)
character, 30
characteristic function
  of a bag, 16
  of a set, 6
child, 61
Chomsky normal form, 331–336, 375, 389
  definition of, 336
Chomsky's hierarchy, 354–355
  definition of, 355
Church's thesis, 444–445, 467, 478
classifier, 276, 279
class of languages, 31
clause, 632
cleaning up, 212
cleanup subprogram, 212, 213
clique, 640
clique problem, 640
closed under an operation, 10
closure of a set, 12
  under concatenation 32
closure property, 279–293, 402–406
  table, 695
  under Boolean operations, 256, 280, 289, 290, 311, 312, 327, 403, 404, 405, 425, 426, 476, 477, 494
  under complementation, 256, 280, 312, 404, 477, 494
  under composition, 288, 290
  under concatenation, 280, 327, 330, 403, 425, 476, 477

with a finite language, 427
with a regular language, 427
under converse, 282
under converse of deterministic finite transductions, 282, 288–289, 404, 416
under converse of unambiguous finite transductions, 415
under DEJAVU, 426–427
under derivative, 290
by regular language, 290
under deterministic finite transductions, 282, 288, 416
under difference 280, 289
under Double-Duty, 424
under finite transductions, 281–284, 288–289, 400, 402, 403
under FIRST-HALF, 308
under HALF-SUBSEQ, 310
under intersection, 280, 289, 290, 311, 476, 477
with regular language, 283, 400, 403–405
under Kleene-closure, 280, 328, 330, 403, 426, 476, 477
under MAX, 426
under MIN, 427
under perfect shuffle, 291, 477
under PERM, 292, 406
under Pratt transductions, 292–293
under PREFIX, 292, 426
under quotient, 280, 290
with regular language, 283, 403, 426
under regular operations, 280, 289, 290, 311, 327, 328, 330, 403, 405, 476, 477
under reversal, 280, 290, 403, 426, 427
under rotation, 310
under shuffle, 290–291, 477
with regular language, 405
under SUBSEQ, 308–310, 405
under symmetric difference, 280, 289
under unambiguous finite transductions, 415
under union, 280, 289, 290, 311, 327, 330, 403, 476, 477
with regular language, 404, 405
used in proving a language is a DCFL, 404–405
used in proving a language is not a DCFL, 424–425
used in proving inherent ambiguity, 416–418
used in proving non-context-freeness, 403, 406
used in proving nonregularity, 284, 297, 304–306, 321
used in proving regularity, 280, 292
CNF formula (*see* conjunctive normal form)
CNF grammar (*see* Chomsky normal form)
co-, 31
co-finite, 31, 534
co-r.e., 468, 473, 488, 494
COF, 597–598
Collatz function, 524–526
coloring, 39–43, 50–51, 651–653
commutative diagram, 158–165, 168–169, 176, 178–180
COMP, 598
complement of a set, 7
complete computation, 135
complete derivation, 343
complete digraph, 235
complete history, 134
complete induction (*see* strong induction)
complete language, 496
for a class, 590, 614
for NP, 614
for Σ_i, 590
complete lattice, 328
complete lower semilattice, 328
complete theory, 570
complete trace, 135
compositeness problem, 604
composite number, 8
computable function (*see* recursive function)
computation, 135
of a subprogram, 177
computationally equivalent programs, 155
concatenation
of languages, 31–32
of sequences, 15–16
of strings, 31
configuration, 118
congruence modulo m, 23
conjunctive normal form, 632
consistent theory, 569–574
definition of, 570
consistent local assignments, 641
constrained set, 625
constraint, 624
context-free grammar, 313–400, 414
ambiguity, 369–372, 374, 414
as rewriting system, 499
decidable problems about, 534, 536, 537

definition of, 330
for English (oversimplified), 316
for Pascal, 317
standardizations, 329–338, 375–389
testing emptiness, 338
testing membership, 389–400
undecidable problems about, 527–537
context-free language, 313–400, 401–406, 414–418, 424, 425, 440–441, 554–555
belong to P, 604
decidable problems about, 534, 536, 537
definition of, 330
inherent ambiguity, 369, 372–375, 414–418
pumping theorems, 356–368
testing emptiness, 338
testing membership, 389–400
unambiguity, 369–375, 414–418
undecidable problems about, 527–537
context-sensitive grammar, 354
context-sensitive language, 355
contiguous regions, 39
continuous from above, 329
contractor, 324
control, 69, 80–82, 166–174
definition of, 80
control set, 69, 80–82, 115
definition of, 69, 115
control state, 69, 80–82
converse of a relation, 21
cost of a path, 37
countable set, 482–486
course-of-values induction (*see* strong induction)
CSG (*see* context-sensitive grammar)
CYK algorithm, 389–391

dangling else, 369–372
Davis–Putnam–Robinson theorem, 539
DCA (*see* deterministc counter acceptor)
DCFL (*see* deterministic CFL)
DCR (*see* deterministic counter recognizer)
dead state, 204–205
decidable problem, 467
decision problem, 112
table, 696
dedicated to a device, 195
defining equation, 462
DEJAVU, 426–427
depth in a tree, 64
derivation (CFG), 342–346
definition of, 343
derivative, 290
derives a string
in a CFG, 342
in a semi-Thuë system, 499
descendant in a tree, 65
destination
of an edge, 36
of a path, 37
deterministic CFL, 353–354, 404–413, 418–427, 441, 528–529, 532–534
deterministic counter acceptor, 82–87
deterministic counter recognizer, 146, 528–534
deterministic finite acceptor, 80–81, 218, 250–253
definition of, 143
for pattern matching, 75–80
deterministic finite recognizer, 146, 218–219, 253, 671, 676–677
minimizing, 258–279
testing membership in language recognized by, 307–308
deterministic finite transducer 147, 218, 282–283, 290, 404–405, 416–418
deterministic program, 99, 139
for oracle TM, 578
deterministic stack acceptor, 73–74, 87–89
definition of, 143
deterministic stack recognizer, 68–73, 404–413, 418–427, 441
definition of, 146
deterministic Turing acceptor, 91–96
definition of, 143
deterministic Turing recognizer, 146
deterministic vs. nondeterministic, 104–106
device, 116
simulation of, 167
DFA (*see* deterministic finite acceptor)
DFR (*see* determinsitic finite recognizer)
diagonalization, 478–490, 615–616
difference of sets, 7
digit relation, 543
digraph (*see* graph)
diophantine equation, 537–553
directed graph (*see* graph)
disjoint sets, 7
disjoint union of bags, 17
disjoint union of sets, 7
disjunctive normal form, 638
distinguish two control states, 262
distinguish two languages, 486

DNF (*see* disjunctive normal form)
domain of a relation, 20
dominating set problem, 650
dovetailing, 474, 477–478
drinking game, 310
DSA (*see* deterministic stack acceptor)
DSR (*see* deterministic stack recognizer)
DTA (*see* deterministic Turing acceptor)
DTA-index set, 561
DTM-index set, 558–563
DTR (*see* deterministic Turing recognizer)
dyadic notation, 34
dynamic programming, 232–237, 389–391

easy as a language, 491
edge in a graph, 36
egrep, 225–229
element of a bag, 16
element of a set, 6
empty sequence, 15
empty set, 6
empty string, 30, 31
  elimination of, from CFG, 332–334
encoding as a number, 471
end-of-line, 227
enter a configuration, 132–133
equipartition problem, 611–612, 661–662
equivalence class, 23–24, 259–279
equivalence closure, 29
equivalence relation, 22–24, 28, 29
equivalent control states, 258–259, 677–678
equivalent programs, 155
equivalent regular expressions, 671
execute an instruction, 133
exponential blowup, 264, 266–267
exponential diophantine equation, 537–553
  definition of, 538
exponential polynomial, 538–539
EXT, 598
extend an operation to sets, 9
extend a partial function, 563, 598

FA, 80
factored form, 195–204
  definition of, 196
fgrep, 225
filter, 149–151, 283, 404
FIN, 593, 595
final configuration, 125
final state, 121
final subprogram, 176
finite automaton, 80
finite machine, 80, 118
finite set, 31
finite state machine, 80
finite transducer, 147–151, 281–284, 288–292, 297–298, 403, 518
  (*see also* deterministic finite transducer)
finite-branching tree, 65–66
FIRST-HALF, 308
fixed point, 322–329
  definition of, 324
fixed-point theorem, 564–566, 568
  Tarski–Knaster, 322–329
FM (*see* finite machine)
∀FA, 257–258
formal definition, 18
formal language, 30
FSM, 80
full binary tree, 64–65
function, 24–27

generalized sequential machine, 281
generate a language
  by a CFG, 330
  by a program, 152, 289, 438
  by a regular expression, 221–222
generator, 152, 289
generic reduction, 621–624
GNF (*see* Greibach normal form)
Gödel's completeness theorem, 526
Gödel's incompleteness theorem, 569–574
go from/to a control state, 195
grammar
  context-free (*see* context-free grammar)
  context-sensitive, 354
  left-linear, 354
  regular, 354
  right-linear, 354
  type i ($i = 0, 1, 2, 3$), 355
  unrestricted, 355
grammar–program equivalences, 690–691
graph, 36–37
  Kleene's theorem for, 229–250
  NP-complete problems for, 639–653
  planar, 50–51
  representation of, 113–114
greatest common divisor, 53–54
greatest lower bound, 322
Greek letters, 681–683
Greibach normal form, 375–389
grep, 225
gsm map, 281
guess nondeterministically, 101, 473

HALF-SUBSEQ, 310
halt, 134
halting problem, 478–480
  for DSM programs, 412–413
  for oracle TM programs, 581
Hamiltonian cycle, 642
Hamiltonian cycle problem, 642–648
  undirected, 651
Hamiltonian path, 642
Hamiltonian path problem, 651
Hamiltonian *s–t* path problem, 651
hard as a language, 491
hard for a class, 590, 614
hardest r.e. language, 496
head, 91
height of a node, 65
height of a tree, 65
Herbrand–Gödel program, 461–466
Hilbert's tenth problem, 537–553
history, 134

immediately derives
  in a CFG, 342
  in a semi-Thuë system, 499
Immerman–Szelepcsényi theorem, 610
inapplicable instruction, 120
inattentive program, 117, 480
independent set problem, 649
index set, 558–569
induction, 39–66
inductive hypothesis, 44
inequivalence problem
  for regular languages, 673–676
  for star-free regular languages, 671–673
inequivalent regular expressions, 671
INF, 593, 595
infinite branch, 66
infinite computation, 138
infinite history, 136
infinite input, 310–311
infinite set, 31
infinite trace, 138–139
infinite tree, 65–66
infix equivalence relation, 265–266
inherently ambiguous CFL, 369, 372–375, 414–418
inherently unboundedly ambiguous CFL, 374–375
initial configuration, 124
initial state, 121
initial subprogram, 176
initializer for a device, 120–126
  table, 123
initializer for a machine, 124–126
  nonstandard, 127–128
input alphabet, 115
input *x*, 473
instance of a problem, 112
instruction, 118–120
  definition of, 119
internal description, 439, 608
internal node of a tree, 62
intersection of bags, 17
intersection of sets, 6
invalid computation, 527–528
invalid trace, 674
isomorphism of graphs, 648

join (in a lattice), 328
join of two languages, 592
jump of a language, 580–581

k-CNF, 634
k-colorability problem, 651–653
k-SAT, 634
k-satisfiability problem, 634
k-tape Turing machine, 447–451
(k, Γ)-SSS (*see* SSS)
(k, Γ)-symbol system (*see* symbol system)
Kleene closure, 32, 220, 327–328
knapsack problem, 662
König's tree lemma, 65–66

labeled digraph, 37
  representation of, 114
Λ-production, 331
  elimination of, 332–334
language, 30–31
  defined by a system of regular equations, 326
  (*see also* context-free language; context-sensitive language; r.e. language; recursive language; regular language)
latency of an infinite sequence, 58
lattice point, 56
leads to a variable, 334
  algorithm for determining, 338
leaf in a tree, 62
least-element principle, 60
least fixed point, 324–329
least set with a particular property, 11–12
least upper bound, 328
left side of a production, 330
left-linear equation, 328
left-linear grammar, 354

leftmost derivation, 343–346
length of a computation, 602
length of a path, 37
  weighted, 37
length of a sequence, 15
literal, 632
live state, 204–208
local assignment, 625, 632, 640–641
local constraint, 625
locality, 624–625
  definition of, 625
lockstep simulation, 156–174
  three conditions of, 161
LR(1) grammar, 353–354, 392–393

m-reducible, 491
machine, 117–118
machine type, 117–118
many-one reduction, 490–498
  polynomial-time bounded, 612–616, 621–679
map (by a partial function), 25
mark characters for Ogden's lemma, 361
match a pattern, 75–80
match a regular expression, 226
Matijasevič's theorem, 551
MCOMP, 598
meet (in a lattice), 322
meet at a control state, 176
MIDDLE-THIRD, 308
milestone, 420
MIN, 427
minimal DFR, 258–279
minimal DTM program, 567–568
minimum separation by DFRs, 664
modulo a number, 23
modus ponens, 521
monochromatic set, 50
monotone clause, 639
monotone function, 323, 327–329
multiple-valued function, 24
multiset, 16
Myhill–Nerode theorem, 261
  used in proving nonregularity, 264

N (natural number), 6
N (new control states), 176
NCA (*see* nondeterministic counter acceptor)
NFA (*see* nondeterministic finite acceptor)
node in a graph, 36
node in a tree, 61
nonblocking program, 141
nondeterministic counter acceptor, 102, 104–107, 440–441, 527–530, 533–534, 554–555
  definition of, 143
nondeterministic finite acceptor, 102–103, 219, 238–258, 264, 266–267, 280
  definition of, 143
nondeterministic program, 99–107
nondeterministic stack acceptor, 101–102, 106, 347–354, 384–387, 389, 402–403, 438
  definition of, 143
nondeterministic Turing acceptor, 468, 469, 471–473, 475, 476
  definition of, 143
nondeterministic vs. deterministic, 104–106
nonrecursive language, 468, 478–480, 490–553, 555, 558–561
nonterminal character, 343
nonuniversality
  of regular expressions, 673–676
  of star-free regular expressions, 672
NP, 603–606
NP-complete language, 611–673, 676–679
  definition of, 614
NP-hard language, 614
NSA (*see* nondeterministic stack acceptor)
NTA (*see* nondeterministic Turing acceptor)
null instruction, 202, 208–212

ω-consistent, 574
ω-DFA, 310–312
ω-language, 310–312
ω-NFA, 310–312
ω-regular ω-language, 310–312
on-line recognition, 418–427
one-one correspondence, 26–27
one-one function, 25–26
one-one reducible, 491
onto function, 26
operation, 116
  table, 108
oracle, 574–581
oracle TM program, 578
ordinary subprogram, 176
origin of an edge, 36
origin of a path, 37
output alphabet, 115

P, 603–606
padding a TM program, 615
padding input strings, 622

palindromes, 33
  not a DCFL, 424
  NSA for, 101–102
palindromes with central marker, 68
  DSA for, 73
  DSR for, 68–70
parent in a tree, 61
parse tree, 318–319, 320, 339–342, 344–346, 369–375
parsimonious reduction, 638
partial computation, 135
partial function, 24–26
  hierarchy of, 692–693
partial history, 133–134
partial match, 75
partial order, 24
partial recursive function, 467, 557–561, 564–569, 597–598
partial trace, 135
partition problem (*see* equipartition problem)
partition a bag, 17
partition a set, 7, 23–24
partitioning tests, 196–199
path in a digraph, 37
perfect shuffle of two languages, 291
periodic sequence, 58
PERM, 292, 406
permutation, 292
phrase, 318
planar DFA, 250
planar graph, 50–51
planar NFA, 250
polynomial, 39
polynomial time, 603–604
polynomial-time m-reduction, 612–616, 621–679
polynomial-time Turing reduction, 613, 616–621, 648
polynomially related resource bound, 608–609
Post correspondence problem, 508–520
postfix notation (for functions), 25
power set, 8
Pratt's theorem, 610–611
precede (in a lattice), 322
predicate, 2
PREFIX, 292, 426
prefix notation (for functions), 25
prefix of a string, 33
prefix-equivalent strings, 260
prefix-free language, 553–554
primality problem, 112, 610–611
prime factorization, 55
prime number, 8
production (in a CFG), 330
production (in a rewriting system), 499
program, 126
program–grammar equivalences, 690–691
PROJ, 312
projection of a language in P, 606
projection of an ω-regular ω-language, 312
projection of a recursive language, 472
proof (in a logical theory), 570
proper subset, 7
pumpable language, 294, 297, 367–368
pumping down, 295
pumping number, 293, 298
pumping theorem, 293, 298, 357, 361–362, 363, 364
  partial converse, 306
pumping up, 295

query an oracle, 575
queue, 78, 520
quotient, 280, 290
  with a regular language, 283, 403, 426

r.e. language, 467–478, 487, 489–490, 491, 494, 539, 551, 555
  in an oracle, 579–580, 581
RAM (*see* random access machine; random access memory)
random access machine, 96–99, 456–458
random access memory, 96
range of a relation, 20
rational TSP, 621
reachability problem, 246
reachable state, 206–208
  determining, 246
real-time NSA, 384, 389
real-time program, 384
realm of a device, 115
  table, 123
REC, 597–598
recognizer, 73, 144–146, 150
  definition of, 144
recursion theorem, 563–569
recursive function (*see* partial recursive function; total recursive function)
recursive language, 467–478, 597–598
  in an oracle, 579–580, 591
recursive predicate, 586
recursively enumerable language (*see* r.e. language)
recursively inseparable sets, 486–489

recursively separable sets, 486–489, 598
reduction, 490
many-one, 490–553
polynomial-time, 612–613
Turing, 576
reduction principle, 490
reflexive relation, 21
reflexive transitive closure, 21–22
algorithm for, 338
regular equation, 314–330
regular expression, 221–229, 238–247
regular grammar (*see* left-linear grammar; right-linear grammar)
regular language, 217–312
definition of, 220–221
regular operations, 31–32, 220
on paths, 231
regular set of paths, 229–247
reject a string, 69
rejecting control state, 69
relate x to y, 18
relation, 18–24
hierarchy of, 694
of representation, 158
relativization, 578–580
reneg, 292
repertory of a device, 116
table, 123
represent a configuration, 158
restricted first-order logic, 521
rewrite a variable, 342
rewriting system, 498–508
RFOL (*see* restricted first-order logic)
Rice's theorem, 558–563
right side of a production, 330–331
right-linear grammar, 328, 354, 355
root of a tree, 61
Rosser's incompleteness theorem, 571–572
rotation, 310
rule (in a Thuë system) 500
rule of inference, 521
run a program, 132–133
running time, 602

SAT, 631–639
reducing, 654–656, 665–668, 672
satisfy a Boolean formula, 632
satisfy a constraint, 625
satisfy a symbol system, 625
satisfying assignment, 625
satisfying local assignment, 640
Savitch's theorem, 609
Schröder–Bernstein theorem, 486
SCM (*see* signed-counter machine)
SECOND-HALF, 308
self-actualized program, 566
self-aware program, 566
self-loop, 36
semantics, 139, 204
semi-Thuë system, 498–508
SEP, 598
separation by DFRs, 664–669
sequel, 135
sequel relation, 135
sequence, 15–16
set cover problem, 654–659
shortest path problem, 246–247
shuffle of two languages, 290–291, 405
signed counter, 86
signed counter machine, 86
simulate a collection of devices, 167, 174
simulation, 153–194
lockstep, 156–174
three conditions of, 161
via subprograms, 174–194
three conditions of, 177
size of a CFG, 336
s-m-n theorem, 493
sound theory, 570
soundness of first-order logic, 521
source of a relation, 18
space, 608–610, 673–676
SSS, 624–631
reducing, 632–633, 635, 640–642
stack, 68, 87–88
stack machine, 87–89, 118
standardization, 194–214
star-free regular expression, 671–673
starless regular equation, 314
start variable of a CFG, 330
state of a device, 115
strictly partial function, 24
string, 29–36
definition of, 30
strong induction, 51–55
strongly prefix-equivalent strings, 439
structural induction, 60–66
definition of, 61
sub-bag, 16
subgraph, 648
subgraph isomorphism problem, 648
sub–parse tree, 318
subprogram, 174
definition of, 176

SUBSEQ, 308–310, 405
subsequence, 308
subset, 7
subset construction, 251–254
subset sum problem, 604, 659–661
substring, 33, 75
subtree, 63
suffix of a string, 33
symbol system, 625–626
symmetric relation, 22
syntactic property, 139, 204

tape, 91–96, 445–453
target of a relation, 18
Tarski–Knaster fixed-point theorem, 322–329
tautology, 638
terminal character, 343
terminator for a device, 121
  table, 123
terminator for a machine, 124–126
  nonstandard, 126–128
test, 75, 116
theorem, 521, 570
theory, 570
3-dimensional matching problem, 663
3-SAT, 634–637
  reducing, 643–647
$(3x + 1)$-function, 524–526
Thuë system, 498–508
TM (*see* Turing machine)
top of stack, 72
TOT, 593, 595
total function, 24
total recursive function, 467, 469, 474, 489–491
trace, 135
transducer, 146–151
transfer function, 558
transfer relation, 135
transitive closure, 21
transitive relation, 21
traveling salesman problem, 611–612, 616–621, 647–648
tree, 61–66
triangle inequality, 648
trivial final subprogram, 176–177
trivial index set, 559
trivial initial subprogram, 176
TSP cost, 616–621
TSP decision, 616–621
TSP search, 616–621
TSP with triangle inequality, 648–649
Turing-complete, 598
Turing machine, 91–96, 443–447, 486–506, 557–569, 590–591
  halting problem for, 478–480
  highly undecidable problems for, 593–598
  k-tape simulation, 447–451
  RAM simulation, 456–461
  used in defining canonical NP-complete problem, 621–624
  used in defining computability, 467–478
  used in defining time-bounded computation, 603, 605–611
  used in generic reduction to nonuniversality of regular expressions, 674–676
  used in generic reduction to SSS, 627–630
  with oracle, 574–581
Turing reduction, 576
  polynomial-time, 613
Turing tape (*see* tape)
2-dimensional tape, 451
type i grammar ($i = 0, 1, 2, 3$), 355

UCM (*see* unsigned counter machine)
unambiguous CFG, 369–375
unambiguous CFL, 369–375
unambiguous NSA, 414–418
unary exponential diophantine equation, 551
unary notation, 34
unboundedly ambiguous CFG, 374–375
uncountable set, 482–486
undecidable language (*see* nonrecursive language)
under the tape head, 91
underhang, 513
undirected graph, 50, 639–640 (*see also* graph)
undirected Hamiltonian cycle problem, 651
union of bags, 17
union of sets, 6
unit production, 331
  elimination of, from CFG, 334–336
universal Turing machine program, 458–461
unreachable state, 206–208
unsigned counter machine, 82–86
use a control state, 176
useless variable, 535

vacuously true statement, 52
valid computation, 470, 527–534
valid statement, 526
variable in a CFG, 314
variable in a regular equation, 314
vector sum problem, 656–661

vertex cover problem, 649–650
vertex in a digraph, 36

weighted digraph, 37
  representing, 114
weighted length of a path, 37
well-behaved terminator, 285
Wiles–Fermat theorem, 538
witness
  for membership in an NP language, 606
  for membership in an r.e. language, 473
word problem
  for a group, 507
  for a semi-Thuë system, 500, 503
  for a Thuë system, 506, 507

yield of a parse tree, 318